OCEAN

SEA OF OKHOTSK

KURILE ISLANDS (Japan)

U N I O N

Novosibirsk

Irkutsk

Khabarovsk

MANCHUKUO (Japan)

Vladivostok

SEA OF JAPAN

Tokyo

JAPAN

NORTH PACIFIC OCEAN

TANNU TUVA

OUTER MONGOLIA

KOREA (Japan)

SINKIANG

Peiping

C H I N A

Shanghai

EAST CHINA SEA

Nanking

Wuhan

FORMOSA (Japan)

Chungking

TIBET

Kunming

Canton

Hong Kong (G.B)

New Delhi

NEPAL

BHUTAN

PHILIPPINES (U.S.)

INDIA (G.B.)

Calcutta

BURMA (G.B.)

Hanoi

Manila

Bombay

Rangoon

THAILAND

Bangkok

FRENCH INDOCHINA (Vichy France)

SOUTH CHINA SEA

BAY OF BENGAL

Saigon

NORTH BORNEO (G.B.)

BRUNEI (G.B)

SARAWAK (G.B.)

BORNEO

CEYLON (G.B)

MALAYA (G.B)

Colombo

Singapore

NETHERLANDS EAST INDIES

SUMATRA

OCEAN

Batavia

JAVA

1941

Also by the Author

1919: The Year Our World Began

1941

OUR LIVES IN A WORLD
ON THE EDGE

William K. Klingaman

HARPER & ROW, PUBLISHERS, New York
Cambridge, Philadelphia, San Francisco
London, Mexico City, São Paulo, Singapore, Sydney

1817

Grateful acknowledgment is given for permission to quote from the following titles:

The Wartime Journals of Charles A. Lindbergh, copyright © 1970 by Charles A. Lindbergh. Reprinted by permission of Harcourt Brace Jovanovich, Inc.

The Diary of Virginia Woolf, Volume Five, Edited by Anne Olivier Bell, copyright © 1984 by Quentin Bell and Angelica Garnett. Reprinted by permission of Harcourt Brace Jovanovich, Inc.

The Goebbels Diaries 1939–1941, copyright © 1982 by Fred Taylor and Hamish Hamilton Ltd. Reprinted by permission of The Putnam Publishing Group.

The Grand Alliance, by Winston S. Churchill. Copyright 1951 by Houghton Mifflin Company. Copyright © renewed 1977 by Lady Spencer-Churchill, the Honorable Lady Sarah Audley, the Honorable Lady Soames. Reprinted by permission of Houghton Mifflin Company.

Breaking In, Breaking Out, by Nicholas Monsarrat. Copyright © 1971 by Nicholas Monsarrat. Reprinted by permission of William Morrow and Company, Inc.

Watching the World, by Raymond Clapper. Copyright 1944 by Raymond Clapper. Reprinted by permission of McGraw-Hill Inc.

FIRST EDITION

Copyeditor: Mary Jane Alexander

Designer: Sidney Feinberg

Index by Maro Riofrancos

Library of Congress Cataloging-in-Publication Data

Klingaman, William K.
   1941 : our lives in a world on the edge.

  Bibliography: p.
  Includes index.
   1. World War, 1939–1945. 2. History, modern—20th century. I. Title.
D755.K56 1988   940.53   87-46150
ISBN 0-06-015948-0

---

88 89 90 91 92 CC/RRD 10 9 8 7 6 5 4 3 2 1

FOR MY MOTHER

Contents

Preface and Acknowledgments

In 1941 the world lived on the edge of hell. As the year opened, the masters of Nazi Germany reigned unchallenged over virtually the entire European continent; Britain stood alone under the bombs of the blitz, with absolutely no hope of victory in the foreseeable future; and the powerful military machine of the Japanese Empire was beginning its fateful march south toward the tempting natural riches of Indochina and the East Indies. On the sideline, the Soviet Union sat patiently waiting for the Axis and the British Empire to batter each other into exhaustion so it could step in at the climactic moment and pick up the spoils. Across the Atlantic, a sense of impending disaster dominated the lives of Americans as the ominous shadow of war loomed nearer the horizon every month, every week, every hour. . . .

The blade fell first across the eastern front. On June 22, Hitler sent the greatest mechanized invasion force in history thundering across the Soviet border, and for nearly six terrible months the Wehrmacht tore a smoldering path through the Russian heartland. Just as the German onslaught finally stalled in the first week of December, literally frozen to a stop within sight of the Kremlin spires, Japanese bombers swooped down upon the United States Pacific fleet at Pearl Harbor, dealing a staggering blow to American naval power and cruelly exposing the American military establishment's appalling lack of preparedness.

Yet these stunning disasters were nothing more than momentary setbacks for the anti-Fascist cause. As Britain's indomitable Prime Minister Winston Churchill gleefully explained to his cabinet colleagues in London, the mobilization of the Soviet Union and the United States—potentially the two greatest military powers in the world—and their entry into the war on the side of the British Empire ensured the ultimate defeat of the Axis. The path to victory would not be easy, but at least the outcome was no longer in doubt.

Insofar as possible, I have tried to use diaries, letters, and journals to trace the events of this crucial year through the eyes of contemporary observers. (Newspapers, alas, were often too heavily censored to provide much useful information.) I should emphasize at the outset that this book is not merely an exercise in military history; although the reader will frequently find himself under attack in the trackless deserts of North Africa, on the frozen Russian steppes, or the jagged mountains of Greece and Crete, I have also looked beyond the battlefields to re-create the atmosphere of life on the home front in a world wracked by total war. Thus we shall encounter Joe Louis and Joe DiMaggio as well as Joseph Stalin; Charles de Gaulle, Ho Chi Minh, and "The Maltese Falcon"; and Franklin D. Roosevelt, Ronald Reagan, and Dumbo the Flying Elephant.

This book might never have seen the light of day without the enthusiasm, support, and friendship of my editor, Daniel Bial. In fact, everyone at Harper & Row has treated me with such unfailing consideration that the entire publication process has been simply delightful.

For their kindness and invaluable assistance in easing my research tasks, I owe a deep debt of gratitude to Dr. Billy R. Wilkinson, director of the Albin O. Kuhn Library and Gallery of the University of Maryland, Baltimore County; Bill Zagar and the staff of the Morris Library of the University of Delaware; and everyone at the microfilm reading room of the McKeldin Library at the University of Maryland's College Park campus. Dr. Raymond Callahan of the University of Delaware provided valuable insights into the course of military affairs in 1941, and a wealth of entertaining stories about the occasionally unconventional behavior of the British military hierarchy. As usual, my wife, Janet, cheerfully read the manuscript and refused to let me get away with anything but my best effort.

Prologue: December 1940

i

The Blitz

"If we can live through this winter unshaken and unafraid,
the rest will be money for jam."
—BRITISH M. P., DECEMBER 1940

The planes came in low over the Channel, through the darkness and the December mist. Tonight the target was London.

Along the Dover coast the watchers heard the familiar monotonous drone of the engines. By the time the warning sirens (known scornfully to Londoners as Weeping Willies) sounded their wailing lament across the beleaguered, blacked-out city, the raiders were almost directly overhead. In the streets there was a fleeting perception of half-seen dreamlike shadows, dark silent shapes hurrying grimly along on their own private missions, and tiny lights that came out of nowhere and suddenly disappeared. Some civilians took refuge underground, some hid in their own flimsy family shelters, and some who long ago had grown weary of the whole routine simply remained where they were, trusting in God and the odds that told them their chances of being the victim of a direct hit were maybe one in a thousand on any given night.

First came the incendiary bombs, nasty little things about one and a half feet long and three inches in diameter and weighing two pounds each, with four metal fins that made them look like miniature torpedoes made out of white limestone. Their thermite cores ignited upon landing (sometimes, said American correspondent Ernie Pyle, when they hit the street the bombs bounced crazily along like footballs) and burned and sparked for ten minutes, long enough to start the flames dancing and scampering across the wooden rooftops that littered the London skyline. Burning at a temperature of nearly two thousand degrees, they could cut through steel as if it were cardboard. The trick was to spot the fire bombs as soon as they landed and extinguish them with sandbags or dirt (water caused the bombs to explode into burning fragments) before any damage was done. "Now come the incendiaries to light you to bed," the children sang each night. "Bring out the sandbags and kill them all dead." Some watchers simply stomped them out with their boots or smothered them with tin garbage can lids. But always there were some bombs that fell on an unattended house or shop, and the flames spread quickly through the narrow twisting streets. This night the first wave of planes flew in parallel formation over the city, dropping long rows of Molotov breadbaskets, the cylinders that held three dozen incendiaries apiece and burst apart at a preset altitude, scattering their load across the target area.

When the fire bombs had done their work, lighting up the city and outlining streets and buildings with lurid guideposts of white and yellow flames, it was time for the heavy planes armed with high-explosive bombs to make their run over London. By now the defenders, too, had come alive: from the ground, searchlights felt for the bombers with broad stalks of light that faded into the mists at the edges; in the suburbs, antiaircraft guns thumped and pounded at the invaders and shells burst like weird blue diamonds below the stars. Royal Air Force fighters—many of which were nothing more than converted twin-engine, lightly built Blenheim bombers—darted in to attack and then danced away before the German Messerschmitt escorts could engage them in combat. Nevertheless the insistent bombers came on and on and on, wave after endless wave with their sinister sawing noise. "It is just like in an Eastern country," remarked a petulant George Orwell in his diary, "when you keep thinking you have killed the last mosquito inside your net, and every time, as soon as you have turned the light out, another starts droning."

Bombs in the distance fell with an odd crumping noise; those that came closer arrived with a gurgling whistle. (It was remarkable, discovered Kenneth Clark, how far and fast one could run when one heard a really large bomb approaching.) Usually there were two or three in quick succession. As a bomb passed through the air nearby, whole houses shook, teacups rattled on the table, electric lights dimmed inexplicably for a second or two. Then the whistle swelled into a scream like a train emerging from a tunnel and the passing bomb suddenly exploded . . . a blinding flash and the earth heaved and shook everything into a heap and debris fell all around. The fear of being trapped beneath the rubble . . . hearing the slow steady drip of the water and smelling the unmistakable odor of escaping gas or feeling the heat of the flames edging closer . . . desperately swimming through the suffocating brick and masonry and wood, until the sharp cold air at the surface finally slapped the mind back to reality. There was a gale blowing through the open gaps in the walls, the air filled with fine white ash and the dank smell of ruined buildings and the pungent odor of cordite, and the accumulated soot of years of undisturbed domestic tranquillity—now rudely dislodged from the crumbled chimney—lay two inches thick over everything. The only other noise besides the wind was the sound of falling glass.

England was at war, and England was alone.

England had, in fact, been at war since September 1939, a condition for which the extraordinarily stupid and wrongheaded British diplomacy of the 1930s bore heavy responsibility. As the Fascist dictators advanced vigorously from one conquest to the next between 1936 and early 1939 (first Spain, then the Rhineland, Ethiopia, and Czechoslovakia), the elderly dilettantes who governed Britain and France fell back in weary resignation, refusing to fight for positions that might have been successfully defended. And even when German military production swung into high gear in the last two years of the decade, the self-righteous and badly mistaken British Prime Minister Sir Neville Chamberlain—who was much more adept at collecting exotic butterflies than judging human nature—refused to launch Britain on an equally ambitious rearmament program. Instead, Chamberlain's government waited until Nazi Germany had grown even stronger, and then in the spring of 1939 arbitrarily and irresponsibly decided to try to stop Hitler's advance by committing Britain to the defense of Poland, a guarantee that in the circumstances—Britain still desperately short of arms, confronting an overwhelming German superiority in Central Europe, with the Russian bear waiting hungrily on the sidelines—could never, even in Chamberlain's deluded imagination, be anything more than a silly bluff. In the end, the government finally decided to take a stand not because it believed the Nazis were evil men bent upon the destruction of European civilization, but rather, quite simply, because Chamberlain and his colleagues had made up their minds that this time Hitler had gone too far. "This," declared Stephen Spender, "was the exercise of a British logic which, like all our attitudes between 1918 and 1939, did not appeal to the French," who were dragged willy-nilly into the confrontation. The outbreak of war following the German invasion of Poland in September marked the culmination of a foolish British policy that deserved to die an inglorious death; the tragedy was that it nearly took all of western Europe down in flames with it.

For six months, during the "phony war" of the winter of 1939–40, as the German military machine completed its preparations for the invasion of western Europe, Chamberlain sat back and complacently assured England that Hitler "had missed the bus," and Britons merrily sang, "We'll Hang Out Our Washing on the Old Siegfried Line." Then, in the spring of 1940, the Wehrmacht's blitzkrieg tore through Europe: Norway and Denmark fell in April, the Netherlands and Belgium in May—whereupon Winston Churchill replaced the discredited Chamberlain as high constable and prime minister of Britain—and disastrously in June, France. With unwonted (and unfounded) bravado, King George VI assured his mother that "personally—I feel much happier now that we have no allies to be polite to & to pamper." The unexpected ease with which German forces rolled over, around, and through the French army into Paris surprised everyone, not least of all the Fuehrer himself, and knocked all the combatants' carefully prepared strategic plans into a cocked hat. ("In a way," said Gertrude Stein, "that is what makes it nice about France. In one war they upset the Germans by resisting unalterably steadily and patiently and valiantly for four years, in the next war they upset them just as much by not resisting at all and going under completely in six weeks. Well that is what makes them changeable enough to create styles.")

The Allies' military fortunes struck bottom in the first week of June, when British and French forces found themselves trapped at Dunkirk with their backs to the sea. Through a combination of courage and good luck, Britain managed to evacuate more than 300,000 of its soldiers to fight another day. "We've got the men away," Churchill reported to the cabinet, "but we've lost the luggage." Understandably, the French considered this panic-stricken retreat to be nothing less than the abject desertion of France at its hour of greatest need. But, in the best tradition of English military lore, wherein glorious defeats have always received far more attention than successful campaigns (Tennyson's magnificent "Charge of the Light Brigade," for instance, celebrates a cavalry unit that charged in the wrong direction), Churchill managed to turn the rout into a moral victory, promising the English people that the struggle would go on even in the face of unmitigated disaster: "we shall fight on the beaches, we shall fight on the landing-grounds, we shall fight in the fields and in the streets, we shall fight in the hills . . ." And for a while it seemed that this was precisely what England would have to do.

After France collapsed like a punctured soufflé, Hitler appears to have expected London to surrender, to agree to a settlement that allowed England to retain its empire at the price of keeping its hands off the European continent. There was a moment of panic in Britain as it became startlingly clear just how nakedly vulnerable the nation was; "all we can do," fretted Harold Nicolson, a member of the Home Morale Emergency Committee, "is lie on our backs with our paws in the air and hope that no one will stamp on our tummies." Churchill briefly considered negotiating with "That Bad Man"—anyone who could read a map knew that Britain was in deep trouble—but decided against it, and never looked back. Accordingly, after a month's delay, the German High Command (i.e., Hitler himself) prepared plans for the invasion of England: Operation Sea Lion. But any attempt to invade the island required that Germany first obtain unquestioned air supremacy over the Channel, and this the Luftwaffe never could do. So, in September Hitler and Reichsmarshal Hermann Göring changed tactics and launched their brutal campaign to bomb Britain into submission. For two months London bore the brunt of the aerial attacks as more than 13,000 tons of explosives fell on the city; then the Luftwaffe pounded the provincial towns (Coventry was virtually wiped off the map in one night of concentrated bombing in mid-November); and by the end of the year London was once again the principal target.

Scenes from the blitz: a grand old house sliced open, a wall cut cleanly away to reveal the interior, like the sectional view of a child's dollhouse

. . . the East End of London a scene of utter desolation, skeleton houses with broken pipes swinging crazily in the wind, streets pockmarked with craters and other streets cordoned off because of delayed-action bombs (which always attracted a knot of sightseers), buses burned out and abandoned . . . a twelve-year-old child burned to death beneath the rubble and the corner policeman shaking his fist at the sky: "I'd like to get my 'ands on the sods wot done it to the poor little nipper" . . . Wimbledon bombed and eighteen people killed . . . a private golf course near London with its own wartime rules: "A ball removed by enemy action may be replaced as near as possible to where it lay, or if lost or destroyed, another ball may be dropped not nearer the hole without penalty; competitors during gunfire or while bombs are falling may take cover without penalty" . . . pulverized glass all over everything . . . a bomb exploding at Broadcasting House just as the BBC commentator began the evening news summary . . . Our Dumb Friends' League, with six ambulances and three hospitals, rescuing and caring for 47,000 pets whose homes had been bombed . . . apocalyptic scenes of churches on fire and blast furnaces . . . a soldier and girl killed by a bomb blast while making love in Hyde Park and the bodies brought in to a West End hospital, where the doctor on duty confessed to an American reporter, "Under the circumstances, I don't know whether to be ashamed or proud of my countrymen" . . . and every night the nation joined in saying a Damn Hitler prayer. A poet wrote that "the city of London acquired an extraordinary, almost regal dignity at the center of the flames." "At this time," mused Winston Churchill, "anyone would have been proud to be a Londoner"; but twenty thousand men, women, and children were already dead.

In this war, unlike the last one, civilians were on the front line right from the start. During the four years of the Great War, from 1914 to 1918, there was only one noncombatant death for every seventy-five military fatalities; the comparable numbers for September 1939 through December 1940 were one civilian for every three soldiers. London found out firsthand what the towns of Belgium and northern France had learned a generation earlier. Windows of commercial buildings in the City were bricked up with only a rifle hole left open for defense; brass-colored gas detectors stood in the parks above the trench shelters; artillery guns perched upon rooftops; and official shelter signs (black metal plates with a big white "S") and bags of loose sand seemed to be everywhere. Government regulations forbade the posting of any signs that indicated the direction or distance to any other place, just in case the invasion ever came. In one park there was a huge mound of bricks and stone, twenty feet high and a hundred yards around, where trucks came every day to dump new loads of debris and rubble from bombed-out homes (palaces and slums together) throughout the city. Alongside the heap of masonry sat a separate dark pyre of burned and broken wood, and then a pile of useless twisted metal: a child's Mickey Mouse pail, something that used to be a sewing machine, a workman's hammer, baby carriages, lead pipes, bathtubs, radiators.

One by one, the cherished landmarks of old London were ravaged by fire or explosion. Six bombs fell on Buckingham Palace while King George and Queen Elizabeth were in a sitting room overlooking the Quadrangle; "we saw the flashes and heard the detonations," noted the king in his journal, "as they burst about eighty yards away. The blast blew in the windows opposite to us, and two great craters had appeared in the Quadrangle. From one of these craters water from a burst main was pouring out and flowing into the passage through the broken windows. The whole thing happened in a matter of seconds." Determined to avoid the fate of the continental monarchs displaced into exile by the Nazi advance through Europe, His Majesty ordered a shooting range built in the palace garden, where he and his family and their servants diligently took target practice with machine guns and pistols. Every morning Queen Elizabeth received special instruction in firing a revolver; "I shall not go down like the others," she calmly told a friend.

On the evening of December 8 (a little late for Guy Fawkes Day), several German bombs fell directly on the Houses of Parliament, barely missing Westminster Hall. But the sixteenth-century Cloister Court, part of the ancient Palace of Westminster and one of the oldest and loveliest sections of the massive building, was virtually demolished. Although some members who had been bombed out of their own houses had recently taken to sleeping at the House of Commons overnight (not to be confused with the members who slept on the back benches during the day), the rooms were empty at the time of the explosion. The bombs destroyed the members' cloakroom; a damp, tattered waistcoat lay disconsolate, half-buried under the rubble of a broken stone staircase. A memorial to the members who had fallen in the last Great War was nearly obliterated. The next morning Churchill, wrapped in a fur-collar coat against the bitter cold, visited the wreckage of the place he loved so dearly and stood close to tears at the sight. "It's horrible," he murmured to a friend, who replied that it was just like the Germans to hit the best part. "Where Cromwell signed King Charles' death warrant," Churchill grunted. Around the corner, in a nearby corridor whose windows had been blasted out, there sat in stony silence a bust of a former minister whose mercurial genius (but not his madness) had been passed on to his son; the nameplate read simply, "Randolph Henry Spencer Churchill, 1849–1895."

But arrayed against this orgy of calculated destruction, there was in the English national character a rather stolid, unspectacular, and altogether admirable ability to absorb a tremendous amount of physical and psychological punishment and never break. That trait never showed itself to better advantage than in the bitterly cold autumn and winter of 1940.

After a brief moment of shell shock in September at the start of the blitz, the nation made up its mind that the bombs were nothing more than an ordeal to be endured, something that made life decidedly dangerous and damnably unpleasant for a while, but something that sooner or later must pass away; and in the end there still would be an England. The nation's mood, one observer found, was based upon "a quaint old British idea that nobody is going to push them around with any lasting success." American journalists like Edward R. Murrow visited England and sent home frantic messages of horrible death falling from the skies; Englishmen reacted far less emotionally to the blitz and the threat looming across the Channel. "Have you heard any of these stories about the possibility of an *invasion?*" murmured Lord Halifax, Churchill's foreign minister. "That would be a great bore." At most there was a universal feeling of living through a crucial moment in the world's history, not unlike Paris during the French Revolution. The urbane British diplomat and author Harold Nicolson compared it to "falling down a mountain. One is aware of death and fate, but thinks mainly of catching hold of some jutting piece of rock. I have a sense of strain and unhappiness; but none of fear. One feels so proud."

From his lofty observation perch, George Orwell looked out over England after the bombs had fallen and decided that "when all is said and done one's main impression is the immense stolidity of ordinary people, the widespread vague consciousness that things can never be the same again, and yet, together with that, the tendency of life to slip back into the familiar pattern." Hotel doormen proudly informed visitors of the number of raids their city had endured and scoffed at the Germans' poor aim ("It's appalling how bad the Germans shoot—you wouldn't believe anybody could be so unfortunate"). Old women refused to panic and explained to inquisitive reporters, "What's the use to bother? Either the bomb has your name on it or it hasn't." "Dearie," boasted a cockney lady, "my uncle that's ninety-two was bombed right out of his bed and his false teeth that was in a water jar on the table fell on the floor and broke." "Blime me," replied her companion. Lunching at Sibyl Colefax's flat with Somerset Maugham and Lady Diana Cooper when the bombers appeared, H. G. Wells refused to leave the table until he had finished his cheese: "I'm enjoying a very good lunch. Why should I be disturbed by some wretched little barbarian in a machine? This thing has no surprises for me. I foresaw it long ago. Sibyl, I want my cheese." One day a low-flying Luftwaffe fighter drove Alec Guinness and his unoffending bicycle into a ditch, whereupon the young actor picked himself up and dusted himself off and declared himself "outraged and ready for anything." There was a marked increase in children's dreams about firemen; but they were reassuring dreams, not nightmares. And Agatha Christie witnessed three farmers near her home outside of Dittisham standing around an unexploded bomb. "Dang it all," said one of the farmers, giving the device a contemptuous kick, "regular nasty it is, I call it, sending those things down—nasty!" Another kick. "Can't even explode properly," he muttered disparagingly.

They were all heroes, and they knew it, and it made them proud.

Churchill, too, was proud of them, and told them so at every available opportunity. Few politicians have ever had the common people of England as completely united behind them as Churchill had at the end of 1940. After a decade spent wandering lonely in the political wilderness, distrusted by his colleagues in the Conservative party as excessively ambitious, and derided by his enemies as "a fire-eater and a militarist," Churchill now stood thoroughly vindicated as all of his dire predictions about the consequences of British military unpreparedness suddenly came true in the spring of 1940—although some dilettantes still suspected that Winston loved war a little too much, and that his words sometimes were a bit too lighthearted and irreverent when discussing human tragedy.

"Life is a whole and luck is a whole," Winston was fond of saying, "and no part of them can be separated from the rest," and of no man was this more true than Churchill himself. Until September 1939, his political career had been, in the words of his foremost biographer, "a study in failure." After entering Parliament in 1900 and enjoying a decade and a half of nearly uninterrupted advancement, Churchill had been cast out of office after the disastrous Gallipoli campaign of 1915, resurrected at the end of the war, and then shunted aside once more by Baldwin and Chamberlain in 1929. After four decades of political life, he had, remarkably, failed to acquire any significant personal support from either his parliamentary colleagues or the country at large. At the age of sixty-six, Churchill had at last landed at Number 10 Downing Street in May 1940 not because he had altered the beliefs that had helped keep him out of office since 1929 (and which were, in many ways, drawn straight from mid-Victorian England and the glory days of the empire), but because the times had changed and his convictions now were shared by the vast majority of his countrymen. "He is a man who leads forlorn hopes," Harold Nicolson had written prophetically of Churchill in 1931, "and when the hopes of England become forlorn, he will once again be summoned to leadership."

More than anything else, Churchill was a romantic; for him, it was "always the hour of fate and the crack of doom." (This trait often revealed itself in posturing and playacting. Winston allegedly was the only British prime minister ever to wear a military uniform—at times an R.A.F. suit, or an admiral's cockade—while in office.) Restless, supremely self-confident, emotional, courageous, excitable, and above all savagely tenacious, he represented precisely the sort of larger-than-life persona that could inspire England when the nation was fighting for its very life. What Englishmen loved most about Churchill, thought Mollie Panter-Downes, "is his great gift for making them forget discomfort, danger, and loss and remember only that they are living history." Americans, too, were vastly impressed; *Time* magazine named Churchill as its "Man of the Year" for 1940. (Hitler, who had won the award in 1938, came in second.) Certainly power seemed to agree with the Prime Minister. Contemporaries noted that Winston had never looked better than at the end of 1940: "the pale and globular look about his cheeks has gone," wrote Nicolson, who was serving in the Ministry of Information at the time. "He is more solid about the face and thinner." And yet there was something about Churchill's eyes that haunted Nicolson:

> . . . The lids are not in the least weary, nor are there any pouches or black lines. But the eyes themselves are glaucous, vigilant, angry, combative, visionary and tragic. In a way they are the eyes of a man who is much preoccupied and is unable to rivet his attention on minor things (such as me). But in another sense they are the eyes of a man faced by an ordeal or tragedy, and combining vision, truculence, resolution and great unhappiness.

Wrapped in a fur coat and topped with an odd little black Homburg hat, clenching a large cigar firmly between his teeth, hurtling through the cities in a bombproof armored car (which someone said looked like "a huge painted thermos bottle"), Churchill's stout, thickset figure became a common sight wherever the land had been especially hard hit by the German bombs. Walking with a careless slouch, his heavy shoulders hunched and his large head bent forward, he strode along like a charging rugby player through the rubble and puddles half a foot deep, marveling at the resilient capacity of his people, reassuring them that their sacrifices were winning the war; it was, after all, the first time that Hitler's will had been thwarted since the fighting began. "Stick to it, Winnie! We won't crack up!" they called out confidently. "No sir," the P.M. replied, "we won't crack up." By the end of the year, Churchill was living in a heavily reinforced annex to his principal residence. There was a splendid view of London from the rooftop (where an overhead cover protected him from flying splinters), and on clear nights the Prime Minister liked to "walk in the moonlight and watch the fireworks."

Unfortunately, much of the rest of London was stuck in considerably less attractive surroundings during the nightly raids. Very little had been done before September to provide clean, well-lit shelters from the bombs, and decent sleeping arrangements evolved slowly and haphazardly. At first many Londoners slept under railway arches, in warehouse or brewery basements, or church crypts. By the end of December there were about one million people spending their nights underground in various parts of the city. There were the tube shelters, of course, where people hauled their bedding to the subway platforms every night. "The tiresome part," Kenneth Clark decided, "was not fear of death, but dragging one's mattress up and down every day (one couldn't leave it, as it would immediately have been stolen by the messenger boys). Then it was miserable to go out in search of breakfast with the smell of burning in the air, and the clink of broken glass under one's feet."

In some districts there were also great basement vaults, divided into special "married" sections (with double beds) and "snoring" and "quiet" areas (nurses stood by in the quiet sectors, ready to give a firm turn to the heads of any snorers who had inadvertently chosen the wrong side). Official shelters provided narrow wooden bunks—some infested with vermin—fitted to the walls, two or three tiers high, with barely enough room for the already foul-smelling air to circulate in between. It was an arrangement especially inconvenient for mothers holding infants all night long. Most people slept in their day clothes or specially designed "siren suits" that resembled oversized rompers, waiting until they returned home the next morning to bathe and don a fresh outfit. There was, of course, no privacy at all, no opportunity for families to live as a separate unit. Night after night, there were always other people living just an arm's length away. People slept sprawled over chairs or on the floor; every square inch of space was taken. Lice seemed to be everywhere, and health authorities constantly feared an epidemic of diphtheria. Usually there was no running water, and the only latrines were buckets behind tattered makeshift curtains. (The government predicted that conventional toilets would be available in five or six months.) Conditions were worst in the East End, the most heavily bombed-out part of the city, where many who had lost their homes were forced to live in long lines of small, damp, cold, dark cell-like structures (originally built to shelter coal supplies) with cement seats for beds. Ernie Pyle nearly wept at his first sight of life in the shelters:

> A bombed building looks like something you have seen before—it looks as though a hurricane had struck. But the sight of thousands of poor, opportunityless people lying in weird positions against cold steel, with all their clothes on, hunched up in blankets, lights shining in their eyes, breathing fetid air—lying there far underground like rabbits, not fighting, not even mad, just helpless, scourged, weakly, waiting for the release of another dawn—that, I tell you, is life without redemption.

T. S. Eliot, misanthropic and high-strung to begin with, could not bear the claustrophic sensation of being shut up all night with strangers. "I would feel the need to get out as quickly as possible, to escape all those faces gathered there, to escape all that humanity." Finally, at daybreak, bystanders on the surface experienced a ghostly visitation, the emergence of what Malcolm Muggeridge described as "grey dishevelled figures carrying blankets, sometimes draped in them, emerging in the pale light from below ground. Like a Brueghel painting of Resurrection Day—pre-destined souls rising from their graves."

No matter where they spent their nights, nearly everyone was perpetually short of sleep. Fatigue made the inevitable material shortages (food, fuel, and clothing) even more annoying. Living in the country, Virginia Woolf found herself weighing and measuring every spoonful of sugar and every ounce of fat. "How one enjoys food now," she confided to her diary. "I make up imaginary meals." One day in late December she took a long look at the ways the war had changed her life: "It changes it when I order dinner. Our ration of margarine is so small that I cant think of any pudding save milk pudding. We have no sugar to make sugar puddings: no pastry, unless I buy it ready made. The shops don't fill till midday. Things are bought fast. In the afternoon they are often gone. Meat ration diminishes this week. Milk is so cut that we have to consider even the cats saucer. . . . Petrol changes the day too. . . . All prices rise steadily. The screw is much increased since the summer. We buy no clothes but make do with the old. These are inconveniences rather than hardships. We don't go hungry or cold. But luxury is snipped off, & hospitality. It takes thought & trouble to feed one extra. The post is the most obvious inconvenience perhaps. It takes 2 days to get a London letter: 4 to get a parcel. Turkeys impossible. The pinch is said to be worse than the last war. If it increases much we shall be hungry, I suppose. . . . Then the black out—thats half an hour daily drudgery. We cant use the dining room after dark. . . . A certain old age feeling sometimes makes me think I cant spend force as I used. And my hand shakes. Otherwise we draw breath as usual. And its a day when every bough is bright green & the sun dazzles me."

In fact, by December the greatest threat to England came not from the air, but from German attacks on British shipping: nearly four hundred merchant vessels—two million tons—had been sunk by the end of 1940. "Tonnage became an obsession, a tyrant dominating everything," observed Charles de Gaulle, who arrived in London at the end of November. "The life and glory of England were staked every day, upon the sea." Facing an alarming shortage of shipping capacity, the government reduced food imports to make room for men and munitions, and Churchill put out an urgent call to the United States for relief.

All the wartime privations seemed especially poignant during the holiday season. For the many Londoners who had sent their young sons and daughters into the countryside or across the Atlantic to Canada or America for safekeeping, it was a Christmas without children; by late December, 80 percent of London's children had left the city. Despite a last-minute plea from the archbishop of Canterbury, it was also a Christmas without bells, since the government had decreed months before that church bells should be rung only to sound the alarm in case of invasion. No bright-colored holiday lights shone from behind the blackout curtains at night. It was a Christmas when shoppers passed by expensive silks and perfumes in favor of more practical gifts such as fleece-lined sleeping bags with hoods, or beaver or skunk coats, or stainless steel wrist watches with waterproof luminous dials for men on active service. Toys were in short supply, and children had to be content with books and paint boxes instead. There was plenty of homegrown English holly, but no mistletoe from France. Turkeys were almost impossible to obtain, as was the traditional roast beef, forcing cooks to rely upon imaginative recipes using carrots, cabbage, and mutton. The Ministry of Transport urged the public to refrain from traveling to family reunions over the holidays, to keep the railway system free for the war effort.

Nevertheless, the nation did its best to keep its yuletide spirits up. Signs in shop windows read, CHRISTMAS IS 1,940 YEARS OLD AND HITLER IS ONLY 51. HE CAN'T SPOIL OUR CHRISTMAS, and THERE'LL ALWAYS BE A CHRISTMAS, or, defiantly, OPEN AS USUAL. (In what used to be the front window of a bombed-out tea shop, the owner had placed a placard: MORE OPEN THAN USUAL.) Greeting cards bore best wishes for "anything but a Jerry Christmas"; King George's own Christmas card featured a photograph of the royal family standing in front of the bombed-out portion of Buckingham Palace. The *Times* of London reported a brisk business in its satirical Hitler Calendar and its eight-page booklet of extracts from the speeches and writings of Mussolini, either of which was available for a shilling.

Christmas Day itself was quiet, due to an unofficial three-day bombing truce arranged through Washington. Churchill spent the day with his family at Chequers; his daughter Mary wrote in her diary that "this was one of the happiest Christmases I can remember. Despite all the terrible events going on around us . . . I've never before seen the family look so happy—so united . . ." The king and queen, with their two young daughters, Elizabeth and Margaret, attended church services in the country in the morning, and then after lunch sponsored a children's party. (George VI was a firm believer in keeping Christmas celebrations simple; the family had never had a Christmas tree, and this year was no exception.) Later in the afternoon, the king read a Christmas message to the empire as part of a special one-hour Christmas Under Fire program on the BBC, which also featured a choir of Allied troops in Palestine singing "O Come, All Ye Faithful" from an olive grove near Bethlehem, a group of London mothers and children thanking their hosts for a wonderful old-fashioned Christmas in the country, a broadcast from an R.A.F. patrol over the Channel, and a celebration of Holy Communion from the six-hundred-year-old crypt beneath the ruins of Coventry Cathedral. Those who had lost their homes, or who had made warm friendships underground, spent their Christmas in the shelters, where unwrapped gifts (there was also a shortage of paper) lay under makeshift trees adorned with cotton and toy balloons, and carolers sang "Silent Night" to children who lay wrapped in patched-up quilts on the hard cold cement floor. A last-minute hookup between the BBC, the Canadian Broadcasting Company, and NBC in New

York gave a dozen children a few brief moments to speak with their parents in Britain; the young ones urged their folks to keep their "thumbs up" until they could all be together again, and then a small boy brought out his accordion and the children all sang "There'll Always Be an England."

Before Parliament adjourned at the end of the year, Churchill stood in the House of Commons and reminded the country that a long hard struggle still lay ahead: "It is no good hoping and asking for immediate conclusions. We are still a half-armed nation fighting a well-armed nation, a fully armed nation, a nation which has already passed the saturation point in its armaments. But," the Prime Minister predicted, "in the course of 1941 we shall become a well-armed nation too, and that will open possibilities to us which have not been opened up to the present." And he left his audience with the reassurance that Britain's position at the end of December 1940 was immeasurably improved from the chaotic, perilous days of May and June. No one, Churchill said, could look back on the terrible events of the past year "without a feeling of thankfulness that we have been preserved so far and that we have made progress after a moment when many in the world, including our best friends abroad, despaired of our continued power of resistance, that we have maintained ourselves, that our resistance has grown, that we have preserved ourselves secure in our Island home and reached out long and strong hands across the seas to discharge the obligations which we have undertaken to countries which have put their faith in us."

Then the bombers returned. On the night of Sunday December 29, flying embers fell like snow as thousands of fire bombs descended in a merciless three-hour barrage upon the City of London. It was the most destructive attack of the year. Hitler and Göring had timed their assault well; at the end of the holiday weekend, there were virtually no watchers on the rooftops, and the fire patrols were late in arriving at their stations. The old wooden buildings in the City burned like piles of kindling, the flames fanned by southwesterly winds that grew to gale force before the evening was over. Then the bombers dropped high explosives upon the fires. Were it not for the bad weather over northern France that kept many German planes grounded, the destruction would have been even worse.

At first the flames lit up the sky almost to a daytime brilliance. "The smoke rose over the roof tops like a tumultuous sea of scarlet and gold, with here and there momentary green flashes as a new shower of incendiaries fell into the furnace," reported one witness. "Westward, towards the Law Courts, the white Portland stone glowed a lurid pink in the glare. On the jagged skyline of roofs black figures moved to and fro, silhouetted against the flames, as the firemen waged their unending battle. Every now and then, as the hateful billows of glowing cloud blew away, one saw dimly through them the shape of the dome of St. Paul's, like a ship sailing steadfastly through a stormy sea." Water cascaded into the sky in a hundred fountains of spray. Injured firemen were borne away in ambulances driven by women volunteers; some firemen died under falling buildings. The air was filled with flying glass. Firefighters were finally forced to use dynamite to stop the spread of the blaze. Ernie Pyle, appalled and entranced by the inferno, wrote of "the monstrous loveliness" of London on fire: "These things all went together to make the most hateful, most beautiful single scene I have ever known." For a time London's largest shelter, in which fifteen hundred people were living, was almost completely surrounded by flames. "Tonight," said Edward R. Murrow on his evening radio broadcast, "the bomber planes of the German Third Reich hit London where it hurts the most—in the heart."

The night became known as the Second Great Fire of London, rivaling the fearsome destruction wrought by the disaster of 1666 during the reign of Charles II. On Monday morning, the narrow streets remained choked with smoke and bits of masonry and brick that fell from wrecked buildings; the heat was still intense, making the gusty December winds warm against the faces of the people who stumbled over the smoldering rubble and the shards of broken glass and the long winding firemen's hoses as they made their way to work, or to the morning prayer service which was held as usual at St. Paul's. Cheapside and Newgate were gutted. The house in Fleet Street where Dr. Samuel Johnson had compiled his dictionary was burnt out. Eight Wren churches (seven of which had been built on the sites of ancient churches destroyed in the first Great Fire) were severely damaged, including St. Lawrence Jewry, the church of the Corporation of London, with its richly paneled oak vestry; St. Bride's, a "madrigal in stone," whose slender tower had been the highest spire in the city; and St. Mary-the-Virgin, where John Milton had married his second wife in 1656. The eleventh-century parchment charter granted to the City of London by William the Conqueror had vanished into smoke. Guildhall, the seat of the Corporation of the City of London, was a shell of blackened, twisted ironwork and charred wood, although along the north wall of the Great Hall the monuments to Wellington and Chatham stood mostly undamaged. Over the ruined building a huge Union Jack flew above the porch.

Churchill and his wife spent two hours walking through the streets that morning. The people greeted them with cheers and shouts of "God bless you, sir." One woman ran up to the Prime Minister and asked, "When will the war be over?" Churchill paused, and then he turned to look her in the face and replied without smiling, "When we have beaten them."

"You Gave Us Our Fuehrer"

"He who does not keep moving is lost."
—BENITO MUSSOLINI

Christmas Day, Berlin: brilliant sunshine and bitter cold. On the gaily decorated trees inside the houses there hung the latest version of a children's game called We Sail Against England. The government distributed free apples and candy to the poor. By early afternoon, theaters and restaurants were crowded to capacity, despite the continuing official restrictions on all private automobile travel. From the radio came the voice of Rudolf Hess, Hitler's deputy, with a Christmas prayer: "Almighty God, you gave us our Fuehrer. . . . Now give us the power to help him."

Germany entered its second winter of war—and its eighth winter under Nazi rule—victorious and yet vaguely discontented. After the astonishing success of the springtime blitzkrieg, the people believed the fighting would be over by the end of the year; but since Britain stubbornly held out against the New Order being forged across Europe by the force of German arms, the war went on month after dreary month, and the fatherland required still more sacrifices. Between the British blockade and the normal rigors of wartime rationing, the weekly official allotment of meat in Germany had been reduced to a pound a week, along with four ounces of margarine or butter and one egg. There was no coffee or tea in Berlin (having long since been replaced by ground roast barley), no citrus fruits, and very little chocolate or sugar. But for the present generation of Germans, many of whom had known real hunger during the Great War and its aftermath, and most of whom—especially those who had grown up in Berlin—had suffered to some degree from malnutrition when they were children (living primarily on bread, potatoes, cabbage, and turnips, and very little milk or meat), the food shortages in December 1940 did not seem unduly harsh. In fact, this winter even provided a few more luxuries than the last, thanks to the imports of food requisitioned from the conquered countries of western Europe.

Civilian morale thus remained relatively high, although in the capital there was certainly no overwhelming popular support for the war, or for the Nazi regime in general. The American diplomat George Kennan believed the people of Berlin to be the least Nazified people in Germany: every day they greeted each other with a conventional "Guten Morgen" instead of the prescribed Nazi "Heil Hitler" salute; by October, when it had become obvious that Operation Sea Lion would never get off the beaches of France, the words to the battle song, "We are marching, marching, marching against England" ("Wir fahren, wir fahren, wir fahren gegen Engeland") had been replaced by the mocking, sarcastic lyrics, "We are marching, marching, marching; we have for years been marching, with hair whitened by the passage of time we go on marching, against England." The news of the fall of France was greeted with remarkable reserve in Berlin; riding on the upper deck of an enclosed bus in the city that afternoon, Kennan could hear the conversation of nearly all the passengers, but he heard no one give the slightest attention to what was undoubtedly the greatest victory of German arms since 1870. Instead, "the talk was all of food cards and the price of stockings." Indeed, continued Kennan, "what struck one most about wartime Berlin was the undemonstrative but unmistakable inner detachment of the people from the pretentious purposes of the regime, and the way in which ordinary life went on, as best it could, under the growing difficulties of wartime discipline." This war belonged to the government, not the people.

And yet it was not quite that simple. One day Gertrude Stein sat on a hillside in France and spoke about the war with an elderly farmer, who said of the Germans, "Do not say that it had to do with their leaders, they are a people whose fate it is always to choose a man whom they force to lead them in a direction in which they do not want to go." Beneath the reserve and the flippant cynicism there was undoubtedly a national sense of satisfaction in Germany that the defeats of 1918 and the disgrace of Versailles had at last been avenged. Hitler already had added 140,000 square miles of territory to the German Reich, and soldiers of the fatherland occupied another 290,000 square miles. William Shirer, then stationed in Berlin as a CBS radio correspondent, reported that the Wehrmacht's stunning victories, along with the long-sought political unification of the German people (achieved through the incorporation of parts of Austria, Poland, and Czechoslovakia), had "knitted the German nation together, given the people self-confidence and a sense of historical mission, and made them forget their personal dislike of the Nazi regime, its leaders, and the barbaric things it has done. Also—coupled with the rebirth of the army and air force and the totalitarian reorganization of industry, trade, and agriculture on a scale never before realized in this world—it makes the German feel strong. For most Germans this is an end in itself . . ."

For Hitler, though, it was not enough. Discouraged by the logistic difficulties of mounting a full-scale invasion of the English coast, frustrated by the Luftwaffe's inability to defeat Britain—by the end of December,

Germany had lost more than three thousand planes (and most of their crews), either shot down or crippled during the bombing raids across the Channel—and enraged by the retaliatory attacks by the R.A.F. on Berlin and the heavy industrial areas of the Ruhr (raids that accomplished little in the way of material destruction, but which dealt a heavy psychological blow to German civilians forced to spend five or six sleepless hours every night in a bomb shelter), Hitler turned instead in the autumn of 1940 to the east, to the homeland of the Bolshevik ideology he despised so fervently: to the Soviet Union of Joseph Stalin.

If Hitler was already disposed to strike against Russia, the visit of Soviet Foreign Commissar Vyacheslav Molotov (the Number Two man in the Kremlin) to Berlin in November clinched the decision. When Hitler and his own foreign minister, the widely detested Joachim von Ribbentrop, laid before Molotov the glittering prospect of untold riches in the Middle East and India once Britain was defeated and the spoils of empire divided among Germany, Russia, Italy, and Japan, Molotov stubbornly insisted upon discussing matters of more immediate concern: specifically, Soviet security interests in Finland, the Balkans, and the Baltic. What, Molotov wanted to know, were Germany's intentions in those regions? What provisions would be made to guarantee Soviet control of the areas along Russia's western border? Hitler, who had his own plans for the Balkans, tried to wave aside these issues as trivial details that could be settled later, but Molotov would not be distracted by vague promises of rewards in the none-too-certain future. (The fact that the talks were interrupted by a British air raid on Berlin did nothing to persuade Molotov that the British Empire was tottering on the verge of collapse.) Stalin apparently believed that he held enough bargaining chips to force Hitler into territorial concessions, but he was wrong. Hitler informed Martin Bormann that by the time Molotov had boarded a train for Moscow, the acrimonious discussions had convinced him that Stalin would eventually betray Germany and join the enemy: "War with Russia had become inevitable, whatever we did; and to postpone it only meant that we should later have to fight under conditions far less favorable. I therefore decided, as soon as Molotov departed, that I would settle accounts with Russia as soon as fair weather permitted." On December 18, Hitler issued Directive Number 21, ordering the German armed forces to "be prepared, even before the conclusion of the war against England, *to crush Soviet Russia in a rapid campaign.*" Code name: Operation Barbarossa.

But first Germany deserved a moment to rest and celebrate the victories of the past year. (The Wehrmacht had, in fact, already been resting on its laurels for six months.) Hitler reportedly spent Christmas Day with his troops, visiting a long-range battery on the Channel coast and a bomber squadron in western France, and distributing yuletide gifts— mostly autographed photographs of himself or, to special friends, his own watercolor paintings. The Fuehrer's Christmas card this year featured a reproduction of the Winged Victory of Samothrace (German troops had recently appropriated the original from the Louvre to decorate Hitler's office in Berlin), accompanied by a bevy of German bombers and Messerschmitts; inside was the inscription "Our Winged Victory." Minister of Public Enlightenment and Propaganda Dr. Joseph Goebbels (Heidelberg U., class of 1921), the clubfooted ex-journalist who had forsaken a less than promising literary career for the pleasure of serving the Nazi cause, cheerfully assisted Kris Kringle in handing out presents to the poor children of Berlin, or at least to the *Kinder* who remained in the city. Like their counterparts in London, many German children had been evacuated from Berlin and the Ruhr as a precaution against the British air raids. Goebbels apologized to their parents for the inconvenience, "but that is the way things happen in wartime. We must all make big sacrifices. Every mother must rest assured, however, that no matter where her child may be today it is surrounded by love."

Goebbels, whose parents had hoped that he might make the priesthood his vocation, also did his best to ensure that this Christmas fully reflected the peculiar Nazi brand of public morality. The holiday celebrations, he decreed, should be limited to Christmas Eve and Christmas Day; "a sloppy Christmas tree atmosphere lasting several weeks is out of tune with the militant mood of the German people." There would be little holiday leave for troops on active duty. Children in evacuation billets would not be allowed to return to their parents for the day. The government forbade all nude shows and performances of strip dancers in the countryside, in the small towns, or in front of German soldiers; "lewd erotic jokes" were likewise prohibited. (Hitler and Goebbels believed this sort of thing should be permitted only in the larger cities, where people's morals had already been irremediably corrupted.) And behind the doors of a castle outside of Stuttgart and a medical institute near Dresden, the "mercy killings" of thousands of "mentally deficient" German citizens went on silently and secretly. (Begun in November 1939, this horrifying Nazi euthanasia program, code-named *Aktion t 4,* involved the execution, without public hearing or appeal, of nearly 100,000 helpless victims— those whom the government classified as retarded, insane, or incurably ill—before it was ended in August 1941 following a heroic protest from the pulpit by Catholic Bishop Clemens Count von Galen. In many ways, *Aktion t 4* served as a testing ground for the methods of mass murder employed several years later in the Nazi annihilation camps.)

On New Year's Eve, the Fuehrer—brilliant, obsessed, and alone— promised his troops that 1941 would at last bring them total victory over "the democratic warmongers and Jewish capitalists." "A momentous year in German history has come to an end," he proclaimed, and now Germany was ready and armed as never before. "Up to now the Lord God has given

his approval to our fight. If we carry out our duty loyally and bravely he
will not desert us in the future. . . . Soldiers of the National Socialist armed
German forces of the Greater German Reich! The year 1941 will bring
consummation of the greatest victory in our history."

France was a confused tangle of conflicting loyalties, clashing egos,
collaboration, resignation, and resistance. Physically, it was not even one
country any longer. Faced with the collapse of the nation's armed forces
in June, the corrupt and incompetent Third Republic had simply voted
itself out of existence, and in its place there was a crazy quilt of military
and political jurisdictions: the northern two-thirds of France and the entire western coastline were occupied by the Nazi conquerors; the region
surrounding Calais and Dunkirk, where the forces for Operation Sea Lion
were being assembled (albeit halfheartedly), was set apart as a "prohibited
zone"; a "Zone Rouge" was carved out of the northeast, stretching from
the Franco-Swiss border north to the German frontier (roughly, from the
Ardennes to Poligny), wherein the German government established internment camps for enemy aliens; most of the long-disputed territories of
Alsace and Lorraine had already been assimilated into the Greater German Reich; and, finally, there was the southern sector, as yet unoccupied,
governed from the collaborationist capital of Vichy.

When Simone de Beauvoir visited Paris in June, shortly after the
German troops had entered the city, she found it extraordinarily deserted.
Nearly half the population had fled in panic before the invaders. (And
many who had been a part of that mass exodus now were dead from
German bombs dropped indiscriminately upon the long columns of refugees.) De Beauvoir, then a relatively unknown thirty-two-year-old writer
whose constant companion, Jean-Paul Sartre, was one of the million and
a half French soldiers captured by the Germans, noticed a sad feeling of
death and stagnation in the Paris air: "I shall sit here and rot for years,"
she wrote in her journal. "Passy and Auteuil are utterly dead; there's a
smell of lime blossom and leafy greenness about them that reminds me
both of the coming holidays and of time past. Even the concierges have
packed up and gone." The German soldiers, she remarked, "have dull
faces, and look like tourists. . . . I observe them but register nothing."

At first the German occupation troops behaved with exaggerated
courtesy and consideration toward the civilian population; no one, not
even the scrupulously correct French, could accuse them of improper
behavior. By December, however, the veil had been lifted. Food grew
ever more scarce and rationing more stringent throughout the occupied
zone; French workers were rounded up and sent into Germany to serve
the Reich's industrial machine (according to the blueprint of the New
Order, France was to be primarily an agricultural nation); Communists
and trade union leaders were arrested and imprisoned. Nothing was sa-

cred: twelve million bottles of the finest French champagne were requisitioned by the German administration. The Reich forbade public celebrations of Armistice Day (November 11, the day Germany had surrendered in 1918); when French students demonstrated in the streets of Paris anyway, Nazi soldiers fired warning volleys from submachine guns and then tossed hand grenades into the crowds. At the end of December a French civilian was shot for showing disrespect to a German officer. "For the first time," wrote de Beauvoir, "the 'correct' Occupants had officially announced that they had executed a Frenchman guilty of not having bowed the knee." The border into Vichy France was closed.

Although foreign observers often deprecated the importance of the line of demarcation between the occupied and unoccupied zones, those who lived in the south understood the difference. "One might not be very free in the unoccupied," reported Gertrude Stein from her villa at Bilignin, "but we were pretty free and in the occupied they were not free, the difference between being pretty free and not free at all is considerable." When the bewildered leaders of the Third Republic had finally stopped running from the German blitzkrieg, they selected Vichy as the capital of unoccupied France largely because the resort city had so much room already available for offices and accommodations in its innumerable gambling casinos, music halls, hotels, and villas. "It seemed wryly appropriate," remarked the young American diplomat Robert Murphy, "that the government of defeated France should choose a place hitherto celebrated only for its rather disagreeable medicinal waters used to treat unpleasant but not necessarily fatal diseases." By the end of the year more than seven million refugees—Jews, Spanish exiles, and assorted enemies of fascism—had found an uncertain, temporary haven in the southern third of France.

Vichy France was governed by one man: Marshal Henri Philippe Pétain, former commander in chief of the French army, the hero of Verdun who had inspired France in the spring and summer of 1916 with the immortal words, "They shall not pass," and the man who also had made the final decision to surrender in the summer of 1940—"It is with a broken heart that I tell you today that fighting must cease . . ." It was a decision undoubtedly supported by the vast majority of Frenchmen at the time; the nation—spiritually bankrupt and racked with government corruption—had no intention of suffering the loss of a million more men, as it had in the long years between 1914 and 1918. Like many of his fellow countrymen, Pétain believed that the armistice had bought France valuable time, and that his Gallic ingenuity would eventually outwit the German conquerors and turn their overwhelming military victory into a political defeat. (When someone asked him who he thought was winning the war, Germany or England, Pétain pointed to his chest and replied, "Moi.") Meanwhile, he would rebuild France in his own stern image. Now eighty-four years old, the Marshal sat in a spacious, well-heated corner office in the Hôtel du Parc (where wealthy invalids had whiled away the winters in years past) and serenely informed an American visitor in December that the ideals of individual liberty fashioned during the Revolution of 1789 had at last come to the end of a long run; the disastrous military defeats of 1940 had revealed the rottenness and decay at the heart of the French Republic. France, he said, required a new revolution dedicated to communal discipline and sacrifice for the good of the state. To ensure that the people fully understood the direction in which he was leading France, Pétain ordered the slogan, "Liberté, Eqalité, Fraternité" erased from the public buildings in his domain and replaced with the words (in French), "Work, Family, Fatherland."

Pétain was, without question, the most popular man in France in December 1940. He was the omnipotent father figure the French people believed they needed to restore order in a time of crisis. As Gertrude Stein explained in her own inimitable way, "the French love to talk about discipline, they always think their country is very disorderly as a matter of fact they are so traditional, and they love so passionately to grow vegetables that they can really only be orderly, and never anything else but they like to think there is no order and that there should be." Every day the Marshal, with his massive head of snow-white hair and an impassive expression on his face, would emerge from the Hôtel du Parc for a walk, usually alone, but always under the adoring gaze of pilgrims who had come to pay homage to the Father of France. "The men would uncover their heads while their eyes filled with tears," recalled one witness to the ceremony; "once, the members of a whole family even crossed themselves. Only rarely were there cries of 'Vive le Maréchal!' for usually utter silence reigned—a churchlike hush." Every morning, the schoolchildren of Vichy would sing their tribute:

> All the children who love you
> And hold your years dear
> To your supreme call
> Have answered smartly, "Here!"
>
> Marshal, here are we
> Before you, O savior of France,
> We your little buddies swear
> To follow where you advance
>
> For Pétain is France,
> And France is Pétain.

Across the Channel, General Charles de Gaulle sat in a shabby suite of offices on the third floor of St. Stephen's House in London. From behind a secondhand desk, in an uncarpeted room, the General received callers who wished to pledge their services to the cause of Free France. These recruits—and there were not yet very many—saw a tall, very pale, rigid man with tired-out eyes and a close-cropped mustache, stray strands of dark brown hair falling across his forehead, and pale lifeless hands that seemed almost effeminate, seemingly without muscles or arteries; they heard a clear, arrogant, and more than slightly brutal voice spit out his disgust at the betrayal of his country. "He does not like mankind," concluded one visitor, "but he loves history, especially that of France, for whom he is creating a chapter, writing it progressively in his head."

Virtually ostracized from the mainstream of the French military establishment during the 1930s for his insistent and occasionally insubordinate advocacy of autonomous, modernized armored forces (General Weygand scornfully considered him "more a journalist than an officer," and Pétain—under whom de Gaulle had served following his graduation from the military academy of St-Cyr in 1912—called him "an arrogant man, an ingrate and surly"), de Gaulle had been hurriedly appointed undersecretary of national defense by a desperate Prime Minister Paul Reynaud in that chaotic first week of June 1940, just before the final collapse of the Third Republic. Determined to continue the fight from abroad, de Gaulle arrived in England in the middle of June with two pairs of pants, four shirts, a photograph of his family, and very little else. In August he had wangled a grudging agreement from Churchill to work together to restore "the independence and greatness of France"; the British government, however, was not yet totally convinced that de Gaulle was the right man to lead the liberation of France. (The king was not overly fond of him, and around the Foreign Office in Whitehall the General was often referred to as "that ass de Gaulle.") He had burned his bridges behind him; for his defiance of the New Order in France, the Vichy government had sentenced de Gaulle to death. He could return only as a savior, or not at all.

The first step was to create a government-in-exile. So, on October 22, in Brazzaville—the capital of French Equatorial Africa, and one of the few French colonial cities that welcomed de Gaulle—the General proclaimed the existence of the Council for Defense of the Empire, and presented himself as the man who would liberate France. The royal "we" began to appear in his directives; "La France entière, c'est la France Libre. C'est moi!!!" he shouted at Harold Nicolson during dinner one evening at the Savoy in London. And on New Year's Day, he urged the people of France to remain indoors for an hour of meditation in the afternoon as a symbolic "silent protest of crushed France," leaving only the enemy in the streets. It was de Gaulle's strength that he knew well the use of symbols. "A man is not de Gaulle without a great deal of luck, without recourse to magic and to a sense of the fabulous," wrote Jean Lacouture. "A man is not de Gaulle if he does not know how to 'make use of dreams to lead the

French.' " Slowly the Resistance appeared in France under the cover of darkness.

Christmas Eve, Rome: Benito Mussolini arose at 6:30 A.M. as usual. After a brief workout on his favorite jumping horse (a gift from Hitler), a quick shower, and a glass of prune juice for breakfast, the Duce took a quick look at the latest news from the war fronts in Greece and northern Africa, and his day was ruined. At noon, snow began to fall steadily over the city, a rare white Christmas in southern Italy. As he watched the crowds trudge through the slush on their way to afternoon mass (blackout restrictions precluded the traditional Christmas Eve midnight mass), Mussolini nodded his shaved heavy head in approval. "This snow and cold are very good," he said. "In this way our good-for-nothing Italians, this mediocre race, will be improved." (One of Mussolini's most cherished, albeit harebrained, projects was the reforestation of the Apennine Mountains; he hoped this would make Italy's climate colder and snowier, thereby toughening the Italian nation and making it better prepared for the rigors of martial life.) For Christmas 1940, however, the government had decided to appease the bourgeois sentiments of the people by lifting the ration restrictions on meat and pastries, and so there were turkeys, fruitcakes, and sausages for those who could afford them. Many Italian families also had set aside part of their monthly spaghetti ration for a special Christmas Eve dinner.

It had not been a particularly pleasant or rewarding year for Mussolini; in fact, the last six months had been one of the most difficult and humiliating periods since the square-jawed ex-schoolteacher and former journalist had forcibly seized power with the aid of his blackshirt legions following the famous march on Rome in October 1922. Italy had officially entered the war in June—after the Germans had routed the French army—in hopes of gaining several valuable chunks of French real estate at a discount price. Since then, almost nothing had gone right for the Italians. Angry because Hitler had failed to inform him before invading France, Mussolini (*Time's* choice as "flop of the year" for 1940) decided to turn the tables by launching an invasion of Greece without telling the Germans. At six o'clock on the morning of October 28, Italian troops rolled across the border into Greece. "Fuehrer," Mussolini grandly announced to Hitler at a meeting that morning at a railway station in Florence, "we are on the march! Victorious Italian troops crossed the Greco-Albanian border at dawn today!" Hitler was furious, although he did not let the Italians know it; the attack threw his own plans for the Balkans into total disarray. He would have been even more irate had he known that virtually no advance preparation had been made for the invasion. Mussolini had dispatched his troops on the understanding that the campaign would be short and relatively bloodless. For several months, Greek politicians and army officials had been accepting bribes from Rome—reportedly close to $20 million—to ensure that the Italian invaders would encounter little resistance. Mussolini did not know that the Greeks had willingly pocketed the money and now were preparing to doublecross the Italians. Always disdainful of advice from professional military men, Mussolini gave his commanders only two weeks' notice of the invasion and warned that "if anyone makes any difficulties about beating the Greeks I shall resign from being an Italian." (Apparently no one took him up on the offer.)

For a week everything went smoothly. But when the Italians reached the mountains, the Greeks stiffened and stopped the advance. Then, in mid-November, a Greek counterattack actually started pushing the Fascist blackshirts back toward the sea. (Around the British Foreign Office, this was known as "whacking the dirty ice-creamers.") The Greeks were fighting on their own territory and were properly equipped for a winter campaign in the mountains of Epirus, where the rains turned the narrow tracks to mud, where the snow was often eight or ten feet deep and only a mule could pull artillery through the treacherous passes. The Italians, on the other hand, were caught wretchedly ill-prepared. Many of the Fascist soldiers had only summer uniforms (and no gloves) to shield them from the subzero temperatures in the evenings. Their tanks, designed mostly for showing off in parades, broke down in the rugged terrain. Rifles misfired and ammunition was in short supply. There were no bandages in some of the field hospitals. Nor did the Italian army suffer from an overabundance of aggressive leadership; one general at the front spent his evenings composing music for the movies. Forced to fight a defensive war to save themselves from annihilation, twenty thousand Italians died in Greece and Albania, forty thousand more were wounded, twenty-six thousand captured, and eighteen thousand suffered serious injuries from frostbite. One battalion of 550 men returned with only thirty-six survivors. General Badoglio, the Italian chief of staff, told Mussolini that the attack had been an absurd mistake from the beginning; for his candor, the general was pronounced a traitor and an "enemy of the regime," and relieved of his duties.

Meanwhile, the campaign in northern Africa was yielding equally dismal results. An initial series of Italian successes in the autumn had pushed the British back to Cairo, but Marshal Rodolfo Graziani—a master of procrastination—refused to go any farther without massive reinforcements of men and supplies. The unexpected respite permitted the British forces to regroup and launch their own lightning counterattack in December. Led by General Sir Archibald Wavell, the taciturn, one-eyed classical scholar-poet-soldier who had learned how to fight in the desert during his service under Allenby in the First World War, the British caught the Italians completely offguard, and one after another the Italian bases in the desert fell as the retreat turned into a rout. Thousands of Italian soldiers surrendered; British casualties remained remarkably low. The victories bolstered morale back in London, and helped dispel the prevailing suspicion that the British army still thought it was fighting some other long-ago war—the Crimean, perhaps.

Looking westward toward Libya, British troops saw the desert stretching away in an infinity of identical brown ridges, where nothing grew except the tough stringy plants that could survive for months without rain. Sandstorms arrived every day at the same time; the wind cut like a knife, and at night the men huddled in holes in the sand or behind an improvised stone windbreak, wearing three greatcoats against the cold. "It's fine, and I'm all for it," vouched one hawk-faced Australian infantryman, "but I wish you'd tell the cooks not to put so much ——— sand in the ——— stew." "I like it fine," agreed one of his friends. "A man can see so much without moving from where he is standing. All you have to do is wait for the wind to spring up and you can see the whole of the flaming Western Desert go past you in five minutes."

Alan Moorehead, serving as a war correspondent in northern Africa, followed Wavell's troops and witnessed the remarkable sights of deserted Italian outposts and subterranean dugouts filled with luxuries almost unimaginable in wartime: "Officers' beds laid out with clean sheets, chests of drawers filled with linen and abundance of fine clothing of every kind. Uniforms heavy with gold lace and decked with the medals and colours of the parade ground hung upon hangers in company with polished jackboots richly spurred and pale blue sashes and belts finished with great tassels and feathered and embroidered hats and caps. . . . We sat down on the open sand and ate from stores of bottled cherries and greengages; great tins of frozen hams and anchovies; bread that had been baked somehow in the desert; and wines from Frascati and Salerno and Chianti, red and white, and Lacrimae Christi from the slopes of Vesuvius above Naples. . . . The spaghetti was packed in long blue paper packages and stored with great sacks of macaroni and other wheat foods as numerous as they used to be in the shops of Italy before the war. Parmesan cheeses as big as small cart-wheels and nearly a foot thick lay about in neat piles except where some hungry soldier had slashed one open with his sword. Ten pound tins of Estratto di Pomidoro—the tomato extract vital to so many Italian dishes—formed the bulk of the tinned stuff. . . . We sampled one package that seemed at first to contain dry grass, but brewed itself over a stove into a rich minestrone soup." Above ground, all the abandoned provisions were covered with two days' layer of sand.

The Italians had tried to conquer the desert and civilize it with material comforts. In the end, the desert had defeated them. By Christmas, over 35,000 Italian soldiers—including 1,704 officers and five generals— had been taken prisoner (many of them spent the holidays teaching their

British captors how to cook spaghetti properly); British losses totaled 72 dead and 738 wounded. Wavell was besieging Bardia, thirty miles inside the Libyan border. And Mussolini was complaining about the miserable material he had to work with. "Even Michelangelo had need of marble to make statues," the Duce told Count Ciano, his son-in-law and foreign minister. "If he had had only clay he would have been nothing more than a potter. A people who for sixteen centuries have been an anvil cannot become a hammer within a few years."

In November 1940, Japan began withdrawing its veteran divisions from China, where they had been battling Chiang Kai-shek's Nationalists since 1937, in preparation for a thrust southward into Indochina. The Japanese already had wrung concession after concession from confused and frightened French colonial officials; ports in the Gulf of Tonkin had been occupied and transformed into staging areas for a southern invasion; Japan was encouraging Thailand to cross the Mekong into Laos and Cambodia, and had even supplied the Thais with the aircraft and machine guns to do the job. Claire Chennault, the American aviator serving as an adviser to Chiang, guessed that the Japanese themselves were heading for the harbor of Saigon.

From Tokyo, Ambassador Joseph Grew informed his superiors in Washington that Japanese extremists were "definitely in the saddle and are supported by at least a substantial section of the public." The Imperial Japanese Government had already pledged itself to a military and economic alliance with Nazi Germany and Fascist Italy—an action that convinced Washington that Japanese aggression should hereafter be viewed "as part of the general assault of the dictators against the free world"—and now, Grew reported, it had prepared a program to sweep through Greater East Asia and the South Seas and obtain political and economic control of the region as quickly as possible. Grew believed that Japan's greatest fear was Anglo-American cooperation in the Far East, and that no one was yet certain which way the Soviet Union would jump if and when it finally left the fence. "But we do know," concluded the veteran ambassador, "with almost mathematical certainty, that if the United States follows a policy of laissez-faire, allowing that forward sweep to continue as fast as it can continue in the light of other obstacles, it will sooner or later constitute for us a problem not merely of maintaining our intangible interests in the Far East but of preserving the safety of our outlying possessions. . . . The precise problem facing our Government, as I see it, is to determine not *whether* we are going to act, but at just what point in the Japanese advance we are going to act."

iii

"The Country Is in Danger"

"And if it weren't for the generally diseased condition of
the world, we would feel that our cup runneth over."
— E. B. WHITE, CHRISTMAS 1940

Late on the afternoon of December 24, President Franklin D. Roosevelt
leaned forward on his crutches on the dry brown winter grass of the
Ellipse, several blocks away from the White House, and pressed a button.
At once there was an audible gasp from eight thousand people and a
brilliant flash of light as seven hundred hand-dipped electric candles burst
into sparkling red and green starlight and six mercury vapor lamps cast
a blue-green glow across the thirty-four-foot tall red cedar that was the
1940 National Community Christmas Tree. Then the President, his words
going out over the radio to millions of Americans preparing Christmas Eve
dinner in their homes, made his annual holiday speech to the nation. This
year there was little joy in his voice. "Sometimes," he said, "we who have
lived through the strifes and the hates of a quarter century wonder if this
old world of ours has abandoned the ideals of the brotherhood of man.
. . . Mankind is all one—and what happens in distant lands tomorrow will
leave its mark on the happiness of our Christmases to come." Roosevelt
urged the people to make this Christmas a merry one for the little children, despite the sad fact that "for us of maturer years it cannot be merry.
But for most of us it can be a happy Christmas if by happiness we mean
that we have done with doubts, that we have set our hearts against fear,
that we still believe in the golden rule of all mankind, that we intend to
live more purely in the spirit of Christ . . . In that spirit I wish a Happy
Christmas to all, and happier Christmases yet to come." At the end of the
ceremony, Roosevelt suggested that the annual celebration would seem
more "homey" if the tree were placed within the White House grounds
next year, so he could address the nation from the White House porch on
Christmas Eve, 1941, "if we are all here." (Some Americans were starting
to worry about all the somber "if" remarks the President had been making
lately. When he left Warm Springs, Georgia, after a brief vacation in
mid-December, Roosevelt had promised to return for the usual two weeks
in the springtime, "if the world survives.")

Following a quiet supper at the White House, the Roosevelt family and their friends gathered to hear the President's traditional dramatic rendition of selections from Dickens' *A Christmas Carol.* It was nearly as entertaining as the concert provided earlier that morning at the White House by a group of Austrian exiles—the famous singing von Trapp *(The Sound of Music)* family, who together sang "Home on the Range" and, in German, "Silent Night" in a special performance for the President's wife, Eleanor. On Christmas morning, Eleanor had to leave the family festivities before nine o'clock to attend a series of parties for the poor children of the city, but the rest of the Roosevelts continued the White House celebration by inviting Crown Prince Olaf of Norway and his wife and three children—who had been living at the Pooks Hill estate in Bethesda, Maryland, since fleeing the Nazi invasion of their homeland in April—to "come over and see the tree."

The weather in Washington was warmer than it had been for any yuletide celebration since 1932, when the icy Herbert Hoover still occupied the White House. And, as far as the American economy was concerned, it was the gayest Christmas since the Great Depression began in 1929. Retail sales volume skyrocketed, and the *New York Times* reported that gift buying in department stores approached "an orgy of spending, as if customers were determined to show there was at least one country that enjoyed peace and good will." At Saks Fifth Avenue, the latest styles for women included V-necked blouses (some cut all the way to the waist, which was fine as long as you sat perfectly still); prim, round-necked houseboy jackets of white drill; gabardine suits in shades of masculine gray; and "saronglike things" in printed black and brown cottons with short-sleeved tops that were knotted between the breasts. A great debate was raging over the propriety of wearing rhinestones on evening clothes, but the weight of conservative opinion was firmly against the notion.

For children, it was a Superman Christmas. The Man of Steel, whom *The New Yorker* described as "an upstanding fellow who wears what the theatrical profession calls 'strip tights,' covered with a cloak, [and] can do anything—*anything:* lift ocean liners with one hand, outrun bullets, put up folding deck chairs even," was the creation of a pair of twenty-five-year-old Cleveland cartoonists named Jerry Siegel and Joe Shuster. Superman had taken the country by storm in 1940; already the caped crusader had earned the distinction of being the largest figure—a balloon filled with $1,000 worth of helium—in Macy's Thanksgiving Day parade. Now, just in time for Christmas, the stores were full of Superman merchandise: Superman costumes, Superman underwear, Superman toy tanks, jigsaw puzzles, cut-out dolls, coloring books, schoolbags, pins, bracelets, dolls, jackets, badges, handkerchiefs, neckties, raincoats, sweat shirts, play suits, suspenders, belts, and milk-bottle caps.

In years to come, many Americans would remember December 25,

1940, as one of the happiest Christmases of their lives. Stretching out behind was the decade of the Depression, now coming to an end at last; stretching out ahead was a future that was uncertain at best, but somehow the notion of Messerschmitts strafing Long Island golf courses and Nazi storm troopers goose-stepping down Bourbon Street seemed too far-fetched for serious consideration, particularly during the holiday season. Out on the West Coast, where the Japanese menace was taken slightly more seriously, all was very well indeed in Hollywood. The movies were at the zenith of their popularity, and fans eagerly devoured the latest news of their favorite film stars. Eleven-year-old Shirley Temple was about to sign a new contract with MGM—$2,500 a week for forty weeks—in an effort to get her career back on track after a one-year layoff to attend school full time (she had found the experience "kinda dull"). Lucille Ball and Desi Arnaz were trying to find time amid their hectic schedules to take a honeymoon after their surprise elopement to Greenwich, Connecticut, at the end of November. (Desi: "We goin' upta Greenwich an' get married." Lucy: "I didn't know." Desi: "I tole you las' night between rumbas.") Joan Crawford had just returned to Hollywood to enjoy her first Christmas with her newly adopted daughter. Clark Gable and his wife, Carole Lombard, were packing for a trip to the East Coast, ostensibly for an examination of Clark's ailing shoulder by specialists at Johns Hopkins in Baltimore; actually, the two stars were going to have fertility tests done to determine why they had been unable to start a family. Ronald Reagan and Jane Wyman, on the other hand, were spending a quiet Christmas at home, expecting a visit from the stork any day.

And F. Scott Fitzgerald was dead. The spokesman of all the sad young men of the postwar years who now were grown-up and forced to take on the responsibilities of life in a treacherous world had suffered a fatal heart attack in Hollywood on December 23. He was forty-four years old, he was haunted by ghosts of years of glory past, and when he died many Americans did not remember who he was.

But Ernest Hemingway was very much alive, and his latest novel, *For Whom the Bell Tolls,* was moving rapidly up the best-seller lists. "It's selling so fast it's ridiculous," Hemingway told a reporter who caught up with the author during a visit to a gymnasium on West 57th Street in New York. "It's a better book than I can write, actually," he admitted with a grin. "I just made up the whole book as I went along. I used to say to my wife, 'I think that son of a bitch Pablo is going to steal the dynamite exploder,' and she'd say, 'Don't you know?' " Hemingway laughed and stepped into the ring (weighing 219 pounds stripped; yes, he did put on trunks and a sweat shirt before he entered the ring) to spar a few one-minute rounds with an old friend who used to train prizefighters. In the middle of the third round, Hemingway stopped to greet a bullfighter buddy from Spain who had wandered into the gym. As they relived old times ("That time going to Spain on the Paris," Hemingway was saying, "the time that obscenity from Hollywood crawled out of that obscenity porthole"), the ex-trainer told the reporter that Hemingway was "the strongest guy I ever had, except Firpo. His arms are like iron and his right forearm is something terrific. It's from all that big-game fishing."

Another hero from the twenties had more on his mind than fishing and boxing. Colonel Charles A. Lindbergh, the Lone Eagle, the aviator who in 1927 had brought Europe closer to the United States with his solo transatlantic flight, had spent most of 1940 trying to undo the damage and keep America isolated from the conflict raging across the Atlantic. His message was simple; as he explained to the nation in his Christmas address, "the important thing is that we unite on the destiny of America; on the necessity of building strength at home and keeping out of war abroad." No one, he argued, would invade the United States unless the United States first meddled in foreign quarrels which were none of its business. With Europe dying in a holocaust born of the Old World's stupidity and selfishness, America's duty was to keep itself aloof and strong, to preserve the light of Western civilization, and then step in when the war was over to rebuild the devastated continent. But there was a darker side to Lindbergh's speeches as well, one that crept in when he issued thinly veiled threats to the American Jews, who, he said, owned or influenced "our motion pictures, our press, our radio and our government." (Lindbergh could also be downright silly sometimes, as he was when he proposed that the United States prohibit the export of *offensive* arms and sell only *defensive* weapons to belligerents abroad.)

The Department of War reportedly had tried to silence Lindbergh by creating a new position of secretary for air especially for him; he refused the bribe. At the end of December 1940, Lindbergh believed there still was a fighting chance of keeping America out of war, "if enough of us are willing to fight and say what we believe, regardless of consequences. Also," he added brightly, "I think it quite possible that the war will be over in Europe before this country can really get into it." The stoic pilot spent a quiet Christmas with his wife, Anne, and their three children. Although he (and the British people) would have deplored the comparison, Lindbergh's views on Christmas celebrations mirrored those of King George VI: "It seems to me that Christmas has deviated as much from the birth of Christ as Christianity has from his teachings," Lindbergh wrote in his diary on Christmas night. "The keynote at the birth of Christ was simplicity. The keynote of Christmas today is luxury. . . . One should eat too little rather than too much, see no one rather than everyone, spend it in silence rather than in communication. Christmas should be a day that brings one closer to God and the philosophy of Christ." Anne Morrow Lindbergh, whose latest book, *The Wave of the Future,* was nesting securely at the top of the best-seller list despite its darkly pessimistic tone, had done her best toward this end by broadcasting a Christmas Eve appeal for public support of the efforts of relief organizations, including the Friends' Service Committee, to alleviate the suffering and starvation in Europe. Although such charitable activities appeared, on the surface, to be altogether commendable and quite uncontroversial, the British government was convinced that any food and medical supplies sent into Nazi-occupied territories, or even into Vichy France, would be appropriated by Germany for its own purposes, and so Churchill refused to allow such shipments to pass through the British blockade.

The whole isolationist-interventionist debate in the United States was shot through with equally difficult choices, and public opinion was not so much divided as it was schizophrenic. Even Anne Lindbergh confided that "I wish I could feel wholehearted about this war, in any way. . . . I am not on the side of evil. I want evil to be vanquished as much as they—only my mind tells me, perhaps wrongly, that it cannot be done the way they think it can." A Gallup poll in December revealed that a clear majority of Americans favored military aid to Britain; when asked, "Which of these two things do you think is the more important for the United States to do—to keep out of war ourselves, or to help England win even at the risk of war?" 60 percent readily replied, "Help England win." And yet 88 percent of those polled also said that they would vote against American entrance into the war if the question were raised in a national referendum. Both figures had actually increased since October; British gains in North Africa and the Luftwaffe's failure to crush Britain had convinced a growing number of Americans that the country could avoid war by the simple expedient of providing arms and ships to Churchill's government. Much to the dismay of Lindbergh and his associates in the isolationist ranks, however, this line of reasoning obviously created a psychological link between the fate of Great Britain and the United States, a link strengthened in September by the Anglo-American deal in which Roosevelt sent fifty ancient destroyers to Britain in return for ninety-nine-year leases on British air and naval bases in the Western Hemisphere. On the surface, the trade so clearly favored America's security interests that isolationists could not openly criticize it.

So, to thwart what they saw as an ominous drift toward war in the last six months of 1940, prominent isolationist leaders announced the formation of the America First Committee in September and the No Foreign War Committee in December. The former group had originated in the fertile minds of two precocious Yale graduate students: R. Douglas Stuart, Jr. (later the president of Quaker Oats), and Kingman Brewster (who went on to become president of Yale and, ironically, U.S. ambassador to Great Britain). By the end of the year, America First had enrolled over sixty thousand members in eleven local chapters, and its period of greatest growth still lay in the future. The committee was headed by General

Robert Wood, chairman of the board of Sears, Roebuck and Company—an extremely able administrator, and a progressive businessman who had voted for Roosevelt in 1932 and 1936. Alice Roosevelt Longworth, Eddie Rickenbacker, Lillian Gish, Henry Ford, and novelist Kathleen Norris served on the national committee of America First at one time or another. (Ford was dropped in the autumn of 1940 because of his violently anti-Semitic views.) The group's platform was based upon the following assumptions: first, the primary obligation of the United States was to build an impregnable defense structure in the Western Hemisphere; second, no foreign alliance could successfully attack a well-armed and prepared America; and third, extensive military aid to Britain would only weaken the American defense effort and threaten to drag the nation unnecessarily into a foreign war.

"They were convinced," concluded Wayne Cole in his excellent study of America First, "that even a successful American intervention would be more disastrous for the United States and the whole world than a British defeat. They predicted that the American people would lose their democracy and freedom if they entered the war. Many believed American intervention would result in national bankruptcy and the collapse of the American system of capitalism and free enterprise. They feared it would result in a prolonged war which would leave both Europe and Great Britain in ruins . . . they predicted that the chaos and destruction left by the war would result in the spread of fascism or communism in Europe."

Not surprisingly, isolationists found thousands of willing recruits to their cause among the undergraduate population of colleges across the country. Few students perceived a Nazi threat to America at the end of 1940; in fact, the results of a survey by *Atlantic Monthly* magazine indicated that few of them even discerned any outstanding moral issues in the war thus far. All their lives they had been taught that Europe was an unsavory den of "intriguing diplomats, secret treaties, unpaid war debts, and propaganda." American entrance into the last war, they had been told, was "a masterpiece of folly which enriched the munitions makers," ending most unsatisfactorily in the disastrous debacle of the Versailles peace treaty. Now, suddenly, their elders reversed course and told them that the New World needed to save Europe once again; who could blame the younger generation if it received the frantic calls for help with more than a little skepticism?

Meanwhile, American interventionists—those who wanted to give Britain all possible material aid—had formed their own national organization, the Committee to Defend America by Aiding the Allies, headed by progressive Republican editor William Allen White of Kansas (an old ally of the previous Roosevelt in the White House). Not surprisingly, White's committee enjoyed its greatest support on the East Coast, attracting such luminaries as publisher Henry Luce, playwright (and presidential speechwriter) Robert Sherwood, Joe Alsop, Dean Acheson, Rex Stout, and Allen Dulles (although Allen's brother, John Foster Dulles, supported the goals of the rival America First organization well into 1941). Luce had become personally obsessed with the Nazi threat to civilization; he regularly used his magazines to introduce the American public in a most graphic way to the horrors of Hitler's bloody march across Europe, and after the fall of France, he circulated a confidential memorandum among his top editors that read, "Danger. The country is in danger. Danger. Danger. The country is in danger."

In the Midwest, in the heartland of America where the battle for public opinion ultimately would be won or lost, the White committee was ably assisted by dedicated men such as Chicago attorney Adlai Stevenson, who told audiences of men and women who wanted desperately to stay out of war that "we all know, I hope, that you don't escape the Nazis by being good and that Hitler moves exactly when and where he pleases." It was clear, Stevenson added, that "a world that has obliterated time and space can't exist part slave and part free":

> ... We know, in short, that America is on the brink of a long ordeal, military, economic and spiritual, with mighty forces bent on world dominion—unless —and thank God there is an unless—unless Britain wins! For if Britain wins, America can escape a trial, within and without, of a magnitude, character and duration that no man can foretell.

So far in 1940, events had overwhelmingly favored the cause of the interventionist forces. In late August and early September, when the first bombs fell on Britain and Americans reacted with horror to Murrow's live broadcasts of fire and terror, Congress had approved the first peacetime conscription measure in American history. Critics warned that the Selective Service Act was the greatest step toward regimentation and militarism ever undertaken by the Congress of the United States, but Gallup reported that 71 percent of Americans favored the measure—partly because it provided that the 800,000 draftees would not serve outside the Western Hemisphere except in territories of the United States. Roosevelt signed the bill into law on September 16. The first draft call went out six weeks later ("Greetings: Having submitted yourself to a local board composed of your neighbors for the purpose of determining your availability for training and service . . ."); the second was announced on December 23. More calls were set for January.

Then, in the first week of November, Roosevelt won reelection to an unprecedented third term in the White House, handily defeating Republican nominee Wendell Willkie in the electoral vote, although the popular count was closer than the President's advisers would have liked. Britain rejoiced at the election results, even though Roosevelt had made an ill-advised and dishonest remark during a campaign speech in Boston, promising American parents that "your boys are not going to be sent into any foreign wars." (In Berlin, the reaction to Roosevelt was less joyful; a vitriolic Joseph Goebbels muttered dark epithets against the "posturing blabbermouth" in the White House.) Carl Sandburg sent his congratulations to the victorious candidate: "In these hours of ordeal you command loyalties that no one else could. I am glad you are cunning—as Lincoln and Jackson were cunning. I am glad you have had suffering and exquisite pain such as few men have known. I am glad you have had preparations for the awful role you now fill."

The next test was not long in coming. While Roosevelt was enjoying a postelection vacation in the Caribbean, he received an urgent message from London: the British Treasury had nearly exhausted its funds, Churchill said, and soon Britain would no longer be able to purchase arms from the United States on the usual cash-and-carry basis. Lord Lothian, the British ambassador to Washington, put it even more succinctly. "Well, boys," he told reporters, "Britain's broke; it's your money we want." Moreover, Britain desperately needed American ships to help convoy supplies through the U-boat squadrons that infested the Atlantic.

Roosevelt pondered the problem for several weeks, then announced that he would address the issue during one of his famous fireside chats— the fifteenth of his presidency—on the evening of December 29. That Sunday evening, attendance at the movies dropped sharply in cities and small towns across America, as everyone stopped what they were doing and listened for the President's voice from the radio. In a hot little oval room in Washington, a live audience of about twenty people sat in wobbly chairs jammed closely together on a dark red carpet; most of those in attendance were cabinet members and their wives, and the President's mother was there, too, but attention seemed to be riveted upon the *real* celebrities in the front row, where Clark Gable (dressed in a chalk-stripe gray suit) and Carole Lombard (in a simple black dress and black hat with a veil) sat waiting politely for the President to begin.

Roosevelt looked tanned and well rested after his vacation; Secretary of the Interior Harold Ickes noticed that the President's hands displayed no signs of the telltale nervous movement that signaled fatigue. Wearing his usual pince-nez and black bow tie and a blue serge suit, with an open pack of Camel cigarettes lying next to the radio network microphones (CBS, NBC, Mutual Broadcasting System) on the table in front of him, Roosevelt began by assuring his listeners that "the nub of the whole purpose of your President is to keep you now, and your children later, and your grandchildren much later, out of a last-ditch war for the preservation of American independence and all of the things that American independence means to you and to me and to ours." He spoke of the Nazi masters who wished to enslave Europe and dominate the rest of the world. He warned that "European and Asiatic war-makers should not gain control of the oceans which lead to this hemisphere." He pointed out that if England went down, the United States would be "living at the point of a gun—a gun loaded with explosive bullets, economic as well as military." He spoke of German spies in America, and of the isolationists who unwittingly abetted the Nazi cause. He rejected the course of negotiation: "There can be no appeasement with ruthlessness. There can be no reasoning with an incendiary bomb. We know now that a nation can have peace with the Nazis only at the price of total surrender." And he promised Americans that they stood less chance of getting into war if they did everything they could to assist Britain right now, than if they waited until the dictators had conquered the rest of the world and then turned their sights upon the United States.

What, then, did the President plan to do? Once again, Roosevelt reaffirmed that he had no intention of sending American troops anywhere outside the nation's borders. Instead, he called upon the country to redouble its efforts to produce more armaments, to become, in his memorable phrase, "the great arsenal of democracy." And America's new planes, ships, guns, and shells, the President vowed with grim determination, would be shipped at once across the ocean to Britain, no matter what threats the dictators might make against the United States in response. Roosevelt frankly admitted that he would not require Britain to pay cash for these arms. Instead, they would be loaned or leased to the British government, much as a man might loan a garden hose to a neighbor whose house was on fire. There was no quibbling about price tags or finance charges when an emergency threatened; when the fire was out, the hose would simply be returned to its owner. (This was a rather disingenuous analogy, of course. Roosevelt neglected to explain what the United States was going to do with planes after they had been shot down or ships after they had been sunk.)

Public reaction to the President's speech was almost unanimously favorable. Letters to the White House ran nearly a hundred to one in support of the lend-lease proposal. The *New York Times* decided that the President had reaffirmed "a doctrine intrinsically as old as the Republic"—the determination not to allow the seaways to fall under the control of powers hostile to the United States—and described the speech as "one of the historic landmarks of American foreign policy." Democratic elder statesman Al Smith, who had not always seen eye to eye with FDR in domestic matters, now heartily applauded his former protégé's bold declaration of "dynamic non-belligerence." On the other hand, America First's General Wood condemned the speech as "virtually a personal declaration of war on Germany."

Two nights later, Americans cheerfully bade farewell to the old year, a year of contentment at home and disaster abroad. In Times Square, miles of neon lights blinked down upon one of the greatest and most enthusiastic crowds ever to celebrate a new year. Police estimated the raucous throng at over a million merry people; to help control the mob, the city had installed for the first time a new mechanical device mounted on each of the four corners of 45th Street. Known as a pedestrian signal box, it flashed WALK and STOP signals in harmony with the automobile traffic lights. "They're good things if people pay attention to them," said a police department spokesman. (Pause) "But they won't."

At his home in Los Gatos, California, John Steinbeck thought about the new year, 1941, and wondered "if any year ever had less chance of being happy." The weather was cold and clear, Steinbeck told a friend, the trees were bare, and the earth was so full of moisture that water was seeping out of the ground everywhere. "So we go into this happy new year, knowing that our species has learned nothing, can, as a race, learn nothing—that the experience of ten thousand years has made no impression on the instincts of the million years that preceded. . . . Not that I have lost any hope. All the goodness and the heroisms will rise up again, then be cut down again and rise up. It isn't that the evil thing wins—it never will—but that it doesn't die."

Part One   The Winter

1

The Reich Triumphant

"It is a queer life one leads in a modern war, every day
is just the same and is mostly food, food and in spite
of all that is happening every day is food . . ."
                                        —GERTRUDE STEIN

As the city clock of Vilna struck midnight on the last night of the old
year, Menachem Begin sat silent and still on a straw mattress in a cell in
the black fastness of Lukishki prison. He and his two cellmates drank a
toast to the new year of 1941 with half a mug of cold bad coffee they had
saved from the previous day's ration. Since June 1940, Lithuania had been
under the political and military domination of the Soviet Union; during
most of that time, the twenty-seven-year-old Begin had been high com-
missioner of the Betar, an aggressive, activist Zionist organization engaged
in smuggling Jewish refugees out of Europe to Palestine. As part of their
campaign to suppress all separatist movements, the Soviet authorities
finally decided that they would no longer tolerate Begin's Zionist activities, and so the NKVD—the secret police—had arrested Begin during one
of its purges late in 1940 and charged him with the crimes of being an
agent of British imperialism and a threat to the prescribed social order.
For nearly sixty hours they had interrogated him, keeping him without
food, water, and sleep, before placing him in Lukishki. Now Begin looked
around at the walls of his cell, at the single shelf that held all the belongings
he was permitted to keep, at the small bowl that never held enough food
and the bucket that the three men used for a toilet, and he listened to the
clock strike twelve and wondered if he would ever be set free. "We did
not know that we were entering not just a new year but a new epoch.
. . . We did not know. But we drank, draining our glasses to the bottom."
        The new year swept across Europe on a wave of snow, sleet, and bitter
cold. Temperatures plunged past twenty-five degrees below zero in Moscow; Hungary was in the grip of the worst winter since 1825. Avalanches
trapped travelers in the southern Balkans, trains were marooned on high
Alpine passes, and the snow mounted to a height of eleven feet along the
Pyrenees. A hard frost covered most of the ravaged, starving Spanish
peninsula. In Zurich, James Joyce was dead, a refugee from Nazi-occupied

France and the moral bankruptcy of Vichy. Blinding snowstorms struck southern France and swept northwestward to the English Channel. The Dover coast was frozen. Traveling with his new bride in an unheated railway car, Albert Camus tried to leave Lyons for Marseilles and the more hospitable climes of Algeria, but a massive snowdrift blocked the train on the way through Provence, and the writer was forced to disembark and seek shelter from the icy winds. Vichy suffered its worst blizzard in fifty years; in the evenings the city was blacked out, cold, and cheerless.

Nor was any place on the Continent free from German control or the chilling prospect of Nazi domination. Anxieties mounted early in the new year as German troops and munitions poured into Romania, as many as twenty-five trains a day loaded with tanks, cannon, and soldiers—the advance guard arriving in the guise of "tourists" who took up their stations along the left bank of the ice-covered Danube. By the second week of January there were reports of 500,000 Nazi occupation troops in the area, Romania's reward for having meekly agreed to join the Axis pact. But no one expected the Wehrmacht to stay in place for long. Churchill feared a German strike across the Mediterranean, through Turkey and Egypt, and then southward into India. To forestall such a move, Britain endeavored to persuade Turkey, Bulgaria, Yugoslavia, and Greece to form a united front against German aggression. One look at the overwhelming strength of Hitler's armored divisions poised on the borders, however, was enough to convince any rational observer that Churchill's scheme constituted a singularly unappealing invitation to national suicide. Moreover, ethnic divisions within the Balkan states provided an inviting opening for Nazi diplomatic penetration. "My ministers are pro-German, my wife is pro-Italian, and my people are pro-Russian," complained the bewildered Bulgarian King Boris III from Sofia. "I am the only neutral in the country." Less than two months later, Bulgaria joined the Axis.

In Greece, food supplies dwindled and the government ordered the civilian population to observe four meatless days a week. Bread in Athens was hard and tough; butter was scarce. On the frozen Albanian front, the war against Italy continued to bring hard-won victories, though the pace was slowed by the weather and a constant flow of reinforcements from Rome. Save for the still, dark waters of the lakes, everything in the battle zone was white, from the snow-covered mountain roads to the isolated valleys and the uniforms of the Greek regular forces. In the dead of winter, most of the fighting was done at long range by artillery, the melting snow dripping through the camouflage nets and sizzling on the hot breeches of the guns. The only large-scale hand-to-hand engagement of January resulted in a devastating loss for Mussolini's vaunted "Lupi di Toscana" division, the Wolves of Tuscany. The Duce received the sobering news of the defeat ("a kick in the pants," in Count Ciano's inelegant phrase) on his way to a meeting with Hitler at Berchtesgaden; the entire Greek misadventure had become an inexplicable drama to Mussolini, Ciano reported, "so much the more serious because it is inexplicable." Hitler stoutly reassured his discomfited Italian ally with the news that German troops would soon enter Greece from the east. Anticipating precisely such an attack, the Greek government of General Ioannis Metaxas urged the United States (in the person of special presidential envoy Colonel William "Wild Bill" Donovan) to send a wide range of supplies without delay: planes, trucks, mountain guns and ammunition, uniforms, socks, shoes, and donkeys.

From snowbound Vichy, Marshal Pétain sternly advised his subjects during a ceremonial New Year's Day radio address that for the foreseeable future, "we shall be hungry." The Marshal blamed the British blockade for the food shortages that plagued southern France, but impartial observers noticed that plenty of cargoes of beef, pork, fruits, and wine were being unloaded at Marseilles, only to be appropriated by German and Italian military commissions who sent the precious foodstuffs back home. Black English crows found it dangerous to make their annual winter migration to the south of France; in Lyons, crow carcasses were sold in the city market for ten francs apiece, the meat and bones used for soup because nothing else was available. Newspapers carried advertisements placed by "horse butchers" who would "travel any distance to buy animals killed accidentally." For lack of bread and milk, two million French children faced the long-term prospect of severe malnutrition. It was even worse for the thousands of foreign refugees (including twenty thousand Jews from Germany) crowded into hurriedly constructed camps in southern France, where prolonged exposure to the cold produced widespread sickness.

"A nation vanquished cannot, without presumption, cherish too many hopes," Pétain admitted to an American correspondent. Still, the old man hoped that France would collaborate loyally in the reorganized postwar European order, "with the hope of establishing a lasting and solid peace both in Europe and the world. The better to prepare herself for this role, France must first of all devote her efforts to her own reconstruction." To this end, the government at Vichy urged its people to spend more time in athletic pursuits. To ensure that the rising generation of Frenchmen received a sound physical and moral education, the army established and administered the *Chantiers de jeunesse,* work camps where young people were taught military discipline, respect for the ancient traditions of rural France, and self-sacrifice for the greater glory of the community. And, following the blueprint for the New Order as drawn by the Nazi conquerors, Vichy also began to enforce its recently enacted regulations excluding French Jews from high-level posts in the government, the armed forces, in universities, the press, and the theater; strict quotas limited Jewish entry into the liberal professions as well. Alien Jews were forbidden to own any business or send their children to French schools.

In the occupied zone to the north, workers of the German Labor Corps dismantled the pathetic remains of the Maginot Line: tank traps, barbed-wire entanglements, and concrete trenches, all the classic monuments to military futility. The coal stoves, mattresses, and wooden bunks from the underground bunkers along the line were shipped to Berlin for use in air-raid shelters; the vast untouched stocks of food and ammunition were likewise appropriated. Once the ground above was cleared, the Germans planned to transform the region into a patchwork of vegetable farms and small orchards. In the celebrated forest at Compiègne, all the monuments commemorating the German surrender of November 1918 already had been removed, except for one lonely statue of Marshal Foch.

"We were the spoiled children of a country worth all the others put together," mourned Sidonie Gabrielle Colette, "and now her portraits of yesteryear break our hearts." From her frigid room at the Palais-Royal in Paris, the sixty-seven-year-old novelist recalled the beauty of French life before the war—when she had created such beguiling, winsome characters as the flirtatious Cheri and the vaguely autobiographical Claudine (Gigi would not appear until the war was over)—and then she looked out upon a city where life had become "narrow, confined, [and] bridled," where the thermometer reached nine below zero and the hunt for nourishment consumed all one's energy. "It's cold here," Colette wrote with brittle fingers, "it's colder than last year because the building on the right and the building on the left, identical twins to the one I occupy, are also empty of coal and warmth." To keep from losing their toes to frostbite, some desperate French women stuffed thick woolen stockings into their small shoes, a procedure that succeeded only in producing an epidemic of chilblains. The more effective procedure (much favored by enterprising streetwalkers) was to wrap old newspapers around one's legs, using string garters to hold them in place.

For much of the winter there was no coal at all; Parisians were forced to uproot trees from the city's parks and public gardens for fuel. The clocks in the occupied zone were set on Berlin time, which meant that it was still dark and cold when Paris went to work in the mornings. German troops requisitioned bed linens throughout the city, leaving each household with only two sets of sheets, one blanket, and one mattress for every bed, a policy that worked a special hardship upon those like Simone de Beauvoir who had to survive the winter in unheated rooms: "I inserted myself between icy sheets wearing ski trousers and a sweater," de Beauvoir explained, "and shivered horribly while washing." In Pablo Picasso's cavernous seventeenth-century studio in the rue des Grand-Augustins, the only source of heat was a secondhand kitchen stove, which unfortunately also emitted obnoxious clouds of black smoke from time to time. Unable to paint on the coldest days because his fingers were too stiff, and facing a severe shortage of bronze for sculptures (though the stuff, like almost everything else, eventually became available through the black market), Picasso spent much of the winter writing an avant-garde play, *Le Désir attrape par la queue,* in which the characters suffered terribly from the penetrating cold; sometimes Picasso made their feet literally cry out, "Oh my chilblains, my chilblains!" The paintings that Picasso did complete in early 1941 revealed a preoccupation with all sorts of food, typified by the almost sensual portrayal of a simple dish of black pudding in *Le Buffet de Savoyard.*

Out of necessity, other Parisians shared the Spanish artist's obsession that winter; despite occasional shipments of produce from Vichy, food became ever more scarce in Paris (primarily because the Germans appropriated it here, too), and the breadlines seemed to grow longer every day. Admiral Patrick Leahy, the retired chief of naval operations and old navy crony of Roosevelt's whom the President had appointed in December 1940 as the new American ambassador to Vichy, informed the State Department that families in the working-class suburbs of Paris reportedly had received no meat at all for the first two weeks of 1941. Only very dark bread was available in the shops, eggs were virtually nonexistent, and housewives fought pitched battles over several pounds of potatoes. Milk was sold only to mothers of babies, pregnant women, and people over seventy, a restriction that induced women to rent babies or grandparents for trips to the dairy shop; some girls stuffed pillows under their apron fronts before they went to stand in the interminable queues. Starch was so scarce that one needed a doctor's certificate to obtain rice. Amid a thriving black market, hatred of the grocer (who never seemed to have what one wanted, at least not at the prescribed price) became a national obsession. A severe shortage of gasoline brought hordes of bicyclists into the streets, riding in orderly single file as required by German traffic regulations. Every month unemployment rose another notch. Anyone who requested relief was invited to go and look for work in Germany.

Although most Parisians retained their barely disguised attitude of superiority and disdain toward the less fortunate members of the human race (i.e., everyone else in the world), the atmosphere of life in the city clearly had changed under the Nazi occupation. "In general, a strained air of venality hovers over Paris," wrote the correspondent for *The New Yorker.* Like ravenous termites who had been on a forced diet for years, German soldiers advanced steadily through the Paris shops, "absorbing, munching, consuming lingerie, perfume, bonbons, leather goods, sweet silly novelties—all the chic, charm, and *gourmandise* of Parisian merchandise." Perusing the lists of goods taken from France after the armistice, Joseph Goebbels chuckled: "No cause for anyone to complain on that score. We took a good swig from the bottle. France certainly had cause to notice that she had lost the war."

Nazi officers and the ubiquitous "gray mice"—female German auxiliaries, so named for the color of their drab uniforms—dined at Maxim's, the Tour d'Argent, Drouant, and Carton, and attended shows at Carrère's, the "in" nightclub. Together with obsequious French businessmen and ambitious girls who engaged in "horizontal collaboration," this was the new elite which now assumed control of the city's social and economic life. (Paris mistresses were reserved for the officers; ordinary German soldiers were sternly discouraged from sexual adventures by official warnings that all French women were diseased. The troops were also forbidden to attend church services in Paris.) Fraternization with Nazi officials over dinner and champagne could be quite profitable, of course, for compliant French industrialists willing to turn their factories into munitions plants for the Wehrmacht.

With the nightclubs full of Germans and the movie theaters closed or restricted to German films (American movies were banned by the occupation authorities), most of the rest of Paris very seldom went out in the evenings. Instead, people stayed at home and read, or listened to the radio—usually shortwave broadcasts on the BBC, a recreation the Germans had not yet gotten around to prohibiting. There was virtually no other way to obtain information from the outside. Before the war, Paris had boasted eighteen major daily newspapers; by January 1941, most of those had vanished beneath the heavy hand of Nazi censorship, and the public ignored the journals that remained because everyone knew they were full of lies. News of the continued British resistance seemed to surprise and even irritate many Frenchmen. The city assuaged its wounded pride during that long winter by reading and rereading the chefs d'oeuvre of French literature. One bookstore owner reported that she had never sold so many editions of the classics, three thousand copies of Montaigne in a single month. "We may believe," Colette wrote optimistically, "that a very sure instinct inclines a sorely chastened people, ignorant of its future condition, to interrogate its past, to desire an acquaintance with the foundations which assured its greatness and may yet be accountable for its future."

Life was no easier in the occupied countries of northern Europe. Following the time-worn dictum of conquerors, "First the street, then the State," German military authorities (aided by the Schutzstaffel, the notorious SS guards) were attempting to terrorize the people of Holland and Norway into submission. By the start of the new year, prisons and concentration camps in both countries were already full to overflowing with political prisoners. Public meetings and dancing were forbidden; universities were closed after students led a series of political protest demonstrations; a severe eight o'clock curfew was enforced. Vidkun Quisling, the paranoid leader of Norway's collaborationist regime (who was trying to resurrect the nation's ancient pagan sun rites as part of his National Concentration Party festivals), decreed that doctors, priests, and lawyers would henceforth be required—under pain of imprisonment—to tell police everything told to them in confidence that might affect the security of the regime. One hundred thousand Dutchmen already had been transported to Germany to serve in the Labor Corps, and unemployed agricultural workers were being registered toward the same end. In Amsterdam, the ration of meat was down to four ounces, with bone, per week.

With their liberties and their country stolen from them, ordinary citizens could only try to salvage their self-respect, and so persistent pinpricks of sabotage continued to bedevil the occupation forces. Railroads and bridges used to transport German military equipment suffered with distressing regularity from landslides and avalanches. Civilians punched tiny holes in canned food requisitioned for German troops. Underground groups formed revenge clubs that adopted the slogan "We Remember"; in anticipation of Bijltjesdag—"Hatchet Day"—they assigned each of their members to keep one prominent collaborator under surveillance, to obtain evidence of treason to be used after the war when the Germans were finally gone. When a German entered a Dutch café, the rest of the patrons got up, paid their bills, and left without a sound. In the movie houses, whistling and rude noises greeted the appearance of German newsreel films, until the authorities decided to leave the house lights on while the films were being shown. During the evening blackouts, anonymous handbills and placards urging unity and perseverance were pasted on walls. In the streets of Oslo anti-Quisling slogans appeared nightly, drawn on the snow with charcoal. And after the BBC broadcast of January 14, 1941, a new symbol—a V—began to appear on walls, sidewalks, national monuments, and the automobiles of German officials.

The idea came from a Belgian lawyer and politician named Victor de Lavelye, a devout anti-Fascist who had fled to London in the spring of 1940. He had heard that people were scribbling "R.A.F." on the sidewalks of Brussels; three letters seemed a little unwieldy to Lavelye, especially when speedwriting might be a matter of life and death, and so he proposed the V symbol instead. In French, it stood for *Victoire;* in Flemish, it stood for *Vrijheid,* and in Polish, *Wolny*—"Free." "Let the enemy see this sign so often, so infinitely repeated," urged Lavelye in this memorable radio broadcast, "that he will feel surrounded, encircled by an immense army of citizens eagerly awaiting his first moment of weakness, watching intently for his first defeat."

Berlin greeted the new year in silence. By ten o'clock on New Year's Eve the city was a deserted shadow, with searchlights filling the sky instead of colored rockets, and buses with dim blue lights gliding silently and ghostlike over the thin layer of snow that lay on the unmarked streets. No revelers thronged the Tiergarten or strolled tipsily down the Unter den Linden; all the parties were held behind shuttered windows.

It was an eerie and inauspicious beginning to what the German people fervently hoped would be the last year of the war. The customary oppressive dinginess of Berlin in January did nothing to raise their spirits. Veteran foreign observers stationed in the German capital fell victim to an overwhelming sense of depression that winter, brought on by the suffocating pressure of life under the Nazi regime, combined with the knowledge that the world inevitably would suffer still more agony before the military tide was reversed. "I vegetated on through the long black night of the second war-winter," wrote Howard K. Smith, then a young correspondent for the United Press. "I was losing my eagerness to see and learn in a tidal wave of despair. My lethargy was not unique. Already old names, long connected with news from Berlin, were disappearing for the simple reason that their owners were sick at heart. . . . The pressure that forced them, one by one, to desert Berlin was finally christened with a name. Those of us who remained called it the 'Berlin Blues.' The name stuck, to describe those awful pits of spiritual depression each of us fell into with periodic regularity, and which grew more severe as the war wore on." William Shirer already had departed in December after fifteen years as a correspondent on the continent, sailing away from Europe and the war and "the Nazi blight and the hatred and the fraud and the political gangsterism and the murder and the massacre and the incredible intolerance and all the suffering and the starving and the cold and the thud of a bomb blowing the people in a house to pieces, the thud of all the bombs blasting man's hope and decency."

There were those in the German military command, too, who felt ill at ease that winter. Hitler had shelved Operation Sea Lion completely, although a marvelously successful campaign of disinformation kept the rest of the world—and particularly London and Washington—unaware of the Fuehrer's decision. Now all his attention was riveted upon the forthcoming invasion of the Soviet Union, scheduled for May. "When Barbarossa commences," Hitler confidently informed his generals, "the world will hold its breath and make no comment!" The ostensible purpose of Barbarossa was to "force a radical settlement of the Continental issue as soon as possible," to strengthen and consolidate Germany's position in Europe so the Reich could withstand a lengthy war against Britain and, probably, the United States. Hitler sought control of the Balkans primarily for the oilfields of Romania and to protect his army's flank as it advanced toward Moscow; otherwise, the Mediterranean—and especially North Africa—held little intrinsic interest for him.

The prospect of fighting a two-front war had long terrified the German General Staff, and the Fuehrer's growing obsession with the destruction of Soviet power did little to inspire confidence in his unorthodox strategic judgment. General Franz Halder, chief of the General Staff and a soldier of classic Prussian military virtues, wondered in his diary what rational purpose Operation Barbarossa might serve: "We do not hit Britain that way. Our economic potential will not be substantially improved. Risk in the West must not be underestimated. It is possible that Italy might collapse after the loss of her Colonies, and we get a Southern front in Spain, Italy, and Greece. If we are then tied up in Russia, a bad situation will be made worse." But loyalty remained the predominant Prussian military virtue, and so Halder and his colleagues accepted the Fuehrer's decision and looked toward the future with more than a little apprehension.

Indeed, the combination of adroit propaganda and actual military success had raised the cult of Hitler the World Conqueror to terrifying proportions within Germany. The unbroken chain of triumphs across Europe led many otherwise rational people to wonder whether Hitler really might possess some sort of supernatural talents. Certainly Hitler himself appeared to believe it. An American reporter watched as the dictator drove through the gates of the Chancellery in an open car: "From a distance of ten feet, his eyes appeared no longer the eyes of the funny little man, not yet entirely certain of himself, but were calm, hard, and cruel, like the Apotheosis of the Military Man, which he had become."

On January 30, the eighth anniversary of his accession to supreme power, Adolf Hitler strode across the platform of the Sportspalast on the Potsdamerstrasse in Berlin and stood before more than twenty thousand wildly cheering admirers. Behind him, above the stage, loomed a gigantic golden eagle against a red backdrop garnished with black swastikas, the last resembling nothing so much as blood-swollen spiders. Storm troopers in full battle dress stood at attention below the eagle; storm troopers occupied every aisle seat, and still more stood guard outside the sports palace for several blocks in every direction. The speech started off slowly, softly, with warnings to Britain that the U-boat war in the Atlantic would commence in earnest in the springtime. Then the Fuehrer warmed to his subject and cast a vehement challenge to the impudent upstarts who governed America. "Whoever imagines he can aid England must, in all circumstances, know one thing," he shouted, shaking his fist in the general direction of Washington, the words like a whirlwind. "Every ship, whether with or without escort, that comes before our torpedo tubes will be torpedoed." (*"Heil* Hitler! *Sieg Heil!"* the crowd shouted.) This time next year, there would be no doubt as to the outcome of the greatest struggle in the history of civilization. "I am convinced," Hitler roared exultantly, sweeping his arms wide in a grand gesture of victory, "that 1941 will be the crucial year of the great New Order in Europe." *"Sieg Heil! Sieg Heil! Sieg Heil!"*

2

Off to See the Wizard

"For all I care about this desert, you can have it!
I myself am a poet."
—GENERAL FRANCESCO ARGENTINO
OF ITALY, FOLLOWING HIS
SURRENDER TO BRITISH FORCES
IN NORTH AFRICA

You cannot know what stone is if you have never been to Oran. In one of the dustiest cities in the world, the pebble and the stone are king . . . crumbling stone whose whiteness blinds." Shortly after his arrival from Marseilles in early January, Albert Camus found himself struggling against the emptiness, ugliness, and boredom of life in the commercial city on the west Algerian coastline. It was depressingly familiar territory for the twenty-eight-year-old writer, who had been educated in Algiers and trained to teach literature at the university there until a bout with tuberculosis forced him to relinquish his academic career. As he contemplated the outlines of a novel about a city besieged by a remorseless plague, Camus amused himself in cafés, eating lobster, bits of seasoned meat skewered on sticks, and snails with sauce so hotly spiced it scalded the roof of his mouth. Yet under the "magnificent and implacable sky" of North Africa, from time to time the writer found nature unexpectedly bursting through the lifeless rocks: "In the midst of these bones of the earth, the occasional red geranium grows, looking like new blood and life . . ."

Across the desert to the east, thirty miles from the border with Egypt, the picturesque, white-walled Libyan city of Bardia was under attack. For more than two weeks, British ships had been lobbing, in a rather desultory manner, fifteen-inch shells over the cliffs that guarded the seaward side of the city; at night, the explosions threw sheets of colored lightning across the dark Mediterranean waters. Inside Bardia, approximately 25,000 Italian troops were entrenched behind a seventeen-mile perimeter of concrete pillboxes with steel shutters, artillery batteries, barbed-wire entanglements, minefields, machine-gun nests, and antitank trenches.

All through the last week of the old year, British troops had been moving up the desert road from Cairo, assembling for the final assault. The attack would be led by the irrepressible Australians of the XIII Corps, commanded by Major General Iven Giffard MacKay, a former Sydney school headmaster whom the men had affectionately nicknamed "Ming the Merciless." At dusk on January 2, R.A.F. planes from the Mediterranean command launched a blistering series of bombing runs over Bardia that lasted until the dawn. Except for a few halfhearted sorties against the British lines, the Italian air force was nowhere to be seen. Then, at 5:30 A.M. on January 3, the Australian advance began.

But not too quickly at first. The poor men had been so overburdened with heavy clothing, huge boots, supplies, and equipment that it was a considerable achievement even to stand upright. "The men were heavily laden," recalled the official Australian account of the battle, with considerable understatement. "Each wore his woolen uniform with a sleeveless leather jerkin over or under the tunic, and most had also a greatcoat with skirts turned back to allow freedom of movement. They wore steel helmets, with respirators hanging on their chests; some carried sandbags wrapped round their legs; and, in pouches, pockets and haversacks, 150 rounds of ammunition, one or two grenades and three days' rations of tinned beef and biscuits. They set out carrying picks and shovels but the combined load was too heavy and the tools were abandoned." Tank officers wore thick corduroy trousers and lambskin overcoats lined with black lamb's wool, and knitted cowls to keep out the sand; one poor fellow said that he had been in the desert without a bath for more than two months, and itched like hell all over.

Nevertheless, off they went into the winds and the flying sand, the sappers blowing in the sides of the antitank trench, cutting the wire and throwing stones to explode the mines. The big tanks rolled through the openings, then came the lighter armor, and finally there appeared waves of ferocious Aussie foot soldiers singing—for reasons best known to themselves—the chorus of "The Wizard of Oz" ("We're off to see the wizard, the wonderful wizard of Oz"). By noon they had driven a wedge three thousand yards deep into the Italian defenses. In the harbor, British warships kept pounding Bardia from the rear.

After a day and a half of not particularly spirited resistance, the Italian garrison surrendered. Most of the defenders had stopped shooting and laid down their weapons as soon as the Australians got close enough to fire back. ("We would have gone on shooting," shrugged one captive Italian officer, "but where was the point when your guns are twice as good as ours?") As the grinning Aussies marched into the city, cigarettes dangling from their mouths and steel helmets pulled low across their faces against the sun, they shouted, "What time do the pubs shut?" and promptly settled down to enjoy some Italian delicacies washed down with Chianti. The Via Benito Mussolini was officially renamed Churchill Street, and the Italian Officers' Club became the press correspondents' headquarters.

Frightened by Rome radio broadcasts that had scornfully berated the Australians as half-savage barbarians running amok in the desert, many of the 45,000 Italian prisoners clearly were petrified by their captors; one correspondent accompanying the campaign saw a number of them go up to touch the leather jerkins of the Australian infantrymen, to see if the rumor was true about their clothes being bulletproof. They might as well have been. During the entire operation, the number of British and Anzac soldiers killed or wounded totaled fewer than five hundred.

Churchill, naturally, was ecstatic at the news from Bardia. He christened January 5 Bardia Day, and urged Wavell to pursue the retreating Italian forces with all due haste. "If I may debase a golden phrase," chirped the obsequious Anthony Eden (who had just reassumed control of the Foreign Office) in a message to the Prime Minister, " 'Never has so much been surrendered by so many to so few.' " In Rome, Mussolini took the defeat with a minimum of grumbling, although the Duce conceded that Italian morale had suffered another damaging blow. "It will take at least a week for this washing to dry," he muttered. He tried to speed up the healing process by announcing over the radio that Bardia was actually a Pyrrhic victory for Britain, and that "the great British offensive has proved a fiasco." For his part, Hitler responded to the fall of Bardia by ordering the Luftwaffe detachment that was assembling in Sicily (designated as Fliegerkorps X) to extend its range of patrols to support the Italian forces that remained in North Africa. Although he remained convinced that North Africa was a peripheral theater at best, and "not the scene of war upon which the fate of a powerful conflict can rest," Hitler also realized that Germany could not afford to have its Axis ally paralyzed by discontent in Rome over the loss of the Fascist colonial empire. And so the Fuehrer also dispatched a light panzer division to the western desert to initiate a counteroffensive, Operation Sonnenblume ("Sunflower"), under the command of General Erwin Rommel.

Although six Italian generals had surrendered at Bardia, the commander, General Bergonzoli—known as Electric Whiskers for his bushy, bristling beard, parted neatly down the middle—had walked away from the battle on the last day when he realized the cause was hopeless. He and several of his officers then traveled across the desert by night, strolling right through the British lines in the darkness, hiding in caves during the day, until they reached Tobruk five days and seventy miles later. They arrived shortly before the main body of British troops.

Tobruk was a pleasant coastal city sandwiched between the Mediterranean and the desert. It was also the only first-class natural harbor on the long Libyan coastline between Alexandria and Benghazi, and in a desert war where supplies were often difficult to come by (and living off the land was wholly impossible), the value of such a port could hardly be overestimated. Driving across the flat, straight asphalt highway designed and constructed by Mussolini's engineers toward the greater glory of Italian fascism, British forces were in place around Tobruk by January 15. Wavell decided to employ again the siege tactics that had worked so well at Bardia, but the assault was held up for several days by a vicious sandstorm that uprooted telegraph poles and tossed trucks on their sides; soldiers lay helplessly on the ground, blinded by the whirlpools of lemon-colored dust that seemed to swirl in every direction at once.

Finally, on the bitterly cold night of January 20, the navy and the R.A.F. began a devastating bombardment of the city, and again the grimy, unshaven Australians attacked on the following dawn. Crossing the twelve-foot-deep ditch that extended along the entire thirty-mile length of the defense perimeter, they found many Italian defenders still asleep in their dugouts. Marched from their beds at the point of a bayonet, tens of thousands of captured Italians in their rumpled gray-green uniforms were herded into makeshift wire compounds. The British were now faced with the very real and entirely unanticipated problem of feeding and caring for these men, nearly one-fourth of whom were suffering from chronic dysentery, until they could be shipped back to permanent prisoner-of-war camps at Alexandria. More than twenty thousand Italians were crammed into prison cages that they themselves had built earlier in anticipation of capturing hundreds of British prisoners; the chaotic conditions in the cages were appalling. "The first attempt to get water into the cage ended in a wild stampede," recalled one eyewitness; "I had not thought that a crowd of men could so resemble a stampeding herd of cattle . . . [We] managed to obtain concrete tubs filled with water and, to some extent, to regulate the rush . . . The sanitary conditions were indescribable. After we had fed and watered the prisoners the greatest possible efforts were made to provide trenches and insist on their use. Drastic punishment was meted out to offenders . . . I don't know how we managed to avoid a major epidemic."

Tobruk represented another brilliant victory for Wavell and especially for Lieutenant General Richard O'Connor, the commander who led the campaign so flawlessly that the British suffered even fewer casualties than at Bardia. But when Alan Moorehead ventured into the smoldering city after the Italian surrender, he found little cause for victory celebrations:

> Sickness, death and wounding enveloped Tobruk. Inside the town fires blazed. Shops, homes, offices, were torn up and their furniture and household goods strewn across the roads. Walking through it, I felt suddenly sickened at the destruction and the uselessness and the waste. At this moment of success I found only an unreasoning sense of futility. The courage of the night

before had been turned so quickly to decay. And now the noise and the rushing and the light had gone, one walked through the streets kicking aside broken deck-chairs and suits of clothes and pot-plants and children's toys. . . . Stray cats swarmed over the rubbish. In the bay a ship kept burning steadily. By its light the wounded were being carried down to the docks.

Now the remnants of the Italian army in North Africa were in full flight. Derna fell to the British at the end of January, and Benghazi on February 6. (In every case, the elusive General Bergonzoli managed to escape just before the British arrived.) Finally, after a magnificent, frantic forced march across two hundred miles of uncharted desert, in the face of storms of sleet driven by gale-force winds, British forces cut off the retreating Italians before they could reach Tripoli. At the climactic battle of Beda Fomm, the Italians at last stood their ground and launched a desperate, last-ditch counterattack. It was no use. A relentless British artillery barrage broke their resistance, and by the morning of February 8 it was over.

More than half of the Italian army in North Africa had been crushed between December and February: ten divisions destroyed, twenty generals and 130,000 soldiers captured, along with more than eight hundred guns and four hundred tanks. Over a thousand Italian aircraft had been rendered inoperative. Italy had lost a land empire as large as Britain and France combined. Wavell and O'Connor had accomplished this remarkable feat with a force that never numbered more than 31,000 men, of whom only 500 had been killed during the entire campaign and fewer than 1,400 wounded. In retrospect, however, this would come to seem the easy part; from this moment forward, British commanders no longer would have the luxury of facing, in Churchill's words, "the sort of enemy against whom any General should be only too happy to be matched."

In the yard of a run-down farmhouse in a small desert village, British correspondents gathered to question General Bergonzoli, who finally had been cornered at Beda Fomm. Moorehead found the exhausted general wearing an undecorated uniform, wrapped in a rug against the cold, shivering uncontrollably in the backseat of a car. "We were grossly outnumbered," he repeated over and over again in a soft voice, trying to convince himself it was true, waving a large diamond ring in the air for emphasis. "You got here too soon, that is all." They put him on a stretcher and flew him back to Cairo.

With Tobruk in hand and the Italians no longer a threat in North Africa, Churchill ordered Wavell to discontinue the offensive. It was time to start shipping men and equipment to Greece to strengthen the Balkan front against the anticipated German offensive, and to East Africa to clear the Italians out of Abyssinia. The British army would try to hold the western desert with a bare minimum of forces. Although Churchill and his military advisers knew that Germany was sending reinforcements to Tripoli, no one thought the Germans would be ready to move across the desert until May at the earliest.

No one anticipated Rommel.

3

Lend-Lease

"I peek at the papers just enough to have about one idea
of my own a week about the war."
—ROBERT FROST

Early in 1941, on a damp, cold, typically gray British day, a slender
ten-year-old girl walked across the Glasgow docks and saw for the first
time the ship that would take her to America. Her mother and brother
would go with her; but her father would not, and at that moment Claire
Bloom suddenly knew what the voyage meant. "Not until I saw the ship
did I understand what we were doing—that we couldn't turn back—and
then I was all at once full of terror," the actress wrote several decades
later. "I had never seen a man cry, until my father, in tears, came on deck
carrying in his hand a packet of biscuits he had just bought. . . . I cannot
remember having felt so solitary and abandoned ever before. It was the
last moment of something, probably of my childhood."

They were part of a convoy of ships that was evacuating women and
children from Britain to safety in the United States. But first they had to
evade the U-boats that were claiming a mounting list of casualties in the
North Atlantic. For ten days that seemed an eternity to a frightened little
girl, the ship swerved and dodged through the ocean; lifeboat drills filled
the days and at nights the passengers slept in their clothes, "dressed for
disaster." Occasionally a sympathetic adult would try to distract the children by organizing an impromptu quiz contest or talent show. The cloying
smell of oil seemed to pervade everything on board, particularly the food.
Like most other evacuees, the Blooms had obeyed the British government's command to take no more than a minimum of currency out of the
country (the young actor Paul von Hernried deftly evaded this restriction
by concealing a roll of banknotes under a mirror built into his traveling
case), and so upon their arrival in New York the Blooms found themselves
virtually helpless, totally dependent upon their family and friends in the
States.

Most Americans welcomed British refugees like Claire Bloom in 1941.
In the popular mind, England remained the first line of defense for the
United States; when George Gallup asked American voters if they thought

the future safety of the nation depended upon England's winning the war against Hitler, 68 percent still agreed that it did. (Most of those who answered "no" were midwesterners who confidently believed the U.S. could always take care of itself.) "It is the courage of the British people which has won the hearts of the people here," Walter Lippmann assured Harold Nicolson in January. "The effect has been immense—no one dares to be anti-British, and the overwhelming majority are for the first time in my lifetime really pro-British."

And so Americans sent their prayers and best wishes across the Atlantic, along with more tangible expressions of support in the form of several millions of dollars' worth of private charitable donations and supplies. As coordinated by the hugely successful Bundles for Britain organization (with 922 branches from coast to coast), American volunteers knitted thousands of woolen sweaters, scarves, seaboot stockings, gloves, socks, caps, and afghans for British soldiers, sailors, and airmen; all garments were supposed to conform to precise army and Admiralty specifications. In Princeton, New Jersey, Albert Einstein agreed to participate in a program to benefit British refugee children and shyly played a few selections—an Indian song, a Russian dance, a Bach minuet, and part of a Mozart sonata—on his violin. Others donated secondhand clothes for bombed-out English civilians. Bundles for Britain fund raisers sponsored watermelon eating contests in South Carolina and bake sales in Oregon, took up special collections in Boston churches and took in washing in West Virginia, all the proceeds going to purchase ambulances, children's cots, X-ray machines, shoes by the ton, sleeping bags, blood transfusion kits, surgical instruments, and children's overcoats for shipment to Britain. (This was precisely the sort of bleeding-heart sentimentality that Charles Lindbergh deplored; "we must not permit our sentiment, our pity, our personal feelings of sympathy to obscure the issue, to affect our children's lives," the pilot reminded his fellow Americans. "We must be as impersonal as a surgeon with his knife . . .")

Knit woolen seaboots were one thing; the weaponry of modern war was quite another. If Britain was to survive another year, it needed American guns and planes, and for that Churchill needed Roosevelt, and Roosevelt needed Congress.

So, shortly before two o'clock on the afternoon of January 6, the President's car pulled into the wide semicircular driveway at the south end of the Capitol and Roosevelt emerged, surrounded by a small army of police and Secret Service men. There was a scattering of applause from the hundreds of spectators who stood watching from the plaza beyond the ropes. At 2:03, Roosevelt, dressed in a gray morning suit, entered the House chamber and made his way to the podium to stand before a joint session of Congress. Some of the veteran congressmen who awaited his words had been present when Woodrow Wilson had asked for a declaration of war against Germany in 1917. Eleanor sat in the President's box in the gallery, accompanied by Princess Marthe of Norway, who looked the epitome of continental elegance in a fashionable black coat and silver fox. From a seat on the House floor, directly below the First Lady, Alice Roosevelt Longworth—widow of former Speaker of the House Nicholas Longworth—impatiently raised her lorgnette, the better to look upon "Cousin Franklin."

Roosevelt began his State of the Union address in a somber, matter-of-fact tone of voice that the three major radio networks carried across the country and to stations around the world. This year his message dealt exclusively with foreign affairs and the totalitarian danger from abroad. "At no previous time," he said, "has American security been as seriously threatened from without as it is today. . . . As your President . . . I find it necessary to report that the future and the safety of our country and our democracy are overwhelmingly involved in events far beyond our borders." There was none of the usual lightness in Roosevelt's voice that afternoon. "Our national policy is this: First, by an impressive expression of the public will and without regard to partisanship, we are committed to all-inclusive national defense." The President admitted that he was not at all satisfied with the lagging defense effort thus far, and he insisted upon a "swift and driving increase" in production to supply a greatly expanded American military machine. There were hearty cheers from the Democratic side, but only a lukewarm response from the Republicans.

"Second," Roosevelt went on, "by an impressive expression of the public will and without regard to partisanship, we are committed to full support of those resolute peoples, everywhere, who are resisting aggression and are thereby keeping war away from our hemisphere." Roosevelt threw his head back and waited for the applause. This time most of the Republican congressmen remained markedly silent. At his home on Long Island, Charles Lindbergh wrote in his diary: "In other words, we seem to want to have Britain win without being willing to pay the price of war. We are indulging in a type of wishful thinking that must lead us, sooner or later, to an impossible position."

Roosevelt continued reading from the oversized black leather binder in front of him. "Let us say to the democracies: 'We Americans are vitally concerned in your defense of freedom. We are putting forth our energies, our resources and our organizing powers to give you the strength to regain and maintain a free world. We shall send you, in ever-increasing numbers, ships, planes, tanks, guns. This is our purpose and our pledge.' " Then the President concluded with a vision of a world founded upon, in the words of his speechwriters, "four essential human freedoms": freedom of speech, freedom of worship, freedom from want, and freedom from fear. "To that high concept," he promised, "there can be no end save victory." (In Germany, the influential newspaper *Deutsche Allgemeine Zeitung* sarcastically dismissed the President's message as "Eccentric Arguments for a Lost Cause.") By 2:48 Roosevelt was done, and when Speaker of the House Sam Rayburn dissolved the joint session with a sharp stroke of an ornate mesquite-wood gavel donated by his constituents, the gavel promptly cracked and splintered into pieces.

Immediate reaction in Congress and the press was generally but by no means universally favorable to Roosevelt's speech and the Lend-Lease legislation itself, which was introduced in the House on January 11 and felicitously titled H.R. 1776, apparently at the suggestion of Supreme Court Justice Felix Frankfurter. Urging Congress to approve Lend-Lease, erstwhile Republican presidential candidate Wendell Willkie declared that "we shall not keep America out of war by mere strong statements that she is to stay out of war. We will keep America out of war if we supply to the fighting men of Britain sufficient resources so they may crush and defeat the ruthless dictatorship of Hitler." The American Federation of Labor assigned the Lend-Lease program first place on its list of legislative priorities for 1941, and leading Wall Street financier Winthrop W. Aldrich, chairman of Chase National Bank and head of the British War Relief Society, publicly declared his support for the measure as well.

But to the most zealous of the bill's opponents, almost all of whom were confirmed Roosevelt haters or Roosevelt baiters of long standing, the Lend-Lease resolution sounded the death knell of the American republic by providing the President with an unprecedented set of dictatorial powers. As originally submitted, H.R. 1776 gave FDR virtually unlimited power to sell, trade, transfer, or give outright an initial appropriation of $7 billion worth of defense material (which was defined so vaguely as to include anything from tanks to corned beef sandwiches) to any foreign government if the President believed the transaction would benefit the national defense. Thomas E. Dewey, the young New York district attorney whose prosecutions of the murder squads of organized crime syndicates had thrust him into national prominence (although he had lost his premature bid for the Republican presidential nomination to Willkie in 1940), charged that "the President's so-called Defense Bill would bring an end to free government in the United States and would abolish the Congress for all practical purposes. . . . This bill is an attempt to abolish free government in the United States." Senator Hiram Johnson of California deemed Lend-Lease a "monstrous" program, and the Chicago *Tribune* warned its readers that "this is a bill for the destruction of the American Republic." General Robert Wood decided that "the President is not asking for a blank check, he wants a blank check book with the power to write away your manpower, our laws and our liberties." And Senator Burton Wheeler of Montana, a liberal whose personal feud with the President over domestic political issues already had turned him into the most vehement and vituperative isolationist critic of all, accused Roosevelt of attempting "to frighten the American people to a point that they would surrender their liberties and establish a war-time dictatorship in this country."

Wheeler's attack reached its nadir in a radio speech on the evening of January 12, when he charged that Lend-Lease represented a "New Deal triple-A foreign policy—plow under every fourth American boy." His words struck a raw nerve in the White House; instead of treating Wheeler with the customary Roosevelt weapons of sarcasm and ridicule, the President responded with uncharacteristic violence at his press conference two days later. Wheeler's comment, he said, was "the most untruthful, the most dastardly, unpatriotic thing that has ever been said. Quote me on that," Roosevelt demanded, his voice rising in anger. "That really is the rottenest thing that has been said in public life in my generation." FDR scoffed at the notion that the Lend-Lease bill would make him a dictator, or that he would give away the American navy to Churchill; as an experienced sailor and a former assistant secretary of the navy, he insisted he was far too fond of his nation's ships to send them all away to anyone.

With Roosevelt's advisers keeping watch over Britain's ever-lengthening list of war matériel requirements, H.R. 1776 was promptly assigned to the House Foreign Affairs Committee, a group of typically undistinguished but well-meaning congressmen led by Chairman Sol Bloom of New York and ranking majority member Lyndon B. Johnson of Texas. ("They are as American as apple pie," wrote journalist I. F. Stone, who added that Lyndon Johnson had impressed him as "the brains on the Democratic side.") Hearings began less than a week later. The administration trotted out the big guns from the cabinet to testify before the committee: Cordell Hull, the longtime congressman from Tennessee who was now entering his ninth year as secretary of state; Secretary of War Henry L. Stimson, a seventy-two-year-old Republican Wall Street lawyer whose cabinet service dated back to the days of William Howard Taft and included a term as Hoover's secretary of state; Secretary of the Navy Frank Knox, the former publisher of the Chicago *Daily News* who had been brought into the administration after waging an unsuccessful campaign as the Republican vice-presidential nominee in 1936; and Treasury Secretary Henry Morgenthau, a financial expert whose friendship with the Roosevelt family went back for decades. Most of their testimony consisted of dire warnings about the threat to America if Britain succumbed to the Axis attack. Some skeptics scoffed at these scare tactics; at one point, Republican Hamilton Fish (a fabled football star during his collegiate days at Harvard, and now the representative from FDR's own Hyde Park district) asked the secretary of war if he actually believed the United States was in imminent danger of invasion. The patrician Stimson rose to his full height (which was considerable), thrust forward his jaw, and, stabbing his finger toward Fish with each phrase, replied in a deliberate, measured voice, "I think we are in very great danger of invasion in the contingency the British Navy is destroyed or surrendered."

Then a procession of opposition witnesses followed Roosevelt's right-hand men to the stand. First came former Ambassador to Great Britain Joseph Kennedy, whom the scornful British had nicknamed Jittery Joe for his nightly habit of fleeing London for a safe haven in the country during the blitz. Even before Roosevelt recalled him from his post in October 1940, Kennedy had made numerous public statements, and more in private, casting doubt upon the ability of Britain to withstand a determined German assault. "Mr. Kennedy," responded one member of the Foreign Office, "is a very foul specimen of double crosser and defeatist. He thinks of nothing but his own pocket." Kennedy was fond of warning his friends that "Roosevelt and the kikes were taking us into war," and he went so far as to urge Hollywood producers (many of whom were personal friends whom he had met after founding RKO studios with David Sarnoff in 1928) to stop making films that might be offensive to Hitler. Nor was Daddy the only Kennedy willing to attempt an accommodation with Nazism. His eldest son and heir apparent, Joe Jr., helped organize isolationist rallies at Harvard, and announced in a Boston speech in early January 1941 that the United States would be better off accepting Nazi domination of Europe than engaging in a quixotic, all-out crusade with Britain against Hitler. (Young Joe apparently feared that the American capitalist economy and free enterprise system was too fragile to withstand the burden of a lengthy war.) Second son Jack, however, reportedly did attempt to enlist in the navy and was rejected because of his bad back.

Isolationist spokesmen implored Joseph Kennedy to lead the crusade against Lend-Lease, but since the millionaire Wall Street speculator—who had made his fortune by knowing when to buy and when to sell—was not in the habit of burning his political bridges unnecessarily, he refused to make any public attack upon the President. Instead, Kennedy waffled in his congressional testimony and in a nationwide radio address, and ended up simply urging the nation to build up its own defenses to deter any prospect of aggression from abroad.

That left it up to Charles Lindbergh to carry the opposition banner into battle. Lindbergh had absolutely no use for Roosevelt. "I have tried to analyze his thinking," the flier complained, "but it is extremely difficult, for the man is so unstable. . . . I feel sure he would, consciously or unconsciously, like to take the center of the world stage away from Hitler. I think he would lead this country to war in a moment if he felt he could accomplish this object."

So Lindbergh arrived in Washington in late January to present his views to the House Foreign Affairs Committee. Like other visitors to the nation's capital that winter, he had a hard time finding a hotel room; already the city was crowded with businessmen seeking lucrative defense contracts. On the morning of January 23, he walked up to the Hill. Hundreds of excited spectators were lined up outside the hearing room doors, hoping to get a glimpse of the hero. Lindbergh followed a phalanx of police officers into the room:

> . . . It was jammed; probably 1,000 people were inside. The room was flooded with brilliant lights for the motion-picture cameras, and there were two or three dozen still photographers gathered around the table where I was to sit—almost all the things I dislike and which represent to me the worst of American life in this period. Up above me, extending in a curve to either side of the room, sat the committeemen; there must have been twenty or more of them.
>
>   *   *   *
>
> I read my statement and then attempted to reply to the questions of the committeemen until about 12:30, when an adjournment was made for lunch. I had expected to encounter great antagonism, but found relatively little of it, to my surprise. In fact, on the whole, they were extremely courteous. . . . And to my amazement, I found that the crowd was with me. They clapped on several occasions!

In response to a direct question, Lindbergh stated—and repeated several times—that he wanted neither Britain nor Germany to win the war: "I think it would be a disaster for Europe if either side won." Indeed, he believed that further fighting was senseless, since Germany could never overcome Britain's control of the seas, and Britain could never launch a successful invasion of the European continent. A protracted struggle to the death inevitably would devastate Europe and reduce it to a point of total exhaustion. By encouraging Britain to continue its futile struggle for world supremacy, therefore, Lend-Lease would wreak havoc abroad while impoverishing the United States. Like many other isolationists, Lindbergh favored a negotiated conclusion to the war, and he was astounded and appalled by Roosevelt's flat rejection of a compromise peace. When Lyndon Johnson asked him for his personal opinion of Adolf Hitler, Lindbergh refused to abjure the Fuehrer. "There are a lot of things going on abroad that I don't like," he said. "But, publicly I feel I should maintain a position of absolute neutrality."

There was little evidence that the hearings in Congress swayed public opinion to any appreciable extent. Every new Gallup poll revealed the same results: Americans wanted to aid Britain even at the risk of war; they supported the Lend-Lease bill because they believed it would keep the United States out of war; but they rejected the idea of American ships and American crews carrying Lend-Lease supplies across the Atlantic, even though it was difficult to see how else military aid could ever reach Britain in appreciable amounts. Amid the confusion in the public mind, two things were certain: Americans still loved and trusted Roosevelt—on the eve of his third term, the President's "vote of confidence" rating in the Gallup poll reached an all-time high of 71 percent—and they had absolutely no intention of fighting in any "foreign war." Across the spectrum of American opinion, from Kansas Republican editor William Allen White to the Communist *Daily Worker,* the rallying cry of "The Yanks are *not* coming" met with nearly universal approbation.

Inevitably, the tension of the endless debate over war and peace proved too much for some Americans, and occasionally nerves snapped and panic ensued. After listening to FDR's ominous fireside chat of December 29 in person, Clark Gable and Carole Lombard fled back to their ranch in southern California. Fearful that war was right around the corner, they promptly began to lay in extensive stores of food supplies: "hundred-pound sacks of sugar, cases of canned goods, bottles of oil and molasses," and ten four-foot-high, galvanized metal trash cans which Lombard filled with dried beans to satisfy her husband's culinary cravings.

Rumors of extramarital affairs plagued the Gables in early 1941, particularly after Clark started filming *Honky Tonk* with sexy starlet Lana Turner in March. No such problems worried Ronald Reagan and Jane Wyman, who were still groggy from the birth of their first child, Maureen, on January 4. Although Jane reportedly was upset that the baby was a girl—"Oh, Ronnie," someone heard her tell her husband at the hospital, "it took so long, and it's *still* only a girl"—he didn't seem to mind at all. "You know," Reagan said later, "the nice thing about having a girl is that you have a sort of picture of the girl you married, the girl you're in love with as a child and a young girl—you kind of watch her grow up. I know it's silly, but it gives you a kick."

Although Jane was still stuck in B movies, typecast as a wisecracking chorus girl who never got the leading man, Ronnie's film career was advancing nicely; fan magazines chose him as one of Hollywood's "stars of tomorrow," and the studio rewarded him with a new contract at $3,000 per week. In January 1941, audiences could see Reagan as the youthful George Armstrong Custer in *Santa Fe Trail,* a rather improbable action melodrama about abolitionist John Brown's freewheeling exploits in the years immediately preceding the Civil War. The star of the film, Errol Flynn (who, the FBI noticed, seemed to be spending an inordinate amount of time consorting with suspected Nazi agents in California and Mexico), played the dashing cavalryman Jeb Stuart. With more hearty camaraderie than they felt offscreen—Flynn reportedly feared that the studio was grooming Reagan to take his place—Stuart and Custer chased John Brown (played with terrifying intensity by Raymond Massey) from Kansas to West Virginia, climaxing with the bloody confrontation at Harpers Ferry. The film was something less than a smashing critical success. "These pictures of early turbulence are actually getting so slipshod," complained one disgusted reviewer, "that even their wild west hoorah makes no sense. Thirty sharpshooters at thirty paces fire thirty rounds into Errol Flynn without spoiling the crease in his trousers; yet any pretty boy fresh from Senior Year can take a snapshot with an 1860 pistol from a galloping horse over rough country and bring down stone dead anything up to a more expensive character actor at 200 yards. . . . Men besieged in arsenals use revolvers at long range, rifles for close combat and, wading through piles of looted guns and ammunition all the time, get a click out of old Deerslayer and throw the whole gun at somebody as a last resort." Others complained of the excess of blood, "blood by the washtubful," spilled during the picture.

For moviegoers of more literate sensibilities, *The Philadelphia Story* was setting attendance records at New York's Radio City Music Hall following its debut in the last week of the old year. Although Jimmy Stewart's wonderful performance as a lovestruck reporter won him an Academy Award as Best Actor of 1940 (actually, the award was more for his previously unrewarded work in *Mr. Smith Goes to Washington* in 1939), *The Philadelphia Story* was primarily a personal triumph for the indomitable Katharine Hepburn, whose Hollywood reputation as "box office poison"— and as an extremely difficult and demanding woman to work with—had kept her out of films for nearly two years. To revive her career, playwright Philip Barry had written *The Philadelphia Story* especially for Hepburn. Hepburn's former suitor Howard Hughes provided financial backing, and Hepburn personally selected Stewart and Cary Grant as her male co-stars. Grant, who still retained his English citizenship, donated his entire fee for the picture ($137,500) to British war relief.

Broadway patrons celebrated the new year with the debut on January 10 of *Arsenic and Old Lace,* the hilarious and wildly successful murder farce produced by Howard Lindsay and Russel Crouse, and written by the hitherto not very distinguished Joseph Kesselring. The story of two kindly, genteel spinsters (Aunt Abby and Aunt Martha Brewster) who routinely served fatal doses of poisoned elderberry wine—out of the purest charitable motives—to homeless old men who had no families to look after them, *Arsenic* drew high praise from *New York Times* drama critic Brooks Atkinson, who described it as "swift, dry, satirical and exciting"; the Second Nighters, an informal group of Broadway reviewers who regularly attended the second performance of new plays, voted it "the most entertaining play of the season." Josephine Hull and Jean Adair played the elderly aunts to perfection, John Alexander threw himself enthusiastically into the role of their daft brother Teddy (who, for no discernible reason, suffered from the delusion that he was actually Teddy Roosevelt and spent much of the play charging up San Juan Hill—the front staircase—waving an invisible saber), and Allyn Joseph appeared as the nephew (a drama critic, no less) who, upon discovering what his aunts were up to, tried to have them committed while covering up from the authorities the evidence of their latest charitable venture (a corpse hidden rather unsuccessfully under the window seat).

The play owed much of its success to the presence of one formidable personality who kept the audiences frightened at the proper moments and prevented the story from degenerating into sheer silliness: the man best known as Frankenstein's monster, Boris Karloff, a fifty-four-year-old veteran of Hollywood films making his first appearance on Broadway. Christened William Henry Pratt, the youngest son of a relatively prosperous British family, he had been groomed at King's College to follow his seven older brothers into the British consular service until he suddenly decided that he did not particularly care to spend what remained of his youth in the stuffy isolation of a diplomatic post in Hong Kong. William thereupon betook himself to the bustling metropolis of Kamloops, British Columbia, where he bought himself a farm and began to dabble in amateur theatrics. Less than a year later, he was offered a professional acting contract at $30 per week, but after his first performance, his pay was immediately cut in half. Undeterred, Pratt changed his name to Karloff and set out across Canada doing odd jobs and joining up with an occasional traveling troupe of entertainers. By 1918 he had landed in Hollywood, where he worked as an extra and bit player until the urbane and properly tweedy Englishman received his first big break in 1931, in *Frankenstein,* followed by a series of equally frightening roles. When Lindsay and Crouse had approached him about *Arsenic,* however, it was Karloff's turn to be scared; "I was frightened out of my wits," he admitted, and during rehearsals his throat got so dry he could hardly speak. Nevertheless, his nerves had settled down nicely by the time the play opened, and it continued to run on Broadway for 1,444 performances.

Two weeks after *Arsenic* opened, Broadway welcomed the debut of *Lady in the Dark,* a musical play written by Moss Hart, with lyrics by Ira Gershwin and music by expatriate German composer Kurt Weill, who had been living in the United States since 1935. It was an intriguing collaboration of creative talents: after a string of successful but numbingly conventional hits, Hart was looking for an innovative critical triumph; Weill, who had settled comfortably into the New York cultural scene, was searching for a vehicle that would earn him some much needed cash without sacrificing his artistic integrity; and Gershwin needed a challenge after spending too many easy months in sun-drenched Southern California. They all found what they needed. Filled with spectacular dream-sequence production numbers, brilliant choreography, and lavish costumes, and featuring a stellar cast that included Gertrude Lawrence, Macdonald Carey, the "unobjectionably handsome" Victor Mature, and a young and inimitably exuberant Danny Kaye (in the first major stage role of his career), *Lady* was an immediate success. "A work of theatre art . . . a feast of plenty . . . a feather in the cap of the American theatre," gushed Brooks Atkinson;

Weill's music, the *Times* critic said, was "the finest score written for the theatre in years. Ira Gershwin's lyrics are brilliant. . . . As for Gertrude Lawrence, she is a goddess: that's all." Despite Ms. Lawrence's fabled and incendiary dramatic prowess, however, the one performance that invariably brought down the house was the "Tchaikowsky" number, Kaye's hilarious fast-talking comic recitation of the names of fifty-two "legitimate" Russian composers in the space of only fifty frenzied seconds: "Malichevsky, Rubinstein, Arensky, Tchaikowsky, Sapellnikoff, Dmitrieff, Cherpnin, Kryjanowski . . ." and so forth, with nary a stumble nor pause for breath.

Clearly Americans were in the mood for a good laugh. In January 1941, the most popular radio program in America was "The Jack Benny Show," sponsored by Jell-O; every Sunday evening at seven o'clock, an estimated eleven million listeners tuned in to hear the latest zany adventures of Jack, Mary, Don, Dennis, and Rochester. For thirty half-hour radio programs a year, the forty-six-year-old Benny reportedly earned $350,000. Close behind was Fanny Brice, the temperamental comedienne who played Baby Snooks—an obnoxious juvenile character if ever there was one—on Maxwell House's "Good News" show. (Despite her poor eyesight, Brice refused to wear glasses while doing the show because she was afraid the spectacles might spoil Snooks' appearance to the radio audience; consequently, her script had to be written in triple-size type.) On the fiction best-seller list, *For Whom the Bell Tolls* was still selling, as Hemingway put it, "like frozen daiquiris in hell." *New Yorker* cartoonist Peter Arno won the Custom Tailors Guild award as the best-dressed man in America; Arno's wardrobe consisted of seventeen suits (costing an average $125 apiece), fourteen pairs of shoes, and thirty-six shirts. He told inquiring reporters that he just dressed to be comfortable. The Guild's runners-up included Guy Lombardo (sixth place) and former winner Adolphe Menjou (who slipped all the way to twelfth). The Guild fearlessly predicted that men's fashions in 1941 would include "natural shoulders, slightly suppressed waistlines, and a generous fullness in the chest and in the width of the lapel. Trousers will be perfectly straight. Narrow bottoms, exaggerated knees and thighs are taboo and positively out." One would hope so. Tailors at Brooks Brothers and Abercrombie and Fitch, meanwhile, were busy fashioning uniforms for the well-dressed prospective officer in the United States Army, where considerable differences in the cut and style of uniforms still were officially tolerated, if not encouraged.

Down Beat magazine, the bible of American jazz, announced the winners of its latest readers' poll in January: Benny Goodman's combo took top honors as best swing band, Glenn Miller's aggregation was voted the best sweet band, and the ubiquitous and unfortunately irrepressible Guy Lombardo was named King of Corn. Clarinetist Goodman also won an award as the fans' favorite soloist, while Bing Crosby and newcomer

Helen O'Connell were selected as best vocalists. The blond, dimpled, twenty-year-old O'Connell, known as Button Nose to the boys in Jimmy Dorsey's band, admitted to reporters that she had never taken voice lessons, and that she practiced her whiskey-voiced singing style while lying in bed.

In deference to the nation's newfound—but still halfhearted—preoccupation with defense production, the moguls of Detroit's automobile industry agreed not to waste design time and factory capacity on the frivolous development of completely new passenger models during 1941; nonetheless, the rising tide of prosperity in the United States created a year-long boom consumer market for autos. The latest popular innovation was the automatic transmission: for an advertised price of merely $825, customers could drive home from the showroom in a brand new Oldsmobile coupe with "Hydra-matic drive" and a 110-hp "Straight-Eight" engine. "See at first hand what it's like to drive for hours on end without ever shifting gears," trumpeted Chrysler's advertisements. "Glide up to traffic lights and stop by simply putting on the brake!" To prove their claims, Chrysler executives chose two average American girls to drive a new De Soto equipped with "Fluid Drive" and "Simplimatic Transmission" from coast to coast: "Not once did they shift or use the clutch . . . *yet a conventional car, over the same route, had to be shifted 4,097 times!*"

Out on the West Coast, Orson Welles, the brilliant bad boy of the entertainment world, was putting the finishing touches on a highly unconventional movie entitled *Citizen Kane*. In collaboration with writer Herman Mankiewicz, who was reputedly even more troublesome than Orson himself, Welles had developed a complex screenplay that told the story of the rise and fall of a media tycoon through the eyes of a number of the great man's friends and enemies. Although much of the material was fiction, there were far too many similarities to the lives of newspaper publisher William Randolph Hearst and his mistress, Marion Davies, to fool anyone. (It is still a mystery how Welles discovered that "Rosebud" was the nickname Hearst used for a certain sacrosanct region of Miss Davies' anatomy.) Early in January, Welles' studio, RKO Radio, gave a private screening of the $800,000 film to critics from *Life, Look,* and *Redbook*. In high dudgeon at being ignored, movieland gossip maven Hedda Hopper showed up at the screening anyway; several hours later, she walked out of the theater in disgust, proclaiming that *Kane* was a "vicious and irresponsible attack on a great man."

In an effort to browbeat RKO into scuttling the film, Hearst ordered his newspapers to refuse all the studio's advertising, and instructed his own syndicated columnist, Louella Parsons, to boycott all RKO movies. This comic-opera brouhaha was precisely the sort of valuable publicity that money couldn't buy. To keep the controversy alive, Welles (who was treading on thin ice, having an illicit affair of his own with Dolores del Rio at the time) blandly told reporters that *Citizen Kane* was "not based upon the life of Mr. Hearst or anyone else. On the other hand, had Mr. Hearst and similar financial barons not lived during the period we discuss, *Citizen Kane* could not have been made." Meanwhile, as attorneys for each side wrangled over real and threatened lawsuits, RKO postponed the public premiere of the film, which had been scheduled for February 14 at Radio City Music Hall.

Already the war in Europe had provided the inspiration for dozens of plays and movie scripts. Alfred Lunt and Lynn Fontanne were touring the United States with their production of Robert Sherwood's *There Shall Be No Night,* the story of a Scandinavian scientist who abandons his pacifist beliefs to take up arms against an invasion by a ruthless totalitarian power (in this case, the Soviet Union). Despite a rash of newspaper boycotts, pickets, and isolationist accusations that the play was a piece of warmongering propaganda, the production regularly played to capacity houses wherever it appeared. "It's something like playing in *Uncle Tom's Cabin* before the Civil War," was Lunt's feeling. Audiences were deeply moved by the dramatic experience. Cynical New York critic Alexander Woollcott wept openly after one performance. The Lunts received scores of letters during the tour: "Nobody could come out of that theatre and still be afraid," said one; "You have given us something to hope for in these frightening times," read another; and, "I walked out of the theatre feeling somehow braver and stronger." "When I started to write this play," explained Sherwood, who doubled as a speechwriter for President Roosevelt, "I had come to the conclusion that the isolationists were leading us into a position of really awful peril for this country. I certainly do not say in this play or anywhere else that we should plunge into this war with full force."

Movie studios were deluged with scripts about the war or life in the army. Forthcoming titles included Bob Hope's *Caught in the Draft* and *You're in the Army Now,* a comedy that featured what purported to be the longest on-screen kiss in Hollywood history (three minutes and five seconds, between Jane Wyman and the ineffable Regis Toomey). *Buck Privates,* with Lou Abbott, Bud Costello, and the Andrews Sisters (singing "Bounce Me Brother with a Solid Four"), already was doing surprisingly solid box-office business, as was *Night Train to Munich,* which featured Rex Harrison as a dashing young British Intelligence officer trying to outwit a devious Nazi admiral (Paul von Hernreid). Hollywood's persistent inclination to characterize German military officers as villainous scum caused considerable consternation within isolationist circles; in January, Senator Wheeler took time out from his attacks upon Lend-Lease to threaten a legislative crackdown on the film studios for "carrying on a violent propaganda campaign intending to incite the American people to . . . war."

Probably the most famous example of the genre was Charlie Chaplin's anti-Nazi satire *The Great Dictator,* for which Chaplin won the New York Film Critics' Best Actor award for 1940. (Chaplin promptly refused the award, citing his opposition to the entire notion of competition among actors.) Although Chaplin had expended two years of creative effort and $2 million of his own money upon the movie, it never achieved the resounding success he had expected, at least not in the United States, where moviegoers preferred not to think about Hitler at all. Harry Hopkins had predicted as much when he saw the film at its advance press showing; "It's a great picture," he told Chaplin, "a very worthwhile thing to do, but it hasn't a chance." British audiences, who were a great deal closer to the subject at hand, received the film with much more enthusiasm.

Nevertheless, Chaplin received an invitation to deliver the dramatic closing speech from *The Great Dictator* at the inaugural ceremonies in Washington in January. The afternoon before he was scheduled to perform at the inaugural eve celebration, Chaplin went to the White House to pay his respects to the President. There he met Roosevelt in his study, a room stuffed with knickknacks, models of ships, and, on such social occasions, an elaborate display of cocktail implements—bottles of liquor, an ice bucket, glasses in a variety of sizes and shapes, a plate of lemons with a squeezer, dishes of olives and nuts, and a gleaming, oversized silver shaker—with which Roosevelt could display his renowned prowess as an expert bartender. "Sit down, Charlie," the President said, and then, almost as an afterthought, he added rather impolitely, "Your picture is giving us a lot of trouble in the Argentine." (In fact, Argentina's pro-German government had decided that *The Great Dictator* was blasphemy and banned it, but special excursion boats ran back and forth across the Plata River to theaters in Uruguay.)

The evening's festivities, held in the patriotic environs of the Hall of the Daughters of the American Revolution, included appropriately inspirational performances of patriotic material by Ethel Barrymore, Mickey Rooney, and Nelson Eddy. Raymond Massey, with tears in his eyes, recited selections from Robert Sherwood's *Abe Lincoln in Illinois,* and Irving Berlin led the audience in singing "God Bless America." Then Chaplin, in his role as the Jewish barber in *The Great Dictator,* walked to the center of the stage and delivered the film's closing plea for peace, tolerance, and world freedom.

> Hannah, can you hear me? Wherever you are, look up! Look up, Hannah! The clouds are lifting! The sun is breaking through! We are coming out of the darkness into the light! We are coming into a new world—a kindlier world, where men will rise above their greed, their hate and their brutality. Look up, Hannah! The soul of man has been given wings and at last he is beginning

to fly. He is flying into the rainbow—into the light of hope. Look up, Hannah! Look up!

Traditionally, the weather in Washington on Inauguration Day ranges from deplorable to absolutely atrocious. But January 20, 1941, dawned crystal clear and bracingly cold. At least a million spectators lined Pennsylvania Avenue to watch the presidential procession from the White House to Capitol Hill. They saw a squadron of fifteen motorcycle policemen driving in V-formation leading the way; then came Roosevelt himself, waving a silk hat, his car surrounded by four army scout cars equipped with heavy machine guns, and a crew of five soldiers in each car. Eleanor sat beside her husband, wearing a vermilion wool tailored dress and matching hat. Police subdued and hustled away a man who was swinging a sword in a wide arc, shouting that he was "protecting Roosevelt." Another man with a gun who said he was "on duty to guard the President" also was taken into custody.

Upon the freshly painted wooden pavilion on the Capitol steps, Chief Justice Charles Evans Hughes administered for the third time the oath of office to Franklin Delano Roosevelt, who stood with his hand on his family's three-hundred-year-old Bible, opened to the thirteenth chapter of First Corinthians. As the Marine Band, attired in overcoats against the cold, played "Hail to the Chief," reporters noticed the deep lines in Roosevelt's face that had not been there eight years before. Once more there was only a passing reference to domestic affairs, and again the mood was somber, almost depressing. "We do not retreat," Roosevelt vowed. "Democracy is not dying." His speech lasted only sixteen minutes. At the German Embassy several blocks away, a brilliantly colored swastika flag flew in honor of the ceremonial occasion.

Then Roosevelt reviewed the inaugural parade, led by Army Chief of Staff General George Catlett Marshall, the honorary grand marshal, riding on horseback. There were none of the usual imbecilic antics of political marching clubs, no donkeys, elephants, or Indian tribes, no fraternal lodge members in silly hats frolicking along Pennsylvania Avenue. This year, virtually the entire parade was composed of units of the armed forces: "soldiers, sailors, marines, Coast Guardsmen, big guns, little guns, bayonets, tanks, trucks, horses, flags, brass bands, nurses and ambulances . . . and squadrons of airplanes roaring overhead." It was, observers agreed, the greatest display of armed might ever witnessed in Washington. Because so much of the procession was motorized, it took only forty-five minutes instead of the usual three to four hours. Someone said it was the most ominous atmosphere surrounding an inaugural ceremony since Abraham Lincoln was made president in 1861.

Perhaps the parade impressed naive spectators, but to those well

Lend-Lease
(71)

acquainted with the arsenals of Germany, Russia, and Japan, U. S. forces remained pitifully inadequate to the demands of modern warfare. At the end of 1938, two months after the Munich debacle, *Life* magazine had published a lengthy critique of the state of American defense preparations. "Among the armies of the major powers," it concluded, "America's is not only the smallest but the worst equipped; most of its arms are outmoded World War [One] leftovers; some of its post-War weapons are already, in the military sense, obsolete; it has developed up-to-date weapons, but has far too few of them for modern war; if America should be attacked, it would be eight months before the nation's peacetime industry could be converted to production of the war supplies which the Army would need; whether there would be any Army left to supply at the end of those months is disputable."

Although George Marshall later claimed that the lessons of Munich and the *Life* article had prodded the army into significant reforms to improve its combat readiness, the situation remained basically unchanged two years later. American military officials were stunned by the speed and power of the Nazi blitzkrieg in the spring of 1940. "The coordination between air and ground, tanks and motorized infantry, exceeded anything we had ever dreamed of in the U.S. Army," recalled Omar Bradley, then a rising officer on George Marshall's administrative staff. "We were amazed, shocked, dumbfounded, shaking our heads in disbelief. . . . To match such a performance, let alone exceed it, the U.S. Army had years of catching up and little time in which to do it."

The appalling contrast seemed even more desperate after Bradley witnessed the United States Army's spring infantry maneuvers in Louisiana in May 1940. Disgusted with the "undistinguished and unimaginative leadership" displayed by the generals conducting the exercises, Bradley and his colleagues recognized that the nation's armed forces had an urgent need for more tanks, more armored vehicles, more powerful artillery, more antitank and antiaircraft weapons—in short, practically all the paraphernalia of modern warfare.

In large part, American defense deficiencies were due to the Roosevelt administration's well-documented allergy to long-range planning. "In the United States," wrote British historian A. J. P. Taylor, "improvisation still ruled. American war production, like the New Deal before it, was built up by guess, and its leaders had little idea what was coming until it happened." The abiding reluctance of Congress to spend any money until the need was desperately obvious played its part, too, as did the desire of American consumers to enjoy the long-deferred benefits of a healthy economy.

With civilian production and purchasing power finally recovering from the Depression, there was tremendous public resistance in the

United States in the winter and spring of 1941 to any plans that would convert a large segment of the nation's industrial plant to military purposes. "Business as usual" became the slogan of corporate executives unwilling to surrender their profits—at least, not until they won enough lucrative defense contracts to make up the difference. This attitude was made all the more dangerous by the indisputable fact (of which the average American adult remained blissfully unaware) that it was going to take American industry a long, long time before it was prepared to mass-produce modern mechanized armaments. "Assembly-line setups for automobiles have little to do with what an assembly line for tanks should be," explained Charles Kettering, president of General Motors Research Corporation. "Caterpillar treads aren't wheels, light cannon aren't windshield wipers, machine-gun mountings aren't rumble seats, and the relations among these various elements are another story altogether."

A comparative analysis of the industrial output of Germany, Great Britain, and the United States revealed that, on the average, German and British workers spent four hours per day in the production of war goods; in the United States, on the other hand, only about thirty minutes out of every eight-hour day was devoted to defense production (fifteen minutes for the nation's own military forces, and fifteen minutes for Britain). Experts estimated that if the U.S. adopted the same production scale as the European belligerents, it could produce $50 billion worth of arms annually. And if half of that total—$25 billion—were sent to Britain, it would equal ten times the actual rate of war matériel exported in January 1941. "It is better to produce too much than too little," warned the editors of the liberal journal *The New Republic;* "if we produce too little, it is the last mistake free America will ever commit."

While the Wehrmacht had made its mechanized divisions the vital pivot of Hitler's blitzkrieg strategy, American military planners had paid little attention to the tremendous advances in modern tank design since the end of the First World War. Production of all sorts of airplanes was lagging in the United States; as late as 1938, the nation had more people employed in making knit underwear than in the aircraft industry. Most of the navy's 2,590 existing planes were trainers, and only a very few were modern combat types. Development of bombers had lagged badly in the United States, partly because American public opinion—which always thought of defense planning in terms of actually *defending* the nation against attack—had little use for an avowedly offensive weapon designed to inflict heavy damage upon defenseless civilian populations. At the start of 1941, only two flight groups in the entire U.S. Army Air Corps were fully equipped and properly staffed. Most army planes were suitable only for hauling freight. There was a desperate shortage of aircraft engines, exacerbated by an interservice dispute over the relative merits of air-cooled engines (favored by the navy) and liquid-cooled engines (which the army employed). Secretary Knox reported that the U.S. Navy trailed far behind the Axis powers in combat tonnage; the relative strengths were especially disproportionate in the areas of cruisers (37 for the U.S., 75 for the Axis), destroyers (159 to 271), and submarines (105 to 284). For the first time in more than twenty years, the navy was not even going to engage in large-scale maneuvers. Instead, most of the fleet was being held as a unit in Hawaiian waters, taking gunnery practice—many of the battleships were still equipped with antiaircraft guns whose range was limited to only 20,000 yards—and participating in simplified exercises designed somehow to make it "the most efficient naval fighting force in the world." It still had a long way to go, although at least some of the ships stationed at Pearl Harbor were scheduled to receive new armor and guns with longer ranges. Few Americans realized precisely how vulnerable the navy was to the sort of ruthless surprise aerial attacks that already had been employed so profitably in the war. "Every battle unit in the fleet," reported the *New York Times* naively at the start of 1941, "has been overhauled and is ready for instant action in any emergency, no matter how sudden."

Nor was the manpower situation in the armed forces particularly encouraging, either. Inexplicably, the War Department appears to have been taken completely by surprise as draftees and members of the reserves and the National Guard descended en masse upon army training camps that winter, 608,000 men by January 1941, a threefold increase in twelve months. "A gigantic mess ensued," admitted Omar Bradley. "Despite all the years of planning—the files bulging with mobilization plans—the army was simply not prepared to assimilate such vast numbers of new manpower. There were no organized basic training camps for draftees. Recruits were sent directly to existing or organizing Regular Army units for basic training, even though those units might be engaged in maneuvers. The Guard units . . . were ill-equipped and in some instances so ill-trained that the officers in charge had not the slightest idea of their jobs or how to train the men in their units. There was as yet no equipment for the newly recruited men. The much-publicized photos of recruits carrying broomsticks for rifles or using stovepipes to simulate artillery—and the slogan 'Hurry up and wait'—were all to the point."

Local Selective Service boards applied wildly divergent standards in deciding whom to draft and whom to defer. Some boards granted deferments to policemen and firemen as essential civic employees, but others did not; some boards drafted men with working wives, while others deferred them on the grounds that a woman should not be required to support a family all by herself. The chairman of one New York draft board cheerfully deferred husbands who were happily married, and drafted those whose marriages were on the rocks. The chief clerk of another district in Manhattan confided that the army did not want many of the applicants in his district: "You'd be surprised about those interior decorators." Often an original decision to defer was reversed. One twenty-five-year-old in Chicago had been given a clean bill of health by his local board; when he arrived at the army induction center, an officer discovered that the man had a wooden leg. Jimmy Stewart received a I-B classification (available only for limited service) purportedly because he was underweight (145 pounds), so he went on an eating binge and gained enough weight to make himself presentable to his board in Los Angeles. Hank Greenberg, the Detroit Tiger slugger who had won the American League's Most Valuable Player award in 1940, received a low draft number and appeared as requested for his physical examination. The first time around, a physician near the team's spring training camp in Lakeland, Florida, decided that Greenberg's flat feet (a case of "second-degree bilateral pes planus") rendered him unfit for active service; in fact, his feet were so flat that some baseball scouts had predicted he would never make it to the big leagues. When his draft board ordered a second examination, however, a team of less finicky doctors declared him perfectly sound, and so Hank prepared to trade his $55,000 salary for a private's $21 per month allowance. (Greenberg was not, however, the first major leaguer drafted in 1941. That honor went to Hugh "Losing Pitcher" Mulcahy of the Philadelphia Phillies, who was inducted on March 8.)

Along with his uniform, every newly arrived soldier received a copy of the new official Army Song Book, from which all of the old songs suggesting service abroad—including "Mad'moiselle from Armentieres"—had been carefully excised (although such dubious standards as "Bombed," "Seven Long Years," and "Where Do We Go From Here?" were still included). The soldiers' repertoire also had been cleaned up; the cheerfully obscene "Bastard King of England" was laundered and renamed "The Minstrels Sing of an English King." Each recruit also was given a pocket-sized publication known as the Soldier's Handbook, which told him everything he needed to know about life in the army, including the care and maintenance of small arms, how to read a map, proper dental care (brush your teeth twice a day), and the ins and outs of military courtesy (never salute an officer in a public place or when you are carrying a heavy package in your arms). Most draftees, fortunately, were unaware that the army had awarded a contract to the Animal Trap Company of America to supply $71,000 worth of folding cots to the training camps.

Very early in the game, army officials discovered that peacetime budget cuts and the dismal prospects for promotion between wars had left them with a dearth of junior officers to train the hordes of draftees. To produce the maximum number of second lieutenants in the minimum amount of time, Omar Bradley devised a plan for an Officer Candidate School at Fort Benning, Georgia, which soon became the prototype for the rest of the services. Fort Benning also was the home of the army's first full parachute training battalion, and the headquarters of one of only two modern armored divisions. It was there that Bradley first came to know well the flamboyant commander of the Second Armored Brigade, Colonel George Smith Patton, Jr.—"the Old Man"—who, his men said, seemed to have the damndest way of showing up when things went wrong . . . just like God.

Listening to radio reports of the endless waves of bombs descending upon England in the winter of 1940–41, officials in numerous American cities prudently decided to prepare civil defense plans in anticipation of an Axis invasion by air or by sea. Even Milwaukee, whose strategic importance was limited largely to the city's breweries, organized an Air Raid Warden Corps; every residential block had one warden who had been trained in the proper use of gas masks and the disposal of incendiary bombs. Nor were the anti-invasion preparations limited to the nation's major metropolitan areas. Way down in Oxford, Mississippi, novelist William Faulkner (who liked to pretend that he was an expert aviator) organized a local aircraft warning service unit and recruited spotters to man Lafayette County's air raid observation posts. Across the country, owners of the estimated forty thousand homing pigeons in the U. S. were requested to register their lofts with army headquarters in Washington, D.C., just in case the government needed to draft the birds to maintain emergency communications during a Nazi blitzkrieg.

On January 20–21, civil defense officials held the first test of the East Coast's air raid warning system from New York to Boston. Nearly ten thousand volunteer observers, armed with telephones, two-way radios, and binoculars, manned their observation posts and waited for the mock attack. On the first day, almost all the "enemy" bombers were spotted and their positions relayed to a central tracking station. (In fact, some of the "bombers" reported by overzealous observers turned out to be commercial airplanes or Weather Bureau balloons.) During the second day of the exercise, however, foggy weather and a breakdown in radio communications allowed some raiders to slip through the net and simulate destructive attacks upon New England's industrial centers. One plane flew completely undetected over the industrial city of Salem and reached New York; another enemy bomber "destroyed" Boston's airport.

In Washington, meanwhile, government officials launched an intensive antiespionage campaign to beef up security precautions at all federal office buildings. Any private citizen who wished to visit the White House on business was required to submit to interrogation and fingerprinting by the FBI. Employees and visitors at the War and Navy departments had to wear photographic ID badges at all times, and security officers kept a detailed log of everyone who entered or left any government office building after the usual business hours. J. Edgar Hoover asked Congress for

$970,000 to hire seven hundred additional special agents to protect defense plants against saboteurs and spies. Combined with the droves of businessmen scurrying about the city, endeavoring to obtain government contracts, it all seemed disturbingly reminiscent of the feverish wartime atmosphere of 1917–18.

4

"Fire Is Not a Very Good Game"

"The newspapers give so much space to the great crusade to
rescue England that they have little left for events in other
quarters. Thus there is not much in them about the doings of
the Jap infidels in the Far East, though there is good reason
to suspect that something unpleasant is afoot there."
                                    —H. L. MENCKEN, JANUARY 1941

General Hideki Tojo, minister of war in the Imperial cabinet of the
Japanese Empire and a dedicated man of infinite discipline and patriotism,
believed that his nation was facing perhaps the gravest emergency in its
glorious 2,600-year history. After four years of brutal and merciless war,
a million Japanese soldiers were still bogged down on the Chinese mainland. The United States and the British Empire stubbornly refused to
recognize the legitimacy of Tokyo's blueprints for a Greater East Asia
Co-Prosperity Sphere, and in recent months both Western nations had
defiantly implemented stringent restrictions upon trade in strategic
materials, aviation gasoline, and scrap iron to Japan. In his New Year's
address to the Japanese people, Tojo sternly urged them to make greater
sacrifices and still greater exertions, to display an unbroken front of national unity for the crusade that lay ahead. "Supreme determination and
extraordinary efforts are necessary," the iron-willed Tojo proclaimed, "before the task of establishing a Greater East Asia is completed."

Tojo's exhortation notwithstanding, extraordinary efforts already
were being made to mobilize the entire population of the Japanese islands
in support of the government's military and diplomatic objectives—
which, incidentally, varied from week to week, depending upon events
abroad and the latest political intrigues in Tokyo. Price fixing, censorship,
conscription, and gasoline rationing had gone into effect long ago. "Dangerous thoughts" were expressly forbidden, as was membership in left-
wing or Communist political organizations which tended to oppose the
national drift toward militarism. In the face of government opposition to
independent organized labor activities, union membership declined
precipitously; lacking any power or purpose, the Japanese General Federation of Labor had simply dissolved itself in 1940.

As part of a ten-year plan to encourage Japanese couples to produce more children (preferably at least five per family) to ensure Japanese racial supremacy throughout East Asia, the government prohibited birth control devices and abortion, and implemented a program of tax incentives, rationing privileges, loans, and propagation propaganda ("Having babies is fun"); nevertheless, the birthrate continued to decline due to the large numbers of working women and the difficult economic situation. As prices rose and shortages developed in consumer goods, civilians were subjected to relentless official pressure to limit expenditures and put their money into government bonds instead.

Fish was scarce in the winter of 1940–41. Japan's rice supply was so adulterated with inferior imported grain that nearly half the civilian population seemed to be suffering from chronic indigestion; the government's only solution was to advise everyone to drink more water before meals. Thousands of public baths in the nation's cities were forced to close down altogether or reduce their water temperature drastically as fuel supplies dwindled. Prescription drugs were in chronically short supply, and nails, leather, and matches were nearly impossible to find. Precious stocks of cotton were reserved largely for infant garments; adults wore clothes made of *sufu,* a flimsy fiber that reportedly disintegrated after two washings. (There were irreverent stories of a half-dozen suicide attempts that failed because ropes made of *sufu* simply snapped.)

A growing feeling of paranoia among military and political officials meant that Western customs and contacts were viewed with considerable suspicion. Japanese girls were forbidden to wear their hair in the decadent American style of permanent waves. Men were discouraged from playing golf, although baseball was permitted to continue for the time being. In mid-January, the government staged antiespionage maneuvers in vital industrial districts, to instruct the public on the best methods to thwart sabotage and foreign intelligence gathering. At the same time, the Imperial cabinet approved urgent plans to install antiaircraft weapons around all defense establishments in the Tokyo, Yokohama, and Osaka-Kobe areas. Observing the rising tide of militant nationalism, the State Department had advised Americans in the Far East in October 1940 to return home as soon as possible; by January 1941, nearly seven thousand of the eight thousand Americans in Japan had departed the islands.

Throughout the decade of the 1930s, Japanese youth had been subjected to a relentless indoctrination in the virtues of patriotism and selflessness. Nearly three million young men belonged to an organization known as the Seinendan, an association founded by a retired Imperial Army general to stem the moral decay that purportedly plagued modern Japanese society. One evening every week, members of the Seinendan gathered at their local youth center to hear lectures, watch morality plays, participate in patriotic ceremonies, or attend classes in wholesome thinking and civic responsibility. The movement was particularly strong in rural villages, where membership often reached 100 percent; in Tokyo, where the attractions of individualism held rather more appeal than the altruistic ideal of self-sacrifice, less than 20 percent of the city's youth joined up.

Children absorbed the same lessons, albeit in a less structured manner, from a series of popular magazines published by a marketing genius named Noma Seiji. Seiji's magazines were directed toward readers with a sixth-grade education, which meant that many older boys read them as well. His avowed aim was to make "real men" out of the younger generation by constantly feeding them adventure stories with patriotic morals and tales of martial glory. Seiji's most famous hero was a comic-strip character known as "Nora-Kura" (Black Mutt), a dog-soldier who worked his way up through the ranks by his spectacular exploits against the Chinese swine (who were literally portrayed as pigs). By reducing complex issues to a simplistic struggle between virtue (Japan) and evil (China and the West), Seiji's wildly popular publications exerted an incalculable influence on impressionable young minds. "In retrospect," Seiji admitted after the war, "it could be said that I was in the vanguard of military aggression."

Still, the fact that Japanese officials found it necessary to continue to attempt to instill these same virtues by every available means in early 1941 indicated that the entire nation had not yet learned its lessons to the satisfaction of the authorities. For the benefit of those soldiers who required further instruction, General Tojo issued the *Field Service Code* to Japanese Imperial troops shortly after the start of the new year. The product of six months of learned debate among military officers and civilian scholars who sought to succinctly define the national spirit and mission of Japan, the *Code* instructed soldiers to accept each assignment from a superior officer as a sacred duty, to rely upon and trust one another implicitly, and to maintain an attitude of absolute obedience and filial piety toward the state. "The mission of the Imperial Army lies in making the Imperial virtues the object of admiration through the exercise of justice tempered with mercy," it advised. "In defense, always retain the spirit of attack and always maintain freedom of action; never give up a position but rather die."

Frustrated by the army's inability to subjugate China, the cabinet—led by the sophisticated and cynical Prime Minister Prince Fumimaro Konoye—planned to move southward instead, to assume control of the enticingly vulnerable treasure house of French Indochina, with its valuable resources of rice, minerals, and rubber. Between 1860 and 1907, France had consolidated its control over this sprawling empire of 286,000 square miles, absorbing the ancient kingdoms of Laos, Cambodia, and Annam into a loosely structured union notable primarily for its flagrant corruption and the fabled greed of the French officials who governed it from Hanoi. It was an empire of exploitation, hatred, and prejudice; "the French made money out of Indo-China," wrote Theodore H. White, who in 1941 was a free-lance correspondent in the Far East, "and they despised the people who lived there." In fact, Frenchmen were so busy extorting riches from their "balcony on the Pacific" that they neglected to develop any viable defenses against invasion from the north.

Thus Tokyo launched its campaign to rescue 23 million Indochinese from the racist, exploitative clutches of the white man. Faced with Japanese diplomatic and military pressure, the stalwart leaders of Vichy France, hard pressed to handle the troubles that sat on their own doorstep, left the governor-general in Hanoi to his own resources, which were far from considerable. Consequently, the government of French Indochina permitted Japanese "observers" to settle in at Hanoi and Haiphong (whereupon Japanese communications specialists installed a military telephone link between the airports of the two cities); Japanese army engineers began building a permanent 25,000-man barracks near Hanoi; the Japanese navy obtained a base at Cam Ranh Bay, and the Imperial air force received free use of air bases in northern Indochina. To supplement these military footholds, civilian representatives from Tokyo arrived at Saigon to negotiate economic concessions and a trade pact favorable to Japan.

Desperately short of men and weapons, French authorities could not resist Japanese demands; but what was left of their imperial pride would not allow an armed incursion from Thailand to go unchallenged. Throughout January, Thai forces battled Foreign Legionnaires in the mountains and jungles along the western borders of Laos and Cambodia. Although French ground forces (mostly demoralized African colonial troops) were steadily driven back by artillery and air attacks, French warships sank nearly half the Thai fleet in a single engagement in the Gulf of Siam.

At the end of the month, the Japanese government—which had supplied and encouraged Thailand's advance—announced that it was stepping in to "mediate" a settlement. To ensure that both sides accepted its role as mediator, the truce talks were held aboard a Japanese warship that had serendipitously arrived in Saigon harbor for the occasion. The ensuing treaty assigned the disputed border provinces along the Mekong River to Thailand, but, as a reward for its intervention, Japan emerged as the real victor. Ostensibly to enforce the terms of the settlement, the Japanese navy obtained the right to occupy certain Cambodian ports, which, as the British noted nervously, provided it with excellent staging areas for an invasion of Singapore, Burma, or the Dutch East Indies. In London, an alarmed Anthony Eden therefore wasted no time in delivering a harsh warning to the Japanese ambassador about the distressing fate that awaited little nations whose appetite for territory exceeded their grasp. Afterwards, Eden feared that he had gone too far in hectoring the poor man, but the permanent undersecretary of the Foreign Office, Alexander Cadogan, reassured him that "a little of that medicine was good for them." (Cadogan, who had personal experience as an ambassador in the Far East and fancied himself an expert on Oriental psychology, went on to express himself as openly suspicious of "the machinations of these beastly little monkeys.")

Adding to the general instability of Southeast Asia was the presence of a small but potentially disruptive body of Communist partisans operating out of the hill country of northern Indochina. After an absence from his native land of nearly three decades (during which time he had lived in Paris, studied in the Soviet Union, and taught the finer points of guerrilla warfare to Chinese troops), a thin, soft-spoken man known to his Maoist friends as Ho Quang (one of many aliases he would later discard for the name Ho Chi Minh) slipped quietly back into Cao Bang province in early 1941. Ho made his home and his headquarters in a cave cut deep into the face of a mountain he named after Karl Marx; the stream nearby was known as Lenin. He knew the time was not yet right for full-scale Communist insurrection, but he watched closely as Japan knocked the props out from under the rotting structure of French imperialism, and he pondered the useless piles of fallen rock outside the entrance to his cave, fallen rock that once had been part of the mountain.

Across the Chinese border, the Communist armies of Mao Zedong had made an uneasy truce with the man they scornfully called a "son of a turtle," Chiang Kai-shek, to establish a united front against Japanese aggression. Although Mao had prudently kept his own military forces separate from Chiang's Kuomintang armies, Chiang retained nominal control over all Chinese military operations. It was the Communists' misfortune that Chiang viewed Mao as a greater threat to his regime than the Japanese. (In fact, Chiang needed a large-scale Japanese presence in China to frighten Washington into giving him the money and weapons he needed to exterminate his internal enemies.) The most worrisome Communist presence was the New Fourth Army, a superbly capable force of more than 100,000 soldiers which the Kuomintang viewed with the gravest apprehension. Unable to obtain all the supplies they needed from the central government, the men of the New Fourth Army lived off the land, stealing food from the peasants in the countryside and appropriating weapons from the Japanese or the fractious, imperious Chinese warlords who roamed and ravaged the hinterland, or even from Chiang's Kuomintang troops. After repeated confrontations between the New Fourth Army and the other anti-Japanese units in the area immediately south of the Yangtze River, Chiang first cut off supplies to the Communists and then ordered them to move the army back to its original territory, north of the Yangtze, late in 1940.

Most of the New Fourth Army obeyed Chiang's command—the broad outlines of the movement to the north had been agreed upon by Zhou Enlai himself—but the army's military and political command staff procrastinated, apparently fearing (correctly) that the withdrawal route chosen by the Nationalist government would lead them straight into a Japanese ambush. So, on January 14, the Communist commander and the remainder of his troops, about ten thousand men, started off upon a different path across the Yangtze. On the pretext that the Communists had thereby violated the withdrawal agreement, Chiang's lieutenants waited until the New Fourth headquarters force was most vulnerable, and then struck mercilessly, attacking with sixty thousand troops. Between four and eight thousand Communist soldiers were slaughtered before the carnage ended. At once Mao sent a chilling response from Yenan: "Those who play with fire ought to be careful. We formally warn them. Fire is not a very good game. Be careful about your skull. . . . Our retreat has come to an end. We have been struck with a hatchet and our first wound is a serious one. . . . We have to give this warning for the last time. If things continue to develop this way, the whole people of the whole country will throw you into the gutter. And then if you feel sorry, it will be too late."

From that point on, effective cooperation between Chiang and the Communists ended, although both sides still maintained a facade of unity for the outside world. From that point on, there were two separate, independent Chinese governments. Those who were not fervent supporters of the Kuomintang were appalled by the Fourth Army massacre, as were Western diplomats stationed in China. "As for me," recalled Han Suyin, the unhappy wife of a high Kuomintang official, "it was such a shock that I could no longer contain myself. I shouted at Pao, 'This is awful, awful.' I felt suffocated, walking up and down Chungking's ladder streets—oh how suddenly I saw, clearly, too clearly, that Chiang would have to go! From that day on, I was convinced inside myself, morally certain, that Chiang would go, and there would be a 'great change' in China, a big, wished-for, longed-for change."

But if Chiang knew anything, he knew how to manipulate American policy and public opinion to his benefit. Americans liked to think of China as the land of *The Good Earth*, populated by simple, earnest peasants suffering under the weight of rapacious landlords, European exploitation, and Japanese atrocities, all of which created a very deep reservoir of sympathy in the United States for the Chinese people. Chiang and his seductive wife played upon these emotions like a pair of virtuosos, flattering and cajoling visitors from America, and dispatching emissaries such as Madame Chiang's brother, T. V. Soong, and aviator Claire Chennault to Washington to prod the Roosevelt administration into sending more and more funds and defense matériel.

Soong and Chennault faced an uphill task in January 1941. Despite the presence of a powerful China lobby within the White House—including Lauchlin Currie (one of the President's special advisers on Far Eastern affairs), Secretary Knox, Secretary of the Treasury Henry Morgenthau, and Tommy Corcoran—the Far East always took a backseat to affairs in Europe in the administration's strategic plans. Endeavoring to obtain U.S. planes and pilots to defend China against Japanese bombers, Chennault found to his disgust that "the American people were like an ostrich with its head buried in the sand, attempting to peck vigorously through its tail feathers. The few American eyes focused abroad were centered on Europe where England was fighting for survival. The Orient was completely forgotten."

Well, perhaps not completely. To Roosevelt, Japanese aggression in Asia was part of a single worldwide assault upon vital American interests; the same strategic outlook that impelled the passage of the Lend-Lease legislation required America to protect British lines of trade and communication in the Far East, too. As the President explained in a "Dear Joe" letter of January 21, 1941 to Ambassador Grew in Tokyo (having been classmates at Groton and Harvard, the two men were certainly entitled to call each other by their first names): "The problems which we face are so vast and so interrelated that any attempt even to state them compels one to think in terms of five continents and seven seas. . . . I must emphasize," Roosevelt continued, "that, our problem being one of defense, we can not lay down hard and fast plans. As each new development occurs we must, in the light of the circumstances then existing, decide when and where and how we can most effectively marshal and make use of our resources."

One of the most intriguing American resources vis-à-vis Japan was a mechanized bundle of wires and wheels known simply as Purple. In the world of international espionage, the successful construction of the Purple machine by a team of cryptographic experts headed by Lieutenant Colonel William Friedman, the founder of the U.S. Signal Intelligence Service, represented a coup of no mean proportions. To safeguard the most important official communications between Tokyo and its diplomatic missions abroad, the Japanese government employed a cipher machine that, through a series of spinning wheels set to precise specifications—changed at frequent intervals—coded and decoded its messages. By the autumn of 1940, following a brilliant, painstaking research effort, Friedman's team had broken the Japanese diplomatic code and constructed a duplicate cipher machine that returned the messages to their original text. (The constant strain and fatigue broke Friedman's health, however, and he landed in Walter Reed Hospital suffering from a nervous breakdown.)

With Purple performing almost flawlessly from the moment of its first success on September 25, 1940, a highly select group of American military officials thus were able to read nearly every Japanese diplomatic dispatch to and from the Foreign Office in Tokyo. The clandestine operation was known as Magic—but the magicians guarded their secrets far too closely for the good of the nation. Fearing that a careless leak or deliberate betrayal by State Department employees or White House advisers—many of whom seemed to military minds to possess less than total allegiance to the United States—might jeopardize the operation by alerting Japan to the existence of the Purple machines (the army and navy each had two by early 1941), General Marshall instituted a restrictive distribution system that limited any knowledge of Magic intercepts to about a dozen top army and navy officials. The only civilians who were let in on the secret were Secretaries Stimson and Knox.

It was precisely this obsessive concern with security that robbed Magic of much of its potential value to American policymakers. The military men who read the intercepts lacked the detailed knowledge of international politics to understand the nuances and intricate shadings of diplomatic messages; nor was there any central agency to receive, coordinate, and evaluate the information obtained. Not until Stimson and Knox took matters into their own hands in late January 1941 was any information from Magic passed on to the White House or the State Department, and even then the President usually received only those summaries that the War Department deemed appropriate. No messages concerning the Japanese advance into Indochina in the first months of the year were forwarded to the State Department. Besides, there were difficulties in translating the messages in a timely manner. "Above all," noted Ronald Lewin, "nobody in the United States had yet grasped the need for making such secret intelligence swiftly and comprehensively available to commanders whose decisions, whose fleets and armies might be vitally affected by it."

One must also remember that these were *diplomatic,* and not *military* dispatches; the Japanese army and navy employed a far more secure system of communications. Taken as a group, diplomats can be a notoriously unreliable and misleading source of information. Many Magic messages were full of speculation by Japanese consuls about their government's intentions, full of uninformed rumors and gossip that revealed little or nothing about the real plans of the military clique that called the shots from Tokyo. Actually, more trustworthy information regarding Japanese intentions came from experienced observers such as Joseph Grew, who picked up a disturbing tip from the Peruvian ambassador in Tokyo (who had heard it from a drunken Japanese officer) near the end of January; Grew immediately passed it on to Washington. "There is a lot of talk around town," warned Grew, "to the effect that the Japanese, in case of a break with the United States, are planning to go all out in a surprise mass attack on Pearl Harbor. I rather guess that the boys in Hawaii are not precisely asleep."

Grew himself put little credence in these rumors. If Japan should decide to attack any American possessions, the Philippine Islands looked like a far more inviting and likely target. Indeed, in the winter of 1941 it almost seemed as if the U. S. War Department was determined to keep the Philippines as vulnerable as possible, to offer them as a sacrifice if Japan suddenly burst the bonds of peaceful conduct and began a rampage of aggression through the Far East. After years of neglect, the islands' defenses were in such a dismal state of disrepair that President Manuel Quezon publicly admitted that "it's good to hear men say that the Philippines can repel an invasion, but it's not true and the people should know it isn't." His painfully vulnerable country, Quezon added candidly, "could not be defended even if every last Filipino were armed with modern weapons," which they certainly were not.

Commanding the Philippine armed forces was the flamboyant former U. S. Army chief of staff, Field Marshal Douglas MacArthur. MacArthur had first gained a national reputation during World War One, as leader of the celebrated Rainbow Division on the Western Front, but his vainglorious posturing and insufferable pomposity had earned him numerous powerful enemies within the armed forces and Congress. At the end of 1937, the War Department—fearing that MacArthur, in his role as head of the American military mission in Manila, might somehow embroil the United States in unwanted commitments in Asia—had ordered him to give up his post and return to the United States for reassignment, where they could keep an eye on him. MacArthur huffily refused; instead, he retired from active duty in the U. S. Army and accepted Quezon's offer of a field marshal's baton to remain as commander of the native military forces.

Realizing just how woefully unprepared his newly acquired army really was, MacArthur sent his chief of staff, Major Dwight David Eisenhower, to Washington to beg or borrow modern weapons and ammunition. Nothing doing, replied the War Department. For one thing, MacArthur was no longer a member of the U. S. armed forces; for another, the Philippines had been clamoring for independence and, as Eisenhower regretfully informed his boss, "as long as the Philippines insisted on being independent, the War Department's attitude was that they could jolly well look out after their own defenses." Besides, the army was having enough trouble obtaining equipment and men from Congress for its own purposes. So there would be no grants, no loans—the Philippines were not made eligible for Lend-Lease assistance—and no special treatment. And although MacArthur was probably unaware of the fact, the War Department already had recommended adoption of a strategic plan that essentially abandoned the Philippines to the Japanese in the event of a two-ocean war. There was never much doubt that the Far East would be relegated to second or even third place in the priorities of U. S. military planners; the danger in Europe always took precedence.

5

The Cold Hour

"The war slowly enacts itself on a great scene: round our
little scene. We spend 59 minutes here; one minute there.
. . . It is a cold windy winter day."
—VIRGINIA WOOLF

Early in the new year, shortly after the death of her lover, F. Scott
Fitzgerald, journalist Sheilah Graham boarded a Pan American Airways
seaplane and flew eastward across the Atlantic. Embarking on an assignment to cover events in Europe for the North American Newspaper Alliance, Graham had asked to cross the ocean in a bomber to provide her
readers with a more colorful story, but the authorities refused her request.
As Lord Beaverbrook delicately explained to her afterward, bombers
were equipped with only one toilet, a bucket, used by the men; besides,
the cabin of a bomber was extremely cold and not pressurized, and any
passengers on board often found that the bomb rack was the only place
to stretch out and sleep during the journey across the ocean.

So Sheilah traveled in the relative comfort of a Pan Am Clipper until
her arrival in Lisbon, where she spent one night before continuing on to
London. As the central transfer point for flights to and from the rest of the
Continent, the neutral Portugese city with its picturesque white-stuccoed
houses was "an international whirlpool into which were swept from every
direction, people of all nationalities, races, colours and tongues, none
wishing to stay, but all forced to remain long days, weeks, and sometimes
months awaiting transportation." There was an unwritten agreement
among the European belligerents not to shoot down one another's commercial flights; so, at Lisbon's Cintra airport, British DC-3s—painted dark
green with blue camouflage patches, flying the Union Jack—sat on the
airstrip between heavy gray Junker transports adorned with black swastikas on a crimson background and airmail planes with the Italian tricolor
painted on their noses. (The Italian pilots of Ala Littoria had much the best
uniforms: powder blue, with waves of gold braid and brass buttons. They
far outclassed the dark blue German coats with gold Lufthansa wings on
the shoulders, or the blue-black British outfits crisscrossed by polished Sam
Browne belts.)

Notwithstanding any gentleman's agreement among the pilots, Lisbon was crawling with spies and an assortment of unsavory and unscrupulous characters, and so the cautious British consul in Lisbon advised Graham not to inform anyone of her flight plans for the morrow. Before dawn the next morning, the reporter joined a group of exhausted British soldiers, who had been wounded in the recent North Africa campaign, as they were stealthily loaded aboard a seaplane. Graham saw that "the windows of the plane had been covered with black cloth. Warned in a whisper to make no sounds, we boarded in complete darkness. Packed tightly together in the flying boat, and quietly chugging towards the open ocean, we took off for England. For the first time I realized that there was a war on."

When Graham arrived in England, the nation was once again bracing itself for the long-awaited invasion from across the Channel, completely unaware that Hitler had already called off Operation Sea Lion. Visitors to London found the city's inhabitants unusually high-strung, talking much louder than normal, as if to cover up the apprehension. The lull in the Luftwaffe's nightly excursions to Britain and the marked decline in U-boat attacks in the North Atlantic seemed an ominous portent of Great Things to Come. (In fact, the respite was due largely to the miserable winter weather.) Everywhere one heard anxious predictions that "he"—the British public invariably referred to Adolf Hitler by that impersonal pronoun—was up to Something. "Not long ago," reported an American correspondent, "the rumor got around that the German High Command was only waiting for three and a half days of good weather before giving the word to go. No one could explain the significance of the half-day, but the story had all sorts of Londoners solemnly counting the hours and scanning the stormy heavens, which remained reliably seasonable." Churchill himself doubted that the Germans would make any attempt to land while they knew they could not dominate the air during the daytime or maintain secure lines of communication; having dispelled his own fears of a successful invasion, Churchill told his private secretary that he now "woke up in the mornings, as he nearly always had, feeling as if he had a bottle of champagne inside him and glad that another day had come." But since the rest of his cabinet and most of the military commanders lacked the courage of the Prime Minister's convictions, the government issued warnings advising housewives to keep their larders well stocked, the Ministry of Food hid canned goods in old meeting halls, theaters, police stations, and barns, and everyone was advised to carry a gas mask. (The cabinet asked members of Parliament to bring their masks along to the House, to set a good example, but it did little good; a random survey of travelers at a London railway station revealed that virtually no one was carrying a gas mask, and a mock gas attack in the middle of the city brought only a lethargic response from bystanders.)

Rumors abounded of insidious German plans to turn England into the cradle of the Third Reich. Supposedly authentic articles from a German newspaper told of an "ungentlemanly" Nazi scheme to require all healthy English females to bear at least one German baby every year; English males would be sterilized. Official paranoia already had reached such a point that foreigners living in England—including Jewish refugees from Nazi persecution—were being rounded up and trucked off to internment camps. "It was a terrible time," recalled actor Paul von Hernreid, a native of Austria who had been assigned to the third and last class of aliens to be interned. "We jumped at every ring of the doorbell, and each time a friend or neighbor went off to internment, an apprehensive dread took hold of us. How long before it was our turn? From a friend, or the pretense of friendship, the local policeman became threatening, and we knew it was only a matter of days before our papers reached the top of the pile." Arthur Koestler, the former war correspondent and repentant Communist who had arrived in England on a Dutch aircraft from Lisbon late in 1940 without proper immigration papers, was placed in Pentonville prison for safekeeping for six weeks while British authorities tried to decide whether he was a German spy. (Despite Pentonville's disreputable plumbing system, Koestler gave his English prison accommodations three stars in comparison to the jails he had known on the continent.) He was still lodged securely in Pentonville when *Darkness at Noon* was published.

At the end of January, the British army staged an exercise known as Operation VICTOR as a dress rehearsal against invasion. A secret hideout was prepared at Madresfield in Worcestershire for King George and Queen Elizabeth (who recently had acquired a three-coach armored train sheathed in bulletproof steel); the Princesses Elizabeth and Margaret kept a set of luggage packed at Windsor, ready for an emergency flight to Liverpool. The crown jewels lay wrapped in newspaper, hidden deep for safekeeping within Windsor Castle. The government purchased 25,000 revolvers from the United States to distribute to constables and policemen to repel Nazi invaders. If the attack ever did come, Churchill had already decided upon the final sentence of his call to eternal resistance: "The hour has come; kill the Hun." To free regular army forces from some of the more routine coastal defense duties, the government had organized the Home Guard, consisting primarily of unpaid volunteers, supplied with weapons and uniforms of a sort, who drilled on village greens by day and spent their nights guarding bridges and watching the moorlands and downs for any sign of enemy paratroopers. (Some enterprising Home Guardsmen wore rollerskates while on patrol, to enable them to spread the alarm more quickly.) Nearly two million Englishmen—many of whom already had extensive experience with firearms from service in the previous war, from years of hunting or chasing four-legged predators off their farms, or from military training at school—joined the Guard before the government finally called a halt to the flood of applications. Then they were taught the techniques of modern military sabotage, such as how to use beer bottles filled with gasoline to stop or at least slow down a mechanized invasion force.

Of course the U-boat attacks and the air raids had not ceased entirely. The Luftwaffe killed another 1,502 Britons in January. (By way of comparison, approximately 800 people lost their lives in traffic accidents in the United States every month.) Losses in the Atlantic in December, combined with the diversion of shipping capacity to support the army's offensive in North Africa, produced more food shortages in Britain in January. As the Ministry of Food worked with canners to supply the island with a plentiful supply of a special high-nutrient liquid concoction known (rather unpalatably) as "blitz soup," individual meat rations were cut all the way back to 1 s./1 d. per week, enough to purchase only one pound of beef or two pounds of mutton. Pork and tripe were added to the restricted list for the first time; although chickens were not rationed, they were so expensive that few could afford them. "Would you rather have meat," asked Lord Woolton, the minister of food, somewhat defensively, "or would you rather have Bardia?" Woolton appealed to housewives to make do with home-grown produce and "go easy with the tin-opener. . . . Don't eat cheese unless you need it." He told England that it was eating too much bread made with imported white flour and not enough potatoes (which were plentiful), too much imported breakfast foods and not enough stout English oats and porridge. Woolton urged gardeners to plant more onions, which were lamentably (or perhaps not) scarce. "The onion shortage," reported George Orwell, "has made everyone intensely sensitive to the smell of onions. A quarter of an onion shredded into a stew seems exceedingly strong."

Until January, restaurants had been allowed to serve virtually unlimited quantities of whatever meat and produce they could obtain. The public outcry against this shameful state of affairs (which obviously discriminated in favor of upper-class stomachs) forced restaurant owners to adopt an informal agreement to limit each patron to one of five main dishes for each meal: meat, fish, cheese, eggs, or poultry. Actually, the rationing system was producing a marked improvement in the diet of Britain's poor, who had always favored the sort of less nutritious canned goods and processed foods that were now unavailable. Everyone benefited from eating more fish and less red meat, and from limiting their intake of tea to just three or four cups a day. Certainly there were still far more comestible luxuries available in London than in Berlin; chocolate was reasonably plentiful in Britain but virtually nonexistent in Germany, and Englishmen could still enjoy a single lump of sugar with each cup of tea. But in early 1941, British razor blades were scarce, silk stockings nearly unobtainable, alarm clocks and tobacco prohibitively expensive, pill bottles sold out, and pipe cleaners completely unavailable (having been pressed into use by women as makeshift hair curlers). All the department stores' stocks of folding cots had been appropriated by the Admiralty, and evacuees long ago had purchased every available piece of secondhand luggage.

Manpower mobilization proceeded apace, as the government lowered the draft age to nineteen on one end and raised it to thirty-seven on the other. (Tea tasters, funeral directors, and underhand puddlers, among others, were still exempt from military service.) But, apart from North Africa, there really was no place for the army to display its well-disguised prowess in the first months of 1941; certainly the British army had not yet been (and never was) subjected to the withering losses of the last war. Instead, serious personnel shortages appeared in the munitions factories, where industrial plant capacity finally had caught up with military demands. "We are now about to enter, for the first time in this war, the period of man-power stringency," Churchill advised the nation, "because for the first time we are going to have the apparatus and the lay-out which this man-power and woman-power will be required to handle." The continuing expansion in defense production already had brought unemployment to its lowest point since the government began keeping records in 1921. In January, Labour Minister Ernest Bevin shocked some of the more somnolent members of the House of Commons by announcing plans to register every able-bodied working man and woman in the country, to create a "permanent mobile labour force" that could be conscripted and reassigned from nonessential work to vital defense industry tasks.

By the end of January 1941, approximately sixty thousand British citizens had died in the war, nearly half of them civilians. The blitz was producing some curious side effects. The divorce rate in Britain reportedly was down by fifty percent, but the cities witnessed a distressing jump in the rate of juvenile crime, attributable primarily to the destruction of schools and social centers, and the relaxation of parental authority as fathers went off to military service or worked overtime in defense factories. Londoners became much more willing to speak to strangers in the street. Telephone wires in the city repeatedly got crossed, allowing callers to listen in on one another's conversations. Odd bits of nonsense doggerel kept flashing through George Orwell's mind:

> And the key doesn't fit and the bell doesn't ring,
> But we all stand up for God Save the King

and

> When the Borough Surveyor has gone to roost
> On his rod, his pole or his perch.

Accidents abounded during the nightly blackouts: pedestrians kept getting poked in the eye by passersby with raised umbrellas; bicycles careened into one another or against unexpected obstacles, leading the government to post placards and take out newspaper ads warning people to wear white at night:

> When Billy Brown goes out at night,
> He wears or carries something white.
> When Mrs. Brown is in the blackout
> She likes to wear her old white mack out.
> And Sally Brown straps around her shoulder
> A natty, plain white gas-mask holder.
> The reason why they wear this white
> Is so they may be seen at night.

People who had never cared a whit about history or the destiny of the English race were overcome with grief when they contemplated the gashed remains of familiar old buildings long taken for granted. "These days," reported Mollie Panter-Downes, "people find themselves looking at England with a new eye, almost as though they were seeing it for the first time, and discovering once again that deep, inarticulate love for it . . ." "Dear London! So vast and unexpectant, so ugly and so strong!" marveled Harold Nicolson. "You have been bruised and battered and all your clothes are tattered and in disarray. Yet we, who never knew that we loved you (who regarded you, in fact, like some old family servant, ministering to our comforts and amenities, and yet slightly incongruous and absurd), have suddenly felt the twinge of some fibre of identity, respect and love. We know what is coming to you. And our eyes slip along your old untidy limbs, knowing that the leg may be gone tomorrow, and that tomorrow the arm may be severed. Yet through all this regret and dread pierces a slim clean note of pride. 'London can take it.'"

Others, however, grew melancholic at the realization that a long-cherished way of life was coming to an end at last. "Its the cold hour, this, before the lights go up," wrote Virginia Woolf in her diary. "A few snowdrops in the garden. Yes, I was thinking: we live without a future. Thats whats queer, with our noses pressed to a closed door." Woolf thought of Walter de la Mare's poignant words, "Look thy last on all things lovely," and she recalled with silent admiration the simple, untroubled beauty of life in her parents' generation, and she gazed upon the wintry English countryside, over the burning blue frost:

> An incredible loveliness. The downs breaking their wave, yet one pale quarry; & all the barns & stacks either a broken pink, or a verdurous green; & then the walk by the wall; & the church; & the great tithe barn. How

England consoles & warms one, in these deep hollows, where the past stands almost stagnant. And the little spire across the fields . . . And I worshipped the beauty of the country, now scraped, but with old colours showing.

Six months of living under the shadow of the bombs had made some Londoners recklessly belligerent. They looked forward to throwing Herr Hitler's cutthroats back into the Channel, they said; when the Luftwaffe launched an incendiary raid upon the city early in the new year, they snuffed out the bombs and chanted defiantly, "We want more! We want more!" Occasionally life on the edge revealed the primitive emotions and love of violence hiding just beneath a veneer of civilization. "I felt a terrible joy and exaltation at the sound and taste and smell of all this destruction," recalled Malcolm Muggeridge; "at the lurid sky, the pall of smoke, the faces of bystanders wildly lit in the flames. . . . Walking in the night it seemed as though the Book of Revelations had veritably come to pass."

After the devastating incendiary attack of December 29, the government organized fire watchers on a compulsory basis, and considered proposals that provided for the imprisonment of businessmen who neglected to take the necessary precautions to protect their industrial buildings. Air raid precaution wardens were sent to the country for brief vacations on a rotating basis, to keep their spirits up and their vision clear. Even this, however, was not enough for the sensitive soul of T. S. Eliot, who, suffering badly from lack of sleep, resigned his part-time post as an air raid precaution warden and moved out of the city temporarily to avoid a nervous breakdown. Disoriented by the disappearance of old London landmarks, his concentration and will to work gone, beset by anxiety and the relentless monotony of uncertainty, day after day, never knowing when the bombs would strike, Eliot took to bed with a severe case of influenza in January 1941.

Ensconced in various embassies and in several of the finer hotels of London, there were more refugee monarchs than had ever before been gathered in one city. (And that was not even counting the former government of Belgium, Czechoslovakia's President Eduard Beneš, and nearly the entire Polish government-in-exile.) King Zog of Albania was living at the Ritz. King Haakon of Norway—a man of imposing stature made still more imposing by his habit of wearing a full-dress military uniform for nearly all his waking hours—divided his time between the Norwegian embassy and Claridge's, where he was joined during the spring by King George of Greece. Claridge's also served as a home away from home for Queen Wilhelmina of the Netherlands, who could be seen in the evenings slowly descending the curving staircase in the front hall, wearing her hair in long braids, dressed in a flannel nightgown and woolen bathrobe, but somehow retaining an air of regal dignity nonetheless, carrying a folded blanket and heading for the air raid shelter in the hotel basement.

But the most important visitor to Claridge's, and to all of Britain in the first months of the new year, was a decidedly nonregal figure: Harry L. Hopkins, the perpetually rumpled ex–social worker from Iowa and former secretary of commerce who had become Franklin D. Roosevelt's most trusted confidant. (Hardly anyone else in Washington seemed to like Harry; favorites typically have few friends. Cabinet members—particularly Harold Ickes—resented his intimacy with the President, and the mere mention of Hopkins' name on Capitol Hill was akin to waving a red flag in front of a sizable bloc of conservative congressmen.) To ensure that the United States was not squandering precious defense resources, Roosevelt wanted Hopkins to bring him a firsthand report on Britain's capacity to withstand the German assault, and a detailed list of military goods the British forces would need and could profitably employ in the near future. The State Department strenuously objected to being bypassed in favor of an amateur envoy, but Roosevelt trusted Hopkins' judgment far more than that of any professional diplomat, and the President knew that Hopkins was totally devoted to him personally. It was all part of what John Patton Davies called "the helter-skelter Rooseveltian style of doing business," although the choice of Hopkins for this particular task almost wrecked the mission before it began.

A cynical, iconoclastic man by nature, Hopkins had already heard so many overblown tributes to Churchill's indomitable fighting spirit that he was heartily sick of the man—a rival to his beloved Roosevelt—before he even met him. For his part, the Prime Minister apparently had never heard of Hopkins ("Who?" Churchill asked in bewilderment when first told that Harry was coming to visit), and he wondered why Roosevelt, whom he thought was his friend, was sending a welfare expert to England at a time when the fate of the world hung in the balance.

Cadaverously thin and in notoriously poor health to begin with ("a soul that flamed out of a frail and failing body," as Churchill later described him), Hopkins endured a grueling four-day trip on a Pan Am Yankee Clipper via the more circuitous but supposedly safer South Atlantic route and arrived in Britain on January 9, disheveled and much the worse for wear (Harry had always passionately detested air travel). On his first night in London, he was greeted by air raid sirens and the thumping of antiaircraft guns; then, walking innocently along a city sidewalk, Harry was unceremoniously pushed face first into the gutter by a blitz-hardened bystander when the bombs began to fall.

It was not an auspicious beginning to his mission. Shortly after his arrival, Hopkins informed General Raymond A. Lee, the American military attaché in London, that despite all the rhetoric about the world's two great democracies marching shoulder to shoulder against the dictators, and Anglo-American cooperation "rolling on like the Mississippi," Roosevelt was adamant that Britain expend all its financial and material resources first, holding nothing in reserve before the United States stepped in to help. Hitler or no Hitler, America would not be suckered in any business deal. "We want to help them to the limit," Hopkins explained, "but the President is going to insist that they must prove they are doing their best before we go all out for them." For instance, the administration insisted that Britain provide collateral for all loans from America. Lee agreed wholeheartedly with this hardheaded Yankee-trader method of doing business. "There is no use blinking the fact that the British are going to look out for themselves primarily," the general decided, "and if they can hold out something on us to use after the war, there is no question about it that they will do so. No one can object to that." (Ivan Maisky, the Soviet ambassador to Great Britain, observed these bargaining shenanigans with considerable interest and wonderment. "In the capitalist world," Maisky marveled, "very tough rules and customs prevail in this respect.")

Of course Churchill's government had little choice but to accept American terms, albeit with occasional bad grace and subtle efforts to soften the blow. "It's hard to fall to the position of a junior partner after you've owned an independent business so long," muttered Home Secretary Herbert Morrison to a friend. "Sometimes your blood boils and you clench your fists. But now there is no other way." At one point, Churchill asked Hopkins, only half-jokingly, what the United States would do when it had "accumulated all the gold in the world and the other countries then decided that gold was of no value except for filling teeth." "Well," Hopkins replied, "we shall be able to make use of our unemployed in guarding it!"

On the day following his arrival, Hopkins went to the Foreign Office to call upon Anthony Eden. "I told him that everything the United States could deliver before May was worth double anything after," Eden recalled in his memoirs. "This seemed rather to depress him," and no wonder. Unlike his British hosts, Hopkins knew that the United States was producing only insignificant amounts of defense matériel as yet, and he was appalled by the desperate shortages of virtually all sorts of military hardware in Britain. He found both the British public and cabinet officials unrealistically optimistic about America's capacity and willingness to help; no one in London appeared ever to have heard the word "isolationist." Following his meeting with Eden, Hopkins visited Number 10 Downing Street and came face to face with Churchill for the first time. "A rotund— smiling—red-faced, gentleman appeared—" Hopkins recalled, "extended a fat but none the less convincing hand and wished me welcome to England. A short black coat—striped trousers—a clear eye and a mushy voice was the impression of England's leader as he showed me with obvious pride the photograph of his beautiful daughter-in-law and grandchild." After a brief exchange of courtesies, the two men met again the following evening at Ditchley, the estate that was serving as Churchill's weekend home in the country during the blitz. By this time Churchill had been informed by a subordinate that Hopkins was well worth cultivating, that he was closer to FDR than any other man alive. So the Prime Minister, in an attempt to get on the right side of Hopkins by appealing to his lifelong interest in social justice, began the evening's discussion by mentioning his own plans for postwar social reform in England. "I don't give a damn about your cottagers," Hopkins replied sharply. "I came here to see how we can beat that fellow Hitler." "Mr. Hopkins," replied Churchill with a sigh of relief, "we had better go into the library."

From that time on, the two men got along quite famously, although their conversations were always dominated by Churchill's interminable eloquence, compared to which Hopkins seemed a faltering, fumbling speaker, even in private. They spent much of the next four weeks together ("I suspect," commented Ickes sourly in his diary, "that if, as his personal representative, the President should send to London a man with the bubonic plague, Churchill would, nevertheless, see a good deal of him"); they inspected defense installations, visited the batteries at Dover, and at one point journeyed north through a driving blizzard of snow and sleet to the naval base of Scapa Flow off the northern tip of Scotland, where they got a firsthand look at the British fleet. Churchill, even in the grip of a bad head cold, was buoyantly in his element on the water, but the midwesterner Hopkins, whose ideas of recreation ran more to racetracks and poker than ships pitching about in high seas, became quite queasy on board a destroyer, nearly tumbled into the sea, and finally sat down, exhausted, upon a fully armed depth charge. Before they left Scapa Flow, the two men bade bon voyage to Lord Halifax, the ascetic, humorless aristocrat who had recently resigned as foreign secretary to replace the late Lord Lothian as ambassador to the United States. (Despite his previous service as viceroy in India, Halifax retained a rather insular state of mind. Just before departing for Washington, his lordship decided he ought to improve his knowledge of American history and culture, and asked General Lee between courses at a farewell dinner why the President's mansion was called the White House. Lee patiently explained that originally it had been made of brick, and then plastered and painted white after the British had burned it during the War of 1812. "Lord Halifax looked shocked and puzzled," observed Lee, "and I got the distinct idea that he did not know the War of 1812 had ever happened." This did not bode particularly well for the future of Anglo-American relations, of course, but if Roosevelt could send Harry Hopkins to London, Churchill was certainly entitled to send Halifax to Washington.)

On the way back to London, the Prime Minister stopped in Glasgow to deliver a bracing speech to the people—"Before us lie sufferings and tribulations. I am not one of those who pretend that smooth courses are open to us or that our experiences during this year are going to be deprived of terrible characteristics. But what the end will be—about that I cannot have the slightest doubt." He also gave a thinly veiled hint to the United States: "All that we can pay for we will pay for, but we require far more than we shall be able to pay for." In return, Hopkins privately assured Churchill that Roosevelt and the American people would stand by Britain no matter the danger; he quoted from the Book of Ruth, " 'Whither thou goest, I will go; and where thou lodgest, I will lodge,' " and then, softly, he added, "Even to the end."

When Hopkins returned to the United States in February, he confidently assured reporters that he harbored no doubts about the British people's ability to withstand anything Hitler could throw at them. He urged the nation to send Britain scores of planes, thousands of guns, tons of ammunition, and ten destroyers a month (ships that presumably would be replaced by an immediate and drastic expansion of the administration's latest shipbuilding program). Privately, however, Hopkins communicated to the President his apprehensions about the deep, deep trouble Britain was in, and refused to recommend that Roosevelt endanger American vessels by using them to convoy supplies across the Atlantic.

Churchill himself was under no illusions about the difficult passage that awaited Britain in the days to come. "Looking back upon the unceasing tumult of the war," he wrote several years later, "I cannot recall any period when its stresses and the onset of so many problems all at once or in rapid succession bore more directly on me and my colleagues than the first half of 1941. . . . No part of our problem in 1941 could be solved without relation to all the rest. What was given to one theatre had to be taken from another. An effort here meant a risk there. . . . After shooting Niagara we had now to struggle in the rapids."

One of the most hopeful signs for the immediate future, though, was the continuing expansion and combat experience of the Royal Air Force. By the beginning of 1941, the number of both bomber and fighter squadrons had increased by more than 50 percent over the previous year; Britain now possessed more than half a million trained pilots and officers, and nearly three thousand first-line planes. This still left the R.A.F. considerably below the strength of the Luftwaffe, particularly in the numbers of the newer types of aircraft, but British production was climbing steadily while Germany's was not. For this satisfactory—at least in the short run— state of affairs, the nation owed a considerable debt to one man: publishing baron Maxwell Aitken, Lord Beaverbrook. Appointed to office as minister of aircraft production in May 1940 (for the sake of his executive abilities rather than any expert knowledge of airplanes), Beaverbrook had prodded, cajoled, threatened, and run roughshod over the British military establishment to accomplish his objectives. All the generals' closely reasoned strategic policy studies, with their hidebound assumptions and neat rows of statistics, were unceremoniously chucked out the window. The professional military men did not take this with particularly good grace; Sir Alan Brooke, commander in chief, Home Forces, wrote of Beaverbrook, "The more I saw of him the more I disliked and mistrusted him. An evil genius who exercised the very worst influence on Winston." With single-minded fervor, Beaverbrook subordinated everything to the production of fighter planes, to prevent the Luftwaffe from dominating the skies; bombers took a backseat until the Battle of Britain was won, or until the United States joined the fray, whichever came first. R.A.F. career officers, who fretted if their service's carefully rationed supply of spare parts dwindled below a comfortable level, watched in horror as Beaverbrook cannibalized damaged planes for the parts that kept a maximum number of fighters in the air at any given moment. "Lord Beaverbrook, to put it bluntly, played hell with the war policy of the R.A.F.," complained Air Marshal Joubert. "But he most certainly produced the aircraft that won the Battle of Britain. What he did in the summer of 1940 set back the winning of the air war over Germany by many months. The bomber production programme was disrupted to allow of high-speed production of fighters. And who can say that he was very wrong?" Certainly not Churchill.

Beaverbrook ran his ministry the same way he ran his newspaper empire. He pushed everyone full speed ahead until production hit a bottleneck; then he focused all his attention on that problem until it yielded to a solution; then they all resumed their breakneck pace until the next snag appeared. They called it "management by crisis," and the remarkable thing was that it worked. But by January 1941 the crucial Battle of Britain had been won, and no one seemed to know quite what to do with all those fighter planes. For the time being, many of them made themselves useful by accompanying bomber sorties on "rhubarb" runs over the Continent, striking stray targets across the countryside, attacking trains, engaging an occasional German Focke-Wulf Condor or Messerschmitt in a dogfight, and making a general nuisance of themselves. At least it kept the pilots entertained. "When I am chasing a Hun," admitted one R.A.F. squadron leader, "I bounce up and down on the seat and bay like a beagle until I can get him in my sights. Then I squirt. If he catches fire or explodes, I cheer and yell, 'Sieg heil!' All this time I am scared to death. I must say that I get a certain thrill out of terror. But the real thrill comes when you get home safely. It is a wonderful feeling. I guess the process is something like beating yourself on the head with a club, so that you can appreciate the contrast when you quit."

Bombers, on the other hand, were Churchill's chosen weapon to bring Germany to its knees. "The Navy can lose us the war," he once had said, "but only the Air Force can win it. Therefore our supreme effort must be to gain overwhelming mastery in the air. The Fighters are our salvation, but the Bombers alone provide the means of victory." Naturally, Churchill had no intention at any time of sending the British army out alone to engage the German army in full-scale ground combat anywhere on the European continent. Even with full mobilization, Britain would never be able to throw more than 90 divisions into combat; Hitler already had over 150 divisions in the field. So Britain was forced to rely upon its bombers, the blockade (which already had sizable holes in it), an occasional ground foray with limited objectives upon carefully chosen terrain, and the hazards of fortune to wear down the seemingly omnipotent Nazi military machine. Still, Air Secretary Sir Archibald Sinclair remained optimistic. "It will be no easy task to defeat Nazi Germany," Sir Archie informed the House of Commons, "but it can and will be done, and my confidence is primarily based on the achievements of the R.A.F. and sister services."

After spending 1940 in a defensive role, harassing the ports across the Channel to impede the halfhearted preparations for Operation Sea Lion, Bomber Command began to emerge in 1941 to take—though not without a struggle—its assigned place in Britain's strategic plans. Sir Charles Portal, chief of the Air Staff, directed the bomber force to concentrate its operations during the coming months upon two primary tasks: the demolition of the central and eastern European oil fields that fed the Wehrmacht, and the destruction of the morale of the German populace. "There is one thing that will bring [Hitler] back and bring him down," Churchill had advised Beaverbrook (who, incidentally, entertained serious doubts about the prospects of achieving victory by relying primarily upon long-range bombers), "and that is an absolutely devastating, exterminating attack by very heavy bombers from this country upon the Nazi homeland. We must be able to overwhelm them by this means, without which I do not see a way through."

Churchill's vision notwithstanding, the R.A.F. as yet possessed neither the navigational technology nor adequate stocks of heavy bombs to strike an effective blow at the oil refineries, located far behind Germany's defensive lines and, for the most part, far away from any cities. Nor did the attacks upon civilian targets produce the desired results. British strategists appear to have convinced themselves by some perverse method of reasoning that the fighting spirit of the German people—whose army had, after all, conquered virtually the entire continent of Europe in less than a year—would crumble precipitately when subjected to a few well-placed British bombs. "The German nation is peculiarly susceptible to air bombing," argued one veteran R.A.F. commander in a lengthy memo to Portal. "The ordinary people are neither allowed, nor offer, to play their part in rescue or restoration work; virtually imprisoned in their shelters or in the bombed area, they remain passive and easy prey to hysteria and panic without anything to mitigate the inevitable confusion and chaos. There is no joking in the German shelters as in ours, nor the bond which unites the public with ARP and Military services here . . ."

Meanwhile, nearly ignored by the strategists and always assigned less than its share of available resources, the British army—"The Old Contemptibles"—was slowly (very slowly) being transformed into a credible, professional fighting force. Between the wars, it was said (and not really in jest) that there were two great conservative powers in the world: the Catholic Church and the British army. When General Brooke assumed command of Britain's Home Forces in July 1940, he had been shocked and dismayed at the dearth of trained men and equipment. To make matters worse, Brooke also inherited anti-invasion plans that called for the static defense of isolated beachfront positions, an obsolete strategy that appeared to nimbler minds to hold about as much chance of success as the French reliance upon the ill-fated Maginot Line. Realizing that the heyday of trench warfare was long gone, vanished forever after the blitzkrieg of the spring of 1940, Brooke set out to develop a force of mobile reserve units that could strike quickly and effectively at the vanguard of an invading army before it established a foothold on the British coast. Assisted by younger, tougher officers such as Bernard Law Montgomery, the ambitious strategist-schoolmaster who would shortly be given command of the crucial anti-invasion front in southeast England, Brooke began to forge a motley collection of regulars, conscripts, and reserves into a hardened modern army capable of fighting in any sort of weather or terrain. Until this time, winter training always had been confined to indoor exercises. But in Montgomery's training camps and those in the desolate north country, recalcitrant recruits were put through endless physical training drills in the worst winter weather the British Isles had to offer, accompanied by blustering barracks-room profanity and false jocularity from the officers ("Come on, men, one more for the King and Queen"), interrupted only by long-distance runs across frozen hills and fields. In some perversely designed camps, the men had to slog up a steep muddy incline just to reach the latrine. "The Army in England was not fit and it must be made so," declared Montgomery. "In rain, snow, ice, mud, fair weather or foul, at any hour of the day or night—we must be able to do our stuff better than the Germans . . . Commanders and staff officers at any level who couldn't stand the strain, or who got tired, were to be weeded out and replaced—ruthlessly. Total war demanded total fitness from the highest to the lowest." What Montgomery wanted were troops who were "imbued with that offensive eagerness and infectious optimism which comes from physical well-being."

Some obdurate recruits, such as the young author Anthony Burgess, failed to discern any guiding purpose behind this boorish insistence upon physical exercise and mental discipline. "Never in the whole history of human conflict, as Winston Churchill ought to have said, have so many been buggered about by so few," complained Burgess four decades later. "Soldiers love the official enemy, seeing the mirror image of their own buggerings about in men they have no desire to kill. They learn hate from their own side. I still lie awake at night plotting vengeance on Corporal Newlands, a little Glasgow lout who, in allusion to my overgrown hair, a barber not yet being available, called me 'Currrrly.' He was one of the physical training instructors who, for a fancied insolence, made me run, to his jeers of 'Peck yer fuckin' feet up,' three times round the square with arms held high. PT was always a torment."

During his six weeks of recruit training, Burgess encountered army food that was "mostly overcooked slop with all the bones removed"—he decided that "the army's first aim was to implement chronic dyspepsia and dry up the bowels"—and endured tedious classes in first aid and anatomy, taught by sergeants who were incapable of pronouncing the word "corpuscle" ("the white buggers and the red bastards," they called them). Among NCOs who had little education and less regard for educated recruits, Burgess's copy of Joyce's *Finnegan's Wake* was widely presumed to be a code book of suspicious origin. Bored, fed up with the routine of army life and interminable administrative delays while awaiting his posting to a field ambulance corps in early 1941, Burgess was not at all certain how the endless stretcher drills and thirty-mile route marches were going to contribute to the ultimate victory. "The Germans had to be beaten sometime," he noted sarcastically, "though nobody was quite sure when . . ."

Meanwhile, hoping as always to garner favorable publicity, Montgomery scheduled a series of full-scale war game maneuvers in late 1940 and early 1941. In anticipation of future action in North Africa, Salisbury Plain was turned into a "desert," and the river Kennet was temporarily christened the Nahr-el-Kennet. It was all quite an elaborate production, but during the night exercises, units collided with one another in the mud and the darkness, and traffic across the plain came to a complete standstill until the mess could be sorted out. "The new British Army that has largely been created since Dunkirk has just carried out the most ambitious exercise in the field that has ever taken place in this country," reported the *Times* with a straight face. "Certainly nothing like it has ever been seen before in wartime conditions." Not since Dunkirk, anyway. "We have today," Montgomery reported in despair in February, "divisional commanders and divisional staffs who have never handled a division under 'full sail' at any time, not even on the training area. Administration is weak and coordination of staff at Divisional HQ is inclined to be sketchy."

It was going to be a long road to El Alamein.

Part Two   The Sea

6

Watching and Waiting

"Of course there are a good many times when there is no war
just as there are a good many times when there is a war. . . .
And when there is no war, well just now I cannot remember
just how it is when there is no war."

—GERTRUDE STEIN

At the beginning of 1941, the Japanese ambassador in Berlin, Saburo Kurusu, offered the German people a poem to celebrate the coming victories of the new year:

Look, the morning is approaching over the Holy Shrine.
The Day of East Asia is coming.
Merrily the swastika and the red, white, and green banner are
    flying in the wind.
It will become spring in Europe's countries.

Spring could not arrive too soon for Joseph Goebbels, the lame little skirt-chasing, anti-Communist fanatic who controlled the German press. "The last days of winter are crawling by like years," Herr Goebbels grumbled in his diary. "The entire nation's nerves are stretched to the breaking-point." Everyone who mattered (except perhaps some particularly obtuse British army commanders) knew that Hitler would move against the Balkans as soon as the weather permitted; as Churchill explained to Hopkins in mid-January, there really was no other place for the German army to go. But Hitler generally preferred to try to achieve bloodless victories through diplomatic pressure and intimidation before unleashing the Wehrmacht; "like the robber," an American observer commented, "who generously will not shoot you if you hand over all your possessions quietly." And so the watching and waiting continued throughout the rest of the winter. "It was one of those periods of preparation during which the Nazis made ready," recalled Harry Flannery, who had recently arrived in Berlin to replace Bill Shirer as the new CBS radio correspondent, "and we all heard so many rumors and were so long awaiting the spring of the beast that, when it did come, many of us were looking the other way." Back in the last days of December, Hitler had decided to occupy at

(103)

least the northern part of Greece, in order to secure his southern flank
before launching Barbarossa; such a move also would prevent the R.A.F.
from acquiring bases within striking range of the Romanian oil fields—
which were rapidly becoming the most important source of fuel for the
Wehrmacht—and keep the British army from gaining a secure foothold on
the Continent. (Hitler never forgot how difficult it had been to dislodge
British soldiers from entrenched defensive positions in the previous world
war.) And, not least important, the operation would rescue Mussolini from
further embarrassment in Albania. "Reports from Italy mention profound-
est defeatism," muttered a thoroughly disgusted Goebbels in February
1941. "These days, the Fuehrer is their only hope. Ciano is absolutely
finished, and the Duce's popularity is approaching zero level. Added to
this are disorganisation, corruption, in short, a state of affairs verging on
chaos. We must soon make a move, or Italy will crumble into nothingness."
So preparations for Operation Marita were set into motion: eighteen divisions of General Sigmund Wilhelm List's Twelfth Army would assemble
in Romania, then cross the frontier into Bulgaria (preferably with the
consent of King Boris, but if not, then without), and invade the plains of
northern Greece at the end of March. The German General Staff expected
List to clean up the Greek mess and prop up Italy within four weeks,
whereupon the Twelfth Army would return to the Russian frontier and
prepare for Barbarossa.

All was not well atop the Third Reich's military hierarchy in early
1941. Actually, this was not an unusual state of affairs, since Hitler encouraged a certain measure of infighting and backbiting among his subordinates. Justifiably suspicious of many of his generals' loyalty to the Nazi
regime, and convinced that his strategic judgment was sounder than theirs
(which it often was), the Fuehrer never allowed any one of his commanders to grow powerful enough to challenge his control of the German
military machine. But the widespread misgivings about Barbarossa and
the petty recriminations that inevitably followed the failure to defeat
Britain in 1940 deepened dangerously the rifts that already existed among
the individual service chiefs and the general staff.

At first glance, General Franz Halder, venerable chief of the German
General Staff, appeared to be a colorless, bespectacled, obedient function-
ary who would never pose a threat to any superior's authority. The stolid,
crew-cut Halder was considered to be the embodiment of the traditional
Prussian military virtues of efficiency and obedience; yet before the war,
he had scornfully referred to Hitler as a madman and a criminal, "a
blood-sucker" who had deliberately maneuvered the fatherland into war
to gratify the bloodlust of his "sexually pathological constitution." Paralyzed by the tension between his loyalty to Germany and his distaste for
the Fuehrer, Halder was growing gradually more querulous and uncooperative; he would finally be dismissed by Hitler in the fall of 1942.

A much more compliant soldier, Field Marshal Wilhelm Keitel, tall, blue-eyed and silent, headed the Armed Forces High Command, the Oberkommando der Wehrmacht (OKW), which Hitler had established in 1938, ostensibly to coordinate "the unified preparation of Reich defense in all areas" according to the Fuehrer's personal directives. In reality, Keitel, whose selfless and tiresome devotion to Hitler earned him the derisive nickname of "the lackey," was little more than a cipher who faithfully carried out the Fuehrer's commands and shielded him from bad news.

Below Keitel on the Nazi military organization chart came the chiefs of the three fighting services: Field Marshal Walther von Brauchitsch, commander in chief of the Army High Command (OKH), who generally tried to stay out of the ceaseless internal squabbling; Grand Admiral Erich Raeder, a devout Christian and commander of the navy, who repeatedly tried (and usually failed) to convince Hitler to concentrate Germany's resources in the Mediterranean theater and strike at Britain through the imperial lifeline at Suez; and the inimitably brutal and bemedaled Reichsmarshal Hermann Göring, head of the Luftwaffe, heir apparent to the Fuehrer, and a man whom many mocked but few dared challenge. To incredulous foreigners who wondered how such a mad, grossly overweight buffoon as the Reichsmarshal—who spent much of his time vainly preening himself in his outrageously baroque uniforms—could acquire such immense power in a supposedly sophisticated twentieth-century nation, one anti-Nazi German conservative explained:

> Goering was the Falstaff of our mass epoch. His particular trick consisted in magnifying on a gigantic scale a characteristic phenomenon of our epoch. The Wilhelmine bourgeoisie, who lacked all resolution, faith, and profundity, found in this pompous, boastful, power-mad, bloodthirsty man all those traits of character with which they were familiar in their own selves. They saw their dilettantism represented in his possession of a hundred offices and titles; their own escape into make-believe from the poverty of reality; their own elevation of trash to the status of fine art; their own superficiality which so soon became a menace to the commonweal; their own degenerate externalization, brutalization, and corruption of the old military traditions.

The Reich's civilian leadership was, if anything, even more disunited than the military. Within the Nazi Party, tension was growing between Goebbels, Deputy Fuehrer Rudolf Hess, Hess's cunning assistant, Martin Bormann (who soon would become party secretary), and Heinrich Himmler—former police chief of Bavaria and erstwhile chicken farmer, now chief of the Gestapo and leader of the sinister SS. The lull in the war in the late winter of 1941 provided an opportunity for each of these ambitious men to try to strengthen his position against the others, and to obtain the Fuehrer's consent for a variety of pet schemes that might have seemed outlandish in a different time or place.

Casting a covetous glance at the eastern empire already conquered by the Wehrmacht—and already being exploited by corrupt local Nazi officials who stole the property and savings of the victims they murdered in the name of racial purity—Heinrich Himmler advanced his plans to deport and Germanize those Poles whom he deemed "racially valuable," leaving the rest to serve the Reich as common laborers; they would be taught only "simple arithmetic up to 500 at the most, how to write their name, and that it is God's commandment to be obedient and honest, hard-working and well-behaved toward Germans." Bormann, on the other hand, proposed to kill every intelligent Pole (the remarkable thing was that he admitted there even were any), and reduce the rest of the country to the status of a work camp. Intermarriage between Poles and Germans would be strictly forbidden; the "lowest German peasant," Bormann insisted, "must still be ten percent better off than any Pole." To keep the Polish peasants "dull and stupid," he recommended that they be permitted to retain their Catholic priests.

This was not Bormann's only slap at the Catholic Church. Aided by the rabidly anti-Christian Dr. Alfred Rosenberg, the official National Socialist Party theorist, Bormann launched a campaign to appropriate the wealth of the monasteries in Germany and Austria. "Experience has shown," Bormann wrote to all the gauleiters (the Nazi Party chiefs in the provinces) on January 13, "that the public has expressed no indignation when monasteries were converted to generally accepted useful purposes." Backed by no law or official decree, Bormann arrogantly proceeded to loot Church property anyway, ejecting the priests and nuns and turning the buildings into barracks, homes for unwed mothers, Party offices, rest homes, hospitals, or youth indoctrination centers.

Although Hitler himself was not yet prepared to launch a final assault upon the churches, official Nazi propaganda repeatedly hammered home the message that Christianity had failed to make good on its promises. "For two thousand years the church had time to begin moulding mankind into a cleaner, high-striving race," proclaimed *Gott und Volk,* a Nazi tract published in support of Bormann's monastery-sacking campaign. "The church not only did nothing but has degenerated into a restraining impediment. But now the Fuehrer and his movement, decried as heretic, have come to perceive and form the true divine will. Christianity has failed and thus rung in its death hour. . . ." The government attempted to lock Christianity into a ghetto: the dates of religious holidays were arbitrarily changed or canceled altogether; theological students were drafted into the army or assigned to compulsory labor; schoolteachers in Bavaria—for centuries a stronghold of the Catholic Church—were ordered to remove all crucifixes from their classrooms and replace them with portraits of

Hitler; and bishops and ministers who defied the Party were arrested, tortured, and shot.

In these circumstances, German Christians appeared to be in a considerable quandary, faced with a choice between loyalty to their government and to their religion. The fact that the government had the guns and the Gestapo, while the church did not, made the decision no easier. Actually, most German Christians probably never made a conscious choice at all; the path of least resistance led straight to obedience to the state in all but the most extraordinary circumstances. Besides, the German ecclesiastical establishment pointedly refused to become an active center for organized opposition to the Nazi regime despite the government's anti-Christian provocations; the churches seemed to be suffering from what one critic termed the chronic disease of German Christianity—"its unfortunate tendency to support faithfully any sort of government." The Lutheran emphasis upon authority, the churches' inability to rise above the myth of "Reich, people, and fatherland," an aversion to liberalism, and a widely shared reservoir of latent anti-Semitism rendered the German churches poor vehicles for any resistance movement. Mostly the church hierarchy confined its anti-Nazi activities to resisting government attempts to encroach upon its authority, and some Christians engaged in individual acts of quiet bravery, perhaps sheltering Jews or assisting fugitives to escape.

There were only a few who went farther along the road to heroism. In January 1941, Dietrich Bonhoeffer, a young pastor in the evangelical German Confessing Church—an openly anti-Nazi sect established in the 1930s by Martin Niemoeller, a cleric for whom Hitler held a deep and abiding personal hatred—became a confidential agent in the Munich office of the Abwehr, the military espionage and counterintelligence agency headed by Admiral Wilhelm Canaris. Under the leadership of Canaris and his deputy, Colonel Hans Joachim Oster, the Abwehr had become the heart and soul of the anti-Nazi resistance within the military, although of course not everyone employed by the Abwehr opposed Hitler. Bonhoeffer's position as an Abwehr "V-Mann" afforded him a valuable degree of protection from his political and ecclesiastical enemies, and allowed him to travel abroad to restore and maintain communications with his contacts in occupied Europe and Britain, and to explore potential avenues toward a negotiated settlement of the war. It was his firm belief that so long as the war continued, the German people faced a set of terrible alternatives: "either to hope for the defeat of their nation in order that Christian civilization might survive or to hope for victory entailing the destruction of our civilization." For their part, the top ranks of the Abwehr leadership recognized how valuable Bonhoeffer's foreign connections could be for their own political objectives within Germany.

The resistance was then at the dead season of its fortunes. Ever since the Nazis consolidated their power by eliminating (often lethally) their leftist political opponents in the mid-1930s, the key to any successful internal revolt against Hitler always rested in the hands of the church (which, as we have seen, refused to take any positive action) and, more significantly, the generals—many of whom, like Halder and Canaris, had opposed the drift toward war in 1939, believing that Germany was not yet adequately prepared for an all-out conflict. Following the startlingly successful spring blitzkrieg of 1940, however, the Wehrmacht—sated with success and hiding comfortably behind its oath and the tradition of the nonpolitical soldier who loyally served the fatherland—had temporarily bowed out of any active role in the resistance. Now, in the early months of 1941, with German forces triumphant across the Continent, any attempted anti-Nazi coup inevitably would revive accusations of a second *dolchstoss,* a reverse "stab-in-the-back" that betrayed Germany at its moment of greatest triumph. "It almost seems to me that we shall have to resign ourselves to this for a long time," wrote Bonhoeffer sadly to his mother, "to live more on the past and the present, and that means more on thankfulness, than on any view of the future."

Certainly Canaris was not yet prepared to do much more than lend his prestige and protection to isolated acts of resistance behind the scenes. A profoundly pessimistic and perplexing man who had come to hate the entire Nazi system and its leadership, Wilhelm Canaris was one of the most enigmatic figures of the Third Reich. He despised military pomp and reportedly kept his own decorations and honors locked away in a drawer. Nervous and oversensitive, Canaris constantly complained of poor health and suffered from insomnia; wrapped in an overcoat in the summertime, he never seemed to be warm enough. Highly intelligent and a devoted student of philosophy and the arts, he adored animals ("Anyone who does not love dogs I judge out of hand to be an evil man") and detested the wastefulness of war and unnecessary violence. He knew this war would end in apocalyptic disaster for Germany.

From his office on the tree-shaded, elegant Tirpitzuferstrasse, Canaris ran the Abwehr by whim and impulse, often issuing contradictory instructions to his subordinates, refusing to delegate authority, restlessly wreaking havoc throughout the military and political bureaucracy in his frequent unannounced official tours through Germany. "Like Ahasuerus fleeing from himself and other men, he journeyed from town to town, everywhere spreading unrest and disorder in the Nazi system," wrote one of his former associates after the war. "Some of his intimates would then always have to put in order the things that Canaris had jumbled as might an overgrown child his toys." Outwardly a loyal servant of the Nazi regime, he regularly sabotaged Himmler's operations and secretly revealed to some of the more scrupulous army officials the sordid depths to which SS brutality had brought the fatherland. Around him, and almost in spite of his own wishes, there gathered an underground circle of idealists, adventurers, intellectuals, mystics, Jews, anti-Fascists, and conservatives, all of whom were united only by their opposition to Nazism.

Canaris was not a man to fight openly against Hitler, which explains why he was so successful for so long, nor could he ever bring himself to betray his country. But until he broke under the strain in 1942, he consistently employed his power in passive ways to shield the resistance, to rescue those threatened by the Gestapo, and to prevent the men he despised from realizing their twisted dreams.

"For all decent people, the dominating factor is their own inner tragedy," lamented Ulrich von Hassell, a veteran German diplomat who also counted himself a member of the resistance to Hitler. "They can wish neither for defeat nor for victory; they cannot wish for the latter because the victory of these people [the Nazis] opens up terrible perspectives for Germany and Europe." In the first month of 1941, von Hassell wrote in his diary that "there is growing awareness of the developing evil, too, but no rift in the clouds which conceal the way out." Doubtless even this dismal view was too optimistic. Among the common people of Germany, the Fuehrer remained an unassailable figure. Certainly there were plenty of ribald jokes about the personal peccadilloes of the Nazi leadership, and foreign correspondents in Berlin regularly heard outspoken criticism of the regime late at night in certain cafés. But, contrary to wishful British thinking, Germany's air-raid shelters were not filled with huddled masses yearning to overthrow Hitler; there were no legions of eager conspirators who needed only a good push to bring down the National Socialist Party.

Instead, there was only the leaden silence of winter. "Except for the outbursts from the Nazi orators, over the radio and in the press, and except for the reports of feverish diplomatic activity and rumours of troop movements," recalled Harry Flannery, "we in Berlin hardly knew a war was on during the early part of 1941." Snow lingered on the ground well into February. The colorful window displays in the department stores disguised the fact that the advertised merchandise had long been out of stock. Streets were filled with sightseers and endless streams of tanks, military trucks, and artillery bound for the front. The meat ration was down to one pound per person per week (pork and sausage were the most plentiful choices), fish was available only twice a week and chicken almost never, and tea was brewed from virtually every sort of foliage except tea leaves. But bread was plentiful, potatoes were not yet scarce enough to be rationed, and fruit was usually available on the black market to the highest bidder. Sales of bottled beer had skyrocketed since the air raids began, forcing the government to demand the return of empties to alleviate a potential bottle shortage. In the absence of cowhide, Germans were using rabbit or fish leather for their shoes, and wooden soles.

Children received more generous food rations than adults. Like their

counterparts in Tokyo, German officials had instituted a program to stimulate the birthrate, to provide more and more children who would grow up
to meet the challenges that time and destiny were thrusting at the Thousand Year Reich. "Do not forget," Himmler reminded the people as he
banned the sale of contraceptive devices, "that the strength of arms alone
cannot assure a people's existence into the distant future, but that an
inexhaustible fountain of fertility is also necessary. . . . Conduct yourselves
accordingly so that the victory of German arms may be followed by a
victory of German children." Couples received government loans when
they married; with the birth of each child, one-fourth of the loan was
written off, so that a family with four children never needed to repay
anything. Families with three or more children also received special
monthly payments from the government until the children turned
twenty-one. Children were virtually the only tax deduction permitted by
the government. Large families usually received priority in obtaining
suitable housing in the cities. (As an interesting by-product of the Reich's
procreation policies, the mothers of illegitimate children found themselves the unwitting recipients of awards for unflagging service to the
fatherland; the Fuehrer welcomed *all* newborn citizens of the Greater
Germany, whether their parents possessed a marriage license or not.
"Outside of marriage," proclaimed the demented Dr. Rosenberg, an ardent proponent of sexual promiscuity, "the mothers of German children
must be esteemed. Adultery on the part of the male of the species must
be regarded in a new light, for those relations which result in an increase
in the birth rate—in the procreation of more German children—cannot
be and will not be considered a breach of the marriage contract.")

As winter faded at last into spring, the Wehrmacht awoke. Hitler
descended from the mountain at Berchtesgaden. Civilian railway traffic
leading to the border of Bulgaria was halted. On March 1, Bulgarian Prime
Minister Bogdan Philov signed the Tripartite Pact, formally aligning his
country with Germany, Italy, and Japan. The next day, General List's
Twelfth Army crossed the Danube and advanced toward the Greek frontier "in order to prevent England's threat of spreading the war to the
Balkans and to protect Balkan interests." Now only Yugoslavia stood between Greece and the Wehrmacht. Watching from the Kremlin as German troops poured into a traditional Russian sphere of interest, Joseph
Stalin was not at all pleased with the ominous trend of events.

Across the Mediterranean, Lieutenant General Erwin Rommel had
arrived in Tripoli on February 20, at the head of the Deutsches Afrika
Korps. Despite his notable success in leading the Seventh Panzer Division
in its springtime gallop through France in 1940, the fifty-year-old Rommel
had not yet been accepted as a member of the inner circle atop the
Germany military establishment. In fact, he was regarded as something of
an unpredictable upstart who definitely required close supervision. (On

the other hand, his status as a non-Prussian outsider struck a responsive chord in Hitler, who admiringly described Rommel as "an incredibly hard man.") After spending several weeks gathering firsthand impressions of the tactical situation in North Africa, Rommel returned to Berlin in the middle of March to receive long-overdue military honors and to confer with Hitler, Halder, and Brauchitsch. He reported that conditions appeared favorable for an immediate advance—before the oppressive summer heat returned—to reconquer the territory Italy had lost; but his superiors instructed him to wait for reinforcements and refrain from any rash actions. With the army's resources fully and irrevocably committed to the coming campaign in Greece and the glorious enterprise of Barbarossa, with the nation's stocks of fuel oil and rubber dwindling to a precariously low level, Germany could ill afford to support any reckless enterprise in North Africa. So Rommel returned to Tripoli and, characteristically, proceeded to implement his plans for an advance across the desert anyway.

While Rommel assembled his panzers in Libya, Anthony Eden, the British cabinet's resident matinee idol, was winging his way back and forth across the Mediterranean to inaugurate one of the most disastrous and ill-conceived British military adventures of the war. Since the first week of January, when Whitehall obtained apparently irrefutable evidence that Germany was planning a move into the Balkans, Churchill's government had been urging Greece to allow British troops to be stationed in Salonika; this would, presumably, frighten the Wehrmacht into staying put. Besides, Britain considered itself honor bound by the unequivocal guarantee that Chamberlain's government, during one of its periodic attacks of entirely worthless generosity, had given Greece in 1939. General Metaxas, the redoubtable Greek prime minister—dictator, in fact—who was no one's fool, rejected the offer on the grounds that a British military presence in Greece would only provide Germany with an excuse to attack his beleaguered nation. Unless Britain could provide enough troops to repel a Nazi invasion (which it obviously could not), Metaxas quite frankly preferred to go it alone, at least until Germany posed a more imminent threat by moving into neighboring Bulgaria.

Meanwhile, Eden tried to persuade Turkey and Yugoslavia to join Greece in a united Balkan front against Hitler, the prospect of which brought the high-strung Prince Paul Karageorgevich of Yugoslavia to the verge of nervous collapse. Having succeeded to the throne as regent upon the assassination of his cousin during a trip to France in 1934, Paul wanted nothing more than to abandon his official responsibilities and turn over the nation—preferably still intact—to his nephew, Peter, as soon as the boy turned eighteen (which he would do in the autumn of 1941). Paul was scrambling desperately for any means to placate Germany and keep the

Wehrmacht from invading Yugoslavia; "on the face of it," Churchill informed the cabinet in London, "Prince Paul's attitude looks like that of an unfortunate man in a cage with a tiger, hoping not to provoke him while steadily dinner-time approaches." Already mistrustful of Eden—there was something about the foreign secretary, perhaps his patent shallowness and his incessant preoccupation with his own career, that struck contemporaries as distasteful—Paul reportedly flew into a rage upon learning on January 12 that General Wavell was due shortly in Athens to encourage and coordinate resistance to Germany; the regent reportedly shouted at the British ambassador, "This stinks of Anthony!" (As a graduate of Eton and Oxford and a recipient of the Order of the Garter, the prince was on a first-name basis with most of the British political establishment.) Nor did Paul display any more willingness to defy Germany openly during a luncheon with American emissary Wild Bill Donovan on January 23, despite Donovan's naive assurances that the United States intended to provide all possible assistance to small nations willing to fight for their independence against the Nazis. Probably Paul knew precisely how much that promise was worth in the circumstances; Roosevelt had previously pledged to send thirty planes to Greece, but the U.S. Navy refused to give them up.

But still Churchill (who was in a vile mood these days, suffering from a succession of bad colds) and his advisers labored onward, exploring the available diplomatic and military options, of which there were depressingly few. Although the Prime Minister was determined to take the offensive wherever possible, there seemed little more to gain in the Libyan desert; besides, the British troops who had chased the Italians out of Cyrenaica had already dangerously overextended their lines, making any advance upon Tripoli a risky proposition. And by now the Luftwaffe's Fliegerkorps X had arrived in Sicily in force, threatening British convoys and destroyers in the Mediterranean. So Whitehall decided that Greece, that little land of great people (as Churchill liked to think of it), must be supported to the utmost, encouraged to resist the temptation to make a separate peace with Italy. Most important, the Wehrmacht divisions that were gathering so ominously in Romania could not be allowed to endanger the vital approaches to Suez or the British oil fields in Iraq. If only the British army could recover a foothold on the Continent, in the Balkans, in Greece, it might be able to hold the Wehrmacht at bay, buying time to rally anti-Axis forces in the region, and thereby proving to America that Europe was not yet doomed to Nazi domination. Besides, Churchill decided that it was time for the main show to begin, for British forces to confront Germans instead of Italians. But what Winston never quite seemed to realize—and none of his military advisers reminded him of the fact—was that Germany had sufficient surplus military power (if not surplus time) to engage in sideshows successfully without endangering its vital interests; Britain did not.

Then, on January 29, General Metaxas died suddenly and unexpectedly of a combination of ailments (allegedly including pneumonia and a heart attack) after a very brief illness. His successor as prime minister, Alexander Koryzis (who did not really want the job in the first place), was a well-meaning banker of unassailable integrity who had little practical political experience, and none of Metaxas' prodigious ability to weld the disparate elements of the Greek government into a cohesive unit. Although King George II remained solidly pro-British—after all, his son, Prince Philip, was betrothed to young Princess Elizabeth and was serving in the Royal Navy—the Greek cabinet started to disintegrate into quarreling factions, and the army began to display distressing signs of indecision.

Into the breach flew, literally, Eden and Sir John Dill, chief of the Imperial General Staff. Actually, Eden would have preferred to make a stand farther east by concentrating British assistance and entreaties upon Turkey, but since the Turks had understandably evinced no inclination to fight until Germany actually invaded Anatolia, the British cabinet had decided that Eden and Dill should travel to Athens to have another go at working out an agreement with the Greeks. Carrying sealed orders from Churchill granting him considerable authority to commit British resources as he deemed necessary, Eden left England on February 14, embarking upon a harrowing airplane ride over the Iberian peninsula through violent storms that knocked out the plane's navigational instruments. ("It was a queer sensation," remarked Eden afterward, "sitting trussed in one's lifebelt and contemplating the alternatives of internment or drowning. One felt strangely detached and could review it all dispassionately and conclude that one had had a very good full life. But the crew were all such boys.") Upon landing safely at Gibraltar, the dismal weather kept the envoys confined to the island for several more anxious days. Eden used the delay to send a message from Gibraltar to Prince Paul requesting a face-to-face meeting; Paul curtly refused.

By the time Eden and Dill finally arrived in Cairo, they discovered that Wavell had abandoned his earlier opposition to the Greek project; having convinced himself that a minimal defensive force could hold the vital positions in the North African desert, the general had already begun preparations to send his exhausted and ill-equipped troops across the Mediterranean from Alexandria to Piraeus. On February 20, Eden and Dill held a strategy conference with Wavell, Sir Arthur Longmore, commander of the R.A.F. Mediterranean force, and Admiral Andrew "Uncle Ned" Cunningham, commander of the Mediterranean fleet of the Royal Navy. Remarkably, considering Eden's Turkish bent and the paucity of military resources available, everyone present agreed that Britain should do its utmost to assist Greece as soon as possible. And precisely what help could Britain provide? Wavell offered three divisions (primarily infantrymen from Australia and New Zealand) and the better part of one armored division to stand against an estimated eighteen veteran German divisions; Cunningham, as usual, was woefully short of destroyers; and Longmore's planes looked more like relics of the First World War (and some of them reportedly were) than suitable rivals for the Luftwaffe. "Many good troopers are still mounted on wretched ponies," was Eden's flippant comment about Longmore's decrepit aircraft.

Upon receipt of Eden's account of this meeting, Churchill—who was alternately enthusiastic and doubtful—immediately dispatched a disingenuous message to Cairo: "Do not consider yourselves obligated to a Greek enterprise if in your hearts you feel it will only be another Norwegian fiasco. If no good plan can be made please say so. But of course," he added slyly, "you know how valuable success would be." Indeed they did, and so the commanders in Cairo declined to change their decision. Back came Eden's reply: "It is, of course, a gamble to send forces to the mainland of Europe to fight Germans at this time. No one can give a guarantee of success, but when we discussed this matter in London we were prepared to run the risk of failure, thinking it better to suffer with the Greeks than to make no attempt to help them." Perhaps.

So Eden and Dill (a scholarly sort of soldier whom the abrupt Cadogan considered a "ninny") journeyed on to an Athens bereft of Metaxas' wisdom. There, even before Eden could open his mouth, Koryzis issued the long-coveted invitation, a product of the Greeks' mounting concern at the Wehrmacht's infiltration of Bulgaria. During the ensuing discussions, the British envoys *thought* they reached an agreement with General Alexander Papagos to assemble a joint Anglo-Greek defense force upon the Mount Olympus–Aliákmon line. Assuming the Germans allowed them sufficient time to transport and equip these troops, both the British and Greek military commanders felt almost confident that they could actually pull it off. Nevertheless, when all was said and done, the British decision to make a stand in Greece was a political one, pure and simple. After receiving a "full steam ahead" signal from Churchill on February 24, Anthony was giddy with self-satisfaction at his diplomatic triumph; he could not have been more pleased if the whole Greek enterprise had been his idea right from the beginning.

Then the wheels started to come off the cart. Any lingering hopes that the Anglo-Greek agreement might inspire Turkey to climb down off the fence were dashed when the Turks politely but firmly told Eden to go away and leave them alone. "You appear to have got nothing out of the Turks," Churchill petulantly cabled to Eden in Ankara. Cadogan wondered, "What the hell is A. going to say to Greeks and Yugoslavs? It's a diplomatic and strategic blunder of the first order. . . . Germans have swarmed over Bulgaria, and there we are. I confess everything looks to me as black as black." Indeed, the Germans were moving troops more quickly through Bulgaria than British intelligence had expected, and Yugoslavia, too, was moving, but in precisely the wrong direction. On March 4, Prince Paul made a secret journey to Berchtesgaden for a five-hour meeting with Hitler. Despite the Fuehrer's threats and bribes of territories on the Adriatic, Paul refused to give a definite answer. He could not make the decision on his own, he said, because Yugoslavia was deeply divided between the pro-German Croats and Slovenes and the pro-British Serbs. If he signed the pact now, he feared he would be overthrown at once, and the country plunged into civil war. So Paul (who had learned the techniques of appeasement from Neville Chamberlain) asked for and received additional time to discuss the dilemma with his cabinet.

Two days later, despairing of any effective British assistance, his nerve completely broken, Paul changed his mind and his government agreed to sign the Tripartite Pact, on the condition that Germany pledge to respect Yugoslavia's territorial and political integrity and refrain from requesting Yugoslav troops or transporting German troops through Yugoslavia. Negotiations over these conditions—which Paul later claimed he did not expect the Germans to accept—dragged on for another two weeks. Berated by the American ambassador in Belgrade for capitulating to Nazi pressure, Paul replied wearily, "You big nations are hard; you talk of our honor, but you are far away." In the capital, the Yugoslav government launched a press campaign to encourage public acceptance of the Axis alliance, and stepped up its arrests of political dissidents.

Meanwhile, upon his return to Athens, Eden discovered to his dismay that the Greeks had not yet begun to move their troops to the Aliákmon line, as they presumably had agreed to do. General Papagos retorted that he had never consented to do any such thing, at least not until Eden sent him definite word about the final results of Prince Paul's anguished vacillations; since Yugoslavia possessed by far the most superior army and air force of any Balkan state (with a maximum strength of 700,000 men and perhaps seven hundred planes), its decision either to resist or to acquiesce in the German advance would have a significant impact on the strategic placement of the Anglo-Greek forces. Besides, Papagos was reluctant, for political reasons, to withdraw all his troops from their forward positions in Thrace and Macedonia, thereby leaving the vulnerable plains of northern Greece open to the German invaders. Disgusted with the delay—although the misunderstanding was at least as much their responsibility as Papagos's—Eden and his military advisers conferred among themselves and finally decided to have a go at the match anyway. "We decided to carry on," recalled Wavell much later, "although obviously we were on a much worse wicket." In London, where misgivings were multiplying daily, the cabinet nevertheless steadfastly refused to step in and call a halt to the expedition, on the grounds that the decision should be left to Wavell and Dill, the senior military officers on the scene who presumably were in a superior position to make an informed decision. Besides, no one wanted to abandon yet another small nation willing to resist Nazi aggression. "The Greeks have done better than anyone could have expected," noted General Jan Christian Smuts, the aged prime minister of South Africa. "The public opinion of the world is strongly on their side. If we do not stand by them, we shall be held up to public ignominy. . . . It may be said that a German victory in the Balkans will result in a great setback to our cause; but the setback will probably be greater if we stand aside and don't help."

Eden, who by now was desperate to return to London, confessed that "this is as tough a proposition as ever I have known," but Churchill put on a lighthearted air now that the decision had been irrevocably taken. Over lunch with Beaverbrook, Churchill maliciously suggested that he might keep Eden in the Middle East for a while longer; "the PM was vituperative about everyone," said an eavesdropper (who heard him refer derisively to Prince Paul as "Palsy"), "but he kept his gems for Wavell whom he likened to a man one might propose as President for the local Country Golf Club." Upon learning that Britain would be supplying several hundred fewer airplanes than originally proposed, and that its own army was desperately short of men and ammunition, the Greek government panicked and secretly asked Germany to mediate the conflict between Greece and Italy. Hitler refused. In Bulgaria, Germany was massing heavily armed troops on the approaches to the Greek frontier, and Wehrmacht engineers were erecting pontoon bridges across the Danube, anchoring them to withstand the weight of tanks and heavy trucks. "I am afraid that there will be a lot of bloody noses this spring in the Aegean," Dill confessed to a friend.

7

"It Is Not My Fault"

"One doesn't have to be a Jew to be anti-Nazi. All one
has to be is a normal decent human being."
                                    —CHARLIE CHAPLIN

On January 21, 1939, Hitler turned to a high-ranking official of the
puppet government of Czechoslovakia and promised, "We are going to
destroy the Jews. They are not going to get away with what they did on
November 9, 1918. The day of reckoning has come."

Yet before 1941, the Third Reich still had not adopted an official
policy with regard to the ultimate disposition of the four million Jews who
resided in the areas under its direct control. Hitler knew he wanted to get
rid of them, but he was not certain of the most effective means of doing
so. Thus far the Nazi regime had been experimenting with various expedi-
ents as circumstances dictated. Although the Foreign Office had not completely abandoned its fantastic plans to ship all of Europe's Jews to
Madagascar as an ultimate solution to "the Jewish problem," other more
practical solutions were being tried in the meantime. For a while, resettlement within Europe had seemed to be the answer. First in Vienna, and
then in Prague, Adolf Eichmann had supervised a very successful operation to force Jews to emigrate to regions outside the Nazi sphere of influence; by periodically unleashing the SS terror and ordering wholesale
deportations to the forced labor camps of Dachau and Buchenwald, Eichmann made emigration appear a relatively attractive option, despite the
exorbitant fees his office charged Jews for exit visas. In effect, Eichmann
forced the Jews to leave and stole their money in the process. By September 1939, nearly 150,000 Jews had left Austria, and in March 1941 Goebbels was able to report that "Vienna will soon be entirely Jew-free. And
now," he added, "it is to be Berlin's turn," for on February 2, the Fuehrer
had confidently predicted that there would be no Jews left in Germany
after the war. Indeed, half of Germany's Jews already had fled the country
since the Nazis came to power in 1933; the total number of Jewish emi-
grants from Germany, Austria, and Czechoslovakia numbered nearly
600,000.

The Reich could not yet afford to eliminate Jews from the capital,

however; there were still some thirty thousand Jews working (for starvation wages) in munitions factories in Berlin, fashioning the weapons that
were spreading the Nazi ideology across Europe. For many Jewish workers, it was the only means of earning a livelihood that was still open to
them. Since 1938, Jews in Germany—at that time, they made up slightly
less than one percent of the population—had been forbidden to engage
in virtually any form of business or commerce; they were not eligible for
government benefits, nor were they permitted to socialize with Aryan
Germans or walk along the main streets of the cities or enter most public
places, including theaters, beaches, resorts. They could not send their
children to public schools; they were allowed to enter stores only after four
o'clock in the afternoon, when most of the shelves were empty anyway.
And in April 1941, Goebbels prepared a decree requiring all Jews in Berlin
to wear a distinctive badge with a Star of David. "Otherwise," he groused,
"they are constantly mixing with our people, pretending to be harmless,
and making trouble."

Goebbels' complaints and the Nazi program of economic and social
discrimination against the Jews found widespread public acceptance
within the German nation (and a sizable portion of Austria as well). Anti-
Semitism had roots deep within the traditions of modern German thought
and culture; Richard Wagner held a place of honor in the Third Reich's
pantheon of cultural heroes, and Martin Luther's frenzied diatribes
against the Jews were well documented. Hitler insisted that Jewish intrigues had caused Germany's downfall in November 1918, and had subjected Germany to the shame of Versailles. As historian Richard Grunberger pointed out, "ever since the early thirties, there had been a
national consensus of opinion favouring the elimination of Jewish influence from German life, which meant that—irrespective of how people
might judge the actual means employed—the broad ends of Nazi policy
were essentially approved." If most Germans did not share the Nazi regime's obsessive hatred of Jews, they certainly made no objection to the
systematic despoliation of their Jewish neighbors. (This does not mean,
however, that the German people were aware of the existence of the
death camps that began their hellish work in the later years of the war;
that question lies outside the scope of this book.)

As a practical matter, resettlement schemes had to be postponed after
Germany conquered Poland—and its two and a half million Jews—in
1939. ("If only I knew where to put those few million Jews," Hitler muttered.) Some Polish Jews, together with many of the nation's leading
Socialists and Communists, were shot by the SS; at the "village of death"
of Palmiry, fifteen miles outside Warsaw, there were already more than
six thousand nameless graves at the beginning of 1941. But as yet there
was no coordinated official effort or master plan to annihilate the Jewry of
eastern Europe. In fact, as late as February 13, 1941, Reinhard Heydrich,

the chief of SS security who soon would assume control of the Third Reich's most barbaric anti-Semitic operations, was explicitly writing about a "final solution" in terms of "sending them off to whatever country will be chosen later on." So, as a more or less temporary measure to isolate them while Nazi officials debated their ultimate fate, the Jews of Poland were evicted from their land and their homes—sometimes seized in the middle of the night and dragged by SS guards to the local freight depot— and herded into ghettos in the largest cities in the *Generalgouvernement,* the eastern region of Poland, which had not been absorbed directly into the Greater German Reich. As Himmler later informed his comrades, these operations sometimes were carried out "in weather forty degrees below zero, where we had to haul away thousands, tens of thousands, hundreds of thousands. . . . Gentlemen, it is much easier in many cases to go into combat with a company than to suppress an obstructive population of low cultural level, or to carry out executions or to haul away people or to evict crying and hysterical women."

First at Lodz in May 1940, then in Warsaw and Lublin at the end of the year, thousands of Jews were sealed into reservations in the poorer districts of the cities. Their synagogues were destroyed, the universities closed, and teachers arrested. Everyone over the age of thirteen was required to wear a white armband with a blue Star of David. Jews were forbidden to own radios, although most of the time there was no electrical power anyway. (When the decree banning radios was published, witnesses saw people obediently dragging their radio sets to the police station at the end of ropes, as if the radios were dogs.) In Warsaw, 400,000 Jews were crammed into an area of less than seventy acres—including a cemetery— that later would be reduced even further in size. Those fortunate enough to find housing often squeezed twelve or more people into a room; thousands were homeless. Sanitary facilities were primitive or nonexistent. Not surprisingly, the city suffered a severe epidemic of typhus, and corpses littered the streets during the harsh winter of 1940–41. Others in the ghetto simply starved to death. Janina Bauman, a young girl living in the Warsaw ghetto, told her diary of two small boys she had seen begging in the street:

> I see them every time I go out. Or they might be girls, I don't know. Their heads are shaven, clothes in rags, their frightfully emaciated faces bring to mind birds rather than human beings. Their huge black eyes, though, are human; so full of sadness . . . The younger one may be five or six, the older one ten perhaps. They don't move, they don't speak. The little one sits on the pavement, the bigger one just stands there with his claw of a hand stretched out. I must remember now to bring them some food whenever I go out. This morning, on my way to lessons, I gave them my bread and butter meant for lunch.

Amid the darkness, people turned to despair or mysticism; seances became one of the most popular forms of entertainment in the ghettos.

Across the European continent, the fate of the Jewish population varied widely at the beginning of 1941. In Bucharest, Jews were being systematically slaughtered in a pogrom instigated by the Iron Guard forces of the Romanian crypto-Nazi leader Horia Sima. Jewish shops and synagogues in the Bucharest ghetto were set afire, Jews were shot or burned with gasoline or had their throats cut in grotesque imitations of ritual butcherings in kosher slaughterhouses. Thousands were arrested and subsequently assassinated in their prison cells.

But in Italy, such massacres were entirely unthinkable. Fascist officials gave lip service to Nazi racial policies, and anti-Semitic legislation that had been approved in 1938 excluded Jews from the civil service, the army, and the schools, limited their ownership of property, and forbade intermarriage with Christians. But over the past century, Italian Jews—all sixty thousand of them, about one-tenth of one percent of the total population—had assimilated themselves into the mainstream of Italian society, eschewing the orthodox observances of Judaism; they were among the most fervent supporters of the *Risorgimento* that created the modern Italian nation-state, most were members of the middle or upper middle class, and for decades many of them had sent their children to be educated at convent schools. So, despite pointed Nazi urgings, there were no wholesale roundups or deportations. Besides, the Italian people were already thoroughly sick and tired of being bossed around by Germany.

Although the question of public and official attitudes toward Jews in wartime France is still a matter of considerable controversy (rekindled by the trial in 1987 of Nazi war criminal Klaus Barbie, "the butcher of Lyons"), certainly the vigorously anti-Semitic record of Vichy France has been amply documented. As Michael Marrus and Robert Paxton have demonstrated, the Nazis had no need to impose a cult of anti-Semitism upon Pétain's government; there already existed among certain sectors of the French public—though not necessarily among a majority of the people—an indigenous reservoir of popular hostility toward Jews, and particularly toward the thousands of foreign refugees from central Europe who had been forcibly settled by Nazi authorities in the south of France. Like their Italian brethren, native French Jews generally had been assimilated thoroughly into the nation's culture over the past several centuries; but in the wake of a sudden, unexpected, and (for many) otherwise inexplicable military defeat, latent anti-Semitic sentiments burst into the open, and Jews were made the scapegoats for France's military misfortunes and the high prices, the food shortages, and the rest of the hardships that plagued France in the winter and spring of 1941 (and which were, of course, the result of life under the Nazis' New Order). Headlines in the collaborationist press screamed that the Jews must be exterminated, and articles told readers how to recognize Jews on the street. England was roundly condemned as the headquarters of international Jewish capitalism.

As an integral part of the plan to resuscitate the French nation through Pétain's National Revolution, the government at Vichy decided that it must first reduce the numbers of Jews in France—that is, get rid of the refugees already there and bar the door to any more—and subsequently eliminate any diabolical (literally) influence that the remaining Jews might exert over French society. Accordingly, in October 1940 Vichy enacted the *Statut des juifs,* legislation that reduced Jews to an inferior position in civil law, established quotas that limited Jewish participation in certain liberal professions, and excluded them entirely from the highest levels of the army, the civil service, and all professions that exerted influence upon public opinion (including education, journalism, radio broadcasting, and filmmaking). Individual exceptions were routinely made, however, for native Jews of exceptional fame and influence, who were allowed to remain in important positions. Although he could be stirred to protect individual Jews with whom he or his friends were acquainted, Pétain seems to have remained basically indifferent to the fate of Jews as a group—the Marshal seldom took a clear-cut stand on any controversial issue. "I remember some one coming it was in the end of '40," recalled Gertrude Stein, "and they said they had just come from America and they had just seen Maréchal Pétain and Pétain had wanted to know how they felt about him over there and the man answered and said they did not like his persecuting, and he [Pétain] said, as for free-masons I hate them, as for communists I am afraid of them, as for the Jews it is not my fault."

Vichy's policies worked special hardships upon the refugees. Local magistrates were given summary authority to intern foreign Jews in unoccupied France's eight concentration camps, one of the most notorious of which was located at Gurs, in the Pyrenees, where sixteen thousand people languished behind barbed wire in filthy overcrowded windowless barracks. "It is dark here, in the truest sense of the word," wrote one inmate. "There are many sick persons and many funerals—yesterday seventeen and today twenty-four." "The landscape around Gurs was beautiful, the food and sanitary conditions horrendous; and the death rate was enormous," recalled a survivor after the war. "When you came out of the barracks in the morning, you had to be careful to stay on the plank walks; otherwise you would sink up to your knees in swamp. The whole complex was built over a swamp, the barracks forming little islands. The prisoners were separated according to sex and origin, and you needed a pass to go from one island to the next." (In fairness, it should be noted that the French officials who supervised the camps were generally sympathetic to the refugees' plight, but were helpless to do very much about it.)

In March 1941, the Vichy government permitted a team of foreign reporters to inspect five of the refugee camps. Prisoners took the opportunity to thrust notes and written pleas for help at the visitors. "It is a fact," reported the *New York Times* correspondent, "that these people have been detained for reasons they, in many instances, do not understand and that they are without the slightest information about what is to be their future. Some of them do cherish the hope that some day they will be allowed to emigrate, but for the majority the maximum of anticipation is the chance that they will be moved to still another camp where conditions may be better." In the end, most of the internees remained shut away in camps such as the one at Gurs until the Gestapo came and began to take the Jews away to the east in 1942.

By the early spring of 1941, American newspapers were carrying— though usually not on the front page—reliable reports of the recurrent pattern of anti-Semitic discrimination and persecution across Nazi-occupied Europe. Yet there was no widespread public revulsion in the United States, and surprisingly few impassioned outcries against Germany's racial policies. (No one could know the horrors that lay in the future.) Certainly Jews were not the only victims of the Nazi regime's disregard for human life; every day, innocent civilians in Britain were dying in the blitz, and freedom fighters in Holland and Denmark were being imprisoned or shot by the thousands. As yet, there was little reason for Americans to suspect that the Nazis' treatment of Jews would be of an entirely different and murderous order.

The State Department did respond to the systematic violation of the Jews' basic human rights by registering protests with individual governments, but there was little else it could do under the circumstances. The most helpful thing that the United States could have done would have been to throw open the doors to vast numbers of refugees, who were being denied asylum in America by a series of extraordinarily tight federal immigration restrictions—as of January 1941, the quota for Germany was 37,-000 people per year. Any attempt to loosen these restrictions would have provoked substantial popular and congressional resistance, however; the public was worried that a flood of immigrants willing to work for low wages would send unemployment skyrocketing among native-born Americans who were just recovering from the Depression, and there was rising concern about the presence of clandestine Nazi agents in the United States. Some influential American officials feared that the Gestapo was placing its own agents among the refugees—nearly one thousand per week—who were being brought to America by private Jewish aid societies (who paid a handsome fee to the Nazis for the privilege). "It is sinister," Assistant Secretary of State Breckinridge Long felt, "because the German Government only gives permits to the persons they want to come to the United States. It is a perfect opening for Germany to load the United States with agents." Besides, both Britain and Switzerland already had effectively barred their frontiers, too, to Jewish German refugees, and the infamous British White Paper of May 1939 had first restricted and then prohibited further Jewish immigration into Palestine. So, for the time being, the gates to freedom remained open to only a fortunate few.

And, of course, the United States (including, conspicuously, Congress itself) had never been entirely innocent of either overt or passive anti-Semitism. In fashionable society, subtle discrimination was almost de rigueur; in less exclusive circles, bigotry wore no mask. Congressmen regularly received letters such as: "I see from the papers that 200,000 Refugee Jews in Hungary will not live through the next few weeks. Thats too Damn Bad what in the Hell do we care about the Jews in Hungary. What we want is the Refugee Jews brought to this country returned where they come from"—and—"I am writing to you to protest against the entry of Jewish refugees into this country. Their lack of common decency, gross ignorance and unbelievable gall stamps them as undesirables even if they could be assimilated into a common society, which they can't." In March, the American Export Line, which operated one of the last remaining regular passenger services between Lisbon and New York, announced that it was closing down its ticket offices for an indefinite period. Unable to arrange sufficient tonnage to accommodate the thousands of refugees who sought to escape to the United States, the company's books revealed a backlog of more than ten thousand people with valid tickets awaiting passage. No more tickets would be sold until June at the earliest.

Walking along Fifth Avenue in New York in January, Charlie Chaplin observed a small group of people gathered on the sidewalk, listening to a slick, handsome young street-corner orator who was praising Hitler as a modern-day prophet who had discovered that Jews had no place in twentieth-century society. "What kind of talk is that?" screamed a woman in the crowd. "This is America. Where do you think you are?" The young man looked down and flashed a condescending smile. "I'm in the United States," he replied, "and I happen to be an American citizen." "Well, I'm an American citizen, and a Jew," the woman said, "and if I were a man I'd knock your block off." Chaplin heard one or two others in the crowd second the motion, but most of the people just stood there silently, wholly indifferent. A nearby policeman calmed down the agitated woman. Chaplin was shocked and disillusioned by the crowd's apathetic attitude toward this blatant advocacy of bigotry. "I came away astonished," he said, "hardly believing my ears."

On March 1, 1941, Heinrich Himmler journeyed to Auschwitz, a small, dismal town built around a swamp and a nineteenth-century Austrian cavalry barracks. During the previous spring, the Nazis had erected on that site an especially barbarous concentration camp which they filled with Polish political prisoners, some of whom were put to work to serve the Reich in the nearby I. G. Farben synthetic-rubber and coal-oil plant. After inspecting the camp, Himmler ordered the commandant to expand its dimensions many times over to accommodate a total of 130,000 inmates. Even then, Himmler suspected, the additional space would be filled in no time at all.

8

The Convoy

"Being in a ship is being in a jail, with the chance
of being drowned."
—DR. SAMUEL JOHNSON

On Convoy Duty in the North Atlantic: The main body of the convoy
left from Liverpool; the rest of the ships departed from smaller ports along
the southern and western coasts of England. As they swung into the open
sea they followed the course set by the minesweepers of the Royal Naval
Volunteer Reserve, small trawlers officered by amateur yachtsmen who
strove to maintain a safe path through the shipping channels along the
coast. Then the big ships turned north past the Mull of Galloway, and the
places with magical names out of the olde ballads: the Isle of Islay, Sker-
ryvore and Tiree, Dunvegan and the Butt of Lewis. All along the route
more vessels waited to join the grim parade—"like anticipant girls," a
sailor said, "some of them very old girls." Finally the sea-swept craggy
outlines of Cape Wrath faded from view, and the procession set a northwest course for Iceland.

There were fifty-eight ships in the convoy: most of them excruciat-
ingly slow-moving, eminently vulnerable merchantmen arrayed in eight
columns, along with one passenger vessel which was painted a dull camouflage gray all over, even the funnels. Protection was provided by seven
corvettes of a thousand tons or less, armed only with four-inch guns and
braces of depth charges that looked like glorified trash cans. The corvettes
had a rough time of it, struggling to maintain their positions in the choppy
waters, trying to form a defensive ring around the outer edge of the
phalanx. Ideally, there would have been a half-dozen destroyers (affectionately known as "old tin cans") to escort the convoy, but on this voyage
there was only one, and ancient it was, a veteran of the maritime battles
of the previous generation. For the first few days out of England, the
convoy was also accompanied by a Sunderland seaplane, a cumbersome
craft that looked very much like a flying whale, and was known to sailors
for some obscure reason as a "steam chicken."

The weather in the North Atlantic was violent, as it had been for most
of the winter, the storms raging almost continuously; the sailors said the

wind was strong enough to blow the balls off a bull. The good news was that the same storms made the sea much too rough for the U-boat wolf packs, and rendered visibility too poor for the dreaded Focke-Wulf Condors that swung out in a great arc from the coasts of France and Norway on their search and destroy missions. The bad news was that there were no guarantees that the more dilapidated ships in the convoy would necessarily survive the high seas, either. Unlike the predators beneath the ocean, a convoy did not enjoy the luxury of waiting for better weather. Limited by the merchantmen's inefficient engines, progress was agonizingly slow, the maximum speed six and a half knots. Any straggler that fell behind or got lost in the darkness or a storm was easy prey for the Germans. Gesturing toward the columns of merchant ships (which, all things considered, were doing a remarkably good job of staying in line), the captain of the destroyer said, "We are the shepherds and they are the sheep. And you know how sheep are sometimes. If they get lost, the wolves are on them." A torpedoed ship's chances of survival depended greatly upon the nature of the cargo it was carrying: those with timber belowdecks might survive for a while; those with steel or iron ore in the hold sank like stones; any ship with munitions on board exploded like a shooting star.

On board the passenger vessel, the lifeboats had long since been lowered to the level of the decks, for easy access if an emergency arose. Every morning for the first few days there were lifeboat drills; everyone wore a life jacket (jocularly dubbed Mae Wests) twenty-four hours a day for the entire voyage. The ship pitched and rolled constantly, the action of the seas exacerbated by the sudden evasive changes of course. (The old sailors told the passengers that the only sure cure for seasickness was to find a tree and sit under it.) All the portholes were sealed tight, all the windows on the upper deck boarded up, the rooms overheated and poorly ventilated if at all. At least half of the fifteen hundred passengers were suffering from head colds brought on by walking directly from their stuffy cabins onto the bone-chilling, spray-swept decks.

Security precautions were tight aboard the liner. The name of the ship had been effaced from the menus and the writing paper in the lounges. The purser had confiscated all the passengers' radios, to make sure no inadvertent signals betrayed the ship's position. At night the darkness on deck was absolute; there were double doors and heavy curtains and wooden screens to prevent any light from escaping from the cabins; smoking was forbidden everywhere, and a sign on the bulletin board read, "Passengers are warned that to shine a flashlight on deck at night is suicidal." Just in case, the crew urged the passengers to keep the pockets of their overcoats stuffed with biscuits and chocolate bars, and a bottle of rum if they had one.

January had not been too bad. The vile weather kept the U-boats in their pens at Lorient; Britain lost only seventy-six ships for a total of 320,240 tons that month. But at the end of January, in his speech at the Sportspalast, Hitler had vowed to escalate the attack: "they will notice that we have not been sleeping." And the statistics for February fulfilled the Fuehrer's prophecy—more than 400,000 tons of British shipping were condemned to the bottom of the ocean. "This mortal danger to our life-lines gnawed my bowels," wrote an anguished Churchill. It would only grow worse. As the German High Command realized that the Luftwaffe's indiscriminate attacks upon the enemy's cities would never bring victory, it decided to strike instead at Britain's most vulnerable point: the ports and the seaborne commerce that kept the empire alive and intact. Germany would starve England into submission.

"The decision for 1941 lies upon the seas," Churchill predicted, and if this were true, the odds hardly favored England. British shipping capacity already had plummeted to a dangerously low level, and the Royal Navy—which had suffered serious losses in 1940 at Dunkirk and during an ill-fated expedition in Norway—was forced to extend itself to the limit to protect the communications and supply lines that ran from the Far East to India and Egypt, around the Cape of Good Hope, up to the British Isles, and west across the Atlantic. There was no time to make full repairs when the navy's ships finally reached port, and little prospect of shore leave for the men to repair the psychological damage. "The Germans had the superiority in the air, and were using aircraft against our shipping in the North Sea, the English Channel and the Western approaches," admitted Admiral Cunningham. "In the Atlantic the virulent U-boat war was gradually extending, while enemy surface raiders were operating against our trade in the South Atlantic, the Indian Ocean, and even the Pacific. The public could not be told everything; but the Navy was stretched almost to the breaking point. I doubt if ever in its long history so tremendous a burden had been imposed upon those who manned its ships or directed its world-wide operation."

From mid-February on, Göring's Luftwaffe set its sights upon Britain's shipyards and coastal cities: Portsmouth, Bristol, Hull, Merseyside, Swansea, and Glasgow. Four terrible nights of intensive bombing nearly obliterated Plymouth, blasting into bits the Mayflower stone that marked the spot from which the Pilgrims had sailed to the New World. This vigorous assault on the ports was supplemented by redoubled airborne attacks by the Focke-Wulfs and Heinkels upon British vessels at sea, and surface attacks by the battle cruisers *Scharnhorst* and *Gneisenau*. Buoyed by success, Hitler confidently predicted that Britain would be forced to surrender in two months. "I anticipate the final onslaught with the utmost confidence," the Fuehrer assured a gathering of Nazi Party veterans in Munich. "Wherever the British touch the Continent we will encounter them immediately, and where British ships cruise they will be attacked by our U-boats until a decision comes."

Encrusted by a centuries-old tradition of confident superiority, hidden away in its new operational headquarters fortress in Whitehall (the complex reportedly was built along the lines of an iceberg, with five-sixths of its offices below ground, thus earning it the sarcastic nickname Lenin's Tomb), the British Admiralty was unaware that Germany had broken the British Merchant Ship Code several years earlier, thereby enabling German cryptographers to read the signals that told the U-boats precisely where to find their prey. For a while, the German attacks seemed so well-planned that Churchill suspected that someone within his government was deliberately disclosing secret convoy routes to the enemy. At the end of February, in the early hours of the morning, news came to Downing Street of yet another devastating convoy disaster. Upon hearing the report, Churchill fell silent. "It is very distressing," the Prime Minister's private secretary quietly offered in consolation. "Distressing!" snapped Churchill. "It is terrifying. If it goes on it will be the end of us."

British losses for the week ending March 2 totaled twenty-nine ships with a combined capacity of 148,038 tons. It was the third worst week since the war began. "The strain is growing here," Churchill cabled in desperation to Harry Hopkins. In London, George Orwell noticed that "the feeling of helplessness is growing in everyone. . . . The worst is that the crisis now coming is going to be a crisis of hunger, which the English people have no real experience of. Quite soon it is going to be a question of whether to import arms or food." Aware that a small minority of Englishmen already preferred cheese to Churchill, Orwell wondered how the government would manage to persuade the people "to starve their children in order to build tanks in Africa, when in all that they are told at present there is nothing to make clear that fighting in Africa, or in Europe, has anything to do with the defence of England?" And in the Atlantic, greatly to the benefit of the U-boats, the weather was improving and the seas were getting smoother all the time.

"We must assume that the Battle of the Atlantic has begun," Churchill proclaimed in a terse March 6 directive that signaled the start of the British counteroffensive—at approximately the same time that he and his cabinet made the final decision to proceed with the Greek enterprise. The Prime Minister ordered the R.A.F. to pursue the convoys' enemies whenever and wherever possible: "The U-boat at sea must be hunted, the U-boat in the building yard or in dock must be bombed. The

Focke-Wulf and other bombers employed against our shipping must be attacked in the air and in their nests." Navy vessels were outfitted with catapults to enable them to launch fighter aircraft against German bomber attacks, and—to the dismay of the R.A.F. Bomber Command—seventeen squadrons of British bombers were assigned to Coastal Command to patrol the east coast and the northwestern approaches. (Scorning these patrols as a waste of time, the R.A.F. recommended instead that its bombers would be more profitably employed in raiding German submarine pens and air bases across the Channel and disrupting production in German shipyards and ports, both of which activities eventually were undertaken with a fair measure of success.) Churchill gave the Admiralty first claim on all the short-range antiaircraft guns that could be mounted on merchant ships. Ground defenses surrounding Britain's coastal cities, from the Channel to Clydeside, were strengthened. Within the shipyards, the production of new tonnage that would not be completed until after September 1941 was temporarily postponed to concentrate upon the repair of damaged ships, on the theory that more seaworthy vessels would be available for the short run. And to ensure that these measures were followed through to the utmost, Churchill established a joint civilian-military Battle of the Atlantic Committee, which he chaired, meeting once every week as long as the crisis lasted, thrashing out every issue and leaving no question unresolved.

As Churchill knew, Britain's ultimate salvation lay in America's willingness to adopt a more active role in convoying supplies across the ocean. Throughout the dark hours of the U-boat menace in the winter and spring of 1941, the Prime Minister—in the typically theatrical guise of a Former Naval Person—kept up a steady drumbeat of petitions and exhortations to Roosevelt to extend American patrols ever farther into the western Atlantic, to frighten away the German raiders and relieve the fearsome pressure on the Royal Navy. In the meantime, Britain succeeded in breaking one of the German naval codes, so that each side was secretly reading the other's wireless traffic from the middle of March through the rest of the spring. This, plus refinements in the art of antisubmarine detection technology (known as asdic, a forerunner of sonar), gave the convoys at least a fighting chance, and enabled the navy to sink five U-boats—three of which were commanded by Nazi aces of considerable reknown—during the month of March.

But in that same month, Britain lost 139 more ships. Nicholas Monsarrat, serving as a lieutenant in the Royal Naval Volunteer Reserve, was assigned to duty on one of the corvettes that accompanied the last convoy of March. There was swirling snow in the wind as Monsarrat's ship, the *Campanula*, all 203 feet and 900 tons of her, sailed out of Liverpool. ("By some ludicrous stroke of policy," Monsarrat explained later, "all corvettes

bore the names of gentle and delicate flowers; in *Campanula's* escort
group there were also *Bluebell, Zinnia, Hyacinth, Aubretia, Convolvulus,*
and *Coreopsis.*" The Admiralty discreetly refrained from employing the
name Pansy.)

Through a hard westerly wind the ships—twenty in the Liverpool
portion of the convoy—made their way into the Irish Sea, and then turned
north, picking up another forty-five merchantmen from ports on the west
coast along the way. Somehow, Monsarrat remembered, "in the next six
howling days and nights, with visibility anything from poor to nothing at
all, it still remained a convoy: keeping good station, preserving discipline
and order, turning when it was ordered to turn, showing no lights, making
no betraying smoke." The relentless battering of the raging sea wreaked
havoc belowdecks as armchairs were smashed into kindling against the
bulkheads, and water sloshed through *Campanula's* messdecks. "The food
had gone the same way as the ship; for three days we had been reduced
to a changeless menu, at all meals, of tea, soup, and corned-beef sandwiches. Nothing more ambitious could be made to stay in or on the galley
stove." No U-boat dared venture from its pen in such violent storms, and
so the convoy reached Iceland safely. The *Campanula* then turned south
and met up with an east-bound convoy headed for Liverpool. Shortly
thereafter the horror began.

As the skies cleared and the sea grew calm, the ship's radio received
the first warnings from Liverpool, from the Commander in Chief, Western
Approaches. There were as many as seven U-boats in the surrounding
waters, the Admiralty warned. By now the Germans had nearly perfected
the wolf-pack tactics devised and controlled by Admiral Karl Doenitz,
Fuehrer der U-Boote, a true believer in the Nazi creed and a brilliant,
relentless predator. The key to the admiral's success was the iron-clad
discipline he imposed upon his subordinates. By day his submarine fleet
patrolled the surface of the water along the established convoy tracks;
once a U-boat sighted its prey, it alerted the centralized command post
and Doenitz assumed control, calling in other submarines to join the hunt.
When darkness fell, one or two of the U-boats might lure away the destroyers or the corvette escort by creating a diversion from a safe distance,
thereby opening a gap within the convoy walls through which the remaining submarines could attack. They struck where the convoy was weakest;
this time, said Monsarrat, it started "with an underwater thud reported by
a stunned asdic operator":

> . . . and then a huge sheet of flame, topped by acrid smoke billowing black
> against the stars on the far side of the convoy. It could only be an oil tanker.
> . . . I pressed the alarm-bell for action stations, but already I could hear
> sea-boots, of men in a hurry, men in fear or expectation, drumming and
> echoing along the iron decks. It was not a night for sleeping.

It was the start of a three-day descent into terror, marked by the annihilation of an ammunition ship ("she went up with a great roar, disintegrating from end to end at a single stroke") and two more tankers. To frighten away the Focke-Wulf bomber that had joined the U-boats, a Hurricane fighter was launched via catapult from a freighter; the pilot scoured the sky, found and then lost his quarry, and then ditched the plane and parachuted into the ocean, since there was no other way for him to land. This time, however, he landed too near a small merchant ship, whose propellers snagged the parachute, dragging the pilot slowly and remorselessly through the water to his death.

Monsarrat remembered the third night as the worst. The convoy lost five ships and sank no U-boats in return. Once, by the lurid firelight of a burning ship, Monsarrat could see bobbing upon the ocean "the usual rubbish of disaster: crates, planks, balks of timber, coal-dust, doors, rope-ends, a dead cat, odd bits of clothing, empty life-rafts, and wallowing corpses—all floating in inch-thick stinking oil, all part of the wrecked jumble-sale which was the only souvenir of a wrecked ship." Then he spotted the lifeboats coming toward him, and the dozens of little lights clipped onto life jackets to improve, however slightly, the chances of rescue in the darkness:

> There were the sounds of men thrashing about in desperate terror; shouts of "Don't go away!" shouts of "Help me!" shouts of "Christ!" There were the other sounds, of men dying, cold to the bone but still showing a last hot anguish for life; and the particular throaty gurgle of men swallowing oil instead of air, and trying to cough it up through a scalding gullet, and failing, and giving up life instead.
>
> We did the best we could. . . .
>
> We did the best we could. . . .

The *Campanula* picked up 180 survivors over those three terrible days. Overcrowded, stinking of oil and vomit, filled with the sounds of agony and wounds and dying, the ship resembled "a foretaste of the very marrow of hell. . . . There were men praying, and weeping, and laughing on a cracked note of hysteria, and crooning as they cradled their dead friends; and other men struck dumb, but screaming with their eyes." Among his other duties, Monsarrat acted both as the ship's surgeon for the wounded and as chaplain for the men he could not save, the ones who ended their voyage enshrouded by the cruel sea.

On the fourth day, a pair of Catalina seaplanes, dispatched by Coastal Command, arrived to frighten off the U-boats, and the convoy—with a sad look backward, but with fifty-four merchant ships still afloat, full of food, arms, and all the other supplies that England needed so desperately—

reached the Mersey and Liverpool at last, "coming into harbour like champions."

In Nassau, far away from the agonies of the Atlantic war, the most prosperous, glittering winter tourist season the island had ever known was coming to an end, presided over by the new governor and commander in chief of the Bahamas, the Duke of Windsor and his elegantly charming companion and wife, the former Mrs. Wallis Simpson. "Her smooth dark head looks as if it had come out of a Persian miniature," wrote an admiring visitor. "I think she is the only woman whom the Bahamian winds cannot dishevel." The Duke's repose, however, was shattered by a recurring nightmarish thought that he might be kidnapped by the Germans and held for ransom. But he never was, and life in Nassau rolled on much as before.

9

Franklin and the Lone Ostrich

Late in 1940, Henry Miller purchased a 1932 Buick sedan for $100 in New York City, and after a few unsatisfactory driving lessons the writer headed west to discover America. Henry was a terrible driver. His vision was not good and after a short while he began to suffer from eyestrain and nervous exhaustion. But by the end of March, Miller had managed to navigate his way safely down to New Orleans and back north to Chicago, where he found a worthy subject for his pen in the notoriously sordid underside of the city. "Chicago's South Side," he marveled, "is like a vast, unorganized lunatic asylum. Nothing can flourish here but vice and disease." The rest of the city he discarded as dull and boorish. Throughout his transcontinental journey, Henry sought out the eccentrics of America, the artists and the haunted visionaries, the men driven by dreams. He found very few. "America," he decided, "is no place for an artist: to be an artist is to be a moral leper, an economic misfit, a social liability. A corn-fed hog enjoys a better life than a creative writer, painter, or musician." At last, after more than six months on the road, Miller arrived in the boomtown of Los Angeles, exhausted from his journey, depressed by what he had learned, and in chronic gastric distress from taking most of his meals in cheap dives. Recalling the sights he had witnessed during his wanderings, words like "hideous," "morbid," "suffocating," and "appalling" rolled through his mind like a litany for the dead; America in 1941, he concluded, was nothing more than an "air-conditioned nightmare."

Paul von Hernreid enjoyed a more pleasant journey that spring. After receiving a movie contract from RKO Studios, the Austrian-born actor and his wife left New York and drove across America in a new Chrysler convertible equipped with fluid drive. The trip was "the most memorable experience of our lives," he recalled. "The scenery, particularly in the West, was breathtaking. There was a quality of grandeur that equaled the Alps, though in a different way. The people were generous and friendly, and since we were crossing in the early spring, the weather was rare and fresh and the air fragrant." No doubt he took a different route than Miller.

The only fly in Hernreid's ointment was the food: "It was uniformly horrible. The only gastronomic pleasure between the two coasts was the baked potato, something new to both of us. Done properly, and it was the one food that was always done properly, it was delectable, and we lived for it during the entire trip." When the couple arrived in Hollywood, the studio changed Paul's last name; Teutonic names on the marquee were not calculated to attract patrons to America's movie theaters in 1941, and so Paul von Hernreid became simply Paul Henreid. (One year later, he made his major breakthrough in American films, in the role of intrepid anti-Nazi underground leader Victor Laszlo in *Casablanca*.)

For Béla Bartók, the process of Americanization was far more difficult and more complicated than a simple change of name. The sixty-year-old Hungarian composer had come to America at the end of October 1940 (unfortunately, his luggage did not arrive until three months later) after obtaining a temporary appointment to the faculty of Columbia University, where he embarked upon the mammoth task of cataloging and transcribing an extensive recorded collection of the Balkan folk songs that were so dear to his heart; but Bartók's transition to twentieth-century urban American society was far from smooth. In fact, he was so preoccupied with his personal and financial difficulties that his creative impulses appear to have vanished for nearly three years; between December 1940 and October 1943, Bartók completed no major (or even minor) compositions. The fact that he had to cope with the bewildering tribulations of life in and around New York City did not make the process any easier for him. To his sons, who remained behind temporarily in Budapest, Béla confessed that "my head is bursting with new words of every kind: the names of subway stations and of streets; subway maps, scores of possibilities for changing from one line to another—all absolutely necessary for living here, but otherwise futile." Occasionally Bartók found himself completely overwhelmed; "for instance, the last time we wanted to go to the southernmost part of New York. I did not know exactly where to change (the sign-posts are not exactly conspicuous enough, rather too few, and confusing), so that we travelled for 3 hours to and fro on the subway. At last, simply because we had no more time, we went home again, rather sheepishly and without having done what we set out to do—underground all the way back, of course." Even after several months in America, Bartók complained that he had been thoroughly unable to get used to such American idiosyncrasies as "human beings ruminating like cows (every second person is chewing gum); railway carriages in semi-darkness; [and] the cheque-book system," and he and his wife finally had to move from their apartment in Forest Hills just to preserve their sanity: "We were piano-played and radio-blasted from right to left; a lot of noise came in from the street night and day; every 5 minutes we heard the rumble of the subway which made the very walls shake." So when he was offered the opportunity to make a four-week cross-country concert tour of the United States in March, Bartok leaped at the chance.

There was a fourth noteworthy transcontinental traveler in the spring of 1941, a tall, balding, slightly stoop-shouldered Frenchman with huge hands and feet: Antoine de St-Exupéry, the pioneer aviator and author who had fled the shattered Old World for America, arriving in New York with film director Jean Renoir on an ocean liner from Lisbon on the last day of 1940. As France collapsed in agony during that frantic June of 1940, St-Exupéry had commandeered a plane in Bordeaux and escorted forty young French military pilots across the Mediterranean, in hopes of continuing the battle from North Africa. Following the armistice, he spurned Pétain's offer of a position on the National Council of Vichy France, but neither would he join de Gaulle's Free French; he knew that he could never fight against other Frenchmen, collaborators or not. St-Exupéry's translator in America, Lewis Galantiere, confessed that he had "never known a man so little made for neutrality, for emigration, for exile," but for the winter months of 1941, St-Exupéry had no choice but to spend the dark bitter days brooding in New York, brokenhearted over the fate of his beloved France and a world held hostage . . . sitting in his room, passing the time by doing card tricks to amuse his friends . . . and longing to return to the battle. He permitted no one to speak to him about the war.

In the springtime, St-Exupéry moved to the West Coast to join Renoir in Hollywood. Ill and sad, the man who had taught the world many wonderful things now issued a challenge to test the humanity of the American people. "You who are the voice of an enormously powerful country protected by the oceans, powerful in its navy, army, and fighting men, you who have nothing to fear, should it really be your role to tell your countrymen to wash their hands of any involvement, like Pontius Pilate?" St-Exupéry demanded. "This war does not directly threaten your survival, but it concerns you nevertheless. . . . Even if you inhabit another continent, you nevertheless inhabit the same planet and are heirs to a civilization where men show solidarity."

As the world slid dazedly toward hell, as men drowned in the North Atlantic and Jews starved in the ghettos of Poland and refugees froze in the camps of Vichy France, as Churchill pleaded desperately for American aid and the Wehrmacht prepared to bludgeon Greece into submission, Americans struggled to find an answer to the questions that racked their conscience. "We seem to be in the midst of an era of delirious ferocity, with half of mankind hell bent upon exterminating the other half," wrote H. L. Mencken, and there were still millions of Americans (including Mencken) who were hell bent upon keeping the nation out of the conflict overseas. Was there a meaning behind the struggle, or was the war simply "more waste, more useless waste of lives," as Anne Morrow Lindbergh believed? How many of her fellow countrymen entertained, like her, "a profound compassion for the suffering but not a conviction of the black and white—the complete wrongness or rightness of either side"? "I feel about America," Anne wrote in her diary, "that what is important is not ultimately whether or not we get into this war or whether or not we can avoid suffering (I do not believe we can). But that we pass through our fire still keeping humility and compassion. At the moment we are not headed that way."

Indeed America was not. Compassion was in short supply when grinning women brought miniature coffins to America First rallies and hung signs on them that said BUNDLES FROM BRITAIN, and compassion was quickly disappearing when the female shock troops of the Paul Revere Sentinels and the Women's Neutrality League paraded in front of the British Embassy in Washington, where they hung a grotesque effigy of President Roosevelt upon the gate with placards that read MOVE OVER, UNKNOWN SOLDIER, and BENEDICT ARNOLD HELPED ENGLAND, TOO. Compassion had nearly vanished when Henry Ford could propose that the United States supply both Britain and Germany with "the tools to keep on fighting until they both collapse." "There is no righteousness in either cause," Ford snarled. "If we can keep both sides fighting long enough, until they cannot fight anymore, then maybe the little people will open their eyes. . . . When both nations finally collapse into internal dissolution, then the United States can play the role for which it has the strength and the ability." Ford did not disclose how many millions of men, women, and children would have to perish before America stepped in to pick up the pieces of a shattered civilization.

At a convocation of the American Youth Congress in February in Washington, D.C., three young left-wing balladeers who later became known collectively as the Almanac Singers—Pete Seeger, Lee Hays, and Millard Lampell—sang together for the first time in public. Heavily influenced by the Depression-era social consciousness of Woody Guthrie, their repertoire consisted primarily of antiwar and anti-Roosevelt material, such as "The Ballad of October 16," commemorating the day in 1940 when Congress approved the draft:

> Oh Franklin Roosevelt told the people how he felt,
> We damn near believed what he said.
> He said, "I hate war and so does Eleanor but
> We won't be safe till everybody's dead."

(After listening to the Almanacs' first album, *Songs for John Doe,* released later in 1941, Eleanor Roosevelt decided that their urban-style folk songs were clever, "but in poor taste.")

Of course, those who opposed the isolationists could be equally bitter, underhanded, and unforgiving. America First headquarters regularly received letters suggesting that its members should be put in concentration camps or kicked out of the country and sent back to Berlin where they belonged. "You Maggots from the Slums of Genoa and Berlin," read one particularly colorful message, "you half Baked *imitation of Americans,* Go wiggle back into the manure of your old world ideas. Hang your Swastika Banner around your Neck, and butt your brainless heads against the Bulwork [*sic*] of American ideals which you pretend to support." News commentator and gossip hound Walter Winchell regularly treated his radio audience to violent denunciations of the America First leaders, whom he called "Ratzis"; he described their followers as "members of the German-American Bund and various other groups which sympathize with or admire Hitler and Mussolini."

Roosevelt himself reportedly ordered wiretaps on his isolationist opponents and encouraged the FBI to investigate their activities. (Although he allegedly was aware of what the President was doing, Winchell refused to reveal the extent of these shady surveillance activities; "you don't shoot the soldiers who are fighting on your side," he explained.) Charles Lindbergh and his family were subjected to an almost constant stream of vituperative personal abuse and ridicule from the media and the interventionists. During a press conference, Roosevelt compared Lindbergh (unfavorably) with notorious Civil War Copperhead Clement L. Vallandigham, Winchell referred to him as "the Lone Ostrich," and Ickes called him a Nazi fellow traveler. "He stalks through our friendly American living room with clouded brow, his eyes drawn painfully together, a darkling child at our feast," wrote Washington columnist Sam Grafton. "A glowering boy, history's sulken tot, a corn-fed Spengler now embarked on his longest non-stop flight." In *The New Yorker,* a facetious poet wrote, "Lindbergh, for you I am no rooter, you sulky knight in shining pewter."

Capitol Hill became the scene of some remarkable antiwar dramatics. During House debate on the Lend-Lease bill on the afternoon of February 5, an attractive young woman arose in the visitors' gallery. Garbed in a long black cape and a black hood pulled high over her flowing black hair, wearing a death's-head mask and long white gloves, she walked down to the railing, peered down at the congressmen on the floor below, raised her trembling hands, gave a hollow croaking laugh, and began to chant, "Victory is death!" As her fellow spectators sat stunned, shouts came from the House floor, "Arrest her! Put her out!" Carried off by Capitol policemen, the lissome apparition gave her name as "Andra the Flame"; actually, she was a Vassar undergraduate named Margaret Russell, who appeared to have become temporarily unglued after watching the House debate for the past three days. Police officials questioned and then released her, placing her firmly on board a train for New York City.

Three days later, voting largely along party lines (Washington was still far more conscious of politics than the war), the House of Representatives passed H.R. 1776 by a margin of 260–165. Now it headed for the more querulous Senate, where Wheeler and his isolationist clique planned an all-out, last-ditch effort to stop the President. The struggle had become a personal vendetta for the Montana senator. Returning with renewed determination (and additional scurrilous antiadministration accusations) from a vacation in Florida with Joe Kennedy, Wheeler proclaimed that the United States was being driven toward war by a cabal of Jewish international bankers—the Rothschilds, Warburgs, and Sassoons; he charged that the U.S. Army already had bought a million and a half caskets for its boys. The marginally more rational Republican Senator Arthur Vandenberg claimed that the Lend-Lease legislation would make Roosevelt "the Ace Power Politician of The World," turning the White House "into G.H.Q. for all the wars of all the world," and he bitterly castigated the administration's not-so-subtle arm-twisting campaign "to drive its votes in the Senate into a goose-step—backed by a nation-wide emotion and a nation-wide propaganda of amazing proportions." North Carolina's backwoods spokesman, Senator Robert "Roarin' Bob" Reynolds, proposed sarcastically that the Lend-Lease bill should more accurately be entitled "A Bill for the Defense of the British Empire at the Expense of the Lives of American Men and at the Expense of the American Taxpayer, and for the Preservation of the British Empire Without Any Consideration for the Preservation of the United States."

No one, though, outdid the florid, bitter oratory of silver-haired Pat McCarran of Nevada, whose melodramatic rhetoric on previous occasions had earned him the derisive sobriquet of "Old Bleeding Heart." "My country is about to approach the cross at the end of its rosary," McCarran cried in anguish on the Senate floor. "I see on that cross not the old man, not the man who has chin whiskers, with stripes on his trousers . . . I see through him a young man just pausing on the threshold of his life. I see through him, gibbeted there, a red-blooded youth, the youth of my country, the blood of my nation, the blood of civilization. I look through the old man, Uncle Sam, outstretched upon the gibbet, and I see his son not given an opportunity to be crucified but only given an opportunity to be murdered in mass formation. I see my country going down into a holocaust of hell where others have been bleeding for centuries. . . ."

From his luxury suite at the Waldorf Towers, where a smartly trained band of security men protected the wealthy tenants from unwanted intrusions, Herbert Hoover used all his waning political influence to kill or cripple the Lend-Lease bill. He tried to persuade Thomas Dewey to undertake a cross-country tour to arouse opposition to the measure, but Dewey, seeing which way the wind was blowing, refused to get caught out on a limb with the isolationists and recanted his previous opposition to Lend-Lease. Nevertheless, Hoover persisted. "The American people have been so fooled as to the purpose and character of this bill," he proclaimed in a rare public statement, "that there remains no hope of adequately

amending it. It is a war bill, and yet 95% of the people think it is only aid
to Britain."

On February 5, at precisely the time that Andra the Flame was inton-
ing her incantation in the House, Charles Lindbergh appeared before the
Senate Foreign Relations Committee, which was holding its hearings in
the vast Senate caucus room, where the lights were dim and the stale air
smelled like it had not been changed since the days of Roscoe Conkling.
Once again, the famous aviator received an enthusiastic greeting from the
audience, composed mostly of stylishly dressed middle-aged women; in
fact, their applause and vocal encouragement of their hero finally forced
committee chairman Walter George of Georgia to threaten to clear the
room of spectators. In his prepared statement to the senators, Lindbergh
repeated his assertion that all-out aid to Britain might so deplete American
resources that the nation would soon be vulnerable to invasion. "I do not
believe that it is either possible or desirable for us in America to control
the outcome of European wars," he told them. "An English victory, if it
were possible at all, would necessitate years of war and an invasion of the
continent of Europe. I believe this would create prostration, famine and
disease in Europe—and probably in America—such as the whole world has
never experienced before. This is why I say I prefer a negotiated peace
to a complete victory by either side." Then, his testimony completed,
Lindbergh relaxed by taking a long walk alone, down Pennsylvania Avenue, along the mall and past the ruins of the dingy old Department of
Agriculture buildings that recently had been torn down, pausing to stare
in silent admiration at the gleaming white columns of the brand-new
National Gallery of Art, home of the $50 million collection donated by
former Treasury Secretary Andrew W. Mellon. (Constructed at a cost of
$15 million, housing nearly five acres of rooms filled with art treasures of
the past, the National Gallery reportedly was the largest marble building
in the world.)

While the Senate debated H.R. 1776, Roosevelt himself maintained a
low profile, in an attempt to prevent partisan or personal political quarrels
from diverting attention from the issues involved. He chose to disarm the
bill's critics by soliciting testimony from hand-picked spokesmen from
outside the administration: Republicans Wendell Willkie and Fiorello La
Guardia, and Harvard University President James B. Conant. Conant, a
chemist of international reputation whom Roosevelt was sending to England to establish a formal conduit for the exchange of scientific information (including preliminary research on the feasibility of atomic weapons),
placed squarely before the committee the moral issue posed by the Nazi
threat. Unlike the isolationists, who perversely failed to acknowledge anything extraordinary in the barbarous behavior of the Nazi regime, Conant
believed that the war in Europe resembled a religious war far more than
a conventional war for territorial possessions; Germany, he charged, was

engaged in an all-out crusade to spread "the revolutionary anti-Christian philosophy which is the basis of the Nazi strength."

Conant was followed to the witness table by Willkie, who had just returned from a tour of England, where he had huddled with working-class Britons in bomb shelters, inspected aircraft factories and the Channel batteries at Dover, and conferred with Churchill on the prospects for Anglo-American cooperation. On February 11, lounging carelessly in his chair, wearing a wrinkled suit that looked as if it had been slept in during the Atlantic crossing, Willkie seemed a bit out of place among the room's ornate rococo decorations and stately marble columns. (At least Wendell was not wearing his famous blue tie with the white stripes that spelled out his name.) But if his rumpled figure was something less than statesmanlike, Willkie's willingness to forgo partisanship by openly and responsibly supporting the President's Lend-Lease proposal had earned him new admirers since the election campaign ended, and the audience—twelve hundred people crammed into a room designed to accommodate fewer than half that many—applauded his performance as he deftly turned aside the barbed questions with which the Republican members of the committee sought to damage him.

"Britain needs more destroyers," Willkie told the senators. "She needs them desperately. The powers asked for are extraordinary. But in my judgment, this is an extraordinary situation." He repeated what Churchill had told him, that Britain wanted America to provide weapons and ships, and *not* soldiers. (At the time, this was probably true. It would have taken so long to train and equip an American army for overseas duty that Britain might well have perished in the interval.) Senator Bennett Champ Clark of Missouri, one of the most irreconcilable isolationists, remained unconvinced. "Suppose the Germans got our bombers and used them against us?" he snapped. "If all the hazards of war go against us," Willkie replied candidly, "we will get whipped." To discredit Willkie's testimony, the Republican members of the committee repeatedly quoted his recent (and unsuccessful) campaign speeches in which he had accused Roosevelt of deliberately attempting to maneuver the United States into war. Senator Gerald Nye of North Dakota quoted one particularly relevant passage from a Willkie statement: "On the basis of his [Roosevelt's] past performance with pledges to the people, you may expect we will be at war by April 1941, if he is elected."

"Do you still agree," Nye asked, "that that might be the case?"

"It might be," answered Willkie with a grin. "It was a bit of campaign oratory."

On the day following Willkie's testimony, the Senate Foreign Relations Committee approved the Lend-Lease bill, 15–8, as six of the seven Republicans on the committee voted against the measure. The margin reflected the prevailing sentiment in the rest of the chamber, and the bill's victory seemed assured despite the antics of The Mothers' Crusade to Kill Bill 1776, an isolationist group whose members paraded in front of the White House carrying banners that read KILL BILL 1776, NOT OUR BOYS and staged a sit-down strike in the corridors of the Senate Office Building. ("It would be pertinent to inquire whether they are mothers," suggested Virginia's elderly Senator Carter Glass tartly. "For the sake of the race, I devoutly hope not.") The isolationists tried to talk the measure to death in the Senate—Nye alone raged against the bill for twelve hours—but the administration wisely let them wear themselves out, and in the end, the bill's opponents were able only to weaken it slightly through amendments that permitted Congress to retain tight control of Lend-Lease appropriations. At 7:10 P.M. on Saturday, March 8, the Senate passed House Resolution 1776 by a vote of 60 to 31. "I had the feeling, as the result of the ballot was announced, that I was witnessing the suicide of the Republic," mourned Vandenberg in his diary. "If America cracks up, you can put your finger on this precise moment as the time when the crime was committed."

Three days later, the House of Representatives approved the Senate's amendments to the bill and dispatched it by special messenger to the White House, where Roosevelt, still weak and tired from a bout with influenza, signed it less than ten minutes after it arrived. Five minutes later, the President officially approved a long list of "surplus" defense materials—including bombers, artillery, machine guns, and ammunition—totaling slightly over $1 billion which was now eligible to be transferred from army and navy stockpiles for immediate shipment to Britain or Greece. Roosevelt then announced that he was sending a request to Capitol Hill for authority to ship another $7 billion worth of armaments and supplies abroad.

While Roosevelt was posing, pen in hand, for the newspaper photographers, Wheeler and his colleagues were laying their plans for a cross-country campaign to "arouse the nation to the imminence of war and high taxes." "Now that the bill has passed," warned Wheeler, "there will be a determined effort by the warmongers to get us into the war."

In London, David Lloyd George, the combative old Welsh Liberal who had guided the British Empire to victory in the First World War, exulted over the final approval of Lend-Lease. "This is a big victory for us!" the former prime minister told Soviet Ambassador Maisky. "Now all the financial difficulties and worries involved in carrying on the war have been solved for us. . . . Winston can now concentrate his attention entirely on the purely military side." Churchill received the news with a sigh of relief—"The stuff was coming"—and publicly hailed the bill's passage as "a second Magna Carta."

South Africa's Prime Minister Jan Christian Smuts, who had worked closely with Woodrow Wilson to create the League of Nations at the end of the First World War, said simply, "Hitler has at last brought America into the war."

German thoughts were darker. "If the war ends this year," predicted Joseph Goebbels, "then the damage will not be too great. If it goes on into next year, then naturally the situation will be somewhat more serious."

Now Roosevelt could throw off the self-imposed constraints that had kept him silent for the past two months. At the annual White House Correspondents' Association dinner on March 15, he unleashed a blistering attack upon the rulers of Nazi Germany. First, of course, the cheerfully inebriated reporters performed their irreverent musical numbers and satirical skits aimed in no small measure at the President himself; among the appreciative audience this year were numerous American military officers, all dressed in civilian clothes. A few moments before Roosevelt was scheduled to speak, the official German news agency's representative—who had already read the press release that contained the text of the President's prepared comments—slipped quietly out of the room.

As usual, all three major radio networks sent Roosevelt's speech live to homes across America, but on this occasion, short-wave transmitters were also broadcasting simultaneous translations in French, Italian, German, Greek, Turkish, Norwegian, Dutch, Spanish, Serbian, Albanian, and Czech, among others. In Washington, the face at the speaker's stand was grave; Ickes watched the President that evening and realized that he was "an exceedingly tired man." The words that the world heard sounded ominously like a call to war, a plea for solidarity in a struggle against evil.

"Tonight I am appealing to the heart and to the mind of every man and every woman within our borders who loves liberty," Roosevelt began. "I ask you to consider the needs of our nation at this hour and to put aside all personal differences until the victory is won." No longer could the United States afford the easy life and leisurely methods of a nation at peace. Now America must dedicate itself to producing more armaments than ever before, to supplying ever-increasing amounts of aid to the embattled democracies of the world "until total victory has been won."

The President continued: "We know that although Prussian autocracy was bad enough in the first war, Nazism is far worse in this. Nazi forces . . . openly seek the destruction of all elective systems of government . . . including our own; they seek to establish systems of government based on the regimentation of all human beings by a handful of individual rulers who have seized power by force. Yet these men and their hypnotized followers call this a new order. It is not new and it is not order."

("A blustering, shameless speech," growled Goebbels. "A lackey of the Jews!")

Roosevelt conceded that the road ahead would be difficult, particularly for a nation just emerging from a decade of depression and deprivation. "Whether you are in the armed services; whether you are a steel worker or a stevedore, a machinist or a housewife; a farmer or a banker; a storekeeper or a manufacturer—to all of you it will mean sacrifices in behalf of your country and your liberties. . . ." There would be longer hours, higher taxes, and lower profits, the President warned, and the country would tolerate no war profiteering, no deliberate sabotage of the defense effort, and no unnecessary strikes.

The reporters in the room applauded heartily. For some in the audience, Roosevelt's call to duty recalled the President's prophetic speech in Philadelphia five years earlier, when he had publicly affirmed his conviction that America had a rendezvous with destiny. Now the time had come—the nation's destiny awaited.

"The British people and their Grecian allies need ships. From America, they will get ships. They need planes. From America they will get planes. Yes, from America they need food. . . . They will get food. . . . A halfhearted effort on our part will lead to failure. This is no part-time job. The concepts of 'business as usual,' of 'normalcy,' must be forgotten until the task is finished. Yes, it's an all-out effort and nothing short of an all-out effort will win." And as the clock ticked away the last few moments of freedom, and democracy was snuffed out in one nation after another in Europe and in Asia, Roosevelt called for "speed, and speed now," before it was too late. "We believe that the rallying cry of the dictators, their boasting about a master-race, will prove to be pure stuff and nonsense. There never has been, there isn't now, and there never will be, any race of people on the earth fit to serve as masters of their fellow men. . . .

"Never, in all our history . . . have Americans faced a task so well worthwhile. May it be said of us in the days to come that our children and our children's children rise up and call us blessed."

Even the audience of veteran correspondents, hardened by years of exposure to every species of overblown oratory and rhetorical device that Washington had to offer, heard the President's words and felt something stir inside. They understood that there could be no turning back now. "Everyone who was in the room when Mr. Roosevelt spoke must have heard the leaf of history turning," thought newspaper columnist Raymond Clapper. "Twenty years of isolationism gone. We sought a life as in *Lost Horizon,* where we could shut out the ugly world, but we found we could not stay there. We have come out again."

Over the next several days, the British Broadcasting Company's short-wave operators repeated Roosevelt's broadcast—in thirty-four languages—for anyone who might have missed it the first time around. In Tokyo, the *Japan Times,* the official newspaper of the Foreign Office, responded with a warning that Roosevelt's message represented a virtual declaration of world war. Another popular Japanese journal sarcastically dismissed the United States as a "huge, wealthy, inflated dragon . . . headed straight for war in name as well as in substance."

In Rome, a spokesman for the Fascist government accused Roosevelt of "tyranny, aggression and immeasurable ignorance of history and elementary European conditions," and the Italian press denounced the President as "Franklin Barnum Roosevelt," a charlatan whose "words, gestures, [and] public pronouncements have reached all the heights of democratic buffoonery; the speech was a new intemperate manifestation of the biggest Barnum that America ever had."

But it was the reaction in Berlin that mattered most. Hitler had recently given Goebbels permission to attack the United States openly in the German press, and now the Nazi propaganda chief ripped mercilessly into Roosevelt on the radio and in the newspapers, charging him with warmongering in conspiracy with degenerate Jewish interests. "There is no point in holding back any longer," Goebbels explained. "It only makes the Americans more insolent." The official Nazi Party journal, the *Voelkischer Beobachter,* ran a huge double banner headline: BLOOD GUILT OF JEWISH ANGLO-SAXON CAPITALISM; AMERICAN PAPERS UNMASK ROOSEVELT. Other articles in the Nazi press castigated Roosevelt as a "well-poisoner," "the hangman of young nations," and a "wolf in sheep's clothing." Göring's newspaper, the *Essener National Zeitung,* boasted that Germany, Japan, and Italy would react by drawing closer to thwart the American threat, "and fight back in such a way that it will soon be seen who is resorting to empty threats and gigantic bluffs and who, in reality, can defend himself with available means against objectionable interventionists." Hitler himself replied to Roosevelt during a ceremony honoring the German war dead of 1914–18. "No power and no support coming from any part of the world can change the outcome of this battle in any respect," the Fuehrer confidently assured his listeners. "England will fall . . . International finance and plutocracy wants to fight this war to the finish. So the end of this war will, and must be, its destruction."

In the early spring of 1941, relations between Germany and the United States seemed to be deteriorating every day. When the German consulate in San Francisco unfurled a huge four-by-eight-foot swastika flag from its ninth-story offices to commemorate the seventieth anniversary of the founding of the Second Reich, a crowd of two thousand people gathered in the avenue below to jeer at the Nazi symbol. The manager of a department store across the street dug into his storeroom and hung out an even bigger American flag. Then a pair of irate sailors climbed up the fire escape, past the consulate, to the tenth floor and entered the empty office above the German flag; one of the sailors then let himself down from a window, sat astride the flagpole, and started slashing at the halyard with a penknife. Some of the consulate staff tried to pull the flag back in, but during the ensuing tug-of-war with the sailor the Nazi banner ripped in half. "I couldn't let that flag stay up there," the sailor explained to reporters. "It was up to someone to get it down, so I just went up there." Since the diplomatic offices were, by international law, sovereign German territory, Washington was forced to issue a formal apology to Berlin over the incident. But the knife-wielding sailor became a popular American hero overnight, despite the revelation that he and his partner had just been released from the psychopathic ward of a West Coast naval hospital.

Alarmed by reports of Nazi spies and fifth columnists infiltrating America, the FBI and the nation's press whipped up so much public hysteria that three hundred complaints of alleged un-American activity poured into federal law enforcement offices every day. Then, just before Roosevelt's March 15 get-tough speech, the Justice Department arrested two "correspondents" of the Nazi-controlled Transocean News Service, on charges of violating the Foreign Agents Registration Act by dispensing propaganda without a license. In retaliation, the Gestapo arrested Richard C. Hottelet, who had been working in Berlin as a reporter for the United Press since 1938, and imprisoned him "on suspicion of espionage for an enemy power." (Hottelet apparently was singled out among American correspondents because of his well-known openly anti-Nazi sentiments.) Hottelet remained in an unsanitary cell in Moabit prison for four months, subsisting on a diet of dry black bread, ersatz coffee, and a bowl of soup once a day. He was, however, permitted to purchase a daily newspaper, and the guards brought him two books each week. "But the selection was not always happy," Hottelet complained after returning to the United States late that summer. "One I received was *The Fuel Problem of Canada.* Another was a volume of British verse for young women published in 1867." After interrogating and then releasing other Western correspondents, Goebbels also imposed tighter censorship restrictions on American radio broadcasts from Berlin. "The USA," he vowed, "will have to be shown that our patience and forbearance are now exhausted."

On another front, Roosevelt's patience, too, was fast becoming exhausted with what Walter Lippmann termed the "resistance, reluctance, and inertia" within both the business and labor communities to an all-out national defense production effort. A casual visitor wandering through the endless maze of dingy corridors in the antiquated War Department offices in Washington might have been excused for believing that the frenzied bustle of activity—the litter of contract drafts and duplicate purchase orders cluttering the hallways, harried businessmen scurrying from one crowded office to another, admirals in civilian dress (it was considered bad form to wear a military uniform in Washington except on ceremonial occasions) earnestly discussing input quotas and vessel tonnage and cadet training enrollment—was proof that the United States was rapidly approaching the status of a first-rate military power.

It was not. In fact, American production of aircraft still was less than one-third of Germany's (even discounting the additional output of the recently occupied Balkan countries). The administration's ambitious

$9 million shipbuilding program was hindered by industrial bottlenecks, largely attributable to a scarcity of skilled labor and management expertise and growing shortages in vital materials such as aluminum and steel. In the absence of sufficient satisfactory shipyard production facilities, the U.S. would have to choose between building merchant ships for Britain or modern warships for its own navy; it could not do both simultaneously.

In a speech to the Overseas Press Club in Manhattan during the first week of March, William Bullitt, who, as U.S. ambassador to France when the blitzkrieg struck, had witnessed at close range the deadly efficiency of the Nazi miltary juggernaut, castigated the stumbling American defense effort. "We know that our country is not producing weapons of defense fast enough and that we are not supplying weapons in sufficient quantities to the British, the Chinese, and the Greeks," Bullitt charged. "If we were fully awake to the danger that threatens us, we should at this hour be producing every implement of defense that we need . . . that the British, the Chinese, and the Greeks need, with as great speed as though we were in war. We are doing nothing of the kind. We are making just the effort that it is not troublesome to make. We could double our planned output of airplanes and tanks and merchant ships and guns in 1942 if we would but buckle to the task now."

Emboldened by organized labor's enhanced bargaining position as an essential partner in the national crusade to boost defense output, some union officials chose this moment to force a showdown with management over long-festering wage and jurisdictional disputes. The result was a rash of disruptive strikes that threatened to undermine the President's "speed—and speed now" program at numerous vital points. By the end of February, there were sixteen major industrial strikes in progress, involving 23,000 workers, holding up the production of more than $60 million worth of defense materials. Walkouts closed the Motor Wheel Corporation's plant in Lansing, Michigan, the Bethlehem Steel plant in Lackawanna, four International Harvester factories, and the Ryan Aviation plant in New York. There were slowdowns and strikes in shipyards in Philadelphia and on the Gulf Coast. The largest and most damaging dispute pitted the United Automobile Workers (which, some critics alleged, harbored a number of Communists in its ranks) against the Allis-Chalmers Manufacturing Company, whose president was a staunch supporter of the isolationist America First organization; in two months, the strike cost the nation more than 1.5 million work hours and tied up the production of turbogenerators and engine parts essential to navy destroyers and ammunition plants. "Some friends of labor in the Administration are very deeply troubled," reported Ray Clapper in exasperation. "They are troubled, and I think with good reason indeed, over the fact that labor is working itself into a role of irresponsible obstruction to war production."

Already Congress was considering several bills to prohibit strikes in defense industries.

Not all the fault lay with labor, however. There were still plenty of businessmen who refused to accept the presence of independent unions in their industries, and who stubbornly chose to disregard the legal requirement (spelled out in the Wagner Act and affirmed by the Supreme Court) to engage in good-faith collective bargaining with the duly elected representatives of organized labor. Bethlehem Steel Corporation, for instance, remained implacably opposed to bargaining with independent unions, and continued to promote employee membership in subservient company unions even after the National Labor Relations Board explicitly ordered it to desist. Even more counterproductive was the Neanderthal attitude of Henry Ford's top lieutenant and designated thug, Harry Bennett. "If the NLRB orders an election, of course we will hold one, because Mr. Ford will observe the law," growled Bennett. "C.I.O. will win it, of course, because it always wins these farcical elections, and we will bargain with it because the law says so. We will bargain until Hell freezes over, but they won't get anything."

Ford himself had long ago decided that "labor-union organizers are the worst thing that ever struck the earth." For a long time Ford had been able to resist encroachments by the United Auto Workers upon his dictatorial control over the company, partly because he paid his employees top dollar, but primarily because Bennett and his goons brutally beat organizers who tried to unionize Ford plants. Four jobless marchers had been shot and killed by Bennett's men during a demonstration in 1932 at River Rouge, and Walter Reuther was among the union men who suffered severe beatings outside Ford's gates several years later. By 1941, though, General Motors and Chrysler (both of which had accepted the UAW as spokesman for their workers) paid better wages than Ford, and the courts had upheld an NLRB ruling that Ford had violated the Wagner Act. The Roosevelt administration was not going to stand idly by and allow Ford to provoke a prolonged strike while his company held millions of dollars' worth of defense contracts to produce airplane engines and Army reconnaissance cars known as Blitz Buggies.

From his 85,000-acre plantation in Ways, Georgia, where he passed the time tending his sweet potatoes, his cane fields, and his 100-acre lettuce patch, the crusty seventy-seven-year-old Ford insisted that Communists were instigating the current round of strikes. ("It would be surprising if the Communists were not in it," mused one veteran observer of the labor scene. "Ford has been one of their best assets in stirring up discontent among American workers.") Henry, his wife, and his son, Edsel, owned the Ford Company outright, which made them the richest family in America. (Ford's U.S. branch alone was valued at nearly $625 million.)

Henry had always been much more comfortable communing with nature or tinkering with machines than dealing with his fellow human beings. His anti-Semitic beliefs were well-known in America and Europe and had earned him the profound respect of the Third Reich, but some of his other utterances were equally unconventional: "To say it plainly, the great majority of women who work do so in order to buy fancy clothes. . . . Salt is one of the best things for the teeth. And also for the hair. . . . Reading can become a dope habit. . . . If you will study the history of almost any criminal, you will find he is an inveterate cigaret smoker. . . . Most of the ailments of people come from eating too much."

As Ford attempted to delay any serious bargaining with the UAW, as Allis-Chalmers refused to accept an arbitrator's proposed settlement and labor organizers struck one defense plant after another, critics wondered what the hell Washington was waiting for. Where was the big, strong government that was supposed to assert the national will and make it effective above the selfish interests of management and labor groups alike? Much to Roosevelt's embarrassment, his administration had not yet discovered how to enforce discipline in its own defense program; the Office of Production Management, established early in 1941 to ride herd over the mobilization effort, suffered from the sort of indecision one might expect from a creature with two heads—one drawn from management (William S. Knudsen of General Motors) and one from labor (Sidney Hillman, head of the Amalgamated Clothing Workers Union)—while the members of the much-ballyhooed Defense Mediation Board seemed to spend most of their time having their pictures taken for the newspapers and deciding not to get involved in labor disputes. And when the government did intervene, its recommendations often were flouted with impunity by one side or the other. So Roosevelt did precisely what he had always done when faced with intractable economic problems in the early years of the New Deal: he set up yet another agency to study the situation. This time the new kid on the alphabet block was known as the PPB, the Production Planning Board, headed by Samuel R. Fuller, president of the North American Rayon Corporation. (Veteran New Dealers in Washington were beginning to grow a bit uneasy at Roosevelt's newfound fondness for employing millionaire business executives to oversee the defense production effort.) Assisted by a nine-man board that included the ubiquitous Harry Hopkins and AFL treasurer-secretary George Meany, Fuller's assignment was to assume a long-range view of the defense effort, to foresee bottlenecks and shortages down the road and advise the administration on ways to avoid such pitfalls.

As if Roosevelt did not already have enough trouble, whispers soon reached Capitol Hill of widespread corruption in the defense procurement and camp construction programs. In January 1941, Harry S Truman (recently elected to his first full term in the Senate) received a flood of letters from irate constituents who claimed to have witnessed appalling waste and malfeasance in the army's hasty expansion of Fort Leonard Wood in Pulaski County, Missouri. These complaints did not exactly come as a surprise to the senator; Truman's own experiences as a captain in the army during the First World War had left him with a deep-seated skepticism of the military's ability to manage even the simplest projects honestly or competently, and his apprenticeship in local Missouri machine politics had taught him how to recognize a payoff or contract scam when he saw one. But when he made informal inquiries in Washington about his constituents' allegations, the Quartermaster Corps treated him to a gold-plated runaround. This, of course, only aroused Harry's suspicions further, and so he quietly set out on a tour of defense projects in the South and Midwest to discover the truth for himself.

Truman returned deeply disturbed by what he had seen and determined to curb the obvious waste of millions of dollars of federal funds. Competitive bidding was a joke; contracts consistently were awarded on the basis of favoritism, to cronies of army officials or multimillion-dollar corporations on the coasts. Consortia of small companies in the rest of the country were being unfairly and systematically shut out of the procurement process. Furthermore, the army was issuing far too many contracts on a cost-plus basis, which were notoriously susceptible to abuse by profiteers and almost impossible to manage effectively.

Truman received little satisfaction when he raised his concerns with President Roosevelt during a thirty-minute conference on February 3. "I don't know whether I made any impression or not," Harry admitted to a friend after the meeting, "because the President is always courteous and cordial when anyone calls on him, and when you come out you think you are getting what you wanted, when nine times out of ten you are just getting cordial treatment."

Undaunted, Truman took his case to his Senate colleagues, a move that did not earn him any points for loyalty with the White House. "He did not want to embarrass the President at this crucial period, when the isolationists were looking for ammunition to smear him," explained Harry's daughter, Margaret, some years later. "But he was convinced that the corruption and misdirection of the defense program could wind up wrecking the Democratic Party." So, on February 10, a quiet day when not much else was happening in the Senate, Truman formally proposed the creation of a special committee to investigate defense spending. Roosevelt, who did not fully appreciate Truman's patriotic or partisan motives, tried to kill the proposal before it reached the Senate floor. He failed. On February 21, the Military Affairs Committee approved Truman's resolution, although the President did succeed in limiting the inquiry to a budget of $15,000. Truman adroitly evaded this restriction by placing his hand-picked staff members on the payrolls of other government agencies, and blocked the administration's efforts to pack the committee with safe, loyalist senators.

Harry then unleashed his investigators on the army camp construction program. "The dirt he turned up stunned Washington and the country," recalled one insider. "The government was letting architects and contractors earn as much as 1,669 percent above the average annual profits. Time-and-a-half and double-time wages at Fort Meade in Maryland cost $1,802,280." A brigadier general in the Corps of Engineers admitted that the army had already wasted $100 million in the $1 billion camp-building program due to the absence of suitable detailed plans for an orderly expansion. When Truman went back to the Senate for more money, they gave him an additional $85,000 to work with.

As America's heavy industries started to gear up, however haphazardly, to meet the nation's defense needs, toy manufacturers rushed to convert their own product lines to war-related games. Demand for toy planes and boats skyrocketed as children enthusiastically pretended to bomb each other into oblivion. Youthful fantasies found a new and disturbing theme. One ten-year-old in Philadelphia calmly informed his teacher that he had invented a poison gas that killed dictators, a development that would not have pleased the scores of unruly children who defied their mothers with taunts such as, "I am Hitler. I don't have to eat my vegetables if I don't want to." Comic books—which were selling at the phenomenal rate of ten million per month—featured sordid stories of Nazi murderers and tortured prisoners; even the squeaky-clean *True Comics,* published by *Parents' Magazine,* carried a series of pictorial articles on the world's greatest warplanes in action. In a popular new street game, kids drew a large chalk circle and divided it into segments, like a pie; each segment bore the name of a European country. The child who was "it" stood in the middle of the circle with a rubber ball at his feet. He was Hitler. The other children stood around the circle, one in each segment. "Hitler" then announced, "I declare war on—Poland." The child who was Poland then ran away while Hitler picked up the ball and, without moving from the center of the circle, tried to hit him with it. If Poland was hit, he was conquered and sat down for the rest of the game. This went on until every country had been conquered. It was just a matter of time; Hitler couldn't lose.

To help American children cope with the bewildering course of events abroad, education experts recommended that parents reassure toddlers that Hitler would not take them away, even if they were bad; mothers were advised to keep their preschool youngsters busy with pleasant things and to shelter them from news of the war. Children between the ages of six and eight were considered capable of dealing with sanitized accounts of the war's progress, but not with the brutality and suffering that accompanied it. Older children were encouraged to listen to actual news reports on the radio and discuss with their parents the war's events—and, equally important, the prospects for peace, too. At Pierson High School in Sag Harbor, Long Island, the students celebrated Bill of Rights Week by learning firsthand what it was like to live under a dictatorship. Principal E. Raymond Schneible assumed the role of dictator of the mythical land of Me-Tamia ("Me-Tame-You"); the school band, dressed in their red and black uniforms, served as storm troopers, dispersing gatherings of the proletariat (i.e., all the other students) in the school corridors and yard. Two members of each class were appointed Gestapo agents for a day and dutifully turned in the names of classmates who dared to violate the fuehrer's proclamations that forbade girls to wear makeup and required boys to wear neckties. Red badges with a white "C" (for concentration camp) were pinned on convicted criminals by judges who rendered their arbitrary decisions (always guilty) without trial. By the end of the day, the virtues of liberty presumably had been amply demonstrated, reinforced by speeches from the community's religious leaders about the unique benefits of democracy—although some seniors decided that they *liked* being storm troopers after all.

Playacting could be educational, but an outbreak of late-afternoon giggling among Me-Tamia's teen-aged citizens made it clear that it was all just a game. Despite Fuehrer Schneible's best intentions, the exercise could never be anything else; the realities of life under a brutal dictatorship were altogether too foreign to anything in the experience of American youth. In Europe, the spring of 1941 brought a renewal of war. In the United States, it ushered in the annual rites of Opening Day, when hopes blossomed and all things seemed possible at the start of a brand-new season of baseball. So the *Sporting News* published a symbolic two-part cartoon that captured the feelings of many Americans that spring: in the first frame, a sobbing child stood beside the ruins of his bombed-out home grieving for his grandmother, whose lifeless body lay buried beneath the rubble; in the second frame, a boy in the grandstands at a baseball game cheered exultantly as a runner slid safely into third base. The caption read, "Europe's national pastime seems to be war; America's is baseball."

Certainly the lords of major-league baseball availed themselves of every opportunity to reinforce this distinction, praying that the peace of their realm would not be disrupted by the war clouds looming on the horizon. Their most immediate concern was the draft. Clark Griffith (who, as the longtime owner of the Washington Senators, claimed to know his way around Capitol Hill) proposed that ballplayers be deferred from military service until the end of the 1941 season, in return for an agreement by organized baseball to implement a rigorous physical training program under military supervision. "Every club would be placed under a drill sergeant who would work with the men at least one hour every morning and put the squad through a public demonstration before every game," suggested Griffith hopefully. "When you consider that our players are in fine physical condition to begin with, I feel sure that by October we would show at least as well trained a body of men as you could find in any Army camp across the country."

Alas, Griffith had no more success with Selective Service director Lewis B. Hershey than his ball club had with the rest of the American League. While rejecting Griffith's scheme, Hershey sought to reassure the owners that there would be no wholesale raids on their big league rosters. "Everyone gets frightened when there's a thunderstorm," Hershey joked with dark humor, "but not many houses get hit." Still, everyone in baseball kept a nervous eye on the draft call-ups.

Players signed their contracts earlier than usual that spring. The hands-down winners for highest salary in the majors (slightly over $30,000) were an incongruous pair of pitchers: the 1940 pennant-winning Detroit Tigers' Bobo Newsom—a Grade-A flake who rarely spent more than two consecutive seasons with the same team, but who nevertheless had amassed sixty-one wins in the past three seasons—and straight-arrow Cleveland righthander Bob Feller. In 1940, the fireballing Feller had led the American League in wins (27), complete games (finishing an astounding 31 out of 43 starts), innings pitched, strikeouts, and shutouts. He was certainly worth every penny the Indians paid him; on the days he was scheduled to pitch, ticket sales jumped between 50 and 200 percent.

Cleveland had finished just one game behind the Tigers in 1940, and the New York Yankees had come in third, one game behind the Indians. This year, the Bronx Bombers were counting upon a pair of rookie infielders to put some spark back in the team: second baseman Jerry Priddy, and diminutive shortstop Phil "Scooter" Rizzuto. Rizzuto looked more like a high school sophomore than a major league ballplayer; when he arrived at the Yankees' spring training camp in St. Petersburg, the clubhouse man, Pop Logan, refused to believe that the kid really was a member of the Yankees. He wouldn't let Rizzuto in. "It was embarrassing," Rizzuto recalled. "I'm standing there trying to convince him and he refuses to budge. Now I don't know what I'm going to do. I am really scared. All of a sudden Lefty Gomez comes along. I knew him. I had played a couple of exhibition games against him in Dexter Park. He tells Logan I'm a ballplayer. 'You better let him in, Pop, before the ducks walk all over him.' Finally I'm inside the clubhouse with all these famous Yankees—DiMaggio and Dickey and Ruffing and Gordon."

Joe DiMaggio. Already the name called up magical, almost mystical connotations. "Just say he was the greatest ballplayer I ever saw in my life, the greatest ballplayer any of us saw, and let it go at that," said Tommy Henrich, who played alongside DiMaggio in the Yankee outfield for eleven years. "Joe had a lot of character. He was the most moral man I ever knew. He couldn't do anything cheap; he wouldn't do anything that would hurt his name or hurt the Yankees." The son of an Italian fisherman in San Francisco, Joe was no prima donna. He asked for no privileges, no special treatment. He didn't mix much with his teammates, although he was always there if anyone needed help or advice. Most of the time he went his own way and kept his thoughts to himself. DiMaggio was a high-strung introvert, intense, and much more nervous than the fans ever knew; often he smoked an entire pack of Camels before a game, and sneaked away under the stands between innings to smoke some more. On the road, he spent most of his spare time at the movies, which was the only place he could genuinely relax. Rizzuto: "Joe would sit so still in the movie you would think he was asleep."

Nobody kidded with Joe except his best friend on the Yankees, pitcher Lefty Gomez, another native Californian, whose nickname, the Goofy One, revealed a personality as loose and free as DiMaggio sometimes longed to be. Joe loved to read *Superman* comics, but he feared it would tarnish his image to be seen buying them at a newsstand, so he persuaded Lefty to purchase them for him. "He was just never a guy who could let down in front of strangers," Gomez said. "He was a guy who knew he was the greatest baseball player in America and he was proud of it. He knew what the press and the fans and the kids expected of him, and he was always trying to live up to that image. . . . He knew he was Joe DiMaggio and he knew what that meant to the country. He felt that obligation to the Yankees and to the public."

After a brief and spectacular minor league career with the San Francisco Seals, Joe had exploded upon the American League scene in 1936 at the tender age of twenty-one, hitting a robust .323 in his rookie season. The next year he led the league with 46 home runs and a .673 slugging average, knocking in a staggering total of 167 runs. He won the batting title in 1939 (.381) and again in 1940, despite suffering a series of nagging leg injuries both seasons. In 1941, DiMaggio reported to training camp late, on March 12, after a ten-day holdout over contract terms. Some thought Joe looked thin and pale, but he said he weighed in at his normal 194 pounds. "I feel fine," Joe told reporters. "I exercised at home just enough to keep myself in shape." His draft number was 5,423, high enough to keep him in pinstripes (he wore number 5) instead of khaki for the foreseeable future, but low enough to make Yankee management nervous nonetheless.

Over in the National League, the oddsmakers' preseason favorites were the Cincinnati Redlegs, who returned their 1940 world championship lineup—and the best pitching staff in the majors—virtually intact. On the other hand, Grantland Rice was singing the praises of the Chicago Cubs, who featured one of the most celebrated rookies of recent years: Lew Novikoff, "the Mad Russian," brought up from the Cubs' Los Angeles farm club. Novikoff had won slugging titles in every minor league in which he had played. "Every baseball authority I've talked to in the West," reported Rice, "voices the same prediction—that Novikoff will hit any kind of pitching and some day will be one of the greatest hitters of major league history." Of course he didn't, and he wasn't.

No team, though, presented more intriguing possibilities than the Brooklyn Dodgers, who had undergone the most drastic off-season face-lifting of any club in either league. For years, the friendly confines of Ebbets Field had sheltered a company of colorfully inept castoffs who spent a few faltering years with the Bums as a last stop on their way down and out of the majors. Despite the Dodgers' never-ending tribulations, the fans still loved them; someone compared it to the affection parents might feel for "a child with a D-plus average in school." By 1938, though, the franchise was in deep financial trouble, in debt to the tune of $1.2 million. Telephone service already had been shut off, and bill collectors camped outside the team's offices every morning. Threatened with imminent fore-closure by the Brooklyn Trust Company, which held a $500,000 note from the team, the Dodgers' desperate owners entrusted the operation of the club to a former used car salesman named Leland Stanford MacPhail.

MacPhail was one of the most outrageous characters in baseball's colorful history, a clownish, bellicose, red-haired and red-faced wild man who set new standards of eccentricity in a sport known for its flamboyant characters. He was an unpredictable, self-destructive genius, a beefy, un-couth, vituperative drunkard whose list of accomplishments included in-troducing night baseball to the majors, single-handedly resurrecting a moribund Cincinnati Reds organization, and attempting (with a gratifying lack of success) to persuade the National League to play its games with yellow baseballs. He had been to law school but never had enough pa-tience for the law. In January 1919, he had helped lead an expedition of U.S. Army officers to kidnap Kaiser Wilhelm from a castle in Holland; twenty-two years later, he still carried a purloined Imperial ashtray to commemorate the occasion. MacPhail had spent the decade of the twen-ties refereeing Big Ten football games, trying to earn a fortune in real estate, and supervising the liquidation of a couple of bankrupt glass facto-ries. Then he purchased the Columbus, Ohio, minor league baseball team in 1930; shortly thereafter, he made the acquaintance of St. Louis Cardi-nals' vice-president Branch Rickey, who subsequently recommended him to the owners of the Cincinnati Reds, and then to the woeful Brooklyn franchise.

MacPhail accepted the challenge of reviving the Dodgers on the condition that he would enjoy absolute authority over the entire opera-tion. Promising "to turn Brooklyn inside out, upside down, and win pen-nants every year," he began by refurbishing the stadium: every seat in the stands was repainted, the playing field was resodded with turf acquired from a Long Island polo field, a plush bar with free liquor was erected for the members of the press, and the Ebbets Field ushers acquired flashy gold-and-green uniforms accompanied by a drillmaster who kept them (the ushers, not the uniforms) constantly on their toes. MacPhail also scheduled a half-dozen night games at Ebbets Field each season, which provided the Dodgers' exuberant fans with an excuse to spend an evening hurling empty bottles at one another.

Then MacPhail took a long look at his ball club. It was not a pretty sight. (Which was probably one reason why MacPhail generally went around wearing an anxious expression that resembled a silent appeal for Bromo-Seltzer.) "Some of the players had grown listless," one bemused New York reporter pointed out. "They threw the ball in the wrong direction, took naps in the outfield, and tried to pass each other while running bases; many of them were not on speaking terms with one another." As the first step in reversing this dismal state of affairs, MacPhail hired the irascible and irresponsible Leo "the Lip" Durocher as manager, and then proceeded to wheel and deal and steal ballplayers from his fellow owners until he had assembled a bona fide contender.

Much to the initial consternation of the long-suffering directors of the Brooklyn Trust Company, MacPhail never hesitated to spend money to build a winner. He bought six minor league clubs and made working arrangements with another half-dozen. He hired fifteen talent scouts to scour the bushes for talent, and came away with some remarkable finds. For instance, MacPhail paid $75,000—an unprecedented sum in those days for an unproven ballplayer—to the Boston Red Sox for a promising minor league shortstop named Harold Henry "Pee Wee" Reese (whose nickname referred not to his diminutive stature, but to the "pee wee" marble he used to win the marble-shooting championship of Louisville, Kentucky). From the Detroit Tigers, MacPhail picked up crowd-pleasing outfielder Dixie Walker, who quickly became "the People's Cherce" among the Brooklyn faithful. When Commissioner Judge Kenesaw Mountain Landis (who did not enjoy particularly good relations with either Rickey or MacPhail) invalidated the contracts of ninety-five players within the St. Louis Cardinals farm system, MacPhail swooped in and plucked promising infielder Pete Reiser for $200. Actually, MacPhail was only supposed to hide Reiser on the Brooklyn roster for a while as a favor to Rickey, but when he realized just how good an all-around prospect Reiser really was, MacPhail could not resist the temptation to keep him. Partly to compensate Rickey for swiping Reiser, MacPhail agreed to purchase aging slugger Joe "Muscles" Medwick and light-hitting catcher Mickey Owen from St. Louis; Medwick, however, never fully recovered after a vicious beaning by his former teammates ended his 1940 season prematurely. (When the incident occurred, MacPhail, who allegedly had been drinking at the press bar and hadn't seen the pitch, ran out onto the field screaming that the Cardinal pitcher had deliberately thrown at Medwick's head. Failing to obtain satisfaction from the umpires, who thought he was simply trying to provoke a riot, MacPhail made an unsuccessful but well-publicized plea to the district attorney to throw the offending hurler in jail.)

MacPhail bought slugging first baseman Dolph Camilli and hard-throwing righthander Kirby Higbe from the hapless Philadelphia Phillies, who were always in need of ready cash. To increase ticket sales to help replenish the team's treasury, he put a grossly overweight Babe Ruth on display as a Dodger coach, and hired Red Barber as the club's radio announcer. (It took Brooklyn fans a while to adjust to Barber's noticeable southern accent; some of them apparently thought he was speaking in a foreign tongue—such as English.) Just before the start of the 1941 season, MacPhail added the final piece to the puzzle when he bamboozled the Cubs' front office (reportedly during an all-night drinking bout) into giving him perennial all-star second baseman Billy Herman in return for two utility players and $60,000. When all the dealing was done, MacPhail had acquired a total of three catchers, twelve pitchers, six infielders, and eight outfielders at a cost of eighteen players whom he no longer wanted, and $1 million, most of which was soon recovered from vastly increased gate receipts.

MacPhail had amassed an impressive collection of talent, and potentially an explosive combination both on and off the field. The volatility started right at the top, in the manager's office. When he first came up to the major leagues as a shortstop with the Yankees, the feisty Durocher promptly got off on the wrong foot by allegedly stealing money from his teammates' lockers. Age had not mellowed him much. It was Durocher who coined the phrase "Nice guys finish last." He was a compulsive gambler and often heavily in debt. (He was also a great dresser; he had all of his suits made in Hollywood by George Raft's tailor. MacPhail, on the other hand, dressed like a surrealist's nightmare, in a wild profusion of clashing plaids, checks, and stripes.)

Durocher rode herd on a team which, he freely admitted, contained its full share of "oddballs, night riders, and drinkers." There was an unusually high percentage of southerners on the Dodgers in 1941, and southern ballplayers in those days tended to be just a little bit tougher and more ornery than anyone else. Two of the most cantankerous spirits were Higbe and Hugh Casey, a pair of moody, hard-drinking righthanders who derived special pleasure from sending a batter sprawling from a pitch aimed directly at his ear. Then there was forty-year-old Fat Freddie Fitzsimmons, a knuckleball pitcher with an arm so crooked, Durocher swore, "that he literally could not reach down and pick anything up, he had to bend from the knees. He was so crooked that it threw his balance off and gave him a kind of rolling, swaggering gait." Off the field, Fitzsimmons was a pleasant, cheerful fellow. But once he got out on the mound, he turned into a raving lunatic. Durocher: "You just couldn't talk to him. He'd snap his head at you and stomp around and snarl out his words like a lion chewing meat."

The champion flake on this team of all-star flakes, however, the man who inspired more baseball ballads than you could shake a policeman's nightstick at, was the tragic figure of Van Lingle Mungo. During the hard times in Brooklyn in the early 1930s, Mungo was the ace of the Dodger pitching staff, the favorite of the Ebbets Field faithful. He possessed nearly as good a fastball as Dizzy Dean, but Van's talent was undone by a unquenchable fondness for booze that was considered excessive even by the liberal standards of Brooklyn ballplayers. (Mungo also had an almost unintelligible southern accent and a peculiar mushmouthed way of talking that sounded, Durocher swore, "like Edgar Bergen doing Mortimer Snerd from the bottom of the well." Once when he missed the bus to the ball park, Mungo explained to Durocher that "ya bush wen'of alevme," which the manager took to mean "the bus went off and left me.") By the end of the 1940 season, Mungo seemed to be washed up, on his way out of the big leagues for good. During the offseason, however, he went on the wagon in an effort to make one last comeback, and he showed up at the Dodgers' training camp in Havana in excellent shape.

Up to that point, MacPhail's decision to train in Cuba had been a public relations bonanza (except for the fact that backup catcher Babe Phelps, who often walked around with lighted cigar butts in his pockets, refused to make the trip because he was afraid of traveling by air or by water, which pretty much exhausted the available alternatives). A brass band had welcomed the team at the Havana airport; the Dodgers received a special invitation to visit President Batista's palace; and MacPhail hired a rumba instructor to help the players limber up before practice. Alas, shortly before he was scheduled to pitch in an exhibition game against Feller and the Indians, Van fell off the wagon and spent several nights in the company of an exotic singer named Lady Vine and the female half of the illustrious tango team of Gonzales and Gonzales. When Mungo showed up drunk at the ball park on the day he was scheduled to pitch, Durocher ordered him back to the hotel and told him to catch the next boat for Miami; but Mungo disobeyed and chose to spend another evening with his unconventional ménage. All hell broke loose that night when Señor Gonzales broke in on the fun and discovered the trio in bed. When Durocher went down to Mungo's hotel room at six o'clock the next morning, he found several policemen, a couple of soldiers with bayonets, and an enraged Gonzales (who had a black eye and was wielding a butcher knife), all of whom were looking for Mungo. His Dodger teammates hid Van in a vegetable bin in the cellar until the storm subsided, then they smuggled him down to the wharf and shoved him, just a few steps ahead of the police, onto a seaplane bound for the mainland and safety.

10

"That Lovely Spirit"

"You don't know where you go from here. At moments the
nonsense and thin airy fantasy is not ridiculous but sublime."
—CARL SANDBURG, ON THE DEATH OF
VIRGINIA WOOLF

She left her home and went for a walk. "A curious sea side feeling in the
air today. It reminds me of lodgings on a parade at Easter. Everyone
leaning against the wind, nipped & silenced." Tall and gaunt and brittle,
she walked stiffly to the banks of the River Ouse. "This windy corner. And
Nessa is at Brighton, & I am imagining how it would be if we could infuse
souls . . ."

On Friday, March 28, Virginia Woolf lay down her walking stick on
the river shore by the little bridge at Southease, and walked into the river
and was borne away by the tide and became a part of the sea for a time.

Once before she had gone mad, in 1915, during the last war. She was
not mad when she drowned herself, nor had she been since that first time.
But since the new year began she had felt the familiar horror returning,
pulling her mind and her soul toward the abyss, and she feared that this
time she could not withstand it.

She despised the war, the inhuman slaughter that St-Exupéry had
condemned as "a giant charnel house, where man is crushed under the
weight of machinery." She believed that five hundred years of darkness
awaited mankind at the end of the bloodletting. She mourned for the
beloved past, for her dead parents and the young men slain in the carnage,
for the old world she had described so lovingly now crumbling in ruins
around her. "Every beautiful thing will soon be destroyed," she had predicted. "We were in London on Monday. I went to London Bridge. I
looked at the river; very misty; some tufts of smoke, perhaps from burning
houses. There was another fire on Saturday. Then I saw a cliff of wall, eaten
out, at one corner; a great corner all smashed; a Bank; the Monument
erect; tried to get a Bus; but such a block I dismounted; & the second bus
advised me to walk. A complete jam of traffic; for streets were being blown
up. So by tube to the Temple; & there wandered in the desolate ruins of
my old squares; gashed; dismantled; the old red bricks all white powder,

something like a builders yard. Grey dirt & broken windows; sightseers; all that completeness ravished & demolished."

She hated her tedious wartime life, isolated in her cottage, Monk's House, in a dreary country village. She despised human contact; the women she saw in the village reminded her of repulsive fat white slugs, "something scented, shoddy, parasitic about them . . . shell encrusted old women, rouged, decked, cadaverous at the tea shop." She went to see a Charlie Chaplin movie and found it boring. Day after wearisome day the routine continued, "sleep & slackness; musing; reading; cooking; cycling . . ." She could not write the words she sought, could neither understand nor describe what she saw around her. "Why was I depressed? I cannot remember." Morbidly self-critical, she scorned her recent writings as unworthy of her lofty standards; tired of time, she sought solace in the eternity of history. "Oh dear yes, I shall conquer this mood. It is a question of being open sleepy, wide eyed at present—letting things come one after another." Then the dreaded voices returned.

She had written before of suicide in *Mrs. Dalloway,* through the eyes of a shell-shocked veteran of the first Great War: "Human nature, in short, was on him—the repulsive brute with the blood-red nostrils. . . . The whole world was clamouring: Kill yourself, kill yourself. . . ."

Her husband knew, had often feared she would suffer another bout with insanity. On March 18 he realized that she was ill. Several days later, Virginia wrote to her sister of the horror that tore at her mind. On March 24 Leonard Woolf thought his wife seemed slightly better.

She left him a note when she walked away to join the dead. "Dearest," she wrote,

> I want to tell you that you have given me complete happiness. No one could have done more than you have done. Please believe that.
>
> But I know that I shall never get over this: and I am wasting your life. It is this madness. Nothing anyone says can persuade me. You can work, and you will be much better without me. You can see I cant write this even, which shows I am right. All I want to say is that until this disease came on we were perfectly happy. It was all due to you. No one could have been so good as you have been, from the very first day till now. Everyone knows that.
>
> V.
>
> Will you please destroy all my papers.

Harold Nicolson was shattered by his friend's suicide. "I simply can't take it in. That lovely mind, that lovely spirit."

" . . . In this hour of the world, the British Empire, and the smoke and stench over Europe," wrote Carl Sandburg in sadness, "I hesitate about inquiring into the motives of Virginia Woolf. I can't help wondering what a book she would have written about why she wanted to belong to the sea forever, to be no more on the land. . . . Why she walked into tidal waters of the sea for a fade-out no one can tell. My reverence for her mind and heart goes on. She represented things money cannot buy nor children be taught."

11

A Visit from Hell

"Yugoslavs seem to have sold their souls to the Devil.
All these Balkan peoples are trash. Poor dears . . ."
—SIR ALEXANDER CADOGAN

At the forsaken hour of two o'clock on the morning of March 27, heavy tanks and antiaircraft guns rumbled through the streets of Belgrade. Led by officers in midnight blue air force uniforms, troops in full combat gear rushed to their assigned positions, seizing strategic points throughout the city, setting up artillery in the streets, stringing barbed wire across the primary approaches to the royal palace on the Kralja Milana. They surrounded the police stations and the homes of top government officials. Premier Dragisa Cvetkovic and Foreign Minister Alexander Cincar-Markovic, who had returned from Vienna the day before after finally signing the treaty that committed Yugoslavia to the Tripartite Pact, were arrested and forced to resign their posts. At 7:00 A.M., seventeen-year-old King Peter proclaimed the end of the regency; his uncle, Prince Paul, abdicated and fled to Greece.

Yugoslavia had just signed its own death warrant. And, arguably, Hitler's as well.

The lightning military coup that overthrew the irresolute Cvetkovic cabinet was led by a group of nationalist Serbian military officers headed by General Dusan Simovic, the tall, handsome, gray-haired vice-marshal of Yugoslavia's air force. Simovic had contemplated a coup at least as early as January, when Colonel William Donovan had visited him during the colonel's tour of the Mediterranean theater. During the course of their meeting, Donovan had sought to use vague promises of American favors to stiffen Simovic against concessions to Germany. Already inspired by the stirring anti-Nazi rhetoric of President Roosevelt's public statements, Simovic told Donovan what he wanted to hear. "He stated that Yugoslavia would not permit the passage of German troops through its territory as . . . the people would not stand for it." But Simovic apparently played little active part in the tactical planning for the takeover, allowing his subordinate officers, notably Brigadier General Bora Mirkovic, to take the lead.

Mirkovic had watched as the government in Belgrade turned and twisted through the month of March, trying to avoid the Nazi net without antagonizing Germany. Everything went back to Barbarossa. For Hitler, it was essential that Germany control northern Greece; he feared that a British foothold in Salonika would imperil the southern flank of the Barbarossa invasion force, and might provide air bases from which the R.A.F. could bomb the oil fields in Romania. So Operation Marita had to succeed, and Hitler desperately needed Yugoslavia's cooperation to make Marita work. If Germany were forced to invade Greece only from Bulgaria, through the narrow, barren deathtrap of the Struma River Valley, the Wehrmacht could expect heavy casualties; but if it could move simultaneously through Yugoslavia's broad Vardar River Valley into Salonika, it could quickly crush any resistance in northern Greece.

To encourage popular resistance to any diplomatic demarche with Germany, agents of the British Special Operations Executive flooded Yugoslavia with propaganda opposing the Tripartite Pact. The American ambassador, Arthur Bliss Lane, conferred with Prince Paul and Dr. Cvetkovic and promised Lend-Lease aid if Yugoslavia withstood German pressure. The patriarch of the Serbian Orthodox Church urged Paul to stand firm. There were threatening rumors that the government would be overthrown if it signed "as much as a dinner check" in Germany. The British minister in Belgrade made a hurried trip to Athens to confer with Eden and returned with further inducements for resistance. But when the Germans—to Paul's surprise—yielded to Belgrade's conditions for joining the pact, Cvetkovic found himself out of time and options, facing a Nazi ultimatum. Despite the resignation of three cabinet ministers in protest, he departed for Vienna on March 24 to bind Yugoslavia formally to the Axis alliance. In London, Cadogan shook his head in dismay: "Jugs are signing—silly, feeble mugs . . ."

Reaction followed swiftly. Less than forty-eight hours later, schoolchildren in Belgrade staged a series of spontaneous demonstrations against the government's decision to sign the pact. They tore down pictures of Hitler and ripped them to shreds. They scribbled revolutionary slogans on handbills and passed them out to startled bystanders in the streets, they scrawled anti-Cvetkovic slogans on classroom walls; refusing to obey their teachers' orders to disperse, they barricaded themselves behind the schoolhouse doors. Behind the scenes, the British minister scurried to carry out Churchill's latest instructions: "Continue to pester, nag and bite. Demand audiences. Don't take *NO* for an answer. . . . Do not neglect any alternative to which we may have to resort if we find present Government have gone beyond recall." The British air attaché secretly met with Simovic to discuss emergency aid in the event a coup touched off a German invasion.

Milovan Djilas had been in Belgrade since early March; the young Communist found the capital suffocating under an atmosphere of pressure and persecution, as if Yugoslavia were already at war. Police raided the headquarters of the opposition Democratic Party, confiscated its literature, and arrested its leaders. To goad the people into direct action against the government, the Communists launched their own propaganda campaign, charging Cvetkovic and his colleagues with cowardice in their dealings with Germany. But the military coup on March 27 caught Djilas and the rest of the inner circle of the Yugoslav Communist Party completely unaware.

Amid the confusion at dawn, as Belgrade awoke and blinked in wonder at the sight of tanks and machine guns and bayonets in the squares, as the voice of young King Peter (who had escaped from his regency custodians by sliding down a drain pipe) came over the radio, the streets filled with people shouting, *"Bolje rat nego pakt!"* and *"Bolje grob nego rob"* ("War is better than the Pact!" "Better the grave than slavery!"). Patrons in the city's cafés smashed their champagne glasses against walls and fireplaces in triumph. In the impromptu parades that wound through the city, joyous citizens danced the *kolo* and men's voices sang over and over again the Serbian battle anthem, *"Oj Srbjo,"* and songs of martial fervor:

> Listen, girl I love,
> Hitler has come to our frontier,
> But the Serbs are ready with their guns.

> The British are sending the navy;
> Roosevelt is sending the planes;
> And we, the battalions!

Rioters burned German flags, hissed and spat upon the car of the German minister to Belgrade, and demolished the German Tourist Bureau, which had been the center of the Nazi propaganda campaign in Yugoslavia. As rumors spread of well-equipped British divisions landing in Greece, hawkers sold thousands of tiny tin British flags, which men displayed proudly in the buttonholes of their coats. "Mobs of people were running down the street carrying Yugoslav flags, drunk with enthusiasm," reported Djilas. "The springtime had awakened new life in us. It was good to be a Serb that day." Temporarily forsaking the strictures of ideology for the sake of national unity, the Communists organized mass demonstrations in the capital; that evening, Djilas addressed a crowd of fifteen thousand and called for the establishment of a free press and free trade unions, the release of political prisoners, and a treaty of friendship with the Soviet Union, because only Moscow—not Britain and its paltry four divisions in Greece—could protect Yugoslavia from the wrathful German reaction that appeared inevitable.

In London, Churchill was overjoyed. "Early this morning the Yugoslav nation found its soul," he informed a gathering of the Conservative Party hierarchy. " . . . This patriotic movement arises from the wrath of a valiant and warlike race at the betrayal of their country by the weakness of their rulers and the foul intrigues of the Axis Powers. . . . The British Empire and its Allies will make common cause with the Yugoslav nation, and we shall continue to march and strive together until complete victory is won." Poor Anthony Eden, who had gotten as far as Malta on his way home, was sent back to Cairo to join Wavell and Dill in keeping an eye on the swiftly changing situation. King George VI sent his congratulations to young King Peter. "The whole country is in ecstasies," reported John Colville, the Prime Minister's private secretary.

("It is pathetic to see London rejoicing so prematurely," sniffed Goebbels scornfully.)

Huge popular demonstrations in Marseilles mocked the Axis diplomatic defeat. From Washington, Roosevelt cabled America's enthusiastic support for the new Yugoslav regime. "At this moment," he assured King Peter, "when Your Majesty has assumed the full exercise of your royal rights and powers and the leadership of a brave and independent people, I wish to share with the people of the United States in the expression of our sincere and genuine wish for the health and well-being of Your Majesty and for the freedom and independence of Yugoslavia." Soon the President's words of encouragement were shouted through the streets, amid joyous cries that the "arsenal of democracy" would provide the wherewithal to ensure Yugoslavian independence.

Hitler received the news of the Simovic coup just moments before he was scheduled to meet with Japanese Foreign Minister Yosuke Matsuoka. He later said that he had thought it a joke at first, a bad joke. Hitler had received no advance warning at all of the reverse; his intelligence services—the Abwehr, the Foreign Office, and the SS Security Service—had let him down completely. He flew into a convulsive rage. He shouted that the coup was a personal affront, a calculated insult which he would repay by wiping the nation of Yugoslavia off the map. He sent for Brauchitsch and Halder and told them, "I have decided to strike Yugoslavia down. What forces do you need? How much time do you need?" He turned to Jodl and Keitel. "Now I intend to make a clean sweep of the Balkans—it is time people got to know me better." During brief conferences with envoys from Hungary and Bulgaria, he promised to divide up the Yugoslavian booty among Germany's faithful allies.

Before the day was over, Hitler had signed Directive Number 25, Operation Punishment, to send wave after wave of bombers against Yugoslavia until Belgrade and the nation's military installations were mercilessly demolished. "Politically it is especially important that the blow against Yugoslavia is *carried out with unmerciful harshness* and that the military destruction is done in a lightning-like undertaking. . . . The main task of the air force is to start as early as possible with the destruction of the Yugoslav Air Force ground installations and to destroy the capital, Belgrade, in attacks by waves." Then, long after midnight, he wrote to Mussolini, advising his ally of the impending assault and advising him in no uncertain terms to watch his rear in Albania. Goebbels rejoiced at his Fuehrer's decision to show no mercy: "It is the best thing. Then, at least, we can have *tabula rasa* in the Balkans. There is no other way we can quieten this witches' cauldron."

Preparations for Operation Marita (the attack upon Greece) and Barbarossa had progressed so far that the diversion in Yugoslavia disarranged the German High Command's carefully laid plans. It took a full week to transport additional forces and matériel from the north and readjust the schedules of List's army in Bulgaria. Now Hitler decided that the invasions of Yugoslavia and Greece would proceed simultaneously with a four-pronged attack.

In the end, Hitler's rage that day would cost him everything. By ordering a full-scale annihilation of Yugoslavia, he advised his generals that they would have to postpone the start of Operation Barbarossa—originally scheduled for May 15—by five weeks, until June 22. It was the most fateful delay in the history of the war.

In the meantime, Churchill conducted a desperate campaign to prod Simovic to strike at Italy in Albania while he still had the chance. It was no use. After basking in the adulation of the frenzied crowd for several glorious days, the officers of the new regime suddenly realized that they were in imminent peril of annihilation. The Croats, who formed a majority of the population in the northern regions of Yugoslavia, were pro-German to begin with, and had no intention of cooperating with or dying for a government dominated by the hated Serbs. In fact, Croatian separatists had already been promised an independent state once Yugoslavia had been crushed. To the east, Turkey still refused to commit itself openly to assisting Yugoslavia, despite repeated British requests. Nakedly alone in the path of the Wehrmacht (there were now 680,000 German troops in Romania), paralyzed by fear of internal revolt and the German avalanche poised to descend upon it, the government in Belgrade would do nothing to provoke Hitler. In fact, Simovic now sought to apologize for the anti-Nazi excesses of the March 27 rising, and reassured Berlin through intermediaries that he still intended to maintain amicable diplomatic relations; he even promised to sign a nonaggression pact and hinted that Yugoslavia would honor the Tripartite Pact after all. Too late. "They are clutching at last, desperate straws," laughed Goebbels. "Nothing will save them."

Yugoslavia's military forces finally, belatedly completed full mobilization, but Simovic was too frightened to move until Germany crossed the border. By April 5 the Wehrmacht was ready. Hitler appeared calm and relaxed, as he always did when his plans were about to unfold (although he did admit to a moment of fear that Russia might take this opportunity to launch a preemptive assault against Germany). The Fuehrer put away his elegant black Mercedes touring car and his beloved phonograph records of Wagner and Bruckner; there would be no time during the campaign for such self-indulgent luxuries. Himmer issued a decree forbidding dancing as an unseemly display of frivolity during the offensive in the Balkans. Goebbels commissioned appropriately "snappy" martial songs for broadcast over the state-controlled radio networks of the Reich.

At one o'clock on the morning of Sunday, April 6, Hitler summoned his propaganda chief. They discussed the texts of the official statements announcing the invasion that was scheduled to begin at 5:20 A.M. "The hours pass with painful slowness," Goebbels confided to his diary. "I drink tea with the Fuehrer and we chat about other things." They talked of the Reich's recent film productions and the prospects for future cinematic ventures. "Filmically, we are on the march," boasted Goebbels. Four thirty. Five o'clock. Finally the moment arrived. "The Fuehrer's thoughts are with his soldiers. He cherishes them with every good wish. As if he were thinking of each individually. It is quite moving," decided Goebbels. "Then he retires."

The Wehrmacht stormed into Yugoslavia from Bulgaria, from Romania, from Austria and Hungary. Communications between Belgrade and Athens went dead. Italian troops fell upon Yugoslavia from the west. Despite British warnings, Simovic's government had not expected the blow to fall quite so quickly; the general had scheduled his daughter's wedding for later that morning. In the markets of Belgrade, peasants went about their business, haggling over prices, suspecting nothing. At seven o'clock, as the pink sky turned bright red, groups of workers in a festive mood gathered on the city's street corners to celebrate the treaty of friendship signed with the Soviet Union only a few hours before.

Goebbels delivered Hitler's message: "Soldiers of the Southeastern Front: Since early this morning the German people are at war with the Belgrade government of intrigue. We shall only lay down arms when this band of ruffians has been definitely and most emphatically eliminated, and when the last Briton has left this part of the European Continent, and when these misled people realize that they must thank Britain for this situation, they must thank England, the greatest warmonger of all time. . . . Soldiers of the Southeastern Front: Now your zero hour has arrived."

Someone shouted to the crowd in the streets of Belgrade that the German radio station had just announced a declaration of war against Yugoslavia; but previous rumors of Nazi invasions had proved false, so Milovan Djilas and his comrades paid little attention and went on with their celebration. "But then we heard a powerful explosion, the buzzing of motors, and the howling sound of a siren. People in the street were running, bent over, like rags carried by the wind. Soon the streets were deserted." Ray Brock, the *New York Times* correspondent in Belgrade, heard the ominous sound: "It was a steadily growing vibration from the east, a swiftly increasing throb that, in a few seconds, grew to a mounting, uneven drone that echoed everywhere and seemed to fill the air all about. My binoculars were ready . . . Then I saw the bombers. They were coming on in perfect formation, flanked by fighters, and in a sudden glint of sunlight I spotted more fighters high above them."

It was a visit from hell. To deliver Hitler's message, German pilots had been ordered first to destroy Belgrade's air fields and its water system, and then to unleash a devastating attack of incendiaries and heavy explosives. They did their work well. The first attack—Heinkels, Dorniers, and Stuka dive-bombers with their devilish screeching whine—lasted for ninety minutes; the bombers dropped their loads and entire blocks of the city erupted in streaks of smoke and flame. Men, women, and children still dressed in their nightclothes ran out of their homes in search of cellars or shelters. The Stukas dove nearly to the level of the rooftops before they released their cargo. Ray Brock ducked instinctively "as bombs whistled down nearby, exploding in the familiar boom-Boom-BOOM-BOOM-BAM! Up the street two blocks away a blinding flash ripped outward and the blast blotted out the street. . . . Far out and up through the swiftly gathering haze, I saw another bomber wave coming, headed directly over our end of the city. I ran out onto the landing and downstairs and into the street. The next sticks started coming down like a clattering of tin trays. I made the last ten yards at a sprint and dived for the ground. I felt, rather than heard, the thudding of the bombs beyond the hotel, and the atmosphere about me seemed to explode in a series of deafening roars."

Nothing was spared, not hospitals, nor churches, nor schools. In the marketplace, the force of the explosions tossed corpses of peasants like rag dolls atop counters piled high with heads of fresh green lettuce. A wedding party of two hundred people sought refuge in a shelter close by the Church of the Assumption; the Stukas hit the shelter directly on center and everyone inside was killed. A mother wept as she walked dazedly through the streets, carrying the severed arm of her dead daughter. Djilas: "Fleets of planes flew overhead. The city howled with wounds. Bombs came down attached to parachutes. Someone yelled: 'Parachutists!' 'Parachutists!' echoed on all sides. In the air the 'parachutists' twisted and turned. They were gigantic bombs designed for special surface action. Every time one exploded—they were falling some distance away now—the earth would painfully heave under us. . . . The city lay in fire, smoke, and ruins."

As the first raid ended, the survivors—including most of the generals and the bureaucrats—rushed toward the suburbs where they thought to find safety. Oxen, horses, carts clogged the roads. The second attack began at eleven o'clock that morning, and was even more thorough than the first.

The city was gashed open and anarchy followed. Gypsies rampaged through the city and stole everything they could carry. Wild animals fled the municipal zoo as it went up in flames, and ran screaming in pain through the burning streets toward the river. Thick black smoke billowed up and covered the sky. Twisted telephone poles lay across the broad Kralja Milana. There was no electricity, no water, no first aid, no defense against the terror. Bodies and smoldering bits of broken masonry cluttered the squares. From a clearing outside the city, Djilas watched Belgrade die. He watched his lover, Mitra, cry for the city, "as if it were her child, her youth, her beauty. The poor and the rich were passing by, cursing, the poor because they hardly deserved this kind of beating, and the rich because they couldn't decide whether to save their lives or their possessions. . . . Most of those with cars had escaped in the morning, leaving in an instant this thousand-year-old city . . ."

Still the planes kept coming. The death toll could never be established with precision because many who were buried beneath the rubble were not uncovered until weeks later. But it has been reliably estimated that seventeen thousand people died during these three days of raids upon Belgrade. (By comparison, about eighteen thousand people died during more than four months of the blitz against Britain in 1941.) After the bombing was over, Admiral Canaris visited the city. Appalled by the devastation, he turned away in horror. "I can't take any more of this," he whispered in his quiet, lisping voice. "We're flying out of here." Those who survived the bombs then suffered through a reign of terror as the Yugoslav police and their Chetnik allies—the irregular Serbian monarchist troops—tried to reestablish order in the capital by purging it of suspected deserters or traitors. Actually, they shot anyone they chose, often on the flimsiest pretext. Communications were cut within the city and between Belgrade and the rest of the country. Hunger and paranoia gripped the capital, and many people prayed for the Germans to enter and restore at least a measure of order.

While the Luftwaffe ravaged Belgrade, the Wehrmacht swept through the countryside as resistance disintegrated all along the line. On the first day, German forces tore gaping holes through Yugoslavia's frontier defenses; neither Cvetkovic's cabinet nor Simovic's officers had bothered to construct antitank ditches along the approaches from Bulgaria. Confronted with the same sort of rugged mountain passes and wretched road conditions that had thwarted Italy's invasion of Greece, General List and his staff had chosen to employ light tanks armed with 20-mm machine guns and 47-mm cannon, motorcycles, flamethrowers, pack artillery, and short-wheeled trucks to lead the way; the invasion force also included an inordinately high proportion of engineering units to surmount the treacherous terrain. (The troops were even provided with portable chlorinating plants to help prevent amoebic dysentery.) An awkward, slow-moving giant of a man who, like Rommel, came from Swabia—the land of the Black Forest—the sixty-one-year-old List was an expert in the art of mechanized warfare in mountainous territory. He had led the conquest of southern Poland in 1939, and commanded the Twelfth Army when it broke through the French defenses at Sedan, rendering the Maginot Line useless. One of his favorite gambits was to push around a defensive stronghold and then return to capture it later.

He needed no inspired strategy to conquer Yugoslavia. Only isolated groups of Serbs and Communists put up a spirited resistance. There were no real front lines and no unified military command. Most of the Yugoslav army, which by now was shot through with apathy and defeatism, had been trained to maintain order against domestic opponents of the ruling class within the country; its commanders seemed to have no idea how to repel a foreign invasion. Entire divisions surrendered without a fight or fled southward in disarray. After all the brave talk, there were few men willing to die for the fiercely disunited nation. In the north, Croatian units mutinied and welcomed the German invaders. Rows of Croat officers stood at attention at train stations, awaiting the Nazi conquerors. In the cities, Simovic's army commanders refused Communist requests to carry on the battle by arming those workers who were willing to fight. On April 8, forty thousand Yugoslav troops submissively lay down their weapons. Zagreb fell on April 11. One edge of the German advance swung down toward Salonika; another headed for Albania. Churchill regretfully advised the British ambassador, who had fled Belgrade with the rest of the diplomatic establishment, that Britain had no aircraft to spare in the Mediterranean theater to help Yugoslavia. "You must remember Yugoslavs have given us no chance to help them and refused to make a common plan," the Prime Minister chided. Still, from its vantage point in London, the British cabinet saw no good reason why King Peter and the Simovic government should feel the need to flee Yugoslavia, which was, after all, "vast, mountainous, and full of armed men." "You should do your utmost," Churchill urged his ambassador, "to uphold the fighting spirit of the Yugoslav Government and Army . . ."

Surely Churchill had misjudged his Balkan allies. "Germany's early successes cannot discourage us," Simovic boasted in a radio broadcast six days after the invasion began. "Though the present situation is difficult, I believe the justice of our cause, the bravery of our Army, and the help of our powerful allies will assure us victory. . . . Our troops are concentrating on main battle lines to check the enemy's advance." They were doing no such thing, nor was Simovic confident of anything other than his wholehearted desire to get the hell out of Yugoslavia as quickly as he could. The cabinet, the military high command, and a frightened King Peter fled from one town to the next, with a large chunk of the National Bank's gold reserve safely in tow. By the time the unfortunate General Kalafatovic carried out the order of unconditional surrender issued by Simovic on April 13, the government and the gold were all on a plane, heading south across the Mediterranean.

Hitler claimed to have captured 335,000 prisoners during the twelve-day campaign. He made good on his vow to dismember the Yugoslavian nation: Italy seized Montenegro and most of Slovenia and Dalmatia; Bulgaria seized Macedonia and part of Serbia; and Hungary occupied the fertile plains north of Belgrade. Russia stood passively aside as Croatia was made an independent state, ruled by a bloody-handed maniac named Ante Pavelic, the man who had plotted the murder of King Alexander (Peter's father). With Germany's tacit consent and the explicit cooperation of the Catholic archbishop of Croatia, Pavelic launched a mass slaughter of Serbs, Jews, and Gypsies. Bands of Catholic fanatics—the Ustashi—embarked upon a holy mission to exterminate all non-Catholics in the region, slicing throats and herding villagers into mass graves. At the Orthodox Church in the village of Glina, seven hundred Serbs were murdered in one morning.

Germany claimed its share of the loot, too. To control the remanants of Serbia, Hitler established a puppet government which willingly began exporting food and workers to Germany. The Wehrmacht began to turn Belgrade into a Nazi fortress. One day the city's Jews were told to wear yellow arm bands; later, of course, they were killed. Djilas returned to Belgrade near the end of April and discovered that "the city looked small. Corpses were strewn in the wreckage. A sour smell emanated from everything, people and food. The first posters were up announcing the shooting of one hundred Serbs for one German killed. At night shots echoed from different parts of the city. Fear, hunger, and death filled the streets." Forlorn and nearly forgotten, the deposed regent, Prince Paul, who had foreseen the impending calamity, was prohibited by the unforgiving British government from settling in Greece or Egypt, and was unceremoniously shuffled off to an estate in Kenya.

Those who chose to carry on the fight for freedom fled to the mountains. There the Communists—one of the few political groups in Yugoslavia that emerged from the April debacle with its integrity and reputation nearly intact—sought to establish a common front, a broadly based resistance movement against the Germans and their reactionary stooges. The Communist fighters called themselves partisans, the name that had first been used a century earlier to describe the guerrillas who had waged a ruthless struggle against Napoleon's forces behind the lines in Spain and Russia. In the twentieth century, the partisans in the Balkan hills were led by Josip Broz, a former skilled mechanic who had risen through the trade union movement to become general secretary of the Yugoslav Communist Party in 1939. (Secretive by nature and necessity, Broz had long been addicted to the use of different aliases, discarding them like old clothes when they no longer served their purpose; over the past decade, he had been known at various times as Oto, Rudi, John Alexander Carlson, Slavko Babic, Timo, and Jiricek, among others. Stalin knew him only as Valter. Ever since 1937, however, he had employed one name—Tito—almost exclusively, despite the fact that it had no real meaning except as an obscure literary reference in his native province of Zagorje; Broz himself admitted that he adopted it simply "because it occurred to me at the moment.") Despite the Communists' professed willingness to establish a temporary alliance, however, the royalist Serbian nationalist officers who held the western hills refused to cooperate, and in fact swore to turn against the partisans once the Germans were gone.

The politicians' time was past and the old order vanished; now came the hour of the conspirator and the guerrillas who understood the use of darkness.

"A grim prospect now gaped upon us all," murmured an apprehensive Churchill.

Part Three   The Spring

12

The Mission of Yosuke Matsuoka

"Ah . . . ha"
—JOSEPH STALIN, APRIL 1941

Ernest Hemingway had his doubts. Sure, plenty of doubts, you could understand that. But he decided to go to China anyway. As far as Ernest knew, he had never been all that interested in China, or anything else in the immediate neighborhood. Probably he would have preferred to spend the springtime in Havana, where the Brooklyn Dodgers were training. Ernest liked ballplayers in general and especially the Dodgers, who were his kind of people, and he could spend an evening bending an elbow with Kirby Higbe and Hugh Casey and Van Lingle Mungo. "Ernest was at the ball park all the time. He was a tough son of a gun," Higbe once said. "He was just tough. A tough old son of a gun. A big fellow, and quite a writer too. I wish he had been living when I wrote my book, *The High Hard One.* He could have helped me out. That Ernest, he was some writer. . . . Ernest told me and Casey one time that he had seen and done everything in the world. Ole Ernest, I never will forget him."

But Ernest was not in Havana in the spring of 1941. Not anywhere near it, for that matter. Too bad. Instead he was heading for China with his latest wife, Martha Gellhorn, a highly regarded reporter in her own right, who had married the best-selling Hemingway in November 1940. Martha had won an assignment from *Collier's* in January to report on the situation in the Far East, and so Ernest, having finished *For Whom the Bell Tolls,* agreed to tag along in hopes of finding good times and maybe also to kill some time while he waited for inspiration to strike (although it never really did). To help pay his bills along the way he agreed to write some features full of local color and profound insight for the New York afternoon daily *PM,* a newspaper that has become known to posterity as an impressive but short-lived experiment in sophisticated journalism, edited by *Fortune* magazine's Ralph Ingersoll and backed by the millions of moneyed department store mogul Marshall Field.

Martha and Ernest left San Francisco on February 1 and sailed to Honolulu, where they boarded a Pan Am Clipper and headed for Hong Kong. At that time Hong Kong was the Lisbon of the Far East, so perpetually filled with tension and intrigue that no one paid any attention to anything out of the ordinary anymore; where Japanese "tourists" and British and American intelligence agents and Chinese Communists and Chiang Kai-shek's minions all mingled together, surrounded by 1.5 million hungry people whose primary concern was living until the next day. Martha reacted with marked distaste to her first exposure to Asian squalor; China, she decided, was "a hell of a thing, absolutely exhausting and appalling and discouraging and dreary (because there are four hundred million people who live worse than animals and in a state of filth and disease to break your heart)."

Ernest, though, had a pretty good time in Hong Kong. "At present," he informed Ingersoll, "the food is plentiful and good"—not to mention the liquor—"and there are some of the finest restaurants in the world in Hong Kong—both European and Chinese. There's also horse racing, cricket, rugby, association football." Hemingway estimated that there were "at least 500 Chinese millionaires living in Hong Kong," refugees from the war in the interior; and the millionaires had brought their whores with them, "another concentration—of beautiful girls from all parts of China." Less wealthy members of the community had to make do with the fifty thousand prostitutes who prowled through the city streets at night. Indeed, as far as Ernest was concerned, the only serious drawback to life in Hong Kong was the sewage disposal problem. In normal times, coolies collected the waste and sold it to farmers as fertilizer, but during an experimental two-night blackout the stuff was simply dumped in the streets and produced a minor epidemic of cholera.

From the carnal delights of Hong Kong, Ernest and Martha traveled to the Seventh War Zone to get a taste of life at the front. Here, too, Ernest found solace in the unique delicacies of Oriental cuisine. He tasted snake wine—rice wine with small snakes coiled up at the bottom of the bottle— and pronounced it good. "The snakes are dead," Hemingway explained. "They are there for medicinal purposes." He said he liked it better than the bird wine that substituted dead cuckoos for the snakes in the bottom of the bottle. After a month spent rambling about the countryside with the Kuomintang troops, Ernest and Martha flew to Chungking which Ernest saw as a "terraced, gray, bomb-spattered, fire-gutted, grim stone island." There they were granted an audience with the Generalissimo himself (impeccably dressed in a plain gray uniform, but Martha thought he "looked embalmed") and Madame Chiang Kai-shek at Chiang's mountainside mansion known as Ying Wo—"The Eagle's Nest."

Ernest sent back precisely the sort of messages Chiang wanted America to hear. "Anyone who says that the troops of the Central Government armies are not a magnificently disciplined, well trained, well officered and excellently armed defensive force has never seen any of them at the front," Ernest wrote. "But if we ceased to back them or if anything ever happened to the Generalissimo, they would be sold out very quickly." Continued American aid to Chiang, Ernest concluded, was the best guarantee against a successful Japanese move into Southeast Asia and the Dutch East Indies.

Ernest also told his American readers that one of the major impediments to a successful Chinese counteroffensive against Japan was Chiang's lack of a competent air force. The Kuomintang was particularly short of competent pilots. In fact, Chiang's pilots had long been the most atrocious collection of fliers in the world. Until 1941, Chiang had drawn nearly all his pilots from the gentry class, who considered it a sign of weakness to practice. This imprudent patrician reticence undoubtedly went far toward explaining how Chiang's pilots had managed to compile the remarkable record of destroying nearly half of their planes in accidents during takeoff or landing. When Claire Chennault arrived to assume the unenviable task of turning this mockery of modern military aviation into a decent fighting force, he discovered that only ninety-one of the Kuomintang's five hundred planes were in operating condition.

While Hemingway was in Chungking, witnessing firsthand the ineptitude of the Kuomintang air force, the persistence of Chennault and Soong paid off in Washington. Taking advantage of what one former State Department official termed "the gentlemanly collusion of all American officials concerned"—including Roosevelt, Hopkins, and Laughlin Currie—Chennault received a gift of one hundred P-40 fighter planes, and, more important, the administration's permission to recruit pilots and crews from the United States Army and Navy. On April 15, Roosevelt signed the executive order authorizing reserve officers and enlisted men to "resign" from the U.S. armed forces to join Chennault's mercenary American Volunteer Group in China. (Since this action was hardly in accordance with the United States' position as a neutral, Roosevelt's order was kept secret.) By the end of June, Chennault had obtained 112 topflight American pilots who were paid between $250 and $750 a month, with a bonus of $500 for every Japanese plane shot down. Meanwhile, at the special AVG training base established in Toungoo, Burma, the P-40s underwent a transformation that left them with painted snouts that looked like grinning sharks (a symbol borrowed from the R.A.F.'s African squadrons), and sides covered with representations of the group's mascot, a Bengal tiger with wings—the Flying Tiger—as designed by an artist from Walt Disney's studio.

Before they left Chungking, the Hemingways also met Zhou Enlai, the Chinese Communists' envoy to the Kuomintang court and their contact point with the rest of the outside world. Ernest dominated the conversation—Zhou reportedly could hardly get a word in edgewise—but Martha came away convinced that Zhou was "the one really good man we'd met in China." Her sentiments were shared by Theodore H. White, who by then was serving as *Time* magazine's correspondent in China; several decades later, White wrote that "Chou En-lai was, along with Joseph Stilwell and John F. Kennedy, one of the three great men I met and in whose presence I had had near total suspension of disbelief or questioning judgment":

> In all three cases I would now behave otherwise, but most of all in the case of Chou En-lai. I can see Chou En-lai now for what he was: a man as brilliant and ruthless as any the Communist movement has thrown up in this century. He could act with absolute daring, with the delicacy of a cat pouncing on a mouse, with the decision of a man who has thought his way through to his only course of action—and yet he was capable of warm kindness, irrepressible humanity and silken courtesy. . . . He had a way of entrancing people, of offering affection, of inviting and seeming to share confidences. And I cannot deny that he won my affection completely.

The intellectual son of a prosperous mandarin family, Zhou had absorbed the subtle nuances of Eastern culture and Western politics during his education in Japan and Europe. During his sojourn abroad he became a Communist; and upon his return to Shanghai he became a commander in the revolutionary armies and survived, by a narrow margin, the Long March of 1934–35. A tireless organizer behind the scenes, Zhou also was capable of hypnotizing an audience. When Han Suyin heard him speak for the first time, in an open-air gathering in Chungking, she was struck by his simple, spellbinding eloquence. She saw "a slim, thin-faced man with an abundance of black hair, very calm, very handsome, all his gestures supple. . . . When he stood on a table so that he could be seen by the crowd, his eyes went calmly from face to face; all of us were caught, waiting for his words. He spoke for almost four hours, and we listened, untired. He could have gone on forever. It was one of the simplest, least complicated, most unrhetorical, almost painstakingly basic speeches one could have heard. But each word counted."

Now, in the spring of 1941, Zhou was forty-three years old, and arguably the most important figure in the Chinese Communist hierarchy. He had to maintain at least a measure of amity with Chiang, who was an old friend from the days of the revolution, in order to obtain desperately needed supplies for the Communist armies while operating the Marxist underground network in those parts of China controlled by the Kuomintang. And he was responsible for maintaining a favorable image of the Chinese Communist movement in the eyes of the West; hence his gracious invitations to influential foreigners who visited Chungking—including Hemingway, White, and Wendell Willkie—to dine with him at his dilapidated residence at Number 50 in the mud-filled alley of the Tseng Chia, where Zhou (who spoke fluent English) and his guests discussed Chinese and world affairs while sitting in shabby armchairs covered with the plain blue cloth favored by workers and peasants. Outside the house, a small army of spies kept a vigilant surveillance on Zhou's comings and goings.

Some five hundred miles to the south, the Eighth Plenum of the Communist Party of Indochina, chaired by Ho Chi Minh, convened in the mountain fastness of the village of Pac Bo, in the province of Cao Bạng. "Uncle Ho," as he was already known to his friends, was convinced that the inexorable Japanese advance through Indochina was driving the native population farther and farther along the road to revolution. Ho understood that if the Party subordinated its ideology of class conflict and emphasized the nationalist character of the struggle against foreign imperialism (both Japanese and French), it could capitalize upon the rising tide of popular discontent and broaden its base of support, laying the foundation for the class struggle that must inevitably come later. Thus the Central Committee of the Party—meeting in a primitive hut, sitting on blocks of wood around a table made of bamboo—approved the policy of National Salvation (Cuu Quoc) and the establishment of the League for Vietnamese Independence, the Viet Nam Doc Lap Dong Minh, or, more simply, the Vietminh. "In the present stage," read the Committee's resolution, "nation is above all. . . . At this moment, if we do not resolve the problem of national liberation, and do not demand independence and freedom for the entire people, then not only will the entire people of our nation continue to live as beasts, but also the particular interests of individual classes will not be achieved for thousands of years either."

Working first in the villages of the northern strongholds of Cao Bang and Bac Son provinces, along the Sino-Vietnamese border, the Party would organize mass National Salvation Associations, encouraging workers, the bourgeoisie, wealthy peasants, impoverished farmers, and small landowners to unite in the patriotic struggle to free Vietnam from the French imperialists and the Japanese militarists. The estates of collaborators (of whom there were many) would be confiscated and the land distributed among the peasants. In a radio broadcast on June 6, Ho proclaimed the new policy: "The hour has struck! Raise aloft the insurrectionary banner and guide the people throughout the country to overthrow the Japanese and the French! The sacred call of the fatherland is resounding in your ears. . . . Victory to Vietnam's Revolution!"

At that moment, Ho and his Vietminh were among the least of the concerns of the government in Tokyo. Like the rest of the world's major powers, Japan was playing a risky game for the highest stakes in the spring of 1941. It was balancing its desire to reach out and grab the enticing resources of Indochina and the East Indies against its manifest reluctance to provoke the United States. Japan had leaped into the arms of the Axis powers in September 1940 on the assumption that Britain would be knocked out of the war in the near future; now it was gambling that the diplomatic benefits afforded by the Tripartite Pact—notably, Germany's recognition of Japanese supremacy in Asia—would outweigh the adverse reaction the alliance created in London and Washington.

The foremost advocate of the Tripartite Pact in Tokyo had always been mercurial Foreign Minister Yosuke Matsuoka, a former railway executive who passionately insisted that he, and he alone, held the key to the salvation of the Japanese Empire. Matsuoka once claimed to have made the decision to forge an alliance with Germany and Italy while he was on an extended fishing trip. "One of my great passions is fishing," he explained. "No other occupation enables me so completely to detach myself from the world to reach decisions through meditation. When, early in 1939, I returned home from Geneva I went away fishing six months for solitude and reflection. Afterwards I returned to Tokyo firmly convinced that Great Britain and America would eternally oppose Japan's rise in the Far East: consequently our only place is by Germany's side. Since then I have never changed my opinion." To obtain his colleagues' approval of the pact, Matsuoka had made grandiose promises that the alliance would enable Japan to fulfill at last the national vision of a Greater East Asia Co-Prosperity Sphere without recourse to hostilities. So far, nothing of the sort had happened, and so Matsuoka decided to betake himself to Berlin and Moscow in March 1941, to rescue his policy of "virile diplomacy" by obtaining tangible evidence of German and Russian goodwill.

At least, that appeared to be his goal, but Matsuoka was so impetuous and talked so much that he often managed to obscure his real meaning beneath a torrent of words. He was known in Tokyo as the Talking Machine; one bemused American correspondent described him as "a pleasant little man with spiked hair, a black pipe, and a great gift of gab." He was a flamboyant orator who enjoyed making intriguingly paradoxical statements that revealed, depending upon the judgment of the listener, either flashes of brilliant insight or glimpses into a mind on the edge of insanity. Sometimes Matsuoka lapsed into bewildering free-association, stream-of-consciousness monologues that mystified his listeners (including his diplomatic adversaries), but usually there was a calculated method behind his irrational behavior. "On the point of Mr. Matsuoka's intellectual and political honesty I am reluctant to express a doubt," reported U.S. Ambassador Joseph Grew, who had suffered through endless Matsuoka filibusters but still considered the foreign minister a personal friend. "In the political manoeuvring that constantly goes on in Tokyo he is sometimes quoted as saying one thing in one quarter while making a totally divergent statement in another quarter. He talks so flowingly and freely, by the hour if time affords, that it is inconceivable that he should never make conflicting statements."

Matsuoka had convinced himself, if no one else, that he knew the best way to handle the United States. He had spent nearly a decade in America as a young man, earning a degree from the University of Oregon (class of 1900) before returning to Japan. "It is my America and my American people that really exist," he liked to say. "There is no other America; there are no other American people." And as far as Matsuoka was concerned, the only way to earn America's respect was to "stand firm and start hitting back," so that "the American will know he's talking to a man, and you two can then talk man to man." This was where the peaceful path grew treacherous: avoiding war by employing tough talk and intimidating the United States, and restraining the militarists in Tokyo while Matsuoka achieved through diplomacy the objectives they sought—namely, economic and political supremacy in the Far East. The American half of this strategy appeared to have failed already; instead of intimidating the United States, Japan's entrance into the Tripartite Pact convinced many Americans that the government in Tokyo was no better than the despised Nazis, and thereby stimulated steps toward diplomatic confrontation in the Pacific.

As Matsuoka interpreted the delicate, ever-shifting balance of world power, Japan could never frighten the United States into recognizing her rights in South Asia without explicit support from Germany and at least an assurance of neutrality from the Soviet Union. And that was why Matsuoka stood at Tokyo Station on March 12, awaiting with undisguised excitement the train that would take him on the first leg of his mission to Moscow and Berlin. He joked with reporters, telling them that he had decided to take a European vacation because he was fatigued from his onerous official duties. "Now I have some leisure and I am taking this trip to Europe," he said, pushing back the heavy, dark-rimmed glasses he always wore. "I must return as soon as possible, as the Japanese nation seems to be looking forward to what presents I will bring back. . . . The Three-Power Pact is most important to Japan and I would not be doing justice to the Japanese nation if I did not make Hitler's personal acquaintance. . . . Hitler must be desiring to see this face of mine, though it is an uninteresting one." Matsuoka's breezy optimism notwithstanding, there were many in the Japanese nation who were also apprehensive about the commitments the unpredictable foreign minister might incur along the way; one of the leading Tokyo journals warned Matsuoka that "great prudence and mature consideration are required" on such a delicate mission, and the army sent along a watchdog, Colonel Yatsuji Nagai, to make sure Matsuoka made no rash promises regarding Singapore. (Neither the army nor the navy had any intention of attacking Singapore until Japan had either obtained American acquiescence in the move southward, or neutralized the American Pacific fleet.) On the other hand, some of Matsuoka's domestic opponents were glad to get him out of the country; they would have a freer hand to overturn his pro-Axis policy while he was gone.

After a brief stop in Moscow, where he held an inconclusive meeting with Stalin and Molotov, Matsuoka arrived in Berlin on the evening of March 26—just hours before the Simovic coup shook Yugoslavia and Hitler made the fateful decision to postpone Barbarossa. When his train pulled into the Anhalter Bahnhof, the foreign minister—dressed in the traditional black frock coat of European statesmen—was greeted by delegations of the German High Command (led by Keitel) and the Reich's civilian leadership (led by Ribbentrop), and representatives of the Hitler Youth. Off to the side, a cadre of Japanese military officers wearing long samurai swords stood at attention, near a wreath of yellow chrysanthemums arranged in the shape of the Rising Sun. Standing only five feet two inches tall, Matsuoka was almost invisible among the Nazi dignitaries who surrounded him as he walked out of the station into a carefully staged tableau filled with hundreds of thousands of flag-waving Berliners who had been dismissed early from their jobs (all places of business except food shops closed at 2 P.M. that day) and herded into position to cheer their honored Japanese guest. ("The people's welcome is very enthusiastic," noted Goebbels with satisfaction. "The Berliners are well aware of all that depends on the success of this visit.") Stirring songs of martial glory blared from the loudspeakers. The German government had spent five days decorating the Unter den Linden and the Wilhelmstrasse in preparation for Matsuoka's visit, and huge banners adorned with swastikas and the Rising Sun (and, noticeably less frequently, the Italian tricolor) flew from rooftop flagstaffs every five feet along the procession route from the Anhalter Bahnhof to the Bellevue Palace, the summer palace of Kaiser Wilhelm II. Matsuoka responded with a message to the German people, wishing them speedy victory in the war, and assuring them that "the Japanese nation is with you in joy or sorrow . . . and will not lag behind you in fidelity, courage and firm determination to arrange the world on the basis of the new order. . . . We must live in the future, not the past." That evening the Berlin cinema theaters featured the first joint German-Japanese film production, *The Daughter of the Samurai.* Harry Flannery noted that the effusively gala spectacle was in complete contrast to the modest reception afforded Molotov the previous November.

As Matsuoka had predicted, Hitler was indeed eager to see his smiling face the following day (although the interview was delayed for several hours while the plans for Operation Punishment were hurriedly set into motion). Matsuoka's visit provided a golden opportunity for Hitler personally to prod his ally into a more aggressive military stance in the Far East, where Germany had everything to gain and nothing to lose by embroiling Japan with the United States and Britain. "It is in our interest," the German Naval Staff had decided in January, "to encourage Japan to take any initiative she considers within her power in the Far Eastern area, as this would be most likely to keep American forces from the European theater in addition to weakening and tying down British forces." The Fuehrer himself had issued a directive of similar import on March 5, stating that "it must be the aim of the collaboration based on the Three Power Pact to induce Japan as soon as possible to take active measures in the Far East. . . . The seizure of Singapore as the key British position in the Far East would mean a decisive success for the entire conduct of war of the Three Powers." "Japan must take steps to capture Singapore as soon as possible, since the opportunity is more favorable than it will ever be again," the Fuehrer and his generals concluded on March 18, while Matsuoka was still en route to Berlin. "The entire British fleet is tied down; the U.S.A. is not prepared to wage war on Japan; the U.S. fleet is inferior to the Japanese fleet." (Certainly Churchill was not unmindful of the impending threat to the well-being of the British Empire in the Far East. On February 15 he had advised Roosevelt bluntly that "the weight of the Japanese navy, if thrown against us, would confront us with situations beyond the scope of our naval resources," forcing a disastrous diversion of warships from the Mediterranean to protect the empire's trade and communications routes in Asia.)

So Ribbentrop had every reason to greet Matsuoka as an honored guest, assuring him that England was not to be feared, that "Germany was in the final phase of her battle against England. . . . the war had already been definitely won for the Axis." He advised the Japanese army to seize Singapore immediately and ensure Japanese military supremacy in the Far East. The Fuehrer personally guaranteed Matsuoka that Japan need not concern itself with American reprisals. "If Japan got into a conflict with the United States," Hitler promised, "Germany on her part would take the necessary steps at once. It made no difference with whom the United States first came into conflict, whether it was with Germany or with Japan." Eight months later, when he was finally ready to confront America, Hitler would make good on this pledge.

Flattered by the Nazis' attentions, Matsuoka went as far as he dared to pledge Japanese support for Germany's war effort. Personally, he said, he recognized the virtues of an attack upon Singapore. A nation must take certain risks to achieve greatness. But, alas, there were others surrounding the Imperial presence in Tokyo, old men who lacked the courage or the inclination to confront the British, weak-kneed intellectuals who feared the prospect of war with the Anglo-Saxon imperialists. Despite Hitler's assurances, Matsuoka was especially careful not to commit Japan to any course of action that might lead to war with the United States. So, regretfully, he admitted that "at the present moment he could under these circumstances make no pledge on behalf of the Japanese Empire that it would take action. . . . He could make no definite commitment, but he would promise that he personally would do his utmost for the ends that had been mentioned."

As far as the Germans were concerned, Matsuoka was a profound disappointment. Japan appeared to be no more capable of making swift decisions than the Italians were of making wise ones. Hitler came away from his discussions with Matsuoka convinced that his ally was not to be trusted; upon learning that Matsuoka was a practicing Roman Catholic who nevertheless had offered sacrifices to the Sun Goddess before leaving Japan, Hitler decided that the foreign minister combined "the hypocrisy of an American Bible missionary with the craftiness of a Japanese Asiatic." Before Matsuoka left Berlin for a return visit to Moscow, however, Ribbentrop dropped heavy-handed hints of the impending German invasion of the Soviet Union; the Nazis wanted to make certain that their Japanese allies were not taken completely by surprise. If Matsuoka understood what was afoot—and no matter what his critics said, the foreign minister was nobody's fool, except, perhaps, his own—his grand scheme of a world divided among the four totalitarian powers would surely vanish in the aftermath of Barbarossa. It was equally evident that Japan's diplomatic obligations to Germany under the Tripartite Pact would subject any proposed Soviet-Japanese neutrality agreement to serious strain.

Yet Matsuoka decided to continue his quest in Moscow, and there really was no reason why he should not. If a German invasion of the Soviet Union freed Britain to release additional forces to the Far East, Japan doubtless would find it useful to have neutralized the Russian threat to its western flank on the Asian mainland. And a tangible demonstration of Soviet goodwill would give Japan a freer hand to bring the war with China to an end; even more important, it would strengthen Tokyo's position in negotiations with the United States.

For six days in the Kremlin, Matsuoka and Molotov labored to bring forth an agreement, making little headway until, shortly before the Japanese minister was scheduled to depart, Stalin suddenly consented to compromise upon the territorial disputes (centering upon conflicting claims to oil-rich Sakhalin Island off the Siberian coast) that had been blocking an agreement. On Easter Sunday morning, April 13, Stalin called Matsuoka to the Kremlin and offered him a five-year neutrality pact whose terms provided that Japan and the Soviet Union would not attack each other, and if either nation became "the object of hostilities on the part of one or several third Powers, the other . . . will observe neutrality throughout the duration of the conflict." Matsuoka sent an urgent message to Tokyo requesting formal approval to enter into the agreement. (While he waited, he was so excited about his triumph that he took the opportunity to drop in on the American ambassador in Moscow and tell him how devoted he—Matsuoka—was to improving relations between their respective nations.) After Prince Konoye hurriedly obtained the consent of the Emperor in Tokyo, the neutrality pact was signed at a raucous alcoholic celebration in the Kremlin that afternoon.

As he tipsily toasted the treaty, Matsuoka shouted, "Banzai for his

Majesty the Emperor!" and then, turning to Stalin, he added with extraordinary indiscretion, "The treaty has been made. If I lie, my head shall be yours. If you lie, be sure I will come for your head." To threaten Stalin's head, even in jest, was a liberty few men could take and survive; it was a measure of Stalin's desire to consummate the neutrality agreement that he allowed the remark to pass with only a mild rebuke: "My head is important to my country. So is yours to your country. Let's take care to keep both our heads on our shoulders." (Following close upon Matsuoka's lengthy meetings with Hitler in Berlin, the sight of the Japanese foreign minister and Stalin drinking to each other's future well-being did nothing to persuade American State Department officials in Washington of Japan's peaceful intentions.)

Liquor flowed so freely that Matsuoka's train—the venerable Trans-Siberian Express, with its old-fashioned samovars and creaking wooden cars of pre-1914 vintage—had to delay its departure for more than an hour while the foreign minister made his way to the Yaroslavsky station late that afternoon. Henry Cassidy, an American reporter who was waiting on the station platform, witnessed Matsuoka's belated arrival at the head of a procession of automobiles flying the Japanese flag and filled with exuberant (and drunken) Japanese officials. As they stood around congratulating one another before Matsuoka boarded the train, suddenly and quite unexpectedly Stalin and Molotov appeared. The sixty-one-year-old dictator, who was a smaller man (about five feet six) than most people expected, had a distinctive bearlike walk; he swung his arms stiffly and very low by his side, and put his right arm forward at the same time as his right foot, instead of vice versa like most people. "Every time I have seen Stalin," wrote Cassidy, "my chief impression has been that the man does not look real. He has been portrayed and cartooned so often, and resembles so closely all the pictures and caricatures and busts of himself, that he always seems to be an animated figure from a printed page. That day, with his narrow eyes squinting and his sallow face pale in the sunlight, he appeared even more unreal. His uniform, too, of khaki kepi and greatcoat, over black boots, but with no insignia whatsoever, looked like a doll's dress." He wore a brown visored cap over his gray hair.

Never before had Stalin honored a guest by personally seeing him off at the railway station, and his inexperience (and the effects of the vodka) showed in his awkward gestures. After locating Matsuoka, Stalin gave him several affectionate bear hugs ("We shall go together along the same road," Stalin declared with calculated cordiality), then went stiffly around the circle, shaking hands with the other Japanese. Since he knew little Japanese and they knew almost no Russian, most of the conversation on both sides consisted of hearty grins, bows, and repeated grunts of "Ah . . . ha" (with the emphasis on the "ha"), accompanied by enthusiastic backslapping. Stalin gave Colonel Nagai an affectionate smack on the cheek as he bellowed, "The reason England's in trouble today is because she has a low opinion of soldiers." Then Stalin picked out the assistant German military attaché, Colonel Krebs, dressed in a long gray coat and standing rigidly at attention. As he peered intently into the soldier's face, Stalin asked, "German?" The man nodded. "German?" Stalin repeated. "Yes, sir," the officer replied in halting Russian, saluting. Stalin grasped his hand firmly and said in a loud voice, "Ah . . . ha. We shall be friends with you." The German, who apparently had no idea what Stalin's carefully staged performance meant, replied with a brisk salute. Stalin laughed and went on shaking hands.

"There is nothing to fear in the whole world," cried an ebullient Matsuoka as he clambered aboard the train. The Georgia-born Stalin came with him for a moment and said merrily, "You are an Asiatic. I am an Asiatic. Out there," and he gestured to the platform, "are all those Europeans." Then Stalin descended the train and went home in his armorplated Packard with its three-inch-thick bulletproof windows. A few minutes later, after the train pulled out of the station, Matsuoka turned to his traveling companion and predicted confidently, "Now the stage is set. Next I will go to Washington."

As a matter of fact, upon leaving Japan in March, Matsuoka reportedly had declared that he would be willing to extend his tour to London and Washington if the British and American governments invited him; "the best way to solve Japanese-American differences," said the foreign minister's chief secretary, "would be for President Roosevelt or Secty. of State Cordell Hull to meet the Foreign Minister at Hawaii and thresh out the whole problem."

Neither Roosevelt nor Hull, however, had any intention of meeting Matsuoka at Hawaii, in Washington, or anywhere else. On March 14, one day after Matsuoka left Tokyo for Berlin, the recently appointed Japanese ambassador to the United States, Admiral Kichisaburo Nomura, called at the White House to assure Roosevelt and Secretary Hull that most of Matsuoka's belligerent pro-Axis rhetoric was designed "for home consumption because he is ambitious politically, but Japan herself cannot maintain such ambitious plans." The foreign minister's trip to Berlin, Nomura explained, was nothing more than a diplomatic courtesy extended to Japan's most powerful friend in Europe.

Roosevelt replied by reminding Nomura that Japan's alliance with Germany and Italy had cost it considerable sympathy in the United States. (As evidence, Roosevelt could have shown Nomura the results of a Gallup poll released the previous day. Taken in early March, the poll revealed that American public opinion was indeed hardening against Japan; for the first time, a plurality of American voters were willing to risk war with Japan to keep it from taking Singapore and the Dutch East Indies.) Cordell Hull, the former Tennessee congressman who, after eight years of on-the-job training at the State Department, still did not understand what international power politics was all about, listened approvingly as the President informed Nomura that the first step in restoring amicable relations between Washington and Tokyo would be "the removal of suspicion and fear regarding Japan's intentions."

As far as the U. S. State Department was concerned, however, there would be snowball fights in hell long before the Japanese government proved itself trustworthy. Matsuoka could argue that "we want nothing from Americans and leave them alone. They should follow our example, and leave us alone," but in the view of Washington it was not that simple. The top-level Far Eastern experts who labored at Foggy Bottom were, almost to a man, sympathetic toward China and hostile to Japan. Their doubts regarding Japan's sincerity and desire for peace were fueled by the Magic intercepts that first became available to State in January 1941; now they could observe for themselves the gaps (occasionally chasms) that yawned between the Foreign Office's instructions to the Japanese ambassador in Washington and Tokyo's *real* intentions. (Although the temptation to condemn Japanese duplicity probably was irresistible, it was also grossly unfair to the Japanese. The very foundations of civilized diplomatic intercourse would collapse if envoys were deprived of the opportunity to knowingly mislead their hosts.)

The anti-Japanese clique at the State Department was led by Dr. Stanley Hornbeck, the senior political adviser in the Far Eastern Division, and a man who combined a virulent antipathy toward Japan with an almost total lack of personal charm. "In his official capacity Dr. Hornbeck was overbearing and sometimes vindictive," wrote John Paton Davies, who joined the China Desk as a junior officer in October 1940. "I suspect this came from a suppressed realization that his recognition as a great scholar-statesman was thwarted by his own inadequacies. The man was, unhappily, not more than a vigorous pedant." Assistant Secretary of State Breckinridge Long, who had served in the State Department during the First World War, remembered that Hornbeck had been rejected for a diplomatic post at that time; "his temperament and all were unsatisfactory to us," Long claimed. "However, during the Harding regime he was taken in and has been here ever since. And he is a rather dangerous man, in my opinion, when delicate matters are concerned in connection with which he has a violent prejudice." Raised in China, Hornbeck despised the Japanese militarists whom he believed were engaged in a far-reaching plot to turn the Far East into their own private feudal hinterland. Hornbeck's assistant was the fastidious and arrogant Alger Hiss, whom Davies described as "a composed and tweedy young man looking like a college instructor reading through a pile of term papers." Cognizant of Hornbeck's prejudices, Roosevelt occasionally attempted to circumvent him by dealing directly with the titular chief of the Far Eastern Division, Maxwell

Hamilton, but Hamilton was only marginally less China-oriented than Hornbeck.

Together, Hornbeck and Hamilton prodded Hull along the path the secretary probably would have chosen to travel anyway. An old Wilsonian who loved the sound of his own moralistic rhetoric (one cabinet colleague complained that Cordell often assumed the air of a Christian martyr), Hull had long ago judged and condemned the slippery Japanese as transgressors who must not be allowed to prosper from their sinful deeds. Shortly before Ambassador Nomura arrived in Washington in February, Hull sent Roosevelt a lengthy memorandum (drafted largely by Hamilton and Hornbeck), outlining—as if it were a legal brief against a criminal—the State Department's case against Japan. "The first fundamental," it stated, "is that since 1931 Japan has been dominated more and more by the military group—a group which finds adherents in all classes of Japanese society, the soldier, the sailor, the merchant, the industrialist, the farmer, et cetera, et cetera. This group sets a peculiarly high value on the use of force as an instrument both in national and in international affairs. As Japan's military adventuring on the Asiatic mainland and southward has proceeded, the unmistakable trend in Japan has been toward an authoritarian control with the military group coming more and more to the front":

> It seems clear that Japan's military leaders are bent on conquest—just as are Germany's. They demand that this country make concessions: that we give up principles, rights, interests: that we stand aside while Japan proceeds by force to subjugate neighboring areas and, working in partnership with Germany, contributes to the establishing of a new "world order": even that we facilitate their efforts by promising to give them financial assistance for the exploitation of areas which they expect to conquer. Is there anything that can stop this aggressively moving force—other than the resistance of a stronger obstacle or the resistance of a greater force?

These were the men with whom Matsuoka intended to seek peace by "standing firm and hitting back." Nor did Japan have many friends at the White House, where the powerful China Lobby held sway. Even beyond considerations of Japan's dalliance with Nazi Germany, these men cast a jaundiced eye at Matsuoka's neutrality pact with Stalin because it threatened to cut off aid from the one nation—the Soviet Union—that had done more to supply Chiang with military goods than even the United States. All in all, there may well have been more anti-Japanese sentiment in the Roosevelt administration (excluding the President himself) than there was anti-American sentiment in the Konoye cabinet.

Behind the scenes, however, and outside the channels of formal diplomacy, there was one initiative under way in the spring of 1941 to avert a head-on collision between Japan and the United States. Late in 1940, a pair of Roman Catholic missionary priests, Bishop James Edward Walsh and Father James M. Drought of the Maryknoll Foreign Mission Society, discussed the ominous trend of Japanese-American relations with government officials (including Matsuoka, who volubly professed his willingness to improve relations with America) and businessmen in Tokyo. The priests returned to America in January 1941, laden with a series of proposals that their Japanese contacts had put forth—unofficially—as the possible basis for an equitable settlement.

Unwilling to close any avenue to peace, Roosevelt received the priests and passed their memorandum along to Hull, who was not quite certain what to do with it, either. (By this time, Hull was getting fed up with all the semiofficial negotiations going on outside regular State Department channels: Harry Hopkins flying off to England, Laughlin Currie closeted with Chiang in China, and now these New York priests poaching on his turf. But that was the way the President liked to do business; besides, Roosevelt never did have an overabundance of confidence in Hull.) Encouraged by Hornbeck and Hamilton, the secretary concluded that in its present form, which included vague provisions for a Far Eastern "Monroe Doctrine" and Sino-Japanese cooperation against the spread of communism, the Walsh-Drought memorandum could not serve as a basis for negotiations. "I am skeptical whether the plan offered is a practicable one at this time," Hull advised the President, adding later that "it was much less accommodating than we had been led to believe it would be, and most of its provisions were all that the ardent Japanese imperialists could want." Nevertheless, Hull held the door open for future proposals: "I feel that we should not discourage those Japanese who may be working toward bringing about a change in the course which their country is following."

In the meantime, Hull initiated a series of secret conversations with Nomura in the privacy of Hull's room in the Wardman Park Hotel. A man of unimpeachable integrity who had preceded Matsuoka in the Foreign Office, Nomura had known Roosevelt for years; when he paid his first official call upon the President in February, Roosevelt genially told him that in view of their respective naval backgrounds, he would call Nomura "Admiral" rather than "Ambassador." Nomura got along well on a personal level with both the President and Hull. "He was tall, robust, in fine health, with an open face," recalled Hull. "He spoke a certain—sometimes an uncertain—amount of English. His outstanding characteristic was solemnity, but he was much given to a mirthless chuckle and to bowing. I credit Nomura with having been honestly sincere in trying to avoid war between his country and mine." Although he had not sought this posting to Washington—it had been Matsuoka's idea, of course—Nomura was determined to do whatever he could to settle the two nations' differences peacefully. "I am going to the United States for peace and not for war," he told reporters when he stopped in Honolulu en route to Washington.

"There must be an understanding on both sides." It would not be easy, for Nomura had been given the unenviable task of trying to persuade the United States to accept Japan's domination of East Asia.

Early in April, the course of the Hull-Nomura talks was interrupted by the reappearance of the Walsh memorandum in a slightly different form. Unofficially entitled the "Draft Understanding," it remained infuriatingly vague on several points of vital importance, but in its main outlines it required Japan to refrain from the use of force in the Far East, in return for which the United States would restore normal trade relations with Japan (insofar as it was economically practicable), help Japan acquire the raw materials it needed from Southeast Asia, and convince Chiang Kai-shek to make peace with Tokyo on pain of losing all American assistance if he refused. Hornbeck's coterie rejected this entire proposal outright, but Hull insisted on keeping the talks alive, and therein lay the seeds of the series of misunderstandings that destroyed the last remaining vestiges of goodwill between the two nations.

When he next conferred with Nomura, on April 14, Hull suggested that the admiral send the Draft Understanding to Tokyo to see if it might form a basis for negotiations. For his part, Hull had no intention of using it for that purpose, but he neglected to inform Nomura of that fact. Apparently the secretary simply wanted to sound out the Japanese reaction to the priests' proposal. Unfortunately, the Japanese government received the distinct impression that the document was an official American initiative.

Two days later, after the Japanese-Soviet neutrality pact had been publicly announced, Hull handed Nomura another document, so one-sided in its adherence to American diplomatic objectives that it could scarcely be reconciled with the Draft Understanding. It was the sort of unequivocal proclamation of moral rectitude that Hull so dearly loved to deliver. Known to posterity as the Four Principles, the memorandum called upon Japan to join America in affirming its "respect for the territorial integrity and the sovereignty of each and all nations," "support of the principle of non-interference in the internal affairs of other countries," "support of the principle of equality, including equality of commercial opportunity," and "non-disturbance of the *status quo* in the Pacific except as the *status quo* may be altered by peaceful means."

At this point, Nomura compounded Hull's earlier blunder by neglecting to send a copy of Hull's Four Principles to his government in Tokyo. Instead, Prime Minister Konoye received only the Draft Understanding, along with certain suggestions for revisions that might render it more palatable to the United States. Completely unaware of Hull's tough talk of April 16—which represented the *real* American position—Konoye was left with a wholly unwarranted, optimistic view of the negotiations in Washington.

Suddenly it appeared that Japan enjoyed the luxury of choosing from two attractive alternatives. On the one hand, Matsuoka's triumph in Moscow, which ostensibly protected Japan's northern flank on the Asian mainland, encouraged the more aggressive military leaders to embark upon a full-scale assault upon Southeast Asia. Yet this would surely entail a confrontation with Britain (which, contrary to Hitler's and Matsuoka's predictions, was displaying a discomfiting ability to withstand everything Germany could throw at it). More to the point, an all-out move southward probably would embroil Japan with the United States as well. The other option, given new life by the Draft Understanding and Nomura's reports of his conversations with Hull, led toward a reconciliation with the United States. After all, Japan still depended heavily upon imports from America to fuel its military machine; the Imperial Army was still bogged down in the China quagmire and was in no position to fight another major power at the moment; and the U. S. Pacific Fleet stationed at Pearl Harbor was the nearest, most serious threat to the security of Japan's island empire. Even General Tojo was prepared to strike a deal with the United States if it would enable Japan to bring the war with China to an honorable conclusion. But could the United States be trusted? Certainly the Japanese government was completely baffled by the unconventional behavior of President Roosevelt, who with one breath assured Nomura of his friendship for Japan, and with the next belabored the poor ambassador with violent criticisms of the Tripartite Pact.

These were, in the words of veteran diplomat and historian Herbert Feis, the two faces of Japanese diplomacy that were glaring at each other in the spring of 1941: "Two ladders were being built for history; no one knew which would be used." The only course upon which Konoye's government could agree was to move cautiously, keep its powder dry, and await the outcome of events abroad. Hence an April 17 army-navy draft policy proposal recommended with conspicuous equivocation that Japan continue to employ diplomatic means to obtain its objectives in Southeast Asia while strengthening its defense posture "for the sake of the empire's self-existence and self-defense." Japan would employ its military might only if the United States, Britain, or the Netherlands imposed stringent trade embargoes that robbed the Japanese Empire of essential raw materials, or "if the United States, alone or in cooperation with Britain, the Netherlands, and China, gradually increases its pressures to contain the empire, making it impossible for the empire any longer to bear those pressures in the light of its self-defense."

Upon his return to Tokyo on April 22, Matsuoka flew into a rage when he learned of the Draft Understanding and the Washington talks that had been taking place without his knowledge. Any moves toward compromise with the United States would undermine the very foundations of his pro-Axis policy. That evening, he told an emergency session of the cabinet that he flatly opposed the entire concept of the Draft Understanding. "I cannot agree to this, whatever you Army and Navy people say," Matsuoka shouted. "First of all, what about our treaty with Germany and Italy? In the last war the United States made use of Japan through the Ishii-Lansing agreement, and when the war was over, the United States broke it. This is an old trick of theirs." Despite the foreign minister's outburst (followed by his decision to go home and go to bed to recover from his arduous journey), the government formally approved an amended version of the Draft Understanding. As the head of the Foreign Office, Matsuoka had the responsibility of transmitting this decision to Washington, but he obdurately refused to do so and continued to press for a reconsideration of the decision (going so far as to frighten the wits out of poor Emperor Hirohito with irresponsible talk of war) until Konoye, frustrated beyond the limits of his endurance, asked the military chieftains to issue an ultimatum to the recalcitrant Matsuoka.

On May 12, Nomura informed Hull that Japan had accepted the main outlines of the Draft Understanding. Hull was, to say the least, unimpressed with the latest Japanese proposal. "Very few rays of hope shone from the document," he concluded as he searched in vain for any recognition of the Four Principles, the immutable foundations of American Far Eastern policy he had explained so patiently to Nomura. Japan still refused to abandon the Tripartite Pact, refused to get out of China except on Tokyo's own terms, and refused to abjure the use of force in Southeast Asia. "Everything is going hellward," Hull muttered as he sank into a deep funk.

Nevertheless, the secretary decided to carry on his talks with Nomura, to explore each controversial issue in excruciating detail to keep the negotiations alive. Back in Tokyo, meanwhile, Matsuoka—whom Hitler was still prodding about Singapore and Japan's obligations to Germany under the terms of the Tripartite Pact—continued to do everything he could to sabotage the discussions in Washington. The strain was pushing the high-strung foreign minister over the edge; during a conversation on May 14 with Ambassador Grew, Matsuoka blurted out that the "manly, decent and reasonable" thing for America to do would be to declare war on Germany, to stand up and fight like a manly nation instead of provoking Hitler and hiding behind the curtain of neutrality. When Grew protested this characterization of American policy, Matsuoka withdrew his remarks and explained that he had meant to say "discreet" instead of "decent," and besides, he had been speaking as "a world citizen" instead of a diplomat. "He expresses his honest hate of the so-called correct attitudes taken by many diplomats which 'hardly gets us anywhere,' " reported Grew; "he acknowledges that he often indulges in thoughts of one thousand or two or even three thousand years, and if this strikes me as a sign of insanity, he cannot help it as he is made that way." Grew concluded that so long as Matsuoka held office, he would refuse to abandon his pro-Axis policy, and would persist in "a course fraught with the gravest dangers [rather] than to chart a new course which would constitute admission on his part that he had completely misread the character and temper of the American people . . ."

Despite Matsuoka's obstinance, Grew—who was one of the ablest American diplomats of this century—believed that war between the United States and Japan was far from inevitable. "Japan's foreign policy and diplomacy are essentially susceptible to world developments and events," the ambassador informed Washington. "Future trends will inevitably be influenced by the trend of the European war as well as by trends in American policy and action. The outcome in Japan is therefore almost wholly unpredictable but I would express the opinion that under present conditions Japan is highly malleable."

But no less dangerous for that. In the event war with the United States should prove unavoidable, Japan would require some feasible plan to strike a sudden blow to neutralize American naval forces in the Far East. And so, since the first week of January, Admiral Isoroku Yamamoto, commander in chief of Japan's Combined Fleet, had been planning a surprise attack upon the U.S. Pacific Fleet. The assignment was not one from which Yamamoto derived any pleasure; he recognized that Japan would have only the slimmest of chances to emerge victorious from a war with the United States. But, like Canaris and Halder in Germany, Yamamoto loyally carried out his duty to his country. If the Imperial cabinet decided to send the Japanese armies southward toward the stronghold of Singapore and the rich resources of the Dutch East Indies, there must first be an assurance that the American navy would not interfere with the operation. After carefully considering the alternatives, Yamamoto concluded that Japanese forces should "do our very best at the outset of the war with the United States . . . to decide the fate of the war on the very first day." Specifically, Yamamoto recommended that Japanese warplanes "fiercely attack and destroy the U.S. main fleet at the outset of the war, so that the morale of the U.S. Navy and her people" would "sink to the extent that it could not be recovered."

13

Tragedy in Greece

"For the past fortnight, Londoners have been listening
to the unnatural silence at nights and wondering what was
brewing. Now they know . . ."
                    —MOLLIE PANTER-DOWNES, April 6, 1941

Tuesday, March 25. Greek Independence Day. Gray clouds hung low over Athens as King George II laid a wreath on the Tomb of the Unknown Soldier and then spoke to his people via radio, extolling their courage and exhorting them to dedicate all their remaining strength to the final campaign to defeat the Axis enemy that surrounded Greece. Hearing rumors of Nazi panzer divisions poised hungrily on the northern borders, an anxious American observer in Athens wondered, "Still free but for how long?" From London, Churchill sent characteristically effusive congratulations to the valiant people of Greece: "One hundred and twenty years ago, all that was noblest in England strove in the cause of Greek independence and rejoiced in its achievement. Today that epic struggle is being repeated against greater odds, but with equal courage and with no less certainty of success. We in England know that the cause for which Byron died is a sacred cause: we are resolved to sustain it."

Less than forty-eight hours later, the world learned of the Simovic coup in Yugoslavia. This unanticipated bonus from the Balkans, where a felicitous combination of stubborn Greek valor and Serbian bellicosity appeared to have stopped the Nazi juggernaut cold, helped make the last days of March a time for unrestrained rejoicing in Britain, a euphoric week "of almost pure jam." In East Africa, British armies completed the rout of demoralized Italian forces under the Duke of Aosta and restored Emperor Haile Selassie to the throne of Abyssinia. Then, in a totally unexpected coup, the Royal Navy struck the Italian fleet a devastating blow in the Mediterranean, off Cape Matapan. Encouraged (pushed, really) by the Germans to disrupt the British convoys that were ferrying troops from Alexandria to Greece, Italy had put a battlefleet to sea and pointed it toward the Aegean. The Italian naval commanders were entirely unaware that British cryptographers had broken their cipher. Carrying a detailed description of the movements and battle plans of Italy's fleet, Admiral

Cunningham's Mediterranean force slipped secretly out of Alexandria harbor during the night of March 27 and caught the Italians completely by surprise at ten thirty the following evening. Aboard the H.M.S. *Valiant*, Midshipman Prince Philip of Greece was given the honor of turning a searchlight on the enemy cruisers to give the British gunners an illuminated target. "The Italians were quite unprepared," remarked Cunningham in his account of the battle. "Their guns were trained fore and aft. They were helplessly shattered before they could put up any resistance. . . . The plight of the Italian cruisers was indescribable. One saw whole turrets and masses of other heavy debris whirling through the air and splashing into the sea, and in a short time the ships themselves were nothing but flowing torches and on fire from stem to stern. The whole action lasted no more than a few minutes." One Italian cruiser reportedly was struck by at least seven 15-inch shells simultaneously and erupted in a massive burst of flame. It was, Cunningham reported, "not a pleasant spectacle."

Next morning the sea was littered with rafts, wreckage, and corpses, all the debris covered with a thin film of oil. Cunningham's attack force lost only one airplane; but Italy had lost three cruisers, two destroyers, and approximately 2,400 officers and men. Intimidated by this crushing defeat, the remnants of the Italian navy remained within the shelter of their coastal defenses for the remainder of the year, a development that, as it turned out, gave the British Mediterranean Fleet an invaluable breathing space in the chaotic days to come.

It was the worst naval disaster in Italy's brief national history, and the most spectacular British victory in the Mediterranean since Nelson defeated Napoleon's fleet at the Battle of the Nile in 1798. Churchill greeted the news with howls of delight. "The tearing up of the paper fleet of Italy," he chortled. "How lucky the Italians came in." The victory inspired him to dispatch a gleeful telegram to Roosevelt, and a stern admonishment to Matsuoka, warning the Japanese diplomat (who had just completed his first round of meetings in Berlin) that Britain was not dead yet. According to Churchill's private secretary, Winston spent the rest of the blissful weekend at his country estate "pacing—or rather tripping—up and down the Great Hall to the sound of the gramophone (playing martial airs, waltzes and the most vulgar kind of brass-band songs) deep in thought all the while."

For Italy, Matapan was one more corrosive link in a long chain of catastrophic defeats. Before the war began, Mussolini had confided to his official biographer that he was "obsessed by this wild desire—it consumes my whole being. I want to make a mark on my era with my will, like a lion with its claw! A mark like this . . ." and he raked his fingernail across the back of a chair. Thus far he had made a mark of a far less savage sort; he had become the most widely ridiculed public figure in the world. During the first week of March, Mussolini had betaken himself to the Albanian front, where he ordered an immediate assault "at whatever cost" upon the entrenched Greek defenses. The Duce knew that Hitler would soon march against Greece, and he yearned desperately to achieve a spectacular breakthrough before the Germans stole the glory (and the ascendancy over the Balkans) that rightfully belonged to Rome. But the Greek lines held fast throughout a week of furious Italian attacks, and Mussolini, dispirited and despondent once more, could only walk through the ranks of the wounded blackshirts, scattering words of consolation: "I am Il Duce, and I bring you the greetings of the fatherland." The soldiers muttered under their breath that their leader's fabled presence had brought them nothing but more bad luck.

Mussolini hid his disappointment behind blustering proclamations that Italy would continue to fight to the last drop of blood. In his distinctive wooden voice, which bore an eerie resemblance to the clicking of castanets, he vowed to remain faithful to his German allies. Not even American aid could save Britain now, the Duce assured the Italian people; he haughtily dismissed the United States as "a political and financial oligarchy dominated by Jewry through a very personal dictatorship." But behind the rhetoric loomed a growing tide of discontent on the home front. Constantly rising prices and shortages of coal, oil, and a variety of consumer goods produced widespread hardship, irritation, and impatience with the Fascist regime. Italians could still purchase new Fiats for a reasonable price ($1,500), but the cars came without tires because there was no rubber; old hot-water bottles were cut up to patch inner tubes. After the invasion of Yugoslavia disrupted normal channels of supply, the civilian ration of gasoline was cut to five gallons per month. Driving after ten o'clock at night was forbidden. Food was strictly rationed: in February, individual allotments of olive oil and butter were cut in half; government decrees forbade the baking of fresh pastry made with milk or fats; ice cream disappeared from the market. Claiming that the consumption of luxury items in wartime was "a voluptuous habit, confined to the well-to-do classes," the government prohibited the sale of panettone, an extremely popular sweet bread filled with raisins. Diners at Alfredo's discovered that the restaurant's famous succulent, golden fettucine was no longer available; all they could get was a hundred grams of gray spaghetti. The magnificent sweeping lawns of the Villa Borghese and the aristocratic ancient parks of Rome were turned into vegetable gardens, crammed with humble beets and potatoes.

To make matters worse, wealthy industrialists were piling up exorbitant war profits while impoverished workers suffered and starved, and the twenty thousand arrogant German "observers" who had invaded Rome (to stiffen Mussolini's resolve, teach Fascist antiaircraft gunners how to shoot, and in general remind the Italian people which side they were fighting on) were getting on everyone's nerves. Nazi women auxiliaries, armed with German paper money, denuded Rome's department stores, and insisted that Italian dressmakers provide them with the latest German styles, which ran heavily to buttons, bows, ribbons, and garish flowers. "The Germans come in," complained one exasperated Roman shopkeeper, "and buy up all our stuff with those tourist marks of theirs. Italians simply haven't the money to buy, so these *bestie* get everything we have on our shelves. As it is, we haven't got much and pretty soon we won't have anything. I'm not just talking about my shop. I'm talking about Italy." During blackouts in the Eternal City, vandals scratched anti-Nazi slogans on the walls: A BASSO I TEDESCHI ("Down with the Germans") and A BASSO HITLER; Marshal Badoglio, the old and not terribly competent soldier whom Mussolini had cast aside for his blunt criticism of the Fascist regime, was forbidden to leave his house because the crowds greeted him with sympathetic cheers whenever he appeared in the streets. "Black days for our Axis friend," noted Goebbels in his diary. "We shall have to take action soon, if only to repair the damage."

When he received Hitler's letter informing him of the Wehrmacht's plans for Operation Punishment, Mussolini rejected the Fuehrer's proposal of a simultaneous Italian advance through Albania. Unwilling to suffer another catastrophic defeat that might totally undermine his sagging prestige, Mussolini decided to wait until Greek resistance started to crumble before launching his own attack, just as he had done in France the previous year.

By April 5, most of the British forces who had been transported from Egypt to Greece—three divisions and an armored brigade, approximately sixty thousand men (over half of whom were Australians or New Zealanders)—had moved into position along the central sector of the Aliákmon line, though most were not yet fully dug in. The odds did not appear promising. A reporter asked an Australian commander along the front what he thought of the prospects for victory. "Oh, all right," came the laconic reply as the officer looked out over his thin lines. "But you like to see a man or two about—and some equipment." The Greek high command still had not made up its mind whether to withdraw all its skeleton force from Thrace and eastern Macedonia, or rush reinforcements to the border regions to try to hold their forward positions against an expected German thrust from Bulgaria. No matter how the Greeks divided their troops, however, the numbers simply were not there. Recent losses in Albania had decimated their reserves, and stocks of ammunition were running perilously low. Poised across the frontier in Bulgaria, ready to push into Greece and southern Yugoslavia, stood General List's veteran Wehrmacht force of fifteen divisions, four of which were armored. Despite the overwhelming German superiority on the ground, the rugged mountainous terrain, so ably suited to defense, might have afforded the British

and the Greeks a fighting chance, were it not for the appalling disparity
in air power. Even though he expected that the battle would be won in
the air, Churchill admitted that the R.A.F. strength in Greece totaled only
seven squadrons—eighty aircraft, many of which, although technically
operative, were frankly obsolescent—against (according to Churchill's
own estimate) nearly eight hundred Luftwaffe planes.

Shortly after five o'clock on Palm Sunday morning, April 6, the German minister in Athens, Victor Prinz zu Erbach-Schonberg, telephoned
Premier Koryzis and requested a meeting. At five forty-five, Erbach-
Schonberg bowed stiffly and read the premier a brief message explaining
that Germany was, at that moment, invading Greece because the Greek
government had forsaken its status as a neutral by permitting British
forces to land upon its territory. The Nazi envoy hastened to add that the
Reich did not really look upon the Greek people as its enemy; the invasion
was aimed solely at the British. Thirty minutes later, the Greek minister
in Berlin listened as Foreign Minister Joachim von Ribbentrop coldly
recited a similar seven-page diatribe, concluding with a pledge to deliver
Greece from the British intruders by driving them (and whatever Greeks
happened to be in the way) into the sea.

In Athens it was a beautiful bright morning, the air full of the sweet-
ness of wisteria in full bloom, a tantalizing promise of spring after the long
long winter. Two hundred miles to the north, along the Bulgarian frontier,
three separate mechanized Wehrmacht columns already had crossed the
border at five fifteen and were grinding south and westward toward the
mountain passes and across the Struma River on the invasion route that
led into Thrace and Macedonia, where the Greek defenses had been left
woefully undermanned. But along the Metaxas Line, at the Rupel Pass and
in the forts that straddled the Struma, 150 Greek volunteers had taken an
oath to die before they let the Germans through the narrow passes. These
men knew that they would have to absorb the full impact of the German
advance with no hope of support, that there would be no reinforcements
to rescue them. In their last days they sent their belongings to their
families and took their last communion and wrote their final messages:
"With our fingers on the trigger, we are following the movements of the
enemy, expecting the ultimatum with the resolution to die and with the
certainty that we will show the Germans what being a free Greek means."
They fought, and they died, and the German advance was delayed for
perhaps forty-eight hours. When they finally captured the mountain dugouts, the Nazis found nothing but corpses.

Under a full white moon that evening, Luftwaffe bombers pounded
Piraeus, the port of Athens that served as the point of debarkation for the
British troops who were still straggling in from North Africa. Laird Archer,
the head of the American Near East Foundation in Athens, was awakened
at 4 A.M. by "a blast of ungodly sound and weird blue light. . . . The whole

southern sky flamed over Piraeus, an unearthly brilliance that silhouetted the calm Parthenon in stark ghostly beauty. . . . From neighboring houses came sounds of maids screaming, and the wild cries of a macaw. Nothing in all the sound effects of catastrophe in Hollywood films could match the crashing thunder, the crackling individual blasts under the greater roar, the howl of the dogs and human shrieks." In the harbor, chaos reigned as ten ships were ripped apart and sent to the bottom. In the confusion, one tanker that had been set afire by the German bombs was left to burn instead of being towed out to sea; within minutes the flames had jumped to the *Clan Fraser,* a British supply ship carrying two hundred tons of TNT. The crew of a British destroyer managed to tow the *Clan Fraser* away from the docks, but before it reached the breakwater it exploded, obliterating the destroyer and flattening most of the buildings along the docks. For the duration of the fighting the port was useless to the British. The explosion shattered windows eleven miles away, creating panic among many Athenians. Refugees started to flee the city.

In the north, List's troops finally broke through the mountain passes and rolled into Macedonia as the unexpectedly swift collapse of the Yugo-slavian troops in the Vardar corridor uncovered the Greeks' left flank. Civilians had been evacuating Salonika for the past several weeks—the fierce resistance of the volunteers along the Metaxas line gave them a few precious extra days—and as the panic-stricken withdrawal was completed, British and Greek demolition squads scuttled everything they could not carry. Bridges, forts, harbor works, unoccupied houses, airport facilities, oil storage depots, warehouses, and munitions dumps were blown sky-high. Flames roared hundreds of feet into the air. The last noncombatants fled in rowboats and caiques; desperate men and women clung to the gangway as it was dragged out to sea. "The last thing we heard was the terrific detonation as the sappers exploded the road bridges leading out of Salonika," recalled Mary Brock, the wife of the *New York Times* corre-spondent, "and then we pulled out into the Aegean Sea, while the refugee Greek passengers on the boat stood silently watching their homes being destroyed."

Fearing that the German advance would swing southward and cut off the supply lines to the Greek troops that remained in the west, General Papagos began withdrawing his forces from Albania. (Fortunately for him, the Italians—perhaps suspecting a trap—obdurately refused repeated German orders to attack the retreating Greeks.) In the face of gusting winds that stung their faces with sleet, Australian troops were rushed forward from the south in a desperate attempt to reinforce the Aliákmon line, anchored at Mt. Olympus. As the Nazis hammered at the Anzac defenses, General Halder (watching safely from German command head-quarters) wondered why the British had not established fortified positions farther north. The Germans dropped two hundred paratroopers behind the Greek lines; every one of them was killed, wounded, or captured. Greek peasants reportedly killed every German soldier who fell into their hands; "tore them to pieces like wolves," one fortunate survivor said.

By now it was obvious that, at best, the defenders could fight only an orderly withdrawal action to slow the Wehrmacht's armored advance; but still more British troops kept arriving from Alexandria. "We begin to realize," remarked one dispirited observer in Athens, "that their effort here is only an honorable and sacrificial gesture."

When the weather cleared in the northern mountains after Easter Sunday, the carnage grew worse. After depleting still further the already impoverished British air strength in Greece by blitzing their airfields and cowing R.A.F. headquarters in the Mediterranean, the Luftwaffe enjoyed almost unchallenged mastery of the air. Some British soldiers reportedly went through the entire campaign without seeing a single friendly plane. (Apparently some R.A.F. commanders refused to run the risk of supporting the Anglo-Greek infantry forces, preferring to save their planes for strategic strikes against Italian air bases.) Stuka dive-bombers swooped down upon the British and Greek columns retreating slowly, painstakingly through the mountains; Messerschmitts sent down a withering hail of bullets. "Every road was blitzed with every type of bombing—high and low level, dive-bombing and ground-strafing," reported Alan Moorehead. "Broken vehicles littered the roadsides. Communications were disorganized. The Stuka was the new artillery—the mechanical device that carried the missile over the mountains to the target and dropped it there. . . . For the Luftwaffe it was just a matter of hopping over from Bulgaria, getting rid of the bombs, and then going back for more. In hundreds the bombers were plying to and fro on their unmolested way." In Athens, a concerned Laird Archer wondered "where on earth the Greeks are going to put all the wounded now coming in on top of those already bedridden from Italian wounds. . . . The combination of bombing concussion which crushes bones, shrapnel splinters which float about in the body, and amputations for frostbite has left the hospitals helpless to free their beds quickly." In the Aegean, at least five Greek hospital ships—clearly marked and brightly illuminated—were attacked and sunk by German bombers; the survivors were machine-gunned as they struggled in the water.

In Berlin, Hitler laughed at the stupidity of the British while he professed his deepest regret at the devastation of Greece. He instructed his commanders to treat captured Greek officers with the respect due a courageous enemy (unlike Serbian officers, who were to be handled "in the worst possible manner"). "Rome and Athens are his Meccas," Goebbels noted admiringly:

> The Fuehrer is a man totally attuned to antiquity. He hates Christianity, because it has crippled all that is noble in humanity. . . . What a difference

between the benevolent, smiling Zeus and the pain-wracked, crucified Christ. The ancient people's view of God was also much nobler and more humane than the Christians'. What a difference between a gloomy cathedral and a light, airy ancient temple. . . .

But back to the war. How wonderful it would be if all this were over. Even the Fuehrer secretly longs for it.

Eden reportedly informed King George of Greece that Britain could send no more aid to his beleaguered country.

News of the latest triumph of German arms stunned Britons, most of whom apparently had not known until the first official announcement (on the morning of April 6) that there even *was* a British army in Greece. Sympathy for the Greeks was mixed with anxiety over the possibility of a Mediterranean-style Dunkirk. "Thinking always of our army in Greece," recorded George Orwell in his diary, "and the desperate risk it runs of being driven into the sea. One can imagine how the strategists of the Liddell Hart type must be wringing their hands over this rash move. . . . The best one can say is that even in the narrow strategic sense it must offer some hope of success, or the generals concerned would have refused to undertake it."

On this occasion, Orwell was far too charitable to the military experts. The Greek expedition had been undertaken for political motives right from the start, and now Britain was paying a severe price in men and matériel for the cruelly mistaken judgment of the cabinet (and the Defence Committee). And the debacle in Greece was not even the most distressing news of that terrible first week of April.

In Libya, Rommel swirled out of the west and wreaked havoc upon the wholly inexperienced, ill-equipped, and undermanned British defenders who had been given the impossible assignment of holding the line at Benghazi and Agheila while nearly sixty thousand of the veterans who had defeated Mussolini's divisions so handily in January and February were shipped off, along with 7,500 vehicles, to face other challenges in Singapore, Iraq, or, mostly, in Greece. "I have to admit to having taken considerable risk in Cyrenaica after capture of Benghazi in order to provide maximum support for Greece," Wavell admitted soon afterward. "I therefore made arrangements to leave only small armoured force and one partly trained Australian division in Cyrenaica." Although British intelligence knew that fresh German troops had landed in North Africa in February, the badly overburdened Wavell—who had to worry about Greece, North Africa, Abyssinia, and the Middle East all at the same time—assumed that the new German commander would not attack until his men had been properly trained in desert warfare and reinforced with fresh supplies and transport. "I do not think that with this force he will attempt to recover Benghazi," Wavell had confidently assured Churchill on March 2. "Shipping risks, difficulty of communications, and the approach of hot weather make it unlikely that such an attack could develop before the end of the summer."

The British general's tactical estimate of the prospects in North Africa was shared by the equally conventional military minds of Halder and Brauchitsch in Berlin, who refused to deprive the far more vital Balkan theater of troops or supplies for the sake of a madcap adventure in Libya; but not by Rommel, whose judgment was the only one that really mattered in this case. After a brief reconnaissance of the environment in the western desert, Rommel immediately recognized that, strategically, "speed is the one thing that matters here." At first unaware of the magnitude of his enemy's shortcomings, Rommel apparently was puzzled and suspicious of the British reluctance to engage in even limited combat. On March 26, the forward units of his Afrika Korps captured Agheila, which Churchill had described as "the gateway . . . the kernel of the situation. If the enemy broke through to Agedabia," the Prime Minister recognized, "Benghazi and everything west of Tobruk were imperiled." Rommel already was enjoying himself immensely in his new surroundings. "Spent our first day by the sea," he wrote to his wife after taking Agheila. "It's a very lovely place and it's as good as being in a hotel in my comfortable caravan. Bathe in the sea in the mornings, it's already beautifully warm." But there was little time for rest and relaxation. To prevent the British from fortifying their new positions to the east, Rommel ordered his troops to keep moving forward.

Upon learning of the unanticipated German advance to Agheila, Churchill telegraphed an urgent message to Wavell: "I presume you are only waiting for the tortoise to stick his head out far enough before chopping it off. It seems extremely important to give them an early taste of our quality." Considering the scanty resources available to Wavell and O'Connor in North Africa, Churchill's exhortation was a striking example of the Prime Minister's willingness to ignore the inconvenient circumstances of reality when they conflicted with his romantic view of himself as the omnipotent commander of the British Empire, dispatching forces right, left, and all over the globe: the first Duke of Marlborough, Pitt the elder, and the Duke of Wellington all rolled into one.

What happened out on the desert when Rommel kept pushing, pushing against the soft British lines ("It was a chance I could not resist," Rommel admitted) should not have surprised anyone. Agedabia fell on April 2, and the recently arrived and ill-prepared King's Dragoon Guards (also known, rather unfairly, as "the King's Dancing Girls") were ordered to retreat to the dubious sanctuary of Benghazi, where there remained only a skeleton reserve force whose tanks were incapacitated by worn treads, missing parts, and a shortage of fuel. During the confusion of the helter-skelter retreat to Benghazi, scores of useless vehicles were abandoned as they broke down in the desert. Even the light British cruiser tanks that were still operative could not withstand the heavier German panzers. Belatedly, British military strategists realized just how far they had fallen behind Germany in the design of mechanized armor over the past two disastrous decades.

Disobeying explicit orders from headquarters in Berlin, Rommel's Afrika Korps "exploded over Cyrenaica like a bomb-burst . . . hurled in every direction, confusing the enemy and seizing at a whirlwind pace the main focal points." Possessed by an almost manic energy, Rommel himself seemed to be everywhere, inspiring and bullying his troops forward in a mad dash toward Cairo, exuberantly exploiting to the utmost his critical advantage in numbers and quality of armor. He had discovered an unexpected weakness and refused to accept any excuse for stopping or even slowing down in pursuing it to the utmost. "One cannot permit unique opportunities to slip by for the sake of trifles" was his famous comment. He knew that a whirlwind attack intimidated a retreating enemy and made his forces appear even stronger than they were. The British lines of communications broke down and individual units found themselves isolated in the confusion, falling over one another in their haste to get away. Discipline disintegrated. Unaware of what was happening, Churchill dispatched another querulous message to Wavell: "It seems most desirable to chop the German advance against Cyrenaica. Any rebuff to the Germans would have far-reaching prestige effects. It would be all right to give up ground for the purposes of manoeuvre, but any serious withdrawal from Benghazi would appear most melancholy."

By April 3, Rommel had concluded that the British "apparently intended to avoid, in any circumstances, fighting a decisive action; so, that afternoon, I decided to stay on the heels of the retreating enemy and make a bid to seize the whole of Cyrenaica at one stroke." Bereft of natural defenses, Benghazi was evacuated on April 4. An Australian division scheduled for assignment to Greece was ordered to remain in Egypt instead (which was a lucky break for the Aussies). "Thus at a single stroke, and almost in a day," complained Churchill, "the desert flank upon which all our decisions had depended had crumpled and the expedition to Greece, already slender, was heavily reduced." The British Army of the Nile suffered a further devastating blow when General Richard O'Connor, the most experienced commander on the scene who had rushed to the front to investigate the rapidly deteriorating situation, was captured when his driver took a wrong turn in the darkness and ran right into a German patrol. By this time Churchill was frantic. He cabled Eden in Athens: "Far more important than the loss of ground is the idea that we cannot face the Germans and that their appearance is enough to drive us back many scores of miles. This must react most evilly throughout Balkans and Turkey. Pray go back to Cairo and go into all this. Sooner or later we shall have to fight the Huns. By all means make the best plan of manoeuvre, but anyhow fight." At the British base at Msus, the local commander nervously blew up a petrol dump prematurely, thereby aggravating the critical shortage of fuel. In Cairo, Eden, Wavell, Dill, Cunningham, and Longmore put on their thinking caps and tried to decide where the fleeing British armies could make a successful stand.

Derna fell on April 7. "You will understand that I can't sleep for happiness," a merry Rommel chortled to his wife. Hitler sent his congratulations to the Afrika Korps. On April 12 the Germans recaptured Bardia. One after another, all the British garrisons along the desert road surrendered or threw away every bit of nonessential matériel and raced for their lives for the one defensible position in the region: Tobruk. The "Benghazi-Tobruk Handicap," the irreverent Aussie soldiers called it; in London they were using other, more forceful words. "You should surely be able to hold Tobruk," Churchill snapped at Wavell, the harsh sarcasm carrying across two thousand miles. The fortress of Tobruk, the Prime Minister decided, "seems to be a place to be held to the death without thought of retirement." Of course Winston was not there at the time.

As Wavell boarded a reconnaissance plane for a firsthand inspection of the situation at Tobruk, he turned to Dill and said, "I hope, Jack, that you will preside over my court-martial." Such a fate might not have assuaged Churchill's anger at the debacle in North Africa. Publicly, the Prime Minister maintained a stout front, telling the House of Commons that since the fate of Britain really rested upon the Battle of the Atlantic, a momentary reverse on the far side of the Mediterranean could safely be shrugged off. He assured Roosevelt that "we are, of course, going all out to fight for the Nile Valley. No other conclusion is physically possible. . . . I personally feel that this situation is not only manageable, but hopeful." Privately, Winston employed stronger words to mask his fears. When a guest at a dinner party advanced the notion that Rommel might soon force Britain to evacuate Egypt, Churchill replied with an ominous growl, "Wavell has 400,000 men. If they lose Egypt, blood will flow. I will have firing parties to shoot the Generals."

At the outset of the Greek adventure, Wavell had denuded the British defenses in Libya to assist Athens; now Churchill's Defence Committee reversed the priorities: any threat to the empire's lifeline at Suez so alarmed Whitehall that the fate of the luckless British expeditionary force in Greece was forced into the background. "Egypt is the base upon which everything depends," concluded Eden, "and to lose it would be worst calamity." Certainly Churchill appeared willing to sacrifice all in Greece to hold Suez. While the British columns retreating from Mt. Olympus were being pounded day after day by the Luftwaffe, Churchill blithely informed Eden that "every day the German Air Force is detained in Greece enables the Libyan situation to be stabilised." And at precisely the time when Admiral Cunningham's fleet was frantically trying to evacuate exhausted British, Australian, and New Zealand soldiers from Greece, the Prime Minister instructed Cunningham that the Mediterranean Fleet's primary responsibility was to interrupt Rommel's supply lines, "to stop all sea-borne traffic between Italy and Africa by the fullest use of surface craft, aided so far as possible by aircraft and submarines. For this all-important objective heavy losses in battleships, cruisers, and destroyers must if necessary be accepted." Already fed up with interference from London, Cunningham ignored the message. "I was beginning to feel seriously annoyed," the admiral later recalled, adding that "we were far too busy with our other commitments" to take the time to frame an appropriate reply.

At Tobruk, meanwhile, Rommel had surrounded the British garrison and launched his first assault on April 11. This time, it was he who received a rude surprise as the attack was thrown back with serious losses. The hard-bitten Anzacs refused to budge from behind their stronghold of concrete and wire. "Tobruk's defences stretched much farther in all directions, west, east and south, than we had imagined," Rommel confessed. When he learned that British ships were on their way to Tobruk harbor, Rommel believed they intended to withdraw the garrison; instead, they unloaded supplies and reinforcements. By the time he realized that he would have to settle in for a lengthy siege of the city, the advance guard of the Afrika Korps had finally come panting to a halt near the Egyptian border. Short of provisions, especially water—their supply officers had assumed that they were engaging only in a limited offensive action when they started out several weeks before—the German forces had outrun their supply lines and had to pull back to regroup. Rommel could advance no further with the British firmly ensconced in Tobruk.

All this time, General Halder had watched in stunned horror as Rommel galloped pell-mell across the desert. It was bad enough that the Fuehrer's decision to punish Greece and Yugoslavia had consumed precious resources and postponed the start of Operation Barbarossa; but the thought of any additional diversions in a peripheral theater such as North Africa was more than the German General Staff could bear. Moreover, Rommel's unorthodox methods were an affront to Halder's orderly Prussian mind. "Rommel has not sent us a single clear-cut report all these days," he grumbled. "I have a feeling that things are in a mess. Reports from officers coming from his theater as well as a personal letter show that Rommel is in no way up to his operational task. All day long he rushes about between his widely scattered units, and stages reconnaissance raids in which he fritters away his forces. No one has a clear picture of their disposition and striking power. Certain is only that his troops are widely dispersed and that their striking efficiency has considerably deteriorated. . . . Apart from that, his motor vehicles are in poor condition from the action of desert sand. Many of his tank engines need replacing. Air transport cannot meet Rommel's senseless demands, primarily because of lack of fuel."

Suspecting that Rommel had gone quite mad, Halder sent the older and ostensibly wiser deputy chief of the General Staff, Field Marshal von Paulus, on a fact-finding mission to North Africa. From the reports sent back by Paulus over a two-and-a-half-week period, Halder concluded that Rommel had "broken up his units in a wild pattern" and conducted "a campaign with very scanty forces on a widely extended front which cannot be measured by European standards." That, of course, was precisely the source of Rommel's greatest strength in the desert; his reckless aggressiveness already had made him a celebrity in Germany and throughout the world. But Halder, concerned about the wasteful expenditure of men and matériel that could not easily be replaced, found only cause for reproach: "By overstepping his orders, Rommel has brought about a situation for which our present supply capabilities are insufficient. Rommel cannot cope with the situation."

After a second coordinated assault of panzers and Stukas against Tobruk was repulsed with heavy casualties, Paulus ordered Rommel to desist from further attacks unless the British decided to evacuate. The panzer troops settled down around the seventeen-mile perimeter: lying motionless under sniper fire, day after day in sandy holes scooped out of the ground; pestered by mosquitoes and swarms of flies and battalions of scorpions and sand fleas and unspeakable varieties of indigenous Libyan insects; always short of water to drink, much less to bathe in; itching constantly and constantly on the lookout for the shells lobbed with cheerful insouciance from within Tobruk; seeking shelter from the sandstorms that covered everything with yellow dust two inches thick. Lacking the sort of vitamin-rich provisions required in the desert—the Germans had even less experience than the British in fighting in this sort of barren, dessicated environment—Rommel began to lose more men to disease, particularly dysentery, than to the enemy's guns. There were no potatoes (normally a staple of the German soldier's diet) in the daily rations because someone at headquarters in Berlin had decided that potatoes would rot during shipment. Instead, the German soldiers subsisted on dried black bread, sausages, and sardines packed in oil—and flies; someone said that the flies were so thick that they covered everything edible no matter how many times you shooed them away, so that you finally resigned yourself to swallowing them along with the food. Rommel's men also had more than enough of an uninviting concoction of Italian tinned meat, sarcastically dubbed "Mussolini's monkey." The portable ovens that arrived belatedly were practically useless because they ran on wood, which was, to the surprise of staff supply officers in Berlin, in noticeably short supply in the desert. "One of the reasons we had so much sickness, especially jaundice, was that our rations were too heavy for the desert," one German war correspondent later wrote to a friend in England. "Our black bread in a carton was handy, but how we used to long to capture one of your field bakeries and eat fresh, white bread! And your jam! For the first four months we got no fresh fruit or vegetables at all."

Life was no easier inside Tobruk, of course. The 25,000 men within the fortress suffered just as much from the sand and the flies and the general shortage of potable water and edible food (although they did receive some shipments of bully beef by sea), and from the added inconvenience of bombs falling by the score from the Stukas and Messerschmitts that flew overhead, unopposed. But at least the besieged garrison enjoyed the consolation of knowing that its obstinate presence in Tobruk was accomplishing some useful purpose: i.e., obstructing Rommel from undertaking any further advance into Egypt. They gloried in their reputation as "the rats of Tobruk," the name first applied to them in derision by a German radio propagandist. "There will be no surrender and no retreat," vowed General Leslie Morshead, as his men settled in for a long stay. "They learned to make a life out of this confinement," remarked Alan Moorehead in admiration. "They played cricket on the sand. They swam. The cooks and orderlies and batmen amused themselves by collecting old pieces of Italian pre-war cannon and ammunition. These they rigged up as best they could on bits of rock and concrete. Having no precision instruments, they poked their heads up the barrels of the guns and sighted them that way before the charge was put in. They achieved elevation and direction by removing or adding another rock to the base of the cannon. And in their spare time they banged away at the enemy, alongside the modern twenty-five pounders. . . . Anti-aircraft guns were lacking, so the garrison turned small arms upon the raiders, and one officer alone brought down six with a Lewis gun. Never was a more timely stand made; never one more vigorously continued."

"Bravo, Tobruk!" shouted Churchill, who now decided that the brave, beleaguered garrison was "a speck of sand which might ruin all Hitler's calculations." His spirits revived by the plucky defiance of the desert garrison, Churchill immediately set into motion a daring plan to enable Wavell to regain the offensive in North Africa, for the Prime Minister's priorities remained unaltered: "Victory in Libya counts first, evacuation of troops from Greece second."

Greece . . . Greece by that time had become a full-fledged disaster. In the middle of April, thrown back in disorganization from the Olympus-Aliákmon line, the retreating Anglo-Greek forces made a vain attempt to hold the Germans at Mt. Parnassus, along a thirty-mile line around the blood-red pass at Thermopylae; the notion of repeating the fabled stand of the Spartans appealed to the romantic warrior in Churchill: "The intervening ages fell away. Why not one more undying feat of arms?" But the Nazi tide came on and on and on, hammering from the ground with tanks and guns and men, strafing from the air with planes that dove and chopped at the weary defenders and then flew back to reload. "For two days I have been bombed, machine-gunned, and shot at by all and sundry," wrote a shell-shocked Australian correspondent. "German Stukas have blown two cars from under me and strafed a third. . . . All day and all night there have been waves of Germans in the skies. . . . Goering must have a third of his air force operating here and it is bombing every nook and cranny, hamlet, village and town in its path." Telephone communications broke down between Athens and the rapidly changing front.

On April 15, with his troops losing miles of ground every day, Wavell conferred with Longmore and Admiral Cunningham and decided that they would have to withdraw all British troops from Greece to save the nation from complete devastation. General Papagos, whose exhausted soldiers were finally crumbling under the Nazi assault, agreed that the British should go as quickly as possible; "the Royal Government is obliged to state that further sacrifice of the British Expeditionary Force would be in vain and that its withdrawal in time seems to be rendered necessary." Absent air cover, it would be a difficult operation at best. In Athens, the minister of war panicked and attempted to flee the capital; several of his colleagues decided further resistance was useless and began making preparations to surrender. King George responded by forbidding all members of the cabinet from visiting general headquarters (where morale was, understandably, already sinking low), and ordered them to remain at their posts. Then the king issued a message to his soldiers: "The honor and interest of Greece and the fate of the Greek race preclude all thoughts of capitulation, the moral calamity of which would be incomparably greater than any other disaster." Broken by the strain of responsibility during the crisis, and deeply shocked by the latest revelations of cowardice, defeatism, and treachery within his government, Prime Minister Koryzis angrily confronted the cabinet with his accusations, then drove home, walked into his bedroom, locked the door, cradled a small beloved icon in one hand, and shot himself in the head.

By April 22, the German columns were only one hundred miles away from the Greek capital. "Roads clear as far as Athens," Halder noted approvingly. The Greek army in Epirus—eighty thousand men who reportedly had gone for five days without food or supplies—surrendered to the German High Command, on the explicit understanding that it was *not* surrendering to the Italian army, which it had in fact defeated. The Greek royal family decided to withdraw to Suda Bay at Crete, and thence to Egypt. The following day, General Papagos resigned his command. Anzac soldiers in Athens invited civilians to take whatever military supplies (blankets, etc.) they could use before the Germans reached the city. On April 24, a caretaker government in Athens signed the articles of capitulation.

The remnants of the British expeditionary force continued to fight a desperate rearguard action through the mountains in the west, demolishing roads behind them, traveling mainly at night to escape the Luftwaffe patrols. As the Germans began to catch up with them, the date for beginning the evacuation by sea—appropriately code-named Operation Demon—was moved up from April 28 to the twenty-fourth. As the weary soldiers made their way to the beaches during the final anxious days, they were warned to keep marching to the beach, even in the midst of a bombing raid. Anyone who took shelter was liable to be left behind. They were told to carry their wounded and leave their dead. Rounding up every available landing craft in the Aegean (including motorboats, caiques, and fishing vessels) to help get the men off the open beaches and the jagged rocky shores, Cunningham had to disperse his fleet to reach all the minor ports to which the troops had fled in the general confusion. To enable as many men as possible to be loaded aboard, Cunningham issued orders that no stores of equipment, however valuable, would be permitted to take precedence over human cargo. The evacuation was carried out under cover of darkness, often in treacherous waters without even the most rudimentary navigational charts; ships were ordered to be away by 3 A.M. at the latest. When there were no ships to take them off the shore, some men swam out to meet the destroyers.

On the first two nights, 17,000 men got away. Then the Germans captured the bridge over the Corinth Canal, enabling them to move into the Peloponnesus and exert even more pressure on the British withdrawal. That night, however, another 19,500 British soldiers were evacuated; but a Dutch ship participating in the evacuation, the *Salant*, tarried too long at Nauplia in a courageous but misguided attempt to bring as many men away as possible. Caught by the Stukas in the daylight, it was bombed and sunk. Two destroyers who went to her rescue were also lost; no more than fifty men survived from the crews and the thousands of troops aboard the three ships.

By the time H.M.S. *Ajax* steamed away from the beaches on the early morning of April 29, twenty-six ships under Cunningham's command had been lost, but more than fifty thousand soldiers had been safely withdrawn: approximately 80 percent of the force originally sent to Greece, considerably more than might have been expected under the circumstances. Another fourteen hundred men eventually found their way back to Egypt. The statistics reflected a heroic effort by the Royal Navy; Cunningham signaled his fleet in appreciation for a job well done: "Throughout these operations, under conditions of considerable danger and difficulty, there was no faltering." "We have paid our debt of honour with far less loss than I feared," commented Churchill brightly. "The concluding stages of the Greek campaign had been a glorious episode in the history of British arms." Other observers were less enthusiastic. Even the

normally Pollyannaish *Time* magazine pointed out that Britain had lost
virtually all of the heavy equipment it had landed in Greece, a severe loss
when its forces in the Mediterranean were already critically short of armor
and artillery. "Wars are not won with return tickets," chided *Time*. "The
British will not win World War II by squeezing miniature forces into
defensive crannies at the last moment, and withdrawing them brilliantly.
Some sardonic wit in London last week figured out what B.E.F. meant:
Back Every Fortnight. There was just enough truth in this interpretation
to point up the real significance of the Battle of Greece. Britons can fight,
but they will not be able to make an expeditionary force stick until some
way, somehow, they get enough men, enough planes and enough tanks to
approximate Nazi strength." Alexander Cadogan's sarcastic reaction was
more to the point. "Evacuation going fairly well," he noted wearily in his
diary. "That's all that we're really good at. . . . Our soldiers are the most
pathetic amateurs, pitted against professionals."

During the evening of April 26, a quiet, dignified voice made a brief
announcement over Radio Athens: "You are listening to the voice of
Greece," it said; and then:

> Greeks, stand firm, be each one proud and dignified. You must prove
> yourselves worthy of your history. The valour and victory of our Army has
> already been recognized. The righteousness of our cause will also be recog-
> nized. We did our duty honestly.
>
> Friends! Have Greece in your hearts, live inspired with the fire of her
> latest triumph and the glory of our Army. Greece will live again and will be
> great because she fought honestly for a just cause and for freedom.
>
> Brothers! Have courage and patience. Be stout-hearted. We will over-
> come these hardships. Greeks! With Greece in your minds you must be proud
> and dignified. We have been an honest nation and brave soldiers.

Then the voice repeated, "You are listening to the voice of Greece,"
and signed off.

On the morning of Sunday, April 27, a Nazi motorcycle column
roared down toward Athens through hills ablaze with wild roses, silencing
the nightingales and scattering the birds deeper into the forests of pine.
By ten o'clock the mayor and the civil governor had formally surrendered
their authority, and German troops were in possession of the capital. A
shepherd watched the scene from a nearby hilltop. "Well, let them come,"
he whispered. "We've had the enemy here before and we've always
thrown him into the sea in the end." The Greek guard who stood watch
upon the Acropolis was ordered to raise the swastika banner next to the
Greek flag as a special tribute to the Fuehrer. The soldier refused the
German command, and then threw himself off the wall, falling five hundred feet to his death.

German occupation authorities immediately issued a series of decrees governing life in a Greek nation under Nazi "protection": civilians were ordered to surrender all weapons, including knives (policemen were permitted to retain their guns); Nazi soldiers were billeted in private homes; farmers were forbidden to harvest their own crops because the Germans feared they might stash some extra food away for themselves; the Wehrmacht commandeered drugs and hospital supplies and all the automobiles, trucks, buses, and bicycles in Athens; the famous market at the Agoronomia was declared off limits to the public and the produce reserved for German officers and their troops; cattle, dairy herds, and sheep were appropriated and slaughtered or driven north; German soldiers "bought" everything they desired in the city's shops, using occupation marks specially printed and distributed for the occasion; industrial raw materials were confiscated; German directors took over control of most of the major Greek corporations and ordered factories to produce goods for German use; and occupation authorities began to plunder the historic treasures of ancient Greece.

"The streets are filled with lean, hard-bitten, glassy-eyed Germans with colorless, expressionless, stony features like sleep-walking automatons," reported Laird Archer, who remained at his post in Athens through the end of July. "They have come to wipe out the Greeks by starvation and disease to save munitions and trouble. But they neither care nor show any scruples whatever. Their uniforms are faded and stained, dull, grimy gray like old mold, fit garb for a foul job. Germans in restaurants gulp food in second and third helpings as if from long want. They stare into the windows of our workshops at the piles of materials being cut into garments with every evidence of coveting what they see. The girls shrink from the stares and have asked us to put up muslin curtains for the first time, at sacrifice of light."

Through the streets of Athens wandered gaunt, starving Greek soldiers who were on their way home from the front after six months of short rations and little sleep. They were joined by bandaged veterans turned out from their hospital beds by the German occupation authorities, who wanted the space to care for their own wounded. Soon the Germans announced that anyone wearing a Greek uniform on the streets would be shot on sight. Nazi machine-gun squads executed any persons convicted of harboring in their attic or cellar any of the British soldiers who had been trapped in the city during the evacuation; undaunted, Greek civilians continued to help the British boys escape by dyeing their hair black and teaching them a smattering of Greek. When R.A.F. planes began to bomb German shipping in the rebuilt Piraeus several weeks later, they were aided by flashlights shining from houses in defiance of the blackout. And the ubiquitous V symbol began to appear at night on the sidewalks of Athens and the gates of the German legation.

As the Wehrmacht began its final round of preparations for Operation

Barbarossa, German occupation troops were withdrawn from Greece and replaced by Italian blackshirts. There had been an embarrassing German-Italian contretemps at the moment of surrender, when Mussolini insisted upon Italian participation in the negotiations despite the fact that his troops still had not yet crossed the frontier into Greece. (For a brief moment, Hitler, who was furious with Mussolini for his refusal to take part in the fighting, apparently entertained the notion of allowing the Greeks and Italians to continue fighting and settle their dispute among themselves in the region west of the Pindus Mountains.) Despite the outraged protests of General List, who sought to conclude the negotiations quickly and present the Duce with a fait accompli, Hitler finally calmed down and overruled his generals, acceding to his ally's request and subsequently permitting Italy to take over the administration of Greece and much of Yugoslavia. When the Italian troops marched stolidly into Athens, the populace greeted them with laughter and ribald cheers of derision, and their German colleagues insulted them whenever the opportunity presented itself.

Although there were indications that the Italian administration sincerely wished to placate its Greek subjects, a shortfall of essential supplies (due in no small part to the efficiency of the German scavenging operations) combined with Italian bureaucratic bungling to leave the country desperately short of food. The bread ration—formerly the staple of the Greek diet—was cut to less than six ounces per person. There was no salt, and meat, fish, and fresh vegetables were virtually nonexistent. Before Greece was delivered from the Axis occupation, hundreds of thousands of men, women, and children would die of starvation. In the mountains of Yugoslavia, meanwhile, Tito's partisans launched a merciless war of attrition against the Fascist occupation troops; when it was all over, Italy reportedly had suffered far greater casualties from the inglorious guerrilla conflict in the Balkans than from the more conventional (though not more successful) warfare in North Africa.

14

"Gone Is That Place"

"How are you bearing everything? The—if anything—
increasing savagery, and horrible sense of waiting for an
attack? The constant anxiety, and feeling of stultification
and personal and general misery?"
—EDITH SITWELL, APRIL 1941

As military reverses in the Balkans and North Africa shattered the euphoria of the last weeks of March, *The New Yorker*'s Mollie Panter-Downes noticed that "Nazi successes seem to have a way of coinciding with those rare and enchanting spells when England really does look like a demi-paradise and not a waterlogged island where nine-tenths of the population have colds in the head. Last year's climatically perfect June was soured for Britons by what was happening in France; this year's April is clouded in much the same way by what is happening in Greece and North Africa, especially Greece." Even Churchill permitted himself a moment of unusually deep despair. John Colville, his private secretary, noted that the Prime Minister was in a "worse gloom than I have ever seen him," contemplating the depressing prospect of "a world in which Hitler dominated all Europe, Asia and Africa and left the U.S. and ourselves no option but an unwilling peace." But, just as he had done after Dunkirk and the fall of France, Churchill exerted himself to stiffen Britain's resolve to carry on against all odds.

Contemporaries noted that Winston's personality was much more appealing at such times of crisis than in the flush of success; when the sky ahead looked threatening and black, his speeches took on a characteristically crisp, almost brutally blunt quality that instilled in his grateful listeners a welcome measure of Churchill's own formidable tenacity. In his radio address to the people on the evening of May 3, after the last ships had gotten away from Greece and Rommel finally had come to a halt before the walls of Tobruk, the Prime Minister began by asserting that Britain had been under an inescapable moral responsibility to do whatever it could to aid Greece. "In their mortal peril, the Greeks turned to us for succor," he said. "They declared they would fight for their native soil ... even if we left them to their fate. But we could not do that. There are rules against that kind of thing." He admitted that the recent reverses had deeply hurt the empire: "You know I never try to make out that defeats are victories." Yet he reminded the people that "we must not lose our sense of proportion and thus become discouraged or alarmed. When we face with a steady eye the difficulties which lie before us, we may derive new confidence from remembering those we have already overcome. Nothing that is happening now is comparable in gravity with the dangers through which we passed last year. Nothing that can happen in the East is comparable with what is happening in the West," meaning, of course, that Britain's salvation lay across the Atlantic.

"No prudent and far-seeing man can doubt that the eventual and total defeat of Hitler and Mussolini is certain," Churchill concluded with unshakable determination. "There are less than 70,000,000 malignant Huns, some of whom are curable and others killable. . . . The people of the British Empire and the U.S. number 200,000,000 . . . They have more wealth, more technical resources, and they make more steel than the whole of the rest of the world put together." Then, just for good measure, Churchill quoted from "Say Not the Struggle Naught Availeth," written nearly one hundred years before by Arthur Clough:

> For while the tired waves, vainly breaking,
>   Seem here no painful inch to gain,
> Far back, through creeks and inlets making,
>   Comes silent, flooding in, the main.
>
> And not by eastern windows only,
>   When daylight comes, comes in the light;
> In front the sun climbs slow, how slowly!
>   But westward, look, the land is bright.

Hitler, for one, was not impressed. In a speech to the Reichstag the following evening, the Fuehrer dismissed Churchill's rhetoric as the ravings of a drunkard, and ridiculed the British decision to send troops to Greece as "one of the most famous strategical blunders of this war." "In London they are being forced to watch one illusion after another crumble to nothing," laughed Goebbels. "All they can do is stutter lame excuses."

Critics within the United Kingdom were only slightly less caustic in their criticism of the cabinet's recent conduct of the war and the silly, vain attempts of the government censors to hide the bitter truth of the defeats in Greece and North Africa from the British people. "In particular," noticed Colville, "people seem to be getting sick of the hearty propaganda of the 'Are we downhearted?' kind, sponsored by the Government." The honeymoon, which had lasted since Churchill assembled his war cabinet in May 1940, was over; now the government had to face "the grim realities of marriage."

"Our ostriches try to persuade themselves—and us—that every Allied triumph is a major triumph, every enemy triumph a sideshow," complained the *Daily Herald*. "Bunk merchants are at it again," agreed the *Daily Express*. "We have been licked in Norway, licked in France, Belgium and Holland, licked in Libya and licked in Greece. Believe nothing good in this war until you see it and until you earn it." Perhaps because it was wholly unexpected, the rout in North Africa proved especially disturbing. "This is no diversion," claimed the *Evening News*. "Glossing it over with vague, official words of comfort—words which long since have lost all their par value on the public market—is mere futility. The blunt truth is that while we were sitting back easily congratulating ourselves on our triumphs over the Italians, the Germans got to work." Most distressing of all was the news that the Nazis had successfully transported a formidable armored force across the Mediterranean, a maneuver announced to a startled British public with no advance warning whatsoever, "in the manner," in one reporter's opinion, "of someone who has just discovered a sinister-looking bundle under a gooseberry bush." It seemed that the Royal Navy was not omnipotent after all, and many Britons began to wonder uneasily whether the Germans might not also be capable of slipping an equally powerful force across the English Channel. "Let us expel the childish notion—the imbecile notion—that the trend of war in the Balkans and Africa can have no weighty effect on the 'real war,'" demanded the *Daily Herald*. "Libya should make an end to all that nonsense that it could not happen here."

Churchill himself remained practically unassailable. Confidence in his leadership was so deep-rooted that it transcended partisanship; it was said that Winston probably could, if he chose, sack every member of his cabinet without provoking a successful party revolt. "When things go wrong, it is the public's trusting habit to expect Mr. Churchill to put them right," remarked an American correspondent in London. The eminent socialist Harold Laski noted prophetically that Churchill's hold over the British people "in a time of adversity is greater, if anything, than his influence in hours of triumph." Colleagues marveled over Winston's capacity to withstand adversity. "It is surprising how he maintains a lighthearted exterior in spite of the vast burdens he is bearing," remarked General Alan Brooke, whose own burdens as commander in chief, Home Forces, were not inconsiderable. One of Brooke's favorite memories of Churchill was the image of the Prime Minister dressed in a powder-blue siren suit, giving an after-dinner exhibition of bayonet exercises in the halls of his ancestral home of Chequers. "He is quite the most wonderful man I have ever met," decided Brooke, "and is a source of never-ending interest to me, studying, and getting to realize that occasionally such human beings make their appearance on this earth. Human beings who stand out head and shoulders above all others." More than anything else, Churchill's resilience was due to his acute understanding and sense of history, his willingness to take the long view, to detach a part of himself from the emotions and difficulties of the present and view events as if he were living a hundred years in the future. "He sees all events taking their place in the procession of past events as seen by the historian of the future," remarked Clement Attlee: "the gallantry of Greece, the heroism of our people, the breakdown of the French are always seen in perspective."

But if the public perceived Churchill as the lone essential member of the government, the rest of his cabinet were fair game, and on the first anniversary of the parliamentary debate which caused Chamberlain's downfall in May 1940, the House of Commons considered a motion of no confidence in Churchill's government. No one seriously expected the motion to pass—the final tally was 447 to 3 against it—but the debate provided the Commons with an opportunity to vent a great deal of pent-up frustration and lash out at the less popular members of the cabinet. Anthony Eden, whom the public had decided was responsible for the muddle in Greece, formed an especially inviting target. At the outset of the debate on May 6, Eden made a vain attempt to defend his ill-starred mission to the Middle East; it was, Chips Channon decided, "an appallingly bad speech; no cheers greeted him and he gave a dim account of his travels and failures. He sat down amidst complete silence." The speakers who followed—including the increasingly nettlesome (and probably senile) Lloyd George, who fulminated for a full hour—indulged in a series of acrimonious attacks upon the beleaguered foreign secretary and his pusillanimous associates. To the accompaniment of ribald laughter and shouts of "hear, hear" from the back benches, Maurice Pethernick, the Unionist member from Falmouth, called for the Prime Minister to bring more ruthless men into the cabinet. "Mr. Churchill," Pethernick agreed, "was a very remarkable leader whom we needed and who appealed almost with an absolutely unshakable confidence to the people of this country and the Empire. Britain could not be beaten. But what we wanted was a panzer and not a pansy Government." ("Savage attacks on Eden in London," noted Goebbels in his diary. "So far as we are concerned, let this pimp stay in office for as long as possible. We could not wish ourselves a better British Foreign Minister.")

If the nation wanted a ruthless man, decided Churchill, it would have one, and so he resurrected the position of minister of state and handed the job to the energetic Beaverbrook, by now affectionately (or not) known as "Lord Spitfire." As the nearest thing to a troubleshooter the government owned, Beaverbrook was made overlord of supply and given responsibility for stimulating production of war matériel, with a roving commission "to kick inefficiency and departmental dawdling hard wherever it is encountered." He had his work cut out for him. British industry (except for Beaverbrook's own aircraft production program) still was not operating at anything near peak efficiency, and had turned in an especially poor performance in the production of the heavy tanks which had come to play such a vital role in the current conflict. A young R.A.F. officer who was also a Member of Parliament informed the Commons that "in Greece 70 to 80 per cent of the British tanks broke down before they ever saw the enemy." Lack of coordination between ministries and between the public and private sectors of the economy, combined with bureaucratic red tape and frequent breakdowns in Britain's transportation system, meant that a large percentage of the defense goods that were produced sat uselessly for days on railroad sidings or on the docks, awaiting shipment—and meanwhile inviting destruction by German bombers.

Churchill's government provided another indication of its newfound ruthlessness when it finally introduced its long-awaited program to draft young women and middle-aged men and assign them to essential civilian jobs. The first call-ups, in April, required all twenty-year-old women, and men between the ages of forty-one and forty-two, to register for labor service. "It is a strange thing to be happening in a country like this," confessed Ernest Bevin, the burly west country trade unionist who served as Churchill's minister of labor, but in the absence of voluntary cooperation (and with unemployment down to 190,000 over the entire nation), compulsory allocation of labor appeared to be the only way to divert essential materials and workers from nondefense industries to labor-starved factories, mines, and farms, thereby releasing more ablebodied young men for military service. No one would be permitted to refuse work or quit his or her assigned job. Production of consumer goods characterized as nonessential—including furniture, stockings, corsets, and musical instruments—henceforward would have to limp along on a drastically reduced scale or shut down entirely.

The government's proposal to enlist middle-aged men caused little furor; there appeared to be widespread agreement with Bevin's comment that "It don't do anybody any 'arm to work a little. After three months of getting accustomed to the toning up of unused muscles any physically competent man of 41 will get along and be useful." Not surprisingly, the drafting of women was a more controversial matter. Bevin had decided to start with twenty-year-olds (of whom there were an estimated 500,000 in Britain, with an equal number of twenty-one-year-olds scheduled to be called next) because he believed they probably would have completed their education, and were less likely to have started families of their own. Pregnant women and mothers with infants were exempt from conscription; for those draftees who had preschool children, the government established special day-care centers (which earned the youngsters the unwanted sobriquet of "Bevin's babies"). When someone asked if recently wed women would be excused for six months "for population reasons," a Labor Ministry official replied, "Oh, there'll be plenty of time for that on the side." But the prospect of sending girls to training camps or factories far away from home raised serious issues of morality at a time when conventional sexual standards already were being enthusiastically violated under the strain of war. Despite the government's assurances that it would keep its young female charges under close supervision, anxious parents were not encouraged by reports that professional prostitutes in Britain were being squeezed out of business by patriotic amateurs who had taken up residence around army camps.

Feminists were appalled when the government admitted that it intended to pay conscripted women workers starting wage rates that were substantially below the salaries of their male counterparts. During their training period, women received a wage of $7.60 per week, compared to $12.10 for the men. (Nevertheless, these rates did accurately reflect the prevailing wage differential in private industry in Britain.) After six months, if a woman was producing as much as a man, she would be paid an equal wage.

If the nation's experience over the past eighteen months with women soldiers was any indication of success, Bevin's labor conscription scheme stood a very good chance of paying great dividends. Although many single girls admittedly had joined the women's branches of the military services for the sole purpose of meeting eligible men, they invariably impressed foreign observers with their efficiency, courage, and versatility. They became expert truck drivers, airplane mechanics, and construction workers. By the summer of 1941, most of the staff personnel at operations headquarters and in war game rooms were women. "Commanding officers of all units and establishments without exception told me women do a better job than men," reported General Ira Eaker of the U.S. Army Air Corps during a tour of the island. "A common expression was heard on every hand, 'The women are the best damned soldiers in England.' " British army commanders reported that their women remained calmer under enemy air attack than many men, and were a good deal more reliable where security matters were concerned: "They do not get drunk at the pub on Saturday night and talk too much."

To ease the transition for those who were not accustomed to eight hours of hard work every day, the Labor Ministry recommended that draftees forgo their customary visits to the beauty parlor and keep their hair cut short, a suggestion that led one contumacious debutante to scoff, "I don't think looking like a convict will help win the Battle of Britain." Despite the Ministry's assurances that it had obtained prodigious quantities of a special protective cream to keep workers' complexions from turning yellow while handling TNT (a common complaint from the last war), socialites were aghast at the notion of spending eight hours a day in a factory or performing manual labor on a farm. The entire social season appeared to be seriously endangered. British matrons already were in a tizzy because of the distressing shortage of competent domestic servants, who appeared to be going the way of the wooly mammoth; Mollie Panter-Downes noticed that "the advertising columns of the morning papers are filled daily with the wails of anguished ladies trying to tempt cooks with details of enormous wages, happy homes, and safe locales, where a bomb is guaranteed to be unknown."

If the inescapable hardships of life on the home front rendered dinner parties tiresomely troublesome, Londoners could still organize outings to the movies. Usherettes had, in fact, been awarded special exemptions from the labor draft as essential personnel, on the grounds that they helped boost the morale of sailors and soldiers who frequented the cinema. In the springtime, the longer hours of daylight allowed West End theaters to remain open until nine o'clock at night (the last show had to be over before the blackout began, so people could find their way home). Every evening, there was an almost interminable series of propaganda newsreel shorts before the feature movie began. The content of these propaganda films had changed dramatically since the war began; like the British people, they were now far more full of hate. General Raymond E. Lee, the American military attaché in London, was shocked to see one newsreel that portrayed British troops being trained to attack the enemy, shouting savagely as they charged, "Kill! Kill! Kill!" "This," noted Lee, "is something which would not have been seen on any screen about a year ago." (It was, however, in line with a comment a military colleague had made about the changed attitude of R.A.F. pilots: "The people in the Air Force have given up the sporting idea now and are grimly determined to kill as many Germans as they can by any means possible.")

One of the most enthusiastic moviegoers was the exiled seventeen-year-old King Peter of Yugoslavia, who liked to sit up in the balcony and watch the latest westerns with an American correspondent from North Carolina; usually Peter got so carried away with the action that he ended up blazing away with his index finger at the bad-guy gunslingers on the screen. Movie fans of less regal heritage (and better taste) flocked to see such American imports as the first anniversary showing of *Gone With the Wind* and the action–love story *Seven Sinners,* featuring John Wayne, Marlene Dietrich, and Broderick Crawford. Miss Dietrich was a special favorite of Lord Beaverbrook, who allegedly sat through *Destry Rides Again* twenty-seven times. Harold Nicolson reported that Churchill "simply loved" *Comrade X,* the jejune American spy farce starring Clark Gable and Hedy Lamarr. There were even a few new British products, including George Bernard Shaw's *Major Barbara;* a satirical anti-Fascist documentary entitled *Yellow Caesar,* in which Mussolini came in for considerable coarse ridicule; and the stately historical drama *The Prime Minister,* starring John Gielgud as Benjamin Disraeli. British movie studios were gearing up to produce a number of wartime action melodramas that spring, but in general, the domestic film industry had fallen on hard times. Actors and skilled cinema technicians of draft age had long ago been lost to the military, and shortages of all sorts of obscure materials (including the hair lace that formed the base of most theatrical wigs, stuff that normally came from the Balkans) restricted the quality and quantity of British film productions. David Niven, a captain in the Royal Army, had recently signed a new contract with a unique clause that read: "Work on any picture will be suspended while any invasion attempt is being made so that David Niven may return to his regiment. Work will be resumed immediately the invasion attempt has failed."

Other arts, too, suffered hardships from the blitz and the increasingly rigorous privations of wartime. Bombs and fire had, of course, destroyed much of Britain's architectural heritage since September 1940, although the National Gallery's art treasures had been evacuated and were nestled safely underground, in a maze of caves deep under a mountain near the town of Blaenau Ffestiniog, in northern Wales. (Some well-meaning civil servants had suggested that the paintings be sent to Canada for safekeeping, but Churchill and Kenneth Clark had insisted that they remain in Britain for the duration. "Bury them in the bowels of the earth," Churchill thundered, "but not a picture shall leave this island.") Ballet companies cut short their London seasons—partly for their own safety and partly because so many people had moved to the countryside—and extended their tours of the provinces. Ballerinas' silk stockings had to be mended again and again to repair runs; for the moment, the new miracle fiber known as "nylon" remained nothing more than a tantalizing rumor. As a token of appreciation for the entertainment, and to sustain the dancers' energy levels, fans sent packets of chocolate and sugar backstage. But even these gifts were not sufficient for some exhausted performers. "We started looking for other sources of energy," recalled Margot Fonteyn, then a twenty-one-year-old prima donna, "and drank lashings of a strange green tonic which was described as 'giving you tomorrow's strength today.' All that happened was that tomorrow one felt even more tired, and drank more green drink."

It seemed that everywhere one went, sooner or later the conversation turned to food. "There is no question but that the food situation is very much worse," reported General Lee. Taking a break from his theological speculations on the existence and nature of a benevolent deity, C. S. Lewis visited Fortnum & Mason's and found the shelves of condiments as full and appetizing as ever. "But," he wondered, "what good were sauces and chutneys if there was no fish or flesh or fowl to put under them?" The meat ration was down to one shilling's worth per week—about half of what it had been in March 1940—which bought only three-quarters of a pound of cheap beef or eight ounces of lamb chops; many Britons chose to substitute less expensive dishes such as liver, sheep's heart, or tripe. Startled housewives saw signs in butcher shop windows that read HORSE MEAT. PASSED FOR HUMAN CONSUMPTION. NO COUPONS REQUIRED. George Orwell was equally amazed to see fishmongers displaying freshwater fish for sale. "A year ago," he remarked in his diary, "English people, i.e. town people, wouldn't have touched such a thing." Biscuits, breakfast cereals, honey, lemons and lime juice, and macaroni were all in short supply, although there was still plenty of beer on stock, and victory gardens provided an adequate yield of fresh vegetables. "I've never been hungry yet," noted Lewis, who was still a little on the pudgy side, "—in fact, the only way it affects me is to plunge me back into the pleasures of early boyhood; I mean, food is a subject infinitely interesting, and every meal a highlight."

Unless something occurred to reverse the terrifying trend of British maritime losses, soon Lewis's meals would become a treasured memory. April 1941 was the cruelest month on the seas since the war began: Britain's losses in the Atlantic and Mediterranean totaled 195 ships and 687,901 tons. And the onslaught had just begun—as yet Germany had no more than thirty U-boats on duty at any given moment. Although April's figures were slightly inflated because of the sinkings incurred during the evacuation from Greece, the average rate of loss since the beginning of March ran slightly over 100,000 tons a week; at that pace, Britain would end the year with a *net* loss of 3 million tons, a wholly unacceptable rate of attrition when one considered that the maximum combined annual output of British and American shipyards probably was no more than 2.1 million tons. "When all is said and done," Churchill declared for the benefit of his friends across the Atlantic, "the only way in which we can get through the year 1942 without a very sensible contraction of our war efforts is by another gigantic building of merchant ships in the United States similar to that prodigy of output accomplished by the Americans in 1918."

The news was so bad that the Admiralty stopped releasing its weekly statistics, to avoid depressing home morale. Churchill and his war cabinet drew up a detailed, bare-bones "budget of imports for the U-boat year 1941": 15 million tons of food, and another 15 million—down from the previous budget's allotment of 19 million tons—for the Ministry of Supply, which included virtually everything else except food. "We must try to import in the most concentrated forms and over the shortest routes," Churchill reminded the cabinet. "This principle must also influence food imports." In growing desperation, Churchill wrote to Roosevelt on May 3: "If you cannot take more advanced positions now or very soon, the vast balances may be tilted heavily to our disadvantage. Mr. President, I am sure that you will not misunderstand me if I speak to you exactly what is in my mind. The one decisive counterweight I can see to balance the growing pessimism . . . would be if the United States were immediately to range herself with us as a belligerent power."

The plain truth was that Britain was in serious danger of being starved and defeated. A wave of mysticism swept the country. Newspapers were filled with prophecies of miracles and disasters. "I suppose it is that in our own minds we can see no way through the wood, but to break it down twig by twig," explained author Vera Hodgson, "and so we look to the stars for aid—and hope a miracle can be worked for us." Churchill, who believed, incorrectly, that the nation as a whole was far less anxious about the future than the House of Commons, might well have wondered how long his battered and bewildered people could stand up against the strain of sinkings in the Atlantic, against the depressing and seemingly endless chain of military disasters abroad, and the relentless pounding of the renewed Luftwaffe onslaught. April brought England the worst bombing raids since the great incendiary attack upon London at the end of December 1940. On clear nights, Elizabeth Longford could hear the hum of an invisible fleet of Nazis above: "It was so high overhead, so utterly disembodied yet loud enough to be placed in space, that I remember it as the most sinister sound I have ever heard. Napoleon's distant troops winding down the hillside before the Battle of Waterloo had had the same effect of the 'supernatural.' . . . I felt more frustrated than a savage shooting arrows at the unseen monster swallowing the sun. At least the savage was doing something."

All Churchill could do was visit the most recent scenes of devastation, ride about on the hood of an open car while waving his square, derbylike hat (which he carried on the end of his cane), look round at the smoldering ruins, tell the grieving survivors more consoling words about the spirit of an unconquerable people and the grand centuries-old traditions of England, and leave them with a promise that "we will give it to them back." He never publicized his plans for visiting a stricken city, and often plunged headlong into the crowd with only a few security men around him. "Stand back," he'd say to his bodyguards. "Let the others see." And the people would call out, "Here's Winnie," and once someone pleased Churchill tremendously by muttering as the Prime Minister walked past, "There goes the bloody British Empire." When he was back in his private car, Churchill's eyes grew moist and he murmured, "They have such confidence. It is a grave responsibility."

There was one night, early in April, when the R.A.F. did, in fact, give it back to Germany; in the most successful raid thus far against Berlin, British incendiary bombs destroyed the State Opera House and damaged a number of other Nazi government and cultural buildings along the Unter den Linden. In retaliation, Göring launched a series of brutal attacks on Plymouth and London. When Churchill made his sad pilgrimage to Plymouth afterwards, he saw that most of the city had been obliterated. ". . . Scarcely a house seems to be habitable," reported Colville. "The whole city is wrecked except, characteristically, the important parts of the naval establishment. . . . I saw a bus which had been carried bodily, by the force of an explosion, on to the roof of a building some 150 yards from where it had been standing." Overcome by the horror and the desolation, Churchill kept repeating under his breath, "I've never seen the like."

On the evening of April 16, nearly six hundred German planes flew across London and dropped 876 tons of bombs upon the city. Six hundred people died, and twice as many were badly injured. "Blind fatalism was probably as good a refuge as any on that night, in which death was democratically making no social distinctions," wrote an American correspondent. "In many cases, well-built shelters deep down beneath expensive brick and concrete proved little better than the kitchen tables under which humble families stoically crouched and listened to hell breaking loose around them." Even the irascible Alexander Cadogan could not fall asleep until the all-clear sounded at 4:30 A.M. "I could not help but think this is a very queer life," remarked General Lee, who spent the evening in the first-floor room of a hotel with a friend, discussing Hugo's *Les Misérables,* the works of Thomas Wolfe, and the merits of Chinese porcelain. "All this time," remembered Lee, "I had a sickening feeling that hundreds of people were being murdered in a most savage way almost within a stone's throw and there was nothing to do about it." Piccadilly, Pall Mall, Lower Regent Street, Jermyn Street, and St. James's Street suffered direct hits in nearly every block. Rescue workers spent the next several days pulling anonymous shapes from the rubble. "It is a curious feeling that overtakes people the morning after a bad Blitz," noted a *New York Times* reporter. "The first thing you do is to pick up the telephone to try to talk to your best friends. All day long you telephone to ask people about other people. You say, 'Glad to see you,' and the phrase has a special meaning. Every familiar face is chalked up as a sort of special personal victory."

There was a huge gash in the above-ground portion of the Admiralty; this, Churchill noted with bleak humor, at least gave him a better view of Nelson's Column. St. Paul's Cathedral was struck by a huge unexploded bomb; Chelsea Old Church was smashed; and St. Andrew's, Holborn, was demolished. The quaint, charming houses of St. James's Place were gutted by fire. Four million dollars' worth of jewelry, scheduled for auction, lay buried beneath concrete and brick at Christie's. "Certainly as I walk through the streets I look at London's landmarks more carefully now," noted Colville, "with a feeling that it may be the last time I shall see them."

Three nights later, another 1,010 tons of explosives fell on London. And, on Saturday evening, May 10, London suffered its most damaging raid of the war. Under a full moon, from eleven o'clock until four in the morning, tens of thousands of fire bombs and heavy explosives ripped through the air, their monotonous, sickening screams mixing with the roar

of the flames and the wail of the sirens as the hours crawled by. General
Raymond Lee watched the inferno from the roof of a hotel:

> It was dark enough, but the whole sky was lit up by a huge yellowish disc
> of full moon, while the horizon was illuminated by a great number of fires
> which extended all around us in a huge ring. As a rule, the fires before had
> appeared like rose red illuminations, but tonight a large number of them had
> huge forked flames leaping up towards the heavens, which indicated to me
> they were buildings which had been ignited on top by incendiary bombs. I
> could count not less than fifteen of them all around us, and it really looked
> as if Claridge's hotel was the exact hub and center of the whole design.
> . . . As we were talking, there was the usual drone of the falling bomb, and
> then over towards Piccadilly there was a huge explosion and a towering pillar
> of dust, debris, smoke and sparks, which shot up like magic to the zenith.

Three thousand people were killed or seriously injured. A bomb
crashed through the roof of a hotel and exploded in the basement shelter
where 140 guests and staff had taken cover. In another shelter, the mayor
of Westminster and thirty-seven other people were killed by a direct hit.
Damage to 150 of the city's water mains prevented firemen from extinguishing all the two thousand blazes, many of which were still raging out
of control the next morning. Five hospitals were hit, including one children's hospital. Nearly all the main railway stations were blocked by the
rubble. A landmine landed on Harrods', and the British Museum was set
afire. Scars that had just begun to heal from earlier raids were torn open
again and lay gaping and filthy, a bitter and ugly sight.

Beyond the loss of life, a beautiful and irreplaceable part of the nation's heritage perished as bombs and fire gutted the historic debating
chamber of the House of Commons. The Commons would not meet there
again until after the war, when the chamber had been completely rebuilt.
Aside from the formalities at the close of the day's debate, the last words
spoken in the chamber had been Churchill's spirited response to the
attacks upon his government in the vote of confidence debate on May 7:
"When I look back on the perils which have been overcome, upon the
great mountain waves in which the gallant ship has driven, when I remember all that has gone wrong, and remember also all that has gone
right I feel sure we have no need to fear the tempest. Let it roar, and let
it rage. We shall come through."

Bombs had ripped through the magnificent roof of Westminster Hall,
the only remaining part of Westminster Palace, built by William Rufus at
the close of the eleventh century; the impact sent the roof's soaring arches
and exquisite oak beams crashing to the ground. The Deanery of Westminster was completely destroyed. A shower of incendiaries upon the roof of
Westminster Abbey started so many fires that the watchers could not
extinguish them all in time. The lantern roof—the low tower directly over

the central portion of the abbey—burned out, and tons of charred beams, broken masonry, cinders, and dust fell through to the floor below, the wreckage damaging the altar, the pulpit, and the platform and coronation chair where George VI and long generations of his predecessors had been crowned. The abbey's graves, including those of Edward the Confessor, Chaucer, and the Unknown Soldier were not disturbed. There was a report that someone found a copy of the Book of Common Prayer lying open on the steps of the choir; scraping away the ashes from the exposed page, the passage read: "They have set fire upon thy holy places; and have defiled the dwelling place of the Name even unto the ground. Yea, they said in their hearts, Let us make havock of them altogether: thus have they burnt up all the houses of God in the land. . . ."

"One cannot comment on such things," wrote Hodgson in her diary:

> . . . I feel we must have sinned grievously as a nation to have such sacrifices demanded of us. Indeed future generations will say we have not taken care of what was handed down to us. We should have been more careful to defend it. We must pay the price now . . . I can see all our ancestors looking down reproachfully, saying: "We gave it you. You have not guarded it and handed it on as you received it. You have failed your trust—even those who loved it best."

On the walls of partially bombed houses throughout the city, enraged Londoners had scrawled chalk messages of unmistakable hate: BOMB BERLIN. In the air raids of 1941, German bombs had killed 18,007 Britons and injured 20,750 more; the total casualties since June 1940 were 43,381 civilians dead and 50,856 seriously wounded. London would not forget.

After breakfast, Colville telephoned Churchill and told him what he had seen. "He was very grieved," said Colville, "that William Rufus's roof at Westminster Hall should have gone," but Churchill also informed his secretary that the Luftwaffe had not escaped unscathed. Using night fighters and the new, highly classified radar technology known to insiders as GCI, the R.A.F. and antiaircraft batteries together had brought down thirty-three German planes, a spectacular haul that equaled 15 percent of the Luftwaffe force employed against Britain that night. With the scheduled start of Barbarossa only six weeks away, such losses were completely unacceptable to Hitler.

After the terrible night of May 10, then, there would be no more air raids over Britain until the long-range V-1 and V-2 rocket attacks of 1944. The blitz was over, and Hitler had lost.

But since no one in Britain could know that the ordeal was over, the sickening results of the raids pushed the battered nation further toward open expressions of defeatism and resignation. People said stoically, "We got over it before. We shall get over it again," but the dull pain from repeated blows on an old wound led many to wonder to themselves,

"What's the use?" A report from the Home Censorship office, which moni-
tored—opened and read—letters sent abroad, revealed a disturbing degree of discontent among the lower and middle classes in Britain, among
people who believed that the aristocracy was "doing well out of the war."
This feeling of resentment was accompanied by an expectation that the
end of the war would—and must—put an end to traditional English class
distinctions and vast inequalities of wealth. "The heirs of Nelson and of
Cromwell are not in the House of Lords," Orwell noted. "They are in the
fields and the streets, in the factories and the armed forces, in the four-ale
bar and the suburban back garden; and at present they are still kept under
by a generation of ghosts. . . . *Laissez-faire* capitalism is dead. The choice
lies between the kind of collective society that Hitler will set up and the
kind that can arise if he is defeated."

But first things first. From his post at the Ministry of Information,
Harold Nicolson observed that "all that the country really wants is some
assurance of how victory is to be achieved. They are bored by talks about
the righteousness of our cause and our eventual triumph. What they want
are facts indicating how we are to beat the Germans. I have no idea at all
how we are to give them those facts."

The answer lay in the east.

15

Stalin Sleeps

"Certainly the Russian has a viewpoint on life far different
from that of the Central and Western European. . . .
We do not expect to understand the outlook of the Oriental,
but the Russian is sufficiently European to mislead us.
We always expect to understand him better than we do."
—CHARLES LINDBERGH, APRIL 1941

There was no springtime in Moscow in 1941. Like a ghost that lingered past the appointed hour, winter tarried until the last snow finally fell on June 6. All through April and May, dark leaden clouds hung low over the towers of the Kremlin, imparting an ashen chill to the already cheerless atmosphere within the city. "The first thing that any visitor remarked, in walking the streets of Moscow, was that the people never smiled," observed Henry Cassidy, who had arrived in the Soviet Union as an Associated Press correspondent in early 1940. There were the customary interminable queues for everything: for milk, bread, flour, and meat, for morning and evening newspapers with the latest reports of the war in Europe, for bus and streetcar tickets, for the privilege of admission to movies such as *Musical Story,* a Soviet-style adaptation of the Fred Astaire–Ginger Rogers classics.

Yet, considering the turbulent decade through which the Russian people had just passed (and which few families had escaped unscathed), the year of 1941 began on a relatively encouraging note. The great purges of 1936–38 were over, and the horrifying ordeal of collectivization and forced industrialization mercifully had run its course. The harvest of 1940 had been a good one and early indications portended an even better yield for the new year. Produce from the gigantic collective farms was abundant and inexpensive in the cities. Soviet factories and coal mines finally were operating at a higher level of efficiency, accounting for approximately 10 percent of the world's industrial production. The USSR trailed only Germany and the United States as a producer of steel, aluminum, and electrical energy; the nation held second place in oil production and machine building, and led the world in the production of synthetic rubber. By the end of 1940, consumer goods appropriated (i.e., stolen) from the recently assimilated Baltic states had begun to arrive in Moscow. Thus far, the war had been profitable for the Soviet Union, bringing territorial gains in Poland, the Baltic, and Romania, which had been compelled to cede oil-rich Bessarabia back to the Ukraine. Russia's western border was protected, ostensibly, by the Nazi-Soviet nonaggression pact of 1939, although the German occupation of Romania and Bulgaria and the Nazi conquest of Yugoslavia and Greece admittedly heightened concern among Soviet strategists, and spurred Stalin to conclude the nonaggression pact with Matsuoka in April; in fact, the Soviet-Japanese treaty was signed on the same day that Belgrade fell.

Ever since it had seized power in 1917, the Communist regime had governed upon the assumption that its capitalist enemies someday would unite and embark on a crusade to crush the Soviet Union. But Stalin never—*never*—acknowledged the probability of a German attack upon Russia in 1941. To all outward appearances, Stalin was convinced that the Soviet Union could escape the ravages of this war until Germany and Britain had decimated each other in a stalemate in the west, and he ordered Party officials to assure the Russian people that it could not happen there. "Of all the major states," proclaimed veteran Bolshevik revolutionary Mikhail Kalinin late in 1940, "the Soviet Union is the only one that is not involved in the war and is observing strict neutrality. . . . When the whole world is in the grip of such a war it is great good fortune to be out of it." Not that the Soviet leaders were taking anything for granted; year after year, they lavished vast expenditures on the armed forces. "Maintain the entire nation in a state of mobilized readiness so no enemy trick can catch us unawares," Stalin had said, and in approving the 1941 economic plan in February the Supreme Soviet had provided for further expansion of the military by allocating one-third of that year's budget of 215 billion rubles for national defense. Naval Commissar Nikolai Kuznetsoff declared that the Red Fleet was "expanding enormously," as Russian shipyards turned out "the most modern of destroyers, cruisers and battleships," and Marshal Grigori Zhukov, recently appointed chief of the General Staff, assured western reporters that the Red Army was equipped with "the latest models of planes, tanks and artillery." At the annual May Day parade, amid a tide of red flags, banners, and patriotic slogans, the military staged an especially imposing display of motorized and mechanized weaponry, warplanes, and thousands of hand-picked well-drilled troops, everything expressly designed to bolster domestic morale and intimidate foreign observers.

It was all a sham. Over the past decade, the Red Army had suffered a series of devastating blows that left it wholly incapable of defending the Russian homeland without suffering terrible casualties. The troubles began at the top. Almost every member of the highest levels of the officer corps—the Old Guard—had been savagely liquidated, imprisoned, or disgraced during the purges. Over the space of three years of undiminished terror, Stalin managed to rid the Soviet Union of virtually every experienced senior officer it had: thirteen of fifteen generals, two-thirds of the corps commanders and commanders of military districts, all but one fleet commander, and approximately half of the army's regimental commanders. In fact, far more Soviet senior officers were killed during the purges than during four years of war with Germany. In all, forty thousand officers of all ranks—more than half of the officer corps—lost their lives or their positions during the terror. Most of those who survived with their lives and reputations intact were thoroughly and understandably demoralized; they owed their careers and their lives to Stalin, and few would ever dare challenge his orders, however mistaken, in the future. Nor had the terror abated entirely by 1941: two weeks before Hitler launched Operation Barbarossa, the chief of the Soviet Air Force reportedly was executed for treason.

To fill the vacancies created by Stalin's paranoid rampages, the Red Army was forced to promote inexperienced junior officers, some even before they had graduated from training school, to positions of responsibility for which they were sadly unprepared. The predictable results were evident during the 1939–40 "winter war" against Finland, when Soviet forces suffered a series of humiliating setbacks that convinced the German General Staff, among others, that the Red Army would make a tempting target: "The Russian 'mass' is *no* match for an army with modern equipment and superior leadership."

Despite its impressive appearance in parades and in paper calculations of numerical strength, an overwhelming preponderance of Soviet military matériel was out-of-date and unreliable. Although new models of tanks, planes, and artillery had been designed and tested, they had not yet been produced in sufficient quantities to fill the needs of even the army units along the western border. As late as January 1941, the Soviet High Command was still mired in a debate over the relative merits of tanks and horses, despite the remarkable successes of the German panzer units during the blitzkrieg across Europe. Antitank and antiaircraft weapons had been virtually ignored. Soviet fighter planes were extremely maneuverable, which made them look wonderful zooming about the sky above parades; they were painfully slow, however, especially when compared to their German counterparts, and had very little firing power and almost no armor. Soviet military aviation experts had pinned their hopes upon the development of powerful four-motor bombers that carried an astonishingly heavy load of explosives; but these ponderous behemoths, too, were far too slow and had a very limited flight range.

Then there was the infantry, "a mass of badly uniformed, badly booted men, whose guns hung from their shoulders by pieces of string," according to an observant young Pole from Cracow who, like many of his fellow countrymen, had been pressed into service with the Red Army. "Even the bayonets, while on the march, were tied by rope to the rifles. Supplies, in great part, came in horse-drawn, flat-bottomed wagons, the harness made of straps of coarse cloth instead of leather. As for the faces of the masses, particularly those of the infantry, of whom a large percentage came from the East, they looked wild, stupid, without a shadow of intelligence. Nor did the officers reveal, as a rule, any great spiritual values." Mobility was severely limited because trucks were in very short supply (hence the horse-drawn wagons), and it has been estimated that the Red Army in 1941 possessed even fewer rifles, though perhaps more reliable ones, than the czar's ill-equipped forces in World War One.

To deploy this unwieldy combination of modern technology and Slavic stolidity, Soviet military strategists had managed to devise a plan that almost guaranteed a series of devastating defeats and heavy Russian losses during the initial stages of a German attack. They had convinced themselves that the Red Army, after a brief period of tactical defensive operations, would quickly be able to stem the tide and launch a counteroffensive against any aggressor. The ruling maxim of the Soviet high command in the 1930s had been: "The Red Army will win any future war with little expenditure of blood and will carry the fight into the enemy's own territory," and no strategic assumption had ever been more mistaken. In the Soviet military academies, such subjects as forced retreat, fighting when encircled, and meeting engagements—precisely the tactics the hard-pressed Red Army would need to employ over the next four years—were given short shrift.

Confident that they faced no imminent danger of invasion from the west in 1941, Soviet officials had dismantled their fortifications along the old line between the USSR and the Baltic states *before* they built similar defenses along the new borders some two hundred miles westward. At the time, this did not seem to be a particularly harmful error; in the unlikely event that Hitler did attack before the spring of 1942, the Soviet high command assumed that he would strike first at the southwest, at the Ukraine with its rich grain fields, oil reserves, and the coal mines of the Donets Basin, and they concentrated their defenses accordingly. Stalin was especially adamant on this point; "Nazi Germany will not be able to wage a major lengthy war without those vital resources," he told Zhukov in the spring of 1941, ignoring (to his peril) the precedent established less than a year before, by the swift German thrusts across Europe which had brought the western half of the continent to its knees in a matter of two short months.

"Stalin was the greatest authority for all of us," wrote Zhukov in his memoirs, "and it never occurred to anybody to question the correctness of his opinion and assessment of the current situation." Certainly not. Sixty-two years old, a native of the southern province of Georgia, near the

Black Sea, Joseph Stalin (né Josif Vissarionovich Dzhugashvili) was a survivor of what George Kennan has aptly termed "the seething, savage underworld of the Transcaucasus." He began his political career as a hired thug, a blackmailer and bandit who joined the Communist Party in 1904 and made himself indispensable by robbing czarist bank messengers to finance Bolshevik activities. By the time of the 1917 revolution, Stalin had climbed close to the upper echelons of the party hierarchy, but he remained a gray blur in the background, dismissed as an uncouth, uneducated tough by the intellectuals who ruled the Party. They paid for their poor judgment with their lives. One of the last to go was Leon Trotsky, who, shortly before he was assassinated in Mexico by one of Stalin's agents, described his former rival as a prototypical Asian despot who displayed "that blending of grit, shrewdness, craftiness and cruelty which has been considered characteristic of the statesmen of Asia." Stalin was, Trotsky wrote scornfully, "a phenomenon utterly exceptional. He is neither a thinker, a writer, nor an orator. He took possession of power before the masses had learned to distinguish his figure from others during the triumphal processions across Red Square. Stalin took possession of power, not with the aid of personal qualities, but with the aid of an impersonal machine."

Insofar as ruthlessness, jealousy, cunning, and vanity may be considered personal qualities, Trotsky was dead wrong. Between Lenin's death in 1924 (Trotsky, incidentally, was convinced that Stalin had poisoned Lenin, and perhaps he had) and his own death in 1953, Stalin exercised supreme power within the Soviet Union by manipulating the police and the Party apparatus, and by his willingness—which at times shaded into a detestable eagerness—to employ terror and murder to eliminate all potential personal rivals. Usually he managed to persuade others to do the actual dirty work, but the gruesome record of his reign speaks for itself. After encountering opposition to his plans from the Seventeenth Party Congress in 1934, Stalin had over half of the 1,966 members of the congress murdered, along with 98 of the 139 members of the Central Committee elected by that congress. Of course, these top officials were only a small percentage of the victims of the great purges. And beyond the clear-cut cases of murder, there were the numberless atrocities committed during the brutal collectivization and forced industrialization programs. "The number of victims here—the number, that is, of those who actually lost their lives—runs into the millions," wrote Kennan. "But this is not to mention the broken homes, the twisted childhoods, and the millions of people who were half-killed: who survived these ordeals only to linger on in misery, with broken health and broken hearts."

In prisons, in concentration camps and forced-labor camps, Stalin had locked away more than twenty million people since assuming supreme power in 1929. Near the end of the spring of 1941, Menachem Begin was removed from Lukishki prison, taken to the train yard of Vilna, and shoved into a crowded freight car along with seventy other prisoners. Then he began the journey north and eastward in his mobile prison, linked with other freight cars bound for an unknown destination, subsisting on bread and salt fish and bad water, nearly suffocating behind closed doors bolted with iron bars. "For days and nights," Begin remembered, "the rhythmic clicking of the wheels over the rails seemed to be repeating the questions: 'Where? Why? Why? Where? . . .' " At last the train arrived in the *taiga*, the northern tundra, the land of the white nights. After a few days in a transit camp, and more hours plodding through treacherous swampland, Begin and his comrades came to the Pechora River, near the shores of the Barents Sea, and the labor camp known as Pechora-Lag, one small link in the chain of the Gulag Archipelago. There they were put to work on twelve-hour shifts off-loading iron sleeper rails from a barge and carrying them on their shoulders to a railway truck, so the bars could be used to build the Kotlas-Varkuta railway. If a prisoner accomplished his daily work quota he would be given a full food ration of bread and soup and occasionally some dried potatoes. Yet even this, Begin learned, was miserably insufficient. "The reward for completing the quota, or even surpassing it, is not satiety, but less hunger, and the hunger in the camp defies comparison with anything we experienced in prison. In Lukishki we sat closed up in a cell; in the camp we were out in the open for sixteen hours a day. The work is back-breaking. The body demands some recompense, but the compensation we were given was smaller than that we received in confinement. We saw what hunger did to people in Lukishki. It is not difficult to imagine, although hard to assess, what hunger did to those living in the labour camps. . . . On the banks of the Pechora I found animals walking on two legs. Hunger. . . ."

Traveling in more comfortable, though perhaps not less hazardous accommodations, Erskine Caldwell made his way from southern China across the Gobi Desert to the Soviet Union via a relay of antiquated aircraft, one of which caught fire while skimming over a rugged range of 5,000-foot mountains. Suspecting that the Wehrmacht would soon turn to the east, the author of *Tobacco Road* and *God's Little Acre* had come to the Soviet Union to obtain a firsthand impression of the country before the cataclysm occurred. Caldwell and his wife arrived in Moscow on May 12, 1941, and to his surprise found the city's hotels still full of German commercial travelers peacefully carrying out their routine business affairs. "Moscow had the appearance of any European capital in peacetime," Caldwell noted. "There were no preparations for war, new buildings were going up all over the city, streets were being widened, and the government was announcing its new Fifteen-Year Plan for Industry and Agriculture. The people of Moscow talked about their summer vacations and their plans for travel abroad when the British-German war was over."

Caldwell could not know that many of the German businessmen in

Moscow were gathering information on Soviet factories, mines, and military installations. The top echelon of German industrialists who were engaged in trade with the USSR had been ordered by Nazi authorities to delay the delivery of supplies to Russia, and step up the pace of deliveries to the Wehrmacht, in preparation for a lengthy military campaign. By the middle of May, so many people had been let in on the secret that anyone with well-placed contacts in Berlin could have known that a German invasion of the Soviet Union was imminent.

Stalin would not believe it. Several Soviet agents in western Europe and Japan—including Dr. Richard Sorge in Tokyo, ostensibly the correspondent of the *Frankfurter Zeitung,* in reality one of Stalin's most dependable and faithful spies—sent reports advising Moscow of the forthcoming danger, but Stalin closed his ears to their urgent warnings. The American commercial attaché in Berlin, an undistinguished political appointee named Sam Woods, was given a verbatim copy of Hitler's December 18 Barbarossa Directive from a reliable, highly placed anti-Nazi contact who passed along the document during a clandestine meeting in a movie theater; Woods relayed the material to Washington, where Hull and the FBI verified its authenticity. Undersecretary of State Sumner Welles reportedly advised Soviet Ambassador Oumansky of the document's contents on two separate occasions, but Stalin chose not to believe it. After mid-April, the concentrations of Nazi troops along the eastern border could no longer be disguised, and German planes repeatedly violated Russian air space on reconnaissance missions, but still Stalin chose to act as if the provocative German actions did not portend an invasion. Instead, he used Matsuoka's departure from Moscow as an opportunity publicly to reaffirm his allegiance to the Soviet-German nonaggression pact, in that memorable scene on the railway platform wherein he embraced the assistant German military attaché.

By the end of March, however, the mounting evidence had convinced Churchill that Hitler was preparing a full-scale offensive against Russia. For one thing, British agents had surreptitiously obtained (from friendly sources in Poland) a copy of the German "Enigma" cipher machine, and ever since the spring of 1940 a team of British experts based at Bletchley Park, sixty miles outside London, had been intercepting and decoding a steadily increasing number of Enigma-ciphered wireless messages to and from Luftwaffe headquarters and the Foreign Office in Berlin (though not, generally, from the Wehrmacht, which employed a much more secure ground communications system). The deciphered products of Enigma, which was the prototype for the Japanese "Purple" machine, were known to a select few British authorities as Ultra intercepts. But while Washington never learned to take full advantage of the gifts bestowed upon it via "Magic," by April 1941 Bletchley had evolved into an efficient center of intelligence interpretation and distribution, regularly supplying Churchill—who reveled in its aura of intrigue like a little boy playing cloak and daggers—with timely translations of Ultra intercepts that often afforded an authoritative insight into German strategic planning.

In its infancy during the Battle of Britain, Bletchley Park had alerted the R.A.F. to the strength and location of incoming air raids, providing commanders with an invaluable margin of minutes to deploy their defenses for action. Now, in March and April, Ultra intercepts of Luftwaffe messages revealed that Germany was moving large numbers of aircraft into the Balkans and enlarging and reinforcing the airfields in Bulgaria, Romania, and Poland. At Bletchley, they knew the ultimate purpose behind these operations; as one British intelligence officer put it, "it occurred to me that this was not being done for the benefit of Lufthansa!"

But beyond the data garnered from his beloved Ultra "eggs," Churchill possessed what he considered to be even more conclusive evidence of Germany's aggressive intentions toward the Soviet Union. "Up till the end of March I was not convinced that Hitler was resolved upon mortal war with Russia, nor how near it was," recalled Churchill. He admitted that "our Intelligence reports revealed in much detail the extensive German troop movements towards and into the Balkan States which had marked the first three months of 1941," but the prospect of Germany opening another major war front before gaining control of the Balkans (and, more to the point, before subduing Great Britain), "seemed to me too good to be true." Then British agents reported that three German panzer divisions which had been ordered north, from Romania toward Poland, immediately after Prince Paul's government signed the Axis Pact, suddenly reversed their course following the Simovic coup and headed south again, to participate in Operation Punishment. The crucial question was why these armored units had been sent toward Poland in the first place, with affairs in the Balkans still unsettled. To Churchill, watching intently from London, this unusual sequence of events "illuminated the whole Eastern scene like a lightning-flash. The sudden movement to Cracow of so much armour needed in the Balkan sphere could only mean Hitler's intention to invade Russia in May. This seemed to me henceforward certainly his major purpose. The fact that the Belgrade revolution had required their return to Rumania involved perhaps a delay from May to June."

Churchill wasted no time in dispatching a warning to Stalin through Sir Stafford Cripps, the British ambassador in Moscow. Stalin received the message but gave no indication that he recognized the danger. Much to Churchill's chagrin, the revelations of German troop movements failed to induce Stalin to support an anti-Nazi front in the Balkans. After the war, Churchill scathingly criticized the Soviet dictator for his stubborn refusal to take appropriate defensive measures:

War is mainly a catalogue of blunders, but it may be doubted whether any mistake in history has equalled that of which Stalin and the Communist chiefs were guilty when they cast away all possibilities in the Balkans and supinely awaited, or were incapable of realising, the fearful onslaught which impended upon Russia. We have hitherto rated them as selfish calculators. In this period they were proved simpletons as well. The force, the mass, the bravery and endurance of Mother Russia had still to be thrown into the scales. But so far as strategy, policy, foresight, competence are arbiters, Stalin and his commissars showed themselves at this moment the most completely outwitted bunglers of the Second World War.

Surely this is too harsh a judgment. Despite the incontrovertible evidence provided by Ultra, Churchill's own Joint Intelligence Committee did not conclude until June 12 that Hitler really intended to invade the Soviet Union.

Besides, Stalin had his own reasons, foolish as they may have been, for disregarding so many insistent warnings. He had long been obsessed by a fear that the western democracies would encourage Nazi Germany to turn against the USSR, and then stand back and watch the two renegade totalitarian nations of Europe decimate each other. To Stalin's paranoid mind, the messages from Britain were part of a devious plot, a dirty trick to incite animosity between himself and Hitler, to encourage him to mobilize Russian forces prematurely as the czar had done in 1914, thereby alarming Berlin and leaving them with no choice but to launch a preemptive strike against the Soviet Union. "This information is an English provocation," he wrote in red ink across one of the warnings of invasion. "Find out who is doing this and have him punished." Stalin's suspicions were fueled by Churchill's well-deserved reputation as a rabid anti-Bolshevik, firmly established by his vociferous support of British military intervention on behalf of White forces during the dark days of the Russian Civil War of 1917–20.

Even if Stalin accepted the inevitability of a war with Germany, he doubted that Hitler would turn eastward before settling affairs with Britain in the west. He obviously believed Russia was safe until the spring of 1942, at least, by which time the Soviet rearmament program would have made much greater progress. The last thing he wanted to do was to provoke a war with Hitler before the Red Army was ready. Hence the flood of rumors that poured into Moscow foretelling a German invasion in the summer of 1941 unnerved an already anxiety-ridden Stalin (who was as cognizant as anyone of the Red Army's glaring weaknesses); the more warnings he received, the more unreasonable he became. So the Soviet dictator accepted—even if he did not entirely believe—German explanations that their troop concentrations were merely a ruse, to trick Britain into thinking that Hitler intended to move east, when in reality he still planned to invade Britain once the island lowered its defenses.

Having successfully deceived Stalin as to its intentions, the German High Command itself fell victim to a brief, panic-stricken moment of uncertainty in the middle of March, when it suddenly realized that the Red Army units along the border, which still greatly outnumbered the Wehrmacht divisions and would continue to do so until April 20, might stumble onto the plans for Barbarossa and launch a preemptive attack before Germany completed its preparations. Once April arrived, most of the top-ranking military officials of the Reich (including Halder) appear to have lost their initial misgivings about the prospects for a successful invasion of Russia. They were reassured by comfortable assumptions of German racial superiority over the dim-witted Russian Slavs, by a steady stream of intelligence reports (which turned out to be disastrously faulty) denigrating Soviet military capabilities, and by Hitler's confident prophecies of swift and easy victory over an enemy armed with obsolete equipment and commanded by incompetent, unimaginative officers. "When one really gets hold of this colossus, it will collapse faster than the whole world suspects," the Fuehrer assured his generals. "The Soviet Union will burst like a soap bubble." Some intelligence estimates predicted that the fighting would be over in as little as four weeks, but certainly no more than four months.

What disturbed some of the generals more than the possibility of failure was the Fuehrer's evident determination to wage a war of annihilation against subversive elements (i.e., Communists and Jews) in the USSR. In a general staff meeting at his office in the Reich Chancellery on March 30, Hitler stormed through a two-and-a-half-hour tirade, during which he vilified Britain (for being so stupid as to reject Germany's peace offer in the summer of 1940) and chastised Italy (for bungling every strategic opportunity in the war). But he saved his most crushing denunciation for bolshevism and the criminal Communist mentality. Exhorting his commanders to crush the Red Army once and for all and shatter the Soviet Union into smaller separatist states, Hitler drew a scenario for Armageddon: "Communism is an enormous danger for our future. We must forget the concept of comradeship between soldiers. A Communist is no comrade before nor after the battle. This is a war of extermination. If we do not grasp this, we shall still beat the enemy, but 30 years later we shall again have to fight the Communist foe. We do not wage war to preserve the enemy."

Then Hitler delivered the infamous Commissar Order, which was only revealed to the outside world during the war crimes trials at Nuremberg. The Fuehrer demanded that every Bolshevik commissar be executed without trial, and the Stalinist intelligentsia wiped out in its entirety. He condemned all Communist officials as criminals and insisted that they be brutally treated as such, with "unprecedented, merciless, and unrelenting harshness." Individual troop commanders were assigned the responsibility for ensuring that these orders were fully carried out. "This war will be very different from the war in the West," he told the generals. "In the East, harshness today means lenience in the future. Commanders must make the sacrifice of overcoming their personal scruples." This was the first time that the Wehrmacht, the proud inheritors of the Prussian military tradition, had been ordered to participate in what were obviously criminal excesses of the twisted Nazi ideology. "I do not expect my generals to understand me," Hitler admitted later, "but I shall expect them to obey my orders."

After Hitler left the room, a few generals reportedly cornered Brauchitsch and pressed him to rescind the order or resign. He did neither. "Nothing in the world," he said, would change Hitler's attitude. Keitel signed the Commissar Order, supplemented on May 13 by another directive excusing from the customary court-martial procedures any German soldier who committed punishable offenses (such as murder) against *any* Russian civilians: "With regard to *offenses* committed against *enemy civilians by members of the Wehrmacht, prosecution is not obligatory* even when the deed is at the same time a military crime or offense."

To the civilian administrators who would rule the conquered Russian territories, Göring and Rosenberg issued directives instructing them to commandeer all surplus food supplies and ship them to Germany. Admittedly this would result in the starvation of at least several million Russians living in industrial areas, but the Nazi administrators were instructed to take no measures to avoid widespread famine. "Any attempt to save the population there from death by starvation by importing surpluses from the black-soil zone would be at the expense of supplies to Europe. It would reduce Germany's staying power in the war, and would undermine Germany's and Europe's power to resist the blockade. This must be clearly and absolutely understood."

No one seemed to object to this inhumane policy, and after their initial protests to Brauchitsch (and despite the misgivings of conscience that some of them evidently felt), the generals of the Wehrmacht declined to organize any coordinated resistance to Hitler's barbarous plans, although eventually they did forbid individual soldiers from conducting reprisals against civilians without explicit orders from a superior officer. Of course there were a few lonely, uneasy souls, like Canaris, who still feared that Barbarossa was nothing more than a suicidal scheme conceived by a madman, a fatal obsession that could end only in disaster. "The German armies will bleed to death on the icy plains of Russia," Canaris predicted in despair, "and two years later there won't be anything left of them." But by May, no one was listening. Keitel curtly dismissed Canaris's warnings: "My dear Canaris, you may know something about military intelligence.

Being a sailor, you surely don't propose to give us any lessons in strategic planning."

There was another member of the top Nazi hierarchy, though, who expressed his dissatisfaction with the course of the war in a more spectacular fashion. Shortly before six o'clock on the afternoon of Saturday, May 10, Rudolf Hess, dressed in the uniform of a Luftwaffe Oberleutnant, took off in a silver-gray ME 110 fighter plane from an airfield near the Messerschmitt factory in Augsburg. The forty-seven-year-old deputy fuehrer, the man who stood second only to Göring in the line of succession to Hitler, pointed the plane north, toward the North Sea. Hess had been a pilot in the First World War, and had won awards for his aerial exploits during peacetime, but this solo flight was perhaps his most dangerous mission. He was headed for Scotland, nine hundred miles away, guided only by two compasses strapped to his pants legs and dance music signals from a radio station in Denmark.

He passed over the North Sea and saw it illuminated by "an evening light of unearthly loveliness, such as is found in the far north. It was utterly lonely. But how magnificent! A multitude of small clouds far below me looked like pieces of ice floating on the sea, clear as crystal; the whole scene was tinged with red. Then the sky was swept clean . . ." Shortly before ten o'clock he recognized the coast of England through a veil of mist. He suddenly dove down through the clouds and, in so doing, unwittingly eluded a pair of British Hurricanes who had come up to intercept him. (This was, unknown to Hess, the evening of the war's most devastating Luftwaffe bombing raid on London.) Flying low to the ground, he watched for the landmarks he had committed so carefully to memory. When he realized he was near his destination—Dungavel House, the county seat of the Duke of Hamilton—he prepared to parachute to a safe landing. Unfortunately, Hess had never before jumped out of an airplane ("I had never asked about how to jump; I thought it was too simple"), and he panicked as he struggled against the crushing air pressure to get out of the Messerschmitt, which by now was running out of fuel and heading for a crash landing. Recalling an instructor's advice that the surest way to escape from an aircraft in distress was to turn it upside down and simply fall out, Hess threw the plane into a tight loop, lost consciousness for a moment, and then dropped out of the cockpit (injuring his ankle in the process) and opened his parachute barely in time. The plane crashed in a field.

Somewhat the worse for wear, Hess drifted to a rough landing on a farm near Eaglesham House. Nearby, a plowman named David McLean, a bachelor who lived with his mother and sister, was performing his nightly routine before retiring to bed when he heard the roar of a plane overhead. Still dressed in his underclothes, he ran out of his house and saw the Messerschmitt crash about two hundred yards away. "I was rather scared," he told reporters afterward, "when I saw a parachute dropping from the sky, and ran back to the house for help. Every one was asleep, however, and, fearing that I might lose the German airman, I seized a pitchfork and ran out again. I found him lying on the ground in a field at the back of the house, and helped him to his feet." McLean naturally had no idea who the intruder was, but he assisted Hess back to the house. As Mrs. McLean prepared tea (which Hess graciously declined, saying, "I never drink tea as late as this. I'll only have a glass of water"), McLean had a chance to study his prisoner at close range. "He was a striking man, standing over six feet in height and wearing a magnificent flying suit. His watch and identity bracelet were made of gold." Hess amiably took out several pictures of his four-year-old son Wolf—named after Hess's pet name for Hitler—and passed them around for the McLeans to admire.

For years, Hess and his wife had been held up to public adulation in Germany as the ideal Aryan couple. The deputy fuehrer was a dark, handsome, square-jawed man, although invariably described by Western reporters as "the beetle-browed Rudolf Hess." He had been wounded while fighting with the right-wing Freikorps units that had savagely ended the brief life of a Bolshevik regime in Bavaria in the spring of 1919; he subsequently fell under Hitler's spell and joined him in the abortive Munich putsch of November 1923. After their release from prison, Hess became Hitler's private secretary and one of his most loyal disciples. He was one of the few people who might have been considered Hitler's friend; after the death of Ernest Roehm, Hess reportedly was the only man to use the familiar "du" when speaking to the Fuehrer.

But by the spring of 1941, Hess had fallen far away from the inner circle that surrounded Hitler. Ever since the war began, the generals and especially Hess's archrival Göring had elbowed him out of the way until he had pleaded with Hitler to allow him to return to active military duty. Hitler refused, and Hess, bitter and envious, was left to spend his time making speeches at factories or gatherings of the Party faithful, or consulting astrologers for more encouraging signs from the stars.

The persistent rumors he heard from more earthly sources in Berlin, however, caused him deep concern. He shared Hitler's detestation of communism, and he realized that the Fuehrer would never rest until the Greater German Reich emerged victorious from the final apocalyptic struggle against the Soviet Union. Although Hitler apparently did not let Hess in on the secret preparations for Barbarossa, it is inconceivable that a man in Hess's position would have been wholly unaware of the ominous rumblings beneath the surface of official life in Berlin in the spring of 1941. Hess had no objections to the conquest of Russia; but he had long believed that Germany and Britain—in his mind, the two great bastions of Nordic civilization—should end their fratricidal conflict and conclude a peace settlement, so that the Reich could devote its full attention to fulfilling its historic mission in the East. Late in 1940, one of his tame astrologers had informed Hess that he was predestined to bring about such a peace. He had planned several times before, in early 1941, to fly to England "in the name of humanity" to initiate negotiations—he said he could not bear the thought of more innocent English women and children dying in air raids—but each time bad weather or mechanical malfunctions had forced him to turn back.

Finally, in May, he had made it. Sipping his glass of water in the McLeans' kitchen, Hess lied and told them his name was Horn, and asked to be taken to the Duke of Hamilton. The Duke, who as the Marquess of Clydesdale had been jocularly known as "the boxing peer," was a well-known amateur sportsman and R.A.F. group captain who, in 1933, had become the first pilot to fly over Mt. Everest. During the Olympic games held in Berlin in the summer of 1936, Hess had observed Hamilton dining with Luftwaffe officers; although the Duke had no recollection of meeting the deputy fuehrer, Hess had convinced himself that Hamilton would understand Hess's mission: to convince the British government that it should overthrow the malevolent Churchill regime, return to its true historical course and come to terms with Hitler *now*, to avoid the needless suffering (mostly British suffering, Hess arrogantly predicted) that inevitably would accompany a fight to the bloody finish. Hess recommended the same terms that Hitler had offered Britain after the fall of France: a free hand for Germany in Europe, in return for which Hitler would permit Britain to retain her empire in Africa and Asia.

After a bevy of nervous and trigger-happy Home Guards and military officials escorted him to a military barracks near Glasgow (they didn't get too many German prisoners up there), Hess finally met Hamilton and revealed his true identity. ("I do not know if you recognize me, but I am Rudolf Hess," and he had photographs to prove it.) Persuaded that the distinguished-looking prisoner probably was the deputy fuehrer, Hamilton telephoned the Foreign Office and asked to see the permanent undersecretary early that evening, but Cadogan—who seemed not to realize the identity of the German pilot—preferred not to be troubled. (For the next week, Cadogan spent nearly all his waking hours dealing with the Hess affair, a situation that made him even more irritable than usual and led him to declare that "if only the parachute had failed to open, he would be a happier and more efficient man.") Fortunately, Jock Colville arrived at the Foreign Office while Hamilton was still on the phone. Colville had awakened that Sunday morning thinking inexplicably of a recent fantasy novel in which Hitler and Göring made a secret flight to England, only to find that no one believed they really were who they said they were. After speaking to the Duke, Colville telephoned Churchill, who was lodged at his weekend retreat at Ditchley, watching a Marx brothers movie. Churchill, who was as incredulous as everyone else when he first heard the news, agreed to meet with Hamilton. After the initial confusion had been cleared away, Hess was debriefed by British military intelligence and lodged in the Tower of London as a "state prisoner."

Although Churchill initially planned to announce the true peaceful purpose of Hess's mission to the rest of a wondering world, others in the cabinet persuaded him to remain silent for a while, to encourage Hitler to believe that Hess had betrayed the Nazi cause and revealed strategic military secrets to Britain. Consequently, for the next several days all the talk in the pubs of London—and the rooms of government officials—was full of speculation about the motives behind Hess's flight. Following a month of bad news, including the Greek debacle, the convoy sinkings in the Atlantic, and the recent air raids, the British public had its first good laugh in weeks. Mollie Panter-Downes reported that the Hess affair "succeeded for several days last week in shifting the war into the key in which war rightly belongs—that of large-scale lunacy. The debt which the nation owed to Herr Hess showed in relaxed, smiling faces everywhere. After the strain and anxiety of recent events, people were glad to open their morning papers and find headlines that weren't tragedy but pure comic opera, with a libretto which might have been better if it hadn't been a trifle farfetched. The subsequent twist, the report that the unexpected visitor had hoped to tumble in on a duke, amused everyone—except, presumably, the duke in question, whose picture snapped by the photographers, showed him shielding his face with a newspaper." (Hamilton feared that people would assume he had some prior connection with Hess—which he did not—and take him for a Quisling, which he was not.)

"London buzzed with the name of Hess yesterday," reported General Lee, "and in White's Club where I lunched, the bar, the lounge and the restaurant were full of sibilants. It sounded like a basketful of snakes." A columnist in the *Daily Express* told his readers, "Your Hess guess is as good as mine," and put forward the suggestion that the deputy fuehrer, a sick man, had come over because he knew that all the best German doctors were in this country as refugees. A London cinema audience cheered when a newsreel commentator, anticipating further Nazi flights, said that even the arrival of Göring wouldn't surprise anyone, and added, "But I hope he brings his ration card."

In Moscow, however, Stalin took a darker view of Hess's mission. Since he had absolutely no idea of what had actually happened, the bizarre incident confirmed Stalin's paranoid suspicions of a compromise peace in the west and an Anglo-German demarche against the Soviet Union, and rendered him more distrustful than ever of British warnings about Barbarossa or anything else. He assumed personal control of Soviet foreign policy, displacing Molotov in the process, and nervously sought to placate Germany with special rail shipments of critical defense materials from eastern Russia, including petroleum, grain, strategic metals, and thousands of tons of raw rubber from Siberia. (Soviet officials never wavered in their conviction that Hess's primary motive had been to plan the destruction of Russia; even after the final defeat of Nazi Germany, they insisted—despite Churchill's pleas that the Allies show mercy to a man who presumably had sought to end the war—that Hess remain incarcerated in solitary confinement for the remainder of his life in Spandau prison. After several bungled suicide attempts, Hess finally succeeded in killing himself on August 17, 1987. He was ninety-three years old.)

Hess's abrupt departure took Hitler completely by surprise. Shortly after ten o'clock on the morning after the deputy fuehrer left Augsburg (and before anyone had noticed his absence), Hess's adjutant, Karl Pintsch, arrived at the Berghof with a personal letter from Hess for Hitler. Hitler, as was his wont, was still asleep. (Hitler had rather unconventional work habits, preferring to work through the night, often until dawn, then sleeping until noon. Churchill, too, usually worked until the early hours of the morning, and caught up on his sleep with a nap in the afternoon.) So Pintsch—who knew that the letter contained Hess's farewell to Hitler—waited nervously in the anteroom, where he was soon joined by architect Albert Speer, who had come to see the Fuehrer on a completely unrelated matter. When Hitler finally emerged from his private rooms, he called Pintsch into the living room. After a few moments, Speer was startled by "an inarticulate, almost animal outcry" from behind the closed doors. Then he heard Hitler roar, "Bormann, at once! Where is Bormann?"

Upon reading Hess's message—"My Fuehrer, when you receive this letter I shall be in England"—Hitler felt personally betrayed. It was, he said later, one of the blackest days of his political career. "The Fuehrer is absolutely shattered," reported Goebbels. "He has been spared nothing. . . . He is very bitter. He had never expected anything like this. One can be prepared for anything except the aberrations of a lunatic." As soon as it became clear that Hess had landed safely in Britain ("If only he would drown in the North Sea," muttered Hitler uncharitably), lunacy became the official explanation for Hess's actions as Goebbels sought to preempt any propaganda from London. "As far as it is possible to tell from the papers left behind by Party Member Hess," read the statement published in identical language in every major German newspaper, "it seems that he lived in a state of hallucination, as a result of which he felt that by getting in touch with some English people with whom he was acquainted he could bring about an understanding between England and Germany. . . . The National Socialist Party regrets that this idealist fell as a sacrifice to his hallucinations. This, however, has no effect on the continuance of the war forced upon Germany. The war will be carried on until, as Der Fuehrer in his last speech said, the British rulers fall or are ready for peace."

More than anything else, Goebbels feared that the British government would release false statements, particularly atrocity reports, under Hess's name, and was pleasantly surprised when London failed to do so. Meanwhile, the Gestapo supervised the removal of all photos of Hess from government and Party offices and all picture postcards with his likeness from news kiosks. The government ordered the arrest of all known astrologers and clairvoyants, on the grounds that Hess had been unwittingly deluded by their mystical nonsense. Hitler abolished the post of deputy fuehrer and established instead a Party Chancellery headed by Martin Bormann, who was himself busy changing the names of his two children for whom Hess and his wife had stood as godparents. The Fuehrer immediately dispatched Foreign Minister Ribbentrop to Rome, to assure a wary Mussolini that Hess had undertaken his peace mission without Hitler's blessing, and that Germany was not really seeking a separate peace with Britain. Mussolini, who by this time was growing quite resentful of the Nazis' arrogant air of superiority in every aspect of the Axis alliance, listened respectfully to Ribbentrop's nervous explanations, but afterward cheerfully informed Ciano that he considered the affair "a tremendous blow to the Nazi regime. He added," said Ciano, "that he was glad of it because this will have the effect of bringing down German stock, even with the Italians."

For once, Mussolini was correct. Even though the Nazi press refused to carry any further news or speculation on Hess's fate, the damage had been done. If Hess really had been as deranged as the official statements suggested, why had Hitler retained him as deputy fuehrer? Jokes about the flight and the government's plight made the rounds of Berlin cafés:

"The 1,000-year Reich has now become a 100-year Reich. One zero is gone."

"That our government is mad, is something that we have known for a long time; but that they admit it, *that* is something new."

"BBC announcement: On Sunday night no further German cabinet ministers flew in."

"German High Command communiqué: Göring and Goebbels are still firmly in German hands."

"Well, if this keeps up," concluded a Berlin society matron well-known for her wit, "we will soon be back among our cosy selves."

Just as Hess's intrepid exploits had brought a welcome measure of comic relief to Britons battered by the blitz and bad news from abroad, so it provided a momentary respite for war-weary Berliners. During the spring of 1941, Germany suffered serious shortages of coal, food, and clothing. In the first week of June, the civilian meat ration was reduced still further, largely because the well-fed Wehrmacht was consuming three times as much meat per stomach as the rest of the population. Staples such as potatoes, tobacco, and beer grew noticeably scarce. Housewives were limited to half a pound of laundry soap a month, and two ounces of a dull, gray, oily substance that passed for toilet soap. Consumers received clothing ration cards, but they were virtually useless because there were never enough new clothes available in the shops. New shoes were impossible to find; old ones were patched with wooden soles, and Gestapo agents searched households to make certain that no one violated the decree restricting everyone to a maximum of two pairs of shoes. R.A.F. raiders continued to pester the capital and northern ports such as Hamburg and Bremen; on the evening of April 9, a shower of incendiaries struck the luxuriously appointed State Opera House on the Unter den Linden in Berlin and left it a burnt-out shell. "How many happy hours I have passed in this building," reflected Goebbels despondently. "And now these ruins." Fortunately, the State Opera and its famous conductor, the darkly handsome thirty-year-old wunderkind Herbert von Karajan—who allegedly had joined the Nazi Party in 1933 and whose agent was a highly placed SS officer—were away on a tour of Italy at the time. (Karajan, incidentally, claims to have had little knowledge of domestic political affairs during the war years; an official biographical summary of his career leaves a large blank space between 1940 and 1945. "I had not the slightest idea of what was going on," Karajan asserted later. "I only wanted to conduct in peace.")

As a symbolic event, the physical destruction of the State Opera House mirrored the aesthetic decline under the Nazi regime of the once-proud German tradition of leadership in the field of classical music. For the past eight years, Hitler and his henchmen had systematically reshaped and corrupted German musical culture to serve their own twisted nationalistic ideology. The works of Jewish composers were banned, of course, and in their campaign to weaken Christianity's hold on the German people, Reichskulturkammer officials even tried to prevent Karajan (whom Hitler deemed an iconoclastic upstart) from conducting a performance of St. Matthew's Passion. Goebbels and Göring waged an incessant and destructive personal battle for leadership in the cultural arena, using conductors and performers as their pawns. The most famous living German composer, Richard Strauss, then seventy-six years old and residing in semiretirement near Munich, suffered through the war years in silence for the most part. With a Jewish daughter-in-law, Strauss could not afford to refuse to cooperate at all with the Nazis, and so he had agreed to compose the Olympic Hymn for the 1936 games in Berlin, and a festival piece in 1940 to celebrate the twenty-six hundredth anniversary of the founding of the Japanese Empire. Repelled by the barbarities of the Nazi regime and disgusted with its philistine attitude toward the arts, Strauss spent much of 1941 scoring his last opera, Capriccio, a light comedy of manners that appears to have provided him with an escape from the depressing realities of wartime. But whenever Strauss's anti-Nazi sentiments—however gently expressed—provoked the displeasure of officials in Berlin,

Hitler and Goebbels issued directives forbidding anyone to honor the legendary composer. Even so, Strauss was far better off than Anton von Webern, the Austrian modernist whose experimental works so antagonized the Nazis that they prohibited any performances of his music and actively suppressed all traces of it.

Throughout the spring of 1941, Berlin swirled with rumors of an impending invasion of Russia. (It was not exactly a well-kept secret; a remarkable number of people outside the government seemed to know that the invasion would be launched in the middle of June.) Beginning in early April, all factory leaves were canceled. Facing a shortage of manpower once Barbarossa began in earnest, Goebbels urged Hitler to institute compulsory female labor ("Our fine ladies will not come voluntarily," Goebbels prophesied correctly), but the Fuehrer gallantly refused. Mothers whose children had been forcibly evacuated from Berlin because of the danger from air raids kept pressing the government to allow them to return, but the bureaucrats told them they needed all available space on the trains to transport troops to the Russian border.

The most disquieting news of the season, however, came from Hitler himself. During a speech at the Reichstag on May 4, celebrating the recent victories in Greece, Yugoslavia, and North Africa, the Fuehrer casually mentioned that "if the German soldier already possesses the best weapons in the world, he will receive still better ones this year and next." This was the first time Hitler had referred to the possibility of a third year of war, and those among his listeners who had believed his New Year's promise that 1941 would witness "the final victory of German arms" were understandably depressed by the gloomy prospect that the conflict might continue into 1942. To bolster morale, Berlin radio stations relaxed their restrictions and began playing lighter popular tunes, and the government lifted the ban on dancing that had been imposed during the Balkan offensive. Although Nazi authorities prohibited German theaters from showing American movies (partly because they did not want people to know that foreigners had succeeded in making movies in color), Berlin movie fans were distracted by a grandiose (and violently anti-British) spectacle of the Boer War, Emil Jennings' epic *Ohm Krueger.* Produced at a cost of 1.5 million marks, *Krueger* featured repulsively oily portrayals of Queen Victoria and the degenerate British aristocrats who surrounded her court, and shocking scenes of sadistic British soldiers raping and torturing innocent Boer women in concentration camps. (The general ban on American movies, incidentally, did not preclude private showings of *Snow White, Gone With the Wind,* and other feature films to Nazi Party officials and foreign correspondents.)

Hitler reportedly enjoyed *Ohm Krueger* immensely; he told Goebbels that the Boer War, which had started Anglo-German relations on their long downhill slide, had made a deep impression on him when he was a boy. The Fuehrer was now fifty-two years old, and in the spring of 1941 he stood at the height of a dazzling career. Since his accession to power in 1933 he had enlarged Germany's territory from 180,976 to 323,360 square miles, plus an additional 290,000 square miles in occupied lands. The Greater German Reich governed 106 million people, a vast increase from the 65 million of 1933. Eleven million young Germans had joined the State Youth (the successor to the Hitler Youth) and the German Girls' League. Before the war, Hitler had revived the German economy and revitalized the nation's transportation system, adding over a thousand miles of new roads and doubling the capacity of the railways (all of which proved remarkably useful for transporting military equipment after 1939). Perhaps most important, he had restored German primacy in Europe; in nearly two years of war, the Wehrmacht had not yet lost a battle, much less a campaign. The swastika flew triumphantly in Paris, on Mt. Olympus and the Acropolis, over the royal palace in Amsterdam, the Maison du Roi in Brussels, and the Hradčany Castle in Prague.

To show their immense admiration for his achievements, the German people honored their Fuehrer with heartfelt gifts on his birthday. From their own meager rations, they sent him parcels of coffee, tea, and cocoa; when it was all combined, the gifts totaled hundreds of pounds of food-stuffs. (The Fuehrer also reportedly received luxurious presents from sympathizers in the United States.) Movie theaters placed busts of Hitler in their lobbies with flowers at the base. Party officials and generals toasted his health, and presented him with more exotic gifts, including a book about Churchill that portrayed the Prime Minister as a drunkard who wore pink silk underwear (an image that amused Hitler immensely), the original of Padua's *Leda and the Swan,* and a collection of one hundred French cartoons of himself. "These he finds killingly funny," Goebbels reported.

Presumably Hitler was unaware of the doggerel composed in his honor by one anonymous British wit: "Napoleon died at fifty-two, / And, Adolf Hitler, so may you." Certainly the Fuehrer did not know that he had already won his last major military campaign.

The town of Coventry in ruins following a night of the Blitz.

Inauguration Day, January 20, 1941. Note the armored vehicles guarding President Roosevelt's car.

JOE DI MAGGIO
Salutes His Bat

Joe DiMaggio, rewarding the bat that carried him to a 56-game hitting streak.

Winston Spencer Churchill, High Constable of England and Prime Minister of His Majesty, King George VI.

Churchill giving the inevitable "V for Victory" sign to workers outside a steel factory in London.

Marshal Joseph Stalin, General Secretary of the Communist Party of the Soviet Union and Chairman of the Council of People's Commissars.

Dr. Paul Joseph Goebbels, Minister of Propaganda of the Third Reich.

Marshal Henri Philippe Petain, Prime Minister of Vichy, France.

Churchill striding across the deck of the H.M.S. *Prince of Wales* on the return voyage from his conference with Roosevelt at Argentia, Newfoundland, in August.

The first family at the Roosevelt home in Hyde Park on July 4, 1941.

President Roosevelt signing the United States' declaration of war against Japan, December 8, 1941.

In the path of the hurricane: a Russian peasant flees before the onslaught of the Wehrmacht.

German panzers frozen on the Russian steppes outside Moscow.

The death of the U.S.S. *California.*

The tragedy of Pearl Harbor:

Rescue efforts aboard the U.S.S. *West Virginia.*

The German High Command: with Adolf Hitler are *(left to right)* Generals von Fritsch, von Brauchitsch, Keitel, and Halder.

16

A Nation Adrift

"The tension has been very high—not only in our life
but in the world. One gets the feeling that it *must* crack—
it cannot go on like this long."
—ANNE MORROW LINDBERGH, MAY 1941

Franklin Roosevelt needed a vacation. Exhausted by the two-month struggle to navigate the Lend-Lease bill successfully through Congress, worn down by a nagging head cold that lingered for weeks, the President left Washington on March 19 for a week-long fishing trip in the Caribbean. Accompanied by his stamp collection and a coterie of his closest advisers—Harry Hopkins, Harold Ickes, General "Pa" Watson, Attorney General Bob Jackson, Press Secretary Steve Early, and his personal physician, Rear Admiral Ross McIntire (surgeon general of the navy)—Roosevelt took a train to Florida and boarded the *Potomac,* the former Coast Guard cutter turned presidential yacht, at Fort Lauderdale on Saturday, March 22. For the first time, the *Potomac* was armed with .50-caliber machine guns both fore and aft. Escorted by a pair of navy destroyers, the President and his friends left their cares behind and headed for an undisclosed location in the Bahamas.

For the first few days, they spent most of their time fishing or playing poker. Hopkins, Early, and Jackson were especially proud of their capacity for liquor and their prowess with cards and, sometimes, with women. "The Hemingway syndrome was strong in the upper ranks of the New Deal in those years," observed John Kenneth Galbraith, who joined the administration later that spring as its resident price-control expert. "It befitted a man to drink heavily, speak always with unvarnished directness, be unadornedly profane, play poker, enjoy the races, frequent the sporting restaurants and bars and, with exceptions, be dominant and successful with women."

On the evening of the twenty-sixth the weather turned bad and the seas grew turbulent, running higher and roughly tossing the small boat like a cork. As they watched the waves break high over the portholes of their cabin, Jackson and Ickes realized that if the *Potomac* should capsize, "there wasn't a chance for a single one of us." Hardly anyone slept that night; next morning, Ickes thought Roosevelt looked "like a boiled owl." After one more bad night, the waters grew calm and the President could resume fishing and playing with his stamps. Whether by design or pure angling skill, Roosevelt ended the trip with considerably more fish than anyone else. He was never permitted to take another pleasure cruise through dangerous waters.

He returned to Washington on March 30 to find the nation embroiled in the same troubling controversies as when he left. If anything, the labor situation had grown worse. The Allis-Chalmers dispute, now entering its eleventh week, turned violent after hot-headed Secretary of the Navy Frank Knox unwisely issued an ultimatum to strikers to return to their jobs; the union men openly defied Knox and engaged in a bloody confrontation with police and non-striking workers when management tried to reopen the plant. Another pitched battle between club-swinging police (who also employed tear gas) and strikers armed with baseball bats, pitchforks, and tree branches took place at the International Harvester plant in Richmond, Indiana. Police charged picket lines at the Bethlehem Steel plant in Bethlehem, Pennsylvania. The UAW called a strike at Ford's River Rouge complex, stopping work on a new factory designed to build over four thousand desperately needed Pratt & Whitney aircraft engines. A wage disagreement between John L. Lewis's United Mine Workers and southern coal operators shut down the nation's production of bituminous coal; this subsequently caused steel production to drop significantly.

All of these strikes eventually were settled—Henry Ford finally agreed to bargain with the UAW for the first time in the company's history, and the Allis-Chalmers dispute ended when the government threatened to take over operation of the plant—but other, equally damaging work stoppages took their place. The public's mood turned dark; a Gallup poll revealed that 72 percent of American voters wanted to forbid strikes in defense industries. Congress debated measures to curb union activity, and set out to investigate Communist influence in the American labor movement. Representative Hatton Sumners, chairman of the House Judiciary Committee, announced in Congress that if the crisis grew much worse, he would not hesitate "one split second" to recommend the electric chair for "enemies of this nation, in the factory or elsewhere." Secretary of War Stimson suggested that patriotic Americans organize Home Guards to suppress labor disorders. "Congress and public opinion are ready to support the Government in overriding private interests in labor disputes," affirmed Ray Clapper. "If the Government cannot prevail over local quarrels between labor and management, then we have a Government without real authority."

After a decade of oversupply, the American economy began to experience shortages in raw materials and consumer goods. Stocks of strategic metals were diverted to defense production. The federal government issued pleas for housewives to turn in used aluminum pots for recycling, and Eleanor Roosevelt advised women to start thinking about doing without new kitchen utensils for the next year or two. Manufacturers were instructed to find substitutes for tin, magnesium, nickel, zinc, and copper. "We are, overnight, in Oz," wrote one bemused observer, "where everything is made of something else." To ensure equitable distribution of scarce commodities and head off a wild inflationary spiral like that which accompanied the preparedness campaign of 1917–18, Roosevelt established the Office of Price Administration and Civilian Supply on April 11 and placed hard-bitten New Dealer Leon Henderson in charge. Two weeks later, Henderson brought in Galbraith to manage the price control effort. Already Congress had voted appropriations totaling nearly $17 billion in 1941. ("Staggering . . . stupendous . . . unrivaled since the dawn of creation," lamented conservative critics.) To make up part of the deficit, Treasury Secretary Morgenthau warned that the government's overall tax intake would have to be increased by one-third. Income taxes skyrocketed and personal exemptions were lowered; experts predicted that the 1940 standard income tax rate of 4 percent would soon reach 8 percent, with nuisance taxes imposed to discourage consumption.

Although the United States Army—which now had 1,210,600 men in active service—had made commendable progress since the summer of 1940, it still had a discouragingly long way to go before it could hold its own against any first-class military power. Few Americans were reassured by the army's decision to wave its century-old rule against allowing ex-felons into the service. Army spokesmen were reduced to bragging about their successful efforts to train homing pigeons as a backup communications system, a program enhanced by the cooperation and presence of famous stripteaser Rosita Royce, whose experience included the expert handling of seven obedient (and very well-trained) birds in her act at the recent New York World's Fair.

Truman, who was not the only politician making a reputation for himself by exposing corruption and inefficiency in the War Department's procurement procedures, told a nationwide CBS radio audience that while "we all have to expect a certain amount of waste because of the emphasis on speed . . . I for one have been amazed at the extent." Thus far, Truman claimed to have uncovered $200 million in waste in the camp construction program. Meanwhile, Thomas E. Dewey embarked upon a cross-country tour to raise funds for the recently organized United Service Organization (USO). As he toured army and navy camps, Dewey was appalled by the primitive living conditions and the lack of suitable recreational facilities for the men. A shortage of housing at Langley Air Force Base forced twelve thousand men to sleep in a converted hangar; at other camps in the south, sailors slept in rowboats. The nearest thing to a town around Fort Monroe, Virginia, was the sleepy (some said comatose) burg of Phoebus—population 3,000—where the evening entertainment consisted solely of a soda fountain and a segregated movie theater. The men at Monroe were lucky; at another camp in Florida, the nearest theater was nine miles away. Local merchants in towns around training camps throughout the South either raised the price of their beer, pool, bowling, and laundry services to make an extra buck off the soldiers, or else banned them altogether from their places of business with signs that read DOGS AND SOLDIERS NOT ALLOWED. Their hostile attitude was not entirely without cause, however. Whenever Dewey asked soldiers at each camp what they wanted most from the USO, someone invariably proposed that the organization provide protection from syphilis epidemics, so the men could see more of "those Southern bellies."

Although the navy was making steady progress in its speeded-up construction program, it remained the slowest fleet afloat—U.S. naval planners had long preferred power to speed—and alarmingly vulnerable to air attacks, especially in light of the Luftwaffe's spectacular success in ravaging British ships. "Our officers appreciated the possibility of air attack," explained Secretary Knox weakly, "but their failure to translate the appreciation into protection for the ships is the one real miscalculation they made during the 20 years of peace." Admiral Ernest J. King, commander in chief, Atlantic Fleet, repeatedly warned Washington that he was short of men, matériel, and vessels; most of the ships he did have would require extensive overhauls and alterations before they would be ready for combat. King's March 24 order to his fleet, a lecture on the virtues of "Making the Best of What We Have," stood as a subtle condemnation of the unpreparedness of American naval forces.

Aircraft production continued to plod along at an agonizingly slow pace, and both the navy and the army air corps suffered a distressingly high percentage of fatal training crashes as pilots were rushed through abbreviated courses of instruction. At the end of April, the long-awaited first B-19 aircraft rolled out of the hangars of the Douglas Aircraft Company in Santa Monica, California. Weighing in at eighty tons, the B-19 was easily the largest and most sophisticated warplane in the world, with a 212-foot wingspan and a bomb load capacity of eighteen tons. But since it had been constructed as an experimental model (it carried risk insurance of $1 million for its first test flight), there were no more of the giant planes in the production pipeline; experts estimated it would take approximately fifteen months to build another one.

During April, the grim news from Europe sharpened the dilemma facing the American people—whether Britain could win the war or even survive without more active U.S. involvement—but the public gave no indication of a willingness to make any clear-cut decision about intervention in the immediate future. A Gallup poll at the end of the month asked whether the United States Navy should be used to convoy supplies across the Atlantic to the beleaguered British Isles; 41 percent replied "Yes," while 50 percent said "No." But in response to a subsequent question, "Should the U.S. Navy be used to convoy if British defeat seems certain without them?" 71 percent answered "Yes," and only 21 percent said "No." Asked how they would vote at that moment on the question of U.S. entry into the war, 81 percent preferred to stay out; but if American entry became essential to defeat Germany and Italy, 68 percent said they would vote to go to war. Reading the results of the polls, one commentator decided that "either people are confused, or the questions of the poll confuse them, or both." In a letter to a friend in Britain, Walter Lippmann tried to explain the seemingly befuddled state of American opinion: "We do not wish to fight a land war in Europe, but our people have now realized that the North Atlantic must be held securely by the English-speaking nations." The question was whether the United States could secure the Atlantic without being drawn into the conflict on the European continent. More than anything else, many Americans prayed for a negotiated end to the war, so the burden of responsibility would be lifted from their shoulders.

At his estate on Long Island, Charles Lindbergh stood and watched a huge, blood-red full moon rise in the evening. "It made me think of Europe and bombed cities," he wrote in his diary. "Whenever I see the moon now, I think of the bombing that is going on over there. As the moon rises here, it is high over Europe, and bombs are almost certainly falling on English and German cities." Convinced that the nation was being stampeded into war by the Roosevelt administration, the press, Jewish interests, British agents, international financiers, and Anglophile intellectuals, Lindbergh's head was filled with the cheers of the crowds in the streets calling out, "Give it to them, Lindy, give us the truth!" and so he flew from city to city, speaking to mass meetings in his cold, clear, dispassionate tone, assuring the people that the United States could not win this war for England and should not even try. Since he really harbored no malice in his own passionless heart, Lindbergh was startled at the ferocious depth of anti-British feeling his comments aroused—the names of Churchill and Roosevelt were roundly booed at every opportunity at America First rallies—and on one occasion he was genuinely embarrassed when raucous cheers greeted his announcement that Britain's cities had been "devastated by bombs."

Perhaps no one understood. Lindbergh longed for the United States to be "on the *right* side of an intelligent war!" "There *are* wars worth fighting," he asserted, "but if we get in this one, we will bring disaster to the country and possibly to our entire civilization. If we get into this war and really fight, nothing but chaos will result. If we enter this war, it won't be like the last, and God knows what will happen here before we finish it—race riots, revolution, destruction; America is not immune to any of these. . . . Sometimes I feel like saying, 'Well, let's get into the war if you are so anxious to. Then the responsibility will be yours.' In comparison to the work I am now doing the fighting would be fun. But my mind tells me that we better face our problems and let Europe face hers without getting messed up in this war. I have an interest in Western civilization, and I have an interest in my race, or culture, or whatever you want to call it, and I have an interest in the type of world my children are going to live in. . . . This war is a mistake; we will only bring disaster if we enter it; we will do no good either to Europe or ourselves, and therefore I am going to put everything I have behind staying out."

Perhaps no one understood, but in Berlin Joseph Goebbels praised Lindbergh as "a man of honour," "a brave lad." And, Goebbels noted, "he has asked us not to give him too much prominence, since this could harm him. We have proceeded accordingly."

When Lindbergh accused the Roosevelt administration of having " 'the bit in its teeth' and hell-bent on its way to war," he was not far wrong. With the exception of Cordell Hull at the State Department, the President's cabinet was nearly unanimous in urging him to lead the nation more forcefully toward an open break with Germany; believing that war with Germany was inevitable, they wished to come in while Britain was still standing, to make the war as brief as possible. In a conversation with Bill Bullitt, Roosevelt revealed that Stimson had told him that he (Stimson) thought the United States ought to go to war immediately. Bullitt was only slightly more reticent. "I then said that I felt we were not handling at all the question of public opinion," the former ambassador recalled. "I believed that it was certain that we would go to war with Germany. We no longer had an easy choice between war and peace." Averell Harriman, who was in London to coordinate shipments of supplies under the Lend-Lease program, openly told Jock Colville that he hoped the United States would soon enter the war on Britain's side. "England's strength is bleeding," Harriman informed Roosevelt. "In our own interest, I trust that our Navy can be directly employed before our partner is too weak." Harold Ickes also favored an open declaration of war, and urged the President to meet the isolationists' challenge head-on. "In every direction I find a growing discontent with the President's lack of leadership," reported the irascible Ickes. "He still has the country if he will take it and lead it. But he won't have it very much longer unless he does something."

Consequently, Stimson, Ickes, Knox, and Bob Jackson met in Ickes' office to discuss the deteriorating situation. According to Ickes' notes, they all agreed that "the country was sadly in need of leadership and that only the President himself could supply the want. We know that the defense program is not anywhere near what it ought to be. . . . We know that there is overlapping waste and inefficiency. . . . We know that public sentiment adverse to the cause of England and to the program of the President has been making headway. We appreciate the fact that Lindbergh has been gaining ground in public opinion. . . . We were unanimous that the country was tired of words and wanted deeds." None of the four cabinet officers, Ickes said, "could account for the President's failure of leadership and all of us felt disturbed by the fact that he is surrounded by a very small group [i.e., Harry Hopkins] and is, in effect, inaccessible to most people, including even members of the Cabinet."

The strain upon the man in the White House was almost unendurable. Even so staunch a Republican partisan as Thomas Dewey privately acknowledged that "Franklin Roosevelt is faced with the most difficult situation and set of choices of any man in our history." Painfully aware of the nation's lack of preparedness, beset by relentless pressure from his cabinet, from the isolationists, and from Churchill ("If you cannot take more advanced positions now or very soon, the vast balances may be tilted heavily to our disadvantage"), alarmed by the relentless German advance through the Balkans to the Mediterranean and across the deserts of North Africa, Roosevelt did what any sensible chief executive would have done. He said the hell with everything and headed straight for the ball park, to throw out the first ball on Opening Day.

A capacity crowd of 33,000 fans filled Washington's Griffith Stadium as the pregame ceremonies got under way at two-thirty on a beautiful April afternoon. This year the Senators' opening-game opponents were the New York Yankees, sparked by highly touted rookie shortstop Phil "Flea" Rizzuto and, of course, Joe DiMaggio, who entered the regular season having hit safely in all nineteen of the club's exhibition games. After the United States Army Band entertained the fans while parading smartly around the infield, a flock of special policemen and Secret Service agents began to emerge from the runway under the grandstand in right field. Then out rolled the President's open touring car, with Roosevelt in the backseat grinning and laughing, enthusiastically waving his fedora to the cheering crowd. For the ninth time ("my ninth year in the majors," he called it), Roosevelt stood in the presidential box and threw out the first ball, an odd little pitch that reporters described as "an eccentric sinker." (Longtime Washington baseball fans generally agreed that Woodrow Wilson had displayed the best pitching form of any president in recent memory.)*

Unlike major league baseball, thoroughbred racing had no fear of the draft in the spring of 1941; all the leading jockeys were too short for military service, most trainers were too old, and the army hadn't gotten around to calling up horses yet. The sport had enjoyed a prosperous winter season at tracks in Florida and California, and anticipation ran high for the first leg of the Triple Crown. In the first week of May, eleven of the

*The Yankees beat the Senators, 3–0.

nation's top three-year-olds gathered at Churchill Downs in Louisville, Kentucky, for the sixty-sixth running of the Kentucky Derby. Bookmakers had made Our Boots, winner of the Blue Grass Stakes, the early favorite, with Porter's Cap a close second; but by post time, the ninety thousand fans at the track had made their own choice: Whirlaway, the chestnut stallion from Calumet Farms who had won the mythical two-year-old championship as the top money winner in 1940.

Whirly, as he was familiarly known to the touts in the grandstand, had displayed consistently uninspired form in the early months of 1941, losing two of his first three races as a three-year-old at odds as low as 3 to 10. He was not an exceptionally handsome animal; his most distinctive physical characteristic was his extraordinarily long, luxuriant tail, which nearly swept the ground when he walked. Purists who disparaged his unorthodox racing style and his lack of self-control had labeled Whirlaway a "halfwit," a swift but unmanageable colt who had the unfortunate habit of running out wide around the turns, invariably giving away three or four lengths to the rest of the field. Sometimes he made up the difference with a burst of speed; sometimes he didn't. "This year it'll be different," vowed trainer Ben Jones. "He's grown up and gotten over all that childish stuff. He'll run anywhere his rider wants him to." And for the Kentucky Derby Jones brought in a new jockey (the eighth one to ride Whirlaway thus far) with an excellent reputation for handling headstrong horses: young Eddie Arcaro.

Mint juleps sold for a dollar at the Churchill Downs concession stands that year. Some veteran Derby observers thought the band played "My Old Kentucky Home" with a little less fervor, perhaps because it was afraid of spooking the notoriously high-strung Whirlaway. The favorite, wearing number four, broke slowly from the gate as Porter's Cap and Dispose took the early lead. At the half-mile pole Whirlaway was loping along five lengths behind everyone else, with Arcaro practically motionless, "sitting still as a bluepoint on the half-shell." He was still well off the pace in the backstretch as half of the field remained in contention. Then, at the top of the stretch, with three horses in front of him, Arcaro took Whirlaway outside and clucked softly in his ear.

"There was a curious sound from the crowd," recalled sportswriter Red Smith, "a sort of deep bass 'whuumph!' of exhaled breath—not a drawn-out 'ooooohhh!' because the horse race didn't last that long." Whirlaway moved around the field with a breathtaking burst of speed. "What he did to those horses was hard to believe even while you were seeing it," said Smith. "He cooked 'em, fried 'em. You could almost hear them sizzle, see them curl like froglegs in the pan." Whirlaway won going away, eight lengths in front. "Johnny," Arcaro called to one of the other jockeys afterwards, "wipe the jam off my mouth, will you? I been on a picnic." Whirlaway's time of 2 minutes, 1⅖ seconds was the fastest ever for the Derby, breaking the old mark by ⅖ of a second; his time of 24 seconds for the last quarter mile was even more remarkable. "He's the runnin'est horse I ever rode," said a grinning Arcaro.

One week later at the Preakness at Pimlico Race Course in Baltimore, Whirlaway drew post position number one and started even more wretchedly, running more like a stable pony than a champion, dead last for more than half a mile. Dreams of a Triple Crown seemed to be fading in the dust. But fortunately for Arcaro, the rest of the field was also holding back, and with three furlongs to go, Whirlaway moved up unexpectedly along the rail, passing the others until there was only King Cole left in front, and so he went around him, too, with almost contemptuous ease at the top of the stretch. He won galloping, by five lengths. "You can throw all them other horses away," Arcaro gloated.

Apparently his competition felt the same way, because only three other horses showed up for the Belmont Stakes on June 7. This time, Whirlaway went to the front quickly. "There was no pace," explained Arcaro. "It was very slow. So I yelled to those other jockeys, 'I'm leaving.'" And he did.

Whirlaway was the fifth Triple Crown winner, the first since War Admiral turned the trick in 1937. When he died in 1953, at the age of fifteen, Red Smith wrote an obituary for the champion: "He wasn't the greatest horse that ever lived, but he was just about the most exciting. Every time he stepped on a track you knew that some time during the race you were going to see that breathless, blinding, tremendous burst which was as stirring a spectacle as any field of sports could produce. He was Babe Ruth, Jack Dempsey, Bill Tilden, Bobby Jones—not just a champion but a champion who was also the most colorful figure in his game."

America was adrift. "I wish I knew more than I know," wrote Carl Sandburg. "I go on drifting. The nation drifts. It is written for a while we must drift. By drifting I mean guessing as to where the national ship of state is going and what will happen to it in the end. Just now I am willing to throw in everything to save Britain. Beyond that I agree with anyone who has a headache."

Certainly that category included the President. The good news at the White House was that Roosevelt's Gallup approval rating had reached an all-time high of 73 percent. The bad news was that the President was ill once again. His face pale, his hands trembling, Roosevelt was confined to his bed for seven days in early May, suffering from a low fever and a case of intestinal flu which left him so weak that he required two transfusions to remedy a severe iron deficiency anemia. "The weight of his burden is plainly written on his face," noted Ray Clapper. "I have never seen him more drawn, and his color was that fatigue gray which comes from long hours of close work and strain."

All the while, the interventionists kept up the steady drumbeat of pressure to force the President into open conflict with Nazi Germany, despite the findings of a Gallup poll that showed that 79 percent of Americans were opposed to sending a U.S. army abroad. "I care not whether you call safe delivery convoying, patrolling, airplane accompaniment or what not," cried Wendell Willkie at a "Freedom Rally" in Madison Square Garden. "We want those cargoes protected . . . at once and with less talk and more action." Bill Bullitt toured the South and the East Coast and returned to tell Roosevelt that "the remark that I heard most often from high and low was 'I don't know what we ought to do. It's too complicated. The President knows.' There is a desire to know the facts—*from you*—and an intense desire to know what you think ought to be done, and a readiness to follow you wherever you may lead. . . . In other words, your personal prestige has never been higher and you have only to lead. The moment seems to be ripe for bold action—and it is 11:59."

Newspaper columnists assailed Roosevelt for his lack of leadership. "The simple truth is that as yet the right kind of spirit does not exist among the people," charged the Baltimore *Sun's* Frank Kent, "and the reason is that the right kind of spirit does not exist among their leaders—or at least is not being displayed by them." Walter Lippmann was even more blunt in his criticism of the President's policy of evasiveness and drift:

> In this tremendous time the American people must look to their President for leadership. They are not getting leadership from the President. They are not being treated as they deserve to be treated and as they have a right to be treated. They are not being treated as men and women but rather as if they were inquisitive children. They are not being dealt with seriously, truthfully, responsibly and nobly. They are being dealt with cleverly, indirectly, even condescendingly, and nervously. They are asked to put their trust in the President, which indeed they must, for he is the President; but in return they must have his trust and they must have his confidence and they must have his guidance.

The immediate question which vexed Sandburg, Lippmann, Roosevelt, and the ordinary people to whom Bullitt spoke, and millions of Americans who read the newspaper accounts of British ships sunk by U-boats and Nazi planes in the Atlantic, was whether the United States should employ its warships to convoy supplies to Britain. This was the bedrock issue that Roosevelt adamantly refused to meet directly, and no power on earth could induce him to change his mind in the spring of 1941. If the United States did nothing to ensure the safety of its Lend-Lease shipments, it was irresponsibly wasting precious defense resources by placing them in inadequately protected British merchant ships and standing by helplessly while German raiders sent them to the bottom. If America had a vital interest in sending vast quantities of war matériel to Britain, then it logically had to accept the responsibility for ensuring their safe arrival. But if Roosevelt ordered the navy to accompany the convoys, American ships inevitably would be sunk and American lives lost, and, just as in 1917, there might be an outcry for war against Germany. But in the absence of any dramatic, overt demonstration of German hostility against the United States itself that might galvanize and unequivocally unite American opinion in defense of the national honor, Roosevelt knew he could not lead this nation into war—even if he wanted to, and the evidence suggests that he did not yet want to go that far—when its armed forces were so pitiably weak, and its people still paralyzed by uncertainty.

Congress probably reflected fairly accurately the schizophrenic mood of the American public. In the first week of May, an Associated Press canvass of the Senate revealed that forty-five senators favored American convoys, while forty (including Foreign Relations Committee chairman Walter George) were firmly opposed. (The remainder were still undecided.) The isolationist clique was led by Republicans Wheeler, Robert Taft of Ohio, and Charles William Tobey of New Hampshire, who introduced a resolution in the Senate forbidding American ships to convoy supplies to Britain. The measure was emphatically buried by the Foreign Relations Committee. The most belligerent of the interventionists was Senator Claude Pepper of Florida, who demanded convoying "without another day's delay or dallying," and once stood up in the Senate and shouted, "Do we want to let millions be crucified later because there is a jeopardy that a few might die an honorable death now?"

This was precisely the sort of clear-cut choice Roosevelt wished to avoid. He could not risk a defeat in Congress if he tried to move too far, too fast. What he needed was an incident, or preferably a series of incidents, to allow him to proceed step by step toward an open alliance with Britain, giving him time to prepare the nation for the ordeal that lay ahead. "The President obviously hoped that he would not have to face an unpleasant decision," observed Averell Harriman, and Roosevelt himself admitted to Treasury Secretary Morgenthau in the middle of May that "I am waiting to be pushed into the situation." So the President poked and prodded, moving like a crab, advancing sideways and retreating into his shell when confronted with opposition. He extended the United States security zone more than halfway across the Atlantic, allowing navy vessels to patrol the ocean to 26 degrees longitude, purportedly to ensure the security of the Western Hemisphere. American ships were allowed to inform British convoys of the presence of Nazi vessels above or below the water, but they were under strict orders not to shoot unless the Germans shot first. Roosevelt sought to keep the patrolling order secret for as long as he could, and when it finally was made public he denied that patrolling (which he said was a traditional duty of the navy) bore any resemblance to convoying. "I think some of you know what a horse looks like," he told reporters during one of his weekly press conferences. "I think you also know what a cow looks like. If, by calling a cow a horse for a year and a half you think that makes a cow a horse, *I* don't think so. Now, that's pretty plain language. You can't turn a cow into a horse by calling it something else; calling it a horse it is still a cow. Now this is a patrol, and has been a patrol for a year and a half, still is, and from time to time it has been extended, and is being extended, and will be extended—the patrol—for the safety of the western hemisphere."

To strengthen British forces in the Mediterranean, Roosevelt issued a proclamation that made the entrance to the Red Sea no longer a combat zone, so American ships could carry supplies directly (via the Cape of Good Hope) to Wavell's beleaguered command in Cairo without stopping in England to transfer the goods to British ships. Roosevelt permitted British warships to be repaired in American ports. He authorized the training of British pilots on American airfields, and allowed American military pilots, including Colonel Curtis LeMay, to ferry warplanes (B-24s) from Canada to Britain. (The detour through Canada was necessary be-cause the terms of the Neutrality Act prohibited American pilots from flying them directly from the U.S. to Britain. The transatlantic flight expe-rience, incidentally, proved quite valuable to LeMay and his colleagues once the United States entered the war.) Roosevelt transferred ownership of two million tons of aged but still seaworthy merchant ships to Britain, along with ten Coast Guard cutters. And he concluded a deal with the Danish minister in Washington to permit the U.S. to establish air bases in Greenland. (The fact that the Danish diplomat actually represented the pre-Nazi government, which had been deposed since his appointment, posed an interesting legal question that bothered Roosevelt not at all.) The President's ultimate objective in taking this series of actions may have been clear, but he was obviously still drifting and searching for the best way to proceed. "He can't bring himself to going in as cold bloodedly as he would be going in if something were done now," reported Ickes. "He is waiting for an incident, fully conscious of the fact that none may come before it is too late." Ickes petulantly complained that Roosevelt had "such confidence in his sense of timing that he has deliberately chosen to run the risk although knowing fully what is involved." Surveying the course of American diplomacy in the spring and summer of 1941, historian James MacGregor Burns succinctly concluded that the President "had no plans."

But the generals did. In consummating the "common-law marriage" between the United States and Great Britain, military representatives of both nations had held extensive and highly secret discussions in Washing-ton from January to March 1941. They agreed that if the U.S. and the British Empire ever found themselves fighting together against both Japan and Nazi Germany, the Atlantic theater would receive top priority; "Hitler must be defeated first," Churchill confirmed. In March, American military representatives visited Britain to choose sites for future air and naval bases, and joint military missions were established in London and Washington. After considerable soul-searching at Bletchley Park, British intelligence officials grudgingly informed their American counterparts of the Ultra secret; by April, there was a regular flow of classified information back and forth across the Atlantic, although the exchange was impeded by London's inability to decide which Americans should get what information, and the continuing British reluctance to share highly sensitive development data and operational statistics with the United States. (For its part, the United States War Department hesitated to send the Royal Army all the equipment it requested until the British were more forthcoming about their operational plans for the future.)

Nor was that all. In June 1940, Roosevelt had created the National Defense Research Committee to coordinate "scientific research on the mechanisms and devices of warfare"; by May 1941, one out of every four physicists in the United States reportedly was active in defense research. Working in complete secrecy under the leadership of Dr. Vannevar Bush, the head of the Carnegie Institution of Washington and a man of excellent administrative abilities, the NDRC established a liaison office in London and initiated a cautious transfer of data between British and American scientists. At first the exchange was very much a one-way street. American defense experts were startled to learn of the British advances in developing radiolocator units (radar), and the results of experiments by British physicists which demonstrated that uranium oxide would produce a self-sustaining chain reaction. "This was the first time that anyone had specifically said that a nuclear reactor would work—in other words that it would really be possible to utilise atomic energy," explained Sir George Thomson, the head of the British nuclear research project. But further research would require an extensive investment of funds, manpower, and equipment, commodities of which Britain was bereft but which the United States could easily supply—if the politicians and generals could be convinced that a financial commitment to atomic energy research would likely provide tangible results within a reasonable period of time.

In 1941, uranium was used primarily as a component in certain types of ceramics and glassware. Most Anglo-American defense officials had never considered using atomic fission as an explosive; if they saw any military applications for atomic energy, it was in terms of providing power for submarines. As Bush pointed out, there was "certainly no clear-cut path to defense results of great importance lying open before us at the present time." To the average American layman, the notion of atomic weapons seemed even more of an improbable Sunday-supplement fantasy. "Luridest field of NDRC work is atomic power—smashing of atoms to release the locked-up voltages which hold them together," reported *Time* magazine in its usual breathless style. "NDRC's Bush expects nothing to come of this work, but there is a slight chance—and that chance has such terrifying industrial and military implications that no nation can risk neglect of the problem. 'I hope they never succeed in tapping atomic power,' says Bush. 'It will be a hell of a thing for civilization.' "

Indeed. Rumors of advances in Nazi atomic weapons research held out a nightmare prospect that could not be ignored, and so in April 1941, Bush appointed University of Chicago physicist Arthur Holly Compton as chairman of a separate committee to investigate the military potential of nuclear energy. When Compton's committee issued its first report on May 17, it concluded that the feasibility of atomic weapons required a more extensive investigation before any firm recommendations could be made; Bush agreed, and Roosevelt accordingly provided the then-munificent sum of $350,000 for a six-month study. No one saw any need to hurry. Even if atomic weapons provided a viable option, the Compton committee predicted that none would be ready until 1945 at the earliest.

17

"A Shameful Episode"

"The British are now in the position of a middleweight boxer
who goes into the ring with a heavyweight who possesses a
longer reach and more strength. If the middleweight boxer
foolishly stands up and tries to swap punches with the bigger
man, he is sure to be knocked out." ·
                    —GENERAL RAYMOND E. LEE, SPRING 1941

The Luftwaffe launched its final assault upon Crete on May 15. Apart
from Malta, this mountainous, barren, 160-mile-long island in the eastern
Mediterranean was the last British stronghold on the sea route that led to
the empire's nerve centers of Cairo and Suez and the oil fields of Iraq.
Göring meant to have Crete; the Reichsmarshal had promised his Fuehrer
he could deliver the island within three or four days at the most. Through
a combination of ferocious bombing raids and the use of parachute troops
on an unprecedented scale, the German conquest of Crete would secure
the reputation of the Luftwaffe within the Reich and remove the last
remaining British base within striking distance of the Romanian oil fields
at Ploesti. So the Nazi bombers softened up the island's defenses, and
prepared the way for the paratroop landings—scheduled to begin on May
17, but postponed for lack of fuel until May 20—by pounding the antiaircraft batteries that ringed the main Cretan airfield at Maleme, on the
western end of the island, and the smaller fields at Heraklion and Retimo.

Once again, the British defenders found themselves in a familiar
position, entirely devoid of air cover. Scanning their Ultra intercepts in
London, the General Staff knew precisely what the Germans were planning, but Dill and his colleagues were powerless to stop it. Incredibly,
there were fewer than two dozen serviceable British warplanes on Crete,
and these were withdrawn to Cairo in early May to keep them from being
needlessly annihilated by the more than twelve hundred German aircraft
based in southern Greece. That left approximately 28,500 men—half of
them English, and the rest Australians and New Zealanders, along with a
few stray Greek units—to face the Nazi onslaught unprotected. Most of
this garrison had come to Crete after the debacle in Greece, where they
had abandoned most of their equipment; hence they were poorly armed,

with an almost total lack of tanks—and Wavell, who had to keep the total strategic picture in the Mediterranean in view at all times, had no intention of sending any additional armor from North Africa to aid the unfortunate men on Crete.

On the morning of May 20, shortly after six o'clock, a contingent of Stuka dive-bombers appeared in the high blue sky over Crete, sounding their insolent, unnatural shrieks that the British remembered so vividly from their nightmare retreat through the mountains of Greece. Then the watchers saw something else, flocks of huge planes in mass formations, and some of the planes were trailing cables attached to weird-looking silver gliders that resembled "young vultures following the parent bird from the roost." From the gliders and the accompanying Junker transports that flew only a few hundred feet above the ground, there spilled hundreds of lazy specks—many white, some red or green or black or yellow—that floated soundlessly down to earth. This was the first wave of German paratroopers, the "Soldiers Fallen from Heaven," most of them zealous young Nazi volunteers from the Hitler Youth movement who had endured months of rigorous physical training, and who now considered themselves the elite of the German fighting force. Among them was Max Schmeling, the burly professional boxer who once had been heavyweight champion of the world. They carried with them inspirational messages, and some of them were drugged to overcome their fear of jumping into combat. Most of the paratroopers hit the ground armed with only a pistol; packages containing disassembled parts of machine guns and mortars were dropped separately. The generals planned to land thirteen thousand soldiers from the Eleventh Air Corps in three equal forces around the three Cretan airfields. They did not know the British were expecting them.

On the average, each paratrooper was drifting helplessly in the air for twelve seconds. During that first day, when the British were lying in wait in their slit trenches with machine guns and rifles and hand grenades, more than a thousand Germans died before they reached the ground; hundreds more were slain as they scrambled for cover, picked off by British sharpshooters at long range. Due to insufficient reconnaissance data, some parachutists were set down in olive groves and impaled themselves upon the trees. Contrary to the Luftwaffe's confident expectations, there were no landing places for the gliders, only craggy mountains where the planes crashed and the crews were killed upon impact. Still the gliders and the Ju-52s kept coming in endless waves, dropping their human cargo, heedless of the inert, crumpled forms that lay below them. Supported by their bombers and fighters, there were enough armed survivors on the ground by the end of the day to challenge the defenders for control of the airfields.

Having expected the garrison in Crete to bolt at the first sight of the airborne invasion, the German High Command was astonished at the heavy invasion losses and the ferocity of the British resistance—Halder noted with horror that the Seventh Air Division had been reduced from nine combat battalions to three and a half—but the decision was made to redouble rather than reduce the aerial assault. Government censors forbade all German newspapers to mention the action in Crete. On the other side, British commanders had not expected the Germans to commit so many troops in so short a time, and after twelve hours of furious fighting under the pressure of almost continuous hostile bombing, their forces on Crete were reeling from the relentless airborne assault. General Bernard Cyril "Tiny" Freyberg, the New Zealander who had been given command (on April 30) of the garrison on Crete, radioed a report to Cairo that evening: "To-day has been a hard one. We have been hard pressed. . . . Everyone here realises vital issue and we will fight it out." Since Churchill was determined to hold Crete "to the death" (though presumably not his), Freyberg was precisely the man he wanted for the job. In his restless youth, Freyberg had practiced dentistry in San Francisco and fought with Pancho Villa before joining the British forces in Europe in 1914; rising quickly through the ranks by his courageous exploits in the war, Freyberg had become the youngest brigadier in the British army at the age of twenty-seven. Before the Second World War, he had already been wounded over a dozen times. He had warned Churchill on May 1 that his garrison could not hope to repel a German invasion without additional support from the navy and the R.A.F., but he accepted without demur Whitehall's decision to fight it out no matter the cost.

Freyberg received a brief reprieve on the evening of May 21, when the Royal Navy chanced to run smack into the defenseless German seaborne convoy that was attempting to ferry nine thousand troops to Crete. Firing at point-blank range, the British warships kept up a murderous fire for nearly three hours; the sea was filled with hysterical Nazi soldiers screaming in agony and fear. It was estimated that nearly half of the German troops in the convoy died that night, and the rest scattered to the Greek islands. None of them landed on Crete alive until the battle was over.

On land, however, the second day of the invasion brought more German paratroopers and more bombers and more Messerschmitts with their strafing machine-gun fire. By May 22, the Germans controlled Maleme airfield, and from that moment on the heavy troop transport planes began to roll in and discharge their human cargoes and head back to Greece for more. German soldiers supported by undisputed control of the air (but no ships) now faced British troops supported by undisputed control of the sea (but no planes). In these circumstances the advantage lay with the Germans. "The battle is most strange and grim," Churchill told the British people. "Our side has no air support and the other side has no artillery and tanks. Neither has any retreat." But that was not entirely true. Worn down by superior numbers of German troops blessed with superior equipment, and by the ceaseless attacks from the air (the Royal Navy did what it could, but it could hardly strafe the German infantry), Freyberg's forces were pushed back, slowly, inexorably, until their backs were up against Suda Bay. Forced to flee for a second time within a month, King George of Greece traveled south across the mountains and boarded a British ship bound for Alexandria.

Offshore, the battered remnants of Admiral Cunningham's Mediterranean fleet, of which only one-third was still undamaged, was suffering terrible losses from German bombers as it sought to prevent further attempts at a seaborne landing. At his headquarters in Alexandria, Cunningham came to dread "every ring on the telephone, every knock on the door, and the arrival of each fresh signal. In something less than twelve hours of fighting against the unhampered Luftwaffe we had lost so much, two cruisers and a destroyer sunk, with two battleships and two cruisers damaged. Most of the ships were woefully short of ammunition, and I very well knew the anxiety and physical strain under which their devoted officers and men were working." Two more destroyers, included Captain Lord Louis Mountbatten's ship, the *Kelly*, were sunk on May 23. As the great-grandson of Queen Victoria, Mountbatten felt that he had a certain tradition of aristocratic responsibility to uphold in such a moment of crisis. "I felt I ought to be the last to leave the ship," he explained later, "and I left it a bit late because the bridge turned over on top of me and I was trapped in the boiling, seething cauldron underneath. I luckily had my tin hat on, which helped to make me heavy enough to push my way down past the bridge screen, but it was unpleasant having to force oneself deeper under water to get clear. Then I started swallowing water. I knew I'd be finished if I didn't stop this so I put my left hand over my mouth and nose and held them shut. Then I thought my lungs would burst. Finally I began to see daylight and suddenly shot out of the water like a cork released." The Messerschmitts promptly began to machine-gun the survivors in the water.

Still Cunningham sent a signal to all his ships at sea: "Stick it out. Navy must not let Army down. No enemy forces must reach Crete by sea."

Churchill was entirely unsympathetic. He had no patience for naval commanders who judged their ships too precious to be risked in battle; when Colville expressed regret at the navy's losses, the Prime Minister snapped, "What do you think we build the ships for?" According to Colville, Churchill firmly believed that "Cunningham must be made to take every risk: the loss of half the Mediterranean fleet would be worthwhile in order to save Crete." But this was precisely Cunningham's point; the admiral shot back that the navy could not, by itself, save Crete, since the Germans were reinforcing their invasion force entirely by air: "It is not the fear of sustaining losses but the need to avoid losses which will cripple the fleet without any commensurate advantage which is the determining factor in operating in the Aegean. As far as I know, the enemy has so far had little if any success in reinforcing Crete by sea. The experience of three days in which two cruisers and four destroyers have been sunk, and one battleship, two cruisers and four destroyers severely damaged shows what losses are likely to be. Sea control in the Eastern Mediterranean could not be retained after another such experience."

A communiqué from Wavell's headquarters in Cairo described the combat in the mountains as "undoubtedly the fiercest fighting in this war." "This battle must have looked like a rat pit," it seemed to General Lee when he read the reports, "with men slaughtering each other all over the island." Certainly the Germans had never encountered anything like it; this time, they were on the receiving end of the atrocities. Cretan peasants—including women—hid near wells and waited for the parachutists to appear, or else dressed themselves in the uniforms of dead German soldiers to lure the enemy. Paratroopers unfortunate enough to fall into their hands were decapitated or castrated. In the hospitals of Athens, some wounded German soldiers raved deliriously about "giant beings who emerged from caves with double-edged swords to behead their victims"; other survivors of the savagery remained "stunned and silent with cold horror in their eyes." "Of course we'll take Crete," muttered one disillusioned German sergeant to an acquaintance in Athens. "That devil in our government doesn't care how many men and planes he throws away. And after Crete we'll take Russia. But what does it mean to me if we take the whole damn world? I haven't seen my wife and children in three years and I know they're suffering for this hellish war." After taking another drink, the sergeant continued his lament. "We have to work like dogs, and live off the country with every man, woman and child hating us like madmen. I went for forty-eight hours during the mountain fighting here on fatigue pills and coffee and those dope pills will ruin the stomach of a man of iron. No, I don't enjoy this war. I'm forty-one years old and I remember the last war. The young fellows, they don't know anything else but der Fuehrer and they still think he is God. They'd just as soon die for him as live!"

On May 23, Churchill telegraphed to Wavell: "Crete battle must be won. . . . Enemy's exertions and losses in highest class troops must be very severe. He cannot keep it up for ever. Following for General Freyberg from me: 'The whole world is watching your splendid battle, on which great events turn.' " As usual, the course of events appeared considerably less heroic from the viewpoint of the common soldier. Evelyn Waugh was a member of the Layforce commando unit (750 men under the command of Colonel Laycock), which had been ordered to reinforce the British garrison on Crete; the commandos were instructed to initiate a measured rearguard action to cover the withdrawal if the regular forces were forced to retreat. The battle had been raging for several days by the time Waugh and his colleagues arrived at Suda Bay, and the retreat from Maleme had already begun. "The first indication which we received of conditions in Crete was the arrival in the captain's cabin, where HQ were waiting, of a stocky, bald, terrified naval commander," recalled Waugh. "He was wearing shorts and a greatcoat and could not speak intelligibly on account of weariness and panic. 'My God, it's hell,' he said. 'We're pulling out. Look at me, no gear. O my God, it's hell. Bombs all the time. . . .' We took this to be an exceptionally cowardly fellow, but in a few hours realized that he was typical of British forces in the island."

By May 26, General Freyberg had seen enough. "I regret to have to report that in my opinion the limit of endurance has been reached by the troops under my command here at Suda Bay," he cabled the Prime Minister. "No matter what decision is taken by the Commanders-in-Chief from a military point of view, our position here is hopeless. . . . I feel I should tell you that from an administrative point of view the difficulties of extricating this force in full are insuperable." Back came the response from Churchill via Wavell: "Victory in Crete essential at this turning-point in the war. Keep hurling in all aid you can."

On his way to the front, which was moving steadily southward in an irregular line, Waugh encountered troops retreating in the darkness with a total lack of discipline, abandoned by their officers who seemed to have driven ahead in whatever motorized transport was available. "Despondent troops," Waugh decided, "were a dead weight on one's spirits and usefulness." It was nearly impossible to move during the daylight. Luftwaffe fighters strafed the stragglers and scattered small fragmentation bombs that spread out for yards, and the men on the ground would lie in zigzag trenches for hours at a time trying to protect themselves from the bullets and the shrapnel. "After a while," recalled one British soldier when it was all over, "you get used to strafing. You're not afraid. You just lie there, your guts tied up inside you into one cold, painful lump. I remember finding an old newspaper lying in the dirt in the bottom of my trench. I pulled it out and started reading an article on agriculture. I read it all through and got drowsy and looked at the chap next to me and he was sound asleep and the Jerries were blasting us with bullets. Funny, isn't it?" Then came the Nazi mortars and the machine guns. Waugh: "As night fell stragglers emerged from the ditches, like ghosts from their graves, and began silently crawling along towards the coast. None that I saw in this area were under any kind of control, but the majority still had their rifles. They had all thrown away their packs, had beards and the lassitude of hunger and extreme exhaustion; a pitiful spectacle."

Wavell telegraphed to Churchill on May 27: "Fear that situation in Crete most serious. . . . Fear we must recognise that Crete is no longer tenable and that troops must be withdrawn as far as possible." Wavell, Cunningham, and Air Marshal Tedder met in Cairo and decided on evacuation, a course endorsed by the chiefs of staff in London, if not by the Prime Minister. "We wearily turned to planning another evacuation," wrote Cunningham, "with fewer ships, far less resources, and in circumstances much more difficult. Our seamen and our ships were worn to the point of exhaustion, and now they were asked for more."

Churchill, too, appeared exhausted; Eden described him as "nervy and unreasonable." For a brief moment during a gloomy and acrimonious cabinet meeting on the evening of May 26, Cadogan thought Churchill seemed almost ready to throw in the towel, for England suddenly found itself facing a terrifying menace on the Atlantic front as well. For the first time since it was completed at the docks of Hamburg in 1940, the giant German battleship *Bismarck* was on the loose.

No ship on any sea approached the *Bismarck*'s firing power—eight 15-inch guns, larger than those of the latest British battleships, along with a host of 5.9-inch guns—or its nearly impenetrable defenses, including a sheath of "Wotan" alloy-steel armor specially designed by Krupp. Despite the fact that it was the largest and most heavily armored warship afloat, the *Bismarck* could still match the speed of the swiftest British battleship. Hitler had deemed it "the pride of the Navy" when he inspected the *Bismarck* at the Polish port of Glydnia on May 5. Having completed its training exercises in the Baltic Sea, the magnificent vessel headed toward the open seas on May 18 with 2,400 men aboard and Admiral Gunther Lutjens in command. Its mission: to break out into the Atlantic and wreak havoc among British merchant ships as part of Grand Admiral Raeder's Operation Rheinubung; already a number of supply vessels were assembling at prearranged stations across the Atlantic to support the raiders.

British naval intelligence had no idea that anything was amiss until May 21, when it learned that two great warships (at first unidentified), escorted by a bevy of destroyers and aircraft, were steaming northwest through the straits between the northern tip of Denmark and the southern edge of Sweden. (Since Bletchley Park could not yet decipher with sufficient speed the code employed to send signals to and from the *Bismarck*, Ultra proved of little use during the ensuing crisis.) When the Admiralty received definite confirmation that the two ships in question were indeed the *Bismarck* and its partner, the 10,000-ton cruiser *Prinz Eugen,* Admiral Sir John Tovey, commander in chief of the Home Fleet based at Scapa Flow, ordered all available ships into action.

Tovey's battle force consisted of two battleships, two battle cruisers, and one aircraft carrier, none of which was a match for the *Bismarck.* The 42,000-ton *Hood* was considered the prize of the Royal Navy, the largest and fastest British capital ship afloat, despite the fact that it was twenty-five years old and poorly armored. Undaunted, the *Hood,* accompanied by the battleship *Prince of Wales* and six destroyers, headed for the Denmark Strait, where the R.A.F. had last spotted the *Bismarck.* In the dense fog and sleet that had settled over the North Sea in the meantime, however, the British reconnaissance planes lost sight of their quarry. No one knew whether the *Bismarck* was already five hundred miles away, steaming toward Iceland, or approaching the southward channels that opened into the Atlantic. Churchill wired an anxious message to Roosevelt, asking for American cooperation in locating the German ships.

Unaware of the frantic British maneuvers being carried on around him, Lutjens was calmly heading toward Greenland when he practically ran into the *Hood* in the midst of a snowstorm on the morning of May 24—Empire Day in Great Britain. Within eight minutes the German ships had found the range from thirteen miles away and a shell struck the *Hood* directly in its munitions magazine. "Almost immediately," wrote a British captain afterward, "the horrified spectators in the British cruisers saw a vast eruption of flame leap upwards between the *Hood*'s masts to a height of many hundreds of feet, perhaps as high as a thousand, in the middle of which a great incandescent ball was seen soaring skywards. The volcanic upshoot of fire lasted but a second or two; and when it had disappeared the place where the *Hood* had been was covered by an enormous column of smoke. . . . The *Hood* had blown up in the middle, had broken in half, and in a couple of minutes or so had completely disappeared." All that was left was a bit of twisted wreckage floating on a film of oil, and the acrid scent of cordite. It had all happened so fast that the crew of more than fifteen hundred men had no time to save themselves; there were only three survivors. Churchill, who was spending the weekend at Chequers, received a running account of the battle as it happened; shortly after seven o'clock, dressed only in a yellow sweater and a short nightshirt that exposed the pink wobbling flesh of his legs, he awakened his American guest, Averell Harriman, and said excitedly, "Hell of a battle going on. The *Hood* is sunk. Hell of a battle." What about the *Prince of Wales,* asked Harriman. "She's still at her," Churchill said, and then returned to his room and went back to sleep. At eight-thirty one of his secretaries entered Churchill's room. "Have we got her?" Churchill asked. "No," the secretary replied, "and the *Prince of Wales* has broken off the action."

It was the first time a German capital ship had met a British warship and emerged victorious. The loss of the biggest ship in the Royal Navy shocked the Admiralty and, of course, the British public, which was already reeling from the dreadful news from Crete. "Poor *Hood,*" mourned Anthony Eden, "the loveliest ship to look at in all the Royal Navy and for many years to millions its emblem." A miserably disappointed Churchill, who seems to have decided (somewhat unfairly) that his naval commanders were a bunch of dangerously incompetent ninnies who had to be pushed into combat, was furious that the *Prince of Wales* had not pressed the attack. (He later absolved the *Prince of Wales*'s officers when he learned that the ship's bridge had been wrecked during the fighting.)

Worse, the *Bismarck,* trailing oil from a wound inflicted by a British shell that landed near one of its fuel tanks, had once again disappeared into the mists. "We did not intend to fight enemy warships," Lutjens told his sailors, "but to wage war against merchant shipping. Through treachery the enemy managed to find us in the Denmark Straits. We took up the fight. The crew have behaved magnificently. We shall win or die." Churchill feared that the German ship would turn northward and return to a safe port; yearning for another shot at the armored giant, the Prime Minister ordered every available ship to sea to hunt the *Bismarck.* In fact, Lutjens would have continued out into the Atlantic to accomplish his deadly mission but for the hole in the *Bismarck*'s fuel tank. Instead, he headed southward, at reduced speed, toward the harbor being specially prepared for it at Brest, when Lutjens made the unforgivable mistake of signaling his victory to his superiors, thereby betraying his position. (Luftwaffe signals ordering air escort for the stricken giant were also intercepted and decoded at Bletchley, confirming what the navy already suspected.) The Admiralty mobilized all its forces in home waters and cast a wide net around the German ship's presumed course. At ten-thirty on the morning of Monday, May 26, thirty-one and a half hours after the *Bismarck* had disappeared, a twin-engine Catalina seaplane (built in San Diego, with a crew of one British pilot and one American observer) spotted the German ship approximately seven hundred miles from Brest. ("What the devil's that?" asked the American, gesturing to a vast, vague black shape in the mist below. "Looks like a battleship," the Englishman replied. "Better get closer.") The battleship *King George V* and the heavily armored *Rodney* pinched in from the northwest; three ships from the Gibraltar squadron, the *Renown, Ark Royal,* and *Sheffield,* approached from the south. Almost all the British ships in the chase were running dangerously low on fuel. Tovey knew that if he did not catch the *Bismarck* soon, his fleet would have to break off the pursuit. Churchill spent that evening nervously watching the progress of the pursuit at the Admiralty's War Room.

In Washington, Roosevelt was only slightly less anxious. He knew that the *Hood* had been sunk and that the *Bismarck* was on the loose. At the cabinet meeting of May 23, Ickes thought the President looked exhausted, and wondered whether he would have the physical strength and stamina to lead the nation through another four turbulent years. In the company of his advisers, Roosevelt wondered aloud what he should do if the *Bismarck* suddenly appeared in the American "security zone" in the western Atlantic, or the Caribbean. He already had scheduled an address to the American people for the evening of May 27; in the light of events in the Atlantic and the Mediterranean, the President's preparations for his speech took on additional urgency.

The occasion for Roosevelt's speech was a gathering of representatives of the Latin American nations to coordinate the defense of the Western Hemisphere. Behind a bank of microphones in the East Room of the White House, Roosevelt sat patiently, dressed in a white evening jacket and black tie, while photographers snapped his picture from every conceivable angle and announcers from the major radio networks began their introductions. Armed with a full pack of cigarettes, the President asked an aide for a half-dozen glasses of water, which were set before him with a silver pitcher. Behind him hung a curtain of crimson velvet topped with flags of the American republics. For the past several days, the country had been full of rumors about a bold presidential initiative that might finally push the United States over the edge into war; 65 million people stopped whatever they were doing and gathered around their radios and braced themselves for the worst. The number of telephone calls in New York City fell by 50 percent during the President's address. Movie theaters set up loudspeakers in their lobbies so patrons could hear the speech live. The baseball game between the Giants and the Boston Braves at the Polo Grounds was halted for forty-five minutes at the end of the seventh inning with the score tied, 1–1, as the players on both clubs sat motionless in the dugouts while the President began talking.

Reading from a large leather looseleaf binder in front of him, stopping several times to mop his forehead from the intense heat of the movie spotlights turned upon him, Roosevelt assured his listeners that the Nazis were fully committed to a campaign to conquer the world. No country, including the United States, was safe from their criminal depredations. He painted a grim, pitiless picture of what a Nazi victory over Britain would mean to the United States. (Somehow, Roosevelt managed to mispronounce the word "swastika," putting the accent on the middle syllable.) Although he revealed no bold new initiatives, the President reiterated his determination to add more ships and planes to the existing American patrols (he explicitly avoided the word "convoys") to guarantee the safety of American food supplies and defense shipments to Britain. "Our patrols are helping now to insure delivery of the needed supplies to Britain. All additional measures necessary to deliver the goods will be taken." The strength of the speech, however, lay in the climax. Roosevelt tapped out the rhythm of the sentences on the table in front of him with a clenched fist:

"As the President of a united and determined people, I say solemnly: We reassert the ancient American doctrine of freedom of the seas. . . .

"We in the Americas will decide for ourselves whether, and when, and where, our American interests are attacked or our security is threatened.

"We are placing our armed forces in strategic military positions.

"We will not hesitate to use our armed forces to repel attack. . . .

"Therefore . . . I have tonight issued a proclamation that an unlimited national emergency exists and requires the strengthening of our defense to the extreme limit of our national power and authority."

Then he went to dinner.

Listening to the speech in the lobby of a hotel in Harlem, heavy-weight champion Joe Louis nodded and told reporters, "We are all with the President." But no one—including Roosevelt's advisers, and the one or two listeners who had rudely fallen asleep while Roosevelt was speaking—was quite sure what the President meant by the term "unlimited national emergency." Some thought it meant that war would come within a matter of days, that the only question was "where and when the fighting will be." "Johnny, get your gun" was a phrase repeated in bars and offices everywhere in America in the ensuing days. "Perhaps some miracle, nowhere visible at the moment, can keep this nation at peace," declared *The New Yorker,* "but if things work out the way we think they will, the brief armed truce that marked the spring and summer of 1941 will shortly be forgotten."

By the time Roosevelt had finished his speech, Admiral Lutjens had sent his final message from the *Bismarck* to the German High Command: "Urgent. Ship unmanoeuvrable. We shall fight to the last shell. Long live the Fuehrer."

Shortly before nightfall on May 26 (Admiral Lutjens' birthday), fifteen Swordfish aircraft, armed with torpedo bombs, had taken off from the aircraft carrier *Ark Royal* in the face of a driving rainstorm, heavy winds, and extremely poor visibility. "Aircraft approached us from all sides," wrote a seaman aboard the *Bismarck.* "I do not know the exact number. I felt two heavy shakings of the ship, one shortly after the other." One or two of the Swordfish crews thought they had indeed hit the *Bismarck,* but no one knew the extent of the damage until shadowing airplanes reported that the German ship was heading, inexplicably, north-northwest. If it still intended to seek shelter at Brest, this was precisely the wrong direction. Tovey concluded that the great ship had been hit and was now wallowing out of control.

He was correct. By a miraculous stroke of fortune, one of the torpedoes from a Swordfish had struck the *Bismarck's* steering compartment, disabling the mechanism and jamming the rudder hard to starboard. The *Bismarck* traveled twice around in a circle, then began to drift. Exhausted after suffering through four days of relentless pursuit, its crew reportedly were falling asleep at their posts. The Fuehrer cabled encouragement: "The whole of Germany is with you." Nearby U-boats who responded to Lutjens' distress signal were unable to prevent the final, inescapable act of the tragedy. At 8:47 on the gray, leaden morning of May 27, the British pursuers opened fire upon the vulnerable giant, which by now was virtually at a standstill. After thirty minutes, the *Bismarck's* gunnery control center was hit; her shots grew erratic and finally ceased altogether, and the *Rodney* and *King George V* swung in to point-blank range and blasted away. "Get closer, get closer," Tovey ordered impatiently, "I can't see enough hits." The carnage resembled a particularly murderous round of target practice, but the target refused to yield. The German ship had absorbed more than a score of the largest shells the two battleships and two cruisers had to offer, nearly a dozen torpedoes from airplanes and destroyers, and hundreds of smaller shells, and it refused to sink. Desperate, almost frantic to bring the giant down, Tovey ordered any ship still armed with torpedoes to open fire. The cruiser *Dorsetshire,* a late arrival on the scene, accordingly closed to close range and the *Bismarck* came into clear view; one of its officers recorded what he saw in the sea ahead: "She was a terrible sight. Her top was blown clear away, flames were roaring out in several places, and her plates were glowing red with heat. Great clouds of black smoke were billowing from her and rising for several hundred feet or so. It was the end." The destroyer fired its torpedoes and struck the battleship abreast of the bridge.

Shortly after ten-thirty, the *Bismarck* turned over and sank with its flag still flying in defiance. She had been alive on the seas for less than seven days. Fewer than one hundred and fifty survivors were rescued from the ocean. "Severe as are the wounds that may be suffered in the maintenance of sea power, it is not challenged with impunity," observed the *Times* of London upon hearing the news.

When Churchill addressed a sullen Commons (which was in an ill-tempered mood anyway from the necessity of meeting in cramped, improvised quarters at the Church House) at eleven o'clock on the morning of May 27, the Prime Minister was still unaware that the *Bismarck* had been sunk. He delivered a dramatic account of the chase, the German escape, the discovery by the Catalina, and the success of the Swordfish torpedo attack. He assured the House that the British fleet had the *Bismarck* surrounded, and its demise was only a matter of time. ("Such is the innate sporting feeling of the House," observed Harold Nicolson, "that we all began to feel sorry for the *Bismarck*.") After the Prime Minister had sat down (leaving the House, Nicolson said, "with a sense of *coitus interruptus*"), his personal secretary, Brendan Bracken, handed him a small slip of paper. Churchill fidgeted uneasily while he waited for an Opposition speaker to complete a question, then finally interrupted as he rose and declared, "I venture to intervene for a moment. I have just received news that the *Bismarck* has been sunk." There was a spontaneous burst of hurrahs. "Still the British Navy keeps the seas," murmured Home Secretary Herbert Morrison; Hugh Dalton called the news "a bright gleam in a dark sky. We have now got a Rook for a Knight and, being ahead before, ought to be winning this naval chess game." Watching Churchill's masterful performance in the Commons, Chips Channon noted dryly in his diary, "The House cheered—and for a moment forgot Crete."

General Raymond Lee visited the War Office that afternoon; as he entered, he passed Sir John Dill, the hard-pressed chief of the Imperial General Staff. Lee thought that Dill looked "very haggard and drawn and evidently was not too elevated by the *Bismarck* news. He said Crete was very bad indeed, and then he went on quietly and almost under his breath, 'I don't see how we can expect to get any of them out.' 'You know,' he went on, 'Freyberg was left with no air support at all.'"

Twenty-two thousand of Freyberg's men were heading southward, most of them making their way over the rugged White Mountains to the small fishing village of Sphakia on the southern coast, where they descended by a narrow zigzag track down a five-hundred-foot cliff to an open beach. It was not a particularly well-coordinated retreat. "Units became divided," wrote Alan Moorehead, "and men lost in the hills had to fend for themselves. There was no hot food and water ran out. Villagers in the mountains led the weary, unshaven, dirty men to wells where they lowered their water-bottles on ropes to the springs below. The walking wounded walked at first, were carried in the end." Freyberg established his headquarters in a cave near the beach. Over the last three nights of May, Cunningham's fleet brought off more than seventeen thousand men; more might have been evacuated had the withdrawal been better organized. When he reached Sphakia on the evening of May 30, Evelyn Waugh found a scene of wild confusion; he could hear sailors shouting, "Any more for the boats?" but in the general melee the ships left with cargo space still empty. The following day, ragged bands of stragglers trickled down the gorge to the beaches, to the accompaniment of yells of "Aircraft! Take cover fuck you!" from the soldiers hiding in caves until nightfall.

Alarmed by the heavy naval losses endured as the Luftwaffe harassed the crowded ships during the return journey to Alexandria, there was considerable sentiment within the Admiralty and army command to discontinue the operation at once. (The General Staff seems to have been under the impression that there were only three thousand troops left on the beaches, when in fact there were more than twice that many.) The government finally decided to go ahead for one more night, and a message was sent to Sphakia alerting Freyberg that May 31 would be the last night for evacuation. "At about 10 o'clock that evening there was no sign of the enemy and the approaches to the beaches were thronged with non-fighting troops," recalled Waugh. "We pushed our way through the crowds who were too spiritless even to resist what they took to be an unauthorized intrusion and arrived at the beach to find that there was no one in charge. . . . As there was nothing further he could do, Bob ordered brigade HQ to embark, which we did in a small motor boat. We reached the destroyer *Nizam* at about midnight and sailed as soon as we came aboard . . . and arrived at Alexandria at 5 in the afternoon, June 1st, after an uneventful voyage during which we were too exhausted to do more than shave."

Cunningham's ships brought back 16,500 men from Crete to Egypt that night. Over 5,000 British troops were left behind on the island, of whom nearly a thousand later escaped with the help of native sympathizers and British commando missions. According to Eden, Churchill wanted to overrule the military chiefs and continue the evacuation for one more evening (June 1), but Wavell already had ordered the shattered remnants of the garrison to surrender. Colville noted that Churchill was greatly perturbed "by the fact that the rearguard, consisting of Royal Marines, was left behind in Crete. He blamed the navy and went so far as to describe it as a shameful episode." British losses—killed, wounded, or captured—totaled 13,000 soldiers, plus another 2,000 sailors drowned when their ships were bombed. Still, Churchill entertained no doubts about the wisdom of defending Crete (unlike the ill-fated adventure in Greece, about which he lately had been having second thoughts). German losses during the invasion had been equally devastating. Berlin admitted to only 4,000 casualties, but Freyberg insisted that the Nazis must have lost at least 17,000 men. With Barbarossa only three weeks away, Hitler could spare no more troops for any further adventures in the Middle East. The Nazi Seventh Airborne Division, which had been so brutally slaughtered during the initial assault, was broken forever; the specter of a German airborne invasion of England vanished.

At the time, however, there was considerable resentment in Britain over the mistakes made during the campaign, particularly the failure to provide any measure of air cover for Freyberg's garrison. There was a flurry of mutual recriminations among the different branches of the Imperial General Staff, each blaming the others for the disaster. The press was in a foul mood and on the lookout for scapegoats, and for the first time the public began seriously to question Churchill's leadership. "On all sides one hears increasing criticism of Churchill," noted Chips Channon (who, it must be pointed out in fairness, was never particularly enamored of Winston anyway). "He is undergoing a noticeable slump in popularity and many of his enemies, long silenced by his personal popularity, are once more vocal. Crete has been a great blow to him." The defeat was not offset by the successful defense of the British position in Iraq against a German-instigated coup led by Rashid Ali, or by the daring dash of a naval convoy carrying desperately needed tanks from England through the straits at Gibraltar and across the western Mediterranean to the army in Egypt. Many Englishmen wondered whether the price for saving the bloody British Empire was too steep after all, whether the nation was paying too dearly for its theatrical Prime Minister's "vivid and fiery imagination," which, one American observed, "discerns a victory at the foot of every rainbow but will not consider the abysses and mountains which lie between him and them." In June 1941, the obstacles to a final victory appeared to have grown even more daunting since the beginning of the year; in General Lee's forthright assessment, "the British are trying to save the Empire with a shoestring of an Army, an outnumbered Air Force, and a Navy which is stretched to the uttermost over the seven seas."

The loss of Crete left the British military position in Malta and at Suez perilously exposed. But the empire's fortunes in the Mediterranean would sink no lower. For the next five months, while Hitler turned his attention to the Soviet Union and the blistering summer heat immobilized Rommel's forces in the deserts of North Africa, the status quo in that theater would remain virtually undisturbed.

"The drama of the Balkan Peninsula is at an end," concluded Soviet Ambassador Ivan Maisky in London. Writing in his diary on June 2, Maisky acknowledged that "Hitler has won a decisive victory. The British as always have acted according to the rule of 'too little and too late.' I am not even inclined to blame them. In the present condition they probably could not do more. And now the fire which began two years ago is extending more and more, and beginning to approach quite close to our frontiers. I don't like the fact that Rumania, Hungary, Bulgaria, and now also Yugoslavia and Greece have joined the 'Axis' or have been turned into German provinces. What can we expect of the coming day?"

18

Waiting

"He can run, but he can't hide."
—HEAVYWEIGHT CHAMPION JOE LOUIS, BEFORE
HIS JUNE 18, 1941, BOUT WITH BILLY CONN

Between June 2 and June 13, Anthony Eden held four meetings with Soviet Ambassador Maisky and advised him that the British government had definite indications that Nazi Germany was preparing to attack the Soviet Union within a matter of days. On June 10, Alexander Cadogan summoned Maisky to the Foreign Office, announced grimly that he had been instructed to "make an important communication" to the ambassador, and asked Maisky to write down the information he would give him. Reading in a monotone voice from documents arranged in order in front of him, Cadogan said: "On such-and-such a date two German motorised divisions passed through such-and-such a point in the direction of your frontier. . . . On such-and-such a date six German divisions were concentrated at such-and-such a point near your frontier. . . . During the whole of May there passed through such-and-such a point in the direction of your frontier from 25 to 30 military trains a day . . ." As Cadogan reeled off the list of precise, concrete statistics of German military movements, Maisky's mind filled with the apocalyptic image of "vast masses of Nazi troops—infantry, artillery, tanks, armoured cars, aeroplanes—which were irresistibly streaming to the east, ever further to the east . . . And all this avalanche, breathing fire and death, was at any moment to descend upon our country!" Although Maisky was well aware that, like all military intelligence, some parts of Cadogan's information might have been inaccurate, the ambassador was sufficiently impressed to forward the details of the British warning to Moscow.

On June 13, the London *Times* published an article predicting a German attack upon the Soviet Union in the near future. On the same day, Chips Channon noted in his diary the persistent rumors of an imminent war between Germany and Russia: "huge German concentrations of troops are reported all along the Russian and Roumanian frontiers." Seven days later, Channon accurately predicted that "Russia will be invaded on Sunday [June 22] by Germany."

On June 16, Raymond Lee reported from London that "a handful of cables originating in the highest quarters both here and abroad this morning shows a universal conviction that the Germans are going to attack Russia." At luncheon that day, Dill told Eden he was convinced that Hitler intended "to smash Russian military power now."

In the United States, Herbert Hoover had been aware for days that Germany would invade the Soviet Union on June 22.

On June 13, *Tass* issued a communiqué condemning as "malicious fabrications" the rumors of impending war between Nazi Germany and the Soviet Union: "In spite of the evident senselessness of the rumours, responsible circles in Moscow have nevertheless thought it necessary, in view of the stubborn circulation of these rumours, to authorise TASS to state that such rumours are clumsily cooked-up propaganda by forces hostile to the USSR and to Germany. . . . Both countries intend to observe the provisions of the Soviet-German pact of friendship."

The following day, Marshals Zhukov and Timoshenko asked Stalin to order the troops on the western border to be placed on alert and deployed to resist a Nazi invasion. "You propose carrying out mobilization, alerting the troops and moving them to the Western borders?" shouted Stalin angrily. "That means war! Do you two understand that or not?"

Nikita Khrushchev, secretary of the Ukrainian Communist Party, was cooling his heels in Moscow in the middle of June, doing nothing in particular except keeping Stalin company. ("He couldn't stand being alone," Khrushchev grumbled.) Khrushchev had recently visited the frontier to inspect the defense works, and was appalled by the decrepit state of Soviet defensive fortifications and the shortages of manpower and ammunition; some of the Red Army's tank units were so short of shells that they could not even take target practice. True to form, Stalin had ignored Khrushchev's urgent requests that additional fortifications be constructed immediately. In fact, Khrushchev decided, Stalin was already in an advanced state of depression: "I didn't like what I saw. He'd obviously lost all confidence in the ability of our army to put up a fight. It was as though he'd thrown up his hands in despair and given up . . ." On June 20, fearful that war might break out at any moment, Khrushchev finally received Stalin's permission to return to Kiev.

On the evening of June 21, Zhukov and several colleagues learned that a German deserter, allegedly a Communist sympathizer, had crossed the border to warn the Soviets of the imminent invasion. Zhukov informed Stalin; the dictator asked Zhukov and the commissar for defense to meet him at the Kremlin. Zhukov found Stalin anxious and alone. "But perhaps the German generals sent this deserter to provoke a conflict?" he asked.

Zhukov said he didn't think so.

"What are we to do?" Stalin asked.

The commissar recommended that the troops in the border districts be placed on alert at once, and read Stalin a draft directive to that effect.

"It's too soon to give such a directive—perhaps the question can still be settled peacefully," Stalin replied tersely. "We must give a short directive stating that an attack may begin with provocative actions by the German forces. The troops of the border districts must not be incited by any provocation, in order to avoid complications."

That evening, as Stalin slept alone with his dreams, every member of the Soviet General Staff and the Defense Commissariat remained at their posts through the night.

Minutes after midnight, the Berlin-Moscow express crossed the border on its usual run, without any untoward incident.

19

Billy Conn's Reckless Gamble

"The plain fact is that homo sapiens enjoys war as he enjoys
no other enterprise. It is unquestionably the king of all sports."
                                        —H. L. MENCKEN

The spring of 1941 had been a bad season for underdogs, as any resident
of the Balkans or the British Isles could testify. But the weight of the odds
meant nothing to Billy Conn (who, by June, was in much better shape than
the British army anyway). Conn was twenty-three years old, handsome
and cocky and restless, the undisputed light-heavyweight champion of the
world. And besides, he was Irish, and nobody had defeated Eire all year
(largely because President Eamon de Valera had kept the Irish Republic
scrupulously neutral, much to the annoyance of his embattled English
neighbors on the other side of St. George's Channel).

So when Billy Conn, clad in a white bathrobe over dark trunks,
climbed into the ring at the Polo Grounds with the whistles and cheers of
the crowd behind him on the sultry evening of June 18, he knew he could
win. Although the bookies did not share his optimism, enough bettors put
down money on Conn to lower the odds against him to 11–5, far less
prohibitive than the usual quotes of 10–1 the oddsmakers gave when other
mere mortals had been foolish enough to challenge Joe Louis. Most ring
experts expected Louis to put Conn away in the early rounds; they agreed
with Whitney Martin of the Associated Press, who conceded that "Billy
Conn is a nice kid. He is handsome, talented with his fists and a credit to
the fight game. But we don't think he can beat Joe Louis." Grantland Rice,
however, was not as certain. Acknowledging that Louis was "still something to whip," Rice pointed out that all of the champion's recent rivals
had possessed about as much speed as a herd of lumbering dinosaurs.
Perhaps Joe, too, had slowed down, during the past four years since he had
won the title from Jim Braddock in Chicago. "There is one point about
which you can be 100 per cent sure in Conn's case," Rice assured his
readers. "He may go out like a flickering candle in a gale, but he won't quit
at any stage."

Ever since he battered Max Schmeling to a bloody pulp in an awesome two-and-a-half-minute display of legalized savagery on June 22,

1938, Joe Louis—popularly known as the Brown Bomber, the Dark Destroyer, or, to less sensitive sportswriters, as Shufflin' Joe—had totally dominated the heavyweight division. In fact, his most formidable challenge had come from outside the ring, from the ubiquitous officials of the Selective Service. Joe had drawn an uncomfortably low draft number ("Looks like Uncle Samuel's got me already, don't it?"), and so his promoter, Mike Jacobs, quickly scheduled a series of bouts with the best challengers he could find, to make as much money as possible before Louis went into the army. Unfortunately, there *were* no other heavyweights who even approached Louis's formidable talents; from December 1940 to May 1941, Louis knocked out six opponents in rapid succession. Scornful sportswriters dubbed the champion's overmatched opponents the Bum-of-the-Month Club. "Louis has never been thoroughly tested," argued former heavyweight champ Jim Jeffries. "He has no competition. . . . Louis may be the greatest of them all, but I doubt it."

By the time of the Conn fight, Joe was visibly tired of the training grind; this would be his eighteenth title defense, and perhaps the lack of a suitable challenge had caused his skills to erode, to lose their fine edge. But he was still the champion, and he carried with him the hopes of millions of black Americans, who, like people everywhere in the world, were looking for a hero in 1941. The son of a southern sharecropper, Louis had fought his way to the top and earned the universal respect of white America. He served as a much-needed role model for the nation's black youth; "every Negro boy old enough to walk wanted to be the next Brown Bomber," recalled Malcolm X years later. As Broadway columnist Ed Sullivan proclaimed, "The fists of Joe Louis are the megaphones and microphones of his race on the nights that he defends his championship. He is, to all intents and purposes, never an individual—he is all the sorrows and joys, and fears and hopes and the melody of an entire race. . . . He is a compound of every little cabin in the Southland, every tenement or apartment in the Harlems of the North; he is the memory of every injustice practiced upon his people and the memory of every triumph." Richard Wright, the author of *Black Boy* and a close friend of Louis, defined the heavyweight champion as "the concentrated essence of black triumph over white. . . . From the symbol of Joe Louis' strength Negroes took strength, and in that moment all fear, all obstacles were wiped out, drowned. They stepped out of the mire of hesitation and irresolution and were free! Invincible! A merciless victor over a fallen foe! Yes, they had felt all that. . . ." In 1941, at the request of legendary talent scout and recording executive John Hammond, Wright wrote the lyrics to a musical tribute to Louis, "King Joe, Part One and Part Two." Backed by Count Basie's band, actor Paul Robeson provided the vocals for the two-sided 78-rpm record:

Black eye peas ask corn bread,
What make you so strong?
Corn bread says I come from
Where Joe Louis was born.

Rabbit say to the bee
What make you sting so deep?
He say I sting like Joe
An' rock 'em all to sleep.

But King Joe had never faced an opponent as fast and as self-assured as Billy Conn. Raised in the brawling East Liberty neighborhood of Pittsburgh, Conn had been boxing since he was fourteen. He had never been knocked out in a professional fight. Conn had an extraordinary ability to block an opponent's punches, and to roll with the few that landed. He enjoyed playing the part of a headstrong rebel against authority; on the eve of the fight with Louis, a grand jury indicted Conn for illegally operating a motor vehicle after his driving license had been suspended on a speeding charge. In fact, the rap against Conn was that he was too reckless, too willing to challenge the odds and to trade punches with a larger opponent when he should have walked away. "I know I have lost my temper in some fights," he admitted, "but you can bet I won't this time."

At the beginning of 1941, Conn had embarked upon what he called a "second helpings campaign" to boost his weight. "I'm going to eat all I possibly can and in between meals I'll just lie around in the sun." He laughed. "I'll gain some more weight and then I'll jab that Joe Louis dizzy. I'll make him so dizzy that he'll think he's on a merry-go-round." Still, by the time of the official prefight ceremonies, Billy weighed only 174 pounds; Louis tipped the scales at 199½. Conn thus became the lightest heavyweight challenger since the "orchid man" from France, Georges Carpentier, got his bell rung by Jack Dempsey in 1921. Some experts advised Conn to wait and train for another year before challenging Louis, but the draft was breathing down Billy's neck, too; besides, he needed the money (20 percent of the gate receipts) to take care of his critically ill mother, and to marry eighteen-year-old Mary Louise Smith, whose father reportedly thought Conn was not good enough (or wealthy enough) for his little girl.

So 54,487 impatient fight fans—including one thousand sportswriters and a generous allotment of soldiers in khaki and sailors in navy blue uniforms—crowded into the Polo Grounds that night. The circle of temporary wooden chairs around the infield was full, and people were packed together solidly in rows in the double-decked steel and concrete grandstands that stretched out into the darkness beyond, as far back as the eye could see. J. Edgar Hoover was present at ringside, along with Mayor

Frank ("I am the Law") Hague of Jersey City, Democratic party power broker James Farley, former presidential candidate James Cox of Ohio, and numerous congressmen, financiers, and entertainers. There were 2,250 policemen on duty in and around the stadium, and nearly a thousand more of New York's finest (including two hundred detectives, sixty-six mounted police, thirty-three motorcycle patrolmen, and two emergency squads) patrolled the streets of Harlem, although the police department admitted that there had never been any serious disturbances in the black district during previous Louis fights. Wagering had been heavy throughout the city; more money had been bet on this fight than on any heavyweight championship bout since the golden days of Dempsey and Tunney.

Thirty seconds after Conn climbed into the ring, Joe Louis appeared, wearing a towel draped over his head, and his familiar blue bathrobe with crimson trim.

Conn was visibly nervous. Shortly after the bell rang, he tripped over his own feet and fell flat on his backside on the canvas. Billy, who had a well-deserved reputation as a slow starter, kept backpedaling, trying to stay out of Louis's range, but once the champion caught him with a right to the ribs that sounded, according to one witness, "like a baseball bat hitting a bag of oats." In the second round, Louis kept pressing the attack, hoping to finish off Conn before the Irishman got started. He trapped Conn in a corner and pummeled him ferociously for thirty seconds, and for a moment it appeared that the challenger would fall; but Conn recovered and threw a few hard hooks of his own to Louis's body. The judges awarded the first two rounds to Louis.

In round three, Conn took the offensive. His quick jabs penetrated the champion's defenses time and time again, keeping Louis off balance. Observers at ringside noticed some swelling under Joe's left eye. The round ended with Louis on the ropes, as Conn landed a flurry of blows to the head. Conn began the next round retreating, luring Louis closer, and then suddenly he stepped forward and lashed a straight left-right combination into the champion's face. Another right to the jaw and Louis's knees buckled. A series of lefts to the head from close range. Louis grabbed and held on. Conn fired more shots to the champion's face; desperately trying to counterpunch, Louis's jabs fell short. Now Conn was grinning.

When the bell rang to start round five, Conn advanced confidently, but Louis suddenly staggered him with a left hook. The challenger began to bleed from cuts over his right eye and under his nose. Conn tried to clear his head; at the end of the round he stumbled to the wrong corner. The two men traded punches through the sixth (won by Louis) and seventh (Conn) rounds, and then Conn launched another furious assault in the eighth. Although his punches had lost much of their steam, the cumulative effect of the blows began to tell on Louis. Conn was piling up an impressive lead on points on the judges' cards. When he returned to his corner at the end of the eighth round, he shouted to his seconds, "I did it! I did it!" In the ninth, he began to taunt the champion. ("I didn't have so much time to talk," Conn said later, "but I talked to him a couple of times. Once I says to him, 'Joe, you're in for a tough night.' And Joe, he says to me: 'Ah knows ah am.'") Louis stalked Conn and took the tenth round with a desperate flurry; Conn came back to win the eleventh.

Now Louis was in the deepest trouble of his four-year reign. He seemed helpless to avoid the rain of blows that Conn showered upon him with renewed energy in the twelfth round. Refusing to run, Conn stayed in and punched furiously at close range, scoring with a left to the jaw that left Louis groggy, pounding with both hands to the body, staggering the champion with three unanswered left hooks, surging relentlessly forward as Louis, badly hurt and legs trembling, covered up and backed away. Between rounds, Louis's handlers told him he was losing the fight. He knew he would have to score a knockout to win.

"As the thirteenth round opened," wrote Grantland Rice the following day, "Conn was only nine minutes away from one of the greatest miracles sport has seen. He was looking into the promised land. He couldn't lose." Perhaps Conn thought he had nothing more to fear from Louis. He had taken the Bomber's best punches in the early rounds and survived. Perhaps he didn't know how to play it safe. He wanted desperately to knock out the champion. He walked right in and smashed a right to Louis's head. Louis countered with a left jab and a right to Conn's chin. Conn fired a left hook that caught Louis flush on the jaw. Louis responded with a combination that hurt Billy; Conn pounded Louis with both hands. The two giants stood against the ropes and flailed at each other, five—ten—twenty punches apiece, slugging away, and the crowd went absolutely mad and stood shoulder to shoulder and fifty thousand people indulged their lust for blood and combat by yelling themselves hoarse. It was bedlam. It had been a hell of a bloody year so far, and most of the men and women in the crowd were cheering frantically for the underdog to win just this one time, and all of them were screaming in exultation and joyous climax as the primitive battle unfolded before them. This was a contest that they could not lose, and most would never see its like again. For a moment everything else fell away, and the world was reduced to two brave men standing and pounding one another relentlessly over and over. But it could not last forever.

As Conn drew back to unleash a sweeping left hook, Louis saw it coming; he stepped in and staggered Conn with a hard right that caught the challenger flush on the jaw, snapping his head back. Conn tried to retaliate, but Louis rocked him with two more rights to the chin. Conn refused to retreat. He took a left to the head, then a right uppercut, then another left. Conn's legs trembled. Another left, and then Louis landed a smashing right to the challenger's open mouth, and Conn spun around and fell—to the stunned crowd it seemed almost as if he were falling in slow motion . . . inevitable like the sand falling silently through an hourglass. He landed hard on the canvas, curled up on his right side. Billy had struggled to his knees and was rising to stand at the count of ten, but the referee waved him off and patted him on the shoulder and pushed him gently toward his corner. The bell would have sounded two seconds later. The fight was over. When Billy's invalid mother heard that her son had lost the biggest fight of his career, she whispered, "I'm very proud of him," and turned her face to the wall. Conn's manager, Johnny Ray, fumed afterwards that if his fighter "hadda Jewish head instead of an Irish one, he'd be the champ."

Grantland Rice wrote sadly of Billy Conn, "His dream was over. He had thrown away his big advantage in speed and smartness on a reckless gamble. He had tossed away his winning lead in the new mad hope of seeing Louis on the floor."

Part Four   The Summer

20

Barbarossa

"Any general who fights against the Russians can be perfectly
sure of one thing: he will be outnumbered."
—PAUL VON HINDENBURG

Hitler had a nasty habit of attacking other countries on Sundays. At 3:30
A.M. on Sunday, June 22, just as dawn was breaking along the Baltic coast
after the shortest night of the year, the vanguard of the most imposing
invasion force in history—three million men, arrayed in 148 divisions,
supported by 3,350 tanks, 7,100 pieces of artillery, and more than 2,000
airplanes—crossed the border into the Soviet Union. It was the first anniversary of France's sudden capitulation to the blitzkrieg. Exactly 129 years
earlier, Napoleon had crossed the Niemen River on the first leg of his
round-trip journey to Moscow. Now, once again, Russia unwillingly became Armageddon. And thousands of people around the world that summer picked up a copy of Tolstoy's *War and Peace* and began searching for
an answer.

With (as John Paton Davies put it) "a Wagnerian blast of brasses and
kettle drums," the Wehrmacht advanced in three main armored columns.
Army Group North, which followed the classical line of Napoleon's invasion, was headed by Field Marshal Ritter von Leeb, the commander who
had led the attack upon the Maginot Line in the spring of 1940; Hitler
expected Leeb's twenty-nine divisions to conquer Leningrad by July 21.
Army Group Center, the most powerful German striking force (slightly
more than 1.1 million men), was commanded by Field Marshal Fedor von
Bock. With the support of nine panzer divisions, Bock planned to roll
through Minsk and Smolensk and across the Dnepr River, crushing all
resistance on the road toward Moscow. Field Marshal Gerd von Rundstedt
was leading Army Group South toward Kiev and the rich oil and grain
fields of the Ukraine. "You have only to kick in the door, and the whole
rotten structure will come crashing down," Hitler had told the marshal,
unaware that the heaviest concentration of Soviet defensive forces lay
directly in Rundstedt's path. And behind the Wehrmacht came the *Einsatzgruppen,* the "Special Units" of the SS, the cold-blooded murder

squads of four thousand men who had explicit orders to liquidate all Jewish and Communist civilians in German-controlled territory.

Speed and surprise were the essential elements of the German attack. Halder and his generals assumed that the Russians had moved—or would move—the bulk of their forces in the west up to the German frontier, to meet the Nazi invasion head-on and avoid frittering away their troops in isolated actions; if everything happened as the German generals planned, their own mechanized divisions would move so quickly that they would outflank the Red Army's positions and close around them in a series of gigantic pincer movements, and the surrounded pockets of defenders would either be destroyed or compelled to surrender. Bock's juggernaut would then roar on toward Moscow, at which point Halder expected the Soviets to pour more reinforcements in the Wehrmacht's path in a desperate attempt to save the city and the armaments plants (most of which were exposed to German attack in the west); thus a Nazi victory in the center would achieve the twin objectives of decimating the Red Army's reserves and capturing the Soviet capital.

Whether through design (which was possible but quite unlikely) or incompetence, the Soviet forces were not, however, where the German High Command expected them to be. It is impossible to determine precisely how many troops the Red Army had at or near the front lines on the first day of battle—not even the Soviet commanders seemed to know for certain—but the best estimates are that there were 170 divisions, nearly 3,000,000 men (slightly more than half the Red Army's total infantry strength of 5,005,000) within four hundred miles of the western frontier. But two-thirds of these apparently were in the rear echelons and lacked adequate weapons anyway; along the border itself, the Wehrmacht enjoyed a crushing superiority in numbers.

By the time his troops crossed the border, Hitler was preparing to leave for the seclusion of his new spartan and heavily guarded command headquarters, the *Wolfsschanze* ("Wolf's Lair"), a wooden hut surrounded by a military complex located deep in a forest outside Rastenburg in eastern Prussia. Earlier that evening, the Fuehrer had composed a letter to Mussolini, explaining that he was invading Russia to neutralize the eastern threat to Germany's security, so he could subsequently concentrate upon bringing Britain to its knees. "Whatever may come, Duce, our situation cannot become worse as a result of this step; it can only improve. . . . Let me say one more thing, Duce. Since I struggled through to this decision, I again feel spiritually free. The partnership with the Soviet Union, in spite of the complete sincerity of our efforts to bring about a final conciliation, was nevertheless often very irksome to me, for in some way or other it seemed to me to be a break with my whole origin, my concepts and my former obligations. I am happy now to be relived of these mental agonies." (Hitler did not ask Mussolini for Italian troops; by now he knew better than that. But Mussolini decided to send some blackshirt units anyway, to share in the expected glory.)

Goebbels, who had dedicated himself during the preceding weeks to the arduous task of selecting a new fanfare for the campaign and supervising the printing of propaganda leaflets to be distributed to the German soldiers, chatted with the Fuehrer one hour before the invasion began. "The Fuehrer seems to lose his fear as the decision comes nearer," Goebbels noticed in unmixed admiration. "It is always the same with him. He relaxes visibly. All the exhaustion seems to drop away." At dawn Goebbels sat before a radio microphone and read the Fuehrer's proclamation to the German people: "I therefore decided today to lay the fate and future of the German Reich in the hands of our soldiers. May God help us above all in this fight!" The words were broadcast over loudspeakers in every major city of occupied Europe that morning.

As the reports of German air assaults upon Sebastopol, Kiev, Odessa, Belostok, Brest-Litovsk, and scores of towns in the Baltic states and the western Ukraine poured into Soviet military headquarters between three and four o'clock that morning, Marshal Zhukov finally summoned the courage to telephone Stalin and advise him of the rapidly deteriorating situation on the border. Stalin said nothing for a long time; all Zhukov could hear was the dictator's heavy breathing at the other end of the line. "Do you understand me?" Zhukov asked. Another long silence. Finally Stalin instructed Zhukov to go to the Kremlin. At 4:30 A.M., the Politburo assembled for an emergency meeting. Pale, stunned, Stalin sat at the table absentmindedly cradling a pipe in his hand. "We must immediately phone the German Embassy," he suggested, hoping that it was all just a bluff or a terrible mistake. Someone told Stalin that Count Friedrich von der Schulenburg, the German ambassador to Moscow, had already requested a meeting with Foreign Minister Molotov.

One hour later, Schulenburg strode into Molotov's office and calmly started to recite a prepared list of German grievances against Russia. As he read, Molotov interrupted and shouted at him furiously, "Heavy bombing has been going on for three hours!" Unruffled, Schulenburg—who himself had learned of Hitler's invasion plans only within the last few days—continued with his recitation for ten more minutes, and then, after an awkward moment of silence, a weary Molotov replied with undisguised bitterness, "It is war. Your aircraft have just bombarded some ten open villages. Do you believe we deserved that?"

Molotov returned to the Politburo meeting and announced, "Germany has declared war on us." Stalin sank deeper into his chair and said nothing. No one said anything, until Zhukov proposed that the frontier units of the Red Army launch an immediate counterattack. Since a large percentage of these forces already had been flattened by the German assault, there was more than a little wishful thinking involved in such an order. Nevertheless, Stalin still clung to the preposterous hope that the German incursions along the frontier were nothing more than a limited action designed by devious Nazi generals to provoke the Soviets into an act of aggression. So he issued a directive ordering the Red Army to resist enemy penetration while stopping short of pursuing any enemy forces into German territory. Stalin also insisted that the radio link with the German Foreign Ministry should remain open; incredibly, he hoped that the Japanese government might be able to mediate an end to the fighting before it got out of hand.

Outside the Kremlin, the rest of the Soviet Union apart from the immediate war zone remained unaware of the invasion—radio stations had been playing their customary Sunday morning music programs—until 12:15 that afternoon, when Molotov's flat, emotionless voice came over the radio and through the loudspeakers in the streets of the cities and towns. He spoke with a pronounced stutter. "Without any claim having been presented to the Soviet Union," the foreign minister announced, "without a declaration of war, German troops attacked our country, attacked our borders at many points and bombed from their airplanes our cities. . . . This unheard-of attack on our country is perfidy unparalleled in the history of civilized nations . . . The Soviet government has ordered our troops to repulse the predatory assault and to drive the German troops from the territory of our country. . . . Ours is a righteous cause. The enemy shall be defeated. Victory will be ours." Stunned, the Russian people absorbed the news in a trancelike silence.

Visiting the resort of Sohumi on the Black Sea, Erskine Caldwell saw "crowds grouped silently around loudspeakers in the streets, staring unbelievingly at the quivering mouths of the amplifiers. At first there was an expression of incredulity on the faces of the people which gradually gave way to fear. But fear was short-lived. It soon wore off completely." Caldwell and his wife, photographer-journalist Margaret Bourke-White, spent that afternoon driving around the collective farms in the region, and Bourke-White noticed that "everywhere there were scenes of the most enthusiastic patriotism. Collective farmers were pledging their support, their work, their lives, to victory of their country. But everywhere there was one question on everyone's lips: where did Great Britain stand?"

Churchill and Eden were spending the weekend at Chequers. At four o'clock on Sunday morning, Jock Colville was awakened by the jangling of a telephone and a message from the Foreign Office with the news from Russia. Since he had standing instructions that Churchill should never be woken up early unless the Germans were actually invading England, Colville waited until eight o'clock to inform the Prime Minister. When he learned the news, Churchill smiled with grim satisfaction and said, "Tell the B.B.C. I will broadcast at 9 to-night." Several minutes later, Churchill's valet waltzed into Eden's room bearing a large cigar on a silver salver, and announced, "The Prime Minister's compliments and the German armies have invaded Russia."

Churchill, the quintessential Bolshevik-hater, had long ago decided that he would give Stalin all available aid to help defeat the Nazis; on the evening of June 21, just hours before the invasion, the Prime Minister had told Colville that "I have only one purpose, the destruction of Hitler, and my life is much simplified thereby. If Hitler invaded Hell I would make at least a favourable reference to the Devil in the House of Commons." His conviction was not altered in the least by the bad tidings brought by Sir John Dill from London. The Luftwaffe had already destroyed a vast number of Soviet airplanes that had been caught unprepared and unprotected on the ground, Dill said, and the Wehrmacht was driving forward with ferocious efficiency. Sir John expected the Soviet Union to surrender in six or seven weeks; "I suppose they will be rounded up in hordes," he added glumly.

Without consulting his cabinet ("I knew that we all felt the same on this issue," he later explained), Churchill spent the rest of the day composing the public statement he would make that evening. "Mr. Churchill listened, questioned, considered, all through the day," recalled Beaverbrook. "Occasionally he sat in the garden in the hot sunshine. Then again he would stride to his office, restless to a degree." He did not finish writing the speech until twenty minutes before nine, and Eden—who had gone off to the Foreign office to assure Maisky of British support—was quite put out when he learned he would not have a chance to review it before Churchill spoke.

"I have taken occasion to speak to you tonight because we have reached one of the climacterics of the war," Churchill told the British people. "At four o'clock this morning Hitler attacked and invaded Russia. . . . All this was no surprise to me. In fact I gave clear and precise warnings to Stalin of what was coming. I gave him warning as I have given warning to others before. I can only hope that this warning did not fall unheeded. All we know at present is that the Russian people are defending their native soil and that their leaders have called upon them to resist to the utmost." No one, Churchill acknowledged, had been a more consistent foe of communism over the past twenty-five years: "I will unsay no word that I have spoken about it. But all this fades away before the spectacle which is now unfolding. The past with its crimes, its follies and its tragedies, flashes away. . . . My mind goes back across the years to the days when the Russian armies were our allies against the same deadly foe," though now they faced an enemy whose unbounded capacity for evil far surpassed the crimes of the German Empire of Kaiser Wilhelm II:

> Hitler is a monster of wickedness, insatiable in his lust for blood and plunder. Not content with having all Europe under his heel, or else terrorized

into various forms of abject submission, he must now carry his work of butchery and desolation among the vast multitudes of Russia and of Asia. . . .

So now this bloodthirsty guttersnipe must launch his mechanized armies upon new fields of slaughter, pillage and devastation. . . . It is not too much to say here this summer evening that the lives and happiness of a thousand million people are now menaced with brutal Nazi violence. That is enough to make us hold our breath. . . .

Then Churchill reaffirmed that the British government had "but one aim and one single, irrevocable purpose. We are resolved to destroy Hitler and every vestige of the Nazi regime. From this nothing will turn us—nothing. We will never parley, we will never negotiate with Hitler or any of his gang. We shall fight him by land, we shall fight him by sea, we shall fight him in the air, until with God's help we have rid the earth of his shadow and liberated its peoples from his yoke. Any man or state who fights on against Nazidom will have our aid." ("This does not mean very much," muttered Raymond Lee. "They made the same promise to Poland, which was too remote for them to reach. Russia is even more remote than Poland.")

"The Russian danger is therefore our danger," concluded Churchill, "and the danger of the United States, just as the cause of any Russian fighting for his hearth and home is the cause of free men and free peoples in every quarter of the globe. Let us learn the lessons already taught by such cruel experience. Let us redouble our exertions, and strike with united strength while life and power remain."

As he climbed into bed early Monday morning, tired but content, Winston kept saying how bloody marvelous it was to have Russia in the war against Germany.

Roosevelt said nothing. He was asleep when news of the invasion first reached Washington, and apparently no one thought it was important enough to wake him. For two days the President acted as if nothing had happened, although Under Secretary of State Sumner Welles did issue a statement on Monday, June 23, expressing the administration's distaste for both Nazism and communism while reaffirming its opinion that Nazi Germany posed a far more serious threat to American security than the Soviet Union. Hence, Welles said, "any defense against Hitlerism, any rallying of the forces opposing Hitlerism, from whatever source these forces may spring, will hasten the eventual downfall of the present German leaders, and will therefore redound to the benefit of our own defense and security." (One enterprising reporter reviewed Welles's statement and checked off the adjectives he had applied to Nazi Germany: "treacherous," "murderous," "deceitful," "brutal," "dishonorable," "hostile," and "desperate." It was not exactly the moderate diplomatic language of a neutral.)

But there was no unequivocal American declaration of support for the Soviet Union, no ringing Churchillian rhetoric about embattled Russian peasants bravely defending their homeland from the bloodthirsty Nazi hordes. Roosevelt was much too cautious for that; "it would be just like him," Ickes grumbled, "to wait for some expression of public opinion instead of giving direction to that public opinion." And public opinion in America clearly was uneasy about the prospect of even a de facto alliance with the Soviet Union. Unlike Britain, the United States was not yet fighting for its life, and could still afford to be choosy about its friends. This was precisely what Hitler had counted on; one of his objectives in invading Russia was to ingratiate himself with conservative Anglo-American capitalist circles by smashing a regime they despised more than they hated Nazism. And to a limited degree, that is what happened in the U. S. "Many people in the United States are confused," reported Assistant Secretary of State Breckinridge Long. "The great majority of our people have learned that Communism is something to be suppressed and the enemy of our law and order. They do not now understand why we can align ourselves even a little with it."

American isolationist spokesmen wasted no time in hammering home the point. "The entry of Communist Russia into the war certainly should settle once and for all the intervention issue here at home," proclaimed the America First executive committee on June 23. "The war party can hardly ask the people of America to take up arms behind the red flag of Stalin." "I would a hundred times rather see my country ally herself with England, or even with Germany with all her faults," argued Lindbergh, "than with the cruelty, the godlessness, and the barbarism that exist in Soviet Russia." "That call to sacrifice American boys for an ideal has been made as a sounding brass and a tinkling cymbal," huffed Herbert Hoover. "For now we find ourselves promising aid to Stalin and his militant Communist conspiracy against the whole democratic ideals of the world. Collaboration between Britain and Russia . . . makes the whole argument of joining war to bring the four freedoms a gargantuan jest." Senator Bennett Clark of Missouri asked rhetorically whether anyone could "conceive of American boys being sent to their deaths singing 'Onward Christian Soldiers' under the bloody emblem of the Hammer and Sickle," and Burton Wheeler made a particularly repugnant reference to Churchill and Roosevelt sleeping in the same bed with "bloody Joe" Stalin. Even Harry Truman admitted that he still thought the Soviets were "as untrustworthy as Hitler and Al Capone."

At Roosevelt's first press conference following the invasion, on June 24, the President made it perfectly clear that he preferred to let Britain take the lead in supporting the Soviets. Asked if he had anything to add to Welles's statement, his response was as typically flippant and evasive as Churchill's was melodramatic and forthright:

THE PRESIDENT: Oh, I think that covers it pretty well. Of course we are going to give all the aid that we possibly can to Russia. We have not yet received any specific list of things, and of course people must realize that when we get a list it will be probably a list of such character that you can't just go round to Mr. Garfinckel's and fill the order and take it away with you. (laughter) . . .

Q: What kinds of things shall we give them, Mr. President?

THE PRESIDENT: Oh, socks and shoes, and things like that. What you can get at Garfinckel's you can probably get at once. That is the easiest way of putting it. When it comes to planes and things that have to be made, we have got orders that will take a long time to fill, of course. Now on the deliveries of those orders, nothing could be changed, of course, except by agreement.

Actually, the question of American aid to Russia was entirely academic for the moment, since there was no way to get the supplies over there; besides, many American military experts and political analysts predicted that the Soviets would surrender in six weeks or less anyway. "I expect little of the Russian resistance, so that any resistance they do put up will be clear gain," wrote Walter Lippmann in a typical comment. "We, on our part, must act on the assumption that they can't last through the summer."

For a few weeks it appeared that they would not. On the first day alone, twelve hundred Soviet aircraft were destroyed as they sat parked in neat rows on the airfields, completely unprotected; within five days, more than half of the Soviet Air Force was gone. "The enemy was surprised by the German attack," noted Halder dryly. "As a result of this tactical surprise, enemy resistance directly on the border was weak and disorganized, and we succeeded everywhere in seizing the bridges across the border rivers and in piercing the defense positions (field fortifications) near the frontier." In Berlin, Howard K. Smith listened as official Nazi radio correspondents, stationed with the troops on the border, provided a blow-by-blow account of the invasion. "The Russians were already collapsing," recalled Smith. "It wasn't war. It was a national sport and the reporters were right on the sidelines giving a play-by-play description."

On June 23, the Red Army began its retreat from Poland and the Baltic states it had seized in 1940. In Vilna, the city where Menachem Begin had spent the early days of 1941 in Lukishki prison, the streets were full of men and women fleeing with children in their arms and bundles of food on their backs. Oddly, recalled the young writer Chaim Grade, the people made almost no sound as they moved; "it was quiet in the streets, awesomely quiet—as though all the people had been transformed into nocturnal shadows on the walls of a dark room illumined from without by a blood-red glow." Outside of town, Red Army trucks laden with officers' wives and furniture sped past the silent column, heading for sanctuary somewhere to the east. The retreating mass hardly looked up to watch them pass. "Soldiers from decimated regiments, peasants from burned-out villages, workers from deserted factories, all mingle together in this multitude—one body with many hands and feet, with bearded faces, caps tilted back. A barefoot peasant from a *kolkhoz* walks beside a Red Army major, also barefoot, his boots tied together and slung over his shoulder to make walking easier. Next to a soldier cradling a lowered rifle is a peasant woman cradling a suckling infant."

"In a few weeks we shall be in Moscow," shouted Hitler exultantly. "There is absolutely no doubt about it. I will raze this damned city to the ground and I will make an artificial lake to provide energy for an electric power station. The name of Moscow will vanish forever." German forces practically ran across western Russia in the first week of the invasion, as infantry divisions often covered twenty-five miles in a day. General Gunther Blumentritt kept in his mind a vivid picture of those late June days, "particularly the great clouds of yellow dust kicked up by the Russian columns attempting to retreat and by our infantry hastening in pursuit. The heat was tremendous, though interspersed with sudden showers which quickly turned the roads to mud before the sun reappeared and as quickly baked them into crumbling clay once again."

Upon learning of the unbroken string of devastating Soviet defeats, Stalin reportedly grew hysterical and wailed, "All that Lenin created we have lost forever," and broke down completely. For several days, as his subordinates struggled to stem the onrushing Nazi tide, he refused to see or talk to anyone. (Some historians have claimed that Stalin never lost control of himself or his grip on the direction of the war; but the argument that a certifiable psychotic, one of the most wildly unstable paranoid personalities of the twentieth century, would have reacted calmly, rationally, and efficiently to the impending destruction of his life's work is ludicrous on the face of it.)

If Stalin maintained a low public profile, however, his uncontrollable rage was soon plainly in evidence. General Pavlov, the discredited commander of the battered and broken Soviet armies in the central sector—crushed by Bock and Guderian's fearsomely efficient panzers—was brought back to the capital, tried for treason, and executed. (Pavlov had spent the night before the invasion at a theater in Minsk, attending a gala production of the comedy *The Wedding at Malinovka;* presumably it was the last amusing time he ever knew.) Their nerves shattered, other Russian officers took their own lives rather than face Stalin's anger and a firing squad. On the southwestern front, where Khrushchev was in charge of the defense of Kiev, the Soviet positions were collapsing in total disarray. "On

the fifth or sixth day of the war," Khrushchev remembered, "the commander of the Front and I sent General Vashugin, one of the members of the
Military Council, to instruct a tank corps in how its resources could best
be used. When he returned Vashugin called on me. He was in a very
strange and confused state. 'Everything is lost. Everything is just as it was
in France. This is the end of everything. I am going to shoot myself,' he
declared. I tried to restrain him: 'You're crazy—pull yourself together!'
But before I had time to do anything, he drew his pistol and shot himself,
right there in front of me."

In the Vatican, Pope Pius XII watched in exultation as the German
armies mercilessly bludgeoned the despised Soviet regime. The overwhelming weight of the currently available historical evidence indicates
that Pius never considered the Nazis as great a threat to civilization and
the Catholic Church as the Communists. That was why His Holiness joined
with Hitler in considering Operation Barbarossa a twentieth-century crusade against the infidels; and that was why, in the course of a radio message
on June 29—one week after the invasion began, while it still appeared to
be devastatingly successful—Pius gratefully proclaimed: "Certainly in the
midst of surrounding darkness and storm, signs of light appear which lift
up our hearts with great and holy expectations—these are those magnani-
mous acts of valour which now defend the foundations of Christian culture, as well as the confident hope in victory."

Suddenly, with no advance warning, at 6:30 A.M. on July 3, nearly two
weeks after the invasion began, Stalin's voice came over the loudspeakers
in the streets and squares of cities and towns across Russia. (The government had seized all privately owned radio sets at the start of the war.) It
was the first time the infallible leader had spoken to his people in three
years. Listeners thought that he sounded exhausted, at the end of his rope;
he spoke slowly and without emotion, his breathing was labored, and he
stopped frequently to drink from a glass that his trembling hand once
bumped against the table in front of him. "Comrades, citizens, brothers
and sisters, men of our army and navy, my words are addressed to you,
dear friends." Although Stalin admitted that "grave danger overhangs our
country," he blamed the Russian defeats on German treachery. He asked
the Russian people to sacrifice everything to save Mother Russia, to form
partisan bands behind the German lines, to mobilize the traditional People's Guard reserve in support of the soldiers at the front. "The enemy is
cruel and implacable. He is out to seize our lands, watered by the sweat
of our brows, to seize our grain and our oil, secured by the labour of our
hands. He is out to restore the rule of the landlords, to restore tsarism.
. . . to germanize [the peoples of the Soviet Union] to turn them into the
slaves of the German princes and barons." But if retreat could not be
avoided, the enemy should find nothing but pain and scorched earth as he
advanced:

In case of a forced retreat . . . all rolling stock must be evacuated, the enemy must not be left a single engine, a single railway car, a single pound of grain or gallon of fuel. The collective farmers must drive all their cattle and turn over their grain to the safe keeping of the authorities for transportation to the rear. All valuable property, including metals, that cannot be withdrawn, must be destroyed without fail. . . . In areas occupied by the enemy, guerrillas, mounted and on foot, must be formed; sabotage groups must be organized to combat the enemy, to foment guerrilla warfare everywhere, blow up bridges and roads, damage telephone and telegraph lines, set fire to forests, stores and transport. In occupied regions conditions must be made unbearable for the enemy and all his accomplices. They must be hounded and annihilated at every step, and all their measures frustrated.

("The bloodsoaked murderers won't find anything," predicted Solomon Lozovsky, head of the Soviet Information Bureau. "They won't be able to find enough wood to build a fire to thaw their frozen hands. They won't be able to find enough food to keep them alive.") Stalin told his people that he and his comrades of the State Committee of Defense had now assumed complete control of the war effort. And he called upon a united Russian nation to "rally around the party of Lenin and Stalin, and around the Soviet government, so as to render self-sacrificing support to the Red army and Red navy, to demolish the enemy and secure victory."

Still the Wehrmacht tore its way through Russian territory. Day after day, the Kremlin issued communiqués that said simply, "We continued to fight the enemy on all fronts," but after four weeks of fighting the Wehrmacht had clawed a path across four hundred miles of Russian territory. Then the twice-daily Soviet communiqués began to read, "Our armies, having inflicted on the enemy heavy losses in men and equipment, have retreated to more advantageous positions, thus shortening the front line." Communications between the Kremlin and the armies at the front— wherever it was—were in a shambles. The Red Army was losing equipment (much of which admittedly was worthless to start with) at an alarming rate; by July 13, Guderian's panzer divisions in Army Group Center had captured 2,500 tanks and 1,500 artillery guns. "The bend of the Dnieper is marked by complete destruction and panic," reported a Berlin radio commentator. "Blazing fields, burned-out oil tanks, dead horses, slaughtered pigs and other animals, destroyed tractors, plundered stables and shops—these are the traces of the retreating Bolsheviks."

By the second week of July, the Nazis were two days ahead of the breakneck pace established by Napoleon a century before. The German High Command estimated that the Wehrmacht had taken approximately 500,000 prisoners and destroyed nearly half of the Soviet divisions near the frontier. (As long as the Wehrmacht was winning, the statistics provided by German military communiqués usually were reliable.) When Stalin summoned Khrushchev to Moscow to explain the Red Army's uninterrupted string of defeats in the Ukraine even after he (Stalin) had given specific orders forbidding any further retreats, Khrushchev was appalled at the dictator's ravaged emotional state and loss of self-control:

> I saw Stalin as I entered the command post, which was then located in the Metro station in Kirov Street. . . . He was completely demoralized. He was sitting on a couch, looking quite exhausted; when I approached, he returned my greeting perfunctorily, shook my hand and asked how things were going. I told him that things were in a bad way—we were in retreat. He retorted grumpily: "Well, they used to talk of Russian gumption. Where is it now, that Russian gumption?" I felt utterly exasperated. How could Stalin . . . reproach the Russian people . . . when it was he, Stalin, who was to blame for the defeat that our troops had suffered because he had destroyed our cadres and had failed to exploit all the material resources that had been created by the labour and sweat of the Soviet people . . . ?

On August 5, the Germans conquered the Soviet stronghold of Smolensk at the head of the Dnepr, only two hundred miles from Moscow, taking 310,000 more prisoners and destroying another 3,200 tanks. The Red Army in the central sector appeared to be very near to collapse. Morale plummeted; over and over again, in one confrontation after another, Russian troops facing battle for the first time broke and ran as soon as the German shells began falling around them. Whole regiments were lost in the chaos of retreat; Soviet losses in mechanized armor became so great that entire tank corps simply vanished.

In the northern sector, Leeb had rolled through the Baltic states in July meeting virtually no resistance; instead, the Red Army simply retreated eastward, giving up territory in vast chunks while maintaining most of its units more or less intact. But by the middle of August, the Wehrmacht had advanced far enough to cut the vital railway link between Moscow and Leningrad, and was now in the process of closing a giant pincers around the second largest city in Russia. Two hundred thousand people were evacuated from Leningrad to the east before the siege began, but three million more men, women, and children remained trapped inside the city. (On two separate occasions, composer Dmitri Shostakovich refused opportunities to leave with most of the other notable resident musicians and artists, vowing instead to stay and defend his native city.) Nearly all the ablebodied young men in Leningrad were drafted and sent to the front, which meanwhile drew closer every day; women, students, and old men were put to work digging tank ditches and defensive fortifications around the city's perimeter.

In the south, Rundstedt had driven to the outskirts of Kiev and was besieging the city, which Stalin obdurately—and tragically—still refused to relinquish.

At this point, if the German army had treated the occupied regions of western Russia with even a minimum of dignity and established viable puppet regimes there, it might well have managed to shorten the war and certainly would have struck a mortal blow at the power and authority of the Soviet regime in those areas. There were many non-Russian nationalists and fervent anti-Communists in the villages of the Ukraine, in eastern Poland, and in the Baltic states who hated Stalin and welcomed the advent of the Wehrmacht—at first. Surely, they thought, the civilized Germans would treat them more sympathetically than the oppressive and corrupt Stalinist regime which had waged such a cruel and unremitting campaign of terror against them over the past decade. Most of the people in these regions knew nothing of Nazism save what the official Soviet news agencies had told them, and in the months following the Nazi-Soviet rapprochement of 1939 all the references had been complimentary; there had been no mention of the wholesale starvation of civilians and the eradication of liberties and the degradation of the human spirit in the nations of Nazi-occupied Europe.

So the Russian people suspected nothing when the black-uniformed SS *Einsatzgruppen,* accompanied by doctors, chemists, transportation experts, engineers, guards, carpenters, and administrators, came to the cities and the villages. With them they brought gasoline, collapsible barracks, and tools for digging. They drew forced labor from the towns to set up their camps, and often they made little distinction between Jews and the rest of the civilian population, primarily because the Nazi ideology classified all Slavs as subhuman. "We do not want to conquer the souls of the Jews, Catholics, and Marxists," proclaimed Reinhard Heydrich, head of the SS security guard. "We want to conquer living space. We want to settle Germanic peasants on that land." The first step was to divide the population against itself. In the Ukraine, the *Einsatzgruppen* encouraged the Jew-hating nationalist militia to instigate pogroms and slaughter thousands of Jews and confiscate their property. In other areas the SS did the work itself. Jews were marched into the forests, stripped naked, and shot. Some were still alive when they buried them. A thirteen-year-old Polish boy watched as "the police surrounded the streets and houses. My father hid my mother, my two sisters, and me, making us lie on the ground, then he went off by himself to see what was happening. We never saw him again. . . . The first people were taken into the forest in cars. . . . A very big grave was dug, and people were thrown into it after being shot." It took more than twenty-four hours to fill the pit. At night, a dozen women and children who had been lying under a pile of corpses crawled out of the grave and ran away. By the end of August, one of the four SS detachments boasted that it had killed 229,052 Jews.

Some Jews and suspected Communists were not murdered right away; rounded up and crammed into ghettoes or concentration camps, they died more slowly of disease, starvation, or exposure. Russian prisoners of war suffered a similar fate. Since Wehrmacht headquarters insisted upon reserving all available rail transport for its own use, to ship supplies to the front and return its own wounded for medical treatment in Germany, there was no way the hundreds of thousands of captured Russian soldiers could be removed to proper accommodations in the west, and so they were placed in crude barbed-wire enclosures that lacked even the most primitive facilities; tens of thousands perished during the last few months of 1941 alone. Bormann instructed the camp commandants to wrap the corpses in oilcloth or tarpaper and stack them tightly in mass graves. (It was later estimated that more than half the Russian prisoners of war in German camps—several million men—died between 1941 and 1945.) After the war, German generals acknowledged that rumors of the fate of Russian prisoners may have encouraged the Red Army to fight to the death. But it should be pointed out that there was no less savagery on the other side, where NKVD agents reportedly carried out their own massacres of Ukrainian political prisoners and suspected saboteurs behind the Soviet lines. Thousands of terrified and bewildered Russian civilians were trapped in the middle of this battle between two equally brutal ideologies.

In mid-July, the Luftwaffe bombers—which now had the luxury of using captured Soviet airfields only several hundred miles away from the capital—visited Moscow for the first time. The city had spent the past four weeks preparing for the blitz, carrying out practice air raid drills and teaching its citizens how to extinguish incendiaries. All children, no matter how young, were evacuated to camps at least sixty kilometers away; government officials wrote identifying marks on each child's hands, but when they arrived at the camps the children were given baths and the marks disappeared, and so the mothers had to be called to sort out the confusion. Great concentric circles of searchlights ringed the city, and antiaircraft batteries disguised with thick coverings of leaves and branches were stationed in nearby clearings. Subway stations were fitted with steel doors against the bombs and air filters against gas attacks. Signs with huge black arrows pointed the way to the shelters, and a constant stream of instructions came over the loudspeakers in the parks; when the government made it mandatory to take cover in a public shelter, thousands of Muscovites stood in line every evening, waiting patiently for the shelters to open. Once you had sat down in a shelter, you were not permitted to stand up or move around for the rest of the night (and there were armed guards to see that you did not).

Sergei Prokofiev watched the nightly raids from his rented dacha in Kratovo, one hour's drive outside of Moscow. "Enemy planes often circled above us at night and lit up the whole area with flares to get their bearings," the composer wrote in his memoirs. "Then Soviet fighters would appear. The skies were flooded with glaring searchlight beams. These shafts of light, the green tracer-bullets of the pursuit planes, and the Germans' yellow flares created a scene of ominous beauty. . . . Occasionally a German bomber would crash, and, still loaded with its undropped bombs, would explode with a huge thundering." Like many Soviet artists, the fifty-year-old Prokofiev put aside the lighthearted project upon which he had been working (a three-act ballet of the fairy tale "Cinderella") and immediately began writing patriotic songs and marches, as well as an ill-fated symphonic suite entitled *The Year 1941.* But his most ambitious project during that war-torn summer—indeed, of his entire career, judging by the time and effort he put into it—was an opera based upon Tolstoy's epic novel *War and Peace;* although Prokofiev had been thinking about writing such a piece for some time, the parallels between Napoleon's invasion and the German assault upon Russia finally convinced him that the challenge could be postponed no longer. What the war provided in inspiration, however, it took away in safety and comfort; almost at once, Prokofiev's work was interrupted when he was evacuated (leaving his wife and children behind) from the capital in August, along with other Moscow musicians and artists, to the small town of Nalchik in the northern Caucasus.

Stalin, on the other hand, let it be known that he was staying in Moscow to face the danger with his people; once Erskine Caldwell spotted him in the backseat of his shiny black bulletproof Packard, speeding sixty miles an hour down a one-way street in the wrong direction. The dictator reportedly spent his evenings in a private shelter—complete with a green-covered conference table for Politburo meetings during the raids—deep underneath the Kremlin.

In an almost comical effort to camouflage vital targets, Soviet officials had repainted the city until Moscow resembled a bad exhibition of expressionist art. The walls of the Kremlin now appeared to be rows of apartment houses; zigzag lines covered Mokhovaya Street between the United States Embassy and the Kremlin; canvas drapes painted with false passageways hung over the Bolshoi Theater; there was a country cottage where the red and black marble of Lenin's mausoleum used to be. "Never in wartime Spain or France had I seen anything like it," reported a vastly amused Henry Cassidy. "The camouflage could have fooled no one in an air-raid but an over-imbiber struggling home through the black-out from a vodka party. It might have deceived for a moment a frightened German private, trying to make his way through a strange city in street fighting, but it certainly meant nothing to a German bombardier, flying thousands of feet above the city, blinded by the searchlight rays and shell bursts rising from the well of blackness below him." Nevertheless, Moscow apparently escaped relatively unscathed, partly because the Germans expected to take the city from the ground. After the last large-scale German air raid in April 1942, Soviet authorities reported that only 1,088 people had died during the raids, with nearly two-thirds of the casualties occurring in the first thirty days.

Having placated the Nazi war machine with shipments of oil, rubber, and strategic metals while the Wehrmacht was overrunning western Europe and while the Luftwaffe blitzed Britain from September 1940 to May 1941, the Soviet leaders now innocently turned to London for succor in their hour of peril. This volte-face struck some British politicians as the ultimate in Slavic chutzpah. "It is no use recriminating," said Colville, "but after all when we were fighting alone and for our lives the Russians were actually supplying Germany with the material means of attacking us." Although Churchill, as has been demonstrated, was not unsympathetic to the Soviet plight, there was no immediate diplomatic rapprochement between the two nations whom Hitler had joined together. After two decades of mutual suspicion, neither could bring itself to speak the word "ally"; "partner" seemed to be better suited to the moment. Churchill dispatched a military mission to Moscow to ascertain precisely what the Soviets needed in the way of equipment, but, he said, he was not about to give up significant quantities of precious supplies when a "harassed and struggling Britain" was struggling to keep its own armies equipped; nor could he agree to the diversion of American defense matériel upon which he had based his plans for the future. For their part, the Soviet military authorities remained wary of their capitalist guests when the British military mission arrived at the Kremlin. "Molotov will tell us nothing beyond what is in the official communiqués," complained one miffed British official. "Now, in their hour of need, the Soviet Government—or at any rate Molotov—is as suspicious and unco-operative as when we were negotiating a treaty in the summer of 1939."

To help break the ice, Churchill opened a personal correspondence with Stalin (a procedure that wounded the amour propre of the sulky Anthony Eden, who thought that all correspondence with foreign heads of state should go through his office). "I was well aware that in the early days of our alliance there was little we could do," recalled Churchill, "and I tried to fill the void by civilities," which no doubt comforted the overwrought Russian leader as he wandered in and out of the depths of depression. "We are all very glad here that the Russian armies are making such strong and spirited resistance to the utterly unprovoked and merciless invasion of the Nazis," chirped Churchill on July 7, in his best "wish you were here" tone. "There is general admiration of the bravery and tenacity of the soldiers and people. We shall do everything to help you that time, geography, and our growing resources allow. The longer the war lasts the more help we can give." (This was a subtle hint not to expect very much of anything in the near future.) "We have only got to go on fighting to beat the life out of these villains." Churchill also moved his most efficient lieutenant, Beaverbrook, to the Ministry of Supply, to spur the production of additional tanks and munitions that might eventually be sent to Russia.

In the Kremlin on July 12, a noticeably weary Stalin signed a vaguely worded agreement with Sir Stafford Cripps, pledging Britain and the Soviet Union to assist each other in the war against Nazi Germany and promising not to conclude a separate peace. Someone asked when the protocol should go into effect. "Immediately," replied Cripps enthusiastically. The next day *Pravda* carried the text of the agreement (complete with photos of the signatories) on its front page. On July 18, Stalin sent his first personal message to Churchill, thanking him for his expressions of support, and reminding the Prime Minister—in case he had not noticed—that hundreds of thousands of Russian troops were fighting desperately for their lives at that very moment. ("It may not be out of place," the Soviet leader remarked plaintively, "to inform you that the position of the Soviet forces at the front remains strained.") Stalin's main objective was—and remained—to encourage Churchill to open a second front, either in western Europe or along the northern edge of the continent.

For his part, Churchill loved the idea of launching smash-and-grab hit-and-run raids on the French or Norwegian coast while Hitler's attention was turned to the east. Now was the time, he told Colville, "to make hell while the sun shines." But Winston had no intention of committing Britain to a full-scale invasion of the Continent in force in 1941, particularly while the coastline bristled with cannon, beach mines, and pillboxes; in fact, he could not envision any assault in force until 1943 at the earliest. "I beg you however to realise limitations imposed upon us by our resources and geographical position," Churchill reminded Stalin on July 20. ". . . You must remember that we have been fighting alone for more than a year, and that, though our resources are growing, and will grow fast from now on, we are at the utmost strain both at home and in the Middle East by land and air . . ." The unimaginative and ultracautious British chiefs of staff were even more pessimistic than the Prime Minister about the prospects for active military ventures on the Continent. Like Dill (and unlike Churchill), most of the War Office experts feared that Russia would not last until the winter, and they insisted upon retaining all available manpower and supplies on the home front in case Hitler once more turned his eyes across the Channel after disposing of the Red Army. Churchill's private secretary complained that the chiefs "seem convinced that their function is to find reasons against every offensive proposal put forward and to suggest some anodyne, ineffective alternative. Their excuse may be shortage of equipment, shipping and manpower; but they show no disposition to improvise or to take risks." The R.A.F. did consent to initiate more frequent raids upon western France, but the navy obdurately resisted pleas to undertake action along Russia's Arctic coast. "The Navy suffer from excessive caution," complained Anthony Eden's private secretary. "They always want to be safe two moves ahead." The army's Home Forces, meanwhile, were sitting on their hands, as they had been doing all spring. "There was never such idleness as in the Home Forces at that time," recalled Anthony Burgess. "They were bored with excessive repetition of drill movements, naming of parts, lectures on syphilis, exhortations about security and the danger of camp-followers. Their evenings were filled with booze and fights. Occasionally a local teacher would give a lecture on beetles, with lantern slides, or a travelling officer would give a reassuring account of Germany's shortage of oil."

Certainly the British public appeared willing to support at least a minor military diversion on the Continent. "The world-shaking din of events on the Eastern Front only accentuates the sad fact that things are all too quiet on the Western Front," reported Mollie Panter-Downes, "though most Britons would give their back teeth to see a series of brisk harassing operations up and down the length of the enemy-occupied coastline. They feel that such a move, in addition to having a healthy effect on the sit-here-and-wait-to-be-invaded jinx which has been perched on many English shoulders since last summer, is the very least that a grateful nation can do to relieve a bit of the pressure on Russia, for whom admiration is steadily increasing." British opinion, which (except for some diehard Conservatives) had never really believed that the Soviets were as black as they were painted, accepted the new partnership with alacrity. (In the Bahamas, the Duke of Windsor still entertained a few doubts: "The war has taken a queer and unexpected turn hasn't it," he wrote to his aunt Bessie, "and I guess we must all be prepared eventually to adopt 'the hammer and the sickle' as our national emblems.") Enthusiastic Londoners turned out in droves to welcome the Russian military mission that arrived in Britain in early July; dance bands played endless swing renditions of "The Volga Boatman"; vodka sales skyrocketed. Newspapers carried pictorial essays on Madame Maisky's horticultural prowess and her praiseworthy efforts to keep the Soviet Embassy's flower bowls full of the Old World cottage roses so beloved of British gardeners.

As Russian resistance continued into August, euphoria in London reached such a point that many Britons began to hope (unrealistically) for victory by Christmas. Churchill grew positively ecstatic with each passing week; Hugh Dalton heard the Prime Minister gloat over the military experts who had predicted that the Soviets would collapse in the first few disastrous days. "He is confident that Russian resistance will continue through and beyond the winter," noted Dalton in his diary, "though they may lose more ground. He thinks that Leningrad may fall, but not Moscow. Never in any nine weeks, either of this war or the last, have the Germans lost anything like these casualties." George Bernard Shaw agreed. "The war situation is amusing though horrible," the irrepressible old radical wrote to a friend that summer. "We have lied to one another about Russia so frantically for twenty years that we have persuaded ourselves that the Bolsheviks, far more than the Nazis, are a gang of thieves and murderers who must be scattered like chaff the moment they come up against a civilized army led by gentlemen. . . . And now," he said, "Hitler is fighting like a rat in a corner without a dog's chance of getting even as far as Napoleon did . . ."

At the beginning of August, the Nazi advance had ground to a temporary halt as Hitler and his generals engaged in a heated debate about the future path of the invasion forces. From the time the formal planning for Barbarossa began, most of Germany's professional military men had recommended that the Wehrmacht concentrate upon a powerful, quick thrust toward Moscow. Hitler, on the other hand, had always cast a covetous eye toward the Ukraine and its bountiful resources of oil and grain; he also entertained a somewhat irrational hatred for Leningrad, the birthplace of the Revolution and a highly visible symbol of industrial progress under the Communist regime. So Hitler and the generals had compromised and decided upon the initial three-pronged advance for the first month of the campaign, at which time they planned to reconsider their ultimate objectives in light of the invasion's progress. But by the end of July, the Red Army had not collapsed as it was supposed to, despite its staggering losses in men and material. The Nazi blitzkrieg had swept hundreds of miles into Russian territory, but Soviet units trapped—apparently hopelessly—behind the German lines obstinately refused to surrender; in some places, the Reds had even launched desperate and bloody counterattacks that bought precious time to allow the Soviet forces behind the lines to regroup. Four weeks had elapsed, and then six weeks, then eight, and still the Wehrmacht had not yet captured Leningrad, or Moscow, or even Kiev. The momentum of the advance slowed as it gradually became clear that there simply were not enough German soldiers to continue the invasion along such a broad front at the same breakneck pace without dangerously dispersing the front-line troops and reserves that were available.

At this point, the German soldiers in the field began to pay the price for the failure of Nazi military intelligence to assess Soviet defensive strength accurately. "I realized soon after the attack was begun that everything that had been written about Russia was nonsense," Rundstedt said several years later. Although the Red Army units along the frontier had not been well equipped at the start of the invasion, Soviet munitions plants were continually producing more and better weapons—including the fearsome, heavily armored T-34 tank and the Katyusha rocket launchers that absolutely terrorized the German troops—and the Kremlin had begun the process of mobilizing a reserve manpower base from the eastern provinces that numbered approximately ten million semitrained men.

A seemingly endless stream of Soviet reinforcements was constantly being shuttled toward the front. "The battle is harder than anything before," admitted Guderian. "It will take some time yet." Halder agreed: "It is becoming ever clearer that we underestimated the strength of the Russian colossus not only in the economic and transportation sphere but above all in the military. At the beginning we reckoned with some 200 enemy divisions and we have already identified 360. When a dozen of them are destroyed the Russians throw in another dozen."

Nor could the finely tuned German military machine function with its customary efficiency amid the uncooperative and antiquated Russian system of transportation. Roads that were barely passable in the best of times degenerated into treacherous quagmires following the heavy rains that struck western Russia in early June. The General Staff discovered, somewhat belatedly, that between many Russian towns there was only a single railway line (which meant that traffic heading in the opposite direction had to wait until an oncoming train cleared the tracks) and that German locomotives would not run on the broad-gauge Russian tracks; since there was a dearth of suitable rolling stock in the areas the Wehrmacht conquered, hundreds of miles of Russian rails—and the sidings, and the repair sheds—had to be converted to the standard Central European gauge, a painstaking and time-consuming process. Trucks carrying fuel supplies often consumed most of their cargo on the way to the distant front. Already showing dangerous signs of wear from the springtime campaigns in the rugged Balkan mountains, German tanks broke down with increasing frequency in the brutish Russian terrain, and replacement parts could not be brought to the front quickly enough to allow the panzer divisions to operate at anything approaching peak efficiency. Already overextended, the Wehrmacht's supply lines were growing longer with each new push into the vast Soviet interior. The absence of suitable airfields inside Russia prevented the Luftwaffe from providing adequate air cover for ground operations. And organized bands of partisans, armed with homemade weapons and fired with an unquenchable determination to inflict whatever damage they could, already were forming behind the Nazi lines—the inevitable retaliation for the SS policy of terror and mass murder.

On the home front in Germany, foreign correspondents thought they discerned the first serious rumblings of discontent as the grandiloquent visions of swift and total victory, promised in the early days of the Russian campaign, failed to materialize. A poor harvest (the result of a cool, wet summer) combined with the diversion of food supplies to the troops at the front to produce shortages of potatoes, vegetables, and meat in the cities. The official Nazi Party newspaper in Berlin, the *Volkischer Beobachter*, advised loyal citizens of the Reich to eat daisies (rich in minerals and vitamin C) and substitute other leafy green plants as fillers in soups, gravy, and vegetable dishes. Mothers were instructed to spend joyous, profitable Sundays with their children gathering edible wild flowers in the woods. Howard K. Smith, who had resigned from UP and was working with Harry Flannery as a CBS radio correspondent in Berlin, noticed that "little items, little amenities, were disappearing from the shops and big items were growing scarcer. The number of letters returned to their senders from the front every day, marked 'Fallen' in red ink, increased portentously. . . . Notices appeared in the newspapers and on boardings calling for fresh volunteers for the *elite* German infantry regiment *Grossdeutschland*. More and more little independent shops were shut and on their doors was hung the information: 'Closed because personnel called up.' "

Now the Resistance, particularly within the German armed forces, began to regain some of its lost momentum. The savage, repugnant cruelties of the SS *Einsatzgruppen* in Russia provoked recurring nightmares for some Wehrmacht officers who witnessed or took part in them; observing a mass murder in progress, one general turned to Himmler and said, "Look at the eyes of those men. Observe how shattered they are. These men's nerves are ruined for the rest of their lives." In mid-August, former ambassador Ulrich von Hassell recorded the story of a young army officer who received an order to shoot "three hundred and fifty Russian civilians, allegedly partisans, among them women and children, who had been herded together in a big barn. He hesitated at first, but was then warned that the penalty for disobedience was death. He begged for ten minutes' time to think it over, and finally carried out the order with machine-gun fire. He was so shaken by this episode that, although only slightly wounded, he was determined not to go back to the front." It was the first time that the Wehrmacht's hands had been tainted with the blood of Nazi atrocities. Added to the heavy losses in the east, especially among officers from old noble Prussian families, and Hitler's stubborn refusal to heed his generals' strategic recommendations over the future course of Barbarossa, a growing number of military officials became willing to discuss privately—though not yet act upon—the possibility of a coup.

Opponents of the Nazi regime were convinced that Hitler's Russian gamble had doomed Germany to defeat, and many took heart from the impending catastrophe. "In their immense vanity, Satan's own have overreached themselves, and now they are in the net, and they will never free themselves again," asserted Friedrich Percyval Reck-Malleczewen, the anti-Nazi scion of a Prussian Junker family. "That is the fact, and this it is that rejoices my heart."

"It's all over now, isn't it?" suggested Dietrich Bonhoeffer to a friend in Switzerland. "I mean that we are at the beginning of the end. Hitler will never get out of this." When someone asked Bonhoeffer what he prayed for in the present situation, he replied, "If you want to know, I pray for the defeat of my country, for I think that is the only possibility of paying for all the suffering that my country has caused in the world." Convinced that the Nazi war crimes would invite divine retribution upon the fatherland, Admiral Canaris turned away from his official Abwehr duties and sought solace in the comforts of mysticism.

But the Wehrmacht had only paused to catch its breath before plunging farther into the vast Russian heartland. On August 17, German troops reached the Dnepr. The panzers of Leeb's Army Group North were approaching the gates of Leningrad. To deliver the knockout blow before the fierce Russian winter set in, Generals Brauchitsch, Halder, Bock, and Guderian favored an all-out drive toward Moscow to demolish the main Red armies, capture vital transportation and industrial objectives, and demoralize the Soviet leadership. But Hitler, who complained that "my generals know nothing about the economic aspects of war," perversely resurrected his initial strategic plan and issued a directive on August 21 ordering Army Group Center to split into two separate groups and turn abruptly to the north, toward Leningrad, and to the south, toward the tempting oil fields and granaries of the Ukraine. "The most important objective to attain before the onset of winter," the Fuehrer proclaimed, "is not the capture of Moscow but the taking of the Crimea, the industrial and coal-mining areas of the Donets basin and the cutting off of Russian oil supplies from the Caucasus. In the north it is the locking up of Leningrad and the union with the Finns." So Guderian's panzers (much to the general's dismay) spun off and slogged southward through the mud to support Rundstedt's siege of Kiev, where 700,000 Soviet soldiers were caught in a steel trap.

21

"John Doe" and Joe D.

"We must always remember that America is composed of many millions
of people who left Europe because they hated it, and that there
are many millions of Italians and Germans whose hearts go out
to their mother countries. . . . What we don't fully understand
in this country is the actual dread of the American soul at
being split. There is always the fear that they will cease to
be a nation, and this is the fear which Roosevelt understands
so perfectly and which he guides with such genius."
—HAROLD NICOLSON, AUGUST 1941

Bertolt Brecht left Helsinki on May 13, 1941, bound for the United States. "Where Columbus succeeded, I'll be successful too," he promised a friend, "though I won't have it as easy as he did." A self-imposed exile from Nazi Germany, Brecht had made his way northward across Scandinavia, pausing first in Denmark, then in Sweden, and finally arriving in Finland in the early months of 1940. By the time he worked his way through the inevitable and seemingly interminable bureaucratic red tape to obtain his coveted American visa, the route west through Europe had been cut off; so Brecht boarded a train for Moscow with his wife, their two children, and his mistress. He remained only a few days in the capital, departing on May 30 aboard the Trans-Siberian railway for the eastern port of Vladivostok. Six days later, he and his family sailed for America on the Swedish freighter *Annie Johnson.* Had he remained in Moscow several weeks longer, he likely would have been arrested with the other German nationals in the Soviet Union following the invasion of June 22; most of those caught in Stalin's retributive roundup were shut away in Siberian detention camps, where they perished before the end of the war.

After six anxious weeks at sea, on the lookout for Japanese submarines, the Brechts landed at San Pedro, California, on July 21. The writer rented a house in Los Angeles near the Paramount studio. In no time at all, Brecht discovered that he despised Southern California. "In almost no other place was my life more difficult than here in this mortuary of easy going," he wrote in his journal several days following his arrival. He hated the superficiality, the neon glamour and the "cheap prettiness" of life in L.A.; he felt anxious and ill at ease in the city he called a "Tahiti in metropolitan form." "The intellectual isolation here is enormous," he complained in misery. "In comparison to Hollywood, Svendborg [Denmark] was a world center." He said he felt like "a chrysanthemum in a coal mine." To make matters worse, Brecht was having a terrible time finding a decent loaf of bread. Forty-three years old, short and gaunt, with two days' stubble of beard that never quite covered the scar on his left cheek, his close-cropped brown hair cut in a severe line across his forehead, dressed in loose-fitting pants and a workman's old flannel shirt, clenching a cheap cigar in his rotting teeth, Brecht was depressed as hell and unable to write anything worthwhile in the summer of 1941. He did not recover from his severe case of culture shock until the following year, when he finally discovered numerous kindred spirits among the ever-growing Hollywood community of refugees from eastern and Central Europe, a remarkable group that included actors Peter Lorre, Oscar Homolka, Paul Henreid, Marlene Dietrich, and Luise Rainer, director Fritz Lang, and director-screenwriter Billy Wilder.

In fact, the influx of creative talent from abroad soon turned wartime Hollywood into a city that expatriate German novelist Thomas Mann (who was also living in Southern California at the time) modestly described as "a more intellectually stimulating and cosmopolitan city than Paris or Munich had ever been," all of which went far toward convincing the flamboyant Russian-born neoclassical composer Igor Stravinsky to make Los Angeles his home, too, when he decided to settle in the United States in late 1940. An elfish little man who almost invariably appeared in public wearing white socks and sandals, Stravinsky received a steady stream of offers from movie producers who wanted him to score their films. Most of them he turned down with barely a second thought; instead, he spent much of the spring and summer of 1941 in a more patriotic pursuit, writing his own variations on "The Star-Spangled Banner." (Although Stravinsky's version of the national anthem was successfully performed in Los Angeles in October 1941, there were those who failed to appreciate his efforts. When the composer tried to conduct a performance of the piece in person in Boston on January 14, 1944, the Boston police confiscated his arrangement from the music stands and gruffly informed Stravinsky that Massachusetts law forbade any "tampering" with national property.)

Like Bertolt Brecht, Charlie Chaplin—the man who had made more people laugh than anyone else in history—spent the better part of 1941 in a creative funk after his disastrous visit to Washington in January. Separated from his wife, Paulette Goddard ("It's just one of those sad things, son," Charlie explained to Charles, Jr. "That's life for you."), Chaplin spent most of his time outside the studio, getting to know his sons, joking with Greta Garbo, battling the Internal Revenue Service, and hosting tennis parties where his Hollywood friends could rub elbows over crumpets, chicken sandwiches, and tea with sports celebrities such as Don Budge, Fred Perry, Big Bill Tilden, and Helen Wills (not yet Moody). Two of Chaplin's fellow Englishmen, Alfred Hitchcock and Cary Grant, suffered their own torment through the summer while shooting *Suspicion,* a film based on a Francis Iles suspense novel in which a woman committed suicide upon discovering that she was pregnant with the offspring of her evil, murdering husband. Since the studio, in its infinite wisdom, doubted that Grant's fans would accept him as a cold-blooded killer (although Grant seemed to enjoy playing the part), Hitchcock had to shoot the film with several endings, leaving the central question of Grant's character—was he a murderer or not?—unresolved until test audiences decided which ending they preferred. (Unfortunately for the sake of cinematic art, they chose the happy ending, which made a mockery of the entire film by blaming the wife's suspicions on a bad case of paranoia.) Production of the movie seemed to drag on interminably through the summer while the studio dithered over the question of the ending; Joan Fontaine (the wife) reportedly grew bored with the whole project and was quite put off by Grant's aloof demeanor; Hitchcock fumed and fussed over the disparity between his relatively small salary and those of his two stars; and the perfectionist Grant (who was already peeved because he had not been nominated for an Oscar for his work in *Philadelphia Story*) constantly haggled with nearly everyone on the set over a host of minor production details.

Another film that suffered from an unsatisfactory ending was Frank Capra's latest exercise in populist social commentary, *Meet John Doe,* a melodramatic response to Nazi Germany's strong-arm, storm-trooper mentality. Working with a dream cast of Gary Cooper, Walter Brennan, Barbara Stanwyck, Spring Byington, and Edward Arnold, Capra began the story by launching the unknown "John Doe"—an unemployed minor league ballplayer described by Capra as "a bindle stiff, a drifting piece of human flotsam as devoid of ideals as he was of change in his pocket"—on a whirlwind political career based upon the slogan "Love Thy Neighbor." Suddenly, Capra jerked the rug out from under Doe (played by Cooper) by revealing that his chief financial backer, a newspaper publisher (Arnold), is a closet Fascist who has been using Doe to get himself elected president. Doe then tries to warn his followers that their trust has been betrayed, but they turn against him instead. Disillusioned, he climbs to the top of City Hall on Christmas Eve and threatens to jump off, whereupon reporter Stanwyck implores him not to give up everything he has fought for . . . and then the director had no idea how to get him down. "For seven-eighths of the film," recalled Capra, "[writer Robert] Riskin and I felt we had made The Great American Motion Picture; but in the last eighth, it fizzled into The Great American Letdown." After experimenting with four different endings during a trial run in six cities, Capra received a letter from someone who signed himself "John Doe," and suggested that the only way to get Cooper down from the tower was to have other "John Does" implore him to come down and continue the fight for truth, justice, and the anti-Fascist way. So Capra shot a fifth ending that was incorporated into the final version, but he remained vaguely dissatisfied. As far as Capra was concerned, his own uncertainty reflected the confusion of current events in the real world. "What our film said to bewildered people hungry for solutions was this, 'No answers this time, ladies and gentlemen. It's back to the drawing board.' And the people said, 'Oh, nuts!' "

Gary Cooper was Hollywood's hottest male star in 1941, though Mickey Rooney (first) and Clark Gable (second) still led the official box-office polls. (The rest of the top ten included Abbott and Costello, Bob Hope, Spencer Tracy, Gene Autry, Cooper, Bette Davis, and Judy Garland.) *Time* magazine, never reluctant to resort to hyperbole, named Cooper "the most popular man in the nation." A native of Montana, Cooper had spent two restless years at Grinnell College in Iowa before embarking upon unsuccessful careers as a cartoonist, a commercial artist, and an electric sign salesman. He said he moved to Los Angeles "so I wouldn't freeze to death," and got a few jobs as an extra in cowboy movies in the mid-1920s while he was trying to decide what to try next. His big break came when he stole a scene in the Oscar-winning World War One aviation drama, *Wings.* Paramount signed him to a long-term contract, and his stock soared with every new picture. Offscreen Cooper moved quickly into the fast lane of Hollywood society, keeping company with (in rapid succession) actresses Clara Bow and Lupe Velez, and socialite Countess Dorothy di Frasso, whom he accompanied on an extended sojourn to Rome in 1930. But his increasingly sophisticated life-style never quite overpowered the down-home, taciturn, natural personality his fans loved so much. By 1941, the forty-year-old actor had settled down in a white Georgian mansion in a fashionable section of Los Angeles with his wife of eight years, the former Veronica "Rocky" Balfe, stepdaughter of the head of the New York Stock Exchange.

Ernest Hemingway thought Cooper was a grand fellow. The two outdoorsmen became boon companions when they met at Sun Valley, Idaho. "Cooper is a fine man; as honest and straight and friendly and unspoiled as he looks," Hemingway wrote to a friend. "We have good times together. He is married to a nice girl too who plays a hell of a game of tennis. . . . Cooper is a very, very fine rifle shot and a good wing shot. . . . We are going to get some gloves and box." (Cooper couldn't play baseball worth a damn, though. After they signed him to play the role of Lou Gehrig in *The Pride of the Yankees,* studio executives were appalled to receive a scouting report that said that their star "couldn't run, couldn't get the knack of fielding, and threw like a girl." "I'm not even sure how many bases there are," admitted Cooper. "I know one's home.")

Hemingway sold the movie rights for *For Whom the Bell Tolls* to Paramount—for a record $100,000—expressly to allow Cooper to play the male lead opposite Ingrid Bergman, who had just finished filming the unsuccessful and unlamented *Dr. Jekyll and Mr. Hyde* with Spencer Tracy and was languishing throughout the summer in Rochester, New York, with her husband Peter and her little girl, Pia. (Lest anyone think that Hemingway was overly impressed with movie celebrities in general, he had absolutely no use for the pretty boys of Hollywood. When he met Robert Taylor at Sun Valley, Ernest decided that Taylor was "sort of a little miniature man. Everything about him would photograph up into manhood and very handsomely, but the actual model that the lens enlarges is neither very gay nor very impressive." Hemingway was only slightly more charitable to Taylor's wife, Barbara Stanwyck, whom he described as "truly ugly in the flesh, wears grease on her face to dinner and is very nice with a good tough Mick intelligence.")

Gary Cooper's most memorable performance in 1941 was his portrayal of America's greatest of the First World War in Warner Brothers' *Sergeant York.* At first, Cooper hesitated to accept the role; the thought of playing someone who was still alive made him extremely nervous. He also felt uneasy playing love scenes opposite sixteen-year-old Joan Leslie, cast as York's girl friend; Cooper later said that every time he embraced Miss Leslie, he felt like a criminal. But Coop was the only movie actor the real Alvin York had ever cared for (York had turned down previous offers to film his life story, and he reportedly refused to give his permission to this project unless Cooper came with it), and so, after meeting the hero at his home in Tennessee, where York was chairman of the local draft board, Cooper reluctantly agreed to accept the challenge. (York promptly turned over the money he received for the screen rights to a local Bible school.)

In the sort of inter-studio swap that was typical of that era, Paramount loaned Cooper to Warner Brothers for one picture in return for Bette Davis's services in *The Little Foxes.* Warner's definitely got the better of the deal; released in July, *Sergeant York* turned out to be Hollywood's biggest moneymaker of 1941. It was also a resounding critical success. The New York Film Critics named Cooper the best actor of 1941, and the following spring he received an Academy Award as well. York himself thought Cooper's portrayal was "perfect." In less talented hands, the film might have turned into a rabble-rousing, jingoistic epic designed to appeal to the baser instincts of a nation on the brink of war. Instead, the strength of the movie resided in its detailed portrayal of the earthy life of the common people in the backlands of the South, where York was saved from a life of hell-raising and corn liquor by his saintly mother, his preacher, and his girl friend. In a moving transformation that once and for all established Cooper's reputation as a serious actor, York became a devout, God-fearing pacifist deeply troubled by the dilemma posed by the apparent necessity of violent struggle against evil, a "simple, deeply religious man who weighs his horror of killing against what he feels is the greater necessity to stop all killing."

At the other end of the box-office scale was the hard-luck champion of Hollywood in 1941, the incomprehensible George Raft, who turned down the male lead roles in *High Sierra, The Maltese Falcon,* and *Casablanca,* all in the same year. In each case, Humphrey Bogart took Raft's place. The picture that Raft did consent to make, *Manpower,* was notable only for the vulgar fireworks and fisticuffs that accompanied its production, when Raft repeatedly hurled verbal abuse at his co-star, Edward G. Robinson, because he thought Robinson was fooling around with Marlene Dietrich, upon whom Raft had his own carnal designs. Exasperated beyond endurance, Warner Brothers finally complained to the Screen Actors' Guild about Raft's behavior, claiming that he had "directed toward [Robinson] a volley of personal abuse and profanity, and threatened the said Edward G. Robinson with bodily harm, and in the course of his remarks directed and applied to Mr. Robinson in a loud and boisterous tone of voice, numerous filthy, obscene and profane expressions."

Raft turned down the role of Sam Spade in *The Maltese Falcon* because he did not want to entrust his career to the inexperienced hands and camera of John Huston, a thirty-five-year-old screenwriter (whose credits included portions of *York*) who was making his directorial debut. On June 6, 1941, Raft formally informed Jack Warner that "I strongly feel that *The Maltese Falcon,* which you want me to do, is not an important picture and, in this connection, I must remind you again, before I signed the new contract with you, you promised me that you would not require me to perform in anything but important pictures." Besides, Raft knew that the story of *The Maltese Falcon* had been filmed twice before already and both movies had sunk without a trace. But Huston realized that the previous versions had strayed too far from the brisk language and dark, world-weary mood of the original Dashiell Hammett novel, and he was convinced that a faithful adaptation—with much of the dialogue lifted directly from the book—would be more successful. Having worked with Bogart on *High Sierra* (for which Huston wrote most of the screenplay), the novice director jumped at the chance to employ him on *The Maltese Falcon.* "Bogie was a medium-sized man, not particularly impressive off-screen, but something happened when he was playing the right part," Huston noted. "Those lights and shadows composed themselves into another, nobler personality." Similarly, Bogart welcomed the opportunity to work with Huston after their collaboration on *High Sierra,* the film that finally allowed Bogie to break out of the series of bad B movies in which Jack Warner had buried him. In fact, Warner still wanted to employ Bogart exclusively as a heavy ("He's a tough guy, not a lady's man," Warner grumbled); in the summer of 1941, Bogart was just emerging from a three-month studio suspension for refusing to play the role of Cole Younger in the notably nondescript *Bad Men of Missouri.*

"I came very well prepared to my first directorial assignment," recalled Huston in his autobiography. *"The Maltese Falcon* was a very carefully tailored screenplay, not only scene by scene but set-up by set-up. If it was to be a pan or dolly shot, I'd indicate it. I didn't ever want to be at a loss before the actors or the camera crew. I went over the sketches with Willy Wyler. He had a few suggestions to make, but, on the whole, approved what he saw. I also showed the sketches to my producer, Henry Blanke. All Blanke said was, 'John, just remember that each scene, as you shoot it, is the most important scene in the picture.' That's the best advice any young director could have."

Although Bogart (who was having a little domestic trouble at the time with his temperamental wife, actress Mayo Methot) often reported to work in the mornings with a dreadful hangover—his usual breakfast routine consisted of cigarettes, orange juice, and coffee, after which he would promptly throw up and then consume more coffee—the shooting of *The Maltese Falcon* proceeded with nary a hitch. Huston had assembled a remarkably cohesive and sympathetic cast. It was the screen debut for sixty-one-year-old Sydney Greenstreet, a 285-pound British actor best known for playing butlers on Broadway. "He was perfect from the word go," said Huston, "the Fat Man inside out. I had only to sit back and take delight in him and his performance." Warner's originally proposed Geraldine Fitzgerald for the role of Brigid O'Shaughnessy, but they settled for Mary Astor, a free-lance actress then in her mid-thirties; Huston called her "the enchanting murderess to my idea of perfection." Peter Lorre was one of the immensely talented refugees from Central Europe who enhanced the quality of artistic life in Hollywood in the late 1930s and early 1940s. Elisha Cook, Jr., who played the part of Wilmer, the young gunsel, lived by himself in the Sierra Nevada, catching trout and tying flies between films. "When he was wanted in Hollywood, they sent word up to his mountain cabin by courier," said Huston. "He would come down, do a picture and then withdraw again to his retreat."

At the end of the day, Huston, Bogart, Astor, Lorre, and character actor Ward Bond often gathered at the Lakeside Country Club for drinks, dinner, and conversation. "We all thought we were doing something good," Huston said, "but no one had any idea that *The Maltese Falcon* would be a great success and eventually take its place as a film classic." The last hurdle was cleared when executive producer Hal Wallis persuaded the studio not to rename the movie *The Gent from Frisco.* Huston had brought the picture in two days ahead of its sixty-day production schedule and slightly under its budget of $381,000. Despite the studio's failure to support it with an adequate publicity campaign, it received excellent reviews—one critic said that Bogart had a "face that seems to have been eroded and battered by harsh words and blunt instruments"—and did great box-office business right from the start. Finally realizing that he had a hit on his hands, Jack Warner promptly asked if Hammett could write a sequel for $5,000 or less. (Hammett, who was busy adapting Lillian Hellman's play *Watch on the Rhine* for the screen, rejected the offer.)

With ticket receipts from *Sergeant York* and *The Maltese Falcon* pouring into its corporate coffers, 1941 was a banner year for Warner Brothers. RKO was not quite as fortunate. In fact, when people in Hollywood talked about building air raid shelters, someone suggested that everyone should head for the RKO studios, where they hadn't had a hit for years. They laughed at RKO for permitting Orson Welles (whom the gossipmongers sarcastically dubbed "Little Orson Annie") to spend $750,000 on a film that remained on the shelf for three months while studio executives debated whether to junk it, or release it and risk the threat of lawsuits from William Randolph Hearst. Through all the months of anxious waiting, Welles's health deteriorated; he suffered from chronic asthma and back pain, his weight ballooned to 218 pounds in spite of the diet pills he swallowed like candy, and he appeared to be on the verge of nervous collapse.

Finally, on May 1, *Citizen Kane* made its debut at the Palace Theater in New York, after Radio City Music Hall refused to show it. Critics who understood what Childe Orson had wrought praised it as a magnificent creative achievement. *The New Yorker* called *Kane* an "extraordinary film" and celebrated its defiance of cinematic conventions: "Something new has come to the movie world at last." *Time* magazine considered *Kane* "the most sensational product of the U.S. movie industry," Hollywood's "greatest creation," "a work of art created by grown people for grown people." *Life* claimed that "few movies have ever come from Hollywood with such powerful narrative, such original technique, such exciting photography"; *Newsweek*'s critic hailed *Kane* as probably "the best picture" ever.

But *Citizen Kane* was a financial disaster. After nine weeks in New York, the movie had lost over $18,000. Unwilling to defy the still powerful Hearst, some distributors refused to carry it. Audiences seemed disconcerted by Welles's unconventional camera techniques, the jarring cuts between scenes, the shock effects that Welles pulled out of his bag of tricks. "People were too scared of it to even know what it was," Welles said later. It won only one Oscar, for best screenplay; at the Academy Award ceremonies in the spring of 1942, the movie community reportedly booed or laughed whenever *Kane* was mentioned. When it was shown at

Churchill's private movie theater at Chequers in July 1941, the Prime Minister was so bored that he walked out before the movie was over. In October, Welles began shooting *The Magnificent Ambersons,* but this time RKO kept the Boy Wonder under stricter control.

One of the hottest starlets in Hollywood in 1941 was Orson Welles's future wife, Rita Hayworth, née Margarita Cansino, a sensuous Latin dancer who received her first big break playing opposite Jimmy Cagney and Olivia de Haviland in the turn-of-the-century period comedy *Strawberry Blonde.* After she turned in an equally stunning performance in *Blood and Sand* (starring Tyrone Power), the Quigley Poll named Hayworth its "Star of Tomorrow." Her fame as a sex symbol was assured when *Life* magazine featured Rita in its August 11 issue, in a pictorial layout that included the famous cover photo of Hayworth kneeling on a bed, wearing nothing but a slinky nightgown of satin and lace and an inviting look. Eventually the photo became one of the best-selling pinups of World War Two, although the most popular cinema goddess among American soldiers in 1941, according to a *Life* survey, was Dorothy Lamour. Believing that an unexamined survey was not worth mentioning, *The New Yorker* decided that the soldiers' choice of Lamour represented a "longing for a female creature encountered under primitive conditions and in a setting of great natural beauty and mystery. . . . She should be in a glade, a swale, a grove, or a pool below a waterfall. This is the setting in which every American youth first encountered Miss Lamour. They were in a forest; she had walked slowly out of the pool and stood dripping in the ferns. . . . Her body, if concealed at all, is concealed by a water lily, a frond, a fern, a bit of moss, or by a sarong—which is a simple garment carrying the implicit promise that it will not long stay in place. For millions of years men everywhere have longed for Dorothy Lamour. Now, in the final complexity of an age which has reached its highest expression in the instrument panel of a long-range bomber, it is a good idea to remember that Man's most persistent dream is of a forest pool and a girl coming out of it unashamed, walking toward him with a wavy motion, childlike in her wonder, a girl exquisitely untroubled, as quiet and accommodating and beautiful as a young green tree. That's all he really wants. He sometimes wonders how this other stuff got in—the instrument panel, the night sky, the full load, the moment of exultation over the blackened city below . . ."

Presumably few draftees kept pictures of Lucille Ball over their beds or in their dreams that summer. A Gallup poll in March revealed that 40 percent of theatergoers claimed they had never seen Miss Ball in a movie, despite the fact that she had made more than thirty-five films. Two-thirds of those polled were unable to identify her from a photograph, and only 58 percent were even aware that "Lucille Ball" was the name of an actress. "It is apparent that so far as the great majority of theatergoers are concerned, Lucille Ball is still a more or less unknown quantity," concluded George Gallup in a marked understatement. "My personal opinion is that she is going to be grievously handicapped by her age . . . Perhaps the most encouraging [!] feature of audience reactions . . . is the prevalence of comments to the effect that she is common, cheap, a hussy, vulgar, coarse . . . or cute, a sweet dish, nice shape, sex appeal, just a blonde, and a homebreaker." What Gallup presumably was trying to say, before he got caught up in this backhanded compliment, was that movie fans saw Ball as a woman of the people, and not a stuck-up ingenue; it was a quality that would help propel her to stardom when television brought actresses into viewers' living rooms. But in the autumn of 1941, her studio, the unfortunate RKO (still reeling from the losses on *Citizen Kane*) was thinking of dismissing her from its rolls.

Gossip columnists had their hands full all summer: they whispered that Lucy and Desi's marriage was already on the rocks; Katharine Hepburn was dumping director George Stevens for her co-star in *Woman of the Year*, Spencer Tracy; twenty-year-old Gene Tierney eloped to Las Vegas to marry Count Oleg Cassini; Brazilian bombshell Carmen Miranda had danced her way through *That Night in Rio* sans underwear; Clark Gable and Carole Lombard were getting a divorce or perhaps Carole was dying of some incurable disease. ("I ain't dying and I ain't divorcing Clark," Lombard replied tartly. "I simply ain't any of the things they say.") On July 26, nineteen-year-old Judy Garland ran off to Las Vegas to marry bandleader David Rose. Garland's story revealed the darker side of Hollywood; after years of being fed pep pills to keep her awake, sleeping pills to knock her out, and black coffee and cigarettes to keep her weight down while Louis B. Mayer ran her through eighteen-hour days, Garland was "overworked, overmedicated, and underfed." After she and Rose returned to L.A., Judy got pregnant. Her mother and the studio persuaded her to have an abortion. Four days later, she was back in rehearsals for her next movie. She was always lonely and at night she could not sleep.

Few dedicated movie fans were surprised to learn in August that Erroll Flynn's wife had initiated divorce proceedings, but most of them had no idea just how perverted Flynn's sexual and political activities really were. Thirty-two years old, Flynn was at the height of his popularity, earning $6,000 per week at Warner Brothers. Behind the glitter, however, Flynn's health was fading fast; he was a drunkard and a drug addict who spent his evenings with teenage prostitutes. He was brought up on a charge of statutory rape after allegedly engaging in sexual relations with a fifteen-year-old girl during a sailing trip to Catalina. As a result of studio pressure and perhaps a well-placed bribe, the charges eventually were dropped. In an effort to evade the persistent attentions of his draft board, Flynn spent much of the latter half of 1941 in Mexico with a succession of young boys and German secret agents. (The FBI had a grand time uncovering the Nazi spy network in Latin America as it followed Flynn around.) When U.S. Navy officials objected to allowing Flynn onto the San Diego naval base to film *Dive Bomber,* Warner Brothers prevailed upon Secretary Knox to overrule the local commanders. Soon thereafter, detailed films of the base reportedly found their way to Tokyo.

While Hollywood hushed up its own worst scandals, the industry's censorship office enforced a rigid code of morality upon directors. In April, chief censor Will Hays (officially the head of Motion Picture Producers and Distributors of America, Inc.) issued a revised list of words and phrases to be omitted from all pictures: alley cat, hot, and broad (all when applied to a woman), fairy (when applied to a homosexual), fanny, lousy, nuts (except when meaning crazy), the sound known as a razzberry, "in your hat," buzzard (because it sounded like bastard), and cries of "Fire!" Of course, "damn" and "hell" were forbidden, as were blasphemous references to the Deity. As John Huston remembered, "there could be no hint of sexual perversion and no mention of drugs whatever. Adultery—indeed, fornication—had to be punished. . . . Kisses were not to be 'protracted.' 'Cleavage' had to be avoided scrupulously." And behind the censors loomed the bluestockings of the Legion of Decency, who had the temerity to condemn *Life Begins for Andy Hardy* (the eleventh entry in the terminally insipid series starring Mickey Rooney and Judy Garland) as "unsuitable for children," primarily because of a scene in which a married woman invites Andy to come to her apartment and "have some fun" while her husband is away. The Legion also condemned Greta Garbo's new film, *Two-Faced Woman,* citing its "immoral and un-Christian attitude toward marriage and its obligations; impudently suggestive scenes, dialogue, and situations; [and] suggestive costumes." The city censors of Boston and Providence banned *Two-Faced Woman* altogether, and Archbishop Spellman castigated it in a letter read at all masses in his archdiocese one Sunday. (Sometimes the men and women with the blue pencils got carried away, of course. The New York State Board of Censors banned *The Forgotten Village,* a documentary of peasant life in Mexico, because it showed such "indecent" and "inhuman" scenes as a mother nursing her baby and a close-up of a woman's face during childbirth. The censors subsequently were overruled by the State Board of Regents.)

Huston claimed that a talented director usually could find a way around any reasonable censorship restrictions, but occasionally a picture ran into serious trouble. When Warner Brothers attempted to film an adaptation of Henry Bellaman's novel *King's Row,* which dealt with such cheerful subjects as sadism, incest, and corrupt medical practices in small-town America, the Hays Office came down on the studio like a ton of bricks. In a letter of April 22, Jack Warner was informed that "before this picture can be approved under the provision of the Production Code, *all the illicit sex will have to be entirely removed* . . . the mercy *killing* will have to be *deleted;* and the several suggestions of loose sex . . . will have to be entirely eliminated." There could be "absolutely no suggestion or inference whatever of nymphomania" on the part of one of the main female characters, and there could be "no suggestion of nude bathing" among children. In a subsequent letter, the censorship board specifically prohibited the following dialogue:

> Then other times she's so different she scares me. She's so wild—as if all she wanted—When she's like that, she's—just a kind of excitement that I dread and wish for at the same time . . .

> Sure, bo—like me and Poppy Ross. Times I could eat her alive, and times I could throw her out on her ear . . .

> Funny she keeps after you. Generally, nice girls—you know what I mean. I think Cassie's nice all right, but generally—well, the ones I've known, like Louise—gosh, you just look at them and they act as if you're yanking their clothes off. Maybe old Cass is cooped up so much that when she does get loose she's all the way loose.

Ironically, Ronald Reagan's performance in this sordid melodrama earned him more critical praise than any other role in his film career.

When they weren't busy on the set, the Reagans spent most of the summer of 1941 supervising the construction of their three-bathroom, pine-paneled, $15,000 dream house (complete with a brick fireplace and a twenty-year FHA mortgage, with payments of $125 per month). Although it was far more luxurious than the average $3,000 American house, the Reagans' new home paled in comparison to Jack Benny's $60,000 mansion or Bob Hope's $80,000 estate. Actually, Ron could have afforded a more expensive house, but he prudently reasoned that an actor's salary could plummet in a hurry. It was the sort of sensible financial attitude his fans had come to expect; after all, Reagan preferred to wear tweed jackets and slacks offscreen, rather than any of the ten tailored suits that hung in his closet. "The Reagans are sensible folk," chirped one trade reporter. "They live on an allowance, and what they don't actually need goes smack into the bank every week and no nonsense."

Unavoidably, dramas inspired by the conflict overseas continued to pour out of Hollywood throughout the summer of 1941. *Underground* traced the activities of the members of a German resistance group who eventually were murdered by the Gestapo. *Man Hunt,* based on the novel *Rogue Male* by Geoffrey Household, followed a British big-game hunter (Walter Pidgeon) as he stalked Hitler at Berchtesgaden. In *One Night in Lisbon,* the ineffable Fred MacMurray played an American pilot flying bombers to Britain who encounters love (Madeleine Carroll) in an empty air raid shelter in London.

Occasionally filmmakers decided that they could best serve their country by putting their directorial talents at the disposal of the government. Veteran director John Ford, who had formed his own corps of technicians to record the history of the war in Europe, accepted a position as chief of the Field Photographic Branch of Wild Bill Donovan's fledgling intelligence service. Ford's first documentary endeavor, dramatically entitled *Sex Hygiene,* was an army instructional film warning draftees of the dangers of venereal disease, including the customary revolting shots of raving syphilitic lunatics and graphic depictions of male organs disfigured by all sorts of gruesome scars.

Frank Capra, too, journeyed to Washington that summer to offer his services to the defense effort. Previously unaware that the preparedness program was lagging far behind schedule, Capra received a rude awakening when he arrived in the capital. "From what I saw and heard," he wrote later, "we were so woefully unprepared for war that Army chiefs dreaded our possible involvement. They hinted that our troops only slightly outnumbered Washington's Continentals—and were as badly trained and ill-equipped. I asked to head a field Photo Company; the Signal Corps offered me a major's commission. Now I knew the Army was hard put." Undaunted, Capra signed up and returned to California to await his nation's call.

Capra was not alone in lamenting the nation's lack of preparedness. "Affairs are frankly in an appalling state," protested Raymond Clapper. Secretary Stimson admitted glumly that "at least a year will pass before we can have an Army and an air force adequate to meet the air and ground forces which could be brought against us." According to House Minority Leader Joseph W. Martin, Jr., the nation had actually produced only $3 billion worth of weapons during the past twelve months, although Congress had authorized $47 billion for armaments. The army reported that it had only 130 light tanks on hand, and it expected no appreciable additional production before October; consequently, only a relative handful of tanks had been sent to Britain, despite the British army's desperate need for armored vehicles. Critics complained that American 37-mm antitank guns had been adapted from obsolescent German models, and that their shells bounced harmlessly off modern tanks. Production of the new 90-mm antiaircraft guns, essential for protection against armored high-flying planes, was down to four guns per month. Small-arms ammunition was in short supply. The production of military aircraft actually *declined* during June and July, and nearly half of the planes that were being built were training planes rather than modern fighters or heavy bombers. Disappointed British newspaper editors complained that the anticipated torrent of Lend-Lease aid had dried up to a trickle. Despite a highly publicized (after the event) visit by Harry Hopkins to Moscow to demonstrate American solidarity with the Soviet Union and to obtain a shopping list of Russian arms requirements, the U. S. had sent the beleaguered Soviets the grand total of five bombers by the end of August. Nor had American military officials demonstrated a grasp of the fundamental strategic lessons taught by the war in Europe; George Patton was openly disgusted by the army's stubborn refusal to recognize the importance of speed and mobility in the age of the blitzkrieg. And it became painfully clear during the army's full-scale summer maneuvers in Tennessee—when antitank crews were forced to employ logs to represent the howitzers they did not possess—that most U.S. commanders still did not fully appreciate the need to integrate air power with infantry and armor.

In the summer of 1941, only 10 percent of the nation's productive capacity was being devoted to defense production; the preparedness program was plagued by apathy, bottlenecks, red tape, indecision, overlapping bureaucratic jurisdictions, and a shocking lack of coordination, all of which created what Senator Harry Byrd of Virginia termed a state of "general confusion and dangerous delay." At a time when the United States was supposed to be turning out unprecedented quantities of military trucks, tanks, and planes, Detroit produced instead nearly three million passenger automobiles in the first six months of 1941—23 percent more than in the same period in 1940, and only slightly under the all-time record established in 1929.

"A great many observers feel that the American people simply will not undergo even the home-front hardships and privations of war so long as they are technically at peace," reported *Newsweek.* "I can see we haven't got the spirit yet," observed William Knudsen, "probably because nobody has dropped a bomb on us." Other analysts were less charitable toward the public's noticeable apathy. "We grow more like the France that was every day, the France that died fat, unable to walk across the street because she had eaten too much," muttered disgruntled Washington columnist Samuel Grafton. But the public's attitude was also a direct result of the Roosevelt administration's failure to define its strategic objectives clearly. There was no unified concept of the military tasks the United States was trying to accomplish. "We are building, we find, a multipurpose Army and Navy," complained Raymond Moley, the well-known New Dealer-turned-columnist. "We are preparing for everything at once, every possible contingency. More, we are making these diverse and indefinite preparations at the same time that our old and new friends are draining away much of the matériel that we manage to put together. We are, literally, preparing for war in the Caribbean and in Alaska, in Iceland and Hawaii and other points west and east. . . . Afraid that we may presently be fighting the most intense specialist the world has seen since Alexander and his phalanxes, we are jacks of all trades in war."

Strikes continued to plague the preparedness program. The number of man-hours lost to walkouts in 1941 was still rising at a near-record pace, surpassed only by the violent labor conflicts that beset the chaotic postwar year of 1919. Frustrated by the powerlessness of federal mediation boards and alarmed by rising public discontent, several cabinet officers seriously advised the President either to deport or to deposit in concentration camps all workers who struck defense plants. Roosevelt himself finally reached the breaking point when the UAW local at the North American Aviation factory in Inglewood, California, defied government mediators and walked off the job in the first week of June, leaving production on some $200 million worth of defense contracts in limbo. It was such an irresponsible action that even national labor leaders condemned the walkout; the CIO quietly launched a drive to comb out Communist saboteurs and Nazi sympathizers from its ranks. Although it was not at all clear that he had the authority to do so, Roosevelt promptly ordered Stimson to take possession of the Inglewood plant. When strike leaders decided to defy the President's order, two battalions of soldiers with fixed bayonets pushed their way through the picket lines on the morning of June 9; within hours, most of the workers had returned to their jobs. Two months later, Roosevelt repeated this performance, seizing the Federal Shipbuilding and Dry Dock Company's yards at Kearny, New Jersey, following the onset of a strike that stopped work on navy and merchant vessel contracts totaling $500 million. And when two thousand CIO members struck an Alcoa plant in Cleveland, Selective Service Director Hershey hinted that the government might decide to draft some of the strikers: "The citizen who has been deferred because of the job he is performing in the national defense program cannot expect to retain the status of deferment when he ceases to work on the job for which he was deferred." In every instance, labor leaders capitulated for the time being, but they complained bitterly about the federal government's strong-arm (some said quasi-Fascist) union-busting tactics; still, administration optimists hoped that Hitler's attack upon the Soviet Union might do more than government coercion to stimulate production and curb the unbridled willingness of left-wing labor leaders to strike defense plants.

After visiting FDR at the White House in June, Noel Coward remarked crossly that "summer always seems to catch Washington unawares, to break over it like an awesome seventh wave, flooding it with sudden, sweltering discontent. There is air-conditioning, of course, and there are iced drinks and sun-blinds and electric fans, but even those fail to dispel, for me at any rate, a feeling that such breathless oppressiveness must herald a cosmic disaster, that some feckless star has changed its course and we are all about to frizzle, curl up and die." John Maynard Keynes noticed that Roosevelt seemed to be bothered even more than usual by the oppressive heat and humidity that pervaded the capital in June and July. (Roosevelt had an old-fashioned air conditioner in his bedroom, but the contraption made so much noise that it kept him awake, so he was no good for anything in the morning.)

Eleanor Roosevelt kept herself almost as busy as her husband. "Mrs.

Roosevelt seems terribly restless and nervous," reported Dorothy Dow, her social secretary. "If she doesn't wear herself to a frazzle it won't be her fault. . . . She is so different from what she used to be. She can't be still or alone for a minute." When she wasn't at Hyde Park driving her new gray Buick convertible, the First Lady (whom Dow said was "a lousy driver") was writing her newspaper column or warning housewives of impending shortages of household goods or traveling around the country supporting liberal causes (including the right of organized labor to strike), thus occasionally creating problems for her husband. But Eleanor's unimpeachable progressive credentials also provided the President with a useful tool in certain ticklish situations.

Since 1933, Roosevelt's civil rights record had consisted primarily of expressions of his own personal goodwill and the more tangible benefits of federal social programs that neither discriminated against blacks nor gave them preferential treatment. During the 1940 election campaign, FDR had pledged his support for further efforts to achieve racial "equality of opportunity," and even though the administration condoned "separate but equal" policies in the armed forces and within federal agencies, there is no reason to doubt that Roosevelt was sincerely sympathetic to the plight of black Americans. But when black leaders threatened to lead a mass march on Washington on July 4, 1941, to protest blatantly discriminatory hiring practices in defense industries, Roosevelt implored them to reconsider. Such an act would give the impression that blacks were trying to coerce the government into concessions at a time of national crisis; surely it would introduce another divisive issue into American life at a time when the need for national unity was paramount. Agitated, the President dispatched Eleanor as an envoy to persuade civil rights leaders to postpone or cancel the march. "I feel very strongly that your group is making a very grave mistake," she dutifully told A. Philip Randolph, head of the Brotherhood of Sleeping Car Porters and one of the organizers of the march. "I am afraid it will set back the progress which is being made, in the Army at least, towards better opportunities and less segregation." (In fact, the Army Air Corps had recently opened its doors to blacks for the first time with the formation of an all-Negro air squadron of thirty-three pilots, complete with twenty-seven planes—and white commanding officers, of course.) But Randolph and Walter White of the NAACP refused to budge until Roosevelt issued an executive order on June 25, establishing a Committee on Fair Employment Practices to ensure that defense contracts were administered on the basis of "full and equitable participation of all workers in defense industries, without discrimination because of race, creed, color, or national origin." Black leaders were disappointed that the committee enjoyed only limited enforcement authority, and most white Americans paid little attention to the entire incident, but the concession exerted under duress from the embattled President provided a precedent that had powerful repercussions over the next twenty-five years.

The fragile facade of American national unity was tested yet again when the administration asked Congress for authority to retain the draftees who were currently in the army beyond their original one-year term of service. Although reporters referred to the resulting furor as a debate over the merits of "the extension of the draft," the issue was not whether the government could continue to use the draft to supply its manpower needs. No one seriously argued that the army could rely on voluntary enlistments. The navy was having a hard enough time attracting qualified candidates, and finally was forced to resort to a newspaper recruitment campaign designed by the Madison Avenue advertising agency of Batten, Barton, Durstine, and Osborn ("Serve Your Country, Build Your Future, Get in the Navy Now"), testimonials by the comic-strip sailor, Popeye ("Sign up wit' me and you'll see th' lands of opportuniky and romansk!" and "The Navy's delicious cookin' builds ya up to a regular tower of Gibraltik!"), and newsreels featuring twenty-one glamorous New York models who cunningly explained the attractions of off-duty life at the Marine base at Quantico, Virginia. Besides, the available pool of healthy manpower was not as large as military officials had expected: approximately 45 percent of the men called for their draft physicals were deemed medically unfit for service. (Mississippi led the nation with a rejection rate of nearly 80 percent.) The leading causes of rejection were bad teeth, venereal disease, and tuberculosis. These statistics were an appalling indictment of the American health care delivery system; most of the men who failed their physical had not been under the care of a physician for years, and many had never seen a dentist. "We are faced with the cold fact that about 40% of the young men of our country at ages 21 to 35 are either considered physically unfit to enter training for military service or are fit for limited service only," reported Dr. George Canby Robinson, chairman of a national defense health conference. To make matters worse, the nation was facing a dangerous shortage of doctors; there were only 160,-000 practicing physicians in the United States in the summer of 1941, and experts predicted that the army would require at least 40,000 doctors of its own once it reached its projected manpower peak.

So the cheerful greetings from hundreds of local Selective Service boards would continue to brighten the lives of young Americans for the foreseeable future. But what Roosevelt now asked Congress to do was to extend the obligations of the men who had already served nearly a year in the army. (Actually, the President already possessed authority under the terms of the 1940 Selective Service Act to retain inductees after their original twelve-month term had expired "whenever the Congress has declared that the national interest is imperiled," so what Roosevelt really needed from Congress was a formal declaration to that effect.) The first group of draftees was scheduled to be released in September; in all, 987,000 selectees, National Guardsmen, and Reserve officers were eligible for a return to civilian status within the next twelve months. The idea of discharging more than half of the 1,443,500-man army and replacing experienced men with raw recruits sent military authorities into a panic; as Army Chief of Staff George Marshall explained under hostile questioning from distraught congressmen, such a graphic demonstration of American military "disintegration" would make the United States Army a laughingstock in the Western Hemisphere and might well encourage Japan to renew its aggressive activities in the Far East.

To emphasize the overriding importance of this issue, Roosevelt delivered a special message to Congress in which he warned the legislators and the people that the peril to America was "infinitely greater" than a year ago. During the course of the speech he also asked Congress for authority to induct an additional 900,000 men into the army. "Time counts," the President insisted. "Within two months, disintegration which would follow failure to take Congressional action will commence. . . . The responsibility rests solely with the Congress."

Predictably, isolationist leaders were outraged. Some swallowed their anger and acknowledged that Congress had no choice, that Roosevelt had taken the nation so far out on a limb that a failure to accede to his request would leave the United States dangerously exposed. The legislative representative of the American Legion, which was rapidly abandoning its opposition to all-out preparedness, declared after Roosevelt's speech that "any man who closes his eyes and denies that this emergency exists is a foolish man." But there were others, including the ineluctable Senator Wheeler, who warned that the President's proposal was just one more step toward the formation of a ten-million-man United States Army that inevitably would be sent into foreign adventures to save the British Empire or "make Russia safe for communism." Wheeler even took the extraordinary step of mailing postcards to thousands of soldiers, asking them to make their feelings known to the administration and their representatives in Congress. (It was this sort of behavior that prompted Stimson to accuse Wheeler publicly of undermining the American defense effort; like Henry II eager to dispose of Thomas à Becket, Roosevelt wondered aloud what might happen if someone kidnapped Wheeler and stowed him away on an outgoing steamer bound for the Congo.)

Despite army regulations that forbade any soldier to attempt to influence congressional legislation, a flood of letters written on cheap pad paper (sold for a nickel at army post exchanges) or company stationery poured into the Capitol from training camps around the country. "How can we have faith in a government that breaks faith with us?" came a plaintive cry from an infantry company at Fort Dix. "What can we do with $30 a month? Outsiders are making a fortune on defense projects. Let us have a chance to do the same." Republican Senator Vandenberg reported the receipt of letters from soldiers in several Michigan companies who complained that "they have not been learning anything, have had enough of it, and want to go home." Morale, which was none too high to begin with, plummeted even further. Angry recruits scrawled "O.H.I.O."— "Over the Hill in October"—on latrine walls. Not without satisfaction, Lindbergh decided that it was "a case of bad leadership, inefficient organization, lack of equipment, and various other factors. Army morale is low all over the country. As nearly as I can judge, the Army is at least three quarters opposed to entering this war." "If morale is poor," countered Lieutenant General Ben Lear, commander of the Second Army, "it is only because the morale of the people is poor."

That was precisely the point. Despite all the President's warnings of grave peril, a substantial segment of opinion in the army, in the public at large, and especially in the halls of Congress refused to accept the administration's contention that the nation's security was seriously endangered. On Capitol Hill, the House indulged itself in several weeks of acrimonious debate, during which many representatives—playing to galleries more crowded with spectators than at any time since the Lend-Lease controversy—argued that the United States was actually in less danger of invasion than it had been in 1940. After a marathon session during which isolationists tried and failed to weaken the draft extension measure with amendments, the House voted on Roosevelt's request shortly after eight o'clock on the evening of August 12. To no one's surprise, Republicans lined up almost solidly against the measure; but administration leaders were stunned when seventy Democrats—slightly over one-fourth of the party's delegation in the House—abandoned their President on a fight which he had defined as vital to the nation's security. The final tally was 203–202, a one-vote margin in favor of the draft extension. When an anxious Roosevelt examined the voting pattern, he discovered that the divisions ran even more along sectional than partisan lines: Midwestern congressmen of both parties cast 111 "no" votes, and only 21 "ayes"; in the South, the balance was reversed, with 120 votes for and only 10 opposed. Perhaps this time the President had jumped too far in front of public opinion; or perhaps he had not exercised the sort of unequivocal leadership that might have better prepared Congress and the people for such a move. Roosevelt appeared to favor the former possibility, for the administration quickly moved to appease the legions of malcontents in the army's ranks by announcing that it intended to limit the term of additional service to eighteen months, and would release men over the age of twenty-eight along with any others whose retention would subject them or their families to "undue hardship."

Apart from the draft extension controversy, which touched millions of American lives directly, the nation descended into a period of profound

apathy about events in Europe during the summer of 1941. Interventionist and isolationist congressmen alike reported that the flood of mail from
constituents that had deluged them during the winter and early spring
had dwindled to a trickle by July. After five long months of living on the
edge of war—from FDR's fireside chat of December 29, 1940, to the May
27 speech declaring an unlimited state of national emergency—most
Americans were tired of it all. They simply wanted a chance to escape
from the constant uncertainty and the approaching holocaust that threatened to disrupt their lives forever and lead them on a path to no one knew
where.

"Two-fifths of our people are more interested in the baseball scores
than they are in foreign news," complained William Allen White at the
end of August. Considering the sensational nature of the events that tran-
spired in major league ball parks that summer, this preoccupation was
hardly surprising. (The charm of the game and all its accompanying pleasures appeared to elude British Ambassador Lord Halifax, however; when
presented with a hot dog during a game at Chicago's Comiskey Park on
May 11, Halifax gave the frankfurter a dubious glance and then placed it
firmly on the ground beside him where it remained for the rest of the
afternoon, thereby precipitating an international incident of no mean
proportions.) On Thursday, May 15, as the Luftwaffe made its final preparations for the airborne invasion of Crete, as London finished digging
through the rubble left by the last major air raid of the year, as dozens of
German divisions crept stealthily toward their positions on the Russian
frontier, the New York Yankees were languishing in fourth place in the
American League with an uninspired record of 14 wins and 14 losses. That
afternoon, the Yanks dropped another game to the Chicago White Sox, but
Joe DiMaggio broke out of an 0–7 slump with a sharp first-inning single.
There was nothing unusual about that, of course; despite the recent dry
spell, Joe was hitting .304 at the time. No one knew that DiMaggio was
about to embark upon the most spectacular individual accomplishment in
the history of organized baseball.

The next day, Joe got another hit, and another on the third day, and
as the hits kept coming, the son of a San Francisco fisherman was off and
running. The hitting streak reached fifteen games, then kept building day
after day to twenty, twenty-five, thirty games in a row. Although Di-
Maggio did slug a dozen home runs during the course of the streak, his
extraordinary success was due in no small measure to his ability (which
modern ballplayers would do well to try to emulate) to make contact with
the ball virtually every time at bat; DiMaggio struck out only thirteen
times *during the entire 1941 season.* Once the ball was in play, anything
could happen, and there were several times when the streak was kept
alive through sheer good luck. On May 30, for instance, DiMaggio got his
only hit of the day when Boston outfielder Pete Fox lost a fly ball in the

sun and it fell right in front of him; on June 17, DiMaggio was 0 for 3 when he hit a ground ball that took a bad hop and glanced off White Sox shortstop Luke Appling's shoulder into left field.

The previous American League record for hitting safely in consecutive games was forty-one, set by George Sisler of the St. Louis Browns in 1922. With a single off Detroit right-hander Dizzy Trout on June 21, DiMaggio's streak reached thirty-four games, surpassing the National League record holder, Rogers Hornsby. "That's when the pressure really started," recalled DiMaggio. "That's when the public, the press, and the pitchers really started noticing." But Joe never let anyone see the tension inside. "He didn't seem to get very excited about it," marvelled teammate Red Ruffing. "He'd come into the clubhouse every day, sit down, get a cup of coffee from Pete, read the paper for a while, get dressed, go out, and get a base hit or two. It was something to see." Lefty Gomez swore that the pressure never bothered Joe. "Joe was probably the least excited guy in America over the streak. Guys would ask me if Joe was nervous as the streak went along and was he sleeping. You could hang him on a coat hanger in the closet and he'd fall asleep. Guys always figured he had to be nervous as the thing went on day after day. I don't know about Joe being nervous but I lost my breakfast a lot." DiMaggio: "I was able to control myself. That didn't mean I wasn't dying inside." His teammates hesitated to talk to Joe about the streak for fear of jinxing him. After each home game, Joe simply relaxed with a beer and went back to his apartment on the West Side and his wife, former movie starlet Dorothy Arnold, who was then pregnant with their first child.

Most opposing pitchers refused to pitch around Joe or walk him intentionally merely to end the streak. "The idea was to make him hit a bad ball if you could," explained the Tigers' Hal Newhouser. "It was a challenge. When the streak really got going, everybody wanted to stop him. It would have been a great honor. I wish I had." "DiMaggio fever" gripped the nation. Players on rival American League clubs asked him for his autograph. Business executives, cabdrivers, schoolboys, even politicians listened eagerly each day for the results of the latest Yankee game. "The question on every baseball fan's lips as he called up a newspaper office or tuned in on his radio for the scores has been, 'Did DiMaggio get a hit today?' " observed the prestigious New York *Herald Tribune.* And radio stations were deluged with requests for the latest hit record, "Joltin' Joe DiMaggio," played by Les Brown and his Band of Renown.

Joe caught up to Sisler during the first game of a doubleheader against the Washington Senators on June 29, smacking a double to the wall off the venerable Elmore "Dutch" Leonard. Between games he changed his uniform, drank some coffee, and smoked another Camel. "Well, how do you feel about it, Joe?" asked one imaginative reporter. "I'm tickled. Who wouldn't be? It's a great thing," replied Joe, who was always good for a colorful quote. Before the afternoon's second game began, someone stole DiMaggio's bat from the dugout, so he had to use teammate Tommy Henrich's bat instead. After going hitless his first three at-bats, he lined a single to left in the seventh inning. Now he owned the record. The Washington fans went wild, and his teammates pounded him so hard they almost broke his back. Still DiMaggio kept hitting, passing the old-timers' mark of forty-four consecutive games set by Wee Willie "Hit 'Em Where They Ain't" Keeler back in 1897. After the annual break for the All-Star game (won by the American League on Ted Williams' two-out, three-run homer in the ninth), Joe picked up where he had left off—fifty games, fifty-five.

Then, when the streak stood at fifty-six consecutive games, the Yankees arrived in Cleveland. As Joe and Lefty Gomez rode out to the stadium in a cab, the driver turned around and said, "Joe, I have a hunch you're going to be stopped tonight. I just feel it in my bones." Gomez told the cabbie to shut up. There were 67,468 fans jammed into Municipal Stadium that night, the largest crowd ever to witness a game under the lights. Al Smith, a journeyman lefthander whose best pitch was a screwball that bore in on right-handed hitters, was pitching for the Indians. On his first trip to the plate, DiMaggio cracked a sharp bouncer over the bag at third and then stumbled getting out of the batter's box. Indian third baseman Ken Keltner, who was playing unusually deep and shaded over toward the foul line (assuming, correctly, that DiMaggio would pull Smith's screwball), backhanded it on a nice play and barely threw Joe out at first. Next time up, Joe walked. He smashed another hard grounder to third in the seventh; again Keltner made an excellent play and nabbed Joe by a step. When DiMaggio came to the plate in the eighth, Jim Bagby had replaced Smith. Joe promptly lined a low shot back through the middle. Shortstop Lou Boudreau scooped it up and tossed it to his second baseman to begin a double play.

The streak was over. Cleveland fans booed Keltner after the game. Jovial Joe McCarthy, the Yankees' manager, saw the president of the Indians' ball club after the game and noticed that "he was so happy and excited that his pitchers had stopped Joe. He was congratulating everyone in sight. But the next day, you know what happened, don't you? The park wasn't half-filled and he was wondering where everybody was." There was silence in the Yankees' locker room. DiMaggio sat by himself for a moment, lit a cigarette, and then said, "Well, that's over." Sportswriters asked Joe if he was happy it was all over. "Heck no, I'm not happy," Joe said. "I wanted to continue to hit throughout the whole season."

Ted Williams once said that DiMaggio's fifty-six game hitting streak might be "the greatest batting achievement of all." Certainly Williams knew whereof he spoke, because while DiMaggio was rewriting the record books (he hit safely in another sixteen consecutive games after the original streak ended), Williams was putting on a remarkable hitting performance of his own. The two greatest hitters of that era had completely antithetical personalities: DiMaggio was quiet and controlled; Williams was short-tempered and brusquely outspoken. A native of San Diego, California, where his childhood heroes had been Charles Lindbergh, George Washington, and Napoleon, Theodore Francis Williams arrived in the majors in 1939 with the Boston Red Sox. "All I want out of life," he once said, "is that when I walk down the street, folks will say, 'There goes the greatest hitter who ever lived.' " At six feet three, 175 pounds, he didn't look much like a hitter, and he was a notably slow, awkward runner besides. "He looks no more like a slugger than a Russian wolfhound resembles a bulldog," one reporter said. But Williams hit .327 in his rookie season and led the league in runs batted in (145) and temper tantrums (nearly as many). He tore up locker rooms, he refused to wear a tie to dinner at Boston's elegant restaurants, he tossed balls into the crowd when he muffed a play in left field. His teammates (including Joe DiMaggio's brother, Dom) knew a good target when they saw one, and they rode him mercilessly. Williams started to sulk. When manager Joe Cronin accused him of loafing in May 1940, Williams—the Beantown Stringbean—announced that he was thinking of quitting baseball altogether to become a fireman like his uncle in Mount Vernon, New York. That inspired the Chicago White Sox to wear papier-mâché fire hats the next time they played Boston; every time Williams came up to the plate, someone in the Chicago dugout rang a fire gong.

Williams subsequently decided that he didn't like Boston or anything about the city, including its streets, its trees, its fans, and most of all its sportswriters. He demanded to be traded, preferably to Brooklyn. Still, he ended the 1940 season with a .344 batting average. When the 1941 season began, Williams informed the world that he was a reformed character. Certainly he seemed to be concentrating even more than usual on his hitting. By June he was hitting a stunning .436. The last major leaguer to hit over .400 had been Bill Terry, who finished the 1930 season with a .401 average. As the season rolled into the last week of August, Williams was still hitting .402.

The 1941 baseball season was marred only by the passing of Lou Gehrig, the Iron Horse of the Yankees, who died of amyotrophic lateral sclerosis at the age of thirty-seven on June 2. For once columnist Westbrook Pegler, usually so acerbic, found himself overcome with emotion. "And here I am, too, still fumbling in an attempt to find words with which to appreciate a man and a player, and coming to the end of the piece with nothing better to offer than something about character. That was what it was that made Gehrig great above and beyond his size and achievements, and it is no credit to the breed that so many of us are so unlike this fine man that we must stand in such awe of his simple virtues."

Although major league owners kept looking over their shoulders at the steadily mounting draft calls, very few players were called into the army that summer; the game lost no more stars of the magnitude of Hank Greenberg, who had been inducted in May and already had risen to the rank of corporal, commanding a five-man antitank crew. In an effort to convince the government of their good intentions, the owners and players jointly agreed to donate the gate receipts from the All-Star game ($53,000) to the USO. Many ball clubs handed out free passes at the stadium to servicemen in uniform. In Brooklyn, staunch interventionist Lee Mac-Phail scornfully rejected a request by America First to stage a rally (including a speech by Colonel Lindbergh) in Ebbets Field.

MacPhail's Dodgers ran neck and neck with the young St. Louis Cardinals all through the summer. Dodger fans began to pray for the chance to watch a World Series, the first in the cozy confines of Ebbets Field since 1920. As the season entered September, Brooklyn home attendance passed the one million mark and seemed certain to surpass the all-time league record of 1,200,000 set at Wrigley Field in the ill-fated year of 1929. Visitors were invariably impressed not only by the number of fans who crowded into tiny Ebbets Field, but by their unfailingly polite and proper behavior as well. Only once, in 1940, had a Dodger fan run onto the field to slug an umpire. It had been three years since two Giant fans were shot and killed in a Brooklyn bar for calling the Dodgers "miserable bums." Out-of-town fans were usually greeted with a cheerful "Ainchu in the wrong park, Buddy?" and only occasionally received a dousing of cold beer from the rows behind. The razzberry-like sound known as "de boid" was usually hoid only after de thoid inning. The zany cast of Ebbets regulars included Hilda Chester, a former bloomer girl who, when not selling song sheets outside a Brooklyn subway entrance, sat in the center-field bleachers and rang a huge bell to celebrate Dodger home runs. And then there was businessman Jack Pierce, unfailingly dressed in a suit and tie, who lodged himself behind the visitors' dugout with his friends and popped balloons all game long.

This sort of silliness seemed perfectly suited to the mood of America that summer. "There has never been a summer when it will be so important to relax," declared one sporting-goods catalog that sold rubber horses for adults to ride in the ocean. "The deluge is coming. Dress up and play." And that was precisely what Americans did.

They dressed up in white sharkskin tennis dresses, with separate shorts and box-pleated skirts that were cut flat and straight at the sides so as not to interfere with ground strokes, and took to the courts with their rackets strung with the new miracle fiber, nylon. There was a new dress fabric called, mysteriously, Pucker Up. Shops along Fifth Avenue featured frothy, peekaboo blouses and sleek evening dresses that made you (if you were a woman) look as if you had been poured into them. Anyone wishing to emulate the Duchess of Windsor could purchase a white shantung suit with a short, four-buttoned jacket, accompanied by a shantung blouse in navy blue. For informal occasions, there were dinner dresses with tailored tops slashed nearly to the waist in front, accompanied by circular skirts with belts and two fat pouches to take the place of pockets. Not for the demure were the daring gossamer dresses of sheer black lace and crepe, worn over "a tiny dead-black brassiere" and a flesh-colored chiffon slip. For the truly daring, the Blue Swan Mills company sponsored a Panty-of-the-Month Club, featuring original designs (priced at 69 cents apiece) to suit each passing season. (Our personal favorite was the olive-drab step-in with "Yoo Hoo" lettered on the thigh.) Although Blue Swan already sold more panties than any other company in America—earning nearly $7 million annually—its executives hoped that their new promotional campaign would reach the 50 percent of American women who went around pantless. If not, Blue Swan could always fall back on its new defense contract to provide $1 million worth of cotton underwear (presumably without "Yoo Hoos") for the army and navy.

Although enlistments and the draft were wreaking havoc on the summer social season by creating an acute shortage of eligible ambulatory young men, the marriage rate was skyrocketing. Based on the number of marriage licenses issued during the first six months of 1941, New York City was headed for a record-breaking year. Analysts attributed the sudden nuptial surge to a desire to sandwich in a brief honeymoon before heading off to training camp. (There was no discernible connection, however, between this phenomenon and FBI reports that arrests of females for drunkenness were up 35.4 percent during the first half of the year.) After complaining for years about the nation's falling birthrate, the Census Bureau proudly announced that 1941 would witness the highest rate in a decade: 18.5 babies per 1,000 population, which brought the U.S. nearly to the impressive procreation level of Nazi Germany.

Former CBS radio correspondent William Shirer's *Berlin Diary* topped the best-seller list that summer, but it faced stiff competition from Alice Duer Miller's sentimental (saccharine, actually) tribute to English stiff upper lips, *The White Cliffs,* and Sophie Tucker's revealing autobiography, *The Last of the Red-Hot Mammas,* which allegedly was bound in asbestos. Hitler's invasion of Russia spurred sales of the new historical novel from Knopf, *And Quiet Flows the Don,* by Mikhail Sholokhov. The all-time fiction champ, *Gone With the Wind,* was still going strong, having run through forty-three printings and six editions by this time, selling a grand total of 2,868,100 copies. (The German translation, incidentally, had sold a brisk half million copies of its own.) Although Pocket Books, the revolutionary and phenomenally successful venture in paperback publishing now entering its third year, had not yet acquired the rights to *GWTW,* it expected to sell a total of nearly ten million copies (at 25 cents apiece) of the books on its constantly expanding list, including the ever-popular *How to Win Friends and Influence People,* the Pocket Bible, *The Good Earth,* and a host of Agatha Christie mysteries.

The most widely broadcast show on radio was "The Goldbergs," created, written, and acted by the indefatigable forty-year-old Gertrude Berg. Three times a day (once each on the CBS, Mutual, and NBC networks), the misadventures of Molly and Jake Goldberg came over the airwaves, subjecting listeners to such snappy dialogue as:

MOLLY: Jake?
JAKE: Jake.
MOLLY: You are home?
JAKE: If I'm here, I'm home.

The *Quiz Kids,* a brigade of relentlessly bright moppets from the Chicago area, were entering their second year on the air, having inspired a remunerative small-scale industry of toys and novelties based on the weekly show. The summer's best-selling records included the latest offerings from the red-hot Ink Spots (who reportedly earned $20,000 per week from their records and personal appearances) and Ethel Merman (singing the ever-popular *Panama Hattie* repertoire in her inimitable ringing style), Duke Ellington's rendition of "Rocks in My Bed" and "Blip-Blip," Benny Goodman's two-sided hit record featuring a brisk "Pound Ridge" and the luxurious "I Got It Bad" (vocals by Peggy Lee), a jazzed-up version of "Clementine" by Bing Crosby, southern songstress Dinah "Honeychile" Shore's "Somebody Loves Me" and "My Man," and the inimitable Noro Morales and his guaracha orchestra playing "Vamo a Jugar La Rueda" and "Bim Bam Boom." Some people even liked the style of a brash young singer named Frank Sinatra (who, one uncharitable critic complained, sang with the ecstatic delivery of a person having his big toenail pulled out without a general anesthetic). The war had not yet inspired any memorable songs of its own; typical of the lackluster attempts was the British ditty "Thanks, Mr. Roosevelt":

And Franklin, by the way, please convey
Our congratulations to the folks in U.S.A.
We're saying, Thanks, Mister Roosevelt, we're proud of you
For the way you're helping us to carry on.

When they weren't reading, going to the movies, or listening to the radio, the average American family pulled out a well-worn deck of cards and dealt another round around the table. A nationwide survey revealed that 83 percent of American families played cards at least once a week; in order of popularity, their favorite games were bridge, poker, pinochle, hearts, and five hundred.

Popular magazines were filled with advertisements that played shamelessly on the theme of national defense. Pall Mall ran a whole series of ads that somehow managed to equate its new "streamlined" cigarettes with modern armaments: "In cigarettes, as in dive bombers, it's modern design that counts!"; "In cigarettes, as in armored scout cars, it's modern design that makes the big difference!"; and so forth. Fleischmann announced "a *new* defense weapon"—Enriched Hi-B₁ Yeast—that could provide an essential first line of defense against "the bomb of vitamin deficiency" that threatened to leave Americans listless, incapacitated, and downright dull. And the United States Rubber Company, manufacturers of "Lastex, the miracle yarn that makes things fit," urged women to engage in "all-out preparedness against summer slump" by wearing its new Nemo Sensation girdles.

Less cynical advertisements asked readers to "open your heart and open your purse: give to the USO." A new crop of army slang was fast making its way into the nation's vocabulary. A motorcycle was a "popsickle," the guardhouse or any place of detention was called "Barrack Thirteen" or "Crossbar Hotel," tanks were known as "hell buggies," radio operators were "static benders" and infantrymen were "gravel agitators," a three-day pass was a "homing device," an attack of mental confusion was liable to leave someone in a "cockpit fog," and if you wanted to get somewhere quickly you "poured on coal."

On the warm, humid Sunday morning of August 3, President Roosevelt decided he had suffered enough cockpit fog in the Crossbar Hotel known as the White House, and so he boarded the presidential train at Union Station and told the engineer to head northward and pour on the coal (well, not in so many words). Reporters had been told that the President was leaving for another fishing trip with his cronies. That night, Roosevelt was helped aboard his 165-foot yacht, the *Potomac,* at the submarine base at New London, Connecticut; contrary to custom, no reporters were allowed to accompany the ship as it swept down the river and vanished into the Atlantic sunset. The following morning, vacationers along the Massachusetts shore could see Roosevelt on deck, accompanied by Princess Marthe of Norway (who, according to Washington gossip, was having an affair with the President) and Prince Karl of Sweden (who was not). On August 5, the *Potomac* appeared again, steaming through the Cape Cod Canal, with a bulky figure seated on deck that, from the shore, looked more or less like the President.

But it wasn't Roosevelt. At first light that morning, in complete secrecy, he had boarded the heavy cruiser *Augusta* in the waters off Martha's Vineyard. Reporters in Washington already had suspected something unusual was afoot when General Marshall, Admiral Stark, Army Air Corps General Hap Arnold, and Under Secretary of State Sumner Welles all suddenly disappeared to unknown locations for vacations or undefined "official business." Still, no one in the capital outside the highest levels of the administration knew where the President was, or what he was up to. "Franklin," Eleanor explained later, "loved little mysteries of this kind."

Hell-bent for leather, Admiral King swung the *Augusta* and its escort of four destroyers northeastward, speeding precipitously and somewhat recklessly through fishing banks shrouded in dense fog. On August 7 the flotilla arrived at Argentia Bay in Newfoundland. Soon it began to sleet. After two days of miserable weather, the British battleship *Prince of Wales* arrived, bearing its precious cargo: Prime Minister Winston Spencer Churchill, a bit shorter and rounder than Roosevelt had expected, but resplendent in a peaked cap and Royal Navy uniform. Since the *Prince of Wales* had maintained absolute wireless silence during the trip across the Atlantic to avoid attracting the U-boats that were cruising the rough waters, Churchill said he had experienced "a strange sense of leisure which I had not known since the war began. For the first time for many months I could read a book for pleasure. Oliver Lyttelton, Minister of State in Cairo, had given me *Captain Hornblower, R.N.*, which I found vastly entertaining. When a chance came I sent him the message, 'I find *Hornblower* admirable.' This caused perturbation in the Middle East Headquarters, where it was imagined that 'Hornblower' was the code-word for some special operation of which they had not been told."

This was the first face-to-face meeting of the two leaders, though they had corresponded for two years; both men felt that the disturbing course of recent events in Europe and the Far East required personal discussions on their part to clear the air of any misunderstandings and ensure that the diplomatic and military policies of the United States and the British Empire were at least proceeding in harmony, if not along precisely the same track. Although Lend-Lease supplies were not arriving very quickly or in the copious quantities that London had expected, at least they were getting there safely. Roosevelt had successfully finessed the convoy issue for the time being; he had ordered American naval vessels to "escort" British convoys as far as Iceland, blithely neglecting to give his commanders more explicit instructions. Admiral Harold ("Betty") Stark, Chief of Naval Operations, repeatedly asked the President for detailed guidance in the event of a confrontation with German U-boats, but received no satisfactory answers. "To some of my very pointed questions which all of us would like to have answered," Stark complained to a friend at the end of July, "I get a smile or a 'Betty, please don't ask me that!' Policy seems something never fixed, always fluid and changing."

Such temporizing succeeded primarily because Hitler had ordered most of his U-boats into the Mediterranean (to assist Rommel and support the campaigns in Russia and the Balkans) and the Arctic Sea (to fend off any attempted British landings in northern Europe). The resulting decline in attacks upon British convoys in the North Atlantic convinced some gullible Britons that the Battle of the Atlantic had been won, but it was nothing more than a false dawn. The U-boats would return in force in 1942. In fact, a U-boat cruising the South Atlantic had sunk the American freighter *Robin Moor* in June, but no lives were lost, and Roosevelt chose to limit the American response to a stiff diplomatic protest to Berlin. It was not yet the right moment to move toward war.

While Churchill spent three days in Argentia Bay explaining to Roosevelt the international situation as he saw it, including the latest ominous turn of events in the Far East (where Japan had taken another giant step toward confrontation by occupying the southern rump of French Indochina), British and American military officials held their own series of strategic discussions. Together, they came to a general agreement on how American defense production should be allocated among the United States, Britain, and the Soviet Union. There were numerous differences of opinion, of course; the American generals suspected that the British cupboard was not quite as bare of armaments as some claimed, they looked askance at the British obsession with protecting the Empire's vulnerable position in the Mediterranean, and they feared that Dill and his chiefs were deluding themselves by presuming that the war could be won primarily by bombing Germany into submission, without engaging in a large-scale invasion of the European continent. Underneath the disagreements, however, both sides readily accepted the strategic proposition that the Atlantic theater was far more critical to British and American security interests than the Pacific. If the United States should enter the war, even as the result of an incident with Japan, the primary target would be Nazi Germany.

Churchill wanted to conclude the conference on a flamboyant note, with a ringing public declaration of Anglo-American unity that would bind the United States even more tightly to the British war effort. Roosevelt, of course, wanted to avoid any specific public commitments; in fact, he told Churchill that he wanted to issue a statement that expressly denied that he or any of the American military chiefs had entered into any binding agreements with the British government that had not already been authorized by Congress. Aghast, Churchill argued that such weak-kneed shilly-shallying would only please the Axis and discourage neutrals who were hoping for some concrete indication of America's commitment to the ultimate defeat of Nazism. "We also would not like it," he added bluntly. As a compromise, the President and the Prime Minister agreed upon a vague eight-point declaration that became known as the Atlantic Charter, proclaiming their dedication to the principles of democracy, freedom of the seas, a circumscribed version of free trade, and general disarmament. It was a pleasant enough document, but rather insipid, and something of an anticlimax to a meeting that, despite its immense symbolic importance, somehow lacked excitement. Certainly future Secretary of State John Foster Dulles was not impressed with the Atlantic Charter's banal generalities. "Unless we propose concrete measures," warned Dulles, "statements of good intentions . . . will be looked upon with grave and warranted skepticism."

Roosevelt went back to Maine on the *Augusta* and then took a train to Washington. Reporters asked if he thought the United States was any closer to war after his meeting with the Prime Minister; Roosevelt replied that he would not say so. Churchill stopped off at Iceland on his way home, and when he finally reached London safe and sound, the British public let out a collective sigh of relief. "Many Britons," reported one American correspondent in London, "seemed to feel that their Premier had gone the dickens of a long way merely to reiterate a stand which, in their simplicity, they thought everyone knew they had been prepared to die for, probably unpleasantly." The eminently respectable *Daily Sketch* charged that unless there were some vital, earth-shaking Anglo-American agreement lurking behind the innocuous Atlantic Charter, the meeting at Argentia Bay would go on record as "the most astounding piece of unjustified recklessness ever recorded in history."

In Berlin, Goebbels dismissed the Atlantic Charter as "a scrap of paper," "insipid chitchat," and "an assault on healthy human intelligence." Ribbentrop's official Foreign Office journal shouted belligerently, "If they want to take our weapons away from us let them come and try!" Mussolini's press spokesman condemned the manifesto as "a gross and clumsy gesture of Anglo-Saxon warmongering," and the semi-official Domei news agency in Tokyo accused the United States and Britain of a "tricky plot" to dominate the world. More to the point, isolationist spokesmen warned that the eight points were a prelude to an American declaration of war. Senator Hiram Johnson of California proclaimed that the objectives of the Atlantic Charter could be achieved only by American entry into the war; "it is as plain as the nose upon a man's face," shouted Johnson, that the Atlantic Charter created "an offensive and defensive alliance between Britain and the United States." "This is the end of isolation," the *New York Times* solemnly declared. "It is the beginning of a new era in which the United States assumes the responsibilities which fall naturally to a great world power."

Invigorated by his exposure to Churchill's ebullient personality, Roosevelt returned to Washington determined to give the American defense program a well-deserved kick in the pants. He forcefully disabused the nation of any thought that the German invasion of Russia had taken the pressure off the United States and Britain. "I give solemn warning to those who think that Hitler has been blocked and halted that they are making a very dangerous assumption," he declared. "When in any war your enemy seems to be making slower progress than he did the year before, that is the very moment to strike with redoubled force." He dispatched Averell Harriman and a bevy of army and navy officials to Moscow, to join Beaverbrook in coordinating aid to the Soviet armies. He expanded the American military mission to Chiang Kai-shek's government in Chungking. And, in a sweeping reorganization of the preparedness program, Roosevelt established a Supply Priorities and Allocations Board, consisting of Hopkins, Stimson, Knox, Knudsen, Hillman, Leon Henderson, and Vice President Wallace, to untangle the confused mess into which the defense effort had degenerated. The SPAB was ordered to forecast the defense production requirements of the nation and to allocate on its own authority all available raw materials to ensure that those needs were fulfilled.

The government ordered Detroit to cut automobile production by 50 percent. To conserve stocks of essential metals, Henderson made similar slashes in the production of household appliances such as refrigerators, washing machines, furnaces, and air conditioners. "It's a dark picture I paint," warned Henderson, "of factories made idle by lack of raw materials, of men made idle . . . of single-industry towns blighted." Railroads in the Southeast were requested to cancel all excursions and reserve their cars for transporting troops. Harold Ickes, who had taken over as coordinator of petroleum supplies, imposed a 7 P.M. curfew on filling stations on the East Coast to conserve the nation's stocks of gasoline and warned that "gasless Sundays" were just around the corner. (While driving around Washington, Ickes also reportedly jotted down the license plate numbers of cars spouting black smoke from their exhaust pipes—presumably wasting oil—and sent the culprits' numbers to the police.)

And to prove that it was finally time to crack down on the nation's business-as-usual mentality, the administration informed the leaders of America's silk industry that they could have no more raw silk without the specific authorization of the Director of Priorities. The armed forces had grabbed the entire available four-month reserve stocks of silk to manufacture parachutes and powder bags for artillery guns. Like nothing else that had happened to date, this threat to the nation's supply of fine hosiery brought the war home to women across America, who purchased silk stockings at the phenomenal rate of 47 million dozen pairs per year. Thousands of frantic female shoppers descended en masse upon the nation's department stores and clothing shops, most of which immediately instituted limits on the number of pairs that could be bought at any one time. When Gimbel's store in Manhattan rashly advertised the unlimited sale of stockings, society matrons launched a frontal assault on the hosiery department counters. "Why aren't there more salespeople here?" one well-dressed lady huffed as she elbowed competitors out of the way. "Give us time," begged the harried sales clerks, who were pinned against the last beachhead by the cash registers. "The government's not giving *me* time," snapped a bosomy matron in response. "I've got three marriageable daughters." It was no use suggesting that middle-aged women go barelegged, as many coeds did on America's college campuses. Cotton lisle replacement stockings were laughed off the market, and there certainly was not enough nylon to go around. (Although it had been introduced commercially in 1938, the synthetic fiber was not yet being produced or employed in great quantities.) Fashion designers prepared to introduce longer skirts as a last resort. From desperate women around the country came the anguished cry, "Do you realize what this country would be like without silk stockings?"

Part Five   The Autumn

22

Stumbling Toward War

"We live under the illusion that all problems are at times susceptible to a reasonably satisfactory solution. They are not."
—ALDOUS HUXLEY, NOVEMBER 1941

Either Yosuke Matsuoka had not understood the heavy-handed hints his German hosts had given him regarding the imminent invasion of Russia, or else he had not expected the blow to fall so quickly. The foreign minister was as surprised as the rest of the Konoye cabinet when the Wehrmacht rumbled across the Soviet border on the morning of June 22. Operation Barbarossa threatened to disrupt Japan's carefully prepared plans to achieve economic supremacy in East Asia; the government in Tokyo had intended to strike southward against the vulnerable European imperialist possessions, to occupy southern Indochina and then perhaps extort concessions from Thailand, British-controlled Malaya, and the Dutch East Indies. But now Hitler, with barely a nod toward his Asian ally, had embarked upon an adventure that would postpone indefinitely the collapse of the hard-pressed British Empire in the Far East, and possibly divert Japanese forces into a war with the Soviet Union as well. No wonder Prime Minister Konoye denounced the invasion as a "perfidious act."

Without missing a beat, Matsuoka, the champion of the Axis alliance, jettisoned his nonaggression pact with Stalin and urged the Emperor to join Nazi Germany in a glorious conquest of Russia's maritime provinces, long coveted by the Japanese army. The foreign minister even advocated that Japan fight the United States, Britain, and the Soviet Union simultaneously, if necessary. Emperor Hirohito, a peaceful man better suited to the tranquil solitude of his marine biology laboratories than the company of high-strung, verbose politicians, did not rejoice at the prospect of a two- or three-front war, and he informed Matsuoka that he doubted the army would approve such a policy. He was right. Although the Konoye cabinet decided to maintain its alliance with Germany, it adopted a wait-and-see attitude toward the conflict in Russia; if the Wehrmacht made short work of the Soviets, then Japan might step in before the end of the war to scoop up territory in the north. (Ironically, the Red Army's refusal to fold in the face of the Nazi blitzkrieg therefore played at least a minor role in the eventual Japanese decision to go to war against the United States.) Otherwise, there was little enthusiasm in Tokyo for a prolonged northern campaign that might swallow up Japanese forces in the Siberian vastness at a time when one million Japanese troops were still tied down in China. Besides, the raw materials Japan needed so desperately—oil, rubber, tin, and rice—all lay to the south.

At an Imperial Conference on July 2, the civil and military leaders of Japan ratified the decision to move southward at once. When Matsuoka, now known derisively in government circles as "Hitler's office boy," protested and pressed once too often for an attack upon Russia, his colleagues finally dumped him unceremoniously from the cabinet and replaced him with a foreign minister of less pro-German—and certainly less voluble— sensibilities. According to the plan adopted on July 2, Japanese diplomats first would attempt to obtain the desired concessions (most important, the unrestricted use of airfields and naval bases) from the Vichy government in Saigon; if negotiations failed, the army would take the objectives by force. Meanwhile, Japan would attack Chiang with renewed vigor to crush resistance in China. "In carrying out the plans outlined in the foregoing article," read the official record of the Conference decision, "we will not be deterred by the possibility of being involved in a war with England and America. . . . We will immediately turn our attention to placing the nation on a war basis and will take special measures to strengthen the defenses of the nation." This bellicose language did not mean that the Konoye cabinet desired war with the United States or Britain; few among the inner circle of the Japanese military chiefs cherished the prospect of a full-scale conflict in the Pacific unless it could not possibly be avoided. The Conference decision did, however, mean that nothing Washington or London might say or do would cause Japan to renounce its designs for hegemony in the Far East. Diplomacy would proceed with a sincere hope that it would succeed; meanwhile, the nation organized for war. Preparations for a conflict with Britain and America—including the refinement of operational plans for attacks upon Singapore and the Philippines, and intensive target practice in Kagoshima Bay that simulated an attack upon Pearl Harbor by dive-bombers armed with torpedoes—went forward at a quickened pace.

Not surprisingly, Vichy France and its governor-general in Saigon knuckled under in short order to virtually all of Japan's demands. On July 21, the government of French Indochina agreed to remove all restrictions on the number of Japanese troops stationed in Indochina; henceforward, the defense of the region was recognized as the joint responsibility of France and Japan. Forty-eight thousand Japanese troops took up strategic positions in the colony, at Saigon, Phnom Penh, and along the border with Thailand. Airfields, railroads, and the ports of Saigon and Cam Ranh Bay were placed at Japan's disposal. Japanese civil administrators promulgated regulations that effectively strangled all foreign trade except with Japan. Now all of Southeast Asia lay within Japan's grasp, if it dared to reach out and take it. "Japan is now in a position of readiness, or will be when the occupation is fully organized, to move aggressively in several directions," acknowledged one Western military analyst. "Camranh Bay is an excellent naval base to serve as the focus of any naval effort, lying only 720 miles from Manila and 690 miles from Singapore. From air bases in Southern Indo-China a sweep of 600 miles puts Singapore, Siam, the coast of British North Borneo and Sarawak, the Malacca Strait, and part of the coast of Burma within striking distance."

Scanning their Magic intercepts in Washington, American officials understood perfectly well that Japan intended to use southern Indochina as a staging area for future conquests. Outraged (but not particularly surprised) by this latest display of Japanese imperialism, the Roosevelt administration decided to respond with a declaration of economic war. For the past year, the United States quietly had been shipping vast supplies of oil to Japan, in hopes that it might thereby deflect Japan from a direct attack upon the oil-rich Dutch East Indies. At a time when the American defense effort required all the fuel oil it could obtain and gas stations on the East Coast were forced to close at 7 P.M. every evening, the notion of sending millions of barrels of oil to a potential Asian enemy (and an ally of Nazi Germany) struck many Americans as hypocritical, if not downright foolish. A Gallup poll revealed that 62 percent of American voters—including a majority in the normally isolationist Midwest—favored steps "to keep Japan from becoming more powerful, even if this means risking war." "The Japanese Navy runs on fuel oil," wrote one outraged Washington columnist. "Correction: it runs on American fuel oil; it bought and we sold 7,500,000 barrels of this handy stuff last year. Perhaps our Navy is roaming too far from home. Perhaps it could protect our Pacific interests better with a yeoman's guard on a few American docks than with ten battle wagons scattered through Eastern seas. The arsenal of democracy is the filling station of fascism."

Not for long. Roosevelt called Nomura to the White House on July 24 and strongly recommended that Japan withdraw its forces from Indochina. The next day, the President put force behind that recommendation by issuing an executive order freezing all Japanese assets (a total of $131 million) in the United States; in effect, this cut off all trade between the U.S. and Japan. Several days later, Roosevelt expressly prohibited the export of American oil supplies to Japan, though he left the door open to renewed shipments if Japan reversed its aggressive course. Since there was no other source from which Japan could obtain such vast stocks of oil on short notice, surely (the State Department reasoned) the militarists in Tokyo would now reconsider their plans.

Upon learning of the freeze, the Tokyo Stock Exchange promptly spun into a decline that sent shares tumbling to their lowest levels since 1931. Japanese military officials professed astonishment at Roosevelt's action, although they probably should have seen it coming. Nevertheless, the government refused to admit it had been shaken; Finance Minister Masatune Ogura publicly affirmed that "Japan cannot retreat even one step from her fundamental policy of constructing a Greater East Asia Co-Prosperity Sphere." And within the Konoye cabinet, the proponents of military action now obtained a new ally: Admiral Nagano, chief of the Naval General Staff. Until the United States threatened to cut off its supply of oil, the Imperial Navy generally had acted as a brake upon the army's expansionist program; it knew it would be hard-pressed to defend the far-flung Japanese Empire (which would be expanding even more in the future) against either the British or the American fleet, and certainly could not challenge both at the same time. Yet, as Nagano pointed out, at that moment the navy possessed fuel reserves for only two more years, even less if war should break out. Thus the American embargo presented Japan with three alternatives, none of them particularly attractive: abide by the United States' demands, which meant an admission of defeat and a humiliating retreat from the Asian mainland; scrimp and stagger along without American oil for as long as possible, with little hope of any improvement in the near future; or defy the Western powers and seize the oil the empire needed. After long deliberation, Admiral Nagano regretfully advised Emperor Hirohito that "under such circumstances, we had better take the initiative."

"From now on, the oil gauge and the clock stood side by side," concluded veteran American diplomat Herbert Feis. "Each fall in the level brought the hour of decision closer."

Desperate to stem the drift toward war, Konoye offered to meet Roosevelt personally, perhaps in Alaska, to find some means of resolving the dispute. Ambassador Grew urged the State Department to give Konoye's proposal serious consideration. "It indicates a determination on the part of the Government to surmount extremist dictation," he wrote. "It may also be true that the Government has been driven to this unprecedented step in the knowledge that Japan is nearing the end of her tether economically and that the nation could not survive a war with the United States. On the other hand, even if Japan were approaching economic disaster of the first magnitude, there can be no doubt whatever that the Government would reluctantly but resolutely face such disaster rather than cede in the face of progressive pressure exerted by any other nation."

Konoye's invitation reached Washington while Roosevelt was moored in Argentia Bay with Churchill. Convinced that only the sternest warning of American retribution would deter Japan from attacking British or Dutch possessions in the Far East, Winston was trying his best to induce Roosevelt to draw a line and dare the Japanese to step over it. (More than anything else, Churchill feared that Japan might launch a Pacific war against the British Empire—specifically, Singapore and Malaya—but not the United States, leaving Britain to fight a two-ocean war without American help.) In the President's absence, Hull decided to spurn Konoye's offer. Concluding that "the invitation to the President is merely a blind to try to keep us from taking definite action," the secretary decided that nothing good could possibly come from such a meeting.

By this time, Hull had been thoroughly conditioned—by the relentless anti-Japanese fulminations of the Hornbeck clique, and the revelations of Japanese duplicity drawn from the Magic intercepts—to assume the worst of any proposal from Tokyo. He firmly believed the Japanese army would never voluntarily withdraw from China or even Indochina no matter what the United States did. "Nothing will stop them but force," Hull told Sumner Welles on August 2. "The point is how long we can maneuver the situation until the military matter in Europe is brought to a conclusion." For his part, Hull was determined not to sign any agreement, even as an interim measure, that left Japan in control of its ill-gotten booty on the Asian mainland. He told reporters that "no settlement with Japan would be acceptable to the Administration unless it involved a cessation of all hostile preparations in the Pacific." At the end of the summer of 1941, Hull was tired, he was ill (several weeks of recuperation at White Sulphur Springs failed to rid him of a lingering throat infection), and he saw no point in flogging a dead horse. For the rest of the year, Hull would simply play out the string and try to delay hostilities until the United States had improved its defensive position in the Pacific. He would make no concessions, and he would utter no threats. Instead, he subjected Japanese envoys to an interminable session of negotiations which one contemporary critic in the Treasury Department described as a series of "subtle half promises, irritating pin pricks, excursions into double dealing, and copious pronunciamentos of good will alternating with vague threats—and all of it veiled in an atmosphere of high secrecy designed or at least serving chiefly to hide the essential barrenness of achievement."

When Roosevelt returned to Washington, he summoned Nomura and expressed his profound disappointment that Japan had chosen to persist in its occupation of Indochina. He then read aloud the carefully worded statement upon which he and Churchill had agreed: "If the Japanese Government takes any further steps in pursuance of a program or policy of military domination of neighboring countries by force or threat of force, this Government would be immediately compelled to take whatever steps might be necessary toward safeguarding its legitimate interests and rights and those of American nationals and toward insuring the security and safety of the United States." Having issued this warning, which still allowed him to retain considerable freedom of action in meeting any hostile Japanese action, Roosevelt chatted amiably with Nomura for the remainder of the meeting, assuring him that he would be willing to resume informal discussions whenever Tokyo desired. He neither accepted nor declined Konoye's invitation.

Frustrated by the American policy of discussion and delay, the Japanese High Command now decided that it could wait no longer. "With each day we will get weaker and weaker," Nagano informed his colleagues on September 3, "until finally we won't be able to stand on our feet. Although I feel sure that we have a chance to win a war right now, I'm afraid this chance will vanish with the passage of time." The admiral compared the situation between Japan and the United States to "a patient with an illness which might require an operation. Avoiding one could mean that the patient wastes away. But there is hope of recovery if a drastic act of surgery is undergone. That is war." Army Chief of Staff General Sugiyama set October 10 as the deadline for diplomacy. "If this fails we must dash forward. Things cannot be allowed to drag out."

At an Imperial Conference three days later, the High Command affirmed its conviction that if negotiations with Washington did not soon succeed in winning at least Japan's minimum demands—an end to American aid to China, the restoration of normal trade relations between the United States and Japan, and an American commitment not to strengthen its military posture in the Pacific—Japan must resort to "aggressive military operations." The Emperor had heard similar confident predictions of success before the invasion of China. At Hirohito's request, the president of the Privy Council pressed the chiefs of staff to declare openly whether they sincerely intended to pursue a diplomatic solution to the dispute. When the questions were followed by a prolonged, uneasy silence, the Emperor rose and, for the first time in five years, spoke at a formal Conference with his advisers: "I am sorry the Supreme Command has nothing to say." One court official noticed that Hirohito's normally placid face was flushed with emotion. His glasses were fogged; after he wiped them dry with his thumbs, he drew a piece of paper from his pocket and recited a poem written by his grandfather, the illustrious Emperor Meiji:

> All the seas, everywhere,
>   are brothers one to another
> Why then do the winds and waves of strife
>   rage so violently through the world?

This extraordinary revelation of the imperial will provided Konoye with the authority he needed to continue his diplomatic initiatives for a little while longer. Nevertheless, the tangible signs of impending war seemed to be everywhere in Tokyo; with half of its one million houses fashioned of paper or bamboo, and its canal bridges made of wood, the Japanese capital was the most vulnerable city in the world to bombing attacks. Workers were building aboveground shelters around the Imperial

Palace. (The subsoil around the palace was too saturated with water to permit the construction of underground shelters.) Ancient trees were ripped up to make room for antiaircraft guns. Tokyo newspapers began to publish articles instructing the public on proper air raid precautions, along with frequent warnings against spies and saboteurs. There were three nights of practice blackout every week. Posters with maps depicting the perfidious Anglo-American attempt to "encircle" the beleaguered Japanese Empire appeared on city walls. The government extended its conscription and mobilization measures to unprecedented levels, and put the entire shipping industry under state control. Eleven of Japan's largest banks formed a syndicate to supply funds for increased armaments production. Several Western correspondents were accused of espionage; Joseph Grew, who was certainly no alarmist, began carrying a pistol for protection when he went out in public. "While there is little free expression of opinion within earshot of foreigners," Grew reported to Washington, "certain indications that the people are apprehensive, alarmed and in dread of war are clear. Four years of inconclusive fighting in China have dulled the patriotic exuberance of 1937. Daily life is increasingly constrained by a [mass?] of restrictions, and queues for bread, sugar, vegetables, and other daily necessities are a common sight on every street." A steadily rising percentage of the nation's mulberry orchards, formerly used for raising silkworms, was converted to grain fields to ease the food shortage. Most ominous, the government prohibited the playing of baseball, the quintessentially American game that had become one of Japan's most popular pastimes.

And while Hirohito wondered aloud why the waves of strife raged so violently upon the seas, the Japanese navy was engaged in its latest series of war games at the Imperial Naval Staff College. Many among the naval general staff had openly expressed their skepticism regarding Admiral Yamamoto's plans for a massive surprise aerial attack upon Pearl Harbor. They watched with amused interest as the first simulation vindicated their doubts; two waves of attack planes were so harried by the island's defenses that they inflicted only minor damage on the harbor, and limped back to the aircraft carriers with heavy losses. Further, pursuit planes from Pearl followed the bombers back to the carriers and managed to sink one-third of the Japanese armada.

Obviously this would never do. So Vice Admiral Chuichi Nagumo, commander of the attack task force, sent his ships on a more northerly course on the second trial run. The revised plan called for his fleet to arrive at a spot approximately 450 miles directly north of Oahu at sunset. Then he would turn southward and increase speed, to approach the target before the first patrol planes took off from Pearl in the early morning. This time the defenders were caught completely by surprise. The Japanese bombers struck at will, demolishing four battleships, two carriers, and three cruisers, and decimating the astonished enemy's air strength that had been trapped on the ground.

If Nagumo's task force could knock out the American fleet at Pearl Harbor while the army neutralized the American base at Manila and the British fortress of Singapore, all serious threats to the southern flank of Japan's proposed advance would disappear. Japanese warships would roam at will through the waters of the South Pacific, protecting the army as it seized the treasures of Indonesia, Malaya, and Thailand (including an almost unlimited supply of oil). Before the British and Americans could recover the initiative, Japan would have safely fortified its new acquisitions.

American naval officials were not oblivious to the possibility of a Japanese attack upon Pearl Harbor, but they generally assumed that Tokyo would strike against other, more readily accessible targets first. (The wide range of choices open to the Japanese misled even the most experienced Far East analysts. As late as mid-October, Sir Robert Craigie, the longtime British ambassador in Tokyo, was convinced that Japan still planned to move northward first, to avoid a clash with America or Britain.) If Japan did choose to attack Pearl, the U.S. naval experts expected that the assault would most likely come by sea, and so that was where the commanders at Oahu concentrated their defenses. Their army colleagues boasted that Pearl Harbor was "the best defended naval base in the world," and certainly any enemy who tried to invade Oahu would have encountered an imposing array of fortifications.

But while the notion of an all-out assault by Japanese bombers had been given serious consideration by U.S. Navy operations staff planners early in 1941, the air defense forces available at Oahu remained grossly insufficient to permit the sort of ongoing, long-range aerial reconnaissance that would give the base sufficient warning of an attack by aircraft. When Lieutenant General Lewis Brereton visited Hawaii in late October on his way to take charge of the American air force in the Philippines, he was "surprised and somewhat disappointed to note the incomplete preparations against air attacks, particularly the lack of adequate air warning equipment. I visited the airfields, air warning service, and interceptor command headquarters, most of which was rudimentary, although energetic efforts were under way to improve it. . . . I had a long talk with General Martin [Air Force Commander of the Hawaii Islands] about the preparedness of the Islands. He was aware that the air warning equipment and program were far short of the requirements. [Naval Air Commander] Admiral Bellinger said that the Navy did not have enough [aircraft] to carry out the necessary reconnaissance of Hawaiian waters." The men at Pearl could only console themselves with the prevailing (and racist) conviction that the Japanese were notoriously poor pilots; the Japanese Air Force reportedly suffered the highest accident rate in the world. As one supercilious American military analyst pointed out, the Japanese "can neither make good airplanes nor fly them well," primarily because the entire race allegedly suffered from myopia and an inner ear defect that impaired their sense of balance.

Instead of wasting American warplanes (of which there were far too few anyway) strengthening an outpost that was already perfectly capable of repelling an invasion, and which was, after all, seven thousand miles across the Pacific from the Japanese home islands, the War Department chose to fortify the Philippines, which lay directly athwart the lines of communication between Japan and its objectives in the South Pacific. On July 27, Lieutenant General Douglas MacArthur, who had been pleading with Washington for years to enhance the Philippines' defenses, was appointed to the new post of Commander, United States Army Forces in the Far East, with headquarters at Manila. Ten native Philippine regiments, totaling 15,000 men, were placed under his control. Then, after hearing reports of the "sudden and startling success" achieved by the American B-17 Flying Fortresses that had been turned over to the R.A.F., Stimson and his advisers managed to persuade themselves that a large force of these heavy bombers stationed on the Philippines under MacArthur's confident command might deter Japan from further aggressive moves toward the Indies. "For twenty years," Stimson claimed, "it had been considered that strategically the Philippines were an unprotected pawn, certain to be easily captured by the Japanese in the early stages of any war between the United States and Japan. Now it began to seem possible to establish in the Philippines a force not only sufficient to hold the Islands but also, and more important, strong enough to make it foolhardy for the Japanese to carry their expansion southward through the China Sea." Although some military officials in Washington warned that the introduction of a strong bomber force in the islands might actually encourage Japan to launch a preemptive strike before the end of the year, the reinforcement program proceeded upon the War Department's confident assumption (shared by MacArthur) that Japan would not attack the Philippines until April 1942 at the earliest, by which time the American preparations would be complete. But far too little was accomplished in the few months that remained. "By December," MacArthur noted, "our operational force had only reached a strength of thirty-five bombers and seventy-two pursuit planes, less than half the strength originally planned for the Philippine defense force. Airfields, accessories, and munitions were almost entirely lacking. . . . Our ground forces consisted of fewer than 12,000 American troops. . . . Our naval forces, including a regiment of Marines, was not under my command or control. The entire fleet comprised only three cruisers, thirteen destroyers, eighteen submarines, and six PT boats."

At its training base deep within Burma, Claire Chennault's American

Volunteer Group was nearly ready for combat. Perpetually short of spare parts and replacements, the unit seemed to be held together with string and baling wire; many of the planes were armed with homemade bombs and incendiaries made from whiskey bottles. But in the autumn of 1941, Chiang was desperate for any air support he could find. Japanese bombers had resumed their devastating raids over Chungking, sometimes sending hundreds of planes in wave after wave at three-hour intervals, for 150 hours at a time. By September nearly half of the city had been flattened. "The raids have almost isolated Chungking from the outside world," reported the *New York Times* correspondent. "Nearly all passenger plane services [practically the only way to reach Chungking] have stopped. Radio and telegraph operations are difficult . . ." The incompetence and disgraceful negligence of Chiang's Kuomintang government compounded the chaos in the capital. In one gruesome tragedy, nearly twenty thousand Chinese civilians suffocated in one of the city's largest public dugouts when military guards locked them in (ostensibly to preserve order and prevent people from constantly running up to the entrance for fresh air) and then went away for ten hours. "It took more than a week to clear the dugout of its corpses," recalled one observer. "Whole families died together. Through the nights of the beginning coolness the lorries came and went, carrying the corpses, and masked men worked with spades removing decomposing debris." Chiang's government attempted to conscript peasants into forced labor gangs to build military roads; when the peasants refused to obey and responded with antigovernment riots in the countryside, the guards fired indiscriminately into the mobs. Then Chiang launched yet another drive to clear the land of Communists. Famine stalked the capital; thousands of workers starved or died of cholera or malaria. As supplies dwindled and prices rose, the government began to evacuate families forcibly from the city.

Prostitution was the only industry that flourished in Chungking; Han Suyin observed that there had never been more prostitutes in the city. They said they were getting ready for the anticipated influx of American pilots and Marines; some enterprising whores, Suyin said, "had even dyed their hair a startling yellow colour."

The United States did, in fact, reinforce its military mission in Chungking in October. Whenever there appeared to be even the slightest chance that Washington would reach an accommodation with Tokyo, Chiang and his wife dispatched a volley of cables to protest and warn (or threaten) that Chinese military resistance might collapse at the slightest indication that America might sell out the Kuomintang regime. This, of course, was precisely what Hornbeck and the rest of the China lobby wanted to hear. Combined with the merciless Japanese bombing raids, which reinforced their image of Japan as a ruthless militarist power that understood only naked force, Chiang's petulant outbursts strengthened the State Department's determination not to agree to any settlement that left Japan with a free hand in China.

This placed the United States and Japan squarely on a collision course. Having invested four years and thousands of lives in what it euphemistically termed "the China Incident," no Japanese government would ever consent to any agreement that did not permit it to settle affairs on the mainland on Japan's own terms. The notion of a Chinese regime hostile to Japan or incapable of crushing Mao's Communist insurgents (whom the Japanese warlords feared almost as much as did Chiang) was intolerable. "I make no concessions regarding a withdrawal!" shouted Tojo during a cabinet meeting of October 14. "It means defeat of Japan by the United States—a stain on the history of the Japanese Empire!" The occupation of Indochina was perhaps negotiable; China was certainly not. Confronted with the sterile intransigence of Hull and the mounting impatience of the Japanese High Command, and having narrowly escaped an assassination attempt by four swordsmen from the fanatically reactionary Black Dragon Society, Konoye at last threw up his hands and resigned the premiership. He was replaced on October 17 by General Tojo, who also retained the offices of war minister and home minister (which left him in control of both the army and the domestic police).

Until this time, Hideki Tojo was best known to the rest of the world as the stern, authoritarian commander of the Kwantung Army that had slashed its way through the Chinese interior in the late 1930s. It was during this campaign that his respectful troops had given him the nickname *Kamisori* ("Razor Blade"). Tojo was a man of action, not ideas, and his entire life had been ruled by the national Japanese principles of filial duty and discipline; he liked to say that "the whole nation should move as one cannonball of fiery resolution." Some optimistic Western observers pointed out that the short, stocky fifty-six-year-old son of a samurai might be the one man who had enough authority to restrain the military extremists, and in fact Tojo did adopt a more conciliatory attitude toward the United States upon his accession as prime minister. In a terse one-minute radio address to the Japanese people (Tojo was a man of very few words), he assured them that he would continue to carry out the policies of the Konoye cabinet.

But the oil gauge was dropping lower, and time was running out. As the original deadline for decision—October 10—passed with no sign of movement in the American negotiating position, the Japanese High Command reluctantly accepted a postponement for another six weeks. A series of final proposals was prepared to be presented to the United States; if no agreement had been reached by November 25, Japan would begin to mobilize its forces for war. Certainly Japanese military intelligence was well aware that the U. S. was reinforcing the Philippines. Suffering terrible hardships under the American trade embargo, the Japanese nation faced economic catastrophe. Government expenditures absorbed nearly three-fourths of the national income. Tojo was shocked to learn that fish was unobtainable in certain sections of Tokyo; fishing boats could not put out to sea because of a lack of fuel oil.

On November 3, the chief of the Japanese Naval General Staff gave final approval to Yamamoto's plan to begin the war against the United States with a surprise aerial attack upon Pearl Harbor.

Armed with their Magic intercepts (which, it should be emphasized, did not include military communications), officials in Washington understood that Japan was moving inexorably toward war. The government advised all American merchant ships in the Pacific to head at once for friendly ports. An administration spokesman publicly acknowledged that "the chances of our having trouble with the Japanese are nine in ten." Watching the deteriorating diplomatic situation from London, Raymond Lee decided that "we may not be heading towards war, but war is heading towards us and at a great rate. Of course, if we manage to get entangled with the Japs we are only playing Hitler's game." More than any other informed observers in the United States, General Marshall and Admiral Stark were well aware that neither the army nor the navy was prepared for a confrontation with Japan; the navy, especially, already had its hands full in the more critical Atlantic theater. On November 5, Marshall and Stark sent a memorandum to Roosevelt flatly recommending that "war between the United States and Japan should be avoided while building up defensive forces in the Far East," and that "no ultimatum be delivered to Japan." That suited Hull fine. He had no intention of forcing the issue; like a crusty old fossil implanted for eternity in a piece of granite, he simply refused to budge. At the same time, however, he warned the War Department—repeatedly—to expect a violent explosion at any moment. "The Administration is prepared to be hard-boiled," reported veteran political commentator Ernest K. Lindley. "The Administration reasons: The Japanese are in a box. Why let them out unless we are reasonably confident they are going to behave?"

On the same day that Marshall and Stark sent their strongly worded message to Roosevelt, the Japanese government announced that it was sending one of its most experienced diplomats, Saburo Kurusu, to Washington to assist Nomura in restoring amicable relations with the United States. If Tojo was sincerely seeking peace, Kurusu was an odd choice for this assignment. Although Kurusu spoke English fluently and had lived for many years in the United States (he had an American wife and an American-born son), the State Department viewed him with deep mistrust because he had been the Japanese ambassador to Berlin when the Tripartite Pact was signed. Kurusu himself seemed to realize his mission was doomed to failure; when he left Tokyo on November 6, he told his son, "Maybe I will not be able to come back. Look after the family." Several days later,

Raymond Lee asked Viscount Kano, a well-connected Japanese financier in London, about his government's motives in dispatching Kurusu to Washington. "Kano said solemnly that it was necessary to have something concrete come from the negotiations which have been dragging along interminably. . . . It was necessary, he said, that something be done because the people in Japan were at a breaking point and could not stand any longer delay. Unless some decision was reached they might fly off the handle and do something foolish."

Kurusu brought with him his government's two final proposals, one of which both sides knew was unacceptable to the United States; the other proposed that Japan withdraw its forces from southern Indochina and refrain from moving further south, in return for which the United States would revoke the freeze on Japanese assets, help Japan find adequate supplies of oil in the Dutch East Indies, and cut off all aid to China. These terms were not terribly satisfactory either, but Hull did not reject them out of hand. He met Nomura and Kurusu for further discussions on November 17, on the eighteenth (for nearly three hours), on the nineteenth, and the twentieth. Meanwhile, Tokyo announced new conscription measures requiring all men who had previously been rejected for military service to be reexamined for possible induction into the army. Vast quantities of tanks, artillery, and trucks were discharged from ships in Saigon and Haiphong harbors and rushed to the frontiers for use against Burma, Thailand, or Yunnan. The *Japan Times Advertiser* proclaimed proudly that "the country is able to move in a number of directions, which requires its potential enemies to be prepared at many places, distributing and decentralizing their strength."

On the twenty-fifth, American cryptographers deciphered a Japanese message warning that November 29 had been set as the deadline for negotiations: "After that things are automatically going to happen." Frustrated, angry, exhausted, beset by anti-Japanese subordinates and pressure from Britain and China to stand firm, Hull decided to "kick the whole thing over." No one else within the administration, including Roosevelt, stepped in to give any firm direction to the drifting American policy. Instead, Hull met Nomura and Kurusu the following day (November 26) and handed them a formal statement that set out in the most inflexible terms the same American demands that Japan already had rejected on numerous occasions: Japan, Hull insisted, must evacuate Indochina and unilaterally give up its hard-won gains in China. Afterwards, Hull saw Stimson and told him, "I have washed my hands of it and it is now in the hands of you and Knox—the Army and the Navy."

On November 27, Marshall informed MacArthur that "negotiations with Japan appear to be terminated to all practical purposes with only barest possibilities that Japanese Government might come back and offer to continue. Japanese future action unpredictable but hostile action possible at any moment. If hostilities cannot, repeat cannot, be avoided, the U.S. desires that Japan commit the first overt act. This policy should not be construed as restricting you to a course of action that might jeopardize the successful defense of the Philippines." MacArthur and Brereton immediately placed the Philippine Air Force on a war footing.

The New York chapter of America First declared that "the Administration, and the Administration alone, will be completely responsible for any breakdown in relations with Japan. The Administration has taken it upon itself to demand actions from Japan that in no way concern the national interests of the United States. None of our territorial possessions are in any way involved." On December 4, Roosevelt rushed back to Washington from his vacation at Warm Springs, Georgia. *Newsweek* magazine reported that "even in far-off Hawaii, the Army was placed on a wartime footing and bayoneted soldiers patrolled docks, bridges, highways, and bases."

On December 5, an official government spokesman in Tokyo announced at a press conference that the negotiations in Washington would proceed: "Both sides will continue to negotiate to find a common formula to ease the situation in the Pacific." Someone asked if the Japanese envoys were sincere in their quest for peace. "If there were no sincerity, there would be no need to continue the negotiations," the spokesman replied.

In his annual report on the state of the Navy Department, released on the evening of December 6, Secretary Knox declared that "I am proud to report that the American people may feel fully confident in their Navy. In my opinion, the loyalty, morale and technical ability of the personnel are without superior. On any comparable basis, the United States navy is second to none."

23

Footsteps in the Hall

"I soon realized that Paris, in 1941, was paralyzed; it would
take a very long time to find men able, or even willing, to risk
their lives for the sake of a vague and remote victory."
—GEORGES BIDAULT

Albert Camus sat under a tent on the dunes near Oran and watched the
sun go down over the southern Mediterranean shore. "At night, the dunes
turn white under the moon. A little earlier, the evening brings out all the
colors, makes them deeper and more violent. The sea is ultramarine, the
road red, the color of clotted blood, the beach yellow. Everything disap-
pears as the green sun goes down, and the dunes glisten with moonlight."
At dawn he saw the young girls, "the naked bodies before the first waves
still black and bitter." They came into flower for one season only; the next
year they would be replaced by other young girls.

Camus felt the wind ("one of the few clean things in the world")
sweeping along the beach, and he watched the sea fade toward the horizon "like a sheet of blue metal," and he thought of the violent absurdity
of Nazism and the ancient gray men at Vichy whom he despised. He was
sick with boredom and despair, sliding toward a recurrence of chronic
tuberculosis. "I am just about hanging on," he told a friend; cut off from
his roots, killing time, methodically pounding into shape his novel of a
civilization beset by plague, *La Peste,* the last volume in the absurdist
trilogy. The writer had uncovered the startling fact that during an earlier
plague, in the time of the Black Death in fourteenth-century Europe, Jews
had been murdered en masse by outraged men searching for a cause for
their suffering. There appeared to be nothing Camus could do to rescue
himself or the world from the blackness that lay ahead. So in September
he sent the manuscripts of the trilogy *(L'Etranger, Caligula,* and *La Peste)*
to his publisher, the Librairie Gallimard in Paris, and turned his back for
a while and joined the staff of a local school in Oran as a soccer coach.

"We are not in a period of great artistic creation," Camus decided,
and it was just as well, for intellectual life in France was smothered by the
occupation. The heavy-handed German censorship of all printed matter
raised a disturbing question for French writers. If they accepted the col-

laborationist ground rules that discriminated against left-wing artists and Jews, they could be accused of lending their moral support to the despised Fascist regime; consequently many anti-Nazi writers simply refused to allow their material to be published by any journal that enjoyed official sanction. The dilemma was even more troubling for performing artists such as Edith Piaf and Maurice Chevalier. Like most Frenchmen, Chevalier preferred to remain in France and suffer the consequences of an uncertain future rather than seek refuge abroad (despite the fact that his friends in the Resistance offered to fly him out of Marseilles to North Africa). He announced his retirement but permitted the occupation authorities to talk him out of it; he submitted to German pressure and returned to Paris to perform at the Casino de Paris before audiences full of Wehrmacht officers and their French mistresses. Like all entertainers, Chevalier had to obtain the consent of the *Propagandastaffel* in the Champs Elysées for the selections on his program, but as a dedicated follower of Marshal Pétain, Chevalier saw nothing wrong in choosing songs that fostered the National Revolution's conservative virtues of work, family, and fatherland. He performed his songs on Radio Paris, despite the fact that the station was one of the Nazis' primary propaganda weapons. "I am torn apart by my love for my country and my profession," Chevalier once admitted. "Have I done wrong?" After refusing repeated Nazi requests to tour camps of French workers who had emigrated to Germany, he finally consented to go in return for the exchange of several French prisoners of war who were natives of his hometown.

Some right-wing French artists, of course, welcomed the Nazi occupation as an unprecedented opportunity to build a Fascist France free of Jews and class warfare. "One must have a short memory," they argued, "not to prefer this June to last June." In fact, many of them wanted the French army to fight openly at Germany's side. Jacques Doriot, an ex-Communist, edited the quasi-Nazi newspaper *Cri du Peuple* and reportedly organized squads of hoodlums to sabotage shops secretly owned or patronized by Jews. Marcel Déat, editor of *L'Oeuvre* and head of the pro-Nazi *Rassemblement Nationale Populaire,* who had openly sabotaged the Third Republic's war effort by ridiculing its decision to declare war over the invasion of Poland (of all places), decided in June 1941 that Nazi Germany was worth fighting for, and so he formed the *Ligue des Volontaires Français en Allemagne,* a French volunteer force that went off to fight the Communists on the eastern front. There was Eugène Deloncle, founder of the underground Fascist society the *Cagoulards;* and the occupation's favorite propagandist, Jean Luchaire, whose young daughter was wooed by the notorious womanizer Joseph Goebbels during Luchaire's famous dinner parties at the Tour d'Argent. Although their egos and overweening sense of self-importance led to so much bickering that they could never work together as a cohesive political force, these collaborationist intellectuals earned the eternal enmity of many of their fellow countrymen. "Never before, I realized, had I known what hatred really was," wrote Simone de Beauvoir. "But now I recognized its flavor, and focused it with especial violence against those of our enemies whom I knew most about. Pétain's speeches had a more inflammatory effect on me than Hitler's; and while I condemned all collaborators, I felt a sharply defined and quite excruciating personal loathing for those of my own kind who joined their ranks—intellectuals, journalists, writers."

In the summer and autumn of 1941, Paris was isolated in time and space. Céline, that violently misanthropic writer who despised Jews and collaborationists alike, observed in June that life in the city was "sickeningly difficult": "One finishes up by shrivelling up like an animal and putting up with almost anything." As factories shut down for want of fuel and materials, and cars disappeared from the city streets, Paris seemed curiously unreal and empty. "It isn't that Paris is ugly," Colette told a friend at the end of July, "its great deserted spaces give us relief, and I can install myself in the Tuileries, where the flowers are beautiful, with no more neighbours than I used to have, once upon a time, in the Bois." Fear, too, rendered the city silent. "No one talks in the Métro any more. No one cares for the exchange of unconsidered words at the top of his voice," noticed one Parisian. There were no frivolous sounds in the streets; children played quietly, with little joy. "France is full of reasonable children," Colette observed, "precociously mature, patient and reserved enough to bring the tears to your eyes." The daily routine revolved around the German restrictions, the *Ausweis* (identification cards) stamped with the eagle and swastika (derisively known as "the crow on pedals"), the omnipresent posters with the latest instructions, and the constant anxiety induced by the Nazi raids in the night.

Author Germaine Beaumont recorded the terror of life in the occupied city:

> . . . the enforced obscurity, the curfew, the watching behind a curtain which one does not dare to lift, the waiting behind a door for footsteps which are late in coming, footsteps one won't hear for a long time, footsteps one may never hear again. The book which falls from the hand, unfinished, broken off in the middle of a line; a tapestry which trembles so much under the fingers that one cannot put a needle through it, and the mouthful of food which stops in the throat, the bread which tastes like sand. . . .

For those who could not afford to purchase additional food on the black market, meat was available once a week if at all. Fats were almost impossible to obtain. It was not uncommon to witness the depressing sight of two hundred women waiting in line for hours to purchase one head of lettuce apiece. Newspapers carried recipes for salads made of wild greens, and housewives sought to make roasts without meat, omelettes without eggs, cream without milk. New expressions crept into the vocabulary of the kitchen: "the 'scrap' replaces the sirloin, the 'chunks' of rabbit deputize for *hare à la royale.* But whence to take the scrap when one has not had the whole article?" De Beauvoir spent her days searching for unrationed foodstuffs, "a sort of treasure hunt . . . what a windfall if I stumbled on a beet or a cabbage." She spent hours culling through her stocks of dried beans to eliminate the ones that had become infested with maggots; when she made "turnip sauerkraut" and covered it with sauce made from canned soup, her lover, Jean Paul Sartre, told her it wasn't half bad. The toll of fifteen months of undernourishment manifested itself in the form of sallow complexions, bad teeth, and an increased susceptibility to minor epidemics. The monthly soap ration was reduced to a cake about half the size of a full pack of cigarettes. Turbans came into fashion because hats and hairdressers were equally difficult to find. "Avoid the mirror," advised one popular women's columnist. "Turn your back to it when writing, sewing or reading. Generally, it will have nothing good to tell you. You are not always capable of appreciating the beauty impressed on feminine features by slackness, enveloping silence, a profitable resignation, melancholy, and the pride of enduring for several hours without seeking the aid of others." As the weather turned colder in the autumn, people drank to stay warm because there was so little coal. Edith Piaf solved the heating problem by moving into the top floor of a *maison close* in the rue de Villejuste, a house where high-priced prostitutes took their clients (and hence was always comfortably warm).

Unemployment continued to rise during the second year of the occupation. Some Frenchmen supplemented their meager incomes by smuggling money, documents, or jewelry across the border into Vichy. Others turned a few extra pennies by supplying the Gestapo with information. On the other hand, the undisguised venality of German occupation authorities, nearly all of whom could be bribed at bargain rates, allowed the French to retain at least a shred of their traditional sense of moral superiority.

Many Frenchmen took to wandering aimlessly through the southern half of the country that year, a sharp departure from previous times when the government travel bureaus had to beg them to leave their own villages. Late in the summer, de Beauvoir and Sartre (who was trying to recruit members for his embryonic resistance group, *Socialisme et Liberté*) crossed into the unoccupied zone for a working vacation. One of the first things they did was to go see a few American movies ("hailing them like very dear, long-lost friends," de Beauvoir said); then they rode their bicycles south, toward the Midi, where Sartre unsuccessfully implored André Gide and André Malraux to join his brotherhood. At Marseilles they saw more American films (including *Dark Victory,* the unrelentingly gloomy melodrama featuring Bette Davis, George Brent, and Humphrey

Bogart). Marseilles was full of French Jews who were on their way out of the country; the Mediterranean city also sheltered most of the nation's intellectual and entertainment community that chose to remain in France but outside of Paris. The residents had to get along without the traditional pleasures of fresh lobsters and bouillabaisse, however, since most of the local fisherman were afraid to venture into the heavily mined Mediterranean.

In the comic-opera capital of Vichy, where the Marshal's Guard dressed in dark-blue uniforms with black leather puttees, long white gauntlets, and motorcycle helmets, where official files of the Foreign Office sat in battered cardboard boxes in the corridors of the Hôtel du Parc and the director general of the Sûreté Nationale ran the government's intelligence activities from a basement room in the Hôtel de Russie, Marshal Pétain was worried. "I have a noose around my neck," he told reporters in November, "and the Germans can pull the rope at any time." Pétain finally had come to realize that the occupation in the north would go on for a long time, and that the slightest misstep might bring the south, too, under the Reich's direct control. Perhaps this sense of impending personal and national catastrophe explained why the aged Marshal had declared, in May, his renewed determination to lead Vichy France loyally into the "new European order." He refused to explain his reasons for following this route of least resistance; yet his defensive speech to the nation announcing his decision revealed an acute sensitivity to the wave of criticism that he knew would follow his proclamation: "It is no longer a question today of public opinion, often uneasy and badly informed, being able to estimate the chances we are taking or measure the risks we take or judge our acts," Pétain said. "For you, the French people, it is simply a question of following me without mental reservations along the path of honor and national interest. If through our close discipline and our public spirit we can conduct the negotiations in progress, France will surmount her defeat and preserve in the world her rank as a European and colonial power." On the other side of the Atlantic, Roosevelt remarked sadly, "Vichy is in a German cage."

As a symbol of France's regeneration under the National Revolution, Pétain removed Bastille Day from the list of national holidays and replaced it with the celebration of May Day. A paternalistic policy toward women gradually took shape: women were forbidden to work if their husbands held jobs, and men on trolleys or buses were required by law to relinquish their seats to pregnant women or women with small children. On June 2, the government revised its *Statut des juifs* and commenced a purge of Jews from the ranks of business, industry, agriculture, and most scientific or liberal professions. Jews could make up no more than 2 percent of Vichy's doctors or lawyers, and no more than 3 percent of its university students. Later in the year, more professions and business activities were added to the restricted list. In an effort to eliminate "all Jewish influence from the national economy," Pétain's government began to confiscate Jewish property. The Ministry of Justice attempted to justify Vichy's increasingly stringent anti-Semitic regulations by stating that Jews "have refused for centuries to melt into the French community. . . . The French government has no intention of assimilating them by force. . . . It is not expelling them. It is not depriving them of the means of existence (which was not strictly true). It is merely forbidding them the functions of directing the French soul or French interests." Although Vichy was usually one or two steps behind occupied France in discriminating against Jews, the government was doing its best to keep up.

Pétain's latest heir apparent (the replacement for the discredited Pierre Laval, whose pro-Nazi sympathies were simply too obvious) was Admiral Jean Darlan, a man whose military career consisted largely of an uninterrupted series of behind-the-scenes political maneuvers aimed always at advancing his own career. Like many French sailors, Darlan thoroughly disliked the British, though his prejudice sometimes reached ridiculous extremes; in denouncing the British blockade that prevented a free flow of foodstuffs from reaching Vichy, he put forth the proposition that "Germans are always more generous and more understanding of the needs of humanity than the English." On May 28, Darlan signed a series of "protocols" designed to consummate the previous halting steps toward military collaboration between France and Germany: Germany was permitted to use French ports and railways in North Africa to supply Rommel's Afrika Korps, and the strategically crucial airfield and port of Dakar, the westernmost point in Africa (1,700 miles from Brazil), was opened to the German High Command, an action that caused a severe anti-Vichy reaction in Washington. "Dealing with Darlan is like dealing with Germany," Churchill warned Roosevelt, "for he will not be allowed to agree to anything they know about which does not suit their book."

In August, Pétain appointed Darlan (already vice premier and foreign minister) to the post of minister of national defense, which gave him control of all French military forces at home and in the colonies still loyal to Vichy. At the same time, Pétain doubled his government's police force, suppressed virtually all independent political activities, and appointed new commissioners of public power to carry out his orders. Shortly thereafter, he forbade his subjects to listen to the BBC or other stations that disseminated "anti-French propaganda," including Boston's shortwave station WRUL, which broadcast General de Gaulle's speeches throughout western Europe. In November, Admiral Weygand, the most visible symbol of anticollaborationist sentiment, was unceremoniously removed from his position as commander of the French armies in North Africa.

For those who wondered how a formerly great and proud nation

could sink to such depths, American correspondent Henry J. Taylor, who
visited Vichy in October, offered a tentative explanation:

> The first and overpowering thought of everyone in unoccupied France
> is food. This overshadows everything, and any other consideration is a very
> poor second. The only way to judge the feelings and attitudes of a Frenchman
> who has not had enough food for a long time is to experience this yourself and
> see how you think and feel and react toward any idea or problem except food.
> Hunger like this is a disease. "I am hungry," is all you can think of, all you can
> feel. There isn't any room for any other thought.

Others were less sympathetic. In November, François Mauriac condemned his fellow countrymen as cowards. Like the bourgeoisie who
stealthily buried their cash boxes in the begonia beds, "so many other
Frenchmen [outside the working class] are moved by an elementary passion: fear! They don't admit it. They idolize the Marshal and invoke Joan
of Arc, but in their heart of hearts everything leads back to what seems
to them the only necessity: saving their privileges and avoiding settling
their accounts—'as long as the Germans are here . . .' A reassuring little
phrase . . ."

But some Frenchmen struck back. As Resistance leader Georges Bidault explained, "from the very start the Resistance was a question of
outlook, perhaps, even more, of character . . . The Resistance was a refusal
to compromise." During its infancy, the Resistance consisted primarily of
amateurs who displayed an appalling disregard for the most elementary
security precautions. It was difficult to distinguish the patriot from the
agent provocateur, or the fighter from the braggart. In Lyons, the city that
became known as the capital of the Resistance, one agent recalled that
"absolute orgies of plotting were going on along the Rue de la République,
and in the No. 7 tramway that went between Perrache and Villeurbanne.
A young man would be standing like a lamp-post at every corner, waiting
for his contact who was late. It was a great mistake to be late and also to
stand conspicuously at street-corners. People went about plotting at the
top of their voices. Talking about plotting was what made it spicy and
pleasurable for many of them." Occasionally they paid for their indiscretion with their lives. The *Comité National de Salut Public,* one of the first
active Resistance groups, consisted largely of academics who smuggled
escaped prisoners of war into the unoccupied zone; betrayed by a double
agent, the circle was soon broken, and the leaders executed after months
of torture in the Cherche-Midi prison.

At first, the Resistance confined itself to publishing defiant manifestos
and gathering information about German military dispositions which it
passed on to the British Secret Service, whose own network of agents had
been shattered during the blitzkrieg in 1940. Then, in the summer of
1941, the situation changed, literally, overnight. Hitler's invasion of the

Soviet Union brought into the Resistance the French political group with the most experienced, ruthless, tightly organized underground structure: the Communists. Now the blood began to flow. During the week of August 13, riots shook the eleventh arrondissement of Paris—a working-class quarter in the shadow of the Bastille—and the occupation authorities (German troops and French police) responded by killing two demonstrators, arresting six thousand "Communist Jews," and banning all Communist activity within occupied France, on pain of death. On August 21 a German naval officer was shot to death on the Paris Métro. General von Stulpnagel, the Nazi military commander in the capital, warned: "First, from August 23 on, all Frenchmen who have been arrested will be considered hostages. Second, should there be another such episode, a number of hostages, depending upon the gravity of the act, will be shot." On August 28, shots were fired in Paris at arch-collaborationists Marcel Déat and Pierre Laval. Two days later, the Germans executed eight hostages. "Make the Boche fall off trains," suggested the underground Radio Syndicaliste. "Make him fall off buses. Make him miss his train. Don't deliver his letters. If you are taking care of his car, ruin it." Scores of mysterious railway accidents piled up in both zones; Vichy broadcast an appeal to railwaymen to refrain from acts of sabotage. Gradually certain segments of the French police became sympathetic to the spreading revolt, and so the Germans cracked down harder. Special military courts were established to order the execution of prisoners accused of offenses against the state. Black-bordered posters appeared on the streets of Paris, announcing the deaths of more hostages. By the end of September the executions numbered sixty-nine. Vichy's minister of the interior, Pierre Pucheu, went to Paris to try to put an end to the reprisals. During the first week of October, several of the most prominent synagogues in the capital were destroyed by bombs, apparently the work of the Gestapo.

On the morning of October 20, the commandant of the German garrison at Nantes was shot and killed while walking to his office; surgeons reportedly found bullets in his body from fifteen different revolvers. The following day, a German major was murdered at dusk on a road in Bordeaux. Hitler and SS security chief Reinhard Heydrich decided that the unanticipated upsurge of resistance required a firm response by the Gestapo, so the Germans lined up ninety-eight Frenchmen against a wall and shot them, and they threatened to execute more if the assassins were not surrendered. "A stream of blood is flowing again over France," cried an anguished Pétain, who reportedly offered himself as a hostage and informed the Germans that he could no longer be responsible for keeping order if the executions continued. The fact that the German army of occupation had been reduced from an estimated 2,000,000 at the beginning of 1941 to 400,000 at the end of October (to feed the Wehrmacht's insatiable need for bodies on the eastern front) made the Nazis extremely nervous and determined to avoid any show of weakness. "To German officers who had been reared with the concept of a 'chivalrous war,' " explained General Keitel, "we were obliged to emphasize the fact that when you are dealing with an enemy who employs such methods, you must not hesitate to retaliate in kind if you wish to remain in control of the situation."

Roosevelt condemned the Nazi executions as "the acts of desperate men who know in their hearts that they cannot win." Churchill warned that they were "but a foretaste of what Hitler would inflict upon the British and American peoples if only he could get the power." And General de Gaulle issued a public appeal to cease all individual isolated anti-Nazi terrorist activities until conditions were more favorable and the struggle could be properly directed (by him).

In fact, until the autumn of 1941, de Gaulle had given little thought to the notion of resistance within Metropolitan France; for him, the critical task was the establishment of an alternative Free French government capable of fighting and winning its own battles, ready to replace Vichy and the occupation when the Nazis had been defeated. "Let us not stay home and merely try to stir up trouble. Let us flee and join General de Gaulle," was the essence of his recruiting campaign within France. He did assemble a rudimentary intelligence network headed by Major Dewavrin, who, like all de Gaulle's agents, adopted the name of a Paris métro station as his pseudonym; in this case, "Passy." But de Gaulle, realizing that he would always be a junior partner in any joint Anglo–Free French intelligence-gathering operation, eschewed active cooperation with the British MI6 and SIS. This happened to suit the British just fine, since they considered de Gaulle's operatives to be nothing more than "dangerously incompetent amateurs" whose headquarters lacked any sense of secrecy. Quite frankly, de Gaulle irritated the hell out of his British hosts, who did not want to antagonize Pétain unnecessarily or push Vichy closer toward active cooperation with Berlin. General Brooke complained that "whatever good qualities he may have had were marred by his overbearing manner, his megalomania and lack of co-operative spirit. He is supposed to have said at that time 'Je suis la France!' Whether he did or not he certainly adopted that attitude." For de Gaulle, who was contemptuous of virtually everyone anyway, this sort of prickly, self-protective posture was essential. He once reportedly said, "The weaker I am, the more intransigent I shall be!" "The grandeur and force of our movement consists exclusively in the intransigence we show in defending the rights of France," de Gaulle sniffed. "We shall have need of that intransigence up to and including the Rhine."

Until the autumn of 1941, de Gaulle's efforts to induce Frenchmen to leave their homeland and join his Free French movement had met with a resounding lack of success. Certainly the General's imperious attitude, his pompous declarations that "whoever is not with us, is against us," his ill-advised personal attacks upon the revered figure of Marshal Pétain, and his unfortunate tendency "to get in other people's hair" (as one American observer put it) hindered his recruiting efforts. Besides, de Gaulle had fled the country while Pétain had remained to share the hardships and humiliations, and that distinction in itself was sufficient to create a serious obstacle to popular support for the Free French movement in the first days after the armistice.

De Gaulle had spent the spring of 1941 searching for suitable employment for the soldiers he had assembled from the garrisons of sympathetic French African colonies. In March, he had landed in Cairo ("And here came I, troublesome and pressing," he admitted), whereupon he urged the embattled Wavell to launch a joint Anglo–Free French invasion of Vichy-controlled Syria and Lebanon: "Sooner or later we would have to go there." This, of course, was precisely what Wavell did not need at a time when he was struggling to juggle inadequate British forces among the Mediterranean, North Africa, East Africa, and the Middle East. So de Gaulle, still straining at the leash, set off on a tour of Equatorial Africa while he continued to badger the British from long range. Following the revolt of pro-Axis forces in Iraq under Rashid Ali in the first week of May, and the subsequent decision by Darlan to grant landing facilities in Syria to the Luftwaffe, Churchill decided—much against Wavell's advice—to prepare a plan for an advance against Syria. Within the next month, Wavell managed to throw together a motley invasion force of Australians, Indians, Free French, and volunteers from the closely knit Jewish settlement in Palestine (which, like the Free French, wanted to validate its political claims by participating in the fighting, while at the same time gaining practical combat experience for use against potential enemies in the postwar world).

Although the British had officially barred the door to further Jewish immigration into Palestine two years earlier, the *yishuv* was already a thriving, vital force. When the young writer Dan Vittorio Segre arrived in Tel Aviv after a comfortable upbringing as the son of a landowner in Italy, he was struck by the sight of barracks made of wood and tattered tar paper perched "like witches' dens" on the sand dunes; all at once he perceived "the dessicated vitality of the place—the power of the people who, from ideological choice rather than from necessity, wanted to appear poorer and rougher than my father's peasants. They exuded an insolent misery; they displayed a life-style that signaled to me unequivocally I had fallen into a world of frenetic action, without reserves or counterweights, with no hiding places for the soul. It was a world devoted to deeds and burned by activism as the flat-roofed, peeling houses were burned by the sun." Recognizing talented fighters when they saw them—the British had, after all, been battling clandestine Jewish military organizations like the

Haganah for several years already—British officials released a large number of Jews whom they had arrested for participating in illegal military activities and assimilated them into the British army for use on special assignments. (Suspicious of any Jews armed with modern weapons, the political administration in Palestine insisted that they be kept under close supervision; the semi-autonomous Jewish Brigade would not be established until 1944. Actually, this proved to be something of a boon in the long run, since their close association with Australian troops provided some Jewish commanders with a model for an army of independent, tough-minded soldiers.)

One member of the Haganah who had been released from Acre prison in February 1941 was Moshe Dayan, who, along with Yigal Allon, became a company commander in the new Anglo-Jewish operations force in Palestine. When the invasion of Syria began on June 8, Dayan's unit was assigned to act as a reconnaissance force for a detachment of Australians. In the ensuing action, a Vichy rifle bullet struck Dayan's field glasses as he stood on the roof of a police station, shattering the lens and ramming bits of glass and metal into the socket of his left eye. After he was evacuated to a hospital in Haifa, a dazed and half-blind Dayan heard his doctor say, *"Two* things are certain. You've lost an eye and you'll live. What is not clear is the condition of your head . . ."

After a week of hard fighting, Wavell called up reinforcements from Iraq, where Rashid Ali's revolt had collapsed. The Australians captured Damascus on June 21, and de Gaulle made a triumphal entry into the city two days later. On July 12, the Vichy commander in Syria surrendered. But when the soldiers of the Syrian garrison were given an opportunity to join the Free French, only 6,000 accepted. The others—25,000—chose to return to France instead. Stung by this rebuke, de Gaulle took out his anger upon the British, verbally lashing them for their refusal to break diplomatic relations with Vichy and recognize Free France as the sole legitimate French government. On his way back to London, he took advantage of a layover in Brazzaville to give an interview to an American correspondent. "England is afraid," he shouted. "England is afraid of the French fleet. What in effect England is carrying on is a wartime deal with Hitler in which Vichy serves as a go-between. Vichy serves Hitler by keeping the French people in subjection and selling the French Empire piecemeal to Germany. But do not forget that Vichy also serves England by keeping the French fleet from Hitler's hands. What happens in effect is an exchange of advantages between hostile powers. . . . If Vichy should lend or lose its fleet to the Germans, Britain would quickly bring the suspense about recognition to an end." Although de Gaulle later claimed that he was misquoted, Churchill responded angrily by refusing to see him for over a month while the British government searched for an alternative leader of a French government-in-exile. There was none. Finally, on October 1, the Prime Minister acknowledged that "General de Gaulle is at present the only possible leader of that movement." But, determined to avoid the spectacle of the uncontrollable General roaming loose about the Mediterranean, stirring up more trouble, Churchill also issued specific instructions that de Gaulle was not to be permitted to leave Britain under any circumstances.

So for the rest of the year the General divided his time between his shabby offices in Carlton Gardens and his home in Hampstead, where he spent his evenings and weekends playing games with his wife and his handicapped daughter, Anne, who adored him. As the incidents of resistance multiplied in France and the execution of hostages fanned the flames of anti-German sentiment, de Gaulle decided that he should place himself at the head of the movement. He recruited a former highly placed civil servant named Jean Moulin to head his network, and sent Moulin back into France via parachute to coordinate the movement. According to Georges Bidault, few of the early Resistance fighters knew very much about de Gaulle, although "the partisans disliked the sound of his voice and the photographs of him that had been parachuted to France." Actually, they probably decided to follow him more from a hatred of Vichy than a love for de Gaulle. His most valuable weapon in the war for the hearts of Frenchman was his ability to draw upon the power and prestige of the BBC. "The British radio, more than anything else, helped to establish de Gaulle's name," Bidault claimed. "The B.B.C. literally made de Gaulle. . . . Distance gave him an aura of mystery, and yet he was in daily communication with us; that was what gave him such prestige."

But there were those who paid no attention to his command to stop the terrorist attacks upon German military personnel. Near the end of November, a bomb exploded in a Montparnasse restaurant used as a mess hall for Nazi troops; on November 28, someone tossed a grenade into a restaurant in Montmartre, killing two German soldiers. The occupation authorities clamped a 5:30 P.M. curfew around the two *quartiers.*

On December 7, General Keitel issued the notorious "night and fog" decree. Henceforth, all non-German civilians in France found guilty of "criminal acts against the Reich or the occupation authorities" would be arrested, and from that time on they would disappear without a trace. Perhaps they would be executed at the discretion of the German authorities; perhaps they would be sent to rot in German prisons. But no news of their fate would ever be announced to anyone.

24

Twilight

"We are able to fight and are not afraid to fight. My only doubt
is whether we need to join in England's fight. I should like it
better if we had it all to ourselves so the issue would be
something I could understand and if we won we would get the loot
the glory and the self-realization. That last is the great thing.
I don't want to see a lot of bloody trouble unless we are going
to bring America out a nation more distinct from all other
nations than she is already."

—ROBERT FROST, NOVEMBER 1941

A British patrol plane alerted the captain of the American destroyer
Greer that a submerged U-boat lay across his path, ten miles ahead on the
route to Iceland on the morning of September 4. The *Greer* promptly set
a zigzag course and established underwater contact with the U-boat—
whose commander apparently did not know whether the destroyer was
an American or British vessel—and then the American ship proceeded to
follow the U-boat around the Atlantic, broadcasting its position to the
British plane, which obligingly dropped several depth charges upon the
submarine. After being shadowed for three hours, the U-boat suddenly
turned and fired a brief flurry of torpedoes at the *Greer*. The destroyer
responded by dropping a dozen depth charges of its own. After this inef-
fectual exchange, during which neither vessel was damaged, the *Greer*
turned back toward Iceland to complete its mail run.

Although it was a relatively undramatic incident, and certainly one in
which the American ship was not entirely an innocent victim of Nazi
aggression, Roosevelt decided to use the U-boat attack to shake America
out of its lethargy. He waited for a week (the delay was due in part to the
death of his mother at Hyde Park on September 6), and then broadcast a
radio message to the nation. Wearing a black armband over the sleeve of
his gray summer suit, sitting next to a sign that read "Keep 'Em Flying,"
Roosevelt told an estimated sixty million Americans that "it is now clear
that Hitler has begun his campaign to control the seas by ruthless force."
It was finally time, he said (again), for Americans to give up the romantic
notion that they could go on living peacefully and contentedly in a world
dominated by Nazism. "There has now come a time when you and I must

see the cold inexorable necessity of saying to these inhuman, unrestrained seekers of world conquest: 'You shall go no further.' " To those who counseled patience and forbearance, the President replied succinctly, "When you see a rattlesnake poised to strike, you do not wait until he has struck before you crush him."

Driving through the lonely hills of Tennessee on an inspection tour of the TVA, White House speechwriter Samuel Rosenman heard Roosevelt's words on the radio. "The atmosphere was quiet and peaceful down there on the shores of the Tennessee River on that still September night," recalled Rosenman. "It seemed so far away from the world of conflict and destruction, from the mass killing of civilians and the cruelties of the Nazis, that the bold, resolute—almost belligerent—tones of the President seemed a little like a voice coming from another planet."

Roosevelt continued. "We have sought no shooting war with Hitler. We do not seek it now. But neither do we want peace so much that we are willing to pay for it by permitting him to attack our naval and merchant ships while they are on legitimate business." And so the President ordered the navy to shoot on sight any Axis submarines or surface vessels it encountered on its patrol routes. "Let this warning be clear: From now on, if German or Italian vessels of war enter the waters the protection of which is necessary for American defense, they do so at their own peril. . . . The sole responsibility rests upon Germany. There will be no shooting unless Germany continues to seek it."

Well, this was as disingenuous a bit of sophistry as Roosevelt ever perpetrated, but for a while it succeeded in rallying the nation behind the commander in chief. It finally got the administration over the convoying hurdle; at the national convention of the American Legion in Milwaukee the following week, Navy Secretary Frank Knox received an enthusiastic reception when he announced that "beginning tomorrow, the American Navy will provide protection as adequate as we can make it for ships of every flag carrying Lend-Aid supplies between the American Continent and the waters adjacent to Iceland. These ships are ordered to capture or destroy by every means at their disposal Axis-controlled submarines or surface raiders encountered in these waters. That is our answer to Mr. Hitler." (Thus challenged, Mr. Hitler—who was busy directing the Russian campaign from his Wolfsschanze retreat—responded through a government spokesman who accused Mr. Roosevelt of having "forced a situation in which the Reich must adopt fitting countermeasures," which remained unspecified. Despite Roosevelt's virtual declaration of naval war against Germany, Hitler informed Admiral Raeder that he wanted no more serious incidents with the United States before mid-October, by which time the renewed German offensive in Russia should have cleared the muddled strategic picture. Besides, there were only ten U-boats on active duty in the Atlantic at the time.)

But once again, having stirred patriotic impulses throughout America, Roosevelt chose to proceed cautiously in Congress. Ultimately, he wanted Congress to repeal the entire set of Neutrality Acts that had been passed in the interwar period; based upon the dubious assumption that American loans and munitions shipments had dragged the United States into the First World War against its best interests, these measures had sought to enforce strict limits on any American economic or military contact with belligerent nations. To avoid a head-on confrontation with the still powerful isolationist bloc in the Senate, Roosevelt decided to request only that Congress permit American merchant ships to arm themselves in self-defense, a measure that would be extremely difficult to oppose while Nazi U-boats allegedly were roaming through the Atlantic, searching for easy targets.

Although a Gallup poll revealed that two-thirds of American voters endorsed Roosevelt's "shoot on sight" policy, the American people remained in a strange twilight mood throughout the autumn of 1941. It was as if they had awakened from their summer slumber to find that they still had an unpleasant chore awaiting them; the war had not gone away. Defense was the number one topic of conversation everywhere. Popular magazines devoted nearly half of each issue to the preparedness program, and every commentator had his own prediction of just how long it would be before America was dragged into war either in the Atlantic or the Pacific. It was becoming difficult to find an advertisement that did not have a defense tie-in: Food for Democracy, Adding Machines for Military Efficiency, Lubricants for Victory.

Isolationist rallies took on a distinct tinge of fatalism. The general sense of lethargy was broken only by two incidents that frankly embarrassed the isolationist cause. At a speech in Des Moines on September 11, Lindbergh charged in his usual cold, unemotional manner that "the three most important groups which have been pressing this country toward war are the British, the Jewish, and the Roosevelt Administration. . . . It is not difficult to understand why Jewish people desire the overthrow of Nazi Germany. The persecution they suffered in Germany would be sufficient to make bitter enemies of any race. No person with a sense of the dignity of mankind can condone the persecution of the Jewish race in Germany. But no person of honesty and vision can look on their pro-war policy here today without seeing the dangers involved in such a policy both for us and for them. . . . Instead of agitating for war, the Jewish groups in this country should be opposing it in every possible way, for they will be among the first to feel its consequences. Their greatest danger to this country lies in their large ownership and influence in our motion pictures, our press, our radio, and our government."

Before the Des Moines meeting, Anne had implored him not to attack the Jews openly. "He will be branded anti-Semite, Nazi, Fuehrer-seeking, etc.," she predicted. "It is a match lit near a pile of excelsior," and she was absolutely correct. From all parts of the political spectrum, a veritable hailstorm of criticism descended upon the former hero; everything else he had said or done over the past year faded into insignificance. (Some accounts of the speech left out the central section quoted above, an omission that made Lindbergh appear even more anti-Semitic.) Wendell Willkie flatly declared that Lindbergh's speech was "the most un-American talk made in my time by any person of national reputation." Huge heart-shaped posters appeared on Los Angeles city streets, saying, "Adolf Loves Lindy." The Texas House of Representatives declared the flier persona non grata in their state. Sergeant York snapped that Lindbergh "ought to be shut up" by throwing him "square in jail"; William Allen White convicted Lindbergh of "moral treason." Thomas E. Dewey charged that Lindbergh had committed "an inexcusable abuse of the right of freedom of speech." Representative Luther Patrick of Alabama brandished a copy of *Mein Kampf* in the House and said that "it sounds just like Lindbergh." One senator received the following sarcastic telegram from a constituent:

HAVE JUST BEEN READING A BOOK CALLED THE HOLY BIBLE. HAS LARGE CIRCULATION IN THIS COUNTRY. WRITTEN ENTIRELY BY FOREIGN-BORN, MOSTLY JEWS. FIRST PART FULL OF WARMONGERING PROPAGANDA. SECOND PART CONDEMNS ISOLATIONISM. THAT FAKE STORY ABOUT GOOD SAMARITAN DANGEROUS. SHOULD BE ADDED TO YOUR LIST AND SUPPRESSED.

Even the isolationist Hearst press jumped on the anti-Lindbergh bandwagon. "The assertion that the Jews are pressing this country into war is unwise, unpatriotic, and un-American," charged Hearst. "This astonishing statement [is] at total variance with the facts." Other isolationist leaders worried that the colonel's "stupid" speech would provide opponents with a tar brush with which to smear the whole movement.

Close upon the heels of Lindbergh's blunder followed the entertaining spectacle of a senatorial investigation of "warmongering" in Hollywood. Charging the heads of filmdom's largest studios with a conspiracy to produce movies that were purposefully designed to inflame public opinion toward American participation in the war in Europe, Senators Wheeler and Nye packed a five-man subcommittee with four die-hard isolationists, including themselves, and launched a Capitol Hill extravaganza that critics compared favorably to *Mr. Smith Goes to Washington.* In self-defense, the studios hired Wendell Willkie to represent them before the committee, but they really needed little help.

It was one of the best shows Washington had seen since Andra the Flame. During the course of the hearings, Nye cited eight films that he claimed were typical examples of Hollywood's anti-Hitler bias: *Sergeant York, The Great Dictator, Man Hunt, Convoy, Flight Command, I Married a Nazi, Escape,* and *That Hamilton Woman.* When freshman Senator Ernest W. McFarland of Arizona, the only nonisolationist on the subcommittee, asked Nye how many of the eight movies he had personally seen, Nye admitted that he had seen only two. Senator Bennett Clark of Missouri, who had accused the movie industry of "turning 17,000 theaters into 17,000 daily and nightly mass meetings for war," said that he had not seen *any* of the films in question and that he really didn't go the movies very often anyway. Meanwhile, Willkie—whom chairman Clark had relegated to the sidelines—grabbed the microphone anyway and charged the subcommittee with "seeking to divide the American people into discordant racial and religious groups in order to disunite them over the United States' foreign policy which has been overwhelmingly approved by the Congress and by the people."

But the most eloquent defense of Hollywood came from the studio executives themselves, who had often rolled over and supinely submitted to political pressures in the past. Harry Warner, whose studio headed Nye's list of suspects, denied that Warner Brothers was attempting to incite the American people to war, or that its movies were inaccurate depictions of current events. "If Warner Brothers had produced no pictures concerning the Nazi movement, our public would have had good reason to criticize," explained Warner. "I tell this committee honestly, I care nothing for any temporary advantage or profit that may be offered to me or my company. I will not censor the dramatization of the works of reputable and well informed writers to conceal from the American people what is happening in the world. Freedom of speech, freedom of religion and freedom of enterprise cannot be bought at the price of other people's rights. I believe the American people have a right to know the truth. You may correctly charge me with being anti-Nazi. But no one can charge me with being anti-American."

From September until December, Congress remained in session, often working around the clock as Washington finally realized that the crisis could be delayed no longer. "We are in the midst of one of those periods of history—and that is what sometimes gives your old man the headache and the pain in the middle," complained Harry Truman to his wife on November 10. "What we do is of vital importance to our daughter's generation and the next one." With a few fitful shudders and false starts (including a disquieting tremor from the shock of 425 new strikes in September), the engines of defense production finally lurched into high gear as Roosevelt asked Congress for a $6.7 billion supplementary appropriation for the War Department. But by now nearly twelve months of precious time already had been lost, and in November 1941 the United States was still woefully unprepared for war.

While Congress debated the wisdom of arming American merchant ships, a somewhat distressed Secretary Knox disclosed that even if the measure passed, there simply were not enough decent deck guns to go around. The best the navy could supply were several hundred 3-inch or 4.7-inch guns of World War One vintage which had long ago demonstrated their inability to ward off determined U-boat attacks; the new, more powerful 5-inch guns were trapped in a severe production bottleneck and the navy's ordnance chief revealed that they probably would not be available even in limited quantities until late 1942. When the Army Air Corps attempted to expand its training program to provide crews for fifty thousand planes, it discovered that most of its aircraft existed only on paper; as the operations officer of the 34th Bomb Group, Curtis LeMay had to try to train his recruits with three obsolete B-18s and two untested B-17s. Reporters discovered that the army was still bound by congressional restrictions that prohibited the use of draftees, National Guardsmen, or reserves—who together made up about two-thirds of the 1,600,000-man army—outside the Western Hemisphere. Since the 537,000 army regulars were scattered throughout various units, this meant that the United States could not send even one complete division abroad without a revision of the Selective Service Law.

But that was not the army's biggest headache, nor its greatest embarrassment. In September, the army staged the most extensive series of field exercises in its history, and the ensuing Battle of Louisiana laid open to public view the alarming deficiencies that still beset the beleaguered service. Lieutenant General Leslie McNair, director of the maneuvers, bluntly acknowledged that the war games proved that the United States Army suffered from poor leadership, hopelessly weak officers, and a lack of discipline. Specifically, he criticized the practice of "sending masses of troops over roads before ascertaining whether they were safe from enemy fire, disregard of blackout orders, spreading forces too thinly over too large a front, inadequate scouting, and the failure to impress troops with the danger of air attack." Lest anyone think that McNair's critique was too harsh, reporters who covered the exercises were even less charitable in their assessments. Hanson Baldwin, the New York Times military correspondent, reported that the army suffered from a lack of coordination between ground and air forces, excessive tactical caution at headquarters, atrocious communications, a serious ammunition shortage, and insufficient initiative on the part of commanders in the field. Baldwin also found little enthusiasm for the whole army experience among the enlisted men; "they have one compelling desire," he reported, "to get out and get home as rapidly as possible." Richard C. Hottelet, who had witnessed the Nazi military machine at close range, concluded that American equipment, leadership, and battle technique were far inferior to Germany's (which was not surprising, since Germany had been at war for two years already).

Less forgivable was the revelation that many American soldiers were still using dummy weapons because real guns were not yet available.

At the conclusion of additional training maneuvers at the end of November, McNair claimed that some American troops might be able to perform at a minimally effective level under actual combat conditions; but, he added, they would suffer unduly heavy losses against an experienced enemy such as Germany.

Isolationist leaders had long argued that no foreign power could successfully invade the United States, but when the government released the disturbing results of October's joint army-civilian full-scale dress rehearsal against an invasion of the east coast, lights must have gone on in military headquarters all over Berlin and Tokyo. Before the ludicrous ordeal ended, six major American cities—including Washington, D.C.—had been attacked, and New York City had been shelled and invaded. According to plan, forty thousand civilian spotters were paired with Army Signal Corps specialists armed with sensitive electronic equipment to track the progress of invading aircraft; when enemy bombers were sighted, pilots of the First Interceptor Command were dispatched to chase away them away. Somehow—the army, of course, would not divulge the details—a dangerous percentage of dive-bombers succeeded in maneuvering through the net and swept down upon the eastern seaboard. A troop of enemy "parachutists" captured Fort Tilden (where the defenders employed passwords such as "Brooklyn" and "Bums") and pretended to lob shells upon Manhattan's skyline for thirty minutes, until the New York State Guard arrived to drive them away. Neither federal, state, nor local governments had provided gas masks for citizens of the vulnerable cities along the east coast; few communities had worked out viable evacuation plans; and there were almost no antiaircraft guns available, nor very much portable fire extinguishing equipment to dampen an incendiary attack. Alarmed, the Office of Civil Defense rushed into publication a sixty-page pamphlet advising civilians to take the following useful precautions during an air raid: don't panic; don't bump other pedestrians off the curb during blackouts; observe all traffic lights; don't become separated from your pets; and "keep your head down, because upturned masses of faces are conspicuous from the air." In an even less practical vein, Buckminster Fuller unveiled his latest invention: a twelve-foot-tall air raid shelter (complete with a skylight, two bedrooms, one living room, a kitchen, and a bathroom) called the Dymaxion Deployment Unit, suitable for combat or civilian use. Fuller swore that his DDU. would survive anything except a direct hit. "It might jump off the ground," he admitted, "but it would come back." The War Department reportedly was giving it serious consideration.

Not all observers were equally distraught about the innumerable deficiencies displayed by the American armed forces. Churchill told American Ambassador John Winant at the end of August that he understood it would take several years before the United States could produce enough trained fighting men to make a substantial contribution to the war effort; Britain counted less upon American soldiers, Churchill said, than the psychological effect an American declaration of war would have upon the rest of the world. Columnist Walter Lippmann, who prided himself on his realistic grasp of international power politics, decided that "I don't think the use of an enormous American army is feasible, desirable, or probable." Working upon the assumption that anti-Nazi nations in Europe and Asia already contained "millions upon millions of trained troops who cannot be equipped," Lippmann contended that the main American contribution to the war should be "the production of weapons and the use of the navy to insure their delivery." In Lippmann's scheme, the United States Army would act as an auxiliary of the navy, to seize and garrison vital naval outposts. "It seems to be, therefore, a misunderstanding to suppose that we are engaged in training a mass army to fight in Europe or Asia, when there are already in being the vast armies of the British Empire, China, and Russia."

China and Russia perhaps; but if the British chiefs of staff (who by the autumn of 1941 were extremely gun-shy) had anything to say about it, their troops were not going to be subjected to any further indignities on the European continent either, despite Stalin's desperate pleas for the establishment of a second front in western or northern Europe. The heart-breaking succession of disasters in Greece, Crete, and North Africa had transformed Sir John Dill into an exhausted, profoundly defeatist personality who was even willing to give up the entire British position in the Middle East (much less aid Russia) rather than jeopardize the defense of the home islands by sending any more armor or aircraft to Egypt. In effect, Dill recommended that Britain withdraw into a shell and hoard all its available supplies. The loss of Egypt, he advised Churchill, "would not end the war. . . . We must not fall into the error of whittling away the security of vital points. If need be, we must cut our losses in places that are not vital before it is too late." "I was astonished to receive this document," remarked Churchill with rare understatement, and before the end of the year Dill had been packed off to Ceylon and replaced by Sir Alan Brooke as chief of the Imperial General Staff. Brooke, who was not Churchill's first choice for the job (largely because he was one of the few British commanders willing to stand up to Winston), was not himself a great deal more optimistic than Dill about the nation's chances of successfully waging a continental war; when he lunched with Raymond Lee in mid-July, Brooke frankly admitted that "the British cannot do a thing against the Reichswehr on land." (It was precisely this sort of negative attitude that led the impetuous Beaverbrook to exclaim in frustration, "The Chiefs of Staff would have us wait until the last button has been sewn on the last gaiter before we launch an attack.") The uneasy relationship between the Prime

Minister and his recalcitrant military advisers reached its nadir at an October 12 conference, when the Chiefs of Staff Committee rejected his impetuous proposal to launch a raid on the coast of Norway. Furious, Churchill berated Brooke for two hours, snapping, "I sometimes think some of my generals don't want to fight the Germans!"

For its part, the Royal Navy was coping, but just barely, with its own far-flung responsibilities, which now included convoying defense matériel to Russia via the treacherous northern route around Norway to Archangel and Murmansk. The navy's nine serviceable capital ships were strung out at strategic points that stretched from Alexandria to Gibraltar to Scapa Flow and the North Atlantic, and then back around to the Indian Ocean and the fortress of Singapore, to which Churchill had recently dispatched the *Repulse* and the mighty *Prince of Wales,* the most powerful battleship in the British fleet. "This ought to serve as a deterrent on Japan," Churchill chuckled in a personal note to Roosevelt on November 2. "There is nothing like having something that can catch and kill anything."

This placed the burden of opening up a second front squarely upon the R.A.F., whose chiefs welcomed the opportunity to move onto the offensive after a year of warding off the blitz and defending convoys in the North Atlantic. Unable to decide whether it should concentrate upon the destruction of German civilian morale or the Reich's transportation system, Bomber Command chose to attempt both. On July 31, the chiefs of staff optimistically informed Churchill that "we believe that if these [bombing] methods are applied on a vast scale, the whole structure upon which the German forces are based, the economic system, the machinery for production and destruction, the morale of the nation will be destroyed . . . It may be that the methods described above will by themselves be enough to make Germany sue for peace and that the role of the British Army on the Continent will be limited to that of an army of occupation."

So Bomber Command stepped up its daylight attacks upon Berlin, the ports of northern Germany, and the Ruhr industrial plants. The thoroughly disheartening result was a horrifying increase in the number of British planes shot down or lost in accidents—525 in the month of August alone. At that rate, the R.A.F. would have been decimated by the end of the year, and Churchill seemed to be ready to call off the raids before the R.A.F. commanders talked him out of it. "The devotion and gallantry of the attacks on Rotterdam and other objectives are beyond all praise," he murmured in deep admiration. "The charge of the Light Brigade at Balaclava is eclipsed in brightness by these almost daily deeds of fame." (It was always a sign of impending disaster when Churchill began making references to the most famous blunder in British military history.)

Even if the bombs had been finding their targets, the sacrifice might have been too great. But in August, a study commissioned by Professor Lindeman (Lord Cherwell), the Prime Minister's scientific adviser, revealed that only one-third of the British bombers who claimed to have reached their target over German-occupied territory actually got within five miles of it. Over Germany itself, the percentage fell to one-fourth; over the Ruhr, just one out of ten. Overall, only one out of every five bombers that Britain sent out managed to drop its load within a seventy-five-square-mile area around its primary target. In other words, most of the British bombs delivered at such a heartbreaking price were falling harmlessly in open country. Although Churchill now began to entertain serious doubts about the efficacy of strategic bombing alone—"All that we have learned since the war began shows that its effects, both physical and moral, are greatly exaggerated," he told the Chief of Air Staff at the end of September—he continued to authorize extensive sorties in the hope that the R.A.F. would at least remain "a heavy and I trust a seriously increasing annoyance" to the Germans.

One reason for the heavy losses and the imprecise bombing lay in the decision made earlier in the year to speed up the training of pilots, to provide more crews for an expanded bomber force. The practice of sending half-trained men, commanded by inexperienced officers, on long-distance missions over the Continent produced especially disastrous results on the storm-ridden night of November 7, when four hundred bombers were dispatched against the Ruhr, Berlin, Mannheim, and Cologne; thirty-seven planes never came back. One hundred and twenty R.A.F. crewmen died in the skies over Berlin; their bombs killed only nine Germans. This wholly unnecessary tragedy finally convinced Churchill to call a temporary halt to the raids. "We cannot afford losses on that scale in view of the shortfall of the American bomber programme," he decided. "Losses which are acceptable in a battle or for some decisive military objective ought not to be incurred merely as a matter of routine. There is no need to fight the weather and the enemy at the same time. It is now the duty of both Fighter and Bomber Command to re-gather their strength for the spring."

Indeed, thoughts of unpleasant things to come in the spring of 1942 preoccupied British minds as 1941 came to a close. Rumors that the Nazis had spent the past year building a vast fleet of landing craft resurrected the nightmare specter of invasion. Might not Hitler pause in his bloody assault upon Russia and turn back toward England with twenty or thirty divisions? It began to dawn upon many Britons that perhaps the government had not made the best use of the valuable months of respite granted by the German invasion of the east. The British public advanced increasingly vociferous demands that the government do more to bolster Soviet resistance or launch a second front on the Continent. "These long, strangely quiet nights are giving everybody plenty of time for talking," reported Mollie Panter-Downes at the end of October. "It's a fact that not since Crete have there been such discussions and such general uneasiness.

. . . The resulting frustration is acute and the public is carrying on like an angry prizefighter who wants to get up and slug somebody somewhere but can't because his manager is sitting on his head." In Hyde Park, demonstrators chanted slogans directed against do-nothing cabinet ministers popularly known as "the better-not brigade": "Go, Get On, or Get Out!" "The political system is bad," acknowledged Harold Macmillan. "The House of Commons is very restive. The Press is hostile." Pulled in different directions by the public outcry, his cautious generals, Stalin's importunate demands, and his own restless desire for action, Churchill began to feel, he said, "like a keeper in the Zoo distributing half-rations among magnificent animals."

The blessed silence that descended upon the island after May's final furious Luftwaffe blitz ushered in an oddly disquieting interlude in the war. As Anthony Eden put it, Britain had won the war for existence, but had not yet started the war for victory. Certainly it was bliss to be able to walk home at night without fear of death; after spending an evening with Sibyl Colefax, Kenneth Clark, and American Ambassador John Winant, a contented Harold Nicolson remarked in his diary, "It was a lovely dinner, and we walked away in the mist with the moon, and felt so pleased to be in London in October 1941." John Dos Passos visited London that fall, in "the most beautiful autumn weather of the century," and thought that the silver barrage balloons that ascended in the late afternoon gave the city "a holiday air." Despite official disapproval, many parents brought their children back to London in an attempt to recreate some semblance of normal family life.

But the same moon that Nicolson pondered so happily cast a sepulchral whiteness over the bombed-out ruins of the city, lending them the air of bleached and bare bones from some ancient civilization. When he arrived in London, Raymond Clapper made a pilgrimage to the statue of Peter Pan in Kensington Garden, a favorite spot for children to visit in times of peace; sandbags still covered the statue, and cobwebs and dust lay thick over the bronze rabbits and mice around it. The high metal gates and fences around Buckingham Palace were torn down and taken away for scrap to build tanks. Gasoline restrictions kept Londoners from taking their customary vacations at the seashore or in the countryside. Clothes rationing limited Britons to sixty-six coupons a year for new garments (a suit required twenty-six coupons, a dress eleven), produced a black market in lingerie peddled by seedy little men in bars, prompted Queen Elizabeth to alter the girls' outfits from last year so Princesses Elizabeth and Margaret could wear them again in 1942, forced thousands of men to walk around with patches on the bottoms of their trousers, and threw hundreds of small clothing shops out of business. ("If you take a walk down any London shopping street," observed one American reporter, "you are likely to see shutters over the windows of dozens of modest businesses

which struggled through the blitz but couldn't survive clothes-rationing.")
The prospect of a renewed blitz when the Luftwaffe returned from the
eastern front kept British nerves on edge, while predictions of a severe
coal shortage—and stricter food rationing (especially of milk)—during the
coming winter cast a pall over the autumn.

But for a brief moment the nation was electrified when the British
Eighth Army in North Africa, commanded by Sir Alan Cunningham
(brother of the admiral), struck suddenly across the desert in the midst of
a violent thunderstorm on the morning of November 18. Both Rommel
and Cunningham had used the summer respite to repair their battered
forces and obtain reinforcements from home in anticipation of an autumn
offensive; in fact, Rommel had scheduled an advance of his own for November 20. Spearheaded by six hundred tanks and (for once) almost complete air superiority because the Axis airfields were waterlogged from the
storms, the British assault, code-named Operation Crusader, took Rommel—who had been preoccupied with the siege of Tobruk—completely
by surprise. As Churchill informed the Commons, this was the first time
British and German forces (actually, a combined German-Italian force, but
Churchill ignored the Italian presence) had confronted one another in
equal strength. In his Order of the Day to the British troops, Churchill had
grandly proclaimed that the desert battle might prove the equal of Waterloo or Blenheim, and he advised the nation that the whole affair "may be
settled one way or the other in the course of perhaps two hours."

For the first three days, the British had much the better of the battle.
But Rommel did not crumble so easily, and Cunningham's imprudent
decision to disperse his forces robbed the surprise attack of much of its
impact. "What difference does it make if you have two tanks to my one,
when you spread them out and let me smash them in detail?" Rommel
chided a captured British officer. In what has generally been regarded as
"one of the most confusing battles ever fought," the R.A.F.'s control of the
air proved less than decisive as swirling clouds of dust made it impossible
to tell from a distance whether the armored columns below were German
or British. Electrical storms knocked out radio communications; in the
absence of recognizable landmarks in the trackless desert, neither side
knew where the other was, or, for that matter, where their own troops
were. The battle degenerated into total chaos. "In brief," declared one
observer, "the peculiarities of desert warfare created an all-pervading
sense of uncertainty of what was happening or had happened on the
tactical battlefield. The dust thrown up by bursting shells, the black billowing oily smoke from burning vehicles and tanks, and the natural desert
hazes made tactical control a matter of battle-instinct and personal judgment. . . . Nothing was ever clear-cut. The successful desert commanders
acquired the 'feel of the battle'; the less successful did not."

Thwarted, as one observer put it, "by their sheer amateurism," the

British forces reeled backward in confusion as Rommel concentrated his panzers as best he could on November 24 and threw them forcefully against the enemy lines. He smashed through and, thinking to destroy British morale once and for all, began a mad dash toward the Egyptian frontier "in the worst manner," said one British critic, "of the Confederate cavalry under General J.E.B. Stuart in the American Civil War." It almost worked. Cunningham lost his nerve and was prepared to give up the fight until General Claude Auchinleck, who had replaced Wavell in June as British commander in chief in the Mediterranean, rushed to the front and took personal command of the British troops. Soon Rommel's "race for the wire" collapsed in a confused mixture of broken-down tanks, garbled communications, and exhausted and thirsty men. He turned around and headed back toward Tripoli.

Although both sides had blundered so badly that neither deserved to win, Britain claimed a victory. It had recaptured Benghazi and relieved Tobruk, at least temporarily. More important, the Eighth Army had acquired invaluable combat experience which would begin to pay dividends when a truly able commander such as Bernard Law Montgomery arrived to take charge of the desert campaign in 1942.

In the chilly waters off the coast of Iceland, the *Reuben James* lay at the bottom of the sea. The destroyer, named for the bosun's mate who had rescued Stephen Decatur from the Barbary pirates in 1804, had been protecting a British convoy when a U-boat's torpedo tore through its unarmored hull on the night of October 30. One hundred and fifteen American sailors drowned. For the first time, a German submarine had sunk a ship of the United States Navy. "Anybody walking along the railroad tracks at night should not be surprised if he gets run over by an express train," sneered a government spokesman in Berlin.

Roosevelt took the news calmly. There was no groundswell of public support for war in the face of this latest Nazi challenge. One week later, the Senate voted on a bill to repeal the Neutrality Act provisions that prohibited American merchantmen from arming themselves and barred them from combat zones. Irreconcilable isolationist Hiram Johnson of California, a veteran of the League of Nations fight two decades earlier, shook his finger at his colleagues and sobbed, "This is a question, after all, of peace and war. I say, declare war tonight and under the providence of God every man who votes to do so will live to regret it to the last day of his life." Then the Senate voted, by the narrow margin of 50–37, in favor of repeal. The House followed suit six days later.

From time to time, Supreme Court Justice William O. Douglas dropped in at the White House for a chat with his old friend the President. ("It's always good to see you, Bill," Roosevelt would say.) "During these days FDR would mull over his problems in the evenings, and he used me as a sounding board," Douglas remembered. "The ugly character of the Nazi regime was a recurring theme as the persecution of the Jews loomed larger and larger. Those barbaric acts and the barbaric quality of the Nazis themselves were the main forces shaping FDR's policies."

25

The Battle for Moscow

"I hope for only one thing, that in this war in the East
the Germans will lose a lot of feathers."
                    —BENITO MUSSOLINI

From George Kennan's viewpoint at the United States Embassy in Berlin, the cataclysmic events that occurred on the eastern front between June 22 and December 7, 1941, spun themselves out in a curious sort of fog. "I remember only a feeling that things were now out of control—not only out of *our* control (we, after all, in our poor overworked embassy, had never at any time had any influence on the course of events) but out of everyone's control. Day by day I followed, on a large map of Russia that hung on the wall of my office, the advance of Hitler's army across the great regions of forest and swamp to the west of Moscow, comparing it at every turn with the similar advance of Napoleon's army in the year 1812. (The similarities in timing and geography were often striking.)"

In the summer of 1941, Zhores Medvedev was a fifteen-year-old boy living in Rostov, the former capital of the North Caucasus republic and one of the largest cities in southern Russia. In July, while the fighting still seemed very far away, he had been sent to work on a collective farm along the Don River to help with the harvest. "The harvest was good and we returned to Rostov at the end of August," Medvedev recalled years later. "The city had changed. People were in a panic. The Germans had occupied Taganrog, an important port on the Azov Sea, only seventy miles away. The Soviet army was retreating and there was no sign of a strong defense. When Rostov was bombed several times, my mother decided to take us out of the city. Nobody seemed to know what was going on. We left Rostov on August 28, only a few days before the German army entered the city."

By the end of August, Hitler already possessed half the Ukraine; German troops had advanced eight hundred miles into Soviet territory at some points; and the fall of Leningrad seemed to be only a matter of time. Against the strenuous objections of Marshal Zhukov (whose willingness to voice his honest opinions cost him his command position), Stalin ordered the Soviet armies on the southern front to hold Kiev at all costs. "You must stop looking for lines of retreat and start looking for lines of resistance, only resistance," Stalin scolded his commanders. But when Khrushchev asked the Kremlin for weapons to arm the workers of Kiev, Molotov told him that "you'd better give up any thought of getting rifles from us. The rifles in the civil defense organization here have all been sent to Leningrad." "Then what are we supposed to fight with?" Khrushchev snapped. "I don't know—pikes, swords, homemade weapons, anything you can make in your own factories," Malenkov replied blandly. "You'll have to do the best you can. You can make fire bombs out of bottles of gasoline or kerosene and throw them at the tanks." Aided in no small measure by this singularly unhelpful attitude on Moscow's part, German troops entered Kiev on September 18; it was the first major Russian city that had not been deliberately destroyed by the Red Army before retreating. The encircled Soviet defenders tried to smash their way out of the steel ring that had closed around them, but 665,000 Red soldiers were forced to surrender. The Germans claimed that they had captured 884 tanks and nearly 4,000 artillery guns as well. Several days later, Stalin ordered the evacuation of Odessa. Soviet resistance all along the southwest front crumbled; the Wehrmacht rolled on toward the east and the Crimean peninsula.

Once inside Kiev, however, the Germans received a series of rude shocks. Instead of burning the city before they left, Soviet troops had left behind concealed land mines triggered by remote radio control, electric light switches, and clock mechanisms. German engineers dismantled ten thousand bombs, but they could not find them all. "Seven thousand of the mines we removed were planted in the most unexpected places where they had no right to be—in museums, cloisters, churches, and administration buildings," complained a distraught Wehrmacht officer. "Some were fixed to explode when the electricity was turned on; others when radio transmission was started. . . . We hesitated to turn on the electricity for fear of throwing switches that would set off mines. . . ." The explosions set off great fires that raged through the city for five days, destroying twenty square blocks, including the ancient white Citadel with its golden domes.

Far to the north, between the shores of the Gulf of Finland and the Neva River, Leningrad had been completely isolated from the rest of the Soviet Union when German troops captured the last remaining railway link to the outside world on August 31. As the German Eighteenth Army penetrated to the Gulf on the western edge of the city and the Luftwaffe strafed the shattered Soviet forces and the Sixteenth Army approached from the banks of the Neva in the east, the city was cut off from its last hope of salvation, the Red Eighth Army, and threatened with imminent destruction. But just as this dazzling prize appeared to be within its grasp, the Wehrmacht cautiously paused to consider the matter; and then Hitler began to pull men and tanks away from Leeb's command, sending them south to take part in what was intended to be the final drive toward

Moscow. The assault upon Leningrad promptly collapsed. The Nazi forces that remained, seriously weakened by fatigue and heavy losses (casualties ran as high as two-thirds in some divisions), were clearly insufficient to take Leningrad by storm, and Zhukov, who had been handed the heretofore unenviable responsibility of stemming the German tide on the northwest front, managed to beat back repeated German infantry and artillery assaults. So, rather than waste valuable troops in a vain attempt to batter his way into the city, Hitler decided to starve Leningrad into submission.

Beginning in early September, heavy artillery barrages pounded the city night and day; air raids, sometimes involving as many as four hundred Luftwaffe bombers at a time, struck the Soviet naval base at Kronstadt and hammered the sole remaining supply route—by water across Lake Ladoga—into Leningrad. Inside the beleaguered city, Zhukov mobilized the population as a civilian defense force and set them to work erecting barricades, digging antitank ditches, watching on the rooftops for the evening raiders, and covering the Winter Palace and other artistic or strategic treasures with sandbags and camouflage. Already facing a perilous supply situation, the unlucky residents of Leningrad suffered a heartbreaking catastrophe when a German bomb struck the central food warehouse and set it ablaze. The heavy, noxious smell of burning sugar, butter, fats, and flour filled the air for days afterward. From that moment on, three million people were trapped inside the city with virtually no food and no practical means of getting it from the outside world.

Everyone was placed upon a near-starvation diet; the regular ration for workers was fourteen ounces of bread per day (children received only a half-portion). To rally morale, the authorities persuaded thirty-five-year-old Dmitri Shostakovich—who was spending his days working furiously, like a man possessed, on the composition of his Seventh Symphony, and his nights searching the heavens for incendiary bombs from his watchman's post upon a rooftop—to broadcast a stirring appeal for resistance over Leningrad radio:

> Life goes on in our city. All of us are now standing militant watch. . . . My life and work are completely bound up with Leningrad. Leningrad is my country. It is my native city and my home. . . . When I walk through the city a feeling of deep conviction grows within me that Leningrad will always stand, grand and beautiful, on the banks of the Neva, that it will always be a bastion of my country, that it will always be there to enrich the fruits of culture.

There may have been an ironic smile upon the composer's thin, hard mouth when he called upon Leningrad to make the supreme patriotic sacrifice in a war to save the Stalinist regime, for no city had suffered more horribly under the Stalinist terror of the 1930s. Tens of thousands of workers, party officials, intellectuals, and students had been arrested and either shot or sentenced to a living death in the hell of the Siberian labor camps during the waves of repression and purges that swept over Leningrad between 1934 and 1938. Although Shostakovich wrote the first movements of his Seventh ("Leningrad") Symphony—so dark, so oppressive and laden with agony and grief—during the German siege of the city, the genesis of the music may be found in the prewar murders that scarred Leningrad's soul. "It's not about Leningrad under siege," Shostakovich wrote several decades later, "it's about the Leningrad that Stalin destroyed and that Hitler merely finished off. . . . The 'invasion theme' has nothing to do with the [Nazi] attack. I was thinking of other enemies of humanity when I composed the theme." (On October 2, Shostakovich himself—as an invaluable national resource—was ordered by City Defense Headquarters to fly out of Leningrad to safety in the makeshift capital of Kuibyshev, where he completed the symphony on December 27. The score was then transferred to microfilm and flown from Moscow via Tehran and Cairo to the West, where its performance by the most prestigious American and British orchestras turned Shostakovich's protest—again, with more than a touch of irony—into a particularly brilliant and effective piece of anti-Nazi propaganda.)

Meanwhile, Leningrad continued to suffer. By the end of November, the bread ration for civilians had been cut to two slices per day. People ate cottonseed oil cake, pine bark, cats, crows, and jelly made from sheep gut. At school, children received 25 grams of bread and a cup of hot water with salt for breakfast. There was no fuel and no power. Water supplies froze; the temperature reached twenty degrees below zero and kept falling. Thousands of men, women, and children died of starvation or exposure. The Richtofen Korps of the Luftwaffe launched more than twenty attacks a day against the tortured city. Telephone contact was cut off. German artillery shells pounded Leningrad without respite, and hospitals reported 4,000 new casualties every day. In December the death toll reached 53,000—approximately the same number as in the entire year of 1940. The poet Vera Inber passed by the city mortuary every morning and never became accustomed to the horrifying sight:

> Each day, eight to ten bodies are brought there on sleighs. And they just lie on the snow. Fewer and fewer coffins are available, and less and less material to make them. So the bodies are wrapped in sheets, in blankets, in tablecloths, sometimes even in curtains. Once I saw a small bundle wrapped in paper and tied with string. It was very small, the body of a child.
>
> How macabre they look on the snow! Occasionally, an arm or a leg protrudes from the crude wrappings. In these multi-coloured rags there still lingers a semblance of life, but there is also the stillness of death. This makes me think of a battleground and a doss-house at the same time.
>
> The mortuary itself is full. Not only are there too few lorries to go to the

cemetery itself, but, more important, not enough petrol to put in the lorries
. . . and the main thing—there is not enough strength left in the living to bury
the dead.

The question has risen about not registering every individual death any
longer. And in order to simplify formalities, a representative of the Registry
will be present in the mortuary, just to count the number of bodies. After all,
there are so many nameless ones.

Convinced that the Red Army was on the verge of collapse in the vital
central sector, the Fuehrer decided to risk everything on a spectacular
gamble. Calling up thirty fresh infantry divisions and vast new quantities
of tanks and aircraft, he ordered his generals to launch a sledgehammer
assault upon Moscow from three different directions at once: "Encircle
them, beat and destroy them," he shouted at his generals. "Today is the
beginning of the last great decisive battle of this year," he told his troops
in his Order of the Day for October 2. At dawn that morning, the Wehrmacht launched Operation Typhoon, spearheaded by three infantry armies, fourteen panzer divisions, and nine motorized divisions. Once again,
Stalin was caught by surprise and reacted far too slowly. The furious
German assault tore and clawed its way through the demoralized and
dissolving Soviet defensive formations. When he finally perceived the
imminent danger to Moscow, Stalin ordered the militia mobilized at once;
Zhukov, the toughest fighter in the Red Army, returned from Leningrad
and was given command of the forces defending the capital. Alerted by
his master spy in Tokyo, journalist Richard Sorge, that the Japanese government had irrevocably decided to move southward instead of north into
Siberia, Stalin stepped up the withdrawal of troops from Russia's Far
Eastern frontier and brought them west over the agonizingly slow Soviet
railway system to plug the huge gaps in Moscow's defenses.

No man had ever witnessed battles like those along the route to
Moscow. Whole villages were obliterated by fire and shell; trees were
splintered and ripped out of the ground, their roots turned skyward; hills
were demolished and new hills arose in a landscape chewed raw by the
clash of giant armored columns. Unusually heavy rains in September had
turned the roads into quagmires; unable to maneuver properly, fifty-ton
tanks slammed headfirst into one another: "Tanks burst into flame; tanks
turned over on their backs like turtles; and tanks clawed frantically at the
soft earth," reported one eyewitness. "Some tankists who escaped from
flaming tanks had their clothing burned from them, and they dashed for
cover behind overturned tanks or tried to get aboard tanks roaring towards the rear for refueling. . . . Gasoline trucks in the act of refueling
tanks burst into flame, lighting up the battlefield for miles around. There
was no letup, day or night. When the dawn came, the tanks were still
roaring across the ground, firing until their gun barrels were red hot."

Behind the German tanks came the infantry columns, twenty miles long, marching numbly through the rain and the slush and the ceaseless sheets of water and the endless ranges of heavily wooded steppe. In a war of merciless butchery, they had long ago lost all semblance of civilized behavior and by now they looked the part: unshaven, unwashed, lice-ridden, sodden soldiers who were living on potatoes and horsemeat. They could not be pushed much farther. Every encounter with the enemy left the field littered with unburied corpses and smoldering metal remains. American correspondent Cyrus Sulzberger visited the scene of one recent fearsome battle and cabled his impressions to the *New York Times:* "This is gray, gloomy desolate territory. Villages have been smashed and leveled and trees ripped apart. The landscape is clothed with stark reminders like shattered tanks and bullet-riddled helmets. It almost always is raining, and even when it is not great clouds rumble across the sky like leaden whales."

The first snow that year fell across Moscow on October 4, far earlier than usual.

At the Sportspalast in Berlin on October 3, the Fuehrer informed the German people that "an operation of gigantic proportions is again in progress, which will help to smash the enemy in the East." It was true, he admitted, that the Reich had underestimated the Red Army's capacity for resistance in the face of the gallant German assault; it was now obvious that the German decision to attack on June 22 had narrowly forestalled a savage Communist invasion of the west. "We had no idea how gigantic the preparations of this enemy were against Germany and Europe and how immeasurably great was the danger, how by the skin of our teeth we have escaped the destruction not only of Germany but also of Europe. . . . This would have been a second storm of Genghis Khan." Even as he spoke, soldiers from nearly every nation on the European continent—Germany, Italy, Finland, Hungary, Romania, Czechoslovakia, France, Norway, Holland, Spain—were fighting side by side against the Soviet foe on a front that stretched from the Arctic Ocean to the Black Sea. "They are fighting on a front of gigantic length, and against an enemy who, I must say, does not consist of human beings but of animals or beasts. We have seen now what bolshevism can make of human beings. We cannot bring to the people at home the pictures we have at our disposal. They are the most sinister that human brains can imagine. The enemy is fighting with a bestial lust of blood on the one hand and out of cowardice and fear of his commissars on the other hand." Hitler went on:

> The German people can be proud today. They have the best political leaders, the best generalissimos, the best engineers and economic organizers and also the best workmen, best peasants and best people.
>
> To weld all these peoples into one indissoluble community was the task

we set ourselves as National Socialists. This task confronts Germany more clearly today than ever before. . . .

Only when the entire German people become a single community of sacrifice can we expect and hope that Almighty God will help us. The Almighty has never helped a lazy man. He does not help the coward. He does not help a people that cannot help itself.

The principle applies here, help yourselves and Almighty God will not deny you His assistance.

For a few days the Fuehrer's speech dispelled the doubts that had crept into the minds of his loyal followers. "He convinced us completely," said one middle-aged Berliner. "The Russians will be routed before winter, and then the war will be over, thank God!" Newspapers called upon peasants in southern and western Germany to apply for grants of farmland in Russia, following the dispossession of the native population. The staggering Soviet losses in the first days of the renewed German offensive raised public morale even higher. According to Howard K. Smith, "The response was electric. There was visible alleviation in faces that for weeks had been dismally drawn. . . . The horrible slaughter of Germany's best sons was nearing an end. The boys were being taken out of the Panzers by Christmas," he noted.

> It is hard to realize what this meant to the German people, unless you have lived through those two years of war with them, and watched them suffer. As the core of strong, steel-willed leadership, they have been remarkably timid and sensitive to trends. They have detested this war from the moment it broke out, and they, the People, have been willing to end it at any juncture. Before it came, they feared it far more than the peoples their leaders and their army threatened with annihilation. On the few occasions on which the end appeared to be in sight, they have been gleeful as children. Dr. Goebbels had not distinguished himself on the score of telling the truth. But when he said, "The German People did not want this war," he knew, for once, what he was talking about.

"As soon as Moscow, Leningrad, and Stalingrad fall," went the popular refrain, "the rest will collapse."

Two weeks later, officials of the Reich launched the first of many drives to collect discarded clothes for the soldiers on the eastern front, many of whom were suffering through the subfreezing nights with only light summer uniforms. (Confident that he could defeat the Soviets before the end of the year, Hitler had planned to keep only one army unit out of five in Russia during the winter; thus most German soldiers were completely unequipped for winter combat.) Train service was cut back again because so much of the rolling stock had been sent to Russia, and many of the cars that remained were being used to transport potatoes to hunger-stricken areas of the Reich. Official permits were required for anything more than local travel; holiday and winter resort trips were banned completely. The government boosted surtaxes to reduce consumption of depleted stocks of liquor and tobacco. Civilians were encouraged to contribute to tax-free "iron savings" accounts, which could not be withdrawn until one year after the war ended. Consumer products followed an inexorable pattern: first a decline in quality, then gradual decreases in quantity.

"Cosmetics disappeared," noticed Howard K. Smith in Berlin. "Tooth paste was chalk and water with weak peppermint flavouring and a tube of it hardened into cement unless used rapidly. Ersatz foods flourished. Icing for the few remaining pastries tasted like a mixture of saccharine, sand and cheap perfume. White bread was issued after the third month of the campaign only on the ration cards formerly for pastry. A red coloured paste called *Lachs Galantine,* resembling salmon in colour and soggy sawdust in taste, appeared in restaurants on meatless days. Several strange bottled sauces made of incredible combinations of acid-tasting chemicals made their appearance in shops to answer the public's growing demand for something to put a taste of some kind in their unattractive and scanty meals." Gasoline restrictions grew more stringent; the speed limit in the country was lowered to 37 mph; there would be no antifreeze for private automobiles this winter. There was no new clothing available, nor shoes, since everything was sent to the soldiers at the front. Shop owners were forbidden to display Christmas decorations until November 29, and those that were used after that date had to be suitable for wartime conditions.

As day after day passed with no conclusive victory on the eastern front, Goebbels bluntly announced "the coming of weeks that will not be easy." In November, the Reich grew increasingly nervous about the domestic reaction to the prospect of a war whose end could no longer be foreseen. Goebbels proclaimed the death penalty for any German subject caught listening to British radio broadcasts; "British lies get into the blood, making listeners weak and tired of carrying on," he explained. At his annual speech commemorating the 1922 putsch planned in the fabled beer hall in Munich, the Fuehrer looked out warily upon his old comrades and shot out a warning: "The fight has become a fight not only for Germany but for all Europe, a fight for existence or nonexistence." He spat out the words. "Should anyone among us seriously hope to be able to disturb our front—it makes no difference where he comes from or to which camp he belongs—I will keep an eye on him for a certain period. You know my methods. There is always the period of probation. But then there comes the moment when I strike like lightning and eliminate that kind of thing." There would be no repetition of the infamous *dolchstoss,* no new stab in the back; in its eternal vigilance, the Fuehrer nodded with satisfaction, the National Socialist Party "reaches into every house and zealously keeps watch that there shall never be another November 1918."

Now the campaign against the Jews in Germany entered a new phase. Beginning September 1, all Jews over six years of age were compelled to wear a Star of David and the word "Jude" on their clothing when they appeared in public. Virtually all remaining Jewish businesses were appropriated by the government, to be distributed to German veterans when the war ended. "The German soldier has met in the Eastern campaign the Jew in his most disgusting, most gruesome form," screamed the *Völkischer Beobachter,* the official Nazi Party organ. "This experience forces the German soldier and the German people to deprive the Jews of every means of camouflage at home." (Besides, the government needed a scapegoat to divert the public's attention from the ceaseless carnage on the eastern front.) In October the mass deportation of German Jews began; in the first wave, approximately twenty thousand Jews in Berlin and other cities in the Reich were informed that their rooms in "Aryan houses" were "scheduled for evacuation." Under cover of darkness on the night of October 16, they were taken away under police guard and sent to the ghettos in the east: Lodz, Warsaw, Lublin. At first they were told they would be used as laborers in the industrial towns or the agricultural colonies of the *Generalgouvernement;* they were forced to sign statements (a ludicrous procedure required by the Germans' compulsive orderliness) that they had voluntarily evacuated their homes, that they had taken part in Communist activities, and that they were transferring all their property to the state. "Almost all maintained a passive attitude toward life and the conditions they found in their new environment," noted a contemporary witness. "Instinctively they defended themselves against identification with the indigenous Lodz Jews, trying to separate by all means from the natives in the belief that this might save them from submerging into the mass of the ghetto population." Like many other ghetto residents, they agreed to work in factories that supplied the German war effort, on the assumption that the Nazis would not kill or mistreat valuable skilled labor.

In Czechoslovakia, Reinhard Heydrich (recently appointed Acting Protector of Bohemia and Moravia) quelled an outbreak of sabotage and anti-Nazi terrorism by establishing special summary courts with Gestapo officers as judges. Four hundred death sentences were carried out within two weeks; four thousand others were sent to prisons or concentration camps. "Racially unfit" elements were sterilized and sent to forced labor camps. Like their brethren in Berlin, the Jews of Prague were told that they were being sent to work as laborers for the duration of the war. Most resigned themselves to make the most of an unfortunate situation. "We were taken to the train station under SS guard, with the Gestapo standing on all sides," remembered one twenty-seven-year-old woman.

> Our route passed through the streets of Prague and thousands of Czechs lined both sides as an expression of their sympathy for the Jews. Many of the

men removed their hats and some of the women wept openly when they saw
how cruelly the Nazis treated us, old and young, and the small children, too.

Even now, no one dreamed they were sending us to Poland. We thought:
Holland, Belgium, Germany—but never Poland. That they were sending us
to Jewish ghettos in other places was very far from our minds.

They loaded us on a regular train, ten to a compartment. The trip was
hard. There was no water or any kind of first aid, but it was hardest on the
children, the babies needing special care.

The SS patrolled the cars for the whole journey, constantly taking head
counts to make sure no one had escaped . . .

It took us over an hour's march till we got to the Lodz ghetto. We were
all put into one building—a transport of over 1,000 people, thirty people to
a room. This is when our hell really began. There was no water in the building,
just a pump in the courtyard, and for these 1,000 people—only four lavatories.
In the meantime, it got colder from day to day, snow began falling and
everything froze solid. Our condition was desperate from the start. Of course,
there was no food anywhere, though the first two days we still had the little
we brought with us from Prague. But after that—we were overcome by
starvation.

Twenty thousand Jews had disappeared from Vilna by the time the
Nazis sealed the ghetto on September 1. Most probably had been machine-gunned at the town of Ponary, ten miles away. Ten thousand more
Jews were gone by the middle of the month. Still more were rounded up
and taken away on October 1, Yom Kippur. By the end of the year, only
twelve thousand Jews remained in the ghetto; nearly fifty thousand had
vanished.

During the summer, the death rate in the Warsaw ghetto exceeded
births by a ratio of 9 to 1. Conditions deteriorated in the autumn when the
ghetto was sealed off even more tightly. At the end of October, the governor for the district of Warsaw decreed the death penalty for anyone
attempting to leave the ghetto without a permit. By then the average
monthly food ration consisted of one-half pound of sugar and four pounds
of bread, the dough mixed with potato peel and sawdust. Children roamed
the streets searching for food. Eleven thousand people died of starvation
in Warsaw that year. Perhaps three-fourths of the apartments in the
ghetto had no heat. Aided by the cold and the hunger, a typhus epidemic
carried away 15 percent of the population.

By the middle of November, the first wild orgy of anti-Semitic violence in the conquered Russian territories had abated. One of the four SS
Einsatzgruppen reported that it had killed 95,000 Jews and Communists;
another claimed 45,467 victims. In Berlin, former German diplomat Ulrich von Hassell heard reports from returning Wehrmacht officers that
confirmed "the continuance of repulsive cruelties, particularly against the

Jews, who were shamelessly shot down in batches." One SS doctor used Jews to carry out experiments with dumdum bullets, gathering evidence to prove that such weapons should be outlawed. Nazi prison-camp authorities discovered that a gas known as Zyklon B produced excellent results in disposing of Russian prisoners of war. It could be stored indefinitely in cans in dry, solid form; when the pellets were exposed to air, they were transformed into a gas that was invariably and almost instantly lethal.

One day Menachem Begin heard the sentry call his voice: "Be—gin!" "Here I am," Begin shouted. "Name and father's name?" asked the sentry. "Menachem Wolfovitch!" "Correct!" the sentry bellowed, and then went on calling other names. "All those whose names I have called, collect your belongings. An order has come to release the Poles. You are going free." Begin had no belongings. He ran for the ship that would carry him away from the gulag.

Desperate for any assistance against the Nazi invader, Stalin had concluded an uneasy alliance with the Polish government-in-exile, headed by General Sikorski in London. The agreement called for the formation of two Polish infantry divisions of five thousand men each; to staff this army, the Soviet government released thousands of its Polish prisoners. Eventually almost 1.5 million Poles were set free, including 400,000 Jews. Begin became a corporal and served in the Polish army for two years, until he arrived in Palestine. But for now, the promise of freedom was all that mattered.

"We went into the boat which carried us to the shore, to a transit camp," Begin remembered. "From there we would travel south.

"I was travelling light, without any luggage.

"I felt very light. I could hear the whirring of the wings of freedom."

On October 7, the Battle of Moscow began. The Wehrmacht broke through at Vyazma and Bryansk, 120 miles southwest of the capital. With the wind whipping the powdery snow into their faces, German troops raced toward Moscow. The Soviet government lost its nerve and ran for its life. On October 10, officials in the Kremlin informed all foreign embassies and correspondents that they should be prepared to evacuate the city. Luftwaffe planes dropped leaflets warning that the German attack would begin that weekend. Muscovites panicked and stormed the railway stations, seeking escape to the east. The Mojhaisk highway, the main road out of Moscow, was black with supply trucks and civilian traffic as two million people fled the city; the air was filled with "black snow," the ash from burning documents. Most of the Soviet government, including the general staff, took up temporary residence at Kuibyshev, 688 miles away, on the Volga River. The British ambassador, Sir Stafford Cripps, burned nearly all his files and flew with Molotov to the new capital. There were rumors that

Stalin, too, had fled, but the dictator remained behind. On October 19, the Kremlin announced a state of siege; spies (anyone who added to the already frenzied state of panic) would be shot summarily. Red Army demolition units mined bridges and railroad tracks on the western approaches, and prepared to disable vital factories "at the first sight of the enemy."

The German army was now within fifty miles of Moscow. There were no Russian reserves available; all had already been thrown recklessly into battle. The Red Army had lost over three million men. Now it was being pounded into oblivion on the outskirts of the capital.

On November 6, Stalin sought to rally Soviet resistance with a speech commemorating the twenty-fourth anniversary of the Revolution. The ceremonies were held in the marbled Mayakovsky Station of the Moscow Metro. "The enemy has seized the greater part of the Ukraine, White Russia, Moldavia, Lithuania, Latvia, Estonia, and a number of other regions," Stalin conceded. "He has penetrated to the Don, hangs like a black cloud over Leningrad, and threatens our glorious capital, Moscow." The German enemy, Stalin said, "cares nothing for the blood of his soldiers. He keeps throwing onto the front fresh units to replace those put out of commission and is straining every effort to capture Leningrad and Moscow before the advent of winter, for he knows that for him the winter has nothing good in store." Denouncing the Germans as "a people who have lost all semblance to human beings and who have sunk to the level of wild beasts," Stalin issued a call for resistance without mercy: "The German invaders wish to have a war of extermination against the peoples of the Soviet Union. Well, if the Germans wish this to be a war of extermination, they will get it! Our task now . . . will be to destroy every German to the very last man who has come to occupy our country. No mercy for the German invaders! Death to the German invaders!"

To the west, the German advance had bogged down again as the ground beneath froze and then suddenly thawed, turning roads into treacherous bogs. "The infantryman slithers in the mud, while many teams of horses are needed to drag each gun forward," wrote General Blumentritt, chief of staff of the Fourth Army. "All wheeled vehicles sink up to their axles in the slime. Even tractors can only move with great difficulty. A large portion of our heavy artillery was soon stuck fast . . . The strain that all this caused our already exhausted troops can perhaps be imagined." Sometimes the battle extended far into the darkness: "We shall never forget that night," wrote a German military correspondent. "It was dark as hell and cold as in midwinter. Even inside the tanks we were bitterly cold. We dreamed mud, mud in our clothes, clinging by the pounds to our boots, in our faces, in our mudguards—it is one heavy hymn of mud."

The temperature plummeted further; Guderian estimated that each

German regiment besieging Moscow had lost about 400 men to frostbite. More died from typhus. By now German casualties had reached 750,000 and the number kept rising. Soldiers tried to erect makeshift log cabins for protection against the cold. They stole jackets, boots, and fur caps from captured Russian prisoners and left their victims to freeze. Trucks whose wheels had been stuck in foot-deep mud were suddenly encased in ice. Guderian: "The tanks could barely move; to get them started we had to light fires under the oil pans. Our automatic weapons jammed in the cold." The bitter cold caused artillery to fire short, and German shells exploded along their own front lines. The spires of the Kremlin loomed ahead, nearly within reach, beckoning them forward, but the German commanders were plunged into despair. Many German units already had lost 50 percent of their combat strength. "Our own troops physically overstrained," reported Halder. "The situation is aggravated by the cold (30 to 35 degrees of frost). Out of five tanks only one was able to fire. Snowfall now would neutralize our tanks."

Russian resistance suddenly stiffened because there was no room for retreat. Siberian divisions, moving almost noiselessly on skis and clad entirely in white against the snow, with even their machine guns painted white, swooped down upon unsuspecting German troops and shot them down. This time it was the physically and psychologically exhausted Germans—devoid of reserves, and already living on the edge of their nerves—who fled from the prospect of hand-to-hand combat. Partisan units ambushed Wehrmacht supply columns in the swamps and forests behind the vastly overextended German lines. Now the Germans, too, panicked. Guderian: "Only he who saw the endless expanse of Russian snow during this winter of our misery and felt the icy wind that blew across it, burying in snow every object in its path; who drove for hour after hour through that no-man's land only at last to find too thin shelter with insufficiently clothed, half-starved men; and who also saw by contrast the well-fed, warmly clad and fresh Siberians, fully equipped for winter fighting . . . can truly judge the events which now occurred."

With German units twenty miles away from Moscow, Hitler—reportedly in "a state of extreme agitation"—refused to allow his generals to stop. He ordered another all-out offensive. On December 1, as the temperature reached thirty degrees below zero Centigrade, the Wehrmacht stumbled forward for several miles, and then collapsed. Pushed beyond any measure of human endurance, German soldiers screamed that they could go no farther. Guderian advised Bock on December 5 that he was retreating; Brauchitsch threatened to resign; Bock told the Fuehrer that "his strength was at an end."

After 167 days, the German invasion of the Soviet Union finally had come to a halt. For the first time, the invincible Wehrmacht had failed. Russia would not be conquered. At the opening of the winter season of the

Moscow circus, the ringmaster announced gleefully that Herr Hitler would be unable to attend.

On December 5, Zhukov launched a massive counterattack all along the central front.

26

"The Dear, Dead Days"

"We say good-by now to the land we have known. Like lovers
about to be separated by a long journey, we sit in this hour
of mellow twilight, thinking fondly of the past, wondering.
Words seem almost an intrusion."

—RAYMOND CLAPPER

Down to the final week of the regular season, the St. Louis Cardinals and
the Brooklyn Dodgers battled for the National League pennant. Leo Durocher was a nervous wreck; "I hadn't had a good night's sleep in three
weeks. I'd wake up in the morning and it would be in my mind that I had
somehow made a decision on my pitching rotation." Like most ballplayers,
the Lip was extremely superstitious. He refused to shave after a Dodger
victory, and decided not to change his clothes until after his club clinched
the pennant. "I had been wearing the same slacks and sport shirt for three
weeks," he recalled, "and—even more important—the same blue necktie.
I knew absolutely that we couldn't win if anything happened to that blue
necktie."

Short-tempered in the best of times, Durocher's gang occasionally lost
control in the heat of the grueling pennant race. On September 18, the
Dodgers led the Cards by only one game when the Bums took the field
against the mediocre Pittsburgh Pirates. The Pirates jumped out to a 4–0
lead that afternoon, but the Dodgers stormed back in the top of the eighth
to make it 5–4. In the bottom of the inning, with Pirate centerfielder Vince
DiMaggio (the third DiMaggio brother in the majors) on third base, home
plate umpire George Magerkurth (who, the previous season, had been
slugged by an overzealous Dodger fan during a game at Ebbets Field)
called a balk on Hugh Casey, letting in the tying run. Casey was so mad
that he threw the next pitch directly over Magerkurth's head; then he
followed that up with two more that whizzed wildly past the umpire's
ears. Magerkurth whipped off his mask and warned Casey that one more
wild pitch would earn him an early trip to the showers. Durocher stormed
the field to complain about this unwarranted treatment of his pitcher who
was simply having a bit of control trouble, and got tossed for his trouble.
(Leo retired to the Dodgers' dressing room, where he proceeded to break

up the furniture.) Eventually the Dodgers lost the game; afterwards, five Brooklyn players confronted Magerkurth under the stands. The next day, Durocher and an Associated Press reporter exchanged blows in a Brooklyn alley.

When the last week of the regular season began, the Dodgers still clung tenaciously to a one and a half game lead, but the Cardinals refused to fold. Decimated by injuries to their starting outfielders, the Cards brought up a twenty-year-old rookie named Stanley Frank Musial who had started the season as a dead-armed pitcher in Class D ball. When Branch Rickey decided to give him a chance in the outfield, Musial started to hit and never quit. He moved up through the entire organization in one glorious summer; when rightfielder Enos Slaughter injured his shoulder and centerfielder Terry Moore got beaned, manager Billy Southworth put Musial in the lineup. In twelve games, he responded with a spectacular .426 batting mark.

But it was not enough. The Dodgers clinched the pennant by sweeping the final two games of the season from Casey Stengel's Boston Braves (who finished in next-to-last place only because the Phillies—who lost 111 games that year—turned in one of the most atrocious seasons of their benighted history). On the train back to Boston on September 25, the Dodgers celebrated with $1,400 worth of champagne, whiskey, and beer; first baseman Dolph Camilli went around the car with a straight razor, cutting off everyone's suspenders or belt while Cookie Lavagetto snipped off their ties with a pair of scissors. When singer Tony Martin, an old Durocher crony, stood up and started to sing a victory song, Pee Wee Reese hit him with a steak and told him to sit down and shut up. A raucous crowd of 25,000 delirious fans greeted the team at Grand Central Station and held their Beautiful Bums captive for two hours. The Cardinals were burned in effigy at two street intersections in Flatbush. A county court judge in Brooklyn adjourned a grand larceny case to celebrate the news of the pennant clinching, and Mayor La Guardia sent Durocher his congratulations, "from one temperamentalist to another."

Over in the American League, the Yankees had clinched the pennant on September 4—the earliest date in league history—and finished seventeen games ahead of the second place Boston Red Sox. Just about the only suspense during the final weeks of the season came from Ted Williams' assault on the .400 batting mark. Going into the final day, when the Red Sox were scheduled to play a double header in Philadelphia, Williams was hitting .39955. Since that figure would be rounded off to .400 under league rules, Manager Joe Cronin offered to let Williams sit out both games. The cranky leftfielder refused. He spent that night pacing restlessly through the streets of Philadelphia (which was not necessarily the smartest thing to do; statistically, his chances of getting mugged probably were better than the odds against raising his batting average), stopping occasionally for an ice cream cone. September 28 was a chilly, dreary Sunday. In the first game, Connie Mack started a young, seldom-used lefthander named Porter Vaughan (0–2, 7.94 ERA) because he knew Williams hated facing unfamiliar pitchers. Mack also reportedly instructed his first baseman to ignore any runner on first and play deep behind the bag when the left-handed Williams was batting. But Williams went four for five in the first game anyway; between games, United Press reporter Jack Mullaney went down to the Boston dugout and announced that Williams was hitting .403. "You want to play this last game?" Cronin asked him. "Sure, I wanna play it," Williams snapped, and he went out and got two more hits in the second game and finished the year at .406. "Ain't I the best hitter you ever saw!" he shouted in the clubhouse afterward.

Oddsmakers installed the Yankees as 2–5 favorites to capture the World Series. After all, the Bronx Bombers had won nine straight World Series games, including four-game sweeps of Chicago and Cincinnati in 1938 and 1939; in their last seven World Series, the Yankee juggernaut had won 28 games and lost only 3. (The Yankees' last Series loss was on October 9, 1937.) Of course, just because people wagered on the Yankees did not mean that they liked them. As John Lardner explained, "The Yankee club is too big and rich and powerful and smooth for my taste. It's not the kind of club that warms the heart and sets the citizens to dancing in the streets. But in the World Series, the Yanks are wolves. They have a quality that is made to order for great issues—and the series is the greatest issue in baseball."

New York City police laid in extra supplies of tear gas and assigned special squads to maintain order during the forthcoming Battle of the Boroughs. A record 68,540 spectators jammed Yankee Stadium for the first game on October 1; among the dignitaries in attendance were Mayor Fiorello La Guardia, Babe Ruth, Jim Farley, Joe Louis, Billy Conn, and Wendell Willkie. President Roosevelt kept his afternoon schedule free and planned to clean up some routine paperwork while he listened to the game on a portable radio in his study. Inside the stadium, black-robed nuns stood patiently collecting contributions for charity; as one heavyset man dropped a coin in the box, he muttered, "Little prayer for the Bums, Sister," and the nun smiled and nodded.

To no avail. Behind a sterling pitching performance by thirty-seven-year-old righthander Charlie "Red" Ruffing, the Yankees captured the first game, 3–2. Afterwards, one rabid Dodger fan who had requested a conscientious objector deferment to delay his induction into the army promptly withdrew his plea. But the Dodgers, led by 22-game-winner Whitlow Wyatt, battled back to take the second game by an identical 3–2 score.

Then, after twenty-four hours of steady rain postponed game three for a day, the Series shifted to the cozy confines of Ebbets Field, which held approximately half as many spectators as majestic Yankee Stadium. The first postseason game in Brooklyn since 1920 took place under a punishing, broiling sun, with oppressive humidity. Before the action began on the field, "Brudda Lou's Dodger Band" from Withers Street, attired in their usual bizarre marching outfits, paraded through the stands playing their patented baroque rendition of "Three Blind Mice" over and over and over again. A black-lettered banner hung over the centerfield railing: WE WAITED TWENTY-ONE YEARS, DON'T FAIL US NOW. The most popular headgear of the day among the perspiring patrons was a tabloid newspaper split down the middle.

Looking out over the residents of the bleachers as the game began, one reporter decided that the hatless, coatless, shirtless, screaming multitude resembled a psychiatrist's nightmare: "If you turned your back on the diamond and looked into the heaving sea of parboiled faces, bare and sweating torsos, fanatically glaring eyeballs, and watched the restless and violent gestures, the effect was startling. . . . An astonishing number of alcoholics roamed through the bleacher sections, exposed to the sun. One slender fellow reduced to a feeble grin and barely able to move, even in first gear, wabbled the narrow aisles calling for Texas Leaguers. 'Tessus ligger,' he'd holler, and then, as if the effort was too great, he'd slide to the concrete in a heap. Cops and ushers worked him up the runways three times, but each time he came back—backward, like one of those teetering toys." Ebbets ushers, who presumably had grown inured to this sort of thing by now, decided that the lunacy in the bleachers that day surpassed all known bounds. One usher looked at the crowd, and then glanced up at Kings County Hospital on the ridge overlooking the stadium and murmured, "They look like someone left open the cages on the hill." Most of the fans remained blissfully unaware that all-star second baseman Billy Herman had pulled a muscle in his rib cage during batting practice, rendering him *hors de combat* for the rest of the Series.

Fat Freddie Fitzsimmons, the forty-year-old knuckleballer from Mishawaka, Indiana, breezed through the Yankee order for six innings, barely breaking a sweat, until disaster (which always seemed to be lurking just around the corner in Ebbets Field) struck the Dodgers with devastating swiftness in the top of the seventh. A line drive back through the box struck Freddie squarely on the kneecap and caromed high into the air. Limping painfully, Fitzsimmons had to be helped off the field; the tough, reliable veteran was through for the Series. The Yankees promptly proceeded to score twice in the eighth off the shaky Dodger bullpen, and went on to win the game, 2–1. "I went home sick," said one dejected Brooklyn fan. "I remember riding on the trolley car that ran from Ebbets Field along Parkside Avenue and throwing up out the window." The odds on a Yankee Series victory now stood at 1 to 5.

But the cruelest blow of all came in game four, when the Bums entered the top of the ninth inning with a 4–3 lead. Hugh Casey, the Dodgers' short relief specialist, easily retired the first two batters, to bring Brooklyn within one out of tying up the Series. Tommy Henrich was the Yankees' last hope for the afternoon. Pitching carefully, Casey ran the count to 3 and 2. It was 4:35 P.M. Employing a considerable amount of poetic license, *New York Times* sportswriter Meyer Berger captured the fateful scene:

> There was ease in Casey's manner as he stood there in the box.
> There was pride in Casey's bearing, from his cap down to his sox.
> And when, responding to the cheers, he took up his trousers' sag,
> No stranger in the crowd could doubt, he had them in the bag. . . .
>
> From the benches black with people there went up a muffled roar
> Like the thunder of dark storm waves on the Coney Island shore.
> "Get him!" "Get him, Casey!" shouted some one in the stand.
> Hugh Casey smiled with confidence. Hugh Casey raised his hand. . . .
>
> Pale as the lily Henrich's lips; his teeth were clenched in hate.
> He pounded with cruel violence his bat upon the plate.
> And now Great Casey held the ball, and now he let it go.
> And Brooklyn's air was shattered by the whiff of Henrich's blow.

To this day, no one knows precisely what sort of a pitch Casey threw. Reporters at the scene said it was a curveball; Pee Wee Reese later described it as "a little wet slider"—a spitball; Durocher swore it was Casey's natural sinker. Casey said he put "everything I had on the pitch." Whatever, it broke sharply just before it reached the plate. Henrich couldn't stop his swing. He missed it by a foot, the home plate umpire bellowed, "Strike three," and dozens of police started to emerge from the dugout to hold back the deliriously happy fans (33,813 of them) who were ready to sprint onto the field.

But the ball eluded Mickey Owen. (Durocher later said Owen reached for the ball instead of shifting his feet, and perhaps he did.) The ball bounced off the edge of his glove and skidded away from the Dodger catcher and kept on rolling. For a second Henrich did not know what had happened. Then, still holding the bat in his hand, he started to run for first as fast as he could as Owen scurried madly in pursuit of the elusive sphere. By the time Owen caught up with the ball in front of the Brooklyn dugout steps, the police were in his way and Henrich was safely perched on first base.

Instead of pausing to calm his shattered nerves, Casey went ahead and pitched to the next hitter, who happened to be Joe DiMaggio. Doubtless Durocher should have taken him out, or at least made a visit to the mound to settle Casey down. DiMaggio singled. With an 0 and 2 count on Keller, Casey grooved a pitch right down the middle of the plate and Keller launched it toward the right field wall for a double, scoring two runs. Dickey walked. Durocher still refused to remove the befuddled Casey. Again, Casey ran the count to 0 and 2 on the next batter, then he grooved another pitch and Joe Gordon sent it flying for another double. By the time the carnage was over, four runs were in and the Yankees led 7–4. The Dodgers went down meekly in order in the ninth. At 4:56 it was all over.

"It couldn't, perhaps, have happened anywhere else on earth," decided the *New York Times*. "Few clubs in major league history have ever had an almost certain victory snatched from them under more harrowing circumstances." There was a weary fatalistic air of resignation in the Dodger clubhouse after the game. "I tell you," muttered Dixie Walker, "those fellows have got all the luck on their side. Never saw a team get so many breaks as they have." Jimmy Wasdell agreed: "There are angels flying around those Yankees, I tell you." Owen refused to make any alibis. Looking squarely at a slightly sheepish herd of reporters, the catcher said calmly, "It was all my fault. It wasn't a strike. It was a great, breaking curve that I should have had." Over in the Yankee locker room, Henrich was ecstatic. "Boy, was that great, or was it great? What a finish! What a game! Never was anything like this. Never will be again, I'll bet."

"Oh, somewhere North of Harlem the sun is shining bright," rhapsodized Meyer Berger. "Bands are playing in The Bronx and up there hearts are light. / In Hunts Point men are laughing, on The Concourse children shout. / But there is no joy in Flatbush. Fate had knocked their Casey out."

Back at Yankee Stadium the next day, a dispirited bunch of Dodgers allowed the fifth Yankee hurler of the Series, 220-pound Ernie "Tiny" Bonham, to hold them to a single run. They got only one hit after the third inning. The most exciting moment of the game occurred when a fire broke out on the roof behind the third-base stands. Pitching on three days' rest, Whit Wyatt could not work two miracles in a row, and the Yankees captured the final game, 3–1.

But the Dodgers had not lost because of Owen's miscue or Casey's mental errors. They lost because they hit a feeble .182 for the Series, hardly enough to beat anyone, much less the powerful Yankees.

A few miles from Yankee Stadium, a short and not particularly powerful Californian named Robert L. Riggs completed a year-long comeback by winning the prestigious United States Lawn Tennis Championship at Forest Hills. The cocky Riggs, who had won the tournament in 1939 and then lost it the following year, was not the most popular men's champion in the annals of American tennis. Known as (among other things) "the counter-puncher of tennis," Riggs never played any harder than he needed to, winning most of his matches by employing a diverse repertoire of spins, lobs, and changes of speed that was not particularly exciting to watch. Besides, he had the annoying (and, back then, almost unheard-of) habit of openly questioning linesmen's decisions. During his semifinal match at Forest Hills in 1941, anti-Riggs spectators cheered every time he made an error. He won anyway. His opponent in the finals that year was Frank "the Clown" Kovacs, who had defeated the 1940 champion, Don McNeill, in the semis. Riggs and Kovacs played the final match in a blustery gale that was strong enough to lift a beach umbrella forty feet in the air at a nearby tea garden. Swirling through the horseshoe-shaped stadium, the wind threatened to disrupt Riggs's carefully placed shots; Bobby also had to overcome the distraction supplied by fans who shouted "Fault!" nearly every time he served and whistled at calls that went against the handsome Kovacs. But after Kovacs took the first set, the rest of the afternoon belonged to Riggs. Countering Kovacs's blistering ground strokes with little drop shots that barely cleared the net and long, high lobs that fell precisely on the baseline (or awfully close to it), Riggs generally gave Kovacs hell and made very few unforced errors himself. He took the last three sets in short order—the final score was 5–7, 6–1, 6–3, 6–3—and began to look around for offers to turn professional.

An atmosphere of uncertainty surrounded the opening of the college football season that fall. Some varsity lettermen already had been drafted ("I do not think there is anything sacred about a . . . college education," grumbled Selective Service Director Hershey), and others had given up football for ROTC, but nothing could dispel the joy of clear, crisp autumn afternoons on the green and golden campuses, with leaves crackling underfoot along the path to the stadium, where alumni packed themselves into the rickety wooden stands and sang the old school songs and leered surreptitiously at the cheerleaders and generally made a vain but genial effort to recapture the special carefree spirit of their own bygone undergraduate days. Despite (or perhaps because of) the uncertain future, college football fans turned out in record numbers to watch the boys play their games that year. Paul Brown was in his first year as head coach at Ohio State; Frank Leahy had just taken over the reins at Notre Dame; and Earl Blaik was starting a long and prosperous coaching career at Army. By the time November rolled around, the top teams in the nation appeared to be the bone-crushing Minnesota Gophers (the consensus number one choice), Texas, Texas A&M, Duke, Fordham, and Duquesne. In the 1941 versions of the oldest traditional annual rivalries, Harvard shut out Yale, 14–0, Michigan and Ohio State battled to a 20–20 tie, and Indiana captured the Old Oaken Bucket from Purdue, 7–0. Almost certainly the worst team in the nation was the Arkansas A & M Boll Weevils, who collectively said the hell with all the rah-rah stuff and just went out and tried to have as much fun as they could on the field. They certainly were entertaining. Since they couldn't decide on a uniform, each man wore whatever color he liked. Their coach was a medieval history professor who doubled as the dean of men, but that was all right because none of the players paid any attention to him anyway, making up their own plays as they went along.

The Boll Weevils were perfectly capable of completing forty-two passes in a game and still losing. Occasionally they tried a trick play to confuse the opposition; once they fell flat on their faces while the opposing team was trying to kick an extra point. (It worked. The kicker was so startled he shanked the ball off to the side.)

"It's been a grand life in America," wrote Raymond Clapper. "We have had to work hard. But usually there was good reward. We have had poverty, but also the hope that if the individual man threw in enough struggle and labor he could find his place. Man has gained steadily in security and dignity, in hours of leisure, in those things that made his family comfortable and gave lift to his spirit. Under his feet, however rough the road, he felt the firm security of a nation fundamentally strong, safe from any enemy, able to live at peace by wishing to. In every one of us lived the promise of America . . .

"Whether we go to war or not, we shall act more and more as if we were going to war. Our lives will all be affected by this. Our ways will change drastically, whether or not a drop of blood is lost.

"Habits must be changed. Peacetime ways have to be sacrificed. For years, dozens of materials will be almost completely monopolized by war needs and there will be little left for civilian purposes. . . .

"I mention only the more pleasant aspects of the future and pass over the heavy hearts, the separated families, the young careers that will have to wait, those inward wounds which are more numerous than the wounds of the battlefield.

"Regimented people. Regimented trade. The waste of war. The millions of days of human labor to make the guns, the shells, the planes, the tanks, and the ships. The huge plants useful only to manufacture weapons of slaughter. That's our future. It will be the same whether we go into the war or not."

In later years, most Americans remembered 1941 as a golden autumn. Coeds never looked better in their shoulder length pageboys and their shaggy sweaters with the single strands of pearls and their pleated houndstooth skirts and felt gaiters and felt pigtails and knee socks and their peasant handkerchiefs they wore knotted around their necks. "Every girl appeared good-looking from behind," recalled Frederick Lewis Allen. There was a marvelous sense of freedom in the air everywhere, sparked by a "who knows if we will live through all this" outlook on the future. While jukeboxes played "Please Give Me Something to Remember You By," the birthrate kept climbing, and baby-food companies and diaper services prepared for a banner year in 1942. For those who could afford the government regulations that placed a stiff new 7 percent excise tax on automobile purchases and required buyers to make down payments of at least one-third of the purchase price, the 1942 passenger car models were generally heavier, longer, more expensive (prices were up about 15 percent even without the taxes) and flashier than ever. The new Packard Clipper model featured a massive radiator grille and "fade-away fenders" that wrapped all the way around to the front wheels; the 1942 Hudson had an ingenious (and potentially dangerous) optional foot-controlled radio station selector button; Chevrolet introduced an interesting gadget that squirted a stream of clean water onto the windshield when you pressed a button; Dodge finally covered its running boards and beefed up its engines from 91 to 105 hp; the new Mercury 8 reportedly was "airplane-engineered, streamlined from the inside out with more power per pound"; Lincoln's latest Continental model had a forward-flaring heavy-barred grille that jutted out from below the headlights like an underslung jaw; Oldsmobile introduced its new, defense-conscious "B-44"; and the 1942 De Soto featured "Airfoil" headlights which were cleverly concealed behind a sliding shutter. But these cars were going to have to last a long, long time. Detroit already had begun to cut production by one-third to concentrate on lucrative defense contracts, and even fewer cars would be produced in 1942. So those who couldn't find or afford a new car might find themselves traveling on the "Magic Carpet" of the Twentieth Century Limited ("Tonight no ups and downs will mar the sweet serenity of your slumber") from New York to Chicago, but they would never find Al Capone in the Windy City; the ex-gangster was spending his retirement playing golf and swimming at his estate in Florida—although his recreational routine had recently been rudely disrupted by government prosecutors who insisted that he was guilty of federal income tax evasion to the tune of $201,347.

October brought American radio audiences a new fall season of shows; this year, there was a noticeable decline in the popularity of serious dramas, and a corresponding increase in the amount of comedy on the air waves. The Great Gildersleeve made his debut, Ozzie Nelson joined Red Skelton's show, Abbott and Costello appeared with Edgar Bergen, and Fibber McGee and Molly returned for one more year to try to straighten up that damn closet. The latest innovation in radio receiving equipment was something called "frequency modulation"—FM—which reportedly provided greatly improved reception for music broadcasts. The FCC already was having trouble regulating the infant television industry. During the autumn of 1941, the agency awarded Channel 2 of the television wave band (the channel heretofore reserved for the exclusive use of the army) to the Columbia Broadcasting System, and ordered CBS to begin broadcasting fifteen hours of television programs weekly, despite the fact that none of the sets owned by civilians in the New York area were capable of receiving Channel 2. (All the sets were tuned to receive only Channel 1, which had already been awarded to NBC.)

By now, the war abroad and the defense buildup at home were creating severe shortages in certain types of consumer goods. Housewives across the nation received a rude jolt when the price of spices skyrocketed (sage, for instance, went from seven cents a pound to $1.35) and stocks dwindled because almost all America's supply of thyme, sage, saffron, poppy seed, bay leaves, marjoram, and caraway seeds came from the Nazi-occupied nations of Europe; husbands were going to be eating some pretty tame meat loaf for the foreseeable future. Although RCA admitted that it was cutting back on the production of phonographs and radios because of raw material shortages, it still proceeded to launch a full-scale promotional campaign for its new "Magic Brain" Victrola, the phonograph with the tandem tone arm "that plays records on both sides without turning them over." Chanel announced that it was still possible to get ... and give ... its famous perfume, although stocks were starting to run low. (Coco Chanel herself was living with a German intelligence officer in Paris.) For women who could not afford the rising price of French perfumes, Bonwit Teller's corset salon offered an alternative that raised interesting possibilities in the minds of men who never knew such a thing was possible: "We mold bosoms ... really, literally, as if they were made out of clay."

Speaking of bosoms, James M. Cain's latest sordid tale of steamy sex (or sexy tale of sordid steam ... or steamy tale of sexy sordity), *Mildred Pierce,* appeared in September and sold eleven thousand copies in the first month before leveling off. *Mildred*'s sudden leap onto the best-seller list caused the *New York Times* to wonder, rather petulantly, whether "we are going to fight a war to save the kind of characters who inhabit the books of Cain and James T. Farrell?" Perhaps the *Times* should have asked that question of James Agee's *Let Us Now Praise Famous Men,* published in August 1941 to mixed (and more than a little bewildered) critical reaction. Agee's story of southern sharecropper families, told in experimental prose and accompanied by Walker Evans' sensitive photographs, sold a grand total of six hundred copies in 1941. For his part, Ernest Hemingway spent the autumn complaining about the tax bite Uncle Sam was taking out of his royalty checks. "If anyone asks the children what their father did in Mr. Roosevelt's war," he complained to his ex-wife, "they can say 'He paid for it.' " On the other hand, young playwright Tennessee Williams, whose latest production, *Battle of Angels,* had closed early in 1941 after a turbulent twelve-day run in Boston, ended the year as an impoverished "companion" to a whacked-out abstract painter in the West Village's warehouse district; from time to time, Williams earned a little extra pocket money by working as a hotel elevator operator or a waiter at a subterranean café known as the Beggar's Bar.

Lillian Hellman, though, stood at the peak of her career as a dramatist in the final months of 1941 at the tender age of thirty-six. Her anti-Fascist drama *Watch on the Rhine* already had won the New York Drama Critics' Circle award as best American play of the year, defeating William Saroyan's *The Beautiful People* (which came in second), *Arsenic and Old Lace,* Maxwell Anderson's *Key Largo, Lady in the Dark,* and Hemingway's *Fifth Column.* Hellman, a short, slim woman who, according to one interviewer, bore "a curious resemblance to the familiar Gilbert Stuart portrait of George Washington," claimed that she wrote the play in just eight months after an extensive period of research in twentieth-century German history. Critics lauded *Watch on the Rhine* for its warmth and humanity (especially after the chilling bleakness of Hellman's previous successes, *The Little Foxes* and *The Children's Hour*), for its penetrating insight into the power of ideology to transform—for better or worse—the hearts and minds of true believers, and for its uncompromising conclusion that the worldwide fight against fascism must take precedence over the lives and welfare of individuals caught up in the maelstrom. Set in a peaceful country house in the suburbs of Washington, D.C., the play follows the changes that occur in the comfortable lives of an American family as the war in Europe (personified by an unscrupulous Romanian nobleman and a German anti-Nazi underground leader) shatters their cherished serenity. "Among other things," noted Brooks Atkinson in the *New York Times,* "Miss Hellman draws a vivid contrast between the simple good will of a normal American family and the dark callousness of Europeans who have grown accustomed to horror, intrigue, and desperation. . . . An intangible political idea from abroad hovers over an American living room and brings a feeling of sadness, apprehension, and restlessness there." Quite an appropriate theme for the autumn of 1941. Yet in the face of the carnage abroad and the gathering storm at home, Hellman could scarcely enjoy her triumphs; despondent over the savage defeats of Soviet forces on the eastern front, she reportedly was seen walking around New York muttering the final lines from T. S. Eliot's "The Hollow Men": "This is the way the world ends / Not with a bang but a whimper."

As November came to a close, Darryl F. Zanuck was preparing to release a grim, bleak film of life in Welsh colliery towns. After paying a record $300,000 for the screen rights to *How Green Was My Valley,* Zanuck insisted that the movie version play down the weighty political and sociological message of the original best-selling novel, and this time his instincts proved sound. Directed by John Ford, who seldom rehearsed and invariably got just what he wanted from his actors on the first take, *Valley* earned more money than any 1941 film except *Sergeant York,* and won six Academy Awards, including Best Picture. (It beat out *Citizen Kane* for best direction and photography.)

For those who preferred more lighthearted entertainment, Walt Disney released his fifth feature-length cartoon, a delightful sixty-four-minute fable about a flying elephant named Dumbo. After experimenting with the spectacular but underappreciated *Fantasia* and *The Reluctant Dragon*, Disney chose to forsake Art and return to the gentler, simpler style that had made him famous. On his way back to Hollywood from a trip to South America, Disney paused in a New York hotel room long enough to explain to a reporter the way the creative process worked at his studios. "I'm the bee that carries the pollen," he said, cupping his hands in front of him. "I've got to know whether an idea goes here" (as he dumped some pollen onto a chair) "or here." He said he didn't show any of his drawings to anyone these days. "I've got too many good artists out there. To draw, you've got to get off to yourself. You've got to have nothing else on your mind. I have to talk so much I can't draw. Suppose I'm making a new character like Dumbo. Well, who the hell *is* he? What's he like? What does he feel? Can you make him fly? You've got to keep experimenting, and you've got to keep talking and throwing away a lot of stuff." Usually, Disney claimed, he produced his movies without the aid of a detailed script. "The best way is to work off the cuff. Don't have any script but just go along and nobody knows what's going to happen until it's happened. That was the way we did with *Snow White*. I'd say to a songwriter, 'Look, at this point we got to have a song that expresses love,' and he'd write one. 'What the hell happens next?' the boys would ask me. 'I don't know, but let's try this,' I would say." After his experience with his last two films, Disney said he had sworn off Art; in fact, he wanted to do a movie with live actors and less animation. "I don't want any more headaches like the *Nutcracker Suite*. In a thing like that, you got to animate all those flowers, and boy, does that run into dough! All that shading. That damn thing cost two hundred thousand dollars—just the one *Nutcracker Suite*. We're getting back to straight-line stuff, like *Donald Duck* and the *Pigs.*"

Salvador Dali, too, was getting back to basics, returning to the classic influences by emphasizing balance, design, and precise technique in his paintings—or so he said. Actually, it was rather difficult to determine exactly what the Spanish surrealist was up to in his latest exhibition at the Julien Levy Gallery in Manhattan. The highlights of the show—where prices ranged from $750 to $5,000—included a *Family of Marsupial Centaurs* (an amusingly self-explanatory venture into the art of modern myth-making) and *Piano Descending by Parachute,* a portrait of a piano sailing majestically off the edge of a cliff. Since their arrival in the United States in August 1941, Dali and his imperious wife, Gala, had been enjoying the bounteous hospitality of Mrs. Caresse Crosby at her Virginia estate, Hampton Manor. There Dali painted from eight in the morning until midnight, taking breaks only for meals, an occasional game of chess, and writing his autobiography (which even included his own prenatal recollections). According to Mrs. Crosby, Dali kept an electric light burning and a radio playing all the time while he was working, and spent most of his time inside the house because he was scared to death of the grasshoppers that lurked menacingly in the grass outside. Not surprisingly, by the end of the year he and Gala were starting to get on nearly everyone's nerves.

After a trip to New York, where Kitty Carlisle entertained nightly at the Persian Room at the Plaza and military planes flew in wedge formation high over the deserted beaches at Fire Island, Anne Lindbergh recounted the rising signs of war. "Soldiers on the train, searchlights in the sky, planes maneuvering in threes. All the billboards have gone 'Defense' mad, with pictures of soldiers and sailors on them. *Vogue* photographs its models in front of Bundles for Britain planes. Longchamps has V's done in vegetables in the windows. Elizabeth Arden gets out a V for Victory lipstick." Still, Anne enjoyed New York in its gay pre-Christmas spirit, "lovely weather, walking down the streets at misty lighted five o'clock with my Paris coat on and my Renoir hat and curls and no one recognizing me! The shops, of course, were nauseating with the richness of material attractions. What appalled me was not so much the unawareness of people skating about on this thin surface of materialism as the insincere attempt to gild the materialism with patriotic motives, especially in advertising. 'Be brave with Diamonds,' 'Defense of good taste—Buy So-and-so's Ale.' 'For the service of America . . .' "

For the discriminating Christmas gift shopper in 1941, F.A.O. Schwarz touted an adult game called Invasion, wherein two, three, or four players started in the middle of the Atlantic and strove to accumulate enough ships and tanks to blast one another off the board. A new perfume from Russia came in a bottle shaped like a tank, with turrets and all. Abercrombie & Fitch featured a service man's game set (with dice, cup, a deck of cards, and a set of rules, presumably limited to legitimate games), and a seventeen-jewel pilot-wing watch "for women to wear as a pilot wears his wings." For kids, Santa's 1941 sack included a mosquito boat kit ("Builds realistic model of the new PT-10 boat with deck and armament material"), metal British toy soldiers with gun emplacements and a howitzer camouflaged with a net, a canopy-topped pedal-propelled field ambulance with U.S.A. MEDICAL CORPS lettered on the olive-drab sides and room for two or three doll casualties in the rear, metal wind-up bathtub battleships with sparks that flashed from the turrets, Red Cross nurses' outfits, and an entire doll-sized army cantonment made of wood.

Of course, not every Christmas gift item reflected the war's influence. There were enough Betsey Wetsy and Dydee dolls to make any parent gag; the most recent innovations—one hesitates to call them advances—in lifelike toys were the Heartbeat dolls (which came with stethoscopes to enable curious little tots to hear the inescapable thudding sound even more clearly) and something called the Magic Skin doll. "The magic skin is a plastic; touch it, and it warms under your startled hand," reported one magazine with distinct repugnance; "pinch it, and it puckers like human flesh; expose it to the sun, and, by golly, it tans! It's all too creepy for us, and you'll simply have to follow your own taste and judgment in this field."

Christmas cards were more subdued in 1941; there was none of the flag-waving patriotism or novelty items that had plagued past years. Along Fifth Avenue, sequins had finally won their fashion battle for acceptance and masses of glitter seemed to be stuck to everything, from V-neck jackets to black crepe evening dresses. Saks Fifth Avenue's latest discovery was a waist-length ostrich cape with crepe lining and a long feather boa that could be dyed any shade one chose. Or, one could choose a thin crepe dress in bright red or peacock blue adorned with tiny glass stars in matching colors; "a soldier beau will have no morale trouble for weeks after he has seen you in it."

For soldiers themselves, gift consultants recommended a shockproof and waterproof wristwatch, writing paper (personalized with name, rank, and address), a down-filled waterproof sleeping bag, inflatable rubber pillows, flannel bathrobes, a rubberized silk money bag, soap (which the army reportedly did not provide), perhaps a Brooks Brothers custom-made jacket in regulation olive drab serge for $75—matching slacks were $27 extra—or a portable radio. Life in camp, as everyone knew, could get terribly dull.

Ray Clapper knew there was no escape. "Now we see the distant fire rolling toward us. It is not being put out. It is still some distance away, but the evil wind blows it towards us.

"So ends our reverie in the twilight, over the dear, dead days."

Part Six   The Lost Island

27

"AIR RAID, PEARL HARBOR"

"Sick at heart. I am so damned mad at the Navy for being asleep at
the switch at Honolulu. It is the worst day in American history."
—ASSISTANT SECRETARY OF STATE BRECKINRIDGE LONG

"AIR RAID, PEARL HARBOR. THIS IS NOT DRILL!"
It was 7:58 A.M. in Honolulu.

Several minutes earlier, the first wave of Japanese Zeros had descended undetected through the thin layer of clouds that had sheltered
their approach toward Hawaii. Below them lay the island of Oahu, sleeping in the early morning sunlight, all green and gold and sparkling blue,
naked and spectacularly vulnerable. The raiders continued on their mission—to seek out and destroy all American air and sea forces they could
find—unchallenged by any patrol planes from the Hawaiian bases. Having
already achieved their initial objective of total surprise, the rest would be
gloriously easy. The Japanese pilots could see clearly most of the ninety-
four ships of the United States Pacific Fleet moored obligingly in neat rows
in Pearl Harbor, wholly unprotected; from the sky, the eight battleships
that were the primary target appeared to be dressed in their gleaming
white virginal Sunday best.

On the ground and on the decks of their ships, bewildered American
sailors looked up to see the sky suddenly filled with Japanese planes, the
red rising sun clearly visible on the underside of the wings. Dive-bombers
(nicknamed "helldivers" by Japanese pilots in sincere admiration of the
recent Clark Gable movie of the same name) screamed through the air
and pulled out of their descent at about three hundred feet; torpedo
bombers leveled off and made their approaches only fifty feet above the
water. Within a matter of seconds the tragically belated warnings began
to sound from the ships' loudspeakers: "Japs are coming!" "Japs attacking
us! Go to your battle stations!" "Man your battle stations! This is no shit!"
There was not even enough time to turn the gun turrets toward the
attackers.

Clusters of torpedo bombs tore through the first battleships in line,
California and the twenty-five-year-old *Oklahoma;* the latter ship

bounced almost completely out of the water after suffering four explosions within the course of sixty seconds, and then settled down and began to roll over slowly, inexorably, on its side, trapping nearly five hundred men below decks where rescue teams could not reach them. The *West Virginia* absorbed direct hits from six torpedoes and two high explosive bombs, one of which sent a piece of shrapnel flying into the stomach of Captain Mervyn Bennion, fatally wounding the commander; as fires spread quickly throughout the ship and Japanese machine guns strafed the survivors, a lieutenant commander took over and ordered the ammunition magazines flooded and the wounded evacuated (although Bennion refused to leave his ship and died minutes later).

The most spectacular tragedy of the morning occurred as a series of bombs struck the *Arizona*, penetrating the fuel storage area where someone—contrary to naval regulations and the dictates of simple common sense—had stored nearly a ton of highly volatile black powder. The powder immediately ignited and set off a chain reaction of explosions in the forward magazine and boiler that culminated in an apocalyptic fireball as the 32,600-ton battleship leaped out of the water and tore sickeningly in half: "It was a dead sound," recalled one witness watching from *Nevada,* "like a big swish of wind going through foliage." At least one thousand men on board *Arizona* died instantly, including Rear Admiral Isaac Kidd, the first officer of admiral's rank to be killed in action in the history of the United States Navy. Severed limbs and metallic debris from *Arizona* were thrown toward the heavens and rained down upon nearby ships, which suddenly found themselves in mortal danger from the holocaust. Moored on the inner side of Battleship Row, *Tennessee* actually suffered more damage from lethal flying shards of red-hot, twisted metal than from Japanese bombs. The heat from *Arizona* was so intense that the crew of *Nevada,* who were frantically trying to guide their vessel through the harbor, had to shield their stores of ammunition with their bodies until they had passed the flaming ship. Mercilessly, Japanese bombers continued to pound *Arizona* until most of the broken battleship lay beneath the sea. As the ship finally settled into its grave, it came to rest directly atop the main that supplied Ford Island with fresh water, severing the pipe.

The Japanese planes turned and began their second run over Battleship Row. By now the sun was blotted out by thick clouds of dense black smoke which actually sheltered the American ships from Japanese view for a few moments. The sea was covered with a heavy coating of oil six inches thick in places, through which hundreds of dazed American sailors, who had jumped overboard to escape the blazing inferno on the ships, struggled desperately to reach the shore; Japanese pilots later remarked that the Americans in the water appeared to be moving in slow motion. Within minutes the oil had caught fire. Between the explosions and the flaming water, 60 percent of the American casualties that day were due to burns.

Meanwhile, in an effort to keep American pursuit and fighter planes out of the air, several detachments from the main Japanese attack force had been strafing and bombing the bases at Wheeler Field, Ford Island, and Hickam Field, knocking out about half of the army and navy planes that sat unprotected in formation on the runways. (Some of the Japanese raiders also reportedly dropped propaganda pamphlets with caricatures of Roosevelt and drawings of battleships exploding, accompanied by slogans such as, "Listen to the voice of doom!" "Open your eyes, blind fools!" "You Damned! Go To Devil!") The helpless airfields were virtually bereft of antiaircraft guns to fight off the enemy raiders, apparently because those in authority had always assumed the island's outer ring of defenses would keep attackers at bay; besides, most of the live antiaircraft shells were securely locked up in warehouses. So the men at the airfields fired back at the low-flying bombers with the only weapons they had: pistols, rifles, and machine guns. Some enraged officers stood out in the open, shaking their fists at the Japanese pilots, who obligingly proceeded to shoot them. Several army pilots eventually did manage to get their planes into the air, however, and shot down a total of eleven Japanese planes that morning. The only other consolation was that many of the American military planes which were destroyed on the airfields had already been declared obsolescent.

During the first incredible moments of the surprise attack, Admiral Husband E. Kimmel, commander in chief of the United States Pacific Fleet, stood on a neighbor's lawn and watched the one-sided butchery in stunned silence. Kimmel soon recovered at least a portion of his senses, and jumped into a waiting car that took him to headquarters to see what could be salvaged from the wreckage.

In the shock and chaos that followed the first wave of explosions across the island, the nearly universal initial reaction of the bewildered resident American community (nine-tenths of whom seem to have been interrupted in the middle of a leisurely weekend breakfast) was that some fools at navy headquarters or the army air corps had taken leave of their senses, launching a Sunday morning drill that had somehow gone madly and inexplicably awry. Joseph C. Harsch, who, as a correspondent for the *Christian Science Monitor,* had lived through numerous air raids in Berlin, told his wife that this was her chance to see firsthand what a practice air raid maneuver was really like, and then the couple headed for the beach for a leisurely morning swim. In fact, hundreds of tourists lay calmly and contentedly on the golden sands of Waikiki Beach enjoying the sun long after the bombs began to fall, blissfully unaware that this was, in fact, the real thing. Most had no idea what was happening until they heard the radio announcements canceling all leaves for sailors, soldiers, marines, and officers, and calling doctors and defense workers to their posts. Then came the terse instructions for civilians: "Hawaii has been attacked. Do not go into the streets. Do not use your phones. Keep calm."

By the time the second wave of Japanese bombers appeared over Oahu at 8:55, all of the eight American battleships in Pearl Harbor were either dead *(Arizona, California, Oklahoma),* dying *(West Virginia),* or ablaze. Later, many witnesses swore that the attack had lasted all morning, but except for a few desultory and futile bursts of antiaircraft fire, it was all over by ten o'clock. The final casualty figures included 2,403 American sailors, soldiers, and civilians dead, and 1,178 missing. Besides the battleships, the navy had lost three light cruisers and three destroyers. Nearly two hundred American planes were damaged beyond repair. The Japanese had lost only twenty-nine planes and one submarine.

"AIR RAID, PEARL HARBOR. THIS IS NOT DRILL!"

The radio alert from Hawaii was intercepted at Mare Island, California, and relayed to the Navy Department at Washington. Shortly after one-thirty that afternoon, Secretary Knox had just completed a meeting with Admiral Stark and was preparing to leave his office for a routine visit to the Washington Navy Yard when a distraught communications officer rushed in and handed a dispatch to Stark. The admiral read it and passed it on to Knox. "What does this mean?" Knox gasped. "This can't be true, this must mean the Philippines." "No, sir; this is Pearl," replied Stark. "It's the beginning."

It was a cold, windy, overcast afternoon in Washington, the first hint of the hard winter to come after an unusually long spell of deceptively mild, sunny weather. The gray city streets were virtually deserted; a sharp breeze swirled the skirts and snapped the overcoats of the few hardy souls who stood shivering in line at the downtown movie theaters.

Roosevelt was sitting in his cluttered study with Harry Hopkins on the second floor of the White House, eating an apple. Fala was munching the lunch leftovers that lay on a tray on the President's desk. It had been a busy morning: for two hours Dr. Ross McIntire had tried to give Roosevelt some relief from a chronic sinus condition that required daily treatments to alleviate the discomfort; a courier had brought the translated intercept of a Japanese message breaking off the Hull-Nomura talks; and Chinese Ambassador Dr. Hu Shih had stopped in for a forty-minute conversation. Now it was time to relax for at least one Sunday afternoon. Roosevelt, hoping to catch up on his neglected stamp collection, told the White House switchboard operator he did not wish to be disturbed.

The telephone on his desk rang at 1:47. The operator apologized and said that Secretary Knox insisted on being put through to the President. In a remarkably calm voice (probably, given Knox's erratic temperament, the result of psychic dissociation following a severe shock), Knox said, "Mr. President, it looks like the Japanese have attacked Pearl Harbor. . . ." He read Roosevelt the radio message from Admiral Kimmel.

When Roosevelt put down the receiver, Hopkins suggested that there must have been some mistake. The Japanese would not attack Honolulu. Yes, the President replied, they probably had.

Roosevelt telephoned Hull, who reportedly received the news with a burst of profanity. In a few moments he was supposed to receive Nomura and Kurusu, who were bringing Japan's formal reply (the document that had already been intercepted and shown to the President) to his November 26 lecture. When they entered his office, Hull did not ask the Japanese envoys to sit down. He glanced at their proffered response for a moment and then said coldly, "I must say that in all my conversations with you during the last nine months, I have never uttered one word of untruth. This is borne out absolutely by the record. In all my fifty years of public service I have never seen a document that was more crowded with infamous falsehoods and distortions—infamous falsehoods and distortions on a scale so huge that I never imagined until today that any Government on this planet was capable of uttering them." Then he waved off Nomura's protest and gestured toward the door. Bewildered, the two Japanese walked out. Nomura, at least, had absolutely no idea what had happened at Pearl Harbor.

It was a cold Sunday in New York, too, but that didn't stop a large, enthusiastic crowd from showing up at the Polo Grounds to watch the Giants-Dodgers football game. Shortly after two o'clock, a message came over the public address system. "Attention, please! Attention! Here is an urgent message. Will Colonel William J. Donovan call Operator nineteen in Washington, D.C." After watching one or two more plays, Donovan (whom Roosevelt had recently appointed as head of American intelligence services) found a telephone and called the capital; he reached the President's eldest son, James, a captain in the Marine Corps, who asked Donovan to return to Washington immediately. In another part of the stadium, *New York Times* reporter Harrison Salisbury stayed on to watch the game, as yet unaware of what was happening.

Film director John Ford, who was working for Donovan as chief of the Field Photographic Branch of the fledgling American intelligence services, spent Sunday afternoon dining at the Alexandria, Virginia, home of Admiral William Pickens, chief of navigation. Their meal was interrupted by a phone call. "It's no use getting excited," Mrs. Pickens told her guests after they learned what had happened. "This is the seventh war that's been announced in this dining room."

At 2:22 P.M., Presidential Press Secretary Stephen Early telephoned the three major press associations from his home on Morningside Drive in Washington and gave them the announcement: "The Japs have attacked Pearl Harbor, all military activities on Oahu Island. A second air-attack is reported on Manila air and naval bases."

In the overheated, garishly lighted White House press room, amid the blaring radio announcements and the ceaseless ringing of twenty telephones, correspondents wondered aloud whether the attack on Pearl Harbor signaled the start of all-out war, or just an isolated, unauthorized incident sparked by a group of impetuous Japanese militarists run amok.

Joseph E. Davies, former American ambassador to the Soviet Union, was having lunch with an old acquaintance, newly arrived Soviet Ambassador Maxim Litvinov, when word came of the attack. "Litvinov asked me how I felt about it," recorded Davies. "I replied that it was a terrible thing, but it was providential. It assured unity in this country. It also assured a united battle front for all the non-aggressor great nations. It was now 'all for one and one for all.'

"I asked him how he felt about it. He said that had the United States come into the war earlier it would have undoubtedly thwarted Hitler. He was not so sure that it was advantageous now. I gathered that what was in the back of his mind was that this development would prevent the delivery of vital war materials to Britain and Russia."

Churchill was spending the weekend at Chequers with American Ambassador John Winant, Averell Harriman, and Harriman's daughter, Kathleen (whose birthday was December 7). At dinner Sunday evening, Harriman thought that "the Prime Minister seemed tired and depressed. He didn't have much to say throughout dinner and was immersed in his thoughts, with his head in his hands part of the time." Shortly before nine o'clock, Churchill's butler carried in a portable radio that Harry Hopkins had given him (Churchill, not the butler). By the time Winston turned it on, the BBC announcer, Alvar Liddell, had already begun the nightly summary of news headlines. Then Liddell returned to the lead story: "The news has just been given that Japanese aircraft have raided Pearl Harbor, the American naval base in Hawaii. The announcement of the attack was made in a brief statement by President Roosevelt . . ." Churchill appeared not to have heard, or understood, what had just been said. Harriman repeated the words: "The Japanese have raided Pearl Harbor." Someone else present said, "No, no. He said Pearl River." Suddenly Churchill arose and slammed down the lid of the radio. One of his secretaries appeared at that moment and said the Admiralty was on the telephone line. Having confirmed the news with his naval advisers (and the butler, who had heard the radio report), Churchill immediately went into his office and called Roosevelt.

"Mr. President, what's this about Japan?"

"It's quite true. They have attacked us at Pearl Harbor. We are all in the same boat now."

"This certainly simplifies things," Churchill said. "God be with you."

Churchill then notified Eden, who was in the north of Scotland en route to Moscow for a meeting with Stalin. Suffering from an attack of intestinal flu, Eden did not particularly feel like talking with the Prime Minister at first, but he cheered up considerably after listening to Churchill's excited message. "I could not conceal my relief and did not have to try to," admitted Eden. "I felt that whatever happened now, it was merely a question of time. Before, we had believed in the end but never seen the means, now both were clear."

Harold Nicolson, too, listened to the nine o'clock BBC news summary. "The Japanese have bombed Pearl Harbour. I do not believe it," Nicolson wrote in his diary. "We then turn on the German and French news and get a little more information. . . . I am dumbfounded by the news. . . . The whole action seems as insane as Hitler's attack on Russia. I remain amazed.

"The effect on Germany will be bad," Nicolson decided. "They will not say, 'We have a new ally.' They will say (or rather they will think in the recesses of their anxious souls), 'We have outraged the most formidable enemy in the world.' Their sense of destiny will begin to hover again as a sense of doom."

Hugh Dalton, head of Britain's clandestine Special Operations Executive: "Nine o'clock news says the Japs are in. They have begun by attacking the Americans. This, from our point of view, is much the best way for them to begin. It will unite all the Americans in one great warlike fury. But this . . . will lengthen the war by two years. We must now begin to make plans for 1946."

General de Gaulle, too, heard the BBC bulletin at his home in Hampstead. He turned to an aide and reportedly said, "The war is over. Of course there are years of fighting ahead, but the Germans are beaten."

At their home near Fort Benning, Georgia, Omar Bradley and his wife were puttering about in a flower bed when a friend stopped by to give them the news. Bradley donned his uniform and hurried to the post. "In event of war, we at Fort Benning had a special duty to perform. The War Department assumed that the enemy would attempt to sabotage key facilities throughout the State of Georgia—electrical generating plants, bridges, dams—and we had orders to protect these facilities." One of Bradley's men had drawn up a plan, "Emergency Plan White," to handle such a contingency. "I ordered Plan White executed, and by four the following morning our troops were deployed statewide guarding the key facilities. I realized, of course, that there was little likelihood of sabotage in the State of Georgia, that what we all of us now faced was far larger; total war with the Axis powers. The U.S. Army was far from ready for that war. Our weaknesses were still many."

Most Americans heard the incredible news over the radio. Anne Lindbergh was in her car, driving to Woods Hole: "Listening to the radio I heard the news. . . . It is the knell of the old world. All army officers all over the United States ordered into uniform. Espionage Act invoked. (If C. speaks again they'll put him in prison, I think immediately.) I listen all afternoon to the radio. I am listening to the Philharmonic, a beautiful concerto of Brahms. But it is interrupted every ten minutes with bulletins about the war. This is what life is going to be from now on, I think." Lindbergh did not react publicly to the attack. But privately he wondered, "How did the Japs get close enough, and where is our Navy? Or is it just a hit-and-run raid of a few planes, exaggerated by radio commentators into a major attack? The Japanese can, of course, raid the Hawaiian Islands, or even the West Coast, with aircraft carriers. But the cost in carriers and planes lost is going to be awfully high unless our Navy is asleep—or in the Atlantic. The question in my mind is, how much of it has been sent to the Atlantic to aid Britain?"

John Dos Passos was driving into New York from Long Island: "No way of forgetting that December afternoon. . . . I went into a Second Avenue ginmill to make a phone call and heard disaster pouring out over the radio." Soon afterward he wrote to a friend, "Damn the Japs, and the wops and the squareheads: gosh it's a big order." Tom Dewey was walking off the Quaker Hill golf course when he heard the news and sighed, "Well, it's a different world now." Curtis LeMay was listening intently to the Giants game while driving home from a morning of work at the airfield at Mt. Holyoke. When the announcer broke into the game with the latest bulletin, LeMay felt "some sense of relief" that the storm had finally broken. LeMay's superior, General Ira Eaker, was taking a nap at his home in Washington. Mrs. Eaker came in and woke him and said, "The Japs have attacked Pearl Harbor." Eaker rolled over and muttered, "You'll have to think of a better story than that to get me out of bed." So she turned up the volume on the radio.

Harrison Salisbury left the Giants game before it was over and went to a friend's apartment for a drink. He heard the radio announcer say something about "additional details on the Japanese bombing of Pearl Harbor." "I had a curious reaction," Salisbury recalled. " 'Those poor little bastards,' I said. 'The suicide boys have got them in the soup. They are finished. They are through. They haven't got a chance.' "

Back in the capital, Margaret Truman was suffering from a bad head cold and her mother wouldn't let her go outside in the chilly Washington weather. "I fiddled with my homework for a while, and then turned on the New York Philharmonic. . . . Suddenly an excited voice interrupted the orchestra to report that Japanese planes were attacking Pearl Harbor. I never was very good at geography, and I thought that was some port in China. When Mother looked in to see how I was breathing, I complained about the way the music was being ruined by bulletins about a Japanese air raid that could just as easily have waited for the six o'clock news. Mother, in closer touch with the international situation, asked me what the Japanese were bombing. When I said Pearl Harbor, she did a vanishing act. I sat there blinking while she raced to the telephone and frantically demanded a long-distance operator" in order to reach Harry, who was asleep in a hotel room in Columbia, Missouri, trying to catch up on his rest after a busy round of inspection tours of defense installations.

John Houseman was in the club car of a train speeding through western Kansas. He later claimed he "stayed there for the rest of the day and night drinking and listening to the news with mixed feelings of exhilaration and terror." Count Basie was sleeping late that day in Wichita on tour with his band; someone woke him up with the news about Pearl Harbor. "My main concern was training and going on those maneuvers. Somebody kept trying to tell me everything was going to be all right because I'd most likely be brought in as a musician and wouldn't have to do any fighting. But I told them I wasn't going anywhere. I said I wasn't going to take all that training stuff. I ain't going out on them maneuvers jumping in foxholes with them g–ddamn snakes and things out there. I said I wouldn't, and I meant that. There was nothing they could do to me that was going to be worse than what them snakes were going to make me do to myself."

Bob Feller was driving to Chicago for the annual winter meetings of major league baseball executives: "Had nothing else to do, and I was going to go in and see all the guys at the Palmer House. It was Sunday, about twelve noon or early afternoon, and I was crossing the Mississippi River at Moline, driving by myself, and just as I landed on the other side of the bridge I heard the thing on the car radio—'Attack on Pearl Harbor.'" Although Feller possessed a valid II-C (food production) draft deferment—after all, he was a farm boy from Van Meter, Iowa—he decided to enlist at once and "throw a few strikes for Uncle Sam"; upon reaching Chicago, Feller telephoned former heavyweight champion Gene Tunney, who supervised the navy's physical fitness program, and offered his services to the naval reserve.

One of the most depressed men in the nation that day was Bill De-Witt, general manager of baseball's hapless St. Louis Browns. The Browns had long been a professional and financial embarrassment to the rest of the American League; for the past ten years, they had drawn an average of fewer than two thousand paying customers per game. So Browns' owner

Sam Breadon, club president Donald Barnes, and DeWitt had spent the summer persuading the rest of the league owners to permit them to move the club to Los Angeles. Such a move would have been a startling departure from tradition; not only were there no major league teams west of St. Louis, but no franchise in either league had changed cities since 1903. Nevertheless, the Browns' front office had obtained tentative approval for the shift, and had even worked out a feasible schedule to bring visiting clubs out to the West Coast via the Super Chief railway line out of Chicago. Bill DeWitt: "December 7, 1941, screwed up the whole thing. We were in Comiskey Park watching the Bears and the Cardinals play football that day, and it was cold as the devil. Somebody came in and said, 'Gee, they just had a flash on the radio that the Japs have bombed Pearl Harbor.' Me, I didn't know where the hell Pearl Harbor was; I never heard of Pearl Harbor." But since the government now would need to commandeer railway space to move troops and supplies across the country, DeWitt's carefully prepared schedule was shot to hell. Besides, the other club owners had no intention of subjecting their ballplayers to the uncertainties of life on the West Coast. When the winter meetings convened, Red Smith watched bemusedly as "magnates kept slipping out of the conference rooms to listen to radio rumors that Jap bombers were over California. They experienced no prodding urge to send their million-dollar chattels junketing into that region." The Browns stayed put. Los Angeles had enough trouble already.

Cecil Travis was every bit as disappointed as Bill DeWitt. Travis, the Washington Senators' shortstop who had led the American League with 218 hits in 1941, thought that he finally had enough leverage to pry a juicy raise out of penurious owner Calvin Griffith for the 1942 season. In the meantime, he got in his car on December 7 and started driving home to Georgia to do some deer hunting. And then: "They were announcing it. Pearl Harbor. There went my big fat contract, and a lot of other things." Phil Rizzuto heard the news while on a visit to Norfolk, Virginia, where he had played minor league ball. "Then I get a call from my mother," he recalled. She frantically informed him "that Lefty had just called and told her the Japs were right outside Brooklyn and I'd better get right home."

Telephone lines were jammed all over the nation. In several cities, there was a wait of three hours before calls could be put through.

In Chungking, Chiang Kai-shek's Military Council was ecstatic. Han Suyin, whose husband was a member of Chiang's inner circle, reported that the generalissimo himself was so jubilant that he walked around singing one of his favorite opera tunes, "and played the Ave Maria all that day. The Kuomintang government officials went about congratulating each other, as if a great victory had been won. From their standpoint it was a victory, what they had waited for, America at war with Japan. At last, at last, America was at war with Japan! Now China's strategic importance would grow even more. American money and equipment would flow in; half a billion dollars, one billion dollars . . ." Chiang's cronies also derived great satisfaction from the fact that an Asian nation had knocked out "the Great White Fleet"; now, perhaps, Washington would not be quite so critical of China's long-standing inability to defeat Japanese military forces. "How the Chinese now laughed at the Americans!" said Suyin. "For it was a Sunday, the week-end, when the 'fat boys,' as the Americans were nicknamed by the Japanese, had been caught. 'They were too busy drinking and whoring,' cried a very drunk Chinese brigadier, raising his glass to toast the future. Now America would *have* to support Chiang, and that meant U.S. dollars into the pockets of the officials . . ."

After requesting guidance from the State Department in Washington, FBI agents and city detectives rounded up Japanese nationals living in and around New York City and interned them at Ellis Island. The entire New York metropolitan district was placed on a war footing.

"This is suicide for Japan," wrote Raymond Clapper in a cold fury. "A desperate, fourth-rate nation, the spoiled little gangster of the Orient will have to be exterminated as a power. Japan has asked for it and now she will get it."

Germany was caught completely by surprise. Foreign Minister Joachim von Ribbentrop heard the news first, from an official of the Foreign Office press department; initially, Ribbentrop thought it was a propaganda trick and refused to believe it: "We had considered the possibility of Japan's attacking Singapore or perhaps Hong Kong, but we never considered an attack on the United States as being to our advantage." Still, by the time he telephoned Count Ciano in Rome, Ribbentrop apparently had decided he liked the idea. "He is so happy, in fact, that I can't help but congratulate him," noted Ciano in his diary, "even though I am not so sure about the advantage. One thing is now certain: America will enter the conflict, and the conflict itself will be long enough to permit her to put into action all her potential strength. This is what I said to the King [Victor Emmanuel III] this morning, when he, too, expressed his satisfaction. He ended by admitting that in 'the long run' I might be right. Mussolini was happy. For a long time now he has been in favor of clarifying the position between America and the Axis." Admiral Dönitz decided that the news of America's entry into the war should be welcomed with "a roll of drums." Now, at last, his U-boats would be free to strike at any target in the Atlantic.

Hitler received news of Pearl Harbor while he was at the Wolfsschanze. The past few days had brought nothing but reports of devastating German defeats on the eastern front. Thus when a messenger read him a telegram describing the Japanese attack, the Fuehrer's face brightened; he grabbed the message and walked over to the bunker that served as the generals' headquarters and thrust the slip of paper at Keitel. "We cannot lose the war!" he shouted exultantly. "Now we have a partner who has not been defeated in three thousand years." Someone pointed out that New York was closer to Berlin than Hawaii was to Tokyo.

In Washington, by four-thirty, cars of curious passersby jammed Massachusetts Avenue around the Japanese Embassy. Several hours before, someone had seen Japanese officials burning documents in the front yard. Now one young policeman stood guard outside the locked embassy gates; within the white stucco building, the shades were pulled down. The crowd in the street seemed to be more dazed than angry.

At 6:50 P.M. Stephen Early, red-faced and sweating profusely under the movie lights, held a press conference and announced that the Japanese had attacked Guam, too. He warned reporters that any relay of news to Japanese sources could endanger the national security. Cordell Hull issued a public statement bitterly denouncing Japan for its "treacherous and utterly unprovoked attack" upon the United States. The national headquarters of America First instructed its chapters to postpone all rallies and released its own statement: "The America First Committee urges all those who have subscribed to its principles to give their support to the war effort of this country until the conflict with Japan is brought to a successful conclusion. In this war the America First Committee pledges its aid to the President as commander in chief of the armed forces of the United States."

Panic struck the West Coast. At Los Angeles, the American city with the largest Japanese population (estimates put the number at about fifty thousand), FBI agents and soldiers from Fort MacArthur took "key" Japanese citizens into custody and interned them in a wire enclosure at the Sixth Street pier. Sheriff Eugene Biscaliuz mobilized the ten-thousand-man Civilian Defense Committee. To the north, San Francisco officials ordered the Golden Gate Bridge blacked out that evening. Someone neglected to turn off the lights at the San Francisco–Oakland Bay Bridge, however. (One woman was shot and critically wounded by an overzealous civilian sentry when she refused his command to halt and dim her headlights at the approach to the Bay Bridge.) Naval authorities at San Diego stationed guards to prevent any Japanese from fleeing into Mexico. Antiaircraft batteries were set up at vital communications and power stations up and down the California coast. Military intelligence hysterically reported the presence of several Japanese planes over San Francisco Bay, but these turned out to be United States Army planes; someone mistook the red circle at the center of the army air insignia for the distinctive rising sun of Japan.

Lucille Ball had been visiting Desi in New York. When she heard the radio bulletins, she apparently decided that California was in imminent danger of invasion, and so both she and her husband rushed back to the coast to be with their families. The news reached the West Coast late in the morning, in time for special editions of the Sunday newspapers. Milton Berle was spending a rather turbulent honeymoon at Lake Arrowhead with his wife, his mother, and his brother. "It wasn't much of a honeymoon," Berle admitted, "but I can't take all the blame. The day after we got to Arrowhead, Joyce and I were sitting around the lawn with Jimmy and Ruthie Ritz, just soaking up the sun and talking. The portable radio I had brought along was on the grass beside me. Suddenly, the music stopped and we got the announcement of the Japanese attack on Pearl Harbor. The next day, I had to leave to get back to the studio. There was a rush on to finish pictures in production. No one knew what the war was going to do to Hollywood, what materials would be available, who would still be in civilian clothes." Milton left his new bride with his mother and sister-in-law at Lake Arrowhead.

From his post at the State Department, Assistant Secretary of State Adolf Berle (presumably no relation) noted that "the political sentiment is swinging behind the President at once. It is just as well: all hands have their work cut out for them. Everyone thinks this is going to be a short picnic. It is not going to be anything of the kind. It is going to be a long, dirty, painful, bloody business."

By the time Japanese warplanes first appeared over Pearl Harbor, it was already the morning of December 8 in Tokyo. Several hours after the attack, Japanese Imperial Headquarters proclaimed that the nation had entered a state of war with the United States and the British Empire. After the people recovered from their initial surprise, they responded with an enthusiastic outburst of patriotic fervor for this sacred conflict to fulfill the two-thousand-year-old dream of eternal peace in Asia; on a more visceral level, many Japanese shared the feelings of novelist Dazai Osamu, who declared that he was "itching to beat the bestial, insensitive Americans to a pulp." In Tokyo, crowds gathered in the streets to sing the national anthem, "Kimigayo," and to chant, "Boku no Tojo" ("Our Tojo"). Newsboys scampered through the city ringing handbells and sounding wooden clappers to announce a flimsy special victory edition just off the presses. Radio stations played patriotic marches, and thousands of Japanese betook themselves to the sacred grounds of the Imperial Palace to pay homage to their divine ancestors and invoke their aid in the coming struggle. After visiting the national shrines in the capital to inform the spirit of his late father that the war had begun with an overwhelming victory, General Tojo spoke to his people over the radio: "I promise you final victory."

A group of two hundred excited Japanese, waving a huge swastika flag, headed for the American Embassy, where the staff had spent the morning burning important documents and copies of the embassy's codes in metal barrels. The police, who kept the crowd away, did not interfere with the work of destruction, but they did seize all radios that might be used to signal enemy aircraft. "While I was burning papers, a relatively minor official of the Foreign Office arrived to read the declaration of war," recalled Charles Bohlen.

> I was asked to help make sure that all personnel of the Embassy were safely moved into the Embassy compound. We were permitted to go to our homes with a Japanese escort and pick up some personal belongings. . . .
>
> We were so busy during the first hours after the news that war had broken out that the full significance of what had happened did not register with most of us. It was not until the Ambassador invited us to his Residence for a drink and we began talking that the full impact of the event stuck us. Only then did I perceive, and only dimly, the long, uphill fight that the United States faced—the sacrifices at home, the uprooting of lives, the casualty lists like those Britain and the Soviet Union had already compiled.
>
> Grew was deeply depressed, feeling that his ten-year mission in Japan had failed. . . .

Before the radios were taken away, Grew heard an American senator say the nation would "lick hell out of the Japanese." "This may be easier said than done," Grew acknowledged; "it may take a very long time and we may get some serious knocks before our full power is able to register. But in the long run, Japan's defeat is absolutely certain, for the American people, once aroused, won't let go. With the United States, Britain, Australia, the Netherlands East Indies, and perhaps Soviet Russia, as well as China, eventually out against her, she will have her hands full before very long."

Although darkness had fallen hours ago, dozens of dazed people were still milling aimlessly about in front of the White House; reporters noted that the crowd still did not seem to realize fully what had happened. It was a cool, crisp, clear night in Washington, the misty half moon shining eerily through the branches of the bare trees. Roosevelt met with his cabinet at 8:30 P.M. and with congressional leaders at 9:45. At 11:20 the dwindling crowd outside suddenly began to sing "God Bless America" as a policeman strolled back and forth in front of the iron railings.

28

Darken the Lights

"Americans can be proud today. We can be proud that we tried
to the bitter end to avoid war."

—RAYMOND CLAPPER

"That day as I left the White House I realized that an armament
program leads irresistibly to war. . . . Preparedness, I realized
that December day in 1941, no more stops war than the death
penalty stops murderers. Man is basically predatory, and
preparedness excites the base instincts that propel man to
killing."

—SUPREME COURT JUSTICE WILLIAM O. DOUGLAS

Now all the doubts had vanished. Early on the morning of December 8,
workmen began pounding steel stakes into the ground while others strung
a heavy wire cable around the House wing of the Capitol to keep the
anticipated crowds at a safe distance. At the gaps in the wire they hung
signs that read SHOW YOUR PASSES. Within the next few hours, a small
army of city policemen and Marines with fixed bayonets took up their
positions around the White House and the Capitol. All the approaches to
those two buildings were blocked. An armored truck stood on M Street in
Georgetown, with its machine gun aimed to sweep the traffic on the Key
Bridge. Another machine gun was strategically planted in the boxwood of
the Lincoln Memorial, overlooking Arlington Bridge and Rock Creek
Boulevard. Elsewhere in the city, the streets of Washington were filled
with people trying to do everything all at once; not since Inauguration
Day in January had there been such a crush of automobiles and pedestrians. At eleven-thirty, two Secret Service cars outfitted with riot guns along
each side pulled up under the White House portico.

Thirty minutes later, precisely at noon, six limousines arrived, the
White House glass doors opened, and President Roosevelt emerged, bun-
dled in a cape and leaning for support on the arm of his son James. Silently
Roosevelt entered the car and it sped off through the East Gate and down
Pennsylvania Avenue.

Marine and army guards with automatic weapons guarded every entrance to the Capitol. Congressmen's identification passes and journalists'

press credentials were checked two or three times along the route to the House chamber. (Apparently believing he was Japanese, the guards refused to allow Chinese Ambassador Hu Shih to pass until Senator Connally interceded on his behalf.) When the President arrived at the Capitol, he went in through the Speaker's entrance immediately, without acknowledging the encouraging applause of the solemn crowd outside the wire rope.

There were a few diplomats and a scattering of soldiers waiting patiently in the House gallery amid the movie spotlights and the cameramen. After the members of the House took their seats, the senators marched in behind Majority Leader Alben Barkley and Minority Leader Charles McNary. (Harry Truman had made it back to Washington just in time for this historic occasion.) Then the nine Supreme Court justices entered in their black robes and sat along the edge of the well. At 12:23 the members of the cabinet arrived and sat on the other side, facing the justices. Speaker Sam Rayburn banged the gavel and announced, "The President of the United States!"

A moment of silence. Then the entire chamber rose to its feet and applauded, the sound growing louder and louder until Rayburn rapped his gavel. Then Roosevelt appeared. Another minute of applause, which finally burst into cheers. The chaplain prayed for the nation.

Under the hot glare of the lights from the gallery, Roosevelt began his speech and the barely suppressed anger was evident to everyone in the chamber: "Mr. Vice President, Mr. Speaker, members of the Senate and the House of Representatives:

"Yesterday, December 7, 1941—a date which will live in infamy—the United States of America was suddenly and deliberately attacked by naval and air forces of the empire of Japan.

"The United States was at peace with that nation, and, at the solicitation of Japan, was still in conversation with its government and its Emperor looking toward the maintenance of peace in the Pacific. . . ."

Now the President continued in a calmer, more dispassionate tone. He was speaking so slowly, Margaret Truman thought, that one might have transcribed the entire speech by hand.

"It will be recorded that the distance of Hawaii from Japan makes it obvious that the attack was deliberately planned many days or even weeks ago. During the intervening time the Japanese Government has deliberately sought to deceive the United States by false statements and expressions of hope for continued peace.

"The attack yesterday upon the Hawaiian Islands has caused severe damage to American naval and military forces. I regret to tell you that very many American lives have been lost . . ."

When Roosevelt vowed that the United States "will remember the character of the onslaught against us," the audience stood and cheered and applauded.

"Hostilities exist. There is no blinking the fact that our people, our territory and our interests are in grave danger. The people of the United States have already formed their opinions and well understand the implications to the very life and safety of our nation. . . . No matter how long it may take us to overcome this premeditated invasion, the American people in their righteous might will win through to absolute victory." Again the audience burst into applause.

Six minutes and thirty seconds after he began (Wilson's request for a declaration of war in 1917 had taken 29 minutes and 34 seconds), Franklin Roosevelt looked up and said, "I ask that the Congress declare that since the unprovoked and dastardly attack by Japan on Sunday, December 7, a state of war has existed between the United States and the Japanese Empire." He did not mention Germany or Italy at all during the speech.

The people gave the President a final standing ovation, and for the only time that afternoon, Roosevelt acknowledged the applause with a wave and a smile. The senators adjourned to their chamber and Roosevelt went back to the White House for an hour's nap. Thirty-three minutes later (a new United States record), both chambers had approved a declaration of war. In the Senate, the vote was 82 to 0; in the House, Jeannette Rankin of Montana voted "No," just as she had done in 1917 (this time, she was greeted with boos and hisses), and so the final vote was 388 to 1.

At 4:10, in the presence of cabinet and congressional leaders in the Executive Office, Roosevelt signed the resolution.

At last America was at war. Ernest Hemingway, for one, was not optimistic about the prospects for the immediate future. "Through our (American) laziness, criminal carelessness, and blind arrogance we are fucked in this war as of the first day and we are going to have ———'s own bitter time to win it if, when, and ever. . . . No matter how many countries you see fucked and bitched and ruined you never get to take it easily. Having to watch all the steps and know them all so well."

That night, the lamps on the White House grounds were extinguished. For every evening during the next three and a half years, the White House lay shrouded in the darkness of war.

Part Seven   The Winter

———————————————————————

29

Toward the Precipice

"We have got where we are through our own weakness and not
through the strength of our enemies. And that weakness runs
very deep, I am afraid . . . In fact, it is a dangerous
disease which has all but destroyed western civilization,
which probably has become incurable except by terrible suffering
and mortal danger."

—WALTER LIPPMANN

On the eastern front, Zhukov's savage counteroffensive slammed into
the exhausted, half-frozen German troops. Blizzards raged day and night;
by the end of the first week of December the snow in the forests west of
Moscow was piled waist-high. On December 8, the Fuehrer publicly admitted that winter would prevent his armies from capturing Moscow
before the end of the year. "The cold is so terrific that even the oil freezes
in motorized vehicles," declared a Nazi military spokesman. "Soldiers and
officers trying to take cover simply freeze to the ground. Fighting under
these conditions is practically impossible." Still, the Fuehrer ordered his
generals to hold the front for the duration of the winter, so the German
army would be able to resume the advance upon Moscow in the spring of
1942. He vetoed all proposals to withdraw, and insisted that the Wehrmacht dig in and defend its positions regardless of the consequences.

It could not. In some parts of the central sector, the Germans were
pushed back over a hundred miles in three weeks. Soviet authorities
permitted Associated Press correspondent Henry Cassidy to view the
highway west of Moscow after the German retreat. Crumbled ruins lay
upon the ground where villages once had stood; hundreds of vehicles lay
in macabre, twisted shapes along the side of the road:

> From that point the road wound like a narrow tunnel through frosted
> pine forests, littered by all that remained of the once-proud German sixth and
> seventh tank divisions. For twenty-five miles stretched this graveyard of the
> panzers, marked by masses of charred vehicles, piles of frozen bodies, and a
> jumble of personal effects. I counted up to one thousand wrecked tanks,
> armored cars, troop-carrying machines, trucks, automobiles, and motorcycles,
> and then grew tired of counting. Hundreds of bodies of the troops who had

once manned those machines could be seen sprawled grotesquely in the snow. Hundreds more lay buried beneath the drifts or beneath white birch crosses. . . . Here, the bodies, in small groups of twelve to fifty, frozen in strange positions, many with arms bent still uplifted as though to ward off the inevitable, seemed more like wax statues than men. The snow and ice clothed their deaths in a merciful cleanliness.

In a desperate attempt to preserve at least some part of his shattered panzer force, Guderian retreated without authorization from Hitler, and for that he was relieved of his command. The Red Army recaptured Rostov in the southern sector. Rundstedt was replaced for impudently refusing to obey a direct order from the Fuehrer to advance. Bock said his health was failing and he, too, resigned under pressure. Bolstered by fresh reinforcements from Siberia, the Red Army launched a second counter-attack; in all sectors, German forces came under heavy pressure. On December 19, after a lengthy argument over the Fuehrer's order to "stand fast" along the eastern front, Hitler removed Brauchitsch from his post and assumed the duties of commander in chief of the German army himself. Halder feared that he, too, would soon be sacked. (And he was.) By the end of the year, Germany had suffered over one million casualties from Operation Barbarossa; in the Red Army, combat deaths approached three million.

And now, much against the advice of his diplomatic advisers, the Fuehrer accepted the challenge of another foe on a different front. Perhaps he thought the occasion might rekindle the German nation's flagging enthusiasm for battle. On December 11, Hitler stood before the Reichstag and declared war on the United States. America already was shooting at German ships, he reasoned, and Berlin's promise of aid to Japan implicit in the Tripartite Pact must be honored. Perhaps the Fuehrer and his Axis allies could forever enshrine the year 1941 in the annals of world history as the glorious year in which National Socialism launched a victorious crusade against the strongholds of both international communism (the Soviet Union) and Jewish capitalism (the United States). He told the Reichstag that Roosevelt, inspired by his "millionaire and Jewish backers," was treading the same path of madness and self-delusion that Woodrow Wilson had chosen more than twenty years earlier: "First he incites war, then falsifies the causes, then odiously wraps himself in a cloak of Christian hypocrisy and slowly but surely leads mankind to war, not without calling God to witness the honesty of his attack." When Hitler announced that he was expelling the American diplomatic mission from Berlin, the audience broke into a roar of approval that blotted out the rest of his speech.

The Fuehrer also employed this occasion once again to warn any potential enemies within Germany that he would brook no opposition. Calling upon his listeners to uphold the German tradition of obedience and duty to the fatherland, he said, "Whoever intends to escape this duty has no claim to being held a National Comrade with the rest of us. Just as we were mercilessly hard in the struggle for national power, we will again be merciless and hard in this struggle for the preservation of our people. At a time when thousands of our best men, the fathers and sons of our people, are falling, no individual at home who blasphemes the sacrifice of the front, can reckon with remaining alive. No matter what camouflage covers any attempt to disturb this German front, to undermine our people's will to resist, to weaken the authority of the government or sabotage the efforts of the home front—the guilty one will fall."

For the enforcement of this threat, he relied upon loyal Party men such as Martin Bormann; they were also permitted to handle most of the Reich's internal affairs, including the persistent and vexing Jewish problem. Hitler had more important matters on his mind. He had convinced himself that he could end the war quickly if he could isolate himself and conduct it without distractions. For the next three years, Hitler seldom emerged from the dark mists that surrounded the Wolfsschanze. He gathered around him a select few whom he knew to be faithful and who shielded him from the outside world. He lived an almost monastic life in the refuge that General Jodl once described as a "cross between a cloister and a concentration camp." Rising around noon, permitting himself only the enjoyment of a fifteen-minute walk with his pet wolfhound along the paths that ran through the nearby pine forest, surrounded by an electrified barbed-wire fence and minefields, working late into the night and sometimes until dawn, the Fuehrer lost virtually all contact with the outside world except for the messages his subordinates brought him. From this time on the lonely man in the Wolf's Lair threw aside pretenses and ruled the Third Reich by personal whim, as an absolute dictator. Slowly his few ties to reality deserted him.

Japan swept through South Asia and made it all look easy. In the December days after Pearl Harbor, Japanese troops landed in Malaya and the Philippines (where more than half of MacArthur's air force was destroyed on the ground), attacked Hong Kong (the colony fell on Christmas Day), swept the Americans off Guam and Wake Island, forced Thailand to capitulate, knocked the British—who had declared war on Japan on December 8—out of Kowloon, bombed Singapore, and, most disastrous for Britain, caught and sank off the Malayan coast on December 10 the fabled battleship *Prince of Wales* (which Churchill had boasted could "catch and kill anything") and the battle cruiser *Repulse,* the only two Allied capital ships in the whole western Pacific. The British ships had been trapped without any friendly air cover at all. "It comes back to Poland, Norway, France, Greece, and Crete," lamented the *Daily Mail.* "Five devastating lessons and still we failed to profit." "For sheer mass misery," reported

Mollie Panter-Downes, "this was probably England's blackest day since the collapse of France. . . . It was as if some enormously powerful and valuable watchdog which had been going to keep burglars away from the house had been shot while exercising in the front yard." Observing the reaction in the House of Commons after Churchill announced the disastrous blow, Chips Channon noted that "a wave of gloom spread everywhere. The House was restive, the Government suddenly unpopular. . . . I could have cried. . . . Thousands of lives lost—it is terrible." Someone asked General Brooke what the loss of the *Prince of Wales* and *Repulse* meant to the British Empire. "It means," he answered, "that from Africa eastwards to America, through the Indian Ocean and Pacific we have lost command of the sea." Two days later, Churchill and his military advisers departed on a ten-day journey across the Atlantic for a series of high-level strategy meetings in Canada and Washington.

"I have a feeling that our nerves are not as good as they were in July 1940," Harold Nicolson observed. "We still face the central issue with courage and faith, but in minor matters we are getting touchy and irritable."

Guerrilla war raged across Nazi-occupied Europe. Fires and explosions wracked munitions plants and oil refineries in Czechoslovakia. Protector Heydrich responded by ordering the execution of 162 civilians, including the mayor of Prague and members of the city council. Polish freedom fighters cut Nazi communications lines to the Russian front and blew up the main railway bridges to the east. The Germans executed another 150 Polish hostages. At the Hague, a special Nazi tribunal was set up to hand out death sentences to Dutch patriots convicted of sabotage. (In a lighter vein, German authorities in Holland warned that "unless there is an end to this practice of publishing dog photos on the front newspages when Der Fuehrer is meeting Mussolini . . . severe measures will be taken against those responsible.")

Tito's Communist partisans waged the most vicious war of resistance. In Belgrade, it began with youths knocking over and burning newsstands that sold collaborationist journals; then it rapidly escalated. Telephone lines were cut, and incendiary devices placed in the gas tanks of German military vehicles. Aided by former Yugoslavian political police, German occupation troops staged mass arrests, imposed a 6 P.M. curfew, and opened fire with machine guns on suspected gangs of Communists in the streets of the city. The pro-Nazi puppet government offered rewards of 2,500 dinars ($75) for every Communist killed or captured. The Communists retaliated by ambushing Yugoslav policemen. The Gestapo hanged partisans in Belgrade's main square and left the swinging bodies to rot. At Zagreb, fifty "Communists and Jews" were executed for allegedly instigating a bombing attack upon the city's telephone exchange.

But most of the fighting took place in the countryside. Stuka dive-bombers and German artillery guns pounded villages suspected of sheltering partisans. Hundreds were slain on both sides during a three-day battle at Doboj. The Germans executed one hundred hostages for every German soldier killed; an entire town of seven thousand inhabitants was wiped out. Serbian nationalists executed six hundred German prisoners in retaliation. In November, Germany was forced to send in a full panzer division—twelve thousand men—to quell the disorder. But Tito reportedly had eighty thousand men under his command in the countryside, and the butchery did not stop.

Europe, December 1941: The Vatican issued a report stating that more than 40,000 Poles had been executed by Germany, and 60,000 taken away to concentration camps, and another 1,180,000 compelled to do forced labor for the Nazis. "In exposing all these facts," the report concluded, "we have tried to be moderate. We need only recall the words of Cardinal Mercier of Belgium in 1914: 'When we speak of German warfare we try to attenuate the impression, for we feel that the naked truth exceeds the limits of what can be believed.'"

Europe, December 1941: In Athens, the cafés were deserted; Greeks were forbidden to enter them. A Greek flag remained atop the Acropolis only because the Germans and Italians could not agree on which of their flags should take precedence. A former Greek army officer smuggled a letter to a friend in Britain: "You would not recognize Athens these days. It has become a city of mourning. People are starving. It is nothing extraordinary to see a man faint in the street from hunger. Everywhere you see our soldiers, back from the war in Albania. Many of them have lost their legs. Amputated because of frostbite. They live by selling cigarettes—if you can call it living. Most of them beg for a livelihood."

Europe, December 1941: Former President Eduard Beneš broadcast a Christmas message of hope to the people of Czechoslovakia over the BBC shortwave network: "You on the home front have suffered one bad blow during the past year. Your resistance against the German invaders brought them to a state of pathological hatred. They sent their hangman Heydrich to Prague to help the Karl Herman Franks, Henleins, Pfitzners who will get what they deserve from the Allies at the end of the war. Hitler has raged against you for the last few months with his Gestapo ogres, with concentration camps, with terrorism and executions. These symbols of German culture in the twentieth century, however, have not broken your faith in victory for freedom and right."

Europe, December 1941: On Christmas Eve, the Jews of the Warsaw ghetto were ordered to surrender all their furs and boots. They did so, handing over enough to fill six large boxcars. One hundred and twenty thousand more Jews were deported. In October 1941, there had been 4,716 funerals in the ghetto (compared to 457 in October 1940); in November 1941, there were 4,801 more funerals in the ghetto; in the past two months, more than 5,500 new cases of typhus had been reported. Complete statistics for deaths and disease in December were still being compiled.

Europe, December 1941: "All Europe is an interminable bread line," reported American correspondent Curt Reiss. "Women stand in line for hours. . . . They wait in the freezing cold, they stay in line, knowing that they will get little today, that they will get less tomorrow, that they will get less and less as time goes on.

"The women of Paris wait in a long queue. They need milk for their children. Their children are pale, almost transparent; at night they cannot sleep for hunger. The women of Paris are clamoring for milk. . . .

"The women of Brussels and Liège, of Warsaw and Helsinki, of Belgrade and Rome—it is the same everywhere. When they wake up in the morning their first thought is: will they get something to eat for their children, for their men, or will they have to stand in line again for hours, in vain. The faces of European women have become mournful and emaciated. They look careworn and bewildered. The women are close to despair."

On December 12, the Gestapo began its first full-scale roundup of Jews in France. Over a thousand people were arrested, including Colette's husband. Gen. von Stulpnagel announced that a billion-franc fine would be levied on the citizens of occupied France to pay for their recent acts of sabotage; "Judeo-Bolshevists" would be deported and set to hard labor; and one hundred more hostages would be shot. One evening Colette heard the sounds in the streets outside, "when the thorough and bureaucratic enemy systematically rounded up all the neighborhood Jewish children, their mothers, separating Jewish husbands from their wives and locking them away in vans, women and children in other vans. . . ." Four days later, a bomb exploded at Gestapo headquarters at Ville Juif ("Jew Villa," an ironic location for such tenants), killing six Nazis.

"I love nothing the war years brought," Colette mourned. "Dry-eyed, I longed like everybody else to return to the days before the war, days we had all thought so dull before we found out what kind of days were to follow. Among other worldly things, I longed for freedom to enjoy my sorrow! Oh, what crying jags I will indulge in when things are all right again! That's what one says."

At Picasso's studio in the rue des Grands-Augustins, where he had to work in the bathroom because it was the only part of the studio that had any heat, the artist fashioned one of his greatest and most disturbing masterpieces of sculpture: a foot-high, dark bronze *Tête de mort*— "Death's head"—a skull hovering between life and the dark decay of death, a face with taut skin and empty eyes that haunted those who were still alive to see it at the end of 1941.

At the end of November, Dr. Vannevar Bush had sent the final report of the Compton committee to the White House. Compton recommended a full American effort toward the development of atomic weapons employing U-235. "A fission bomb of superlatively destructive power will result from bringing quickly together a sufficient mass of element U-235," the report concluded. "The possibility must be seriously considered that within a few years the use of bombs such as described above, or something similar using uranium fission, may determine military superiority." By this time Bush had also received a report from Britain's MAUD committee that concluded that there appeared to be a reasonable chance that an atomic bomb with the estimated destructive power of 1,800 tons of TNT could be produced before the end of the war. Roosevelt appointed a blue-ribbon panel consisting of himself, Bush, Stimson, General Marshall, Arthur Conant, and Vice President Henry Wallace to study the matter.

On December 6, Bush received his answer: a new committee, known as S-1, was to be appointed to cooperate with British scientists and "do everything possible to find out whether atomic bombs could be made and to report back our findings within six months. If at that time the report was favorable, we should expect authorization to proceed with all the resources that the nation could make available." For the immediate future, Roosevelt supplied S-1 with several million dollars from a White House discretionary fund.

Following the outbreak of war the next day, the atomic weapons research effort shifted into high gear. The American military establishment was convinced that Germany and Japan would inevitably be defeated *unless* the Axis succeeded in developing some totally new sort of weapon. To ensure that the United States obtained atomic weapons first, the Army Corps of Engineers was ordered to assist in the construction of a plant for the conversion of uranium into plutonium. In the meantime, Enrico Fermi, the Italian-born Nobel Prize–winning physicist who had exchanged the uncertainties of life in Fascist Rome for a research position at Columbia University, was granted additional funds to continue his work on the construction of an atomic pile employing uranium oxide and graphite, for the purpose of creating a nuclear chain reaction. Although Fermi (aided by the Columbia U. football team, who physically arranged the sixty-pound canisters of uranium according to the physicist's instructions) had succeeded in building a primitive, experimental structure in New York City, Compton decided that the first stages of the nuclear weapons research effort would thereafter more properly be concentrated at the University of Chicago, at a secret location code-named the Metallurgical Laboratory, or, simply, "the Med." Herein lay the origins of the project which later became known as the Manhattan District.

One man who would not be involved in the Manhattan project was the most brilliant and famous scientist in the world, Albert Einstein. Although Einstein had informed Bush through a mutual acquaintance that he would welcome the opportunity to contribute to the nuclear fission research effort, the exceedingly suspicious Bush decided (apparently on his own initiative) that Einstein, an uncompromising opponent of Nazism who had been granted American citizenship earlier in 1941, was too great a security risk. "I am not at all sure," Bush informed Einstein's associate on December 30, "that if I place Einstein in entire contact with this subject he would not discuss it in a way that it should not be discussed, and with this doubt in my mind I do not feel that I ought to take him into confidence on the subject to the extent of showing just where this thing fits into the defense picture, and what the military aspects of the matter might be." Bush apparently was unaware of the fact that two years earlier Einstein had urged President Roosevelt to establish an American research effort into the feasibility of atomic weapons.

"We shall begin to win the war when we give up our pose of injured innocence, confess frankly that we spent the last five years playing a shrewd and, in many respects, a naughty game, and beat our heads to the earth as a mark of repentance and reform," chided Washington newspaper columnist Samuel Grafton that bleak December. "Our cry that we were merely picking daisies and humming a wordless tune when the Axis clipped us is, in itself, a sign of bad conscience. The moment we were socked, we burst out crying, donned a set of false honey-colored curls, and began to sweat out the legend that we were a child victim of atrocity."

And so America went to war, unwillingly perhaps, certainly with more than a little anxiety, and for the most part unaware of the tremendous sacrifices that inevitably would be involved before it was all over. *The New Yorker* voiced a strong (and remarkably naive) sense of relief now that the nation finally had entered the conflict: "We were safe enough up to that disastrous Sunday afternoon, but it was an unsatisfactory kind of safety, humiliating to some, foolish to others, clearly temporary to all but a few. . . . We're sure that a lot of very unpleasant things still lie ahead of us, but we doubt if anything can be much more unpleasant than the uncertainty, frustration, and bitterness that lay between Munich and Manila."

So for a while, much of the nation acted as if it did not fully comprehend the dangers that lay directly ahead. Wall Street greeted the coming of war enthusiastically with a series of million-share days. Auto manufacturers pleaded for time to produce just a few more passenger cars and add to their record-breaking profits; astonishingly, the federal government agreed to give them several additional weeks before imposing a ban on civilian production. In a fireside chat to the American people, Roosevelt declared that every factory that was producing defense material would be placed on a seven-day-week schedule; but the President's plan could not be implemented immediately because the government still had not yet decided how to allocate scarce raw materials among competing demands for the production of antiaircraft guns, tanks, and heavy bombers. Recruiting offices across the nation reported a huge jump in enlistments in the first days after Pearl Harbor, but the army could take in only a limited number of men because it still lacked sufficient training facilities and equipment. Soldiers who had just been discharged were called back and elevated to the rank of second lieutenant to train the new recruits; poor Hank Greenberg, who had been released on December 5 due to a regulation that allowed men over twenty-eight years of age to be discharged after six months' service, decided he might as well reenlist anyway. Charles Lindbergh offered his services to the military, but the administration turned him down; eighty-one-year-old General Pershing offered *his* services, and Roosevelt gratefully accepted.

Meanwhile, American soldiers were dying in the Pacific. As Congress belatedly pushed through a $10 billion authorization for armaments, Ray Clapper reported that the four hundred American Marines stationed on Wake Island were courageously resisting a furious Japanese assault with the aid of only four—*four*—warplanes; in the Philippines, American soldiers were defending bridges with nothing more than hand grenades and rifles. "Read it and weep. . . . It won't be our men out there that lose the Philippines," the columnist warned. "If the islands are lost they will have been lost here, by our lagging war production. For 18 months recordbreaking automobile production has been using up precious chrome. Now chrome mines in the Philippines have been evacuated in the face of the Japanese advance. . . . There is only one point in bringing this up. It is to emphasize that the confusion, divided authority, and hesitant state of mind that caused these failures still exist." British Chief of Staff Sir John Dill, who liked and admired his American counterparts, made a firsthand inspection of U.S. military capabilities when he arrived in Washington in December and promptly warned London that the Americans lacked even "the slightest conception of what the war means, and their armed forces are more unready for war than it is possible to imagine."

"Too many Americans continue to underestimate the danger involved in the attack of the Axis Powers," Raymond Moley observed in the first days after Pearl Harbor. "Infinitely greater dangers lay ahead—dangers the majority of us do not seem to comprehend at all. . . . For there will be losses. There will be setbacks."

Indeed, December 1941 was a month of almost unbroken catastrophe for American military forces in the Far East. Shortly after noon on December 8, approximately nine hours after the attack upon Pearl Harbor, a fleet of nearly two hundred Japanese warplanes launched a devastating raid upon the American military airfields that stretched across the Philippines.

Japanese air force commanders had embarked upon this mission with considerable apprehension, assuming that the Americans would have taken extensive defensive precautions to protect or evacuate the rest of their forces in the Far East following the debacle at Hawaii. But in one of the most bizarre incidents of his tempestuous career, General Douglas MacArthur neglected to take the most elementary precautions to ensure the safety of his planes even after he learned of the surprise attack against Pearl, and despite intelligence reports that indicated that another Japanese strike force was headed in his direction (which should have come as no surprise; after all, the Philippines were precisely the target that the American military command had long expected the Japanese to attack). Searching for a clue to MacArthur's irrational and almost inexplicable behavior, historian William Manchester has concluded that the general suffered a sort of "input overload" immediately after learning of the outbreak of hostilities; faced with conflicting demands on his inadequate resources in the midst of a rapidly changing situation, MacArthur simply froze, withdrew into a shell, and allowed events to overtake him. Whatever the explanation, when the Japanese bombers reached Clark Field (the main American airbase on the islands) on the afternoon of the eighth, they found tidy rows of B-17s and P-40s grouped together, wing to wing on the ground. One hour later, the airfield and virtually every plane that had been stationed there had been utterly demolished. MacArthur had lost more than half of his total air strength in the Philippines. The American military presence on the islands had suffered a crippling blow. "It's all clear to me now except one thing," said General George Marshall two weeks later. "I just don't know how MacArthur happened to let his planes get caught on the ground." Claire Chennault was less charitable in his judgment of MacArthur. Several years later, Chennault swore that "if I had been caught with my planes on the ground, I could never again have looked my fellow officers squarely in the eye."

The effects of the tragedy at Clark Field became all too obvious when another attack force of fifty-four Japanese warplanes—enjoying unchallenged supremacy in the air—arrived over Luzon at noon on Wednesday, December 10, their silver wings glistening in the brilliant sunlight. When they finally departed, the U.S. naval base at Cavite Bay just outside the capital lay in smoldering ruins. In less than seventy-two hours, Japan had succeeded in destroying the two main sources of American military strength in the Philippines. The way lay open for its long-planned conquest of the islands.

At two o'clock on the morning of December 22, the Japanese landed the first wave of an imposing invasion force—43,110 men supported by tanks—at Lingayen Gulf on the northwestern coast of Luzon; encountering only an ill-trained native Filipino battalion, the invaders headed south toward Manila. Bereft of air and naval support, MacArthur realized that

he could not successfully defend the city, and on Christmas Eve he ordered a general withdrawal into the Bataan peninsula on the western edge
of the island; the general himself retreated to an island fortress known as
Corregidor in Manila Bay. The Japanese entered Manila virtually unopposed on January 2.

In Washington, General Marshall summoned the deputy chief of the
War Plans Division for the Pacific and Far East, a fledgling brigadier
general named Dwight David Eisenhower, and handed him the unenviable task of formulating plans to save what was left of the American position
in the Philippines. Driven by his personal conviction that the honor of the
American military establishment required the War Department to do
everything in its power to assist MacArthur, Eisenhower tried every possible stratagem he could devise—including jerry-rigged combinations of
tramp steamers from Australia, converted World War One destroyers, and
United Fruit Company banana boats—to get supplies and reinforcements
to Bataan. "Ships! Ships! All we need is ships!" he cried, but at last Eisenhower realized that there were no ships nor planes available for the task.
The navy, jealously guarding what was left of its battered Pacific fleet,
refused to cooperate in anything more than a cursory way, and by mid-
December the top echelons of the War Department had written off the
Philippines as a lost cause; any large-scale relief efforts were deemed "an
entirely unjustifiable diversion of forces" from the more critical Atlantic
theater. "It will be a long time before major reinforcements can go to the
Philippines," Eisenhower acknowledged in despair, "longer than the garrison can hold out with any driblet assistance, if the enemy commits major
forces to their reduction." So Eisenhower was forced to stand by helplessly
while the Japanese slowly strangled the garrison at Bataan. By the time
the 76,000 men on the rugged peninsula finally surrendered in April 1942
and started on the infamous "death march" to the Japanese prison camps
(during which nearly 10,000 men died), MacArthur was long gone from
Corregidor to Australia, though he had, of course, vowed in characteristically melodramatic fashion that "I shall return."

While MacArthur's forces suffered one setback after another during
the difficult days at the close of the year, the United States Navy was
undergoing its own tortured period of recriminations and resignations in
the aftermath of Pearl Harbor. There was a substantial segment of violently unsympathetic American public opinion which agreed in large part
with Ernest Hemingway when the writer suggested gruffly that "Knox
should have been relieved as Secretary of Navy within 24 hrs of the Pearl
Harbor Debacle and those responsible at Oahu for that disaster shot."
Hemingway's scorn notwithstanding, Knox retained his cabinet post for
the time being, and the beleaguered secretary set off for Hawaii on December 9 for a personal fact-finding tour to determine precisely what had
gone wrong. Horrified by what he saw at Pearl, Knox left for the mainland

after only one day on Oahu. In his hastily assembled report, released on December 15 (and given prominent play in the American press, which was in the midst of its own search for scapegoats for the tragedy), Knox concluded to no one's surprise that "the United States services were not on the alert against the surprise air attack on Hawaii." In the face of this official rebuke, Kimmel could hardly retain his post. The following day (December 16), he was relieved as commander of the Pacific Fleet, and Vice Admiral William Pye took over on an interim basis for two weeks pending the arrival of Kimmel's permanent replacement, Rear Admiral Chester W. Nimitz, a calm and confident commander who had been serving as chief of the Bureau of Navigation. Roosevelt then resurrected the post of Commander in Chief, United States Fleet (which he had abolished eleven months earlier), and handed the job to Admiral Ernest J. King. According to Roosevelt's executive order, King would have "supreme command of the operating forces comprising the several fleets of the United States Navy," and would report directly to the President (which meant that he did not necessarily have to work through Knox). At first, King was not at all certain that he wanted the assignment; when he arrived at his new office at the Navy Department in Washington at the end of December, the crusty admiral realized that "nothing was ready. I had to start with nothing."

While Nimitz and King pondered their plans to resurrect U.S. naval power and prestige, the beleaguered garrison of Marines on Wake Island was staging one of the most heroic and doomed defensive actions in American military history. At first glance, Wake hardly appeared to be the sort of real estate for which brave men might reasonably be expected to die. Actually, it was not one island but a V-shaped trio of tiny volcanic islets covered with shrub and hardwood trees, enclosing a shallow lagoon; the entire atoll was only four and a half miles long and one and a half miles wide. When the United States Navy took possession of the uninviting territory in 1899, it was inhabited only by frigate birds and an occasional visiting albatross.

But Wake was one of the coral stepping-stones that lay almost directly athwart the line from Hawaii to Manila (it had served as a way station for Pan American Clippers on their flights to the Orient), and the Japanese were determined to take the island and fortify it to secure their communications and supply lines in the Pacific. First, however, they had to convince the 377 Marines stationed on Wake to surrender.

Upon receiving a radio message informing them of the raid upon Pearl Harbor, the Marine commanders on Wake—Major Paul A. Putnam and Major James P. S. Devereux—sent four of their twelve single-seated Grumman fighter planes into the air on patrol; their plan was to set up a rotation system that would keep one-third of the force aloft at all times. (This was precisely the sort of precautionary measure that MacArthur should have taken—but did not—at Clark Field.) At two minutes before noon that morning (December 8), a fleet of twenty-four Japanese bombers attacked Wake from the south; within minutes, the airdome was wrecked, along with seven of the eight planes which remained on the ground; twenty-five Marines lay dead. The next day the bombers returned at almost exactly the same time of day. This time they dropped their explosives on the island's tiny hospital and one of the encampments, killing six more men. Between them, the garrison's four remaining fighter planes did succeed in bringing down one of the Japanese bombers.

Apparently the Japanese decided that the raids had sufficiently softened up the defenders, because at dawn on the morning of December 11 a twelve-vessel invasion flotilla containing six destroyers, a light cruiser, and several gunboats and supply ships appeared off the southwest coast of Wake Island. Anticipating just such a development, Devereux had camouflaged a formidable array of 3- and 5-inch artillery behind the shrubs along the edge of the island. The enemy cruiser opened fire at 6,000 yards. Devereux ordered his men to hold their fire until the ships got closer. At 5,000 yards the Japanese flagship ran up signals ordering the Americans to surrender. "Tell them to come get us," Devereux replied. At 4,700 yards, he gave the command to open fire; at the same moment, the four Grummans swooped down and struck the cruiser with hundred-pound bombs, setting it afire and sinking it almost immediately. The coastal artillery continued to pour shells into the rest of the invasion fleet; within minutes, two destroyers and a gunboat turned over and sank. Licking their wounds, the Japanese retreated out of range of the American guns.

Six hours later, the enemy launched a second attack, this time with a force of bombers as the ships remained well off the coast. Although the island's antiaircraft guns shot down two Japanese bombers, the Marines lost one of their four Grummans; now they were down to three planes. The Japanese planes struck again on the twelfth, but by this time the Marines had dug themselves into secure ground shelters, leaving virtually nothing above ground for the enemy raiders to destroy. It looked as if the embattled garrison might be able to hold out after all—if they only received supplies and reinforcements. In the course of a radio conversation, an operator at Pearl Harbor cheerfully asked the Marines what they wanted for Christmas. "Send us more Japs," came the laconic reply.

Although some cranky historians have claimed that this memorable phrase was merely gibberish padding that helped obscure a more serious coded message, the slogan immediately captured the imagination of the American public. At least the Marines, the people thought, were upholding the valiant and defiant tradition established by American military men through two hundred years of victorious combat. In Washington, Roosevelt urged his naval commanders to do everything they could to relieve Wake. On December 15 and 16 a three-pronged task force (including all three American carriers currently in the Pacific) actually set sail from Pearl Harbor with orders to stage a rescue operation and possibly take the offensive against the Japanese. It was scheduled to rendezvous at Wake on December 23. In the interim, however, navy officials in Washington began to entertain serious doubts about the wisdom of committing such a substantial portion of American naval strength to a potentially disastrous expedition. "The General Situation," read one influential and pessimistic estimate, "dictates caution—extreme caution." Thrust suddenly and uncomfortably into a position of full accountability as Kimmel's temporary replacement, a hard-pressed Admiral Pye decided that discretion was by far the better part of valor. "The danger to damaged ships at 2000 miles from base must not be underestimated," Pye concluded. "A loss of a large part of our forces would make possible a major [enemy] operation against the Hawaiian Islands. We cannot afford such losses at present." Obligingly, King and Stark both agreed that in the present difficult situation, Wake had become a liability and was "more trouble than it was worth." So Pye ordered the task force to retire and return to Pearl, and the navy contented itself with issuing the following formal statement: "Probably no military force in American history, not even the defenders of the Alamo, ever fought against greater odds, nor with greater effect in view of these odds."

By December 16, after a week of almost continuous fighting, the Marine garrison was down to two operational planes. On that day, a force of forty-one Japanese bombers razed nearly every building that remained on Wake Island, including a storehouse, the blacksmith shop, and a dynamite dump. Still the Marines refused to surrender. "It must have been a heartbreaking fight, those two hellish weeks on Wake," noted one observer. "Officers and men must have cried for a few more planes, just a few, knowing they could hold out until kingdom come if only they had the stuff to fight with." They did not know that the relief force would never arrive.

Early on the morning of December 22, the Japanese launched their final assault on Wake Island with 830 men supported by bombers, fighters, and naval artillery. By this time, Devereux was nearly out of ammunition. Both of the remaining American planes went up; one was forced to make a crash landing; the second pilot never returned. After hours of bitter combat, Devereux finally walked out onto the beach with a torn piece of white cloth stuck to the handle of a mop. After taking possession of the battered and forsaken piece of volcanic rock, the Japanese promptly renamed it Bird Island.

As one stunning defeat in the Pacific followed another, the American public's shock quickly turned to anger. A wave of anti-Japanese fury swept the nation. By the end of December, 2,340 German and Japanese nationals had been taken into custody by the FBI, far more than the total number of foreign nationals interned during 1917–18. Discarding the customary courtesies of peacetime, newspapers began to use the word "Jap" in their headlines, and some editors wondered—only half-jokingly—if they could get away with the phrase "little yellow bellies." Vandals chopped down four Japanese cherry trees along the Tidal Basin near the Jefferson Memorial in Washington; at the base of one of the stumps, someone scrawled, "To hell with the Japanese." The S. S. Kresge company removed all Japanese merchandise from the counters of its five-and-ten stores. In other shops, Christmas decorations made in Japan went begging. The New York Department of Parks began demolishing the Japanese Pavilion still standing from the 1939–40 World's Fair. The sign on the pen housing the Japanese deer in Central Park was changed to "Asiatic Deer." A flood of anti-Japanese tunes emerged from Tin Pan Alley: "We'll Knock the Japs Right into the Laps of the Nazis" (sung by the inimitable Bert Wheeler), "The Sun Will Soon Be Setting on the Land of the Rising Sun," "Goodbye Mama, I'm Off to Yokohama," and one ditty that made an appearance on Eddie Cantor's radio show:

> We did it before—and we can do it again
> And we will do it again.
> We'll take the nip out of Nipponese
> And chase 'em back to their cherry trees.

(Lyrically speaking, the war was not off to a great start.)

If any Axis planes had ventured to attack the United States in those first few weeks, they might have succeeded beyond their wildest dreams. Seldom in American history had the nation suffered through the sort of wholesale ineptitude and confusion that greeted its first chaotic efforts at civil defense. Few American cities on either coast were equipped with adequate air raid sirens. Los Angeles used a makeshift system of police and fire department vehicles combined with radio announcements; San Francisco had on hand only five low-range sirens used to signal drawbridge openings and special events; and New York tried to get by with only the "super whistle" at the Consolidated Edison East River generating plant. In Boston, merchants urged the mayor not to stage practice alarms until after the busy Christmas shopping season.

Air raid drills and practice blackouts produced chaos everywhere. Invariably some radio stations carried the emergency bulletins and others did not; many citizens went on their way wholly unaware that a drill was in progress. *Newsweek*'s correspondent in San Francisco recorded the remarkable scene during that city's first alarm:

> First air raid alarm caught the city unprepared and uninstructed. The only sirens were on the Ferry Building and two small bridges. Outlying residential districts couldn't hear the alarm. Police and Fire Department

vehicles, racing through the streets as auxiliary sirens, increased the confusion. Neon signs, operating on a time-lock device, could not be doused. Many householders who extinguished lights on hearing the alarm saw these brilliant signs, concluded the alarm was false or over, and relighted. So did Alcatraz penitentiary, making this mid-channel island a perfect beacon.

In Los Angeles, one blackout resulted in five times the normal traffic injuries. Someone in Seattle sounded an alarm on December 23 and a self-appointed Paul Revere jumped on a horse and rode through the city shouting, "Blackout! Air raid! The Jap bombers are coming!" To enforce the blackout, a mob of two thousand patriotic people marched through the downtown area smashing lighted neon signs and shop windows and looting their displays. On Christmas Day in Chicago, naval stations were placed on alert when someone allegedly spotted "strange planes" over Lake Michigan, but no one informed the army, the police, or civil defense officials. During a daylight air raid alarm in New York City, school administrators sent one million children home despite recommendations from the U.S. Office of Civilian Defense that students remain in their school buildings until the raid ended; instead, the children passed the time playing in the streets, shouting "Air raid! "Air raid!" When the city tried again the following day, many principals failed to hear the sirens; those who did sent their students home, but police waiting outside sent them right back into the schools.

Department and hardware stores quickly sold all available stocks of black paint, blackout cloth, portable radios, flashlights, lanterns, candles ("Christmas or blackout?" clerks asked), shovels, hatchets, first-aid kits, oil stoves, thermos bottles, earplugs, lanterns, whistles, waterproof matchboxes, and goggles. Woolworth's put up a special Blackout Necessities counter offering bandages, antiseptics, and masked flashlights. Interior decorators took orders for blackout curtains with hand-painted flowers appliquéd on the inner side. Saks Fifth Avenue reported a run on pea jackets for men and heavy nightgowns for women. Lord & Taylor sold ladies' handbags that contained first-aid kits, flashlights, and phosphorescent camellias to wear in one's hair. Sleeping bags sold out almost immediately; one lady ordered twenty-two mattresses, explaining, "If we're going to have to sleep in the subway, at least we'll be comfortable." She needn't have worried; Mayor La Guardia officially declared the subways unsafe (as air raid shelters, that is).

Anne Morrow Lindbergh saw the world she knew rapidly slipping away. "I feel as if all I believed *was* America, all memories of it, all history, all dreams of the future were marching gaily toward a precipice—and unaware, unaware."

And it was.

30

An Old and Broken Year

"I've changed since the war. I've acquired a complete contempt
for everything that interests *me* . . . I'm curiously sick,
almost all the time, sick with a total indifference. I want to
finish my book—that's all. . . . I need nothing, neither money,
nor pleasures, nor company. I have a vital need for peace."
—ANTOINE DE ST-EXUPÉRY

The war has only just begun," General Hideki Tojo told the Japanese
people on the last day of 1941. "Although the Japanese forces are fighting
with the greatest energy, the war will be long in duration." In Tokyo, the
government announced that through December 31, British and American
troops had lost 3,000 soldiers killed and 9,000 captured; Japanese casualties totaled only 743 dead and 1,799 wounded. But, Tojo warned, let no
one be misled by these easy early triumphs. The British and American
imperialists had started "desperate counter-action to maintain the old
order," and both Western nations were backed by immense wealth and
power. Thus there was no alternative for Japan but "to continue the war
to the end to achieve the great ideals for which she has been striving."

On February 15, 1942, Japanese forces captured Singapore.

During Christmas week in Berlin, Goebbels broadcast another appeal
for warm clothing for soldiers on the eastern front. To emphasize the need
for sacrifices on the home front, the German public was forbidden to send
New Year's cards. As part of their anti-Christian campaign, Bormann and
Himmler ordered German radio stations to refrain from playing all the
traditional Christmas hymns (except the noncommittal "O Tannen-
baum"). Christmas candles were strictly rationed. "What will we do?"
asked one disappointed Berliner. "All we'll have is a Christmas tree with
nothing to put on it. Ach, das leben ist schwer." ("Life is hard.")

Soviet propagandists smuggled taunting Christmas cards into the
Reich: one, entitled "Living Space in the East," portrayed a frozen vista
of wooden crosses topped with German helmets; another depicted a Russian pine tree with the body of a German soldier beside it.

For the first time since the war began, the Fuehrer's New Year's Eve proclamations did not promise victory for the coming year. Instead, he promised only "still harder battles for 1942 if we are to circumscribe the powerful foe which confronts us." "And it is for this reason," Hitler told the German people, "that the year which is now beginning imposes on us the gravest responsibility. Churchill and Roosevelt have delivered Europe to Stalin. The Bolshevist monster to whom they wish to deliver the nations of Europe will finish by destroying them and their people. A light has, however, risen in the Far East, and while those two blasphemers pray to God for their business the European nations will deliver themselves.

"On the threshold of the New Year we can ask of the Almighty that he give to the German people and to its soldiers the strength to resist with valiant hearts for the maintenance of our liberties and our future. . . . The year 1942—and we pray to God, all of us, that it may—should bring the decision which will save our people and with them our allied nations."

"Frenchmen!" spoke Marshal Pétain on December 31. "War has now spread to all corners of the earth. The Continent is in flames, but France remains outside the conflict." Expressing his fervent hope that Germany and France seek a rapprochement, the Marshal condemned the persistence of disorder in France, a condition he ascribed to unbridled individualism, class hatred, and a pervasive distrust between the occupied and unoccupied zones. "The new order which is about to assume its place cannot be founded on anything but a severe internal order, one which demands from all the same discipline founded on the preeminence of labor, the hierarchy of values, a sense of responsibility, respect for justice and mutual confidence. . . . Frenchmen! If the government which has received the legacy of defeat cannot always obtain your support, its acts, nevertheless, tend to perpetuate French history. Its text will be written in those textbooks of your children. Strive that those pages remain written in honor and that those who come after you will have no reason to blush, either for the nation or for its chiefs."

Amid the blackened skeletons of churches and the jagged silhouettes of bombed-out buildings, Londoners cheerfully bade farewell to the old year, the tired and broken year. They had not enjoyed the merriest Christmas of their lives in 1941; besides the depressing news from the Far East, many families spent the holiday separated by thousands of miles, and there were few gift items that remained unrationed. But for now, it was enough to know that 1941 was gone and they were still alive to welcome in another new year. A disproportionate number of the revelers were women, and many were in uniform, but this year there were no air raid sirens, no sinister buzzing of Luftwaffe bombers overhead, no deafening explosions or falling buildings or screams of people buried under flaming rubble. This year there was laughter, and singing, and "Auld Lang Syne" as the clock of St. Paul's Cathedral sounded midnight. Then, rather inexplicably, the crowd gathered around the cathedral began to sing, "She'll Be Coming 'Round the Mountain When She Comes," and yells of "Hi-yi yippee!" filled the air. Then they all went home and went to bed with flashlights and warm clothing close at hand in case the bombers returned. Looking back over the long, heartbreaking days of 1941, General Alan Brooke sighed and said, "We're not doing too badly. We've only lost about a quarter of the Empire."

In Washington, soldiers with fixed bayonets patrolled endlessly in front of the White House. Curious pedestrians were ordered to move along; no one answered their questions. Hidden behind a high fence, East Executive Avenue was blocked to civilian traffic. Police and soldiers inspected every car on West Executive Avenue. Workmen installed slots for blackout shutters on the White House windows. Deliveries were rerouted to a garage six blocks away. Everyone, including presidential advisers who had been with Roosevelt for eight years, had to show credentials to pass through the Secret Service guards.

There was only one exception to the rigorous security precautions: on Christmas Eve, thirty thousand people were admitted to the White House grounds to watch the President light the national Christmas tree. It was a bitterly cold day. From the south portico, Roosevelt delivered a few brief remarks; then the crowd listened in awed silence as Prime Minister Churchill, who had arrived in Washington on December 22, made a short speech of his own. "Let the children have their night of fun and laughter," he said. "Let the gifts of Father Christmas delight their play. Let us grown-ups share to the full in their unstinted pleasures before we turn again to the stern task and the formidable years that lie before us, resolved that, by our sacrifice and daring, these same children shall not be robbed of their inheritance or denied their right to live in a free and decent world. And so, in God's mercy, a happy Christmas to you all." The two men stood side by side as the Marine Band played "God Save the King" and "The Star-Spangled Banner."

It was Franklin's first Christmas without his mother. None of his own children were there—all four sons were in the military—nor could any of the Roosevelts' eleven grandchildren come to Washington for the holiday. Eleanor filled the few Christmas stockings that remained. In the morning, the President took Churchill to an interfaith service at the Foundry Methodist Church. ("It is good for Winston," Roosevelt said, "to sing hymns with the Methodies.") "I am glad I went," Churchill admitted afterward. "It's the first time my mind has been at rest for a long time. Besides, I like singing hymns." Roosevelt and Churchill spent most of the day in meetings with their military advisers. ("Christmas must give way to the necessity of work," Churchill sternly advised Eleanor.) At four-thirty they all opened their presents (Fala's gifts from well-wishers had to wait for another day), and then the President carved the turkey for sixty-one guests, including all the Norwegian royal family, who were beginning to make a habit of this sort of thing. After dinner everyone retired to the auditorium for a movie, a documentary of the war. Churchill, who had to deliver a speech to Congress the following day, retired early, shortly before a visiting band of carolers led the entire presidential party in singing the traditional Christmas songs. Then the President shouted "Good night" to everyone as they wheeled him away in his chair. "He had been like a schoolboy, jolly and carefree," remarked Admiral Moran, Churchill's personal physician. "It was difficult to believe that this was the man who was taking his nation into a vast conflict in which, until Pearl Harbor a few days ago, she had no thought of being engaged."

Veteran observers of New York society claimed that the 1941 New Year's Eve celebration in Times Square was one of the gayest, most uninhibited gatherings they ever witnessed. Under heavy skies that threatened storms for most of the evening, 500,000 partygoers blew their horns and rang their bells and jammed the city's nightclubs and cabarets and movie theaters to capacity. The neon lights of Broadway shone as bright as ever, augmented by the dazzling brilliance of batteries of spotlights set up on rooftops to permit motion picture cameras to capture the scene.

Signs of the war abounded. There was a heavy concentration of men in uniform in the crowd, and MPs on every corner, and sixteen hundred air raid wardens who stood ready to turn off the lights at a moment's notice; mobile loudspeakers adorned lampposts; black and white signs pointed the way to air raid shelters (IN CASE OF ALARM, LEAVE TIMES SQUARE. WALK. DO NOT RUN). Behind the famous statue of Father Duffy at the north end of the Square, a huge white sign asked, REMEMBER PEARL HARBOR and BUY DEFENSE BONDS. But none of this dampened the festive mood. At the honky-tonk parlors along Broadway, the most popular form of entertainment with civilians were the mechanical target practice games with toy antiaircraft guns that brought down phantom enemy bombers.

Just before midnight, the huge fiery ball atop the New York Times building began its descent. Then the loudspeakers came to life as Lucy Monroe, surrounded by policemen and soldiers as she stood in Father Duffy Square, sang "The Star-Spangled Banner." After a moment of hesitation, the crowd joined in the anthem. Radio networks sent the music ringing throughout the nation.

Epilogue

The war ended first in North Africa.

On the night of October 23–24, 1942, 70,000 men and 600 tanks of the British Eighth Army, under the command of General Bernard Law Montgomery, commenced an assault upon the German positions outside El Alamein in the deserts of western Egypt. Although the British enjoyed a vast superiority in manpower (estimated at 6 to 1), Rommel's lines did not break until November 4. In the end, it turned out to be a costly victory for the British, for Montgomery lost approximately 13,000 men and more than 500 tanks; but the power of the Afrika Korps had been broken forever. When the dust had finally settled at El Alamein, Rommel had only about a dozen tanks remaining.

Immediately afterward, the Allies launched Operation Torch, a three-pronged series of landings of British and American troops (accompanied, as it turned out, by considerable confusion and incompetence) at Casablanca, Oran, and Tangiers on November 8. Over the next six months, Allied troops blundered and battered their way across the North African coastline, finally trapping the depleted and exhausted remnants of the German and Italian armies in a narrow strip of land on the Tunisian coast. With the Mediterranean at their backs, retreat was impossible. On May 7, the last two Axis bastions in North Africa fell as two British armored divisions entered Tunis in triumph and the American Ninth Division captured Bizerte; by the time all the scattered resistance ended on May 13, more than 250,000 German and Italian soldiers had surrendered. (But not the Desert Fox. Rommel had departed Africa on March 9 for a period of sick leave in Germany, and never returned to the desert.)

The Allies now controlled the entire continent of Africa; even more significant was the fact they once again possessed a solid foothold in the Mediterranean.

Italy was next. On July 10, 1943, two separate Allied invasion forces landed on the shores of Sicily: the Americans on the western side of the island were led by General George S. Patton; Montgomery commanded the British in the east. Nearly all the resistance they encountered came from the Germans who fought a fierce rearguard action as they retreated across the Strait of Messina. The Italian troops in Sicily regularly surrendered after only a halfhearted fight, and the local civilians, who by now were heartily sick of the Fascist government, Mussolini, and, especially, his German colleagues, generally gave the Allied invaders an enthusiastic welcome.

Mussolini himself was deposed by the Fascist Grand Council on July 24—after King Victor Emmanuel III informed the Duce, rather gratuitously, that he was "the most despised man in Italy"—and was placed under arrest by the army. The aged Marshal Badoglio, whom Mussolini had sacked at the end of 1940, returned to power at the head of a shaky caretaker government. As Badoglio pondered the wisdom of continued loyalty to the Axis, the Allied armies began their drive north from the heel and toe of the Italian boot. On September 8, the Italian government surrendered unconditionally. But in the meantime, Hitler had dispatched thirteen additional German divisions into Italy, and the Allies' painstaking advance up the peninsula did not reach Rome until June 3, 1944.

Mussolini, meanwhile, had been rescued from his "prison" in the Apennine Mountains by a daring Nazi commando raid in September 1943. Out of loyalty to his erstwhile ally, Hitler restored the Duce to power at the head of a puppet government in German-occupied northern Italy. But on April 28, 1945, as his Nazi protectors were retreating into Austria, Mussolini tried to flee by disguising himself as a Luftwaffe officer and hiding among a group of German soldiers. With American troops (who presumably would have spared his life so that he could stand trial for war crimes) just a few hours away, Communist partisans discovered Mussolini's identity and executed him at once. His body was taken back to Milan, where it was strung up by the heels in the Piazzale Loreto to be cursed and spat upon by the mob.

On the eastern front, the Wehrmacht recovered the initiative and drove toward the vital industrial center of Stalingrad in the summer of 1942. Luftwaffe bombers turned the city into a charred ruin; by the middle of September, half of Stalingrad was in the hands of the German Sixth Army of General Friedrich Paulus. But the Soviet defenders maintained a tenacious grasp on the rest of the city, and in savage house-to-house and street fighting they gradually managed to halt the Nazi advance. In a stunning reversal of position, a Russian counteroffensive in November succeeded in surrounding the German forces in and around Stalingrad. At the end of January 1943, Paulus and more than 100,000 German soldiers surrendered; most of the prisoners were sent to camps in Siberia where they died before the end of the war.

Bolstered by massive shipments of Lend-Lease supplies from America, and aided in no small measure by Hitler's decision to transfer thirteen divisions from the eastern front to Italy, Soviet forces won a bloody, spectacular victory over the Wehrmacht in the greatest tank battle in history, at Kursk, in July 1943. That was the Germans' last gasp. From that time on, the Red Army slogged its way westward in a brutal offensive campaign, slowly punishing and pushing the Nazi invaders out of Russia in the spring and summer of 1944. But instead of pursuing a single straight line toward Berlin, Stalin ordered his armies to spread out and advance along a broad front, through the vital centers of eastern Europe, to ensure Soviet military and political domination of the region in the postwar world. By the time Stalin, Roosevelt, and Churchill met at Yalta in February 1945, there was nothing Britain or the United States could do (short of declaring war against the Soviet Union) to liberate eastern Europe from Stalin's ironclad grasp.

After 880 days of agony, the siege of Leningrad was finally broken on January 27, 1944. More than a million and a half people had died of starvation, exposure, or sickness; fewer than 700,000 men, women, and children remained in a city that had numbered more than three million residents when the ordeal had begun in the autumn of 1941. Upon the lifting of the Nazi siege, poet Vera Inber wrote in her diary, "The greatest event in the life of Leningrad: full liberation from blockade. And I, a professional writer, have no words for it. I simply say: Leningrad is free. And that is all."

Throughout 1942 and 1943, Stalin continued to press for the establishment of a second front in western Europe. Finally, on June 6, 1944—D-Day—an Allied force that included 150,000 men, 1,500 tanks, and 12,000 planes landed upon the shores of Normandy. Because Hitler's generals had convinced him that the main Allied strike would fall upon Calais, the British and American invaders were spared the full fury of the Nazi defenses in those first vulnerable moments on the beaches known as Omaha, Utah, Juno, and Sword. By July 14, more than one million Allied soldiers had landed in France. Hitler ordered his commanders on the western front not to retreat, and so they were chewed up where they stood by the vastly superior Allied firepower. On August 26, the Allies entered Paris; de Gaulle marched triumphantly through the liberated city the following day. Marshal Philippe Pétain was subsequently sentenced to death for collaborating with the enemy, but received a pardon and was instead imprisoned for life. Pétain lived for seven more years and died peacefully in 1951, at the age of ninety-five.

In an effort to avert the total destruction of the German nation, a group of Wehrmacht officers led by General Ludwig Beck and Colonel Klaus Philip Schenk (Count von Stauffenberg) entered into a conspiracy to kill Hitler and seek a negotiated peace with the Allies. On July 20, 1944, Stauffenberg placed a bomb hidden in a briefcase beneath a table at a high-level strategy conference at the Wolfsschanze. Unfortunately, another German officer, apparently unwittingly, moved the briefcase just before the bomb exploded, and the blast wounded but did not kill the Fuehrer. In retribution for the attempt on Hitler's life, the SS hanged two thousand alleged conspirators, including Admiral Canaris.

So the war went on. Late in December 1944, German forces under Field Marshal von Rundstedt launched a sudden, desperate, and momentarily successful counterattack against the Allies in the Ardennes Forest. But by then the Wehrmacht was far too weak to sustain any offensive, and on January 9 the bloody Battle of the Bulge—Hitler's final, impulsive gamble—ended in one more Allied victory.

Within Germany, the city of Berlin lay in ruins, the smoldering rubble mute testimony to the devastating efficiency of daylight bombing raids led by American B-17 Flying Fortresses. Dresden had been firebombed; Hamburg, Essen, and Frankfurt suffered far more grievously from bombing assaults than London ever had.

In November 1944, President Franklin Delano Roosevelt won election to a fourth term in the White House. This time his running mate was Senator Harry S Truman, whose investigations into defense scandals in 1941 had catapulted him into national prominence. But Roosevelt was a very, very tired man. Early in the afternoon of April 12, 1945, while vacationing in Warm Springs, Georgia, the President suffered a massive cerebral hemorrhage. Several hours later—at 3:35 P.M.—he died. When the news reached Washington, a crowd gathered in front of the White House. From his office in the nearby Executive Office Building, future Secretary of State Dean Acheson watched the people stare helplessly at the entrance to the President's home. "There was nothing to see," Acheson wrote later, "and I am sure they did not expect to see anything. They merely stood in a lost sort of way."

Shortly after noon on April 30, 1945, Adolf Hitler shot himself in a closed room in a bunker deep underneath the city of Berlin. Joseph Goebbels gave fatal doses of potassium cyanide to his wife and his six children and then swallowed the poison himself.

Germany surrendered unconditionally on May 8, 1945.

As the Allied armies approached Berlin, they discovered the existence of the Nazi extermination camps—Auschwitz, Treblinka, Sobibor, Belzec, Chelmno, and Maidanek—where more than 5,370,000 human beings had been tortured and murdered. Most of them had been killed in gas chambers, and most of the victims had been Jews, including an estimated 3.2

million Poles. In all, more than six million Jews perished in the Holocaust. Perhaps 500,000 more had been brutally torn from their homes and their families.

Physically and psychologically ravaged by Hitler's Final Solution and determined to ensure that such horror would never again be visited upon its people, the Jewish community in Europe and the United States employed every diplomatic and military resource at its disposal to transport these displaced persons to Palestine, where they intended to erect their own national state. When the British refused to allow more than a handful of Jewish immigrants into Palestine (for which Britain still held a mandate) in 1946 and 1947, semi-autonomous Jewish guerrilla organizations—the most uncompromising of which was the Irgun Zvai Le'umi, under the leadership of Menachem Begin—launched a terrorist campaign against British and Arab forces in the region. On November 29, 1947, the United Nations voted to recommend the partition of Palestine into two separate Jewish and Arab states. Less than six months later, on May 14, 1948, Prime Minister David Ben-Gurion proclaimed the establishment of the State of Israel. The following day, Arab armies from Egypt, Syria, Lebanon, Iraq, and Jordan invaded Israel to begin the first Arab-Israeli war.

The first American victory in the Pacific had come at Midway, on June 4, 1942, when navy bombers swept down upon Admiral Yamamoto's combat fleet and destroyed four aircraft carriers, forcing the Japanese to retreat. Then, from August 1942 until February 1943, American and Japanese naval and ground forces waged six separate battles for Guadalcanal; by the time it was over and the Japanese had evacuated their troops from the island, they left behind over 30,000 of their own men dead.

For the next two years, American sailors and marines slugged their way from island to island, winning hard-fought victories at Buna, Bougainville, the central Solomons, Rabaul, Tarawa, Kwajalein, the Marshall Islands and the Marianas, Iwo Jima and Okinawa. They always had to win their battles with whatever matériel could be spared from the primary theater in Europe; often in the early months they fought with surplus World War One weapons. By the spring of 1944, the Japanese had developed a tenacious defensive strategy that exacted the maximum amount of casualties on the American attackers. Still the U.S. troops kept pressing inexorably forward, and after the American victory at Saipan, General Hideki Tojo resigned his post as prime minister in July 1944.

Three months later, General Douglas MacArthur fulfilled his famous promise and returned at last to the Philippines. The last major remnants of the Imperial Japanese Navy were destroyed in a prolonged and bitter engagement at Leyte Gulf, and by March 1945 American troops had recaptured Manila. With the Philippines firmly in hand, U.S. forces were back where they had been in the autumn of 1941, with air bases conveniently near to the Japanese homeland. Now the terror began for the Japanese; in two full-scale B-29 incendiary raids against Tokyo, nearly 225,000 Japanese civilians died.

At 5:30 A.M. on Monday, July 16, 1945, a blinding flash suddenly split the desert sky at Alamogordo, New Mexico. *New York Times* reporter William Laurence described it as "a sunrise such as the world had never seen, a great green supersun climbing in a fraction of a second to a height of more than eight thousand feet, rising ever higher until it touched the clouds, lighting up earth and sky all around with a dazzling luminosity. Up it went, a great ball of fire about a mile in diameter, changing colors as it kept shooting upward, from deep purple to orange, expanding, growing bigger, rising as it expanded, an elemental force freed from its bonds after being chained for billions of years. For a fleeting instant the color was unearthly green, such as one sees only in the corona of the sun during a total eclipse. It was as though the earth had opened and the skies had split. One felt as though one were present at the moment of creation when God said: 'Let there be light.' "

At 9:15 A.M. on August 6, 1945, the bombardier of the *Enola Gay* pressed a button and the first atomic bomb descended upon Hiroshima. Over 60,000 Japanese died immediately; nearly 100,000 more perished later from burns or radiation sickness. Three days later, the United States dropped another atomic bomb on Nagasaki. On August 13, Emperor Hirohito made his final decision to surrender, and after a short-lived and abortive revolt among die-hard Japanese militarists was quelled, the formal surrender ceremonies took place aboard the USS *Missouri* on September 2. Japan passed under the control of an American occupation regime headed by General Douglas MacArthur. Following a lengthy trial, Hideki Tojo was sentenced to death by an Allied war crimes tribunal in Tokyo on November 12, 1948; he was hanged six weeks later.

For the living, the war now passed into the realm of memory. It had been the most bloody conflict in human history: among the major powers alone, over 16 million men had died in combat. Eleven million of those had been soldiers in the Soviet Red Army, a staggering number which far surpassed the losses (which were sufficiently terrible in themselves) among the other combatants—3.5 million German soldiers; 1.3 million Japanese; 292,131 Americans; and 264,443 Britons. Civilian losses in the Soviet Union were equally grim: between 1941 and 1945, 7 million Russian noncombatants died, compared to Germany's 780,000 and Japan's 672,-000 civilian deaths. To these numbers must be added many more millions of casualties among the Chinese and the less powerful nations of Europe,

Africa, and Asia. In the end, between 45 and 50 million men, women, and children died during the Second World War.

After this war, there could be no American retreat into isolation, for the world was a very different place in September 1945 than it had been in January 1941. The British Empire had been badly shaken and was in the final throes of disintegration; Germany lay prostrate and divided; southern Europe was gripped by social and political chaos; and only the most chauvinistic Frenchman would pretend to count France among the world's major powers. Through the installation of Communist puppet regimes in Poland, Hungary, Czechoslovakia, Bulgaria, and Romania, Stalin had drawn an "iron curtain" across eastern Europe, and no amount of moralistic American outrage in the halls of Congress or at any of the postwar major-power conferences could make so much as a minor dent in the Soviet Union's control of half of the Continent. Soon it became obvious to Washington that the military destruction of Nazi Germany had not, in fact, brought about the sort of European political order the United States had sought; the noble democratic principles of liberty, justice, and self-determination enshrined in the Atlantic Charter bore little relation to the realities of international diplomacy in the postwar world. Few American policymakers believed that the organized force of world opinion, as formally embodied in the United Nations—founded in October 1945—could protect the rights of nations threatened by subversion or aggression from abroad. Within eighteen months, influential members of the Truman administration were following George Kennan's lead in using the word "containment" to describe American policy toward Communist Russia; by the summer of 1948, the cold war was well under way.

In the Far East, colonialism was dead or dying. None of the imperialist European powers had the resources—and most lacked the will—to reestablish complete control over their possessions after the collapse of the Japanese Empire. Over the next decade, most of the formerly subject nations of Asia received their independence: the Philippines on July 4, 1946; India on August 15, 1947; Burma on January 4, 1948; Indonesia on December 27, 1949. France stubbornly attempted to regain control of its provinces in Indochina, but a series of demoralizing defeats at the hands of the Viet Minh insurgents (led by Ho Chi Minh), culminating in the siege of Dien Bien Phu in the spring of 1954, finally persuaded the French government to withdraw from Indochina. At a multinational conference in Geneva in July of that year, three separate independent nations were recognized: Cambodia, Laos, and Viet Nam. Viet Nam was temporarily partitioned at the 17th parallel, pending national elections, as a compromise between the Communist Viet Minh in the north and the French-backed Emperor Bao Dai in the south.

After the military defeat of Japan, the sham facade of Chinese national unity collapsed and open civil war broke out between Chiang Kai-shek's Kuomintang and the Communist forces under Mao Zedong. Attempts by U.S. Secretary of State George Marshall to establish a coalition government were doomed to failure, and no amount of American assistance short of open intervention (and perhaps not even that) could prevent the collapse of Chiang's corrupt and inefficient regime. In the end, the U.S. sent more than $2 billion in aid to Chiang—much of which eventually ended up in the hands of the Communists—but refused to risk an open-ended military commitment on the Asian continent. On October 1, 1949, Mao proclaimed the sovereignty of the People's Republic of China; on December 8, Chiang established the Republic of China on the island of Taiwan off the southeast coast of the mainland.

Seven months later—less than five years after V-J Day—the United States was at war once again. At the Potsdam conference in July 1945, the nation of Korea had been divided along the 38th parallel into Soviet and American zones of occupation. On the last weekend in June 1950, North Korean troops—supported by many of the same Soviet T-34 tanks that had broken the German panzer divisions at Kursk in 1943—crossed the border in force, routing the unprepared South Korean and American outposts, and the defenders fled southward in complete disarray. Bolstered by a United Nations resolution condemning North Korea for its unwarranted aggression, the Truman administration organized military force to repel the invasion. A daring amphibious operation of the multinational United Nations forces in September at Inchon, designed and led by General MacArthur, succeeded in chasing the enemy back across the parallel; but then MacArthur blundered by ordering his troops to follow them into North Korea. After MacArthur reached the Yalu, thirty-three divisions of regular Chinese troops struck the United Nations lines. Thousands of Americans and South Koreans lost their lives during the hard retreat southward over the frozen peninsula. Finally the lines stabilized near the original line of demarcation; when MacArthur attacked government policy and insisted once again in April 1951 upon the desirability of carrying the fight to China, Truman sacked him. After two years of peace negotiations, American and North Korean representatives signed an armistice at Panmunjom on July 27, 1953. Over 54,000 American soldiers had lost their lives during the undeclared war.

The Truman administration never seriously considered using atomic bombs to end the war in Korea; one reason for its forbearance was that the United States no longer enjoyed a monopoly on nuclear weapons. At the end of August 1949, Truman had learned of the Soviet Union's successful test of an atomic weapon of unknown strength. The discovery sparked a frenzied American research effort to maintain its lead in nuclear technology by developing a hydrogen (fusion) bomb. On November 1, 1952, the

United States set off its first H-bomb at a remote atoll in the Pacific Ocean; within nine months the Soviets, too, had developed a hydrogen weapon, and Britain had exploded its own atomic bomb. The nuclear arms race had begun in earnest.

During the night of March 1, 1953, after a continued reign of terror, Joseph Stalin suffered a fatal stroke. He died four days later. Many Russians wept when they learned that their leader, their murderous father, was gone.

Winston Churchill had been raised to power by the war; the approach of peace brought his downfall. In the flush of victory in the spring of 1945, British voters ousted Churchill's coalition cabinet and replaced it with a Labour government headed by Clement Attlee, who, like Thomas E. Dewey, reminded many people of the little man atop a wedding cake. Churchill returned as leader of a Conservative government in 1951, and served as prime minister until his resignation in 1955. He lived in retirement for ten more years, filling his days with his paintings, his memoirs, and his account of the history of his nation.

And in the end, what was the meaning of the year 1941?

As we have seen in the preceding pages, numerous perceptive contemporary observers recognized that 1941 was a critical period in the history of the twentieth century, and the passage of more than forty years has abundantly vindicated their judgment. The subsequent course of events throughout the world has revealed to the present generation just how influential the developments of those tumultuous twelve months were in shaping the outcome of the war and the nature of the postwar world. In January 1941, the British Empire stood alone against a European continent dominated by Nazi Germany, and no rational, objective observer would have predicted that Britain could ever win such an unequal fight. Japan was on the threshold of total dominion in the Far East; China was a helpless giant, carved into spheres controlled by Japan, the Kuomintang, and the Communists. And the vast majority of the American people had no intention of ever getting involved in the conflagration overseas.

By the end of December, the combined weight of the Soviet Union and the United States, with their overwhelming manpower and industrial resources, had been thrown unexpectedly (and somewhat unwillingly) into the scales on the side of Great Britain; and from that moment on, despite a multitude of obstacles that needed to be overcome in the short run, the defeat of Hitler's Germany became only a matter of time. In the wholesale murders of Jews and Communists behind the lines on the eastern front, the Nazi apparatus for the Holocaust was being constructed.

The Japanese Empire had sealed its death warrant with the attack upon Pearl Harbor, and American scientists had received a green light from the Roosevelt administration to pursue a full-scale research effort toward the development of an atomic bomb.

Our lives would never be the same.

Source Notes

In the following notes, works are cited by the author's name and a brief title upon the first citation; for a full listing, consult the bibliography. If the note cites an author with more than one work in the bibliography, a brief title for the work is always given in the note. All dates for newspapers and periodicals refer to the year 1941 unless specifically stated otherwise. The following abbreviations are used throughout:

LT	*Times* (London)
MG	Manchester *Guardian*
NAT	*Nation* (U.S.)
NR	*New Republic*
NWK	*Newsweek*
NY	*The New Yorker*
NYT	*New York Times*
SUN	Baltimore *Sun*
T	*Time* magazine
WP	Washington *Post*

PROLOGUE

PAGE

4. "It is just like in . . .": Orwell and Angus, eds., *Collected Essays,* p. 55.

5. "This was the exercise . . .": Spender, *The Thirties and After,* p. 64.

5. "personally . . .": Terraine, *A Time,* p. 169.

5. "In a way . . .": Stein, *Wars,* p. 6.

6. "We've got the men away . . .": Dalton, *The Fateful Years,* p. 341.

6. "all we can do . . .": K. Clark, *Other Half,* p. 19.

7. "I'd like to get . . .": Reiss, ed., *They Were There,* p. 247.

7. "Under the circumstances . . .": ibid., p. 244.

7. "the city of London . . .": Spender, p. 73.

7. "At this time . . .": Churchill, *Finest Hour,* p. 372.

8. "we saw the flashes . . .": ibid., p. 378.

8. "I shall not go down . . .": H. Nicolson, *Diaries,* p. 188.

8. "It's horrible . . .": R. James, ed., *Channon,* pp. 278–79.

9. "a quaint old British idea . . .": Pyle, *Ernie's War,* p. 49.

9. "Have you heard . . .": Dalton, *Fateful,* p. 329.
9. "falling down a . . .": H. Nicolson, p. 194.
9. "when all is . . .": Orwell, p. 54.
9. "It's appalling" and "What's the use . . .": Reiss, ed., *They Were There,* p. 241.
9. "Dearie, my uncle . . .": ibid., p. 243.
9. "I'm enjoying . . .": David Smith, *Wells,* pp. 470–71.
9. "outraged and ready . . .": Guinness, *Blessings,* p. 105.
9. "Dang it all . . .": Christie, *An Autobiography,* p. 471.
10. "a study in failure . . .": R. James, *Churchill: A Study in Failure, 1900–1939,* passim.
10. "He is a man . . .": quoted in ibid., p. 384.
10. "always the hour of fate . . .": A. G. Gardiner quoted, ibid., p. 382.
10. "is his great gift . . .": *NY,* March 8.
11. "the pale and globular . . .": H. Nicolson, p. 196.
11. "a huge painted thermos bottle . . .": R. James, ed., *Channon,* p. 270.
11. "walk in the moonlight . . .": Churchill, *Finest Hour,* pp. 375–76.
11. "The tiresome part . . .": Clark, *Other Half,* pp. 20–21.
12. "A bombed building . . .": Pyle, pp. 53–54.
12. "I would feel . . .": Ackroyd, *Eliot,* p. 261.
12. "grey dishevelled figures": Muggeridge, *Chronicles,* p. 110.
13. "How one enjoys food . . .": Woolf, *Diary,* p. 347.
13. "It changes it . . .": ibid., pp. 344–45.
13. "Tonnage became an obsession . . .": de Gaulle, *Call to Honour,* p. 142.
14. "this was one of the . . .": Soames, *Clementine,* p. 395.
15. "It is no good hoping . . .": *MG,* Dec. 20, 1940.
15. "The smoke rose . . .": *MG,* Dec. 31, 1940.
16. "These things all . . .": Pyle, p. 44.
16. "Tonight, the bomber planes . . .": David Johnson, *The City Ablaze,* p. 95.
16. "When will the war . . .": *MG,* Dec. 31, 1940.
18. "Wir fahren . . .": Kennan, *Memoirs,* p. 130.
18. "the talk was all of . . .": ibid., pp. 108–9.
18. "Do not say . . .": Stein, p. 5.
18. "knitted the German nation . . .": Shirer, *Berlin Diary,* p. 582.
19. "War with Russia . . .": Toland, *Hitler,* p. 884.
20. "but that is the way . . .": Baltimore *Evening Sun,* Dec. 24, 1940.
20. "a sloppy Christmas tree": Boelcke, ed., *Secret Conferences,* p. 110.
20. "the democratic warmongers . . .": *NYT,* Jan. 1.
21. "I shall sit here . . .": Bree and Bernauer, eds., *Defeat and Beyond,* p. 153.
22. "For the first time . . .": Knight, *Resistance,* p. 72.
22. "One might not be . . .": Stein, p. 56.
22. "It seemed wryly appropriate . . .": Murphy, *Diplomat,* p. 48.
23. "the French love to talk . . .": Stein, p. 57.
23. "The men would uncover . . .": Frenay, *The Night Will End,* p. 37.
23. "All the children . . .": ibid., pp. 37–38.
24. "He does not like . . .": Lacouture, *De Gaulle,* p. 78.
24. "more a journalist . . .": Shirer, *Third Reich,* p. 761.
24. "an arrogant man . . .": ibid.
24. "La France entière . . .": H. Nicolson, pp. 198–99.
24. "A man is not de Gaulle . . .": Lacouture, p. 72.

25. "This snow and cold . . .": Ciano, *Diary, 1939–1943,* p. 321.
25. "Fuehrer, we are . . .": Payne, *Life and Death,* p. 409.
27. "It's fine . . .": *LT,* Dec. 23, 1940.
27. "I like it fine . . .": ibid.
27. "Officers' beds . . .": Moorehead, *The March to Tunis,* pp. 67–68.
28. "Even Michelangelo . . .": Ciano, p. 268.
28. "definitely in the saddle . . .": Grew, *Turbulent Era,* pp. 1230–31.
28. "as part of the general . . .": Graebner, *Ideas and Diplomacy,* p. 569.
29. "Sometimes we who have . . .": *WP,* Dec. 25, 1940.
29. "if the world survives . . .": Los Angeles *Times,* Dec. 16, 1940.
30. "an orgy of spending . . .": *NYT,* Dec. 25, 1940.
30. "an upstanding fellow . . .": *NY,* Dec. 28, 1940.
31. "We goin' . . .": Higham, *Lucy,* p. 59.
31. "It's selling so fast . . .": *NY,* Dec. 28, 1940.
32. "the important thing is . . .": *NYT,* Dec. 25, 1940.
32. "our motion pictures . . .": Manchester, *Glory,* p. 220.
32. "if enough of us . . .": C. Lindbergh, *Journals,* p. 429.
32. "It seems to me . . .": ibid., p. 434.
33. "I wish I could feel . . .": A. Lindbergh, *War Within,* pp. 100, 147.
34. "They were convinced . . .": Cole, *America First,* p. 38.
34. "intriguing diplomats . . .": *Atlantic Monthly,* October 1940.
35. "Danger . . .": Wainwright, *Life,* p. 116.
35. "we all know, I hope . . .": Stevenson, *Papers,* p. 471.
36. "posturing blabbermouth . . .": Goebbels, *Diaries,* p. 144.
36. "In these hours . . .": Sandburg, *Letters,* p. 392.
36. "Well, boys . . .": Cadogan, *Diaries,* p. 335, fn.
37. "a doctrine intrinsically . . .": *NYT,* Dec. 31, 1940.
37. "virtually a personal . . .": Cole, p. 43.
38. "They're good things . . .": *NYT,* Jan. 1.
38. "if any year ever . . .": Steinbeck, *Letters,* p. 221.

PART ONE: THE WINTER

41. "We did not know . . .": Begin, *White Nights,* p. 114.
42. "My ministers . . .": *T.,* Jan. 20.
42. "a kick in the pants . . .": Ciano, p. 326.
43. "A nation vanquished . . .": *NYT,* Jan. 18.
44. "We were the spoiled . . .": Colette, *Looking,* p. 107.
44. "It's cold here . . .": ibid., p. 127.
44. "I inserted myself . . .": de Beauvoir, *Prime,* p. 377.
45. "In general . . .": *NY,* Nov. 24, 1940.
45. "No cause . . .": Goebbels, p. 251.
46. "We may believe . . .": Colette, pp. 132–33.
48. "I vegetated on . . .": H. Smith, *Train,* pp. 59–60.
48. "the Nazi blight . . .": Shirer, *Berlin,* p. 605.
48. "When Barbarossa . . .": Toland, *Hitler,* p. 891.
48. "force a radical . . .": Halder, *Diaries,* p. 751.
49. "We do not hit . . .": ibid., p. 765.
49. "From a distance . . .": H. Smith, p. 59.

49. "Whoever imagines . . .": *T.*, Feb. 10.

49. "I am convinced . . .": Toland, *Hitler*, p. 890.

50. "You cannot know . . .": Camus, *Notebooks*, p. 187.

51. "The men were heavily . . .": Jackson, *North Africa*, pp. 58–59.

51. "We would have gone on . . .": Moorehead, p. 97.

52. "If I may . . .": ibid., p. 61.

52. "It will take at least . . .": Ciano, p. 325.

52. "the great British . . .": *NR*, Jan. 13.

52. "not the scene of war . . .": Panter-Downes, p. 131.

53. "The first attempt . . .": Pitt, *Western Desert*, p. 158.

53. "Sickness, death . . .": Moorehead, pp. 90–91.

54. "the sort of enemy . . .": Colville, *Fringes*, p. 331.

54. "We were grossly outnumbered . . .": Moorehead, p. 114.

56. "Not until I saw . . .": Bloom, *Limelight*, pp. 25–27.

57. "It is the courage . . .": Blum, ed., *Philosopher*, p. 402.

57. "we must not permit . . .": H. Douglas, *Life*, p. 172.

58. "In other words . . .": C. Lindbergh, p. 437.

59. "we shall not . . .": *NYT*, Jan. 17.

59. "the President's so-called . . .": *NYT*, Jan. 11.

59. "this is a bill . . .": *NYT*, Jan. 12.

59. "the President is not . . .": Cole, p. 43.

60. "New Deal . . .": *NYT*, Jan. 15.

60. "the most untruthful . . .": ibid.

60. "They are as . . .": *NAT*, Jan. 25.

61. "I think we are in . . .": *NYT*, Jan. 17.

61. "Mr. Kennedy is a very foul . . .": Collier and Horowitz, *Kennedys*, p. 104.

61. "I have tried to analyze . . .": C. Lindbergh, pp. 437–38.

62. "It was jammed . . .": ibid., pp. 442–43.

62. "I think it would be . . .": *SUN*, Jan. 24.

63. "hundred-pound sacks of sugar . . .": Tornabene, *King*, p. 259.

63. "Oh, Ronnie . . .": Morella and Epstein, *Wyman*, p. 44.

63. "You know . . .": ibid., 49.

63. "These pictures . . .": *NR*, Jan. 6.

66. "natural shoulders . . .": *NYT*, Jan. 2.

67. "vicious and irresponsible . . .": Leaming, *Orson*, p. 205.

68. "not based upon . . .": *NYT*, Jan. 11.

68. "It's something like . . .": J. Brown, *Lunts*, p. 293.

68. "Nobody could come out . . .": ibid., p. 293.

68. "When I started to write . . .": ibid., p. 292.

68. "carrying on a . . .": *T.*, Feb. 10.

69. "It's a great picture . . .": Chaplin, *Autobiography*, p. 400.

69. "Sit down, Charlie . . .": ibid., pp. 404–6.

70. "soldiers, sailors . . .": *SUN*, Jan. 21.

71. "Among the armies . . .": Wainwright, p. 103.

71. "The coordination . . .": Bradley, *Life*, pp. 88–89.

71. "In the United States . . .": A. Taylor, *Beaverbrook*, pp. 492–93.

72. "Assembly-line setups . . .": *Saturday Evening Post*, Jan. 18.

72. "It is better to . . .": *NR*, Jan. 6.

73. "the most efficient . . .": *NYT*, Jan. 1.

73. "Every battle unit . . .": ibid.
73. "A gigantic mess . . .": Bradley, p. 91.
74. "You'd be surprised . . .": *T.*, March 17.
77. "Supreme determination . . .": *LT,* Jan. 6.
79. "In retrospect . . .": Hane, *Peasants,* p. 75.
79. "The mission . . .": Dower, *War Without Mercy,* p. 26, fn.
80. "the French made money . . .": T. H. White, *In Search,* p. 106.
81. "a little of that . . .": Cadogan, p. 353.
82. "Those who play with fire . . .": T. H. White, p. 115.
82. "As for me . . .": Suyin, *Summer,* p. 212.
83. "the American people . . .": C. Chennault, *Fighter,* p. 90.
83. "The problems which we face . . .": *Foreign Relations, IV,* p. 8.
84. "Above all . . .": Lewin, *Ultra,* p. 236.
84. "There is a lot of talk . . .": Grew, pp. 1230–31.
85. "it's good to hear . . .": Manchester, *Caesar,* p. 200.
85. "as long as the Philippines . . .": ibid.
86. "an international whirlpool . . .": Flannery, *Assignment,* p. 3.
87. "the windows . . .": Graham, *Hollywood,* p. 110.
87. "Not long ago . . .": Panter-Downes, p. 133.
87. "woke up in the mornings . . .": Colville, p. 341.
88. "It was a terrible time . . .": Henreid, *Ladies' Man,* p. 78.
88. "The hour has come . . .": Colville, p. 344.
89. "Would you rather have . . .": *NR,* Jan. 6.
89. "The onion shortage . . .": Orwell, p. 382.
90. "We are now about to enter . . .": R. James, ed., *Speeches,* p. 6337.
90. "And the key . . .": Orwell, p. 381.
91. "When Billy Brown . . .": *SUN,* Jan. 19.
91. "These days . . .": *NY,* March 8.
91. "Dear London . . .": H. Nicolson, p. 201.
91. "Its the cold hour . . .": Woolf, p. 355.
91. "An incredible loveliness . . .": ibid., p. 346.
92. "I felt a terrible joy . . .": Muggeridge, pp. 104, 106.
93. "the helter-skelter . . .": J. P. Davies, Jr., *Dragon,* p. 212.
93. "a soul that flamed out of . . .": Churchill, *Alliance,* p. 23.
94. "We want to help them . . .": Lee, *London Journal,* p. 222.
94. "In the capitalist . . .": Maisky, *Ambassador,* p. 32.
94. "It's hard to fall . . .": ibid.
94. "accumulated all the gold . . .": Colville, p. 334.
94. "I told him . . .": Eden, *Reckoning,* p. 294.
94. "A rotund—smiling . . .": Sherwood, *Roosevelt and Hopkins,* p. 238.
95. "I don't give a damn . . .": Harriman, *Envoy,* p. 11.
95. "Lord Halifax . . .": Lee, p. 225.
96. "Before us lie . . .": R. James, ed., *Speeches,* p. 6329.
96. " 'Whither thou goest . . .": C. Wilson, *Moran Diaries,* p. 6.
96. "Looking back upon the . . .": Churchill, *Alliance,* pp. 3–4.
97. "The more I saw . . .": Fraser, *Alanbrooke,* p. 191.
97. "Lord Beaverbrook . . .": A. Taylor, p. 431.
97. "When I am chasing . . .": Reiss, ed., *They Were There,* p. 273.
97. "The Navy can lose . . .": Terraine, p. 260.

98. "It will be no . . .": *T.*, March 24.
98. "There is one thing . . .": Terraine, p. 259.
98. "The German nation . . .": ibid., pp. 263–64.
99. "The Army in England . . .": Montgomery, *Memoirs*, pp. 65–66.
99. "imbued with that . . .": ibid., p. 69.
99. "Never in the whole history . . .": Burgess, *Little Wilson*, pp. 242–43.
100. "mostly overcooked slop . . .": ibid., p. 250.
100. "The Germans had to be . . .": ibid., p. 256.

PART TWO: THE SEA

103. "Look, the morning . . .": Flannery, p. 129.
103. "The last days of . . .": Goebbels, p. 242.
103. "like the robber . . .": Flannery, p. 200.
103. "It was one of those . . .": ibid., p. 131.
104. "Reports from Italy . . .": Goebbels, p. 231.
104. "a blood-sucker . . .": Gisevius, *Bitter End*, p. 289.
105. "the unified preparation . . .": Kahn, *Spies*, p. 43.
105. "Goering was the . . .": Gisevius, p. 308.
106. "simple arithmetic . . .": Lang, *Secretary*, p. 151.
106. "lowest German peasant . . .": ibid.
106. "Experience has shown . . .": ibid., pp. 186–87.
106. "For two thousand years . . .": Flannery, pp. 177–78.
108. "It almost seems . . .": Bethge, *Bonhoeffer*, p. 627.
108. "Like Ahasuerus . . .": Gisevius, p. 440.
109. "For all decent people . . .": Hassell, *Diaries*, p. 173.
109. "there is growing awareness . . .": ibid., p. 164.
109. "Except for the outbursts . . .": Flannery, p. 151.
110. "Do not forget . . .": *NYT*, Feb. 24.
110. "Outside of marriage . . .": Flannery, p. 114.
110. "in order to prevent . . .": ibid., p. 201.
112. "on the face of it . . .": Cadogan, p. 349.
112. "This stinks of Anthony . . .": R. James, ed., *Channon*, p. 285.
113. "It was a queer sensation . . .": Eden, p. 222.
114. "Do not consider yourselves . . .": Terraine, p. 330.
114. "It is, of course . . .": Eden, p. 227.
114. "You appear to have . . .": Cadogan, p. 360.
114. "What the hell is . . .": ibid.
115. "You big nations . . .": B. F. Smith, *Shadow War*, p. 52.
115. "We decided to carry on . . .": R. Higham, *Disaster*, p. 159.
116. "The Greeks have done . . .": Jackson, p. 84.
116. "this is as tough . . .": Colville, p. 360.
116. "the PM . . .": R. James, ed., *Channon*, p. 295.
116. "I am afraid . . .": R. Higham, p. 158.
117. "We are going to destroy . . .": Dawidowicz, *The War*, p. 106.
117. "Vienna will soon . . .": Goebbels, p. 272.
118. "Otherwise . . .": ibid., p. 328.
118. "ever since the early thirties . . .": Grunberger, *History*, p. 459.
119. "sending them off . . .": Marrus and Paxton, *Vichy France*, p. 10.

119. "in weather forty degrees . . .": Shirer, *Reich,* p. 664.
119. "I see them every time . . .": Bauman, *Winter,* p. 42.
121. "I remember some one . . .": Stein, p. 60.
121. "It is dark here . . .": *NYT,* Feb. 23.
121. "The landscape around Gurs . . .": Engelmann, *Daily Life,* p. 233.
122. "It is a fact . . .": *NYT,* March 29.
122. "It is sinister . . .": Israel, ed. *Long Diaries,* p. 174.
123. "I see from the papers . . .": Wyman, *Abandonment,* p. 12.
123. "I am writing . . .": ibid.
123. "What kind of talk . . .": Chaplin, p. 404.
125. "like anticipant girls . . .": Monsarrat, *Breaking In,* p. 261.
126. "We are the shepherds . . .": Reiss, ed., *They Were There,* p. 251.
126. "Passengers are warned . . .": *NY,* April 19.
127. "they will notice . . .": Churchill, *Alliance,* p. 118.
127. "The decision for 1941 . . .": Saward, *Victory,* p. 214.
127. "The Germans had the superiority . . .": Cunningham, *Odyssey,* p. 299.
128. "I anticipate . . .": *NYT,* Feb. 25.
128. "It is very distressing . . .": Colville, p. 358.
128. "the feeling of helplessness . . .": Orwell, p. 388.
128. "We must assume . . .": Churchill, *Alliance,* p. 123.
129. "By some ludicrous . . .": Monsarrat, p. 250.
130. "in the next . . .": ibid., p. 261.
130. "The food had gone . . .": ibid., p. 262.
130. "and then a huge sheet . . .": ibid., p. 265.
131. "the usual rubbish . . .": ibid., p. 267.
131. "a foretaste of the very . . .": ibid., p. 268.
132. "Her smooth dark head . . .": Bloch, *Windsor's War,* p. 182.
133. "Chicago's South Side . . .": Winslow, *Miller,* p. 53.
133. "America is no place . . .": ibid., p. 54.
133. "the most memorable . . .": Henreid, p. 102.
134. "my head is bursting . . .": Bartók, *Letters,* p. 292.
134. "for instance . . .": ibid., p. 293.
134. "We were piano-played . . .": ibid., p. 301.
134. "human beings ruminating . . .": ibid., p. 292.
135. "never known a man . . .": St-Exupéry, *Writings,* pp. 57–58.
135. "You who are . . .": ibid., pp. 47–48.
135. "We seem to be . . .": *SUN,* Feb. 2.
135. "more waste . . .": A. Lindbergh, p. 170.
135. "a profound compassion . . .": ibid., p. 169.
136. "MOVE OVER . . .": *T.,* Feb. 24.
136. "the tools to keep on fighting . . .": ibid.
136. "Oh Franklin Roosevelt . . .": Klein, *Guthrie,* pp. 191–92.
137. "You Maggots . . .": Cole, pp. 106–9.
137. "members of the . . .": Klurfeld, *Winchell,* pp. 89–90.
137. "you don't shoot the soldiers . . .": ibid., p. 90.
137. "He stalks through . . .": Grafton, *Diary,* pp. 115–16.
138. "the Ace Power . . .": Vandenberg, *Papers,* pp. 9–10.
138. "My country is . . .": *T.,* March 3.
138. "The American people . . .": R. N. Smith, *Uncommon,* p. 295.

139. "I do not believe . . .": *SUN,* Feb. 6.
140. "the revolutionary anti-Christian . . .": Conant, *Memoirs,* pp. 232–33.
140. "On the basis of . . .": Burns, *Roosevelt,* p. 49.
141. "It would be pertinent . . .": *T.,* March 10.
141. "I had the feeling . . .": Vandenberg, pp. 9–11.
141. "Now that the bill . . .": *NYT,* March 12.
141. "This is a big victory . . .": Maisky, p. 133.
141. "The stuff was coming . . .": Churchill, *Alliance,* p. 128.
142. "Hitler has at last . . .": *T.,* March 24.
142. "an exceedingly . . .": Ickes, *Diary,* p. 459.
142. "A blustering . . .": Goebbels, p. 269.
143. "Everyone who was in the room . . .": Clapper, *Watching,* p. 269.
143. "huge, wealthy . . .": *NYT,* March 8.
144. "tyranny, aggression . . .": ibid.
144. "There is no point . . .": Goebbels, p. 269.
144. "No power and no support . . .": *T.,* March 24.
144. "I couldn't let . . .": *SUN,* Jan. 19.
145. "on suspicion of espionage . . .": *NYT,* March 16.
145. "The USA . . .": Goebbels, p. 269.
145. "resistance, reluctance . . .": Blum, ed. p. 412.
146. "We know that . . .": *T.,* March 10.
146. "Some friends of labor . . .": Clapper, p. 218.
147. "If the NLRB orders . . .": *T.,* March 17.
147. "labor-union organizers . . .": ibid.
147. "It would be . . .": Clapper, p. 223.
148. "To say it . . .": *T.,* March 17.
149. "I don't know whether I . . .": R. Miller, *Truman,* p. 354.
149. "He did not want to embarrass . . .": M. Truman, *Bess,* pp. 198–99.
150. "The dirt he turned up . . .": ibid., p. 199.
151. "Europe's national pastime . . .": W. Mead, *Browns,* p. 9.
151. "Every club would be . . .": Goldstein, *Spartan,* p. 5.
152. "Everyone gets frightened . . .": W. Mead, p. 25.
152. "It was embarrassing . . .": Allen, *Where Have You,* p. 111.
152. "Just say he was the . . .": ibid., pp. 94–95.
153. "Joe would sit . . .": ibid., pp. 112–13.
153. "He was just never a guy . . .": ibid., p. 117.
154. "a child with a . . .": Golenbock, *Bums,* p. 24.
154. "to turn Brooklyn . . .": ibid., p. 31.
155. "Some of the players . . .": *NY,* July 12.
156. "oddballs, night riders . . .": Durocher, *Nice Guys,* p. 165.
156. "that he literally . . .": ibid., p. 143.
157. "like Edgar Bergen . . .": ibid., p. 170.
158. "A curious sea side . . .": Woolf, p. 359. The entry is not from the date of her death.
158. "This windy corner. . . .": ibid.
158. "Every beautiful thing . . .": *T.,* April 14.
158. "We were in London . . .": Woolf, p. 353.
159. "something scented . . .": ibid., p. 357.
159. "Oh dear yes . . .": ibid., p. 358.

159. "Dearest . . .": N. Nicolson, ed., *Woolf Letters,* pp. 486–47.
159. "I simply can't take it in . . .": H. Nicolson, p. 207.
159. "In this hour . . .": Sandburg, *Memo,* p. 54.
161. "He stated that Yugoslavia . . .": A. Brown, *Donovan,* p. 157.
162. "Jugs are signing . . .": Cadogan, p. 366.
162. "Continue to pester . . .": Churchill, *Alliance,* p. 161.
163. "Listen, girl . . .": *T.,* April 7.
163. "Mobs of people were running . . .": Djilas, *Memoirs,* pp. 370–71.
163. "Early this morning . . .": Churchill, *Alliance,* p. 168.
164. "The whole country . . .": Colville, p. 368.
164. "It is pathetic . . .": Goebbels, p. 287.
164. "At this moment . . .": *NYT,* March 31.
164. "I have decided to . . .": Heckmann, *Rommel's War,* p. 104.
164. "Now I intend . . .": Toland, *Hitler,* p. 893.
164. "Politically it is especially . . .": Churchill, *Alliance,* pp. 163–64.
165. "It is the best thing . . .": Goebbels, p. 295.
165. "They are clutching . . .": ibid., p. 299.
166. "The hours pass . . .": ibid., pp. 301–2.
166. "Soldiers of the Southeastern Front . . .": *T.,* April 14.
166. "But then we heard a . . .": Djilas, p. 381.
167. "It was a . . .": Reiss, ed., *They Were There,* pp. 295–96.
167. "as bombs whistled down . . .": ibid., p. 296.
167. "Fleets of planes . . .": Djilas, pp. 381–82.
168. "as if it were . . .": ibid., p. 382.
168. "I can't take . . .": Hohne, *Canaris,* p. 448.
169. "You must remember . . .": Churchill, *Alliance,* p. 223.
169. "Germany's early successes . . .": *T.,* April 21.
170. "the city looked small . . .": Djilas, p. 386.
171. "A grim prospect . . .": Churchill, *Alliance,* p. 224.

PART THREE: THE SPRING

175. "Ernest was at the ball park . . .": Golenbock, p. 51.
176. "a hell of a thing . . .": Meyers, *Hemingway,* p. 360.
176. "At present, the food . . .": W. White, ed., *By-Line,* p. 306.
176. "The snakes are dead . . .": ibid., p. 307.
176. "terraced, gray . . .": ibid., p. 335.
176. "Anyone who says . . .": ibid., pp. 330–31.
177. "the gentlemanly collusion . . .": Davies, p. 220.
177. "the one really good man . . .": Meyers, p. 360.
178. "Chou En-lai was, along with . . .": T. H. White, p. 118.
178. "a slim, thin-faced . . .": Suyin, pp. 220–21.
179. "In the present stage . . .": Duiker, *Vietnam,* p. 256.
179. "The hour has struck . . .": Lacouture, *Ho,* p. 77.
180. "One of my great passions . . .": *LT,* March 27.
180. "a pleasant little man . . .": Cassidy, *Dateline,* p. 8.
180. "On the point of Mr. Matsuoka's . . .": *Foreign Relations, IV,* p. 238.
181. "It is my America . . .": Toland, *Rising Sun,* p. 73.
181. "Now I have some leisure . . .": *T.,* March 24.

182. "The people's welcome . . .": Goebbels, pp. 282–83.
182. "the Japanese nation is with you . . .": *NYT*, March 27.
182. "It is in our interest . . .": Feis, *Pearl Harbor*, p. 180.
183. "it must be the aim . . .": ibid., p. 183.
183. "Japan must take steps . . .": ibid.
183. "the weight of the Japanese navy . . .": Kimball, ed., *Correspondence*, pp. 129–30.
183. "Germany was in the final . . .": Churchill, *Alliance*, pp. 82–86.
183. "If Japan got into . . .": Feis, p. 184.
183. "at the present moment he could . . .": ibid., p. 185.
184. "the hypocrisy of an American . . .": Toland, *Rising Sun*, p. 86.
184. "Banzai for his Majesty . . .": ibid., p. 75.
185. "Every time I have seen . . .": Cassidy, p. 8.
186. "The reason England's . . .": Toland, *Rising Sun*, p. 75.
186. "Ah . . . ha . . .": Reiss, ed., *They Were There*, p. 305.
186. "There is nothing to fear . . .": Toland, *Rising Sun*, p. 76.
186. "You are an Asiatic . . .": Reiss, ed., *They Were There*, p. 306.
186. "the best way to solve . . .": *Foreign Relations, IV*, p. 74.
187. "the removal of suspicion . . .": ibid., p. 79.
187. "we want nothing . . .": *LT*, April 15.
187. "In his official capacity . . .": Davies, p. 210.
187. "his temperament and all . . .": Israel, ed., p. 139.
187. "a composed and tweedy . . .": Davies, p. 211.
188. "The first fundamental . . .": *Foreign Relations, IV*, pp. 22–23.
189. "I am skeptical whether . . .": ibid., p. 25.
189. "He was tall . . .": Feis, p. 172.
189. "I am going to the United States . . .": *SUN*, Feb. 1.
191. "Two ladders were being built . . .": Feis, p. 161.
192. "I cannot agree to this . . .": Toland, *Rising Sun*, p. 84.
192. "Very few rays of hope . . .": Feis, p. 199.
192. "Everything is going hellward . . .": ibid., p. 201.
192. "He expresses his honest . . .": *Foreign Relations, IV*, pp. 236–38.
193. "Japan's foreign policy . . .": ibid., p. 231.
193. "do our very best . . .": Prange, *At Dawn*, p. 16.
194. "Still free but for how long . . .": Archer, *Journal*, p. 162.
194. "One hundred and twenty . . .": Colville, p. 367.
194. "of almost pure jam . . .": Panter-Downes, p. 141.
195. "The Italians . . .": Cunningham, p. 332.
195. "The tearing up . . .": Colville, p. 369.
195. "pacing—or rather tripping . . .": ibid., pp. 369–70.
195. "obsessed by this wild desire . . .": *T.*, March 24.
196. "a political and financial oligarchy . . .": *NYT*, Feb. 24.
196. "a voluptuous habit . . .": *NYT*, Feb. 22.
197. "The Germans come in . . .": *NY*, May 17.
197. "Black days for our . . .": Goebbels, p. 291.
197. "Oh, all right . . .": *LT*, April 29.
198. "With our fingers . . .": Archer, p. 167.
198. "a blast of ungodly sound . . .": ibid., pp. 165–66.
199. "The last thing we heard . . .": *NYT*, April 14.

200. "We begin to realize . . .": Archer, p. 177.
200. "Every road was blitzed . . .": Moorehead, p. 146.
200. "where on earth . . .": Archer, pp. 170–71.
200. "Rome and Athens . . .": Goebbels, pp. 304–5.
201. "Thinking always of our army . . .": Orwell, pp. 390–91.
201. "I have to admit . . .": Churchill, *Alliance*, pp. 202–3.
201. "I do not think . . .": ibid., p. 198.
202. "speed is the one thing . . .": Liddell Hart, ed., *Rommel Papers*, p. 104.
202. "the gateway . . .": Churchill, *Alliance*, pp. 196, 200.
202. "Spent our first day . . .": Liddell Hart, ed., p. 106.
202. "I presume you are only . . .": Churchill, *Alliance*, p. 202.
202. "It was a chance . . .": Liddell Hart, ed., p. 109.
203. "exploded over Cyrenaica . . .": Lewin, *Afrika*, p. 43.
203. "One cannot permit unique . . .": ibid., p. 46.
203. "It seems most desirable . . .": Churchill, *Alliance*, p. 204.
203. "apparently intended . . .": Liddell Hart, ed., p. 109.
203. "Far more important . . .": Churchill, *Alliance*, pp. 205–6.
204. "You will understand . . .": Liddell Hart, ed., p. 111.
204. "You should surely . . .": Churchill, *Alliance*, p. 207.
204. "I hope, Jack . . .": Eden, p. 279.
204. "we are, of course . . .": Churchill, *Alliance*, p. 210.
204. "Wavell has 400,000 . . .": Jackson, p. 111.
204. "Egypt is the base . . .": Eden, p. 277.
204. "every day the German Air Force . . .": Churchill, *Alliance*, p. 229.
205. "to stop all sea-borne traffic . . .": ibid., p. 211.
205. "I was beginning to feel . . .": Cunningham, pp. 348–49.
205. "Tobruk's defences . . .": Liddell Hart, ed., p. 123.
205. "Rommel has not sent us . . .": Halder, p. 885.
206. "broken up his units . . .": ibid., p. 907.
206. "By overstepping his orders . . .": ibid., p. 915.
206. "One of the reasons . . .": Lewin, *Afrika*, p. 50.
207. "There will be no surrender . . .": Heckmann, p. 69.
207. "They learned to make . . .": Moorehead, p. 142.
207. "Bravo, Tobruk . . .": Churchill, *Alliance*, p. 211.
207. "Victory in Libya . . .": ibid., p. 227.
208. "For two days I have been bombed . . .": Terraine, p. 333.
208. "Roads clear as far as . . .": Halder, vol. VI, p. 77.
209. "Throughout these operations . . .": *T.*, May 12.
209. "We have paid our debt . . .": R. Higham, pp. 231–32.
210. "Wars are not won . . .": *T.*, May 5.
210. "Evacuation going fairly well . . .": Cadogan, p. 374.
210. "You are listening . . .": *LT*, April 28.
210. "Well, let them come . . .": Archer, p. 194.
211. "The streets are filled . . .": ibid., p. 203.
213. "Nazi successes . . .": *NY*, April 20.
213. "worse gloom than I have ever . . .": Colville, p. 382.
214. "one of the most famous . . .": *LT*, May 5.
214. "In London they are being . . .": Goebbels, p. 317.
214. "In particular, people seem . . .": Colville, p. 377.

215. "Our ostriches . . .": *NYT*, April 16.
215. "Bunk merchants . . .": *T.*, May 12.
215. "This is no diversion . . .": *T.*, April 28.
215. "in the manner of someone . . .": Panter-Downes, p. 143.
215. "Let us expel the . . .": *NYT*, April 16.
215. "When things go wrong . . .": Panter-Downes, p. 147.
215. "in a time of adversity . . .": *T.*, May 7.
215. "It is surprising . . .": Bryant, *Tide*, p. 201.
216. "He sees all events . . .": Harris, *Attlee*, p. 192.
216. "an appallingly bad speech . . .": R. James, ed., *Channon*, p. 303.
216. "Mr. Churchill . . .": *LT*, May 7.
216. "Savage attacks . . .": Goebbels, p. 323.
216. "to kick inefficiency . . .": Panter-Downes, p. 147.
217. "in Greece 70 to 80 . . .": *NWK*, July 21.
217. "It is a strange thing . . .": *NYT*, March 18.
217. "It don't do . . .": *T.*, March 31.
218. "Commanding officers . . .": Parton, *Eaker*, p. 122–3.
219. "the advertising columns . . .": Panter-Downes, p. 139.
219. "This is something which . . .": Lee, p. 243.
219. "The people in the Air Force . . .": ibid.
220. "Work on any picture . . .": *NWK*, July 7.
220. "Bury them in the . . .": Clark, p. 19.
220. "We started looking . . .": Fonteyn, *Autobiography*, p. 80.
220. "There is no question . . .": Lee, p. 243.
220. "But what good . . .": Griffin, *Lewis*, p. 193.
221. "A year ago . . .": Orwell, *Diary*, p. 393.
221. "I've never been hungry . . .": Griffin, pp. 193–94.
221. "When all is said . . .": *T.*, April 28.
221. "We must try . . .": Churchill, *Alliance*, p. 128.
221. "If you cannot . . .": Kimball, ed., pp. 140–41.
222. "I suppose it is . . .": Hodgson, *Few Eggs*, p. 139.
222. "It was so high . . .": Longford, *Shore*, p. 206.
222. "we will give it to them . . .": *NYT*, April 13.
222. "They have such . . .": Harriman, p. 30.
222. "Scarcely a house . . .": Colville, p. 381.
223. "I've never seen . . .": ibid., p. 382.
223. "Blind fatalism . . .": Panter-Downes, p. 144.
223. "I could not help . . .": Lee, p. 244.
223. "It is a curious feeling . . .": *NYT*, May 12.
224. "It was dark enough . . .": Lee, p. 271.
225. "One cannot comment . . .": Hodgson, pp. 150–51.
226. "The heirs of Nelson . . .": Orwell and Angus, eds., *My Country*, pp. 109, 105.
226. "all that the country . . .": H. Nicolson, p. 207.
227. "The first thing . . .": Cassidy, p. 19.
228. "Of all the major states . . .": R. Medvedev, *Khrushchev*, p. 29.
228. "Maintain the entire . . .": *NYT*, Feb. 24.
228. "expanding enormously . . .": ibid.
229. "The Russian 'mass' is *no* . . .": Bialer, *Stalin*, p. 130.
229. "a mass of badly . . .": Virski, *My Life*, p. 71.

230. "The Red Army will win . . .": Bialer, p. 61.
230. "Nazi Germany will not . . .": Zhukov, *Memoirs,* p. 211.
230. "Stalin was the greatest . . .": ibid.
231. "that blending of grit . . .": Trotsky, *Stalin,* pp. 1, xv.
231. "The number of victims . . .": Kennan, *Russia,* p. 242.
232. "For days and nights . . .": Begin, p. 145.
232. "The reward . . .": ibid., p. 179.
232. "Moscow had the appearance . . .": Caldwell, *All-Out,* pp. 18–19.
234. "it occurred to me . . .": Lewin, *Ultra,* p. 109.
234. "Up till the end of March . . .": Churchill, *Alliance,* p. 354.
234. "illuminated the whole . . .": ibid., p. 357.
235. "War is mainly a catalogue . . .": ibid., p. 353.
235. "This information is an . . .": Garlinski, *Enigma,* p. 112.
236. "When one really gets hold . . .": Kahn, p. 447.
236. "Communism is an enormous danger . . .": Halder, p. 846.
237. "This war will be very different . . .": ibid., p. 847.
237. "I do not expect . . .": Payne, p. 419.
237. "Nothing in the world . . .": Shirer, *Reich,* p. 831.
237. "With regard to *offenses* . . .": ibid. (emphasis in original)
237. "Any attempt to save . . .": ibid., p. 833.
237. "The German armies . . .": Hohne, p. 449.
237. "My dear Canaris . . .": ibid., p. 450.
238. "an evening light of . . .": Manvell and Fraenkel, *Hess,* p. 97.
238. "I had never asked . . .": ibid., p. 99.
240. "I do not know if you . . .": Douglas-Hamilton, *Motive,* p. 158.
241. "succeeded for several days . . .": *NY,* May 17.
242. "an inarticulate, almost . . .": Lang, pp. 154–55.
242. "The Fuehrer is absolutely . . .": Goebbels, pp. 364–65.
242. "If only he would . . .": Lang, pp. 154–55.
242. "As far as it is . . .": Flannery, pp. 270–71.
243. "a tremendous blow . . .": Ciano, p. 351.
243. "That our government . . .": Vassiltchikov, *Diaries,* p. 52.
244. "How many happy . . .": Goebbels, p. 311.
244. "I had not . . .": Vaughan, *von Karajan,* p. 126.
246. "These he finds . . .": ibid., p. 343.
246. "Napoleon died at . . .": *T.,* April 28.
247. "The Hemingway syndrome . . .": Galbraith, *Memoirs,* p. 106.
247. "there wasn't a chance . . .": Ickes, p. 467.
248. "like a boiled owl . . .": ibid., p. 469.
248. "one split second . . .": *NYT,* March 28.
248. "Congress and public opinion . . .": Clapper, p. 221.
249. "We are, overnight . . .": Grafton, p. 93.
249. "Staggering . . .": *T.,* April 28.
249. "we all have to expect . . .": R. Miller, p. 354.
250. DOGS AND SOLDIERS . . . : R. N. Smith, *Dewey,* pp. 336–38.
250. "those Southern bellies . . .": ibid.
250. "Our officers appreciated . . .": *T.,* May 19.
250. "Making the Best . . .": Buell, *King,* p. 136.
251. "either people are confused . . .": C. Lindbergh, p. 478.

251. "We do not wish to fight . . .": Blum, ed., pp. 406–7.
251. "It made me think . . .": C. Lindbergh, p. 474.
251. "There *are* wars worth fighting . . .": ibid., pp. 478–79.
252. "a man of honour . . .": Goebbels, pp. 322, 381, 341.
252. " 'the bit in its teeth' . . .": C. Lindbergh, p. 481.
252. "I then said that I felt . . .": Bullitt, ed., *Correspondence*, p. 512.
252. "England's strength . . .": Harriman, p. 31.
252. "In every direction . . .": Ickes, p. 511.
252. "the country was sadly . . .": ibid., p. 513.
254. "This year it'll be . . .": *SUN*, Feb. 3.
254. "sitting still as a . . .": Red Smith, *Friends,* p. 86.
254. "There was a curious . . .": ibid.
254. "What he did to those horses . . .": ibid., p. 87.
254. " 'Johnny,' Arcaro called . . .": ibid.
255. "He's the runnin'est . . .": *T.,* May 12.
255. "You can throw all . . .": *NY,* May 17.
255. "He wasn't the greatest . . .": Red Smith, p. 87.
255. "I wish I knew . . .": Sandburg, *Memo,* p. 53.
255. "The weight of his burden . . .": *T.,* May 12.
256. "I care not . . .": ibid.
256. "the remark that I heard . . .": Bullitt, ed., p. 520.
256. "The simple truth . . .": *T.,* April 28.
256. "In this tremendous time . . .": ibid.
257. "without another day's . . .": *T.,* May 12.
257. "The President obviously . . .": Harriman, p. 19.
257. "I am waiting to be . . .": Burns, pp. 91–92.
257. "I think some of you . . .": Roosevelt, *Conferences, vol. 17,* p. 286.
258. "He can't bring himself . . .": Ickes, p. 538.
258. "had no plans . . .": Burns, p. 91.
258. "Hitler must be defeated . . .": Churchill, *Alliance,* pp. 137–38.
259. "This was the first time . . .": R. Clark, *Bomb,* p. 121.
259. "Luridest field of . . .": *T.,* May 26.
262. "young vultures . . .": Archer, p. 217.
263. "The battle is most strange . . .": ibid., p. 219.
264. "every ring on the telephone . . .": Cunningham, p. 372.
264. "I felt I ought to be . . .": Ziegler, *Mountbatten,* p. 144.
264. "Stick it out . . .": Cunningham, p. 373.
264. "What do you think we build . . .": Colville, pp. 389, 391.
264. "It is not the fear of . . .": Cunningham, pp. 375–76.
265. "This battle must have looked . . .": Lee, p. 284.
265. "giant beings who emerged from caves . . .": Archer, pp. 218–19.
265. "Of course we'll take . . .": ibid., pp. 219–20.
265. "Crete battle must be won . . .": Churchill, *Alliance,* p. 293.
266. "The first indication . . .": Waugh, *Diaries,* p. 499.
266. "I regret to have to . . .": Churchill, *Alliance,* p. 295.
266. "Victory in Crete essential . . .": ibid.
266. "Despondent troops . . .": Waugh, p. 503.
266. "After a while . . .": Reiss, ed., *They Were There,* p. 302.
266. "As night fell . . .": Waugh, p. 505.

267. "We wearily turned . . .": Cunningham, pp. 378–79.
267. "nervy and unreasonable . . .": Eden, p. 283.
267. "the pride of the Navy . . .": Churchill, *Alliance*, p. 306.
268. "Almost immediately . . .": Grenfell, p. 52.
268. "Hell of a battle . . .": Harriman, pp. 33–34.
268. "Have we got her . . .": Churchill, *Alliance*, p. 309.
268. "Poor *Hood* . . .": Eden, p. 282.
269. "We did not intend . . .": Bradford, p. 204.
269. "What the devil's . . .": Grenfell, p. 135.
271. "We are all . . .": *NYT*, May 28.
271. "Perhaps some miracle . . .": *NY*, June 7.
271. "Urgent . . .": Lewin, *Ultra*, p. 202.
271. "Aircraft approached us . . .": Grenfell, p. 205.
271. "The whole of Germany . . .": ibid., p. 206.
272. "Get closer . . .": ibid., p. 185.
272. "She was a terrible sight . . .": Bradford, p. 207.
272. "Severe as are the wounds . . .": *LT*, May 28.
272. "Such is the innate . . .": H. Nicolson, p. 211.
272. "I venture to intervene . . .": *NYT*, May 28.
272. "Still the British Navy . . .": *NYT*, May 28.
272. "a bright gleam . . .": Dalton, *Diary*, p. 216.
272. "The House cheered . . .": R. James, ed., *Channon*, p. 307.
273. "very haggard and drawn . . .": Lee, p. 294.
273. "Units became divided . . .": Moorehead, p. 161.
273. "Aircraft . . .": Waugh, p. 508.
273. "At about 10 o'clock . . .": ibid., p. 509.
274. "On all sides . . .": R. James, ed., *Channon*, p. 307.
274. "vivid and fiery . . .": Lee, p. 285.
275. "the British . . .": ibid.
275. "The drama of the Balkan . . .": Maisky, p. 130.
276. "On such-and-such a date . . .": ibid., pp. 148–49.
276. "vast masses of Nazi troops . . .": ibid., p. 149.
276. "huge German concentrations . . .": R. James, ed., *Channon*, pp. 307–8.
277. "a handful of cables . . .": Lee, p. 312.
277. "to smash Russian . . .": Eden, p. 311.
277. "In spite of the evident . . .": Maisky, p. 150, and Cassidy, p. 16.
277. "You propose . . .": Zhukov, p. 230.
277. "He couldn't stand . . .": Khrushchev, *Remembers*, p. 167.
277. "I didn't like . . .": ibid., p. 166.
277. "But perhaps . . .": Zhukov, p. 32.
279. "Billy Conn is a nice . . .": *SUN*, June 17.
279. "There is one point . . .": ibid.
280. "Looks like . . .": ibid., Feb. 1.
280. "Louis has never been . . .": ibid., Jan. 17.
280. "every Negro boy . . .": C. Mead, *Champion*, p. 197.
280. "The fists of Joe Louis . . .": ibid., p. 185.
280. "the concentrated essence . . .": ibid., p. 197.
281. "Black eye peas . . .": ibid., p. 203.
281. "I'm going to eat all . . .": *SUN*, Jan. 17.

282. "like a baseball bat . . .": *NYT,* June 19.
283. "I didn't have so much . . .": *T.,* June 30.
283. "As the thirteenth round opened . . .": *SUN,* June 19.
284. "I'm very proud . . .": *NYT,* June 19.
284. "hadda Jewish head instead of . . .": C. Mead, p. 181.
284. "His dream was over . . .": *SUN,* June 19.

PART FOUR: THE SUMMER

287. "a Wagnerian blast . . .": J.P. Davies, Jr., p. 215.
287. "You have only . . .": Payne, p. 429.
288. "Whatever may come . . .": Shirer, *Reich,* p. 851.
289. "The Fuehrer seems . . .": Goebbels, p. 423.
289. "Do you understand me . . .": Zhukov, pp. 235–36.
289. "Heavy bombing . . .": Salisbury, *900 Days,* p. 50.
289. "It is war . . .": Toland, *Hitler,* p. 920.
290. "Without any claim . . .": Cassidy, pp. 41–42.
290. "crowds grouped silently . . .": Caldwell, p. 20.
290. "everywhere there were scenes . . .": Reiss, ed., *They Were There,* p. 307.
290. "Tell the B.B.C. . . .": Churchill, *Alliance,* p. 371.
291. "The Prime Minister's . . .": Eden, p. 312.
291. "I have only one purpose . . .": Churchill, *Alliance,* p. 370.
291. "I suppose they will be . . .": ibid.
291. "I knew that we all . . .": ibid.
291. "Mr. Churchill listened . . .": A. Taylor, p. 475.
291. "I have taken occasion . . .": R. James, ed. *Speeches,* pp. 6428–31.
292. "This does not mean very much . . .": Lee, p. 316.
292. "any defense against . . .": *T.,* June 30.
293. "it would be just like him . . .": Ickes, p. 549.
293. "Many people in the . . .": Israel, ed., p. 208.
293. "The entry of Communist Russia . . .": Cole, p. 85.
293. "I would a hundred times . . .": ibid.
293. "That call to sacrifice . . .": R. N. Smith, *Hoover,* p. 299, and *NWK,* July 7.
293. "conceive of American boys . . .": *NWK,* July 7.
293. "as untrustworthy . . .": Ferrell, ed., *Dear Bess* p. 471.
294. "Oh, I think that . . .": F.D. Roosevelt, pp. 408–9.
294. "I expect little . . .": Blum, ed., p. 407.
294. "The enemy was surprised . . .": Halder, p. 162.
294. "The Russians were . . .": H. K. Smith, p. 74.
294. "it was quiet . . .": Grade, *Memoir,* p. 245.
295. "In a few weeks . . .": Payne, p. 431.
295. "particularly the great clouds . . .": Shirer, *Reich,* p. 855.
295. "All that Lenin . . .": Salisbury, *900 Days,* p. 80.
295. "On the fifth . . .": R. Medvedev, p. 32.
296. "Certainly in the midst . . .": Rhodes, *The Vatican,* p. 258.
296. "Comrades, citizens . . .": Cassidy, pp. 62–63.
296. "The enemy is cruel . . .": Grey, *Stalin,* p. 330.
297. "The bloodsoaked murderers . . .": Caldwell, p. 97.
297. "The bend of the Dnieper . . .": *NWK,* Sept. 1.

298. "I saw Stalin . . .": R. Medvedev, p. 33.
299. "We do not want to conquer . . .": Calic, *Heydrich*, p. 241.
299. "the police surrounded . . .": ibid., p. 240.
300. "Enemy planes often circled . . .": Nestyev, *Prokofiev*, p. 327.
301. "Never in wartime Spain . . .": Cassidy, p. 85.
302. "It is no use recriminating . . .": Colville, p. 431.
302. "harassed and struggling . . .": Churchill, *Alliance*, p. 379.
302. "Molotov will tell us . . .": Colville, p. 408.
302. "I was well aware . . .": Churchill, *Alliance*, p. 386.
302. "We are all very glad . . .": ibid., pp. 380–81.
303. "Immediately . . .": Cassidy, p. 67.
303. "to make hell while . . .": Colville, p. 406.
303. "I beg you however . . .": Churchill, *Alliance*, pp. 384–85.
303. "seem convinced that their . . .": Colville, p. 418.
303. "The Navy suffer from . . .": Harvey, *Diaries*, p. 17.
304. "There was never such idleness . . .": Burgess, p. 256.
304. "The world-shaking din . . .": Panter-Downes, p. 158.
304. "The war has taken . . .": Bloch, p. 199.
304. "He is confident . . .": Dalton, *Diary*, p. 274.
304. "The war situation . . .": Hyde, ed., *Shaw*, pp. 145–46.
305. "I realized soon after . . .": Shirer, *Reich*, p. 855.
306. "The battle is harder . . .": Macksey, *Guderian*, p. 142.
306. "It is becoming ever clearer . . .": Shirer, *Reich*, p. 855.
307. "little items . . .": H. K. Smith, pp. 99, 101–2.
307. "Look at the eyes . . .": Bierman, *Gentile*, p. 12.
307. "three hundred and fifty . . .": Hassell, p. 207.
307. "In their immense vanity . . .": Reck-Malleczewen, *Diary*, p. 122.
307. "It's all over now . . .": Bethge, p. 639.
307. "If you want to know . . .": ibid., p. 648.
308. "my generals know nothing . . .": Macksey, p. 147.
308. "The most important . . .": Shirer, *Reich*, p. 857.
309. "Where Columbus succeeded . . .": Lyon, *Brecht*, p. 27.
309. "In almost no other . . .": ibid., p. 33.
310. "The intellectual isolation . . .": ibid., p. 38.
310. "It's just one of those . . .": D. Robinson, *Chaplin*, p. 510.
311. "For seven-eighths . . .": Capra, *Name*, p. 304.
312. "What our film . . .": ibid., p. 305.
312. "Cooper is a fine man . . .": Hemingway, *Letters*, p. 518.
312. "couldn't run . . .": Swindell, *Hero*, pp. 238–39.
313. "sort of a little . . .": Hemingway, *Letters*, pp. 528–29.
314. "simple, deeply religious . . .": *NWK*, July 14.
314. "directed toward [Robinson] . . .": Behlmer, *Inside*, p. 149.
314. "I strongly feel that . . .": ibid., p. 151.
314. "Bogie was a . . .": Huston, *Book*, p. 79.
315. "He's a tough guy . . .": Hyams, *Bogie*, p. 74.
315. "I came very well prepared . . .": Huston, pp. 78–82.
315. "He was perfect . . .": ibid., p. 79.
316. "face that seems to have . . .": Nolan, *Hammett*, p. 180.
316. "Something new has . . .": *NY*, May 17.

316. "the most sensational product . . .": *T.*, March 17.
316. "few movies have ever . . .": Leaming, p. 215.
316. "People were too scared . . .": ibid., p. 216.
317. "longing for a female creature . . .": *NY*, July 19.
317. "It is apparent . . .": C. Higham, *Lucy,* pp. 62–63.
318. "overworked, overmedicated . . .": Edwards, *Garland,* p. 75.
319. "there could be no hint . . .": Huston, p. 83.
319. "before this picture . . .": Behlmer, pp. 136–39.
321. "From what I saw . . .": Capra, p. 311.
321. "Affairs are frankly . . .": *NWK*, Sept. 1.
322. "A great many observers . . .": ibid.
322. "I can see we haven't . . .": ibid.
322. "We grow more like the . . .": Grafton, p. 122.
322. "We are building . . .": *NWK*, Sept. 8.
323. "The citizen who has been . . .": *NWK*, June 16.
323. "summer always seems to . . .": Coward, *Future,* p. 140.
323. "Mrs. Roosevelt seems terribly . . .": Dow, pp. 135, 138.
324. "I feel very strongly . . .": Burns, p. 124.
325. "We are faced with the . . .": *T.*, May 12.
326. "Time counts . . .": *NWK*, July 28.
326. "any man who closes his eyes . . .": ibid.
327. "they have not been . . .": C. Lindbergh, p. 513.
327. "a case of bad . . .": ibid.
327. "If morale is poor . . .": *NWK*, Sept. 1.
328. "Two-fifths of our people . . .": W. Johnson, ed., *White,* p. 433.
329. "That's when . . .": Allen, *Where Have,* p. 99.
329. "He didn't seem . . .": ibid., p. 109.
329. "Joe was probably . . .": ibid., p. 108.
329. "I was able to . . .": ibid., p. 102.
329. "Well, how do you feel . . .": De Gregorio, *DiMaggio,* p. 98.
330. "he was so happy . . .": Honig, *America,* pp. 240–41.
331. "All I want out of life . . .": Connor, *Baseball,* p. 3.
331. "He looks no more . . .": *NWK*, July 21.
331. "And here I am . . .": *T.*, June 16.
336. "Franklin loved . . .": E. Roosevelt, *Remember,* p. 226.
336. "a strange sense of leisure . . .": Churchill, *Alliance,* p. 429.
336. "To some of my . . .": Buell, p. 139.
337. "We also would not . . .": Churchill, *Alliance,* p. 436.
338. "Unless we proposed concrete . . .": Pruessen, *Road,* p. 194.
338. "Many Britons seemed to feel . . .": Panter-Downes, p. 164.
338. "the most astounding . . .": ibid.
338. "a scrap of paper . . .": *NWK*, Aug. 25.
338. "it is as plain . . .": *NWK*, Sept. 1.
339. "It's a dark picture . . .": *NWK*, July 28.
339. "Why aren't there . . .": *NY*, Aug. 16.

PART FIVE: THE AUTUMN

344. "In carrying out the . . .": Feis, p. 216.
345. "Japan is now in a position . . .": *NWK*, Aug. 4.
345. "The Japanese Navy . . .": Grafton, p. 95.
346. "Japan cannot retreat . . .": *NWK*, Aug. 11.
346. "under such circumstances . . .": Toland, *Rising Sun*, p. 99.
346. "From now on . . .": Feis, p. 244.
346. "It indicates a determination . . .": *Foreign Relations, IV*, p. 382.
347. "the invitation to the President . . .": Feis, p. 259.
347. "Nothing will stop them . . .": ibid., p. 248.
347. "no settlement with Japan . . .": *NWK*, Sept. 3.
347. "subtle half promises . . .": Utley, *War*, p. 170.
347. "If the Japanese Government . . .": *Foreign Relations, IV*, p. 378.
348. "With each day we will get . . .": Toland, *Rising Sun*, p. 108.
348. "a patient with an illness . . .": Mosley, *Hirohito*, p. 215.
348. "If this fails we must . . .": Toland, *Rising Sun*, p. 109.
348. "I am sorry the Supreme Command . . .": ibid., p. 113.
349. "While there is little free . . .": *Foreign Relations, IV*, p. 408.
350. "the best defended . . .": Prange, *Dawn*, p. 97.
350. "surprised and somewhat . . .": Brereton, *Diaries*, pp. 12–13.
351. "can neither make good . . .": Dower, p. 102.
351. "For twenty years . . .": Feis, p. 263.
351. "By December our operational . . .": MacArthur, *Reminiscences*, p. 110.
352. "The raids have almost . . .": *NYT*, Aug. 13.
352. "It took more than a week . . .": Suyin, p. 222.
352. "had even dyed their hair . . .": ibid., p. 224.
353. "It means defeat of Japan . . .": Utley, p. 161.
353. "the whole nation should . . .": *NWK*, Oct. 27.
354. "the chances of our . . .": *NWK*, Nov. 17.
354. "we may not be heading . . .": Lee, p. 428.
354. "war between the . . .": Feis, p. 302.
354. "The Administration is prepared . . .": *NWK*, Nov. 17.
354. "Maybe I will not . . .": Brereton, p. 24.
355. "Kano said solemnly . . .": Lee, p. 453.
355. "After that things are . . .": Utley, p. 174.
355. "kick the whole thing . . .": ibid., p. 173.
355. "I have washed my hands . . .": ibid.
355. "negotiations with Japan . . .": Brereton, p. 33.
356. "the Administration, and the . . .": Cole, p. 193.
356. "even in far-off . . .": *NWK*, Dec. 8.
356. "Both sides will continue . . .": Reiss, ed., *They Were There*, p. 395.
356. "I am proud to report . . .": *NYT*, Dec. 7.
357. "At night, the dunes . . .": Camus, p. 196.
357. "the naked bodies . . .": Lottmann, *Camus*, p. 240.
357. "one of the few . . .": Camus, p. 193.
357. "like a sheet of . . .": McCarthy, *Camus*, p. 170.
357. "I am just about . . .": ibid.
357. "We are not . . .": Camus, p. 199.
358. "One must have a short . . .": Bree and Bernaver, eds., p. 237.

359. "Never before, I realized . . .": de Beauvoir, p. 398.
359. "One finishes by shrivelling up . . .": McCarthy, *Céline,* p. 185.
359. "It isn't that Paris . . .": Richardson, *Colette,* p. 182.
359. "No one talks in the . . .": Colette, p. 115.
359. "France is full of . . .": ibid.
359. "the enforced obscurity . . .": ibid., pp. 115–16.
360. "the 'scrap' replaces . . .": ibid., p. 173.
360. "a sort of treasure hunt . . .": de Beauvoir, p. 399.
360. "Avoid the mirror . . .": Colette, p. 187.
360. "hailing them like very dear . . .": de Beauvoir, p. 392.
361. "I have a noose . . .": H.J. Taylor, *Time,* p. 190.
361. "It is no longer a question . . .": *T.,* May 26.
361. "Vichy is in a . . .": Kimball, ed., p. 139.
362. "have refused for centuries . . .": Marraus and Paxson, p. 99.
362. "Germans are always more . . .": *T.,* May 26.
362. "Dealing with Darlan . . .": Kimball, ed., p. 134.
363. "The first and overpowering . . .": H. J. Taylor, p. 196.
363. "so many other Frenchmen . . .": Bree and Bernauer, eds., p. 64.
363. "from the very start . . .": Bidault, *Resistance,* p. 3.
363. "absolute orgies of plotting . . .": ibid., p. 17.
364. "First, from August 23 . . .": Chambard, p. 25.
364. "Make the Boche . . .": Riess, ed., *They Were There,* p. 85.
364. "A stream of blood . . .": *NWK,* Nov. 3.
365. "To German officers . . .": Chambard, p. 27.
365. "the acts of desperate men . . .": *NWK,* Nov. 3.
365. "but a foretaste . . .": ibid.
365. "dangerously incompetent . . .": Ledwidge, *De Gaulle,* p. 88.
365. "whatever good qualities . . .": Fraser, p. 190.
365. "The grandeur and force . . .": Ledwidge, p. 98.
366. "to get in other people's . . .": H. J. Taylor, p. 197.
366. "And here came I . . .": de Gaulle, p. 172.
366. "Sooner or later . . .": ibid.
366. "the dessicated vitality . . .": Segre, *Fortunate,* p. 111.
367. *"Two* things are certain . . .": Dayan, *Life,* p. 71.
367. "England is afraid . . .": Ledwidge, p. 99.
368. "General de Gaulle . . .": ibid., p. 108.
368. "the partisans . . .": Bidault, p. 19.
368. "The British radio . . .": ibid., pp. 21–22.
370. "The atmosphere was quiet . . .": Rosenman, *Roosevelt,* p. 292.
370. "beginning tomorrow . . .": *NWK,* Sept. 22.
371. "the three most important . . .": *NWK,* Sept. 22, and A. Lindbergh, p. 222.
371. "He will be branded . . .": A. Lindbergh, pp. 220–23.
373. "turning 17,000 theaters . . .": *NWK,* Sept. 22.
373. "If Warner Brothers . . .": Behlmer, pp. 190–91.
373. "We are in the midst . . .": Ferrell, ed., pp. 467–68.
374. "sending masses of troops . . .": *NWK,* Oct. 13.
374. "they have one compelling . . .": ibid.
375. "keep your head down . . .": *NWK,* Nov. 24.
375. "It might jump off . . .": *NY,* Oct. 14.

376. "I don't think the use . . .": Blum, ed., p. 408.
376. "would not end . . .": Churchill, *Alliance,* pp. 421–22.
376. "I was astonished . . .": ibid., p. 422.
376. "the British cannot . . .": Lee, p. 336.
376. "The Chiefs of Staff . . .": A. Taylor, p. 495.
377. "I sometimes think . . .": Fraser, p. 194.
377. "This ought to serve . . .": Kimball, ed., p. 163.
377. "we believe that if . . .": Terraine, p. 291.
377. "The devotion and gallantry . . .": ibid., p. 288.
378. "All that we have learned . . .": ibid., p. 295.
378. "We cannot afford losses . . .": ibid., p. 461.
378. "These long, strangely quiet . . .": Panter-Downes, pp. 176–77.
379. "The political system . . .": A. Taylor, p. 494.
379. "like a keeper . . .": Churchill, *Alliance,* p. 513.
379. "It was a lovely dinner . . .": H. Nicolson, p. 217.
379. "the most beautiful autumn . . .": Ludington, *Dos Passos,* p. 408.
379. "If you take a walk . . .": Panter-Downes, p. 176.
380. "may be settled . . .": ibid., p. 183.
380. "What difference does it make . . .": Jackson, p. 183.
380. "one of the most confusing . . .": Terraine, p. 359.
380. "In brief, the peculiarities . . .": Jackson, p. 154.
380. "by their sheer amateurism . . .": Terraine, p. 356.
381. "in the worst manner . . .": ibid., p. 358.
381. "This is a question . . .": *NWK,* Nov. 17.
381. "It's always good to see you . . .": Farago, *Seal,* p. 342.
381. "During these days . . .": Douglas, *Court,* p. 273.
383. "I remember only . . .": Kennan, *Memoirs,* p. 134.
383. "The harvest was good . . .": Medvedev, *Gorbachev,* pp. 49–50.
383. "You must stop . . .": Grey, p. 334.
384. "you'd better give up . . .": Khrushchev, p. 168.
384. "Seven thousand of the mines . . .": *NWK,* Nov. 3.
385. "Life goes on . . .": Sollertinsky, *Pages,* p. 101.
386. "It's not about . . .": Shostakovich, *Testimony,* p. 156.
386. "Each day, eight to ten . . .": Inber, *Diary* pp. 37–38.
387. "Encircle them . . .": Shirer, *Reich,* p. 859.
387. "Tanks burst into flame . . .": Caldwell, pp. 49–50.
388. "This is gray, gloomy . . .": *NWK,* Oct. 6.
388. "an operation of . . .": *NYT,* Oct. 4.
389. "He convinced us . . .": Engelmann, p. 249.
389. "The response was . . .": Reiss, ed., *They Were There,* pp. 317–18.
390. "Cosmetics disappeared . . .": H. K. Smith, pp. 126–27.
390. "the coming of weeks . . .": *NWK,* Nov. 10.
390. "British lies get into the blood . . .": *NWK,* Sept. 8.
390. "The fight has become a fight . . .": *NWK,* Nov. 17.
390. "Should anyone among us . . .": H. K. Smith, p. 80.
391. "Almost all maintained . . .": Trunk, *Responses,* p. 11.
391. "We were taken . . .": ibid., pp. 106–7.
393. "Here I am . . .": Begin, p. 202.
393. "We went into the boat . . .": ibid., pp. 202–3.

394. "The enemy has seized . . .": *NWK*, Nov. 17, and Grey, p. 338.
394. "The infantryman . . .": Shirer, *Reich*, p. 860.
394. "We shall never forget . . .": *NWK*, Nov. 24.
395. "The tanks could barely . . .": Engelmann, p. 252.
395. "Our own troops . . .": Halder, p. 205.
395. "Only he who saw . . .": Shirer, *Reich*, p. 862.
395. "a state of extreme . . .": Halder, p. 193.
395. "his strength was at . . .": Shirer, *Reich*, p. 864.
397. "I hadn't had a . . .": Durocher, p. 151.
399. "You want to play . . .": Connor, p. 167.
399. "Ain't I the best . . .": ibid., p. 166.
399. "The Yankee club is . . .": *NWK*, Sept. 17.
399. "Little prayer for the . . .": *NYT*, Oct. 2.
400. "If you turned . . .": ibid., Oct. 5.
400. "They look like someone . . .": ibid.
400. "I went home sick . . .": Golenbock, p. 72.
401. "There was ease . . .": *NYT*, Oct. 6.
401. "everything I had . . .": ibid.
402. "It couldn't, perhaps . . .": ibid.
402. "It was all my fault . . .": ibid.
402. "the counter-puncher . . .": *NWK*, Sept. 15.
404. "It's been a grand . . .": Clapper, p. 275.
406. "we are going to fight . . .": Hoopes, *Cain*, p. 314.
406. "If anyone asks the children . . .": Hemingway, *Letters*, p. 525.
408. "I'm the bee . . .": *NY*, Nov. 1.
409. "Soldiers on the train . . .": A. Lindbergh, pp. 232, 239–40.
409. "The magic skin . . .": *NY*, Nov. 29.
410. "a soldier beau . . .": *NY*, Nov. 22.
410. "Now we see the distant fire . . .": Clapper, pp. 275–76.

PART SIX: THE LOST ISLAND

414. "It was a dead sound . . .": *NYT*, Dec. 22.
416. "What does this mean . . .": Reiss, ed., *They Were There*, p. 396.
416. "This can't be true . . .": Prange, p. 527.
417. "Mr. President . . .": Reiss, ed., *They Were There*, p. 398.
417. "I must say that in all . . .": Prange, p. 554.
417. "Attention . . .": A. Brown, p. 3.
417. "It's no use . . .": Gallagher, *Ford*, p. 203.
418. "The Japs have attacked . . .": *NWK*, Dec. 15.
418. "Litvinov asked me . . .": *Foreign Relations, IV*, pp. 730–31.
418. "the Prime Minister . . .": Harriman, pp. 111–12.
419. "Mr. President . . .": Churchill, *Alliance*, p. 605.
419. "I could not conceal . . .": Eden, p. 331.
419. "The Japanese have bombed . . .": H. Nicolson, p. 219.
419. "Nine o'clock news . . .": Dalton, *Diary*, p. 331.
419. "The war is over . . .": Ledwidge, p. 128.
419. "In event of war . . .": Bradley, p. 103.
420. "Listening to the . . .": A. Lindbergh, pp. 239–41.

420. "How did the Japs . . .": C. Lindbergh, p. 560.
420. "No way of forgetting . . .": Ludington, p. 412.
420. "Well, it's a . . .": R. N. Smith, *Dewey*, p. 340.
420. "some sense . . .": Coffey, *LeMay*, p. 9.
420. "The Japs have attacked . . .": Parton, p. 126.
420. "I had a curious reaction . . .": Salisbury, *Journey*, p. 152.
421. "I fiddled with my . . .": M. Truman, p. 207.
421. "stayed there for the rest . . .": Houseman, *Run-Through*, p. 485.
421. "My main concern . . .": Basie, *Blues*, pp. 252–3.
421. "Had nothing else . . .": W. Mead, p. 32.
422. "December 7, 1941, screwed up . . .": ibid., p. 34.
422. "magnates kept slipping . . .": Red Smith, p. 85.
422. "They were announcing . . .": Honig, p. 243.
422. "and played the . . .": Suyin, pp. 235–36.
423. "This is suicide . . .": Clapper, p. 287.
423. "We had considered the possibility . . .": Shirer, *Reich*, p. 893.
423. "He is so happy . . .": Ciano, p. 416.
423. "a roll of drums . . .": Terraine, p. 416.
424. "We cannot lose . . .": Toland, *Hitler*, p. 951.
424. "The America First . . .": Cole, p. 193.
425. "It wasn't much . . .": M. Berle, *Milton*, p. 226.
425. "the political sentiment . . .": A. Berle, *Navigating*, p. 384.
425. "itching to beat the . . .": Dower, p. 242.
426. "While I was burning papers . . .": Bohlen, pp. 112–13.
426. "This may be easier . . .": Grew, p. 496.
429. "Through our . . .": Hemingway, *Letters*, p. 532.

PART SEVEN: THE WINTER

433. "The cold is so . . .": *NYT*, Dec. 8.
433. "From that point the road . . .": Cassidy, pp. 195–96.
434. "millionaire and Jewish . . .": Engelmann, p. 254.
434. "First he incites . . .": Toland, *Hitler*, p. 953.
435. "Whoever intends to escape . . .": H. K. Smith, pp. 80–81.
435. "cross between a cloister . . .": Payne, p. 433.
435. "For sheer mass misery . . .": Panter-Downes, p. 185.
436. "a wave of gloom . . .": James, ed., *Channon*, p. 314.
436. "I have a feeling that our nerves . . .": H. Nicolson, p. 220.
436. "unless there is a . . .": Reiss, *Underground*, p. 103.
437. "In exposing all these . . .": *NWK*, Oct. 13.
437. "You would not . . .": Reiss, *Underground*, pp. 221–22.
437. "You on the home front . . .": ibid., p. 185.
438. "All Europe . . .": ibid., pp. 232–33.
438. "when the thorough and . . .": Sarde, *Colette*, p. 418.
438. "I love nothing . . .": ibid., p. 419.
439. "A fission bomb of . . .": Conant, p. 281.
439. "The possibility must be . . .": Compton, *Quest*, p. 59.
439. "do everything possible . . .": ibid., p. 63.
440. "I am not at all sure . . .": Sayen, *Einstein*, p. 148.

440. "We shall begin to win . . .": Grafton, p. 144.
440. "We were safe enough . . .": *NY,* Dec. 20.
441. "Read it and weep . . .": Clapper, p. 288.
441. "Too many Americans . . .": *NWK,* Dec. 22.
443. "It will be a long time . . .": D. James, *MacArthur,* p. 51.
443. "Knox should have been . . .": Hemingway, p. 531.
444. "nothing was ready . . .": Buell, p. 154.
446. "The General Situation . . .": Hoyt, *How They Won,* p. 21.
446. "The danger to . . .": ibid., pp. 22–23.
446. "It must have been . . .": Holbrook, *None More,* p. 143.
447. "First air raid alarm . . .": *NWK,* Dec. 22.
448. "Blackout! Air raid . . .": *NWK,* Jan. 5, 1942.
448. "If we're going to sleep . . .": *NY,* Dec. 27.
448. "I feel as if all I believed . . .": A. Lindbergh, p. 242.
449. "The war has only . . .": *NYT,* Jan. 1, 1942.
449. "What will we do? . . .": *NWK,* Nov. 17.
450. "still harder battles . . .": *NYT,* Jan. 1, 1942.
450. "Frenchmen! . . .": ibid.
451. "We're not doing . . .": Fraser, p. 236.
451. "Let the children . . .": C. Wilson, pp. 12–13.
451. "It is good for Winston . . .": ibid., p. 14.
451. "I am glad I went . . .": ibid.
451. "Christmas must give way . . .": *NWK,* Jan. 5, 1942.
452. "He had been like a schoolboy . . .": C. Wilson, p. 15.

Select Bibliography

There is so much published material available on the events of the year 1941 that the following list of approximately four hundred volumes can do little more than scratch the surface. Nevertheless, I wanted to express my appreciation to the authors of all these books, which were most helpful to me in writing my own study. For those intrepid readers who wish to learn more about any of the incidents or personalities discussed herein, I should also provide a few words of guidance and warning.

There is more good literature about Great Britain than any of the other participants in the war. Churchill's multivolume study of *The Second World War* is an essential source, although it tends to be surprisingly tedious when read straight through in large gulps. I found the diaries of Alexander Cadogan, Jock Colville, Hugh Dalton, and Chips Channon (even with—or perhaps because of—Channon's tendency to gossip) to be both fascinating and valuable for behind-the-scenes glimpses of Parliament and the Churchill government. George Orwell's relevant volume of collected essays, *My Country: Right or Left,* contains a remarkable number of enlightening revelations about British society and politics in the late 1930s and early 1940s. For two firsthand American views of Britain during 1941, see Mollie Panter-Downes' collected articles for the *New Yorker,* assembled in *London War Notes,* and General Raymond Lee's *London Journal.*

For sheer volume of material, more appears to have been written about Nazi Germany than any other topic in history. Unfortunately, it is not all of sterling quality. Goebbels' diaries—even though they cover only a few of the war years—are invaluable as a relatively candid guide to the propaganda chief's thoughts. I found John Toland's biography of Hitler to be very helpful, and Robert Payne's study of the Fuehrer helped fill in some of the gaps. Harry Flannery, who was Bill Shirer's replacement as the CBS radio correspondent in Berlin, provides a useful eyewitness account of life in the Third Reich in *Assignment to Berlin;* Howard K. Smith's *Last Train from Berlin* is also helpful, but Smith too often allows his quite natural and marked distaste for Nazism to mar his reporter's objectivity.

Toland's *The Rising Sun* provides an excellent introduction to events in Japan in 1941, although it is occasionally disconcerting to encounter discussions of Japanese politicians translated into colloquial or overly melodramatic English. John Dower's psychological study of Japanese and American perceptions of one another is an exceptionally wise and wonderful work, and highly recommended for anyone who wishes to gain further understanding into the bitterness that accompanied the war in the Pacific. Ambassador Joseph Grew's diaries are both revealing and entertaining.

There is no single satisfactory account of the war on the eastern front, doubtless because the subject is simply too large and too complex for one volume. Readers have the choice of drowning in endless accounts of battlefield maneuvers all along the thousand-mile front, or else focusing on one theater at a time. Furthermore, Russian and German sources do not agree on where particular divisions were at any specific time; that is, if one used German sources to plot the movement of the armies in September 1941, and then employed Russian sources to trace troop movements during the same month on the same map, one would obtain two quite different sets of results. Nevertheless, Adam Ulam's biography of Stalin gives an excellent overview of the subject, and Albert Seaton's *The Battle for Moscow* and John Erickson's *The Road to Stalingrad* are two of the best military histories of Operation Barbarossa and its aftermath.

The best biography of Franklin D. Roosevelt remains James MacGregor Burns's two-volume study, *The Lion and the Fox* and *The Soldier of Freedom,* the latter of which includes the events of 1941. Secretary of the Interior Harold Ickes' diary is both acerbic and enlightening. For the isolationist point of view, the diaries of both Anne and Charles Lindbergh (especially the former) provide a valuable glimpse into the sort of mind-set that steadfastly opposed American intervention in Europe. Although Raymond Clapper is virtually unknown today, his newspaper column was quite influential in 1941, and remains a source of considerable wisdom.

On the North African campaigns, please see the studies by W. G. F. Jackson and Wolf Heckman, as well as Alan Moorehead's eyewitness account. Laird Archer and Robin Higham are most helpful on the campaign in Greece. I sincerely hope that no one is ever going to write more about Pearl Harbor than Gordon Prange did in *At Dawn We Slept;* we could, however, use a volume which is written with a more graceful touch.

•

Ackroyd, Peter. *T. S. Eliot: A Life.* New York: Simon and Schuster, 1984.
Allen, Maury. *Where Have You Gone, Joe DiMaggio?* New York: Dutton, 1975.
Archer, Laird. *Balkan Journal.* New York: Norton, 1944.
Arnaz, Desi. *A Book.* New York: Morrow, 1976.
Baker, William J. *Jesse Owens: An American Life.* New York: Free Press, 1986.
Baldwin, Hanson. *The Crucial Years: 1939–1941.* New York: Harper & Row, 1976.
Balfour, Neil, and Sally Mackay. *Paul of Yugoslavia: Britain's Maligned Friend.* London: Hamish Hamilton, 1980.
Bartók, Béla. *Letters,* ed. by Iános Deméney. New York: St. Martin's, 1971.
Basie, Count. *Good Morning Blues: The Autobiography of Count Basie.* As told to Albert Murray. New York: Random House, 1985.
Bauman, Janina. *Winter in the Morning: A Young Girl's Life in the Warsaw Ghetto and Beyond, 1939–1945.* New York: Free Press, 1986.
Beauvoir, Simone de. *The Prime of Life.* New York: Harper & Row, 1962.
Begin, Menachem. *White Nights: The Story of a Prisoner in Russia.* New York: Harper & Brothers, 1957.
Behlmer, Rudy, ed. *Inside Warner Brothers: 1935–1951.* New York: Viking, 1985.

Benchley, Nathaniel. *Humphrey Bogart.* Boston: Little, Brown, 1975.

Bergman, Ingrid, and Alan Burgess. *Ingrid Bergman: My Story.* New York: Delacorte, 1980.

Bergreen, Laurence. *James Agee: A Life.* New York: Dutton, 1984.

Berkow, Ira. *Red: A Biography of Red Smith.* New York: Times Books, 1986.

Berle, Adolf A. *Navigating the Rapids, 1918–1971,* ed. by Beatrice Berle and Travis Beal Jacobs. New York: Harcourt Brace Jovanovich, 1973.

Berle, Milton, with Haskel Frankel. *Milton Berle: An Autobiography.* New York: Delacorte, 1974.

Berteaut, Simone. *Piaf.* New York: Harper & Row, 1972.

Beschloss, Michael R. *Kennedy and Roosevelt: The Uneasy Alliance.* New York: Harper & Row, 1980.

Bethge, Eberhard. *Dietrich Bonhoeffer.* New York: Harper & Row, 1970.

Bialer, Seweryn, ed. *Stalin and His Generals.* New York: Pegasus, 1969.

Bidault, Georges. *Resistance: The Political Autobiography of George Bidault.* New York: Praeger, 1967.

Bierman, John. *Righteous Gentile.* New York: Viking, 1981.

Bloch, Michael. *The Duke of Windsor's War.* New York: Coward McCann, 1983.

Bloom, Claire. *Limelight and After: The Education of an Actress.* New York: Harper & Row, 1982.

Blotner, Joseph. *Faulkner: A Biography.* New York: Random House, 1974.

———, ed. *Selected Letters of William Faulkner.* New York: Random House, 1977.

Blum, John Morton, ed. *Public Philosopher: Selected Letters of Walter Lippmann.* New York: Ticknor & Fields, 1985.

Boelcke, Willi, ed. *The Secret Conferences of Dr. Goebbels.* New York: Dutton, 1970.

Bohlen, Charles E. *Witness to History: 1929–1969.* New York: Norton, 1973.

Bokun, Branko. *Spy in the Vatican, 1941–1945.* New York: Praeger, 1973.

Bradford, Ernle. *The Mighty Hood.* New York: World Publishing, 1959.

Bradley, Omar, and Clay Blair. *A General's Life: An Autobiography.* New York: Simon and Schuster, 1983.

Bree, Germaine, and George Bernauer, eds. *Defeat and Beyond.* New York: Pantheon, 1970.

Brereton, Lewis H. *Diaries.* New York: Morrow, 1946.

Brown, Anthony Cave. *The Last Hero: Wild Bill Donovan.* New York: Times Books, 1982.

Brown, Frederick. *An Impersonation of Angels: A Biography of Jean Cocteau.* New York: Viking, 1968.

Brown, Jared. *The Fabulous Lunts: A Biography of Alfred Lunt and Lynn Fontanne.* New York: Atheneum, 1986.

Browne, Courtney. *Tojo: The Last Banzai.* New York: Holt, Rinehart & Winston, 1967.

Bryant, Arthur. *The Turn of the Tide.* Garden City, N.Y.: Doubleday, 1957.

Bryer, Jackson R., ed. *Conversations with Lillian Hellman.* Jackson: University Press of Mississippi, 1986.

Buell, Thomas B. *Master of Sea Power: A Biography of Fleet Admiral Ernest J. King.* Boston: Little, Brown, 1980.

Bull, Hadley, ed. *The Challenge of the Third Reich.* Oxford: Clarendon Press, 1986.

Bullitt, Orville H., ed. *For the President, Personal and Secret: Correspondence Between Franklin D. Roosevelt and William C. Bullitt.* Boston: Houghton Mifflin, 1972.

Burgess, Anthony. *Little Wilson and Big God.* New York: Weidenfeld & Nicolson, 1986.

Burns, James MacGregor. *Roosevelt: The Soldier of Freedom.* New York: Harcourt Brace Jovanovich, 1970.

Cadogan, Sir Alexander. *The Diaries of Sir Alexander Cadogan, 1938–1945,* ed. by David Dilks. London: Cassell, 1971.

Cagney, James. *Cagney by Cagney.* Garden City, N.Y.: Doubleday, 1976.

Caldwell, Erskine. *All-Out on the Road to Smolensk.* New York: Duell, Sloan & Pearce, 1942.

Calic, Edouard. *Reinhard Heydrich.* New York: Morrow, 1982.

Camus, Albert. *Notebooks, 1935–1942.* New York: Knopf, 1963.

Capra, Frank. *The Name Above the Title: An Autobiography.* New York: Macmillan, 1971.

Caro, Robert A. *The Years of Lyndon Johnson: The Path to Power.* New York: Knopf, 1982.

Carpenter, Humphrey. *W. H. Auden: A Biography.* London: George Allen and Unwin, 1981.

Cassidy, Henry C. *Moscow Dateline: 1941–1943.* Boston: Houghton Mifflin, 1943.

Cerf, Bennett. *At Random: The Reminiscences of Bennett Cerf.* New York: Random House [naturally], 1977.

Chambard, Claude. *The Maquis: A History of the French Resistance Movement.* Indianapolis: Bobbs-Merrill, 1976.

Chandler, Alfred D., Jr., ed. *The Papers of Dwight David Eisenhower: The War Years: Vol. I.* Baltimore: Johns Hopkins University Press, 1970.

Chaplin, Charles Spencer. *My Autobiography.* New York: Simon and Schuster, 1964.

Charles-Roux, Edmonde. *Chanel.* New York: Knopf, 1975.

Chennault, Anna. *The Education of Anna.* New York: Times Books, 1980.

Chennault, Claire. *Way of a Fighter: The Memoirs of Claire Lee Chennault,* ed. by Robert Hotz. New York: G. P. Putnam's Sons, 1949.

Christie, Agatha. *An Autobiography.* New York: Dodd, Mead, 1977.

Churchill, Winston Spencer. *The Second World War: Vol. II: Their Finest Hour.* Boston: Houghton Mifflin, 1949.

———. *The Second World War: Vol. III: The Grand Alliance.* Boston: Houghton Mifflin, 1950.

Ciano, Galeazzo. *Diary,* ed. by Malcolm Muggeridge. London: William Heinemann, 1947.

Clapper, Raymond. *Watching the World.* New York: McGraw-Hill, 1944.

Clark, Kenneth. *The Other Half: A Self-Portrait.* New York: Harper & Row, 1977.

Clark, Ronald. *The Birth of the Bomb.* London: Phoenix House, 1961.

Coffey, Thomas M. *Iron Eagle: The Turbulent Life of General Curtis LeMay.* New York: Crown, 1986.

Cole, Wayne S. *America First.* Madison: University of Wisconsin Press, 1953.

Colette. *Looking Backwards.* Bloomington: Indiana University Press, 1975.

Collier, James Lincoln. *Louis Armstrong: An American Genius.* New York: Oxford University Press, 1983.

Collier, Peter, and David Horowitz. *The Kennedys: An American Drama.* New York: Summit, 1984.

Colville, John. *The Fringes of Power: 10 Downing Street Diaries, 1939–1955.* New York: Norton, 1985.

Compton, Arthur H. *Atomic Quest: A Personal Narrative.* New York: Oxford University Press, 1956.

Conant, James B. *My Several Lives: Memoirs of a Social Inventor.* New York: Harper & Row, 1970.

Connally, Thomas, as told to Alfred Steinberg. *My Name Is Tom Connally.* New York: Thomas Y. Crowell, 1954.

Connor, Anthony J. *Baseball for the Love of It.* New York: Macmillan, 1982.

Cook, Bruce. *Brecht in Exile.* New York: Holt, Rinehart & Winston, 1982.

Coward, Noel. *Future Indefinite.* London: William Heinemann, 1954.

———. *The Noel Coward Diaries,* ed. by Graham Payn and Sheridan Morley. Boston: Little, Brown, 1982.

Crawford, Deborah. *Lise Meitner, Atomic Pioneer.* New York: Crown, 1969.

Creamer, Robert W. *Babe: The Legend Comes to Life.* New York: Simon and Schuster, 1974.

Crosland, Margaret. *Piaf.* New York: Putnam, 1985.

Crozier, Brian. *De Gaulle.* New York: Scribner's, 1973.

Crozier, Brian, and Eric Chou. *The Man Who Lost China.* New York: Scribner's, 1976.

Cunningham, Andrew Browne. *A Sailor's Odyssey.* New York: Dutton, 1951.

Dalton, Hugh. *The Fateful Years: Memoirs, 1931–1945.* London: Frederick Muller, 1957.

———. *The Second World War Diary of Hugh Dalton, 1940–45.* London: Jonathan Cape, 1986.

Daniel, Clifton. *Lords, Ladies, and Gentlemen: A Memoir.* New York: Arbor House, 1984.

Davies, John Paton, Jr. *Dragon by the Tail.* New York: Norton, 1972.

Davies, Marion. *The Times We Had.* Indianapolis: Bobbs-Merrill, 1975.

Dawidowicz, Lucy S. *The War Against the Jews, 1933–1945.* New York: Holt, Rinehart & Winston, 1975.

Dayan, Moshe. *Moshe Dayan: The Story of My Life.* New York: Morrow, 1976.

Dedijer, Vladimir. *Tito.* New York: Simon and Schuster, 1953.

de Gaulle, Charles. *The War Memoirs of Charles de Gaulle: The Call to Honour, 1940–1942.* New York: Simon and Schuster, 1955.

De Gregorio, George. *Joe DiMaggio: An Informal Biography.* New York: Stein & Day, 1981.

Deighton, Len. *Fighter: The True Story of the Battle of Britain.* London: Jonathan Cape, 1977.

Djilas, Milovan. *Memoir of a Revolutionary.* New York: Harcourt Brace Jovanovich, 1973.

Dobroszycki, Lucjan, ed. *The Chronicle of the Lodz Ghetto, 1941–1944.* New Haven: Yale University Press, 1984.

Doenitz, Karl. *Memoirs.* Cleveland: World Publishing, 1959.

Donaldson, Frances. *P. G. Wodehouse: A Biography.* New York: Knopf, 1982.

Douglas, Helen Gahagan. *A Full Life.* Garden City, N.Y.: Doubleday, 1982.

Douglas, William O. *The Court Years: 1939–1975.* New York: Random House, 1977.

Douglas-Hamilton, James. *Motive for a Mission.* London: Macmillan, 1971.

Dower, John W. *War Without Mercy: Race and Power in the Pacific War.* New York: Pantheon, 1986.

Duiker, William J. *The Rise of Nationalism in Vietnam.* Ithaca: Cornell University Press, 1976.

Dulles, Eleanor. *Eleanor Lansing Dulles: Chances of a Lifetime: A Memoir.* Englewood Cliffs, N.J.: Prentice-Hall, 1980.

Durocher, Leo, with Ed Linn. *Nice Guys Finish Last.* New York: Simon and Schuster, 1975.

Dutourd, Jean. *The Taxis of the Marne.* New York: Simon and Schuster, 1957.

Eban, Abba. *Abba Eban: An Autobiography.* New York: Random House, 1977.

Eden, Anthony. *Memoirs: The Reckoning.* Boston: Houghton Mifflin, 1965.

Edwards, Anne. *A Remarkable Woman: A Biography of Katharine Hepburn.* New York: Morrow, 1985.

———. *Judy Garland: An Autobiography.* New York: Simon and Schuster, 1974.

Eisenhower, Julie Nixon. *Pat Nixon: The Untold Story.* New York: Simon and Schuster, 1986.

Ellmann, Richard. *James Joyce.* New York: Oxford University Press, 1982.

Engelmann, Bernt. *In Hitler's Germany: Daily Life in the Third Reich.* New York: Pantheon, 1986.

Erickson, John. *The Road to Stalingrad, Vol. 1.* New York: Harper & Row, 1975.

Farago, Ladislas. *The Broken Seal.* New York: Random House, 1967.

Feis, Herbert. *The Road to Pearl Harbor.* Princeton: Princeton University Press, 1950.

Fermi, Laura. *Atoms in the Family.* Chicago: University of Chicago Press, 1954.

Ferrell, Robert H. *Dear Bess: The Letters from Harry to Bess Truman, 1910–1959.* New York: Dutton, 1983.

Field, Andrew. *VN: The Life and Art of Vladimir Nabokov.* New York: Crown, 1986.

Flannery, Harry W. *Assignment to Berlin.* New York: Knopf, 1942.

Flynn, Errol. *My Wicked, Wicked Ways.* New York: Putnam, 1959.

Fonda, Henry, as told to Howard Teichmann. *My Life.* New York: New American Library, 1981.

Fonteyn, Dame Margot. *Autobiography.* New York: Knopf, 1976.

Fourçade, Marie-Madeleine. *Noah's Ark: A Memoir of Struggle and Resistance.* New York: Dutton, 1974.

Fraser, David. *Alanbrooke.* New York: Atheneum, 1982.

Freedland, Michael. *Maurice Chevalier.* New York: Morrow, 1981.

———. *The Warner Brothers.* New York: St. Martin's, 1983.

Freedman, Max, ed. *Roosevelt and Frankfurter: Their Correspondence, 1928–1945.* Boston: Little, Brown, 1967.

Frenay, Henri. *The Night Will End.* New York: McGraw-Hill, 1976.

Foreign Relations of the United States [FRUS], *Vols. I–V.* Washington, D.C.: State Department, 1956–58.

Fugate, Brian. *Operation Barbarossa.* Novato, Calif.: Presidio Press, 1984.

Galbraith, John Kenneth. *A Life in Our Times: Memoirs.* Boston: Houghton Mifflin, 1981.

Gallagher, Tag. *John Ford: The Man and His Films.* Berkeley: University of California Press, 1986.

Gallo, Max. *Mussolini's Italy: Twenty Years of the Fascist Era.* New York: Macmillan, 1964.

Gann, Ernest. *A Hostage to Fortune.* New York: Knopf, 1978.

Garlinski, Jozef. *The Enigma War.* New York: Scribner's, 1979.

Gary, Romaine. *Promise at Dawn.* New York: Harper & Brothers, 1961.

Gervase, Frank. *The Life and Times of Menahem Begin: Rebel to Statesman.* New York: Putnam, 1979.

Gielgud, John. *Gielgud: An Actor and His Time.* New York: Clarkson N. Potter, 1980.

Gisevius, Hans Bernd. *To the Bitter End.* Boston: Houghton Mifflin, 1947.

Goebbels, Joseph. *The Goebbels Diaries: 1939–1941,* ed. by Fred Taylor. New York: Putnam, 1983.

Goldstein, Richard. *Spartan Seasons: How Baseball Survived the Second World War.* New York: Macmillan, 1980.

Golenbock, Peter. *Bums: An Oral History of the Brooklyn Dodgers.* New York: Putnam, 1984.

Gordon, Lyndall. *Virginia Woolf: A Writer's Life.* New York: Norton, 1984.

Goudeket, Maurice. *Close to Colette.* New York: Farrar, Strauss and Cudahy, 1957.

Grade, Chaim. *My Mother's Sabbath Days: A Memoir.* New York: Knopf, 1986.

Graebner, Norman. *Ideas and Diplomacy.* New York: Oxford University Press, 1964.

Grafton, Samuel. *An American Diary.* Garden City, N.Y.: Doubleday, 1943.

Graham, Sheilah. *Hollywood Revisited.* New York: St. Martin's, 1985.

Grenfell, Russell. *The Bismarck Episode.* New York: Macmillan, 1949.

Grew, Joseph C. *Turbulent Era: A Diplomatic Record of Forty Years, 1904–1945, vol. II,* ed. by Walter Johnson. Boston: Little, Brown, 1952.

Grey, Ian. *Stalin: Man of History.* Garden City, N.Y.: Doubleday, 1979.

Griffin, William. *Clive Staples Lewis: A Dramatic Life.* New York: Harper & Row, 1986.

Griffiths, Richard. *Marshal Pétain.* London: Constable, 1970.

Groves, Leslie. *Now It Can Be Told.* New York: Harper & Row, 1962.

Grunberger, Richard. *A Social History of the Third Reich.* London: Weidenfeld & Nicolson, 1971.

Guinness, Alec. *Blessings in Disguise.* New York: Knopf, 1986.

Guthrie, Woody. *Bound for Glory.* New York: Dutton, 1976.

Haldane, R. A. *The Hidden War.* New York: St. Martin's, 1978.

Halder, Franz. *The Halder Diaries: The Private War Journals of Colonel General Franz Halder.* Boulder, Colo.: Westview Press, 1976.

Hane, Mikiso. *Peasants, Rebels & Outcasts: The Underside of Modern Japan.* New York: Pantheon, 1982.

Harriman, W. Averell, and Elie Abel. *Special Envoy to Churchill and Stalin, 1941–1946.* New York: Random House, 1975.

Harris, Kenneth. *Attlee.* New York: Norton, 1982.

Harrison, James Pinckney. *The Endless War: Fifty Years of Struggle in Vietnam.* New York: Free Press, 1982.

Harrison, Tom. *Living Through the Blitz.* London: Collins, 1976.

Harvey, Oliver. *The War Diaries of Oliver Hardy,* ed. by John Harvey. London: Collins, 1978.

Hassell, Ulrich von. *The Von Hassell Diaries, 1938–1944.* Garden City, N.Y.: Doubleday, 1947.

Hayden, Sterling. *Wanderer.* New York: Knopf, 1963.

Hayman, Ronald. *Sartre: A Life.* New York: Simon and Schuster, 1987.

Hecht, Benjamin. *A Child of the Century.* New York: Simon and Schuster, 1954.

Heckman, Wolf. *Rommel's War in Africa.* Garden City, N.Y.: Doubleday, 1981.

Hemingway, Ernest. *Selected Letters, 1917–1961,* ed. by Carlos Baker. New York: Scribner's, 1981.

Henreid, Paul. *Ladies' Man: An Autobiography.* New York: St. Martin's, 1984.

Henrey, Mrs. Robert. *London Under Fire: 1940–45.* London: Dent, 1969.

Higham, Charles. *Errol Flynn: The Untold Story.* Garden City, N.Y.: Doubleday, 1980.

――――. *Lucy: The Real Life of Lucille Ball.* New York: St. Martin's, 1986.

――――. *Trading with the Enemy.* New York: Delacorte, 1983.

――――. *Warner Brothers.* New York: Scribner's, 1975.

Higham, Robin. *Diary of a Disaster: British Aid to Greece, 1940–1941.* Lexington: University Press of Kentucky, 1986.

Hilberg, Raul, Stanislaw Staron, and Josef Kernisz, eds. *The Warsaw Diary of Adam Czerniakow.* New York: Stein & Day, 1979.

Hodgson, Vera. *Few Eggs and No Oranges.* London: D. Dobson, 1976.

Hohne, Heinz. *Canaris: Hitler's Master Spy.* Garden City, N.Y.: Doubleday, 1979.

Holbrook, Stewart H. *None More Courageous.* New York: Macmillan, 1944.

Honig, Donald. *Baseball America.* New York: Macmillan, 1985.

Hoopes, Roy. *Cain: The Biography of James M. Cain.* New York: Holt, Rinehart & Winston, 1982.

Houseman, John. *Run-Through: A Memoir.* New York: Simon and Schuster, 1972.

Hoyt, Edwin P. *How They Won the War in the Pacific.* New York: Weybright and Talley, 1971.

Huston, John. *An Open Book.* New York: Knopf, 1980.

Hutton, J. Bernard. *Hess: The Man and His Mission.* New York: Macmillan, 1970.

Hyams, Joseph. *Bogie: The Biography of Humphrey Bogart.* New York: New American Library, 1966.

Hyde, Mary, ed. *Bernard Shaw and Alfred Douglas: A Correspondence.* New York: Ticknor & Fields, 1982.

Ickes, Harold. *The Secret Diary of Harold L. Ickes, Vol. II.* New York: Simon and Schuster, 1954.

Inber, Vera. *Leningrad Diary.* London: Hutchinson, 1971.

Israel, Fred L., ed. *The War Diary of Breckinridge Long.* Lincoln: University of Nebraska Press, 1966.

Jackson, W. G. F. *The Battle for North Africa, 1940–43.* New York: Mason/Charter, 1975.

James, D. Clayton. *The Years of MacArthur: Vol. II, 1941–1945.* Boston: Houghton Mifflin, 1975.

James, Robert Rhodes, ed. *Chips: The Diaries of Sir Henry Channon.* London: Weidenfeld & Nicolson, 1967.

———. *Churchill: A Study in Failure, 1900–1939.* New York: World Publishing, 1970.

———. *Winston Spencer Churchill: His Complete Speeches, 1897–1963, Vol. VI.* New York: Chelsea House, 1974.

Johnson, David. *The City Ablaze: The Second Great Fire of London, 29th December, 1940.* London: Kimber, 1980.

Johnson, Diane. *Dashiell Hammett: A Life.* New York: Random House, 1983.

Johnson, Walter, ed. *Selected Letters of William Allen White, 1899–1943.* New York: Henry Holt, 1947.

Jones, R. V. *The Wizard War: British Scientific Intelligence, 1939–1945.* New York: Coward, McCann, 1978.

Jungk, Robert. *Brighter Than a Thousand Suns.* New York: Harcourt, Brace, 1958.

Kahn, David. *Hitler's Spies.* New York: Macmillan, 1978.

Keitel, Wilhelm. *In the Service of the Reich.* New York: Stein & Day, 1979.

Kennan, George. *Memoirs, 1925–1950.* Boston: Houghton Mifflin, 1967.

———. *Russia and the West.* New York: New American Library, 1960.

Kennedy, Richard S. *Dreams in the Mirror: A Biography of E. E. Cummings.* New York: Liveright, 1980.

Khrushchev, Nikita. *Khrushchev Remembers.* Boston: Little, Brown, 1970.

Killorin, Joseph, ed. *Selected Letters of Conrad Aiken.* New Haven: Yale University Press, 1978.

Kimball, Warren F., ed. *Churchill & Roosevelt: The Complete Correspondence, Vol. I.* Princeton: Princeton University Press, 1984.

Klein, Joseph. *Woody Guthrie: A Life.* New York: Knopf, 1980.

Kluger, Richard. *The Paper: The Life and Death of the New York Herald Tribune.* New York: Knopf, 1986.

Klurfeld, Herman. *Walter Winchell: His Life and Times.* New York: Praeger, 1976.

Knight, Frida. *The French Resistance: 1940 to 1944.* London: Lawrence and Wishart, 1975.

Knox, MacGregor. *Mussolini Unleashed: 1939–1941.* Cambridge: Cambridge University Press, 1982.

Koehn, Ilse. *Mischling, Second Degree: My Childhood in Nazi Germany.* New York: Greenwillow Books, 1977.

Krause, David, ed. *The Letters of Sean O'Casey, 1910–1941, Vol. I.* New York: Macmillan, 1975.

Lacouture, Jean. *De Gaulle.* New York: New American Library, 1966.

———. *Ho Chi Minh: A Political Biography.* New York: Random House, 1968.

Lang, Jochem von. *The Secretary: Martin Bormann: The Man Who Manipulated Hitler.* New York: Random House, 1979.

Laqueur, Walter, and Richard Breitman. *Breaking the Silence.* New York: Simon and Schuster, 1986.

Larrabee, Eric. *Commander in Chief.* New York: Harper & Row, 1987.

Leaming, Barbara. *Orson Welles: A Biography.* New York: Viking, 1985.

Ledwidge, Bernard. *De Gaulle.* New York: St. Martin's, 1982.

Lee, Raymond E. *London Journal, 1940–1941,* ed. by James Luetze. Boston: Little, Brown, 1971.

Lehman, John, and Derek Parker, eds. *Edith Sitwell: Selected Letters, 1919–1964.* New York: Vanguard, 1970.

Lewin, Ronald. *The American Magic: Codes, Ciphers, and the Defeat of Japan.* New York: Farrar, Straus & Giroux, 1982.

———. *The Life and Death of the Afrika Korps: A Biography.* London: B. T. Batsford, Ltd., 1977.

———. *Ultra Goes to War.* New York: McGraw-Hill, 1978.

Liddell Hart, B. H., ed. *The Rommel Papers.* New York: Harcourt, Brace, 1953.

Lilienthal, David E. *Journals, Vol. I.* Harper & Row, 1964.

Lindbergh, Anne Morrow. *War Within and Without: Diaries and Letters, 1939–1944.* New York: Harcourt Brace Jovanich, 1980.

Lindbergh, Charles. *The Wartime Journals of Charles Lindbergh.* New York: Harcourt Brace Jovanovich, 1970.

Lipstadt, Deborah E. *Beyond Belief: The American Press and the Coming of the Holocaust, 1933–1945.* New York: Free Press, 1986.

Livingston, Jon, Joe Moore, and Felicia Oldfather, eds. *Imperial Japan: 1800–1945.* New York: Pantheon, 1973.

Loewenheim, Francis L., Harold D. Langley, and Manfred Jones, eds. *Roosevelt and Churchill: Their Secret Wartime Correspondence.* New York: Saturday Review Press/E. P. Dutton, 1975.

Longford, Elizabeth. *The Pebbled Shore.* New York: Knopf, 1986.

———. *The Queen: The Life of Elizabeth II.* New York: Knopf, 1983.

Lottman, Herbert R. *Albert Camus.* Garden City, N.Y.: Doubleday, 1979.

Ludington, Townsend. *John Dos Passos: A Twentieth Century Odyssey.* New York: Dutton, 1980.

Lyon, James K. *Bertolt Brecht in America.* Princeton: Princeton University Press, 1980.

McAleer, John. *Rex Stout: A Biography.* Boston: Little, Brown, 1977.

MacArthur, Douglas. *Reminiscences.* New York: McGraw-Hill, 1964.

McCarthy, Patrick. *Camus.* New York: Random House, 1982.

———. *Céline.* New York: Viking, 1975.

McClure, Ruth K., ed. *Eleanor Roosevelt, An Eager Spirit: Selected Letters of Dorothy Dow, 1933–1945.* New York: Norton, 1984.

McCormick, John. *George Santayana: A Biography.* New York: Knopf, 1987.

MacDonald, Charles B. *The Mighty Endeavor.* New York: Oxford University Press, 1969.

Macksey, Kenneth. *Guderian: Creator of the Blitzkrieg.* New York: Stein & Day, 1976.

Macmillan, Harold. *The Blast of War, 1939–1945.* New York: Harper & Row, 1968.

MacShane, Frank. *The Life of Raymond Chandler.* New York: Dutton, 1976.

Maisky, Ivan. *Memoirs of a Soviet Ambassador: The War: 1939–1943.* New York: Scribner's, 1968.

Manchester, William. *American Caesar.* New York: Dell, 1978.

———. *The Glory and the Dream.* Boston: Little, Brown, 1974.

Manvell, Roger, and Heinrich Fraenkel. *Hess: A Biography.* London: MacGibbon & Kee, 1971.

Marrus, Michael R., and Robert O. Paxton. *Vichy France and the Jews.* New York: Basic Books, 1981.

Marx, Arthur. *Goldwyn.* New York: Norton, 1976.

Mead, Chris. *Champion: Joe Louis, Black Hero in White America.* New York: Scribner's, 1985.

Mead, William B. *Even the Browns.* Chicago: Contemporary Books, 1978.

Medvedev, Roy. *Khrushchev.* Garden City, N.Y.: Doubleday, 1983.

Medvedev, Zhores. *Gorbachev.* New York: Norton, 1986.

Merrill, James M. *A Sailor's Admiral: A Biography of William F. Halsey.* New York: Thomas Y. Crowell, 1976.

Meyers, Jeffrey. *Hemingway: A Biography.* New York: Harper & Row, 1985.

Miller, Richard Lawrence. *Truman: The Rise to Power.* New York: McGraw-Hill, 1986.

Monsarrat, Nicholas. *Breaking In, Breaking Out.* New York: Morrow, 1971.

Montgomery, Bernard Law, Viscount. *The Memoirs of Field Marshal the Viscount Montgomery of Alamein.* Cleveland: World Publishing, 1958.

Moorehead, Alan. *The March to Tunis: The North African War, 1940–1943, Vol. I.* New York: Harper & Row, 1967.

Morella, Joe, and Edward Z. Epstein. *Jane Wyman: A Biography.* New York: Delacorte, 1985.

———. *Rita: The Life of Rita Hayworth.* New York: Delacorte, 1983.

Morley, James William, ed. *The Fateful Choice: Japan's Advance into Southeast Asia.* New York: Columbia University Press, 1980.

Mosley, Leonard. *Hirohito: Emperor of Japan.* Englewood Cliffs, N.J.: Prentice-Hall, 1966.

———. *Zanuck: The Rise and Fall of Hollywood's Last Tycoon.* Boston: Little, Brown, 1984.

Muggeridge, Malcolm. *Chronicles of Wasted Time: Chronicle II: The Infernal Grove.* New York: Morrow, 1974.

Murphy, Robert. *Diplomat Among Warriors.* Garden City, N.J.: Doubleday, 1964.

Nestyev, Israel. *Prokofiev.* Stanford: Stanford University Press, 1960.

Nicolson, Harold. *Diaries and Letters, 1930–1964,* ed. by Stanley Olson. New York: Atheneum, 1980.

Nicolson, Nigel, ed. *Leave the Letters Till We're Dead: The Letters of Virginia Woolf, Vol. VI, 1936–1941.* London: Hogarth Press, 1980.

Nolan, William F. *Hammett: A Life at the Edge.* New York: Congdon and Weed, 1983.

Orlow, Dietrich. *The History of the Nazi Party: 1933–1945.* Pittsburgh: University of Pittsburgh Press, 1973.

Orwell, Sonia, and Ian Angus, eds. *Collected Essays, Journalism, and Letters of George Orwell, 1940–1943.* New York: Harcourt, Brace & World, 1968.

Pack, S. W. C. *The Battle for Crete.* Annapolis: Naval Institute, 1972.

Panter-Downes, Mollie. *London War Notes, 1939–1945.* New York: Farrar, Straus & Giroux, 1971.

Parton, James. *"Air Force Spoken Here": General Ira Eaker and the Command of the Air.* Bethesda, Md.: Adler & Adler, 1986.

Paxton, Robert O. *Vichy France.* New York: Knopf, 1972.

Payne, Robert. *The Life and Death of Adolf Hitler.* New York: Praeger, 1973.

Perlmutter, Amos. *The Life and Times of Menachem Begin.* Garden City, N.Y.: Doubleday, 1987.

Phelps, Robert, ed. *Letters from Colette.* New York: Farrar, Straus & Giroux, 1980.

Pitt, Barrie. *The Crucible of War: Western Desert, 1941.* London: Jonathan Cape, 1980.

Prange, Gordon W. *At Dawn We Slept.* New York: Penguin, 1982.

Pruessen, Ronald W. *John Foster Dulles: The Road to Power.* New York: Free Press, 1982.

Pyle, Ernie. *Ernie's War: The Best of Ernie Pyle's World War Two Dispatches,* ed. by David Nichols. New York: Random House, 1986.

Reck-Malleczewen, Friedrich Percyval. *Diary of a Man in Despair.* New York: Macmillan, 1970.

Reiss, Curt, ed. *They Were There: The Story of World War II and How It Came About.* New York, 1944.

———. *Underground Europe.* New York: Dial, 1942.

Rhodes, Anthony. *The Vatican in the Age of the Dictators, 1922–1945.* London: Hodder & Stoughton, 1973.

Rhodes, Richard. *The Making of the Atomic Bomb.* New York: Simon and Schuster, 1986.

Richardson, Joanna. *Colette.* New York: Franklin Watts, 1984.

Robinson, David. *Chaplin: His Life and Art.* New York: McGraw-Hill, 1985.

Robinson, Harlow. *Sergei Prokofiev: A Biography.* New York: Viking, 1987.

Roosevelt, Eleanor. *This I Remember.* New York: Harper & Brothers, 1949.

Roosevelt, Franklin D. *Complete Presidential Press Conferences, Vols. 17–18.* New York: Da Capo, 1972.

Rosenman, Samuel I. *Working with Roosevelt.* New York: Da Capo, 1972.

Saint-Exupéry, Antoine de. *Wartime Writings, 1939–1944.* San Diego: Harcourt Brace Jovanovich, 1986.

Salisbury, Harrison. *A Journey for Our Times.* New York: Harper & Row, 1983.

———. *The 900 Days.* New York: Harper & Row, 1969.

Sandburg, Carl. *Home Front Memo.* New York: Harcourt, Brace, 1942.

———. *Letters of Carl Sandburg.* New York: Harcourt, Brace, 1968.

Sanders, Marion K. *Dorothy Thompson: A Legend in Her Time.* Boston: Houghton Mifflin, 1973.

Sarde, Michele. *Colette: Free and Fettered.* New York: Morrow, 1980.

Saward, Dudley. *Victory Denied: The Rise of Air Power and the Defeat of Germany, 1920–1945.* New York: Franklin Watts, 1987.

Sayen, Jamie. *Einstein in America.* New York: Crown, 1985.

Seaton, Albert. *The Battle for Moscow, 1941–1942.* New York: Stein & Day, 1971.

———. *Stalin as Military Commander.* New York: Praeger, 1976.

Secrest, Meryl. *Kenneth Clark: A Biography.* New York: Holt, Rinehart & Winston, 1984.

Segre, Dan Vittorio. *Memoirs of a Fortunate Jew.* Bethesda: Adler & Adler, 1987.

Seymour-Smith, Martin. *Robert Graves: His Life and Work.* New York: Holt, Rinehart & Winston, 1982.

Sherwood, Robert. *Roosevelt and Hopkins: An Intimate History.* New York: Harper & Brothers, 1950.

Shirer, William. *Berlin Diary.* New York: Knopf, 1941.

———. *The Rise and Fall of the Third Reich.* New York: Simon and Schuster, 1960.

Shostakovich, Dmitri. *Testimony: The Memoirs of Dmitri Shostakovich,* ed. by Solomon Volkov. New York: Harper & Row, 1979.

Smith, Bradley F. *The Shadow Warriors: The O.S.S. and the Origins of the C.I.A.* New York: Basic Books, 1983.

Smith, David C. *H. G. Wells: Desperately Mortal.* New Haven: Yale University Press, 1986.

Smith, Denis Mack. *Mussolini: A Biography.* New York: Knopf, 1982.

Smith, Howard K. *Last Train from Berlin.* New York: Knopf, 1942.

Smith, Red. *To Absent Friends.* New York: Atheneum, 1982.

Smith, Richard Norton. *An Uncommon Man: The Triumph of Herbert Hoover.* New York: Simon and Schuster, 1984.

———. *Thomas E. Dewey and His Times.* New York: Simon and Schuster, 1982.

Soames, Mary. *Clementine Churchill: The Biography of a Marriage.* Boston: Houghton Mifflin, 1979.

Sollertinsky, Dmitri. *Pages from the Life of Dmitri Shostakovich.* New York: Harcourt Brace Jovanovich, 1980.

Spender, Stephen. *The Thirties and After.* New York: Random House, 1967.

Sperber, A. M. *Murrow: His Life and Times.* New York: Freundlich, 1986.

Spoto, Donald. *The Dark Side of Genius: The Life of Alfred Hitchcock.* Boston: Little, Brown, 1983.

———. *The Kindness of Strangers: The Life of Tennessee Williams.* Boston: Little, Brown, 1985.

Stein, Gertrude. *Wars I Have Seen.* London: B. T. Batsford, Ltd., 1945.

Steinbeck, John. *A Life in Letters,* ed. by Elaine Steinbeck and Robert Wallsten. New York: Viking, 1975.

Stevenson, Adlai. *The Papers of Adlai E. Stevenson, Vol. I,* ed. by Walter Johnson. Boston: Little, Brown, 1972.

Stevenson, William. *A Man Called Intrepid.* New York: Ballantine, 1976.

Sugar, Bert Randolph. *The Great Fights.* New York: Gallery Books, 1981.

Suyin, Han. *Birdless Summer.* New York: Putnam, 1968.

Swanberg, W. A. *Citizen Hearst.* New York: Scribner's, 1961.

Swindell, Larry. *Body and Soul: The Story of John Garfield.* New York: Morrow, 1975.

———. *Charles Boyer: The Reluctant Lover.* Garden City, N.Y.: Doubleday, 1983.

———. *Screwball: The Life of Carole Lombard.* New York: Morrow, 1975.

———. *The Last Hero: A Biography of Gary Cooper.* Garden City, N.Y.: Doubleday, 1980.

Taylor, A. J. P. *Beaverbrook: A Biography.* New York: Simon and Schuster, 1972.

Taylor, Henry J. *Time Runs Out.* Garden City, N.Y.: Doubleday, 1942.

Teichmann, Howard. *Smart Aleck: The Wit, World and Life of Alexander Woollcott.* New York: Morrow, 1976.

Terraine, John. *A Time for Courage: The Royal Air Force in the European War, 1939–1945.* New York: Macmillan, 1985.

Thompson, Lawrence, ed. *Selected Letters of Robert Frost.* New York: Holt, Rinehart & Winston, 1964.

Toland, John. *Adolf Hitler.* New York: Ballantine, 1976.

———. *The Rising Sun.* New York: Bantam, 1971.

Tornabene, Lyn. *Long Live the King: A Biography of Clark Gable.* New York: Putnam, 1976.

Trotsky, Leon. *Stalin: An Appraisal of the Man and His Influence.* New York: Stein and Day, 1967

Truman, Margaret. *Bess W. Truman*. New York: Macmillan, 1986.

Trunk, Isaiah. *Jewish Responses to Nazi Persecution*. New York: Stein & Day, 1979.

Ulam, Adam. *Stalin: The Man and His Era*. New York: Viking, 1973.

Utley, Jonathan G. *Going to War with Japan, 1937–1941*. Knoxville: University of Tennessee Press, 1985.

Vandenberg, Arthur H., Jr., ed. *The Private Papers of Senator Vandenberg*. Boston: Houghton Mifflin, 1952.

Vassiltchikov, Marie. *Berlin Diaries, 1940–1945*. New York: Knopf, 1987.

Vaughan, Roger. *Herbert von Karajan*. New York: Norton, 1986.

Virski, Fred. *My Life in the Red Army*. New York: Macmillan, 1949.

Wainwright, Loudon. *The Great American Magazine: An Inside History of "Life."* New York: Knopf, 1986.

Wansell, Geoffrey. *Haunted Idol: The Story of the Real Cary Grant*. New York: Morrow, 1984.

Waugh, Evelyn. *The Diaries of Evelyn Waugh*, ed. by Michael Davie. Boston: Little, Brown, 1976.

Werth, Alexander. *France, 1940–1955*. London: Robert Hale, 1956.

———. *Moscow '41*. London: Hamish Hamilton, 1942.

Whelan, Richard. *Robert Capa: A Biography*. New York: Knopf, 1985.

White, Elwyn Brooks. *Letters of E. B. White*, ed. by Dorothy L. Guth. New York: Harper & Row, 1976.

White, Theodore H. *In Search of History*. New York: Harper & Row, 1978.

White, William, ed. *By-Line: Ernest Hemingway: Selected Articles and Dispatches of Four Decades*. New York: Scribner's, 1967.

Williams, Tennessee. *Memoirs*. Garden City, N.Y.: Doubleday, 1975.

Wilson, Sir Charles. *Churchill: Taken from the Diaries of Lord Moran: The Struggle for Survival, 1940–1965*. Boston: Houghton Mifflin, 1966.

Wilson, Edmund. *The Forties*, ed., Leon Edel. New York: Farrar, Straus & Giroux, 1983.

Wilson, Richard. *Zhou Enlai: A Biography*. New York: Viking, 1984.

Winnick, R. H., ed. *Letters of Archibald MacLeish: 1907–1982*. Boston: Houghton Mifflin, 1983.

Winslow, Kathryn. *Henry Miller: Full of Life*. Los Angeles: Jeremy Tarcher, 1986.

Woolf, Virginia. *Diary, Vol. V*, ed. by Anne Olivier Bell. San Diego: Harcourt Brace Jovanovich, 1984.

Wright, William. *Lillian Hellman: The Image, The Woman*. New York: Simon and Schuster, 1986.

Wyman, David S. *The Abandonment of the Jews: America and the Holocaust, 1941–1945*. New York: Pantheon, 1984.

Zhukov, Grigori. *The Memoirs of Marshal Zhukov*. New York: Delacorte, 1971.

Ziegler, Philip. *Mountbatten*. New York: Harper & Row, 1985.

Zuccotti, Susan. *The Italians and the Holocaust*. New York: Basic Books, 1987.

Index